HOW TO PAY ZERO TAXES, 2014

Also by Jeff A. Schnepper

How to Pay Zero Estate Taxes
Inside IRS
Professional Handbook of Business Valuation
New Bankruptcy Law
Can You Afford to Retire?

HOW TO PAY ZERO TAXES, 2014

THIRTY-FIRST EDITION

Jeff A. Schnepper

New York   Chicago   San Francisco   Athens   London
Madrid   Mexico City   Milan   New Delhi
Singapore   Sydney   Toronto

1 2 3 4 5 6 7 8 9 10   QFR/QFR   1 9 8 7 6 5 4 3

ISBN	978-0-07-180781-4
MHID	0-07-180781-0
e-ISBN	978-0-07-180782-1
e-MHID	0-07-180782-9

This publication is designed to provide accurate and authoritative information in regard to the subject matter covered. It is sold with the understanding that neither the author nor the publisher is engaged in rendering legal, accounting, securities trading, or other professional services. If legal advice or other expert assistance is required, the services of a competent professional person should be sought.

—*From a Declaration of Principles jointly adopted by a Committee of the American Bar Association and a Committee of Publishers*

McGraw-Hill Education books are available at special quantity discounts to use as premiums and sales promotions or for use in corporate training programs. To contact a representative, please visit the Contact Us pages at www.mhprofessional.com.

This book is normally dedicated to my mogul,
Barbara, who taught me how to love, and to
my children, Brandy, Joshua, Allison, Mario,
and Jonelle, who gave me five more reasons why.

If I had the choice of doing it all over again,
I would begin by loving you again.

Also normally dedicated to the memory
of Frisco T. D. Schnepper, Tiger T. C. Schnepper,
and to Fred and Bruno, who now give me paws,

BUT

Forget it, guys . . . This one's
for my Bianca Rose Conlin,
and her brothers Drew Ethan Conlin, Tyler Evan Conlin,
and Spencer Henry Conlin who redefined my universe!

Contents

CHAPTER 5

Credits—Dollar-for-Dollar Tax Reductions

CHAPTER 6
"Above the Line" Deductions   135

A   **Deductions for Adjusted Gross Income**   139

Acknowledgments

I wish to thank Nancie Crook, Barbara Thomassian, Pat Berenson, Ronnie Smith, and Anne McVay, without whom this book could not have been written, and the U.S. Congress and the IRS, without whom this book wouldn't have been needed.

I also want to thank Sayes B. Block and Paul Malagoli, CLU, AEP, and ChFC, for their encouragement and professional guidance; Sandi Walker, April Napolitano, and Anne Rigney, for their typing and editorial assistance; my editors at McGraw-Hill, Mary Glenn, Jane Palmieri, Tania Loghmani, Zach Gajewski, and Cheryl Ringer; and Sri Haran, CPA, Robert Doyle, Steve Leimberg, Jeff Kelvin, Joel Petchon, John McFadden, Kenn Tacchino, Bill Rotella, George Hasenberg, Frank Kesselman, John Oxley, Stephen D. Leightman, Noeleen McLoughlin, Julian Egnaczyk, Ed Caldwell, CPA, Al Blum, Brian Hans, Harry K. Sorenson, CPA, Patrick O'Rourke, CPA, S. Scott Davison, Zulma Lombardo, Morris Abraham, Richard and Janice Schank, Mark S. Fineberg, CPA, Anthony Lyras, and Ron Campbell for their professional assistance; and Simba T.C. Schnepper Conlin, Bruno T.D. Conlin, and Fred T.C. Schnepper, who give me reason to paws. Special thanks to Stephanie Davison-Thompson and Brian Lance for research and editorial assistance and to Bill Fox for his investment insights.

HOW TO PAY ZERO TAXES, 2014

CHAPTER 1

Tax Insanity

"Our income tax system is overly complex. It distorts investment decisions and encourages people to put money into schemes to reduce their tax bills instead of into enterprises to create jobs and help our economy grow."

BILL BRADLEY, New Jersey senator (1984)

"The words of such an act as the Income Tax . . . merely dance before my eyes in a meaningless procession: cross-reference, exception upon exception—couched in abstract terms that offer no handle to seize hold of—leave in my mind only a confused sense of some vitally important, but successfully concealed, purport, which it is my duty to extract, but which is within my power, if at all, only after the most inordinate expenditure of time. I know that these monsters are the result of fabulous industry and ingenuity, plugging up this hole and casting out the net, against all possible evasion; yet at times I cannot help recalling a saying of William James about certain passages of Hegel: that they were, no doubt, written with a passion of rationality; but that one cannot help wondering whether to the reader they have any significance save that the words are strung together with syntactical correctness. . . ."

JUDGE LEARNED HAND, Thomas Walter Swan, 57 Yale L.J. 167, 169 [1947].

Q: What's the difference between Obama's cabinet and a penitentiary?

A: One is filled with tax evaders, blackmailers, and threats to society. The other is for housing prisoners.

—DAVID LETTERMAN

"I don't believe in a law to prevent a man from getting rich; it would do more harm than good."

ABRAHAM LINCOLN

"Politicians tax the middle class for the same reason some people rob banks. That's where the money is."

FORBES MAGAZINE
May 11, 1992

"If our current tax strucure were a TV show, it would either be 'Foul-ups, Bleeps and Blunders,' or 'Gimme a Break.' If it were a movie, it would be 'Revenge of the Nerds' or maybe 'Take the Money and Run.' And if the IRS ever wants a theme song, mabye they'll get Sting to do 'Every breath you take, every move you make, I'll be watching you.'"

PRESIDENT REAGAN, in remarks to students at
Northside High School, Atlanta, Georgia, June 6, 1985

WHAT'S NEW FOR 2013?

"April is the cruelest month"

T. S. ELIOT

It starts with laughter on April Fool's Day—but by April 15, nobody is smiling. The IRS had some issues in 2013:

- The Internal Revenue Service reportedly posted the Social Security numbers of tens of thousands of people on the Internet before taking it down when a whistleblower pointed out the mistake.

- The Treasury Inspector General for Tax Administration (TIGTA) found that IRS supervisors urged employees to ignore potential fraud when reviewing applications for Individual Taxpayer Identification Numbers (ITINs). The study showed 15,028 ITINs assigned to individuals with the same address in Dallas and $46.3 million in refunds sent to the same address in Atlanta. Another $7.3 million in refunds for allegedly 2,706 taxpayers went to the same single bank account.

- The TIGTA also found that the IRS revenue agents failed to follow procedures designed to protect taxpayer rights during the tax collection process, did not follow guidelines on contacting taxpayers with representatives, and were not efficiently or effectively processing information referrals, including identity theft claims. Identity theft has increased by more than 650 percent from fiscal 2008 to fiscal 2012. At the end of fiscal 2012, the IRS had nearly 650,000 identity theft cases in its inventory.

- Approximately 1.45 million taxpayers who qualified for relief from tax penalties totaling close to $181 million were never told they could get penalty abatement and never got it.

- The IRS could not provide documentation for $394,430 paid for labor hours. Point *that* out in your next audit!

- The IRS failed to save $527 million in erroneous tax credits for the Earned Income Credit and Additional Child Tax Credit due to inadequate IRS controls.

- For the second year in a row, the IRS has failed to comply with the provisions of the Improper Payments Elimination and Recovery Act.

- Accounting errors by the IRS in calculating unpaid tax assessments created a risk of "a material misstatement of the IRS's financial statements."

- The American Civil Liberties Union released documents showing that the IRS criminal division had been reading taxpayers' e-mails without a warrant, in violation of the Fourth Amendment.

- And then there were the IRS *parties*. During one conference, more than $50,000 was spent on receptions, including 28 bottles of wine for 41 guests. Then there was the almost $4,000 spent on giveaway items, including footballs, $418 in Kazoos, bathtub toy boats, and other novelty decorations. IRS credit cards were used to purchase romance novels, steaks, diet pills, and unspecified items from merchants affiliated with online pornography . . . your tax money at work!

- The IRS spent about $50 million on 225 conferences during the 3 years between fiscal 2010 and 2012. The Small Business and Self-Employed division spent $4.1 million alone on a single conference in Anaheim, California. You should have been there. Speaker fees for presentations such as "how seemingly random combinations of ideas can drive radical innovation" totaled $135,350. One speaker was paid $17,000 to create six paintings. Three were donated to charity, two were given to conference attendees, and the sixth was lost. Then there were the videos that cost $50,107 to produce. They included a dance video showing IRS employees learning the "cupid shuffle" and a *Star Trek* parody, for which the set alone cost $2,400 and 11 hours of staff work (estimated to cost an additional $3,100). But, they did get a 1-minute finished video. We won't even talk about the IRS video parody of *Gilligan's Island* used to train 1,900 taxpayer assistance employees in 400 locations nationwide. As Maynard G. Krebbs would say, "WORK?" In addition to these large expenditures, the IRS spent $15,669 of your money on "brief bags" with free gifts and trinkets, $6,060 on lanyards and badge holders, $1,524 on engraved travel mugs and clocks, and $90 on sleeves for puzzle pieces.

- And then there were the *political issues*. The supposedly politically independent IRS was found to have targeted conservative groups seeking tax exemption for extra scrutiny. The TIGTA found the inappropriate conduct "inexcusable" and Attorney General Eric Holder announced that criminal penalties may be sought in a Justice Department criminal investigation. Add that to the 24 IRS employees who were indicted for fraudulently obtaining more than $250,000 in government benefits and you have what some would call a rogue agency out of control.

There was some good news:

- The IRS *was* in compliance with restrictions on the use of enforcement statistics to evaluate employees.

- For fiscal 2012, the IRS collected $2.5 trillion but only spent about 48 cents for every $100 in revenue collected, which is the lowest cost since 2008.

- Among households with incomes of less than $50,000, 55 million or 59 percent didn't pay any federal income tax. Nonpayers made up 41 percent of all households.

- IRS firings for misconduct fell to the lowest level since 2002.

- Between fiscal 2009 and fiscal 2011, the total amount of outstanding taxes collected under the IRS Collection Program was 20 percent higher than before, with even fewer revenue officers on staff. Conversely, the IRS had grown slower in closing Offer-in-Compromise cases during the same period.

2012 WAS WHEN...

SHAMEFUL!

I don't want to get on a rant here but our Congress has all the character of an egg yolk frying on the asphalt road behind my grandfather's barn on a hot summer day. Since when did having a three-digit IQ disqualify someone from running for office? Are our choices limited only to the left-hand leg of the bell curve? As we crawl out of a recession, I'm reminded of my 92-year-old mother-in-law's comment, "Recession? I lived through the depression of the 1930s and this is a *depression*." Does anybody think a sane business person would take the risk and invest and expand when the tax rules keep changing (maybe) and the cost of employee healthcare is subject to a new law that nobody understands and few agree upon.

When I wrote this, we were approaching what some called a fiscal cliff and others refered to as tax Armageddon. If Congress did nothing, we faced the biggest tax increase in the history of the Internal Revenue Code. Between the expiration of the Bush tax cuts (which were extended in 2010 for 2 years through 2012) and the expiration of the "extenders," deductions would be lost, rates would increase, credits would disappear, and the marriage penalty would return in full force. The maximum tax on dividends would jump from 15 percent to as much as 43.4 percent! According to the Tax Policy Center, four out of five U.S. households would face an average of $3,701 more in taxes. Add mandated spending cuts to this tax hike and on January 1, 2013, we were scheduled to suffer an *$8 trillion* hit!

Here's the part that really gets me angry. Everybody agreed on what should be done. But nobody in Congress had the backbone to do anything until *after* the November elections. So once again politics trumped economics and sanity. Once again hundreds of millions of dollars were wasted on reprogramming IRS computers and tax preparation programs at the last minute. More of your tax money was spent redoing IRS forms. It's hard to play the game if the rules keep changing. It's even harder if the rules change in December when the year is already up.

According to the Joint Committee on Taxation in March 2012, the prior cost of "kicking the can" down the road for tax cuts, extenders, estate tax, etc., through fiscal year 2012 was 967.7 billion in wasted dollars. Add to that decreased stability and the inability to properly budget into the future, and you had a framework for economic impotence.

Don't blame the IRS. Then Commissioner Doug Shulman warned, "If Congress can't act by the end of the year, and even starts to think about retroactive legislation of things like the AMT, which have already expired, you could have a real disaster in the filing season, where there is total confusion, where some people are filing under one law and others under another."

Congress finally passed the American Tax Relief Act of 2012 to address these issues. See Chapter 19 for details.

What else happened? Well, the IRS did have some issues:

- The IRS delayed tax refunds early this filing season for 7.8 million tax returns because of fraud detection problems with its computer system.

- It was revealed that the IRS paid $3.2 billion in erroneous American Opportunity Tax Credits during the first 5 months of 2010 to 2.1 million taxpayers.

- The Service either failed to notify or incorrectly notified 61,427 taxpayers about their need to start repaying the First-Time Home Buyer Credit.

- The Tax Inspector General for Tax Administration (TIGTA) reported that the IRS failed to "securely operate its computer network. . . ." The TIGTA also found that the IRS needed to gain tighter control over its wireless technology and improve security to protect data from computer attacker exploits. Weaknesses in the Internal Revenue Service's financial and tax processing systems continue to jeopardize the confidentiality, integrity, and availability of sensitive taxpayer information. No surprise that the number of fraudulent returns jumped to 2.2 million in 2011, up from just 457,369 in 2009.

- Somebody got the math wrong. The IRS sent out 8.6 million math error notices, but almost 138,000 taxpayers disputed the computer-generated adjustments.

- Tax returns that were incorrectly prepared by IRS volunteers, if filed, would have caused taxpayers to pay almost $10,000 more than they owed and would have kept them from receiving legitimate refunds of $4,000 according to a TIGTA study. Of the 36 returns audited, only 14 were prepared correctly.

- Another TIGTA study found more than $697 million in wrongly claimed investment theft deductions causing a revenue hit to the Treasury of over $41 million.

- The percentage of customer service phone calls that actually reached IRS representatives in fiscal year 2012 fell to 61 percent, down from 70.1 percent in 2011. That's what happens when Congress cuts the IRS budget by 2.5 percent, and the IRS responds by eliminating 3.1 percent of its full-time employees.

- TIGTA also found the IRS's new e-file system "error prone" and still unable to ensure the accurate processing of individual tax returns.

There was some good news:

- For 2011, the IRS scored a 73 percent on the American Customer Satisfaction Index survey, way up from only 32 percent in 1998.

- The IRS was ranked third out of 15 large agencies in the Best Places to Work in the Federal Government survey for 2011, up from eighth place as recently as 2008.

- Why is it so much fun to work at the IRS? It may have something to do with a forfeiture relating to a Nevada brothel. I guess the job with the Secret Service was already taken.

- According to the TIGTA, IRS inability to detect identity theft could result in the issuance of $21 billion in fradulent refunds over the next 5 years.

The best "tax tip" of the year? A Cleveland waitress received an erroneous tax refund of $434,712. She had requested a refund of only $754.

WE SURVIVED 2011

Senator Olympia Snowe (R-Maine) hit the nail on the head in 2011 when she said, "It's all political theater. It's not about legislating anymore. It's all for the next election that's coming very shortly." That pretty much described 2011. But we did have an interesting year:

- A Joint Tax Committee Report revealed that 51 percent of households not only owed no federal income tax for 2009, but that 30 percent of all households got back a check for their full income tax bill and more resulting from refundable credits.

- In January the IRS launched IRS2Go, a free application for the iPhone and Android market, an app that lets users check their refunds and access help lines over the phone.

- Having trouble keeping up with changes to the tax law? In April 2011, IRS Commissioner Shulman reported that there have been about 3,500 tax law changes since 2000.

- More than half of small businesses spend at least $5,000 and 40 hours per year just to file their taxes according to a National Small Business Association survey.

Our government tax enforcers are still having problems:

- The IRS improperly transferred hundreds of millions of dollars in taxpayer payments to its Excess Collections File.

- A March Government Accounting Office (GAO) report revealed that taxpayer data are at risk of being disclosed, modified, or destroyed because of material weaknesses in IRS internal control systems. About 74 percent of previously reported information security weaknesses still remained unresolved or unmitigated.

- A June 2011 report by the Treasury Inspector General for Tax Administration (TIGTA) found that IRS databases are increasingly being targeted by attackers and that the IRS needs to increase its security diligence.

- An August 2011 TIGTA report showed that only 19 percent of written inquiries from taxpayers received timely and accurate responses. In another study, the percent dropped as low as 8 percent.

- The TIGTA reported that the IRS has been doing a better job of detecting and preventing fraudulent returns. But, I guess that doesn't apply to prisoners and those with kids. The number of fraudulent tax returns filed by state and federal prisoners in the United States doubled from 18,103 in 2004 to 44,944 in 2009. That allowed $295.1 million in illegal tax refunds. The IRS reported that between 23 and 28 percent of earned income tax credits (EITCs) each year are issued erroneously. For 2009, that was $13 billion in improper payments.

- The IRS didn't do much better with cars or other credits. As much as 20 percent of the $163.9 million in credits claimed for electric and alternative motor vehicles was claimed in error according to a February TIGTA report. The IRS also allowed 125,762 individuals to erroneously receive $111.4 million in stimulus-related tax credits. If this is doing "better," how bad was it before?

- The TIGTA did find that the IRS needs to improve the security of a Web portal used by preparers to electronically file returns. I guess the IRS failed to show its security concerns when it awarded a tax processing contract to a company that admitted to having information on 1.5 million payment cardholders and 1.1 million Social Security numbers stolen by computer hackers.

- The TIGTA found that the IRS also divulged personal taxpayer records and information over the phone without properly authenticating taxpayer identity.

- Because of multiple use of taxpayer identification numbers, the IRS accepted $380 million in erroneous tax exemptions and tax credits in 2007.

- In July 2011, the TIGTA reported that the IRS may have violated over 32,000 taxpayers' tax lien rights with improper notifications.

- The IRS found over 245,000 identity theft incidents last year. Since 2004, there have been 470,000 incidents of identity theft affecting more than 390,000 taxpayers.

- TIGTA auditors found that taxpayers had to wait an average of one hour to receive assistance as per an August 2011 report.

- The good news—the IRS provides a special toll-free phone line for hearing and speech impaired taxpayers. The bad news—the IRS ignores most of the calls! Out of the 350,000 calls made to the special line, only 339 were responded to by the IRS.

- Really? The Center for Plain Language gave the IRS its Grand ClearMark Award for clear language in its simplified notices, as required under the Plain Writing Act signed in October 2010.

2010 WAS WHEN...

2010 was a great year for tax preparers. Congress "solved" any and all economic and social problems with multiple changes in the tax code while shamefully delaying any action on the estate tax and tax extenders by playing politics rather than providing clear and long-term rules for playing the tax game. But, we had fun:

- It's become harder and harder to reach executive level in government service if you actually pay your taxes. New York Congressional representative Charlie Rangel was forced to resign as Chairman of the House Ways and Means Committee, which writes all our tax rules, because he couldn't follow them. I guess anybody could forget to report $75,000 in rental income.

- Lael Brainard was nominated and approved to be undersecretary for international affairs despite late real estate tax payments, questionable home office deductions, late unemployment insurance payments for household employees, and questions as to their legal work status.

- You didn't have to be a senior executive to be bad. IRS employee Lattice Murray pleaded guilty to stealing cash and mail addressed to the IRS facility where she worked.

- IRS revenue officer Albert Bront threatened to kill tax agents who investigated his fraudulent returns and was hit with a 16-count indictment.

- IRS employee Colette Browne was charged with filing 32 fraudulent returns and embezzling over $100,000.

- While it helps, being on the government teat wasn't a prerequisite for cheating on your taxes. In April 2010, the Department of Justice and the IRS announced fraud charges against 26 New York City tax preparers.

And then there were the "successes" of the Internal Revenue Service itself:

- A report by the Treasury Inspector General for Tax Administration (TIGTA) found that errors in the Modernized e-Filing system limited its utility and caused it to erroneously reject tax returns. The $78 million MeF Release 6.1 was deployed in February 2010 and subsequently rejected 23 percent of the electronic returns filed.

- The TIGTA in July 2010 found security weaknesses in IRS contractors which placed "confidential information at risk of unauthorized access and disclosure."

- The IRS also failed to expeditiously process paper checks resulting in the loss of thousands of dollars in interest for the agency.

- The TIGTA also found $20 million in erroneous credits issued by the IRS under the Making Work Pay program.

- Then there was another $20 million in erroneous refunds issued to nearly 14,000 taxpayers as a result of dishonored and bounced checks for payments.

- Then our tax masters failed to make timely and appropriate lien determinations on more than $1.4 billion in delinquent taxes.

- IRS oversight could have been more focused. At least 130 companies that received federal funds under the Troubled Asset Relief Program (TARP) owed taxes totaling $530.8 million at the time they received government funding.

- The IRS didn't do much better with home buyer credits. A TIGTA study reported $636 million in bogus claims, including 500 people under age 18 and one "home buyer" only four years old. One hundred IRS employees filed dubious claims, and 256 filers took the credit for homes at just five addresses. That's your tax dollars at work with a computer system that won't work!

- Putting perpetrators in jail didn't appear to work. 1,295 prison inmates, including more than 200 serving life sentences, received $9.1 million in fraudulent home buyer tax credits. One home was used by 67 inmates to claim credits.

- Taxpayer security is still an issue. The Government Accounting Office (GAO) found control and processing weaknesses that "continue to jeopardize the confidentiality, integrity, and availability of financial and sensitive taxpayer information."

But, there was some good news:

- Laura Schultz, a house cleaner in the Denver area, received an erroneous $122,783 tax refund. Being honest, she voided the check and returned it to the IRS. Being a government agency, the IRS then billed her for $80 in taxes owed.

- IRS Commissioner Douglas Shulman revealed that nine out of ten taxpayers use either a tax preparer or third party software to complete their tax returns. Well, that's good news if you're a tax preparer or sell software.

- The IRS has established a global high wealth industry division to make sure high wealth taxpayers pay their share. These "wealth squads" will go after taxes on income from high net worth individuals regardless of its source or country of origin.

- I think the Tax Court got this one right: William C. Naylor, Jr., set up a foundation to store his sperm and, in conjunction with a sperm bank, distribute it to recipients of his choice. The Tax Court found that the foundation "did not promote health for the community" and denied the foundation status as a tax-exempt organization.

2009 WAS FINE

I'm beginning to understand now. The tax code *is* the Holy Grail—the answer to all our social and economic problems. If we have a problem, it can be solved through the tax code. Need to sell more cars? Simple! Make the sales tax on their purchase deductible, even for those taking the standard deduction, and create a "clunkers credit." But, then again, the government does own General Motors, doesn't it?

Still, I stand by my argument. Your house went down in value? Stimulate the real estate market by making real estate taxes on a principal residence deductible, again, even for those taking the standard deduction.

Oil prices getting too high again? Stimulate "green" energy alternatives with credits that reduce your taxes on a dollar-for-dollar basis.

On June 11, 2009, Rep. Carolyn Maloney (D-NY) introduced a bill that would give an employer a 50 percent tax credit on up to $10,000 for "qualified breast-feeding promotion and support expeditures." Talk about milking the system.

You can't say 2009 was a quiet year taxwise.

The Internal Revenue Service released a Taxpayer Attitude Survey on February 2, 2009, which found that 89 percent of Americans think it unacceptable for people to cheat on their taxes. The other 11 percent appear to be headed for the president's cabinet. President Obama's pick to lead the Department of Health and Human Services, former Senate Majority Leader Tom Daschle, apologized for owing $140,000 in back taxes and interest. In 1998, he was quoted as saying, "Make no mistake, tax cheaters cheat us all and the IRS should enforce our laws to the letter." The president's selection for the first Chief Performance Officer for the federal government, Nancy Killefer, failed to pay tax on her household help. Both had the good graces to withdraw from consideration. And then there was Ron Kirk, nominated to be the U.S. trade representative. He "forgot" to report $37,000 in speaking fees assigned to a charity, but he managed to remember taking a deduction for $7,500 of the donation. And then there was $7,400 in pro basketball tickets without a business purpose.

Cheating on his taxes didn't deter Timothy Geithner from becoming Treasury Secretary. His taxes were found to be underpaid in 2001, 2002, 2004 and 2005. (Nobody looked at 2003?) But then again, who better to put in charge of the IRS than someone who requests a ruling on the law and then ignores it? But, he did pay up, when caught.

Talking about the law, surprise, it changed again! The year started with the American Recovery and Reinvestment Act of 2009 passed on February 17. That was just the beginning. The details of these and other changes, and how to respond to their opportunities, are found in Chapter 18.

GOT STIMULATED IN 2008

Rebate, rebate, rebate!

That's all we heard in 2008. Once again Congress, in its infinite wisdom, decided that you could be trusted to spend your own money and spent many millions of your dollars to send some back to you—to stimulate the economy. The IRS estimated that the reallocation of hundreds of IRS collection staff members to answering taxpayer telephone calls about the stimulus payments alone would result in up to $565 million in foregone enforcement revenue. According to the Treasury Inspector General for Tax Administration, calculations of the economic stimulus payments by the IRS may have been wrong in nearly 400,000 cases. More than 100,000 self-employed taxpayers received larger checks than they were entitled to and 25,000 clergy members didn't get the rebates owed to them. The details of this give-back are covered in Chapter 17 as part of the Economic Stimulus Act of 2008.

Chapter 17 also discusses the tax aspects of three more tax law changes—both 2008's Housing Stimulus Bill and the Hero's Earnings Assistance and Relief Act, as well as the Mortgage Debt Relief Act of 2007, which was passed and signed into law on December 20, 2007. We also had the Emergency Economic Stabilization Act in October 2008 in response to our economic and financial meltdown.

Because of the last minute changes in the law, more than 3 million and as many as 13.5 million taxpayers in 2008 were unable to even file their returns until February 11 because the forms were wrong—*again!* Let's not even think about the cost to update and correct all the tax preparation programs and educate the public. As noted by National Taxpayer Advocate Nina Olson, "When taxpayers do not claim tax benefits because they do not know about them, Congress's intent in providing the tax benefits is undermined and taxpayers understandably question the fairness of the tax system." She was referring to the last minute 2006 changes that resulted in 1.4 million fewer claims for deductions that were extended but weren't even on the forms that finally went out to confused taxpayers.

The IRS computer system remains a mess. The IRS still lacks adequate procedures to identify identify theft victims or adequate systems to even determine the number of tax-related identity thefts that occur. From 2002 to 2006, identity theft related to refund fraud rose by 396 percent, while employment related identity theft increased by 129 percent. Call 800-908-4490 if you have an identity theft issue.

2007 SUCKED BLOOD

I guess the IRS is a great training ground. First they want your money; now they want your blood! Former IRS Commissioner Mark W. Everson left that position in April 2007 to head the American Red Cross. In July, his successor, Kevin M. Brown, declared that he too was leaving the IRS to serve as chief operating officer for the American Red Cross. Unfortunately, Mr. Everson was caught in a tryst with one of his employees and the Red Cross wrote him off.

In December 2006, Congress passed an extenders package that gave renewed life to the research and development credits, deductions for college tuition, above-the-line deductions for teacher expenses, and the sales tax deduction. Unfortunately, the 2006 tax forms had already been printed *without* these changes. The IRS incurred additional costs of $410,000 for printing and $1.3 million for postage for the new sales tax tables alone.

In 2007, the IRS eliminated the telefile program, a free telephone filing service. It had been used by about 2 million taxpayers in 2005. Half of those reverted to filing paper tax returns, slowing the refund process and increasing IRS processing costs. Those who paid tax preparers or purchased software spent nearly $24 million to file their taxes in 2006.

The Treasury Inspector General for Tax Administration revealed that of the 106 million refunds totaling $228 billion issued by the IRS to individual tax-payers in 2004, taxpayers voluntarily returned approximately 51,000 refunds totaling $302 million. The report estimated that about half of those erros were due to IRS mistakes!

It's a good thing the former IRS commissioner was a computer expert. In five weeks to April 13, 2007, the IRS sent upward of $300,000 worth of one time $30 federal telephone tax refunds to a single JPMorgan Chase Bank account in Ohio. Personally, I would have called first. . . .

2007 was a tough year all around. More than 450,000 federal workers and retirees were revealed to owe the IRS a whopping $3 billion in back taxes. You didn't have to work for the government to get in trouble. More than 125 Jackson Hewitt tax preparation branches run by five franchises of the company were shut down for preparing fraudulent returns. That cost the government $70 million in lost revenue. Even Joseph Francis, the creator of *Girls Gone Wild*, was indicted for tax evasion!

2006 WAS NO PICNIC

DUH! Somebody give them a calendar. On May 17, *2006,* President Bush signed a tax bill into law. Its technical name is the Tax Increase Prevention and Reconciliation Act of *2005*! Maybe Congress was so impressed with corporate crooks back-dating options that it thought back-dating laws could generate back-dated votes?

We'll talk about what opportunities and traps that law offers in a later chapter.

The IRS building in Washington, D.C. was closed by a flood costing $13 million. It's almost biblical, isn't it? But, rather than wetting the bottoms of bureaucrats who are only struggling to do an impossible job, I suspect the flood was really a warning to those across the street in the Capitol who create the devilish complexity we call the tax law.

The General Accounting Office reported that the *lowest* available estimate of the cost of complying with federal tax code is $107 billion—a whopping 1 percent of the nation's gross domestic product. In January 2009, National Taxpayer Advocate Nina Olson pegged the cost at $193 billion a year, 14 percent of the total taxes collected.

In 1969, the total number of pages of federal tax rules was 19,500. By 2009, it had increased to 70,320. Back in 1913, it was only 400 pages.

In 2006, the General Accounting Office visited alleged tax preparers at 19 outlets affiliated with major tax preparation chains. They were not happy with the results of their test returns. Nearly all of the returns were prepared incorrectly and were accompanied by "very bad tax advice." Errors ranged from incorrect refunds of almost $2,000 to a liability of $1,500.

Is the tax law complicated? H&R Block, the country's largest tax preparer, blew its own tax liability by $32 million! Couldn't it find someone to help with its taxes?

How about General Electric? In May 2006, it filed a 24,000-page tax return with the IRS.

By 2008, 62 percent of Americans were using professionals do their tax returns. In 2006, that included three of the four senior lawmakers on the Senate Finance and House Ways and Means Committees, the panels charged with writing our tax law. Another 22 percent purchased tax software. By 2010, 90 percent of the tax returns done were prepared by professionals or with computer software. Our code ain't simple!

A NATIONAL DISGRACE

I had a dream last night. I'd died and was taken by the devil down below to suffer my eternal torment. After all, I was an attorney. But, I couldn't believe my eyes. The place was a frozen wasteland, with huge mountains of ice and snow.

I was amazed. Congress had actually passed a *simple* tax law that helped taxpayers!

Then, I woke up. And I woke up mad!

Is the only difference between our government and the Mafia that the Mafia is organized?

If con is the opposite of pro, is Congress the opposite of progress?

Who was the prophetic visionary who designed all the streets in Washington, D.C. to go in circles?

Is *anybody* in charge here?

OUR TAX CODE

Our tax code is a disgrace! Thousands of words dancing without rhythm or connection, failing to make a point. As a tax attorney, I'm embarrassed.

According to former Treasury Secretary Paul O'Neill, ". . . the complexity of our Tax Code is the worst problem facing our society. . . ." Paul doesn't spend a lot of time in hospitals or hang with the homeless. But, I feel his pain.

I'm not the only one who's embarrassed. Rep. Steny Hoyer (D-MD), House Democratic Whip, saw it the same way. "Our tax system is an embarrassment that treats many taxpayers unfairly." His view on the code was no less frank. "The Internal Revenue Code is a Kafkaesque maze of complexity that confounds millions of Americans every single year."

To make sure we don't ever understand the code, Congress changes it each year. We've had over 47 *major* tax law changes in the last 50 years! Remember, it was Albert Einstein who said, "The hardest thing in the world to understand is the income tax." And, he said that way before it became a whopping 70,320 plus page, 25-volume beast.

Here are some numbers directly from the IRS. The average taxpayer who files a Form 1040 needs 16 hours. Add a single rental property or a Schedule C for your business and the hours jump to 23, and that's with about 81 percent e-filing with a computer.

We spend more than 6.1 billion hours and over $350 billion each year complying with the tax code—just to figure out what we owe. That's more hours than are used to build every car, van, truck, and airplane manufactured in America. That's just your time.

Our government wants your money as well. According to the Tax Foundation, the average taxpayer had to work 108 days, until April 18, 2013, in order to earn enough to cover his federal, state, and local tax burden. They call it "Tax Freedom Day." I call it "Get Out of My Pocket Day." The group Americans for Tax Reform includes the cost of regulation. Its "Cost of Government Day" had us working for the government until July 13, 2013!

THE TAX CODE IS DRIVING ME NUTS!

The tax code is driving me nuts! I've got two law degrees and an MBA in finance. I've been licensed by the New Jersey Board of CPAs. I've taught taxation for over two decades, both on an undergraduate and a graduate level. And I still have no idea what they're talking about half the time!

It's been claimed that the only difference between death and taxes is that death, on occasion, is allegedly painless. Wrong! Death doesn't become more complicated every time Congress meets.

Remember the Tax Foundation? If the average middle-income taxpayer's 2013 salary, starting from January 1, went to pay taxes, it would have taken 100 percent of the earnings until April 18 to meet all the federal, state, and local payments due. That's about one-third of the year, 108 days, or about 2 hours and 22 minutes of each eight hours' earnings. In comparison, in 1930 it was only 57 seconds.

Here's some more of the stuff making me crazy:

- On average, Americans now spend more time working to pay their taxes than they spend working to provide food and shelter combined.

- Secretary of State and former presidential candidate John F. Kerry illegally shaved $12,000 off his tax on his 2003 return. He sold a piece of art and reported the gain at the 15 percent rate. But, the profit on the sale of the art, as a collectible, should have been taxed at a 28 percent rate. If the nominee of the Democratic Party for president, with 57 Heinz varieties of tax lawyers and CPAs, got it wrong, what can the IRS expect from the rest of us?

- The IRS audit rate for 2005 was 0.93 percent, up from 2004's 0.77 percent, up from 0.65 percent in 2003, and 0.57 percent in 2002. But who cares if they're auditing the wrong people? The percentage of no change audits grew from 14 percent in fiscal 2001 to 18 percent in 2003, a significant increase and a waste of time and resources. Why? Easy. Their formulas for selecting returns were way out of date. They hadn't been revised since the late 1980s. The IRS has updated its numbers. The data was reflected in IRS audit selection in 2006.

- The fiscal 2006 numbers showed an increase from 0.93 percent to a whopping 0.98 percent. For fiscal 2007, it grew to 1.03 percent and then dropped to 1.01 percent in 2008. In fiscal 2009, it rose to 1.03 percent and 1.11 percent in 2010 and 2011. I am not impressed. And then down to 1.03 percent in 2012.

But, are they "real" audits? According to Senator Max Baucus (Mont.) on April 29, 2004, "I'm concerned that the IRS's audit priorities are misplaced. . . . IRS is trying to bolster its audit figures, not by going after those who are deliberately trying to cheat on their taxes, but by sending out more letters regarding mathematical errors or mismatching of taxpayer information."

In 2011, 76 percent of the audits were correspondence audits, done by mail, with no personal face-to-face contact.

One Treasury Inspector General for Tax Administration's report showed taxpayers received *incorrect* answers to 43 percent of tax questions asked in a special study. The investigators concluded that about 500,000 taxpayers who visited Internal Revenue Service help centers got wrong or incomplete responses!

Our tax code is just too complex. Even the IRS agrees. Former Commissioner Mark Everson has remarked that "Frequent changes to the tax code and rising complexity are perhaps the greatest obstacles to reducing paperwork burden. . . . I am concerned that tax law complexity may discourage taxpayers and adversely impact voluntary self-assessment that is at the heart of our tax system."

Responding to a report of IRS employees incorrectly preparing 19 of 23 tax returns in a December 2003 survey, Everson replied, "Whatever you can do to simplify the code would really help us."

Guess what Commish? It would help the rest of us as well. If the code is too complex for the IRS and Jeff Schnepper, how about those of us who aren't supposed to be tax experts?!

But, let's not jump on the IRS. They don't write the code. It's those brain surgeons we send to Congress who have created this mess. In 1986, I was invited to the White House to consult on the proposed Tax Reform Act. I suggested that it include a provision requiring all members of Congress to do their own tax returns. I also suggested that all elections be held on April 16. Both my suggestions were rejected.

Since 1986, over 15,000 amendments were made to the U.S. tax code—that's about three for each working day, and that doesn't include the 2012 and 2013 changes! From 2001 through 2012, it jumped to more than one change per day.

As I said up front, the tax code is driving me nuts. But, let's see if I can add some sanity to your financial life. Tax planning is not for the timid. The laws are constantly changing and you have to keep up to minimize your tax liability.

You have to know the rules. That's what *How to Pay Zero Taxes* is for. If you don't know the rules, you can't win the game.

According to Jerold Rochwald, "Nuclear physics is much easier than tax law. It's rational and always works the same way."

For 2010, 51,980,000 taxpayers received a total of $160,185 billion in refunds, an average of $3,082 each. In 2011, the IRS paid out more than $288 billion in refunds to over 102 million taxpayers—an average of $2,805 each. For 2012 returns, almost $268 billion was refunded, averaging $2,651. That's a huge, interest-free loan to the IRS.

The source of this nightmare—the Internal Revenue Code—is a quagmire so complicated that former Treasury Secretary Paul O'Neill disdains it as ". . . not worthy of an advanced society."

Even former IRS officials find the tax code confusing. "No, I don't do my own return," says Randolph Thrower, a former IRS commissioner. "It's much too complicated for me." In 1954, our tax code and related material fit into 14,000 pages in 9 volumes. By 1984, it was 26,300 pages in 14 volumes. By 2002, it grew to 52,310 pages in 25 volumes. As of 2009, it had grown to 70,320 pages and more than 3.7 million words! It is now over 4 million words—many meandering without meaning. So much for tax simplification. . . .

This 2014 edition of *How to Pay Zero Taxes* will detail the new tax law changes, the hidden secrets of our tax code, and how you can take advantage of them to keep more of your hard-earned dollars.

According to the Tax Foundation, the United States passed a depressing milestone back in fiscal 1995. Total tax collections exceeded $2 trillion for the first time. That's a two and 12 zeros.

It is April 15, 2014 and the IRS is after your money again. To protect your hard-earned dollars, first turn to the new 2014 edition of *How to Pay Zero Taxes.* It contains all of the new laws, rules, regulations, and court cases to legally minimize your tax outlay. Remember, your objective should be to pay all of the taxes that are due, but not one penny more than the law requires. The law, however, is complicated, convoluted, and constantly changing. The new edition of *How to Pay Zero Taxes* is your guide through the minefield of these changes.

Almost three decades ago, on October 22, 1986, former President Reagan signed a sweeping revision of the tax code that touched the lives of all American taxpayers. The text of the Tax Reform Act of 1986 bulked 10 inches and weighed more than 33 pounds; it detailed changes in 2,704,000 subsections of the tax code, which cost the Internal Revenue Service an estimated $106,485,000 in fiscal year 1988 to implement. The act dramatically cut tax rates and paid for this decline by eliminating or reducing a vast array of tax breaks. The American tax structure for 2012 is vastly different from that in the past and will be different again in 2013.

Taxes have been likened to a plague of locusts on a field of wheat. Yet there are several individuals earning millions of dollars who pay little or no taxes and many more who earn hundreds of thousands of dollars each year whose tax bill is just as small. For the year 1998, filed in 1999, 2,085,211 individual tax returns were filed showing income of $200,000 or more. Of those, 0.07 percent, or about

Tax Freedom Day, Selected Years, 1940–2011

Year	Tax Freedom Day
1940	March 7
1950	March 31
1960	April 11
1970	April 19
1975	April 17
1980	April 21*
1981	April 24
1982	April 22
1983	April 18
1984	April 17
1985	April 18
1986	April 19
1987	April 22
1988	April 21
1989	April 22
1990	April 21*
1991	April 21*
1992	April 20*
1993	April 21*
1994	April 23*
1995	April 24*
1996	April 26*
1997	April 28*
1998	April 30*
1999	May 1*
2000	May 3*
2001	April 30*
2002	April 19*
2003	April 16*
2004	April 17*
2005	April 23*
2006	April 26
2007	April 27
2008	April 21
2009	April 8*
2010	April 9
2011	April 12
2012	April 13*
2013	April 18

*Revised.

1,467 returns, showed *no* U.S. tax liability. For 1999, filed in 2000, 1,605 returns with incomes of $200,000 or more showed *no* U.S. tax liability. For 2000, filed in 2001, 2,328 returns with income of $200,000 or more showed *no* U.S. tax, and 2001 returns, filed in 2002, without a tax liability increased to 2,959. The number for 2002 was 2,551 and for 2003, 2,416 returns showed no tax liability. In 2004, 2,833 filers had no tax liability. For 2005 the number jumped to 7,389 increasing to 8,252 in 2006. For 2007, the number was 13,412, jumping to 22,257 in 2008. In 2009, 1,470 people earned over $1 million and paid *zero* taxes and 20,752 taxpayers with incomes of $200,000 or more paid *zero* taxes. For 2010, the number fell to 19,003 "happy" returns. These people are able to avoid paying taxes by the use of sophisticated tax strategies devised by high-priced and very professional tax planners, who guide their clients along the cracks in the federal tax code.

Many of those cracks have been put there intentionally by Congress as economic and social incentives. For example, to encourage capital spending and to support the U.S. auto industry, a combination of provisions in the tax code allows a knowledgeable average taxpayer to buy a $12,000 car at a net cash cost of only $6,641 (see page 312). If that car is run only 60,000 miles in its first 5 years, the net cash outlay for the car can be reduced to below *zero!* In effect, the taxpayer gets a free car; more important, his costless acquisition is completely legal. Exactly how to do this will be explained later in the book.

As the examples indicate, Congress has created a financial mechanism whereby certain actions substitute for tax payments. Rather than taking the taxpayers' money in taxes and then paying it out in direct support for certain activities, Congress has indirectly accomplished the same goal by granting taxpayers some credits and deductions if they make expenditures in certain defined areas. *How to Pay Zero Taxes* will expose these areas and detail how you, a now enlightened reader, can structure your transactions to benefit optimally from these completely legal strategies and techniques.

You first will learn how our tax system works and how the structure of the system provides opportunities to save money on your income tax. The crucial difference between tax deductions and tax credits will be explained, and the internal IRS chart detailing the average amount deducted for each tax bracket for each category of itemized deductions will be revealed.

You then will be transported into the netherworld of tax shelters and shown what to look for and what to avoid. The section on tax shelter strategies is followed by the fun part of the book—how to take tax deductions for your personal expenses and hobbies. Here you will be shown how to turn your normal living expenses into tax deductions. We all must pay housing and food costs, but *How to Pay Zero Taxes* will show you how to structure these costs to reduce your taxes. We all enjoy vacations—*How to Pay Zero Taxes* will show you how the federal government could pay part of their costs. If you have a hobby—stamp collecting, auto racing, etc.—*How to Pay Zero Taxes* will demonstrate how you can get the Internal Revenue Service to help finance it by converting it into a legitimate business.

Finally, *How to Pay Zero Taxes* will detail and explain those more sophisticated legal 2013 and 2014 tax techniques and instruments that have been developed for shifting income, deferring taxes, and avoiding payment completely. These techniques all have been court tested and approved. Most important, *How to Pay Zero Taxes* will not simply explain and document these tax savings strategies but will show you examples, provide you with guidelines and tax cases to support your deductions, and take you step by step through the creation of these money-saving instruments for your own use. Its objective is not merely to reveal and educate but to demonstrate and guide as well.

Taxpayers who can afford expensive professional tax planning don't pay high taxes. The goal of *How to Pay Zero Taxes* is to provide that planning and those techniques to middle-income taxpayers who are unknowingly overpaying. Supreme Court Justice Sutherland once remarked, "The legal right of a taxpayer to decrease his taxes or to altogether avoid them by means which the law permits cannot be doubted."[1] *How to Pay Zero Taxes* is dedicated to that ideal.

---

[1] *Gregory v. Helvering*, 35-1, USTC Par. 9043, 293 U.S. 463, 469 (1935).

CHAPTER 2

Is It Legal?

"Taxation must not take from individuals what rightfully belongs to individuals."

HENRY GEORGE

In 2008, a record 51.6 million tax returns—36.3% of all returns filed—had no income tax liability because of the available credits and deductions in the tax code. For 2012, the number had risen to 419.

"The purpose of the IRS is to collect the proper amount of tax revenue at the least cost to the public, and in a manner that warrants the highest degree of public confidence in our integrity, efficiency, and fairness. To achieve that purpose, we will: Encourage and achieve the highest degree of voluntary compliance in accordance with the tax laws and regulations; Advise the public of their rights and responsibilities; Determine the extent of compliance and the causes of noncompliance; Do all things needed for the proper administration and enforcement of the tax laws; Continually search and implement new, more efficient and effective ways of accomplishing our Mission." (IRS statement of organization and functions, 39 Fed. Reg. 11,572, 1974)

It has been said that "the Internal Revenue Code is a remarkable essay in sustained obscurity . . . a conspiracy and restraint of understanding." (*All State Fire Insurance Company* [Ct. Cl.], 80-1 USTC-, 45 AFTR 2d, 80-1096)

For 2012, individual taxpayers received almost $268 billion in refunds. That's a $268 billion interest-free loan to the IRS. At a 3 percent rate, that's $8.04 billion in lost interest—enough to cover my kids' spending for most of their teenage years!

When the modern income tax law was introduced in 1913, only one American in 271 was affected; the taxable incomes of the great majority did not exceed the exempt amount of $3,000 for individuals, $4,000 for couples. Those who were affected paid at the rate of 1 percent on taxable income up to $20,000 and, at most, 6 percent on income over that amount. The average tax rate for the 437,036 individual tax returns filed in 1916 was 2.75 percent. For last year, over 144 million individual income tax returns were filed and the IRS processed over two billion pieces of paper—which, if placed side by side, would stretch over 200 miles.

You pay too much in taxes, and it costs too much for you to do your tax returns. Here are a few "for instances:"

- Even after adjusting for inflation, the U.S. government collected twice as much income tax revenue in 2001 as it did in 1981.

- An increase of 250 million hours in the burden on the public of complying with the tax system during 2000 resulted in an overall increase of 180 million hours in the burden on the public of federal agencies' collection of information.

- Let's talk about complexity. By 2009, our tax rules needed 70,320 pages and it contained 3.7 million words. It now has 4 million words. The epic book *War and Peace* has 1,444 pages and 660,000 words, while the Bible contains 1,291 pages and 774,746 words.

According to Daniel J. Mitchell of the Heritage Foundation:

- The paperwork received by the IRS would circle the globe 36 times.

- The IRS sends out 10,000,000 correction notices each year. 5,000,000 of them are wrong!

- The IRS has lost more than 6,400 computer tapes and cartridges.

- In 1948, the average American family with children paid 3 percent to the federal government in income and payroll taxes.

Time is money, and these dollars come out of your pocket and drain your ability to save and invest, while inflation compounds your financial concerns by draining your ability just to keep even.

Even if your earnings can keep even with inflation, you still lose. For example, assume you have a taxable income for 2013 of $87,850 and pay $17,891.25 in taxes. You have $69,958.75 left to spend. With both inflation and a raise of 8 percent, you will now earn $94,878 and pay $19,859 in taxes, leaving you $75,019 to spend. But due to inflation, this $75,019 is worth only $69,017. In real dollars, the progressive nature of your tax structure and the purchasing power decay caused by inflation have together decreased your real buying power by $69,958.75 minus $69,017 = $941.75 on a $7,028 increase in earnings! The impact of state and social security taxes further magnifies your financial dilemma.

What can you do? One simple answer is to try to reduce your taxes, and the rest of this book will tell you how to do so. Some of the techniques found in this book are the result of mixing complicated and convoluted tax code sections, but all of them are completely legal. Some are legal not because Congress intended them to be there but because both Congress and the Internal Revenue Service were lax in their homework and the tax code language allowing them is there. While Congress writes the tax law, that law is read and interpreted by the courts. Quite often the Internal Revenue Service and the courts differ in their interpretations of various code sections and their applications—the courts *always* win. Even if a tax effect is contrary to original congressional intent, the courts must and do support the language of the code. Such effects are the law and can be changed or eliminated only by congressional action. Until such action is taken, it is fully within the legal rights of the American taxpayer to use such code combinations to reduce, minimize, or even completely eliminate taxes. Each individual must pay taxes, but not one penny more than the law requires. If you want to make voluntary contributions to our federal Treasury, you'll have bought the wrong book.

On the other hand, most of the techniques detailed here have been intended by Congress. In many cases, legally reducing your income tax liability is both good for you and good for America. Certain kinds of receipts are intentionally excluded from gross income for tax purposes in order to achieve some economic or social objective. These provisions are frequently referred to as "tax incentives" and are specifically designed to encourage certain types of activity. Tax incentives have the same impact on the federal budget as direct expenditures because they represent revenues not collected by the federal government. These special tax provisions, therefore, have been labeled "tax expenditures" or "tax aids" by the Treasury Department.

These expenditures are revenue losses arising from provisions of the tax code that give special or selective tax relief to certain groups of taxpayers.

These provisions either encourage some desired activity or provide special aid to certain taxpayers. For example, the federal government seeks to encourage certain forms of investment. Thus business investment is encouraged by the accelerated rather than straight-line depreciation. This tax advantage has been legislated so that business will have additional capital to be able to expand. Tax advantaged investment helps create new businesses and new jobs. These new jobs produce more paychecks and these additional paychecks produce more taxes. In the long run, if everything works as it should, everyone wins.

Alternatively, other tax expenditure provisions have been adopted as "relief provisions" to ease "tax hardships" or to "simplify tax computations." For example, the elderly and the blind receive special financial benefits through a deduction called the "additional amount." The other tax benefits for the aged—the retirement income credit and the potential exclusion of social security annuity payments from taxable income—also fall into this "personal or tax hardship" category.

These revenue losses are called tax "expenditures" because they are payments or expenditures by the federal government made through a reduction of taxes rather than a direct grant. Just as a forgiveness of debt is equivalent to a payment, so a remission of tax liability is equivalent to an expenditure.

According to the Congressional Budget Office, in 1980 a total of 92 provisions were considered tax expenditures. These were estimated to cost $206 billion in fiscal year 1981, based on laws in effect at the start of 1980. Projected 2013 individual tax expenditures are $1.36 trillion.

The financial benefits offered by tax expenditure provisions resemble those available through entitlement programs on the spending side of the budget. A tax expenditure provision can provide special tax relief in any of the following ways:

- *Special exclusions, exemptions, and deductions*, which reduce taxable income and thus result in a smaller tax liability—for example, tax-exempt municipal bond interest or the exclusion from taxable income of employee discounts or dependent care assistance programs.

- *Preferential rates*, which reduce liabilities by applying lower rates to all or part of the taxpayer's income—for example, the special reduced maximum tax rate on long-term capital gains income.

- *Special credits*, which are subtracted from the tax liability rather than from the income on which the taxes are figured—for example, the child tax credit or the foreign tax credit.

- *Deferrals of tax*, which generally result from allowing deductions that (according to standard accounting principles) are properly attributable to a future year—for example, accelerated depreciation allowances: The taxpayer, paying later rather than now, in effect receives an interest-free loan of the deferred liability.

Tax spending and direct spending are alternative methods of providing federal subsidies. Nearly any tax expenditure could be recast as a spending program, just as most spending programs could be replaced by tax expenditures. Thus, the choice between tax spending and direct spending is essentially a choice between alternative administrative mechanisms. Once it has been decided that a particular subsidy is worth providing, the question of the best method of providing that subsidy arises. In designing or evaluating any subsidy program, however, the following criteria have been applied:

- *Cost and efficiency.* How much does the program cost? How well targeted is the program—that is, does it reach those and only those it is intended to reach? Does it provide the incentive or benefit it was designed to offer? Does it achieve its goal at the least cost?

- *Fairness and equity.* Is the subsidy benefit fairly distributed?

- *Ease of administration.* How much does the program cost to administer? How quickly can the benefits be distributed? Can the benefits be distributed to those and only those for whom they are intended?

- *Budget visibility and control.* Is each program subject to periodic review by the Congress? Are its costs subject to control by the Congress?

In reality, though, many of these expenditures are the result of pressures applied by special interest groups seeking relief provisions for their own constituencies. For example, why is there an additional "standard deduction" amount for the blind and not for the deaf? The answer, I suggest, may have more to do with the political and lobbying power of the two groups than with any inherent difference between the hardships.

These special provisions also arise out of the political needs of our individual representatives in Congress. These are off-budget expenditures that show up as a reduction of revenues rather than as an increase in congressional spending. In effect they allow our representatives to increase our federal fiscal deficit, to spend more tax money, without appearing to do so. Arguments are made that these tax incentives are simple and involve far less government supervision and detail than direct expenditures. It has also been argued that these incentives encourage the private sector to participate in social programs and promote private decision making rather than government-centered decision making.

Whether these asserted virtues of tax incentives are in fact valid or whether their defects outweigh their claimed advantages is not the subject of this book. The fact that they do exist is critical. In order to minimize or to eliminate your taxes completely, you must first accept the fact that the techniques to be detailed in this book are both legal and, for the most part, specifically intended by Congress. That they have not been publicized or made widely known by the Internal Revenue Service is not surprising. Despite publicity releases and continuous claims to the contrary, the Internal Revenue Service is a revenue collector. While the professed goal is a fair administration of the tax law, the service's job is to collect your tax money. No Internal Revenue agent ever received or ever shall receive a raise or promotion by suggesting to a taxpayer how to arrange a financial situation to reduce or eliminate taxes. To discover those techniques, you either have to pay thousands of dollars to a professional tax practitioner, attorney, or accountant—or you can turn to the next chapter.

CHAPTER 3

How Our Tax System Works

"Kings ought to shear, not skin their sheep."

> English poet ROBERT HERRICK shortly after the
> execution of Charles I, who had imposed numerous
> burdensome taxes on his subjects

*"The greater the number of statutes, the greater
the number of thieves and brigands."*

> LAO-TZU

*"A fine is a tax for doing something wrong. A tax
is a fine for doing something right!"*

*"The 9,500 page tax code, with its endless
convolutions, is an abomination unworthy of our
society. Is it any surprise that some people run
from it? It undermines notions of law of, for, and
by the people, because even those who spend a
lifetime studying can barely understand it.
Certainly ordinary citizens cannot hope to figure
it out."*

> Treasury Secretary PAUL O'NEILL, March 20, 2002

Now that you understand the legal foundation for our tax sheltering and eliminating techniques, it remains necessary first to uncomplicate our federal income tax structure so that you can see where each shelter technique fits into the whole picture. You pay taxes on your taxable income. Your taxable income is your gross income less certain deductions. It is necessary, therefore, to define your "gross" income.

Gross income means *all* income, from whatever source derived, including (but not limited to) the following items:

Compensation for services, including fees, commissions, and similar items
Gross income derived from business
Gains derived from dealings in property
Interest
Rent
Royalties
Dividends
Alimony and separate maintenance payments
Annuities
Income from life insurance and endowment contracts
Pensions
Income from discharge of indebtedness
Distributive share of partnership income
Income in respect of a decedent
Income from an interest in an estate or trust
Unemployment compensation

Income has been defined by the Supreme Court as "undeniable accession to wealth, clearly realized, over which the taxpayers have complete dominion" (348 U.S., 426 [1985]). Everything you receive for personal services must be included in your gross income. This includes many so-called fringe benefits as well as wages, salaries, commissions, tips, and fees. You must report income in any form other than cash at the fair market value of the goods or services received.

Amounts withheld from your pay for income and social security taxes or savings bonds are considered received by you and must be included in your income in the year they were withheld. The same generally is true of amounts withheld for insurance and union dues.

If your employer uses your wages to pay your debt, or if wages are *attached* or *garnished,* the full amount is still considered received by you and must be included in your income. The same is true of fines or penalties withheld from your pay.

Vacation allowances paid to you from a vacation fund are wages and are also included in your income. Severance pay as well is taxable. A lump-sum payment for cancellation of your employment contract is income in the year you receive it.

Rewards and bonuses paid to you for outstanding work are income. These include such prizes as an all-expenses-paid vacation trip for meeting a sales goal and even prizes won on a TV quiz show. If a prize or award is in goods or services, you must include its fair market value in income. However, if your employer merely promises to pay you a bonus or award at some future time, it is not taxable until you receive it or it is made available to you.

If you buy property from your employer at a reduced price, you must normally include in your income as extra pay the excess of the property's fair market value over what you paid for it. If you receive a cash allowance from your employer for meals or lodging, you must include that cash allowance in your income. All tips you receive are also subject to federal income tax; they are not tax-free gifts. You must include in gross income the cash tips you receive directly from customers and the tips from charge customers that are paid to you by your employer.

Any interest that you receive or that is credited to your bank account is taxable income unless it is specifically exempt from tax. This is true even if that interest has not been entered in your bank book—it *has* been credited to you on the books of your bank. Certain distributions commonly referred to as dividends must be included in gross income as interest. You must report as interest the so-called dividends on deposits, withdrawals, or share accounts in:

Cooperative banks
Credit unions
Domestic building and loan associations
Federal savings and loan associations
Mutual savings banks
Money market accounts

In addition, the fair market value of gifts or services received for making long-term deposits or opening accounts in savings institutions is interest and should be reported as income in the year received.

Amounts you receive as rental income must also be included in your gross income. Rental income includes not only the amount you receive for the occupancy of real estate or for the use of personal property but other amounts as well. For example, advance rent must be included in your rental income in the year you receive it regardless of the period covered or the accounting method used. Payments for the cancellation of a lease or the reduction in the principal of a mortgage (even on your home) if paid before due should also be included as income. So, too, are payments made directly by a tenant for any of *your* expenses. For example, if your tenant pays your heating bill in lieu of partial rent, that amount must be included as rental income.

You must also include in your gross income all fees for your services. Examples of these fees are payments you receive for services as:

A corporate director
An executor or administrator of an estate
A notary public
A member of a jury
An election precinct official
An accountant
An attorney
A medical practitioner

Income received in the form of property or services must be included in income at its fair market value on the dates received. If you receive the services of another in return for your services, and you both have definitely agreed ahead of time as to the value of the services, that value will be accepted as the fair market value unless the value can be shown to be otherwise. An exchange of property or services for your property or services is called bartering and should be included in your gross income.

Finally, dividends, capital gain distributions, and all gains on the sale of property also are included in your gross income. Dividends are distributions paid to you by a corporation. You also may receive dividends through a partnership, an estate, a trust, or an association that is taxable as a corporation.

When all of your gains, all of your "accessions to wealth, clearly realized, over which you have dominion," are added together, you arrive at your gross income amount. From this amount you next subtract your allowable deductions to arrive at your taxable income. Your tax is based on that taxable income. Therefore, in order to reduce or eliminate your tax, there are four possible avenues of attack:

1. You can reduce or minimize your gross income figure by converting income that normally would be included in gross income into certain forms of income that can be excluded from the gross. This means that amount of income will never even enter into the tax computation picture.

2. You can arrange your activities so that certain personal expenditures that you would normally make will be allowable as deductions, thus reducing both your gross income and your taxable income.

3. You can take advantage of special credits that the tax code allows as dollar-for-dollar offsets to your final tax liability.

4. You can reduce or eliminate your tax by attacking the progressivity of our tax rates structure through the allocation of family income to different family members and entities.

Chapter 9 discusses how this fourth very special and very sophisticated tax planning technique works.

The following chapters will take you through these tax sheltering and elimination approaches.

CHAPTER 4

Exclusions— Tax-Free Money

"Thank God we don't get all the government we pay for."

WILL ROGERS

"When men get in the habit of helping themselves to the property of others, they cannot easily be cured of it."

"The history of our tax code, in economic terms, mirrors the course of most addictions: advancing dependence, diminished returns, and deteriorating health of the afflicted."

A 1909 EDITORIAL OPPOSING THE VERY FIRST
INCOME TAX
The New York Times

"When Congress talks of tax reform, grab your wallet and run for cover."

SENATOR STEVE SYMMS of Idaho

"You understand it, Stanley. I almost understand it. Now I must go out and teach it to 2,000 agents who have to apply it, and God help the millions of people who have to live with it."

AN INTERNAL REVENUE SERVICE COMMISSIONER,
in response to a technical proposal sponsored
by tax expert Stanley Surrey

In their infinite wisdom, Congress and the courts have decided that some income should not be taxed—that is, it should not even enter into the tax computation picture. The tax code and relevant case law therefore have provided that certain items received by you may be excluded from gross income for any one of the following four reasons:

1. The item may be excluded for constitutional reasons. For example, it has been argued that certain interest on state and municipal bonds is not subject to federal taxation because of the fear that "the power to tax is the power to destroy." Such interest, therefore, is constitutionally exempt from federal taxation.

2. The item received may not be true income but rather a return of cost. For example, when you lend money and then later collect it, the receipt of that money collected is merely a return of your original loan. Alternatively, when you sell property, part of the proceeds of the sale represents a return of your cost, and therefore only the excess of the proceeds over your original cost for that property represents true income.

3. Congress has from time to time seen fit to relieve certain items from taxation for equitable or other reasons. Each exclusion has its own legislative history and reason for enactment. Some exclusions are intended as a form of indirect welfare payments, as when certain injury or sickness payments are excluded from income. Other exclusions prevent double taxation of income or provide incentives for socially desirable activities. For example, scholarships for tuition may be excluded from the income of the recipient. Alternatively, other exclusions have been enacted by Congress to rectify the effects of judicially imposed decisions. For example, the value of improvements to property made by a lessee has been excluded from the lessor's income upon the termination of the lease in reaction to a Supreme Court decision that such value was taxable income.

4. Certain items have been excluded from gross income on the basis of administrative discretion and efficiency. For example, if you buy property from your employer at a reduced price, you normally must include in your income as extra pay the excess of the property's fair market value over what you paid for it. But if such employee discounts are generally available and are not part of negotiated compensation, the discounts are

not generally included in your gross income. This is because of the administrative difficulty the Internal Revenue Service would have in identifying and valuing such discounts. Other employee fringe benefits, such as free parking or nonbusiness use of your employer's facilities, would also be excluded from your gross income for the same reasons.

This chapter will detail those items that are not taxable and explain how you can use the availability of these items to reduce your income tax.

A Alternatives to "Earned Income"

The most important thing that you as a taxpayer can do to reduce your taxes to zero is to convert fully taxable income into excludable income. An exclusion is something that is not included in gross income. It is the best kind of revenue to receive. If you are in the 28 percent tax bracket (single, taxable income over $87,850), each dollar you convert to excludable income is the equivalent of getting a raise of 28 percent! Therefore, in negotiating compensation, you as an employee-taxpayer should examine the following forms of nontaxable remuneration for services rendered as alternatives to fully taxable cash income.

1 Hospitalization Premiums (Sec. 106)

Hospitalization premiums, including premiums for supplementary medical insurance (Medicare) paid by your employer, or your former employer if you are retired, are excludable from your income. However, if you have the *choice* when you retire either to receive continued coverage under your employer's group medical insurance plan or to receive a lump-sum payment and you choose the lump-sum payment, you must include the amount of the payment in your gross income at the time you make the choice to receive it. If you choose continued coverage, and if you qualify for itemization of deductions, you may deduct the amount you include in your income as a medical insurance premium.

For example, if you normally would purchase hospitalization insurance costing $500 a year, and you are in the 28 percent tax bracket, you would require pretax earnings of $694.44 in order to make that purchase. Of that

$694.44, 28 percent, or $194.44, would go to paying your taxes. In other words, having your employer pay the hospitalization premiums ($500) for you is the equivalent of receiving compensation of $694.44 from your employer and then paying your own hospitalization premiums. The savings of $194.44 to your employer can come back to you in *additional* alternative compensation.

2 Group Life Insurance Premiums (Sec. 79)

Group term life insurance coverage of $50,000 or less provided to you by your employer is excludable from your income. This rule applies even if you make an irrevocable assignment of your rights in the policy to another person who agrees to pay your part, if any, of the insurance premiums.

Group term life insurance is term life insurance protection (insurance for a fixed period of time) provided under a master policy or a group of individual policies. The policies must be life insurance contracts and form part of a plan of group insurance arranged for by an employer for all employees. The life insurance protection in a policy of permanent insurance (for example, a whole-life policy) is *not* term life insurance protection.

You are not taxed on the cost of group term life insurance protection of *more* than $50,000 if:

a) the coverage is provided after you have retired and are disabled;

b) your employer is the beneficiary of the policy for the entire period the insurance is in force during the tax year; *or*

c) the only beneficiary of the amount over $50,000 is a qualified charitable organization for the entire period the insurance is in force during the tax year. You do not make a deductible charitable contribution by naming a charitable organization as the beneficiary of your policy.

Where the policy provides only term insurance of $50,000 or less, the payment of premiums by your employer does not create any taxable income for you as an employee. The cost of insurance protection in excess of $50,000 paid by your employer is includable in your gross income according to the following table.

Table I

Uniform premiums for $1,000 of group term life insurance protection as of and after July 1, 1999 (Annual cost per $1,000 of protection)

Age	Amount Included in Income
Under 25	$ .60
25–29	$ .72
30–34	$ .96
35–39	$ 1.08
40–44	$ 1.20
45–49	$ 1.80
50–54	$ 2.76
55–59	$ 5.16
60–64	$ 7.92
65–69	$15.24
70 and above	$24.72

For example, assume you are 47 years old, hired July 1, 2013, and your employer carries a group policy that provides you with $60,000 of term life insurance. You must include only $9.00 ($1.80 × 10 divided by 6 months out of 12) in your income for your employer's payment of premiums. The rest of the premium paid for you is tax-free income. For 2014, you work the whole year and the amount is $18.00. Furthermore, any amount contributed by you toward the purchase of such group term life insurance reduces the amount of gross income that you realize. Had you contributed $9.00 in 2013 toward the purchase of the insurance, you would have had zero included in your income.

If two or more employers provide you with group term life insurance coverage, you must figure the amount of income from this source. Moreover, the cost of group term life insurance provided to you is the cost of life insurance provided to you during the tax year, regardless of when your employers pay the premiums.

For example, assume you are 51 years old and work for two employers. Both employers provide group term life insurance coverage for you. Your coverage with the first employer is $35,000 and with the second is $45,000. You pay premiums of $50 a year under the second employer's group plan. The amount to be included in your gross income is figured as follows:

First employer coverage	$35,000
Second employer coverage	+45,000
Total coverage	80,000
Minus exclusion	−50,000
Excess amount	30,000
Multiply cost per thousand, age 51 (from table)	×2.76
Cost of excess insurance for tax year	82.80
Minus premiums paid by you	−50.00
Amount included in income	$32.80

The cost of employer-provided group term life insurance must now be included in wages for FICA tax purposes to the extent that it is includable for income tax purposes. However, if you need life insurance, the use of this technique provides that insurance at either a tax-reduced or completely tax-free cost.

3 Group Legal Services Plans (Sec. 120)

Amounts paid by your employer for a qualified group legal services plan and the value of the benefits you receive under such a plan can no longer be excluded from your income. This exclusion expired July 1, 1992.

4 Accident and Health Plans (Sec. 105)

Although you realize no taxable income from the benefits of an accident and health policy on which you pay your own premiums, it may be more tax advantageous to have these policies paid by your employer. The general rule is that any benefits received by you as an employee under such policies are includable in your gross income.

There are, however, certain exceptions permitting you to exclude specific benefits that would otherwise be taxable under the general rule:

1. You may exclude benefits received directly or indirectly as reimbursement for medical expenses incurred for yourself, your spouse, or your dependents. If you deducted such medical expenses in a prior year, however, the reimbursement for these expenses must be included in the current year's income.

2. You may exclude benefits received for the permanent loss or the loss of the use of a member or function of the body, or a permanent disfiguration of yourself or your spouse or dependents, so long as the benefits are not related to absence from work.

The value of the exclusion of accident and health benefits can be shown by the following example:

Assume you lost a leg in an automobile accident that was unrelated to your work and you collected $10,000 from an insurance policy carried by your employer. If the payments were computed with reference to the nature of the injury and were not related to the time period that you were absent from work, then the entire $10,000 would be excluded from your income. Furthermore, if you incurred $3,000 in medical expenses that were covered under an employer-sponsored hospitalization plan, those payments would also be excluded from your income.

5 Employee Death Benefits (Sec. 101)

Amounts received as death benefits by your family or by your estate could be excluded up to an aggregate amount of $5,000, whether paid directly or indirectly by your employer.

This exclusion could not be claimed for accrued salary, unused leave, or compensation for past services. Furthermore, it could be claimed for a nonforfeitable amount you had the right to receive before your death *only* if it was received as a lump-sum distribution from a qualified plan or under an annuity contract purchased by an employer that is a tax-exempt organization.

The Small Business Job Protection Act of 1996 repealed this exclusion for decedents dying after August 20, 1996.

6 Merchandise Distributed to Employees on Holidays

Merchandise distributed to you as an employee on holidays, such as Christmas or New Year's Day, is excludable from your income if it is not of substantial value and is given for substantially noncompensatory reasons.

A turkey, for example, or similar merchandise given to you by your employer on a holiday therefore will not be includable in your taxable income. Unfortunately, this does not apply to cash distributions such as bonuses.

7 "Expenses of Your Employer"

The law does not tax reimbursement expenses that are true reimbursements for expenses of your employer rather than income amounts truly compensatory in nature.

Under this category are such items as reimbursements for cab fares and the payment of supper money. Rather than being excludable on the basis of statutory or constitutional language, these items are truly nontaxable as the result of Internal Revenue Service recognition of the impossible administrative verification problems in auditing such expenses. For whatever reasons, therefore, they are nontaxable.

If you as an employee can arrange with your employer to work from 11:00 A.M. to 7:00 P.M. rather than from 9:00 A.M. to 5:00 P.M. and she agrees to provide you with supper money, these personal supper expenses therefore can be converted into nontaxable income. In effect, no matter what bracket you are in, you have arranged for the Internal Revenue Service to buy you dinner.

8 Meals and Lodgings (Sec. 119)

The value of meals and lodgings provided to you, your spouse, and your dependents without charge by your employer is not taxable income if the following three criteria are met:

1. The meals or lodgings are provided at your employer's place of business.

2. The meals or lodgings are provided for the convenience of your employer.

3. In the case of lodging (but not meals), you must accept the lodging at your employer's place of business as a condition of your employment. This means that you must accept the lodging to carry out the duties of your job properly, for example, if you must be available for duty at all times.

Lodging includes the cost of heat, electricity, gas, water, sewerage service, and similar items that are necessary to make lodging habitable.

With reference to meals, you may exclude from income the value of meals provided to you during working hours so that you can be available for emergency calls, or because the nature of your employer's business restricts you to a short meal period. For example, if you are the only receptionist at your place of work, you must be available "at all times." If your employer provides you with lunch every day, that lunch is not includable in your income. Furthermore, the Supreme Court has ruled that such lunches do not constitute "wages" for social security taxes. They are truly *tax-free* (see TAM 9829001 where meals provided by a casino to its food service and security employees were excluded from their income and *Boyd Gaming Corp. v. Commissioner,* 9th Cir., No. 98-70123, 5/12/99 where 100 percent of the expenses of a casino's employee cafeteria were deductible as *de minimis* fringe benefits).

However, if you receive a cash allowance from your employer for meals or lodging, you must include the cash allowance in your income. The solution, therefore, is to have your employer provide the food, not the dollars. The net effect is the same to you but the net cost is substantially less.

Situations in which meals and lodging are furnished for the convenience of the employer normally include the following:

- A waitress is required to eat her meals on the premises during the busy lunch and breakfast hours.

- A worker is employed at a construction site in a remote part of Alaska. The employer must furnish meals and lodging due to the inaccessibility of other facilities.

- A bank furnishes meals on the premises to limit the time tellers are away during the busy hours.

- A hospital provides a free cafeteria for its staff. The hospital's business purpose in providing the meals is to induce employees to stay on the premises in case an emergency arises. These meals are not includable in the income of the staff, even though staff members are *not* required to eat on the premises.

The 1998 Reform Act now provides that *all* meals furnished to employees at the employers place of business shall be treated as "for the convenience of the employer" if more than half of such meals are furnished for the convenience of the employer.

This technique should be used extensively when married couples run their own businesses or professions. For example, assume the situation where one spouse performs the services and the other runs the office. That second spouse needs to be available "at all times" to answer the phone, receive clients, etc., and therefore any meals provided to that spouse would be deductible by the business as an expense but not includable as income to the recipient. The spouse must truly be employed and must be required to be on the business premises during lunchtime or the deduction will be disallowed as a sham (*Weidmann*, 89-1 USTC ¶9197 [DC N.Y., 1989]). In effect, what we have done again is to convert a personal expense—a meal—into nontaxable compensation. Again, the Internal Revenue Service is put into the position of helping to pay for your dinner.

9   Employee Discounts

You need not include as taxable income the discounts or privileges of relatively small value that you, as an employee, receive, where such discounts are given primarily to provide good employee relations and do not take on the character of additional compensation. This exclusion includes the usual courtesy discounts allowed to employees in many retail stores. But the value of discounts beyond a mere courtesy discount would be taxable income to you. Furthermore, if you buy property from your employer at less than fair market value, the amount of that discount is income.

For example, if you pay $2,000 for one of your employer's company cars that has a fair market value of $6,000, you are considered to have earned $4,000 of income on the transaction.

10   Workers' Compensation (Sec. 104)

Workers' compensation received for sickness or injury is fully exempt from tax. If you turn over your workers' compensation payments to your employer, and all or part of your regular salary continues to be paid, the excess of the salary payments over the amount of workers' compensation is taxable income.

For example, assume you are hurt on the job and are out of work for 6 weeks. Your employer continues to pay your salary of $200 a week, or $1,200 for the time you are absent. You also receive $75 a week, or a total of $450, in workers' compensation. Under your employment contract, you turn over all your workers' compensation to your employer. The $75 a week is fully excludable from your income and the balance is taxable income.

11 "Cafeteria" Plans (Sec. 125)

Employer contributions under a written "cafeteria" plan, "salary deduction plan," or "flexible spending or benefit plan," permitting you as a participant to select between taxable and nontaxable benefits, are excludable from your income to the extent that you choose nontaxable benefits.

Nontaxable benefits include medical expenses including nonprescription drugs (but not vitamins), group life insurance (up to $50,000 coverage), disability benefits, dependent care, and accident and health benefits to the extent that such benefits are excludable from gross income.

Such employer contributions may be excluded if the following conditions are satisfied:

- Participation in the cafeteria plan must be restricted to employees.

- The same service requirement must apply to all participants.

- The participant chooses nontaxable benefits.

- The plan's eligibility requirements do not discriminate in favor of "highly compensated individuals."

- Employer contributions and employee benefits do not favor "highly compensated participants."

The deadline for the use of these funds has been extended to March 15 of the next year (Notice 2005-42), but the plan must allow it.

As of January 1, 2011, over-the-counter drugs don't qualify. Payments from these plans are limited to prescription drugs and insulin. As of January 1, 2013, pay-ins to Health Flexible Spending Accounts will be capped at $2,500 a year.

12 Dependent Care Assistance Program (Sec. 129)

For tax years after 1981, the value of the dependent care assistance that an employer provides to employees under a dependent care assistance program is not generally includable in the employee's gross income. However, if payments for child care expenses are made to someone who is a child of the employee under age 19 or who qualifies for a dependency exemption for the employee, the payments are not excludable. If the child is not under age 19 and is not claimed as a dependent, such payments *do* qualify (*Langlois,* T.C.M. 1988–415).

The value of dependent care assistance that you may exclude from your pay is limited. If you are an employee who is not married at the end of the tax year, the limit is equivalent to your earned income for that year. For married employees the limit is the lesser of: (a) the employee's earned income for the tax year; or (b) the employee's spouse's earned income for the tax year. The Tax Reform Act of 1986 put a $5,000 cap on dependent care expenses. Moreover, the Family Support Act of 1988 provides that any amount excluded under a dependent care assistance program reduces the amount of expenses otherwise eligible for the child care credit.

A dependent care assistance program is a plan written by the employer for the exclusive benefit of the employees and that meets the following requirements:

1. *Eligibility.* The program must benefit employees who qualify under a classification set up by the employer, and the Secretary of the Treasury must find it nondiscriminatory in favor of employees who are officers, owners, or highly compensated, or who are dependents of these employees. However, the employer does not have to include in this program employees who are covered by what the Secretary of Labor considers to be a collective bargaining agreement between employee representatives and one or more employers if there is evidence that the dependent care benefits were the subject of good faith bargaining between the representatives and the employer.

2. *Limitation on principal shareholders or owners.* Not more than 25 percent of the amounts paid or incurred by an employer for the dependent care assistance during the year may be for individuals who are shareholders or owners (or their spouses or dependents) each of whom—on any day of the year—owns more than 5 percent of the stock or of the capital or profit interest in the employer.

3. *Funding.* An employer is not required to fund a dependent care assistance program.

4. *Notification of availability.* An employer must provide all eligible employees with a reasonable notification of the availability and terms of the dependent care assistance program.

5. *Notification to participants.* The plan will give each employee, by January 31, a written statement showing the amounts paid for the expenses incurred by the employer in providing dependent care assistance to the employee during the calendar year.

13 Employer Educational Assistance (Sec. 127)

This provision excludes from an employee's gross income employer-provided educational assistance, regardless of whether or not the education is job-related. The provision did not apply to any payment for graduate-level courses (except for those taken in 1995 and those beginning prior to July 1, 1996) taken by an individual pursuing a program leading to an advanced academic or professional degree and is generally not available for any education involving sports, games, or hobbies. Employers are not required to withhold on educational assistance payments, but the exclusion is limited to $5,250 per individual per calendar year. Educational expenses that would be deductible by an employee as trade or business expenses if they had been paid by the employee are not subject to this $5,250 cap.

The plan must provide that not more than 5 percent of the benefits paid or incurred annually will be attributable to owners.

The 2001 Tax Relief Act made this exclusion permanent and it was extended to cover graduate education as of January 1, 2002. Every employer who maintains an educational assistance program must file a return showing the number of employees eligible to participate in the program; the number participating; the total cost of the program; the employer's name, address, and taxpayer identification number; and the type of business in which the employer is engaged.

In PLR 200339017, the IRS validated a law firm's plan for assisting its non-lawyer employees with the cost of attending law school.

14 Employee Awards (Sec. 274)

Under prior law, an employee award such as emblematic jewelry or an engraved plaque awarded an employee for job performance, which was not excludable as a scientific or other achievement award, was generally excludable from gross income if it qualified as a gift. If the employee award was includable in the employee's income, the employer was entitled to a deduction for the award as a business expense. If the award was excludable as a gift, the employer's deduction was limited to a maximum of $25 for the cost of gifts to any one employee in any one tax year.

If a gift of tangible personal property was awarded to an employee for length of service, safety achievement, or productivity, the deduction ceiling was raised from $25 to $400. If a length of service, safety, or productivity award was a *qualified plan award,* the ceiling on the employer's deduction was $1,600, provided that the average cost of all awards provided under the plan for qualified awards did not exceed $400. A qualified plan award was one awarded (a) under a permanent written program of the employer which (b) does not discriminate in favor of officers, shareholders, or highly compensated employees.

The Tax Reform Act of 1986 changed these rules. That law states specifically that employee awards will *not* be excludable from the employee's income as gifts. Since such awards will no longer be treated as gifts (and are therefore fully includable as income to the employee), the limitations described on employer deductions for business gifts will no longer apply. The entire amount of the award (assuming ordinary, necessary, and reasonable tests are met) will be deductible.

Employee awards generally will be includable in the income of the employee and will be deductible by the employer, subject to two limited exceptions. One exception applies to awards that are *qualified plan awards.*

The definition of a qualified plan award under new law is essentially the same as under prior law: one awarded (a) under a permanent written program of the employer which (b) does not discriminate in favor of officers, shareholders, or highly compensated employees. If an award is a qualified plan award, the award is excludable by the employee *and* deductible by the employer only to the extent that the cost to the employer of all such awards made to the employee during the taxable year (whether or not qualified plan awards) does not exceed $1,600. The $400 average cost limitation described for qualified plan awards has been retained: That is, awards will not be considered qualified plan awards unless the average cost limitation is met.

The second exception applies to certain awards that are not qualified plan awards. If the award is not a qualified plan award (for example, if it is awarded under an informal plan or in a discriminatory fashion), the award will be excludable by the employee *and* deductible by the employer only to the extent that the cost of all such awards that are not qualified plan awards provided to the employee during the taxable year does not exceed $400.

Under current law if the cost to the employer of the qualified plan award exceeds the limits just described, then the employee must include in income the *greater* of (a) the excess of the cost of the award over the amount allowable as a deduction (but not more than the award's value), or (b) the excess of the value of the award over the amount allowable as a deduction. If the employer's cost is *not* over the applicable limit, the employee may exclude the award regardless of its value.

Example: If an employer gave an employee one qualified plan award that cost the employer $2,000 and had a value of $1,900, the employee would have to include $400 (cost minus $1,600 limitation) in income. If the award cost $2,000 and had a value of $2,200, the employee would have to include $600 in income (its value minus the $1,600 limitation).

Furthermore, to be excludable under *either* of the exceptions just described, an award must be an *employee achievement award.* Only awards that are length of service awards or safety achievement awards will qualify as employee achievement awards. Professional, administrative, managerial, and clerical employees do not qualify for safety achievement awards for tax purposes. A significant change in the 1986 law is that awards for productivity will no longer qualify for an exclusion. Awards for productivity will simply be treated as compensation.

Also, the 1986 law specifically stated that employee achievement awards must be tangible personal property (not cash, securities, or life insurance). To the extent employee awards are excludable from income, they are also exempt from the Social Security and other employer withholding taxes.

After the 1986 law there would no longer be any need to make the subjective determination as to whether the employee award is a gift. No employee awards will be treated as gifts for income tax purposes.

However, the 1986 law created a double whammy with respect to employee achievement awards that are in excess of the applicable limits. They are not deductible by the employer and must be included in the gross income of the employee. Because of this double whammy, beginning in 1987 employers had to keep employee achievement awards for length of service and safety achievement within the applicable dollar amount limitations.

Example: An insurance company has a program of employee achievement awards provided to employees for length of service achievement, but the arrangement discriminates in favor of highly compensated employees. The company provides a top executive with a computer that cost the company $600. The computer has a value of $700. The cost of the computer is deductible by the employer only to the extent of $400. Since the computer's cost to the employer is more than $400, the executive must include the excess of its $700 value over the employer's $400 deductible portion in gross income. The reportable amount would be $300.

The 1986 law does make it easier to plan employee achievement award programs since the interest of the employer corresponds with the interest of the employee; that is, the employer receives a deduction under the same circumstances that the employee receives an exclusion. The 1986 law is less favorable with respect to employee awards in that the exclusion is not available for awards given for productivity of the employee.

The 1986 law does not change the rules for fringe benefits which are *de minimis* under Sec. 132(e). Under these rules employees may exclude from income employee awards that are of nominal value, such as holiday turkeys or employee picnics. However, the Senate Finance Committee's Report on the Tax Reform Act states that certain employee awards for length of service "such as a gold watch" may be treated under the *de minimis* provision! The rationale appears to be that such an award is the functional equivalent of several smaller gifts made over the course of many years of service. Or perhaps the committee has been too busy in recent years to follow the price of gold.

15 Clergy Housing Allowance (Sec. 107)

If you're a member of the clergy, you can exclude from taxes part of your income that's attributated to housing. The amount you exclude is equal to the fair market value of the property or the amount used to provide the home, whichever is less. You no longer can have more than one house qualify if ministerial services are provided at both (*Driscoll v. Commissioner of IRS,* T.C. No. 1070-07, 135 T.C. No. 27, December 14, 2010, which was reversed by the 11th Circuit, on February 18, 2012.)

16 Miscellaneous Fringe Benefits

An employer can give discount fare cards, passes, or tokens to an employee who takes public transportation to work. If the subsidy provided

is not worth more than $245 per month to an employee, it is considered to be a *de minimis* fringe benefit. The employer can deduct it, but you, as an employee, received it tax-free (Regulation Section 1.132-6T[d][1]). Note, however, that if the employer supplies you with more than $245 a month toward the public transportation commute, only the amount in excess of $245 is taxable as compensation income (Notice 94-3) (Rev. Proc. 2005-70).

Employer-provided free parking, up to a maximum value of $245 per month, is also excludable from income.

An employer can designate $20 per month of your pretax earnings for expenses related to bicycle commuting. But if this occurs, you can't claim the parking or transit benefits, which have the higher per month allowance.

B Donative Items

17 Gifts, Bequests, and Inheritances (Sec. 102)

If you receive money or property by bequest, devise, or inheritance, that receipt does not constitute taxable income to you. (Any income produced by that money or property while in your hands, though, is taxable in the usual fashion.)

Only money and property received from a decedent or as a bona fide gift fall under this rule. For a transfer to constitute a gift, there must be a motive of "detached and disinterested generosity." The exclusion, though, applies only to the donee.

Here you must be careful. For purposes of taxation, a simple assignment of income is ineffective. For example, if you make a gift of salary receivable from your employer to your child, even though that check goes directly to your child, that income is still taxable to you. You were the one who earned it and therefore are the one who is taxed on that earning. Your child, however, will exclude the "gift" and not be taxed on its value.

But once property is conveyed, the impact of taxation does shift to the donee. Thus for example, if you are in the 28 percent bracket and own a bond yielding $1,000 in interest, you must pay taxes of $280, leaving you only $720 of after-tax disposable income. Alternatively, if you transfer that bond to your child and allow your child to receive the income, the first $1,000 of interest to

that child will be completely tax-free. In terms of net family disposable income, the total amount available will be increased by $280.

The advantages of interfamily income allocation will be discussed extensively later in the book. The important thing to recognize under this section is that the transfer of the bond to your child is not at all a taxable transaction—that is, your child will not be taxed on the value of the bonds received. This exclusion of gifts from the gross income of the recipient constitutes the foundation of the income allocation strategies and techniques to be discussed later.

18 Scholarships and Fellowships (Sec. 117)

Under prior law, if you received a scholarship or fellowship grant, you could exclude that amount from your gross income, subject to certain limits, depending upon whether you are a degree candidate. To qualify for this exclusion, the payment had to be made for your education and training. The payment did not qualify, however, if it was made to pay you either for past, present, or future services, or for studies or research conducted mostly for the grantor's benefit.

A scholarship generally means an amount paid for the benefit of a student at an educational organization, to aid in the student's pursuit of studies. An educational organization is any organization that normally maintains a regular faculty and curriculum and has a regularly organized body of students in attendance at the place where its educational activities are carried on. A fellowship is the same as a scholarship, but the individual receiving aid does not have to be enrolled at an educational institution, and research is usually the aim.

Under current law, the exclusion will be limited to scholarships or fellowship grants to individuals who are degree candidates at educational institutions that maintain a regular faculty and curriculum and have a regularly enrolled body of students. There will no longer be an exclusion available to nondegree candidates or for scholarships granted by organizations other than qualified educational institutions. In addition, the exclusion will be available only with respect to payments that are actually used for tuition, enrollment fees, books, supplies, and other equipment required for courses of instruction. Payments for teaching, research, or other services rendered to the institution by a degree candidate will no longer qualify for the exclusion.

The exclusion does apply to *qualified tuition reductions.* A qualified tuition reduction is a tuition reduction for the employees, spouses, and dependent

children of employees of educational institutions for studies below the graduate level, under a plan that does not discriminate in favor of officers, owners, or highly compensated employees of the institution.

Amounts paid to help you in pursuing your studies or research are not excludable if the studies or the research is mostly for the benefit of the grantor. However, if the main purpose is to further your education and training, and the amounts are not payment for services, they would be excludable. This is true even if you must give progress reports to the grantor, or if the results of your studies or research may slightly benefit the grantor.

Payments for your past, present, or future services are not excludable, *but* there is a very important exception that must be kept in mind: If you work for pay for a research project, you generally must include that pay in income. Your pay is not a scholarship or fellowship grant merely because the research can be used for credit toward a degree. However, if similar services are required of all candidates for the degree, as a reasonable condition for it, you may exclude the pay from your gross income.

Your pay for services over and above those specifically needed for the degree must be included in your gross income. Interns, resident physicians, and registered nurses in training in a hospital therefore must include their pay in gross income. But tuition and work payments given to you under a work study program are considered scholarships if your college, under its educational philosophy, requires all students to take part in a work program. These payments, therefore, are excludable from your income. Alternatively, payments you receive for service *not* required by the work program must be included in your income. Furthermore, amounts paid by your employer to you when you are on educational leave also are not excludable.

The following example will demonstrate the value of the potential exclusion of scholarships and fellowship grants from your income: In a contest sponsored by a business firm, you receive a scholarship award of $5,000 that you can use only for tuition, books, and supplies when enrolled as a candidate for a degree at a certain college. You do not include any of the $5,000 award in your gross income if:

a) you are not employed by the firm at the time of the award;

b) you are not being paid for services you provided for the firm in the past; *and*

c) you are not required to provide future services for the firm.

If you are in the 28 percent bracket and desire to enroll as a candidate for a degree, you would have had to earn $6,944.40 before tax in order to have $5,000 after tax to pay for the college tuition and fees. The enormous financial advantage of the exclusion of scholarships and fellowships from taxable income thus becomes very clear. Remember, however, that the same after-tax effect can be achieved if your employer establishes an employee education assistance plan as discussed earlier.

Tax Treatment of Scholarship and Fellowship Payments

Payment for	Degree candidate	Not a degree candidate
Tuition	Tax free	Taxable
Fees	Tax free[1]	Taxable
Books	Tax free[1]	Taxable
Supplies	Tax free[1]	Taxable
Equipment	Tax free[1]	Taxable
Room	Taxable	Taxable
Board	Taxable	Taxable
Travel	Taxable	Taxable
Teaching	Taxable[2]	Taxable
Research services	Taxable[2]	Taxable
Other services	Taxable[2]	Taxable

[1] If required of all students in the course.

[2] Does not include amounts received under the National Health Service Corps Scholarship Program or the Armed Forces Health Professions Scholarship and Financial Assistance Program.

19 Prizes and Awards (Sec. 74)

Prior to 1987, prizes and awards received in recognition of past accomplishments—in religious, charitable, scientific, artistic, educational, literary, or civic fields—were excludable income if the winners were chosen without action on their part and were not expected to perform any future services. For example, if you received a Pulitzer or Nobel Prize or any other award and were selected for your past work, this award was not includable in your income. Under current law, the exclusion for scientific and other achievement awards is repealed. The only exception to the repeal is when the recipient assigns the award to a governmental unit or charitable organization.

The provision in the current law which permits you to exclude the value of the prize or award if you assign it to the government or a charity is of limited benefit. Under prior law an excludable award could be contributed to charity and the recipient contributor could take a deduction for the contribution. Under new law you may exclude the prize or award if you contribute it to a charitable organization, but your contribution is disallowed. The end result is that you have simply given away what you received and have no extra income and no deduction. In effect, this is no different from your having included the prize or award in gross income and then taken a charitable deduction for contributing it.

In addition, if you win a prize in a lucky number drawing, a television or radio quiz program, a beauty contest, or some other event, that prize is taxable. So, too, are awards or bonuses given to you as an employee for your good work or for suggestions. These are not instances where the winners have been chosen without action on their part and are not expected to perform any future services.

Taxable prizes and awards in goods and services must be included in your income at their fair market value to you. This is very important. It is not the general fair market value but rather the fair market value of that prize *to you*. If you already have two attaché cases and win a third on a quiz show, the value of that third attaché case *to you* may be negligible. It clearly would not be its full retail selling price. However, when sold, the amount received for such prizes or awards is normally deemed to be equal to their fair market value. If, for example, you receive an award of a car that retails for $10,000 and immediately sell that car to a third party for $8,000, the amount to be included in your income would be the $8,000 figure rather than the $10,000 figure.

Be careful here. A bargain sale to a relative may be considered part sale, part gift. If you sold that $10,000 car to your brother for $5,000, the Internal Revenue Service might successfully argue that you received income of $10,000 and made a gift of the $5,000 difference to your brother. One technique that has been used to avoid this is to sell the car for $5,000 to an independent third party, who could turn around and resell the car to your brother for the same $5,000. Watch the structuring of such three-party transactions. There must be no prearranged agreement for the third party to resell to your brother, and that third party must be truly independent. Otherwise, if the Internal Revenue Service catches on, it will collapse the two transactions, deem the first sale to be a sham, and successfully establish the true nature of the gift to your brother.

20 Qualified Charitable Distributions (QCDs)

A distribution from an IRA normally results in an increase in adjusted gross income (AGI). This higher AGI can reduce your medical expenses, miscellaneous deductions, total itemized deductions, exemptions, and your qualification for multiple credits.

Passed in 2006, and now extended through 2013, QCDs allow a direct distribution to a charity without the inclusion amount being included in income. Requirements for a QCD are:

- The individual must be older than 70½ when the distribution is made.

- Charities must be eligible to receive tax-deductible charitable contributions.

- The maximum QCD is $100,000, although a spouse can also make a $100,000 QCD if the couple files a joint income tax return.

- The $100,000 maximum QCD does not apply to the overall charitable deduction limit. Individuals may make charitable contributions that exceed 50 percent of adjusted gross income.

- The distribution must be a direct transfer from the IRA to the charity.

- The distribution first comes from taxable funds, then from any nondeductible IRA contributions. Previously, distributions would have been allocated proportionately between deductible and nondeductible contributions.

C Investors

21 Interest on State and Municipal Obligations (Sec. 103)

You can exclude from gross income all interest earned on obligations of a state, territory, municipality, or any political subdivision, except in the case of arbitrage bonds issued after October 9, 1969.

An *arbitrage bond* is an obligation, the proceeds of which are reasonably expected to be used to acquire other securities or obligations that are expected over the term of the issue to yield a materially higher rate of return. This exception prohibits state and local governments from issuing bonds at a low interest rate because of their tax-exempt nature and using the proceeds to buy federal or industrial bonds returning a higher yield. Since the state or local government does not pay an income tax on the difference, this exception prevents the federal government from becoming an unintended source for financing state and local government operations.

If you are in a sufficiently high tax bracket, the advantages of purchasing a state or municipal bond can be substantial. If you are in a 28 percent bracket, a $6\frac{1}{2}$ percent yield on a municipal obligation is the equivalent of a 9.03 percent yield on a nonexempt security. Moreover, the risk factor on a state or municipal obligation will normally be far lower than that on an industrial security.

If Your Marginal Tax Rate Is:	And Your Tax-Exempt Investment Yields					
	4%	5%	6%	6.5%	7%	7.5%
	It Is the Equivalent of a Taxable Investment Yielding:					
15%	4.71	5.88	7.06	7.65	8.24	8.82
25%	5.33	6.67	8.00	8.67	9.33	10.00
28%	5.56	6.94	8.33	9.03	9.72	10.42
33%	5.97	7.46	8.96	9.70	10.45	11.19
35%	6.15	7.69	9.23	10.00	10.77	11.54

The higher the tax bracket, the greater the attraction of a tax-exempt security. The following table shows the tax-exempt equivalent yield to a taxable investment at various marginal tax rates:

Click on www.investinginbonds.com to compare taxable and tax-free yields.

D Benefits for the Elderly

22 Public Assistance Payments

Benefit payments from a general welfare fund in the interest of the general public, such as payments to aid the indigent or the blind, or payments to crime victims, are excludable from your gross income. These welfare payments have been excluded by the Internal Revenue Service, because the IRS sees them in the nature of gifts.[1]

23 Social Security and Other Retirement Benefits

Social Security benefits under the federal Social Security programs may not be taxable. Social Security benefits received from foreign countries, however, are taxable unless they are specifically exempt by treaty.

Basic railroad retirement benefits are also not taxable. Railroad retirement lump-sum payments, commonly known as either the insurance lump-sum payment or the residual payment, are excluded from your gross income as well.

The Internal Revenue Service tax code does not specifically exclude Social Security benefits, but these benefits were declared not subject to tax by the Internal Revenue Commissioner.[2] According to the Internal Revenue Service, these payments are in part a return of the after-tax contributions made by the individual and in part a welfare or annuity payment from the government.

---

1. Rev. Rul. 71-425, 1971–2 CB 76.
2. Rev. Rul. 70-217, 1970-1 CB 12.

These welfare payments have been viewed by the Internal Revenue Service as essentially in the nature of gifts.[3]

Moreover, basic Medicare benefits received under the Social Security Act are also excluded from gross income since they are considered Social Security payments. So also are supplementary benefits covering costs of doctors' services and other items not covered under basic Medicare, as they are in the nature of medical insurance payments.

Note, however, that since January 1, 1984, part of your Social Security benefits have been subject to tax if your income exceeded a specified level determined by formula. There are three factors used in determining how much of your Social Security benefits, if any, will be included in taxable income: (1) your *income,* defined as your adjusted gross income for federal income tax plus any tax-exempt interest, plus any foreign source income you receive during the year; (2) your *half-benefit,* defined as half the Social Security income you (and, if you're married and filing jointly, your spouse) receive during the year; and (3) your *base amount,* which is $25,000 for a single taxpayer, $32,000 for a married couple filing jointly, and zero for a married couple filing separately (unless they have lived apart for the entire tax year, in which case they qualify for the $25,000 base amount).

The amount of Social Security income to be reported, if any, was 50 percent of the amount by which (1) your income plus (2) your half-benefit exceeds (3) your base amount. However, in no event will more than your half-benefit be reported as taxable income.

For example, assume a married couple filing jointly has an adjusted gross income of $20,000 plus tax-exempt interest of $8,000. They therefore have *income* of $28,000. If they have Social Security income of $12,000 they will report $1,000 of that benefit as taxable income as follows:

Income	$28,000
Half-benefit	+$6,000
Total	$34,000
Base Amount	−$32,000
Difference	$2,000
50% of difference	$1,000
Taxable S.S. benefit	$1,000

---

3. Rev. Rul. 71-425, 1971-1 CB 76.

Effective after December 31, 1993, the Omnibus Budget Reconciliation Act of 1993 created a second tier of Social Security benefit inclusion in gross income. Prior law now applies to *income* up to $34,000 for unmarried individuals and $44,000 for married individuals filing joint returns. For taxpayers with *income* above these amounts, the amount included in income shall be the *lesser* of:

1. 85 percent of your total Social Security benefit, or
2. the sum of:

    a) the smaller of (i) the amount included under prior law; or (ii) $4,500 (if unmarried) or $6,000 (if married filing jointly)[4]

    plus

    b) 85 percent of the excess of your *income* over the new applicable second tier threshold amounts ($34,000 and $44,000).

Now that Social Security payments may be taxable, recipients should find out whether their benefits are included as part of their adjusted gross income under the income tax laws of the states where they reside. Eleven states have, in the past, exempted from their income taxes Social Security benefits now included in federal adjusted gross income: Delaware, Hawaii, Idaho, Indiana, Maine, New Mexico, New York, South Carolina, Virginia, West Virginia, and Wisconsin. Minnesota has provided an exclusion from federal adjusted gross income for Social Security benefits in a portion of the calculation of the maximum income exclusion for pensions and retirement benefits. Other states, such as New Jersey, specifically exempt Social Security from taxation. Check your own state rules.

24 Annuities (Sec. 72)

An annuity is a type of investment that requires you to pay a fixed amount in exchange for the right to receive periodic payments for your life or for some definite period. If the annuity payments are based on your life, or the life of another individual, the amounts of such payments are determined through the use of standard mortality tables.

---

4. These amounts equal 50 percent of the difference between the prior and new thresholds: i.e., 50 percent of $34,000 − $25,000 = $4,500; 50 percent of $44,000 − $32,000 = $6,000.

When you receive the income from this annuity, part of what you are receiving represents a recovery of your initial investment. This recovery amount is fully excluded from income. The Internal Revenue Service provides tables with which you can compute your exclusion ratio. This exclusion ratio remains the same and continues to be applied to annuity payments even if you outlive your life expectancy.

For example, assume you have made principal payments into an annuity of $60,000 in return for payment of $500 per month for life. Also assume that the tables show that your life expectancy is 15 years from the annuity starting date. Your investment in the contract is $60,000 and your expected return is $6,000 per year times 15 years, or $90,000. You would exclude two-thirds of each payment ($6,000 × $\frac{2}{3}$) or a total of $4,000 yearly. That $4,000 is a nontaxable return of capital; the remaining $2,000 is taxable income.

In IRS Notice 88-18, the IRS came up with an easier way for some retirees to compute how much of their pension or annuity payments are tax-free. Under this IRS safe-harbor method, the expected number of monthly annuity payments is based on your age at the annuity's starting date, rather than on the life expectancy tables contained in Regulation Section 1.72-9. The same number is used for a single-life annuity or a joint and survivor annuity.

Age of Distributee	Number of Payments
55 and under	300
56 to 60	260
61 to 65	240
66 to 70	170
71 and over	120

For example, if you begin receiving payments at age 65, you would divide your total investment by 240 to find out how much of each payment is tax-free.

The Small Business Job Protection Act of 1996 provided that basis recovery on payments from qualified plan annuities generally will be determined under a method similar to the prior law simplified alternative method provided by the IRS above. The portion of each annuity payment that represents a return of basis is equal to the employee's total basis as of the annuity starting date, divided by the number of anticipated payments under the following table:

IRS Table V—One Life
Life Expectancies

Age	Years Remaining	Age	Years Remaining	Age	Years Remaining
5	76.6	42	40.6	79	10.0
6	75.6	43	39.6	80	9.5
7	74.7	44	38.7	81	8.9
8	73.7	45	37.7	82	8.4
9	72.7	46	36.8	83	7.9
10	71.7	47	35.9	84	7.4
11	70.7	48	34.0	85	6.9
12	69.7	49	34.0	86	6.5
13	68.8	50	33.1	87	6.1
14	67.8	51	32.2	88	5.7
15	66.8	52	31.3	89	5.3
16	65.8	53	30.4	90	5.0
17	64.8	54	29.5	91	4.7
18	63.9	55	28.6	92	4.4
19	62.9	56	27.7	93	4.1
20	61.9	57	26.8	94	3.9
21	60.9	58	25.9	95	3.7
22	59.9	59	25.0	96	3.4
23	59.0	60	24.2	97	3.2
24	58.0	61	23.3	98	3.0
25	57.0	62	22.5	99	2.8
26	56.0	63	21.6	100	2.7
27	55.1	64	20.8	101	2.5
28	54.1	65	20.0	102	2.3
29	53.1	66	19.2	103	2.1
30	52.2	67	18.4	104	1.9
31	51.2	68	17.6	105	1.8
32	50.2	69	16.6	106	1.6
33	49.3	70	16.0	107	1.4
34	48.3	71	15.3	108	1.3
35	47.3	72	14.6	109	1.1
36	46.4	73	13.9	110	1.0
37	45.4	74	13.2	111	.9
38	44.4	75	12.5	112	.8
39	43.5	76	11.9	113	.7
40	42.5	77	11.2	114	.6
41	41.5	78	10.6	115	.5

Age	Number of Payments
Not more than 55	360
56 to 60	310
61 to 65	260
66 to 70	210
More than 70	160

This provision was effective with respect to annuity starting dates beginning 90 days after the date of enactment (August 20, 1996). Therefore, if your annuity starting date is after November 18, 1996, you must use this new simplified method.

For annuity starting dates beginning after November 18, 1996, but before January 1, 1997, the total number of monthly annuity payments expected to be received is based on the primary annuitant's age at the annuity starting date. The same expected number of payments applies to an annuitant whether he or she is receiving a single life annuity or a joint and survivor annuity.

For annuity starting dates after December 31, 1997, the table used to determine the expected number of payments depends on whether payments are based on the life of more than one individual.

For joint and survivor annuities, the total number of monthly annuity payments expected to be received is based on the combined ages of the annuities at the starting date, IRS said. For annuities that are not based on life expectancies, the expected number of payments is the number of monthly annuity payments under the contract (Notice 98-2).

Whichever method you use, once you have received your investment back, your exclusion ratio expires. Although the total tax-free recoupment is the same with both methods, using the optional second method may reclaim your investment faster. For example, under a joint and survivor annuity, payments continue until the death of the second beneficiary. Since two beneficiaries have a longer life expectancy, and therefore more payments over which to recover the investment, using the regular IRS method results in a smaller portion of each payment coming back tax-free. With the optional method, it is irrelevant whether or not the joint and survivor annuity is elected.

The IRS optional second method could have been used for payments from annuities that began distributions after July 1, 1986. If you began receiving payments before then, you must use the old method. New retirees will now use the new method as per the 1996 law.

25 Sale of Your Home (Sec. 121)

You may exclude from your gross income some or all of your gain from the sale or exchange of your main home, if you meet certain ownership and use tests at the time of the sale or exchange.

Prior to May 7, 1997, you could have expected to exclude from your gross income $125,000 (the maximum allowable) of gain on the sale or exchange of your main home *if:*

a) you were age 55 or older before the date of the sale or exchange;

b) you owned and lived in the property sold or exchanged as your main home for at least three years out of the five-year period ending on the date of the sale or exchange; *and*

c) you or your spouse never excluded gain on the sale or exchange of a home after July 20, 1981.

All three tests must be met by one taxpayer. For example, you may be age 55, and your younger spouse may have owned and lived alone in the property for the required 3 year period, but because you are not one taxpayer, you cannot take the exclusion.

These rules were *all* changed by the Tax Relief Act of 1997. *After May 6, 1997* joint filers can exclude, as often as every 2 years, as much as $500,000 ($250,000 for single filers) in gain on the sale of a principal residence occupied for 2 of the 5 years prior to sale. To qualify, you must have used the house as your principal residence for at least 2 out of the 5 years prior to the sale. However, the exclusion will be available once every 2 years, although there are exceptions to that rule too. Those close to retirement or whose children have moved out may be big winners here. They can now sell their old, big houses without the need to reinvest in new, more expensive homes to avoid taxation on the gains. They can now buy smaller residences, or even rent. The prior law provision under Section 1034 that deferred taxation upon a rollover of the sales proceeds into a new home has been repealed.

You can get a partial exclusion based on the time of use and ownership, but only if the sale is required because of a *change in place of employment, health reasons, or unforeseen circumstances.* The IRS has been very flexible in defining "unforeseen circumstances." Even the birth of twins or the hostility of neighbors (PLR 200403049) will now qualify. See page 92 for details.

Unfortunately, the 1997 law was unclear if you owned the property for less than 2 years. The 1998 Act provided the answer. It provides partial relief based on a fraction of the *maximum exclusion,* rather than on the basis of your actual realized profit.

For example, assume you bought a house in 2012 for $250,000 and sell it in 2013 for a $25,000 profit. Because you are married, and lived there 1 year, you are eligible for half the $500,000 exclusion you would have been entitled to had you been there the full 2 years. Half the exclusion is $250,000, greater than the gain of $25,000, and therefore none of your gain is taxable. Had the alternative interpretation applied, you would have been able to exclude half your profit, and paid tax on the remaining $12,500.

Not everybody wins on this one. Miss Fortune bought her home in 2012 for $1.5 million and sold it 1 year later for a $400,000 profit. Since she is single and lived there only half the required 2 years, she gets to exclude $125,000, and pay tax on $275,000 of her gain. Had the alternative interpretation applied, she would have excluded half her $400,000 gain and only paid taxes on $200,000. Note that any "nonqualifying use," such as a rental, reduces your exclusion. See pages 92–93 for more details.

There is no age requirement for this exclusion and the exclusion can be claimed every 2 years. However, if you have a $250,000/$500,000 gain every two years, I want to meet your real estate broker!

E Miscellaneous Individual Exclusions

26 Carpool Receipts

If you form a carpool to carry passengers to and from work, the amounts received from these passengers are not included in your income. These amounts are considered reimbursement for transportation expenses incurred.

Although your cost of commuting back and forth to work has been subject to continually increasing costs as energy prices have risen, commuting costs are neither deductible nor normally excludable from income. But establishing a carpool can help you defray these expenses without incurring additional taxable income.

Therefore, what you should do is establish a carpool in which the passengers pay you amounts sufficient to cover the cost of your repairs, gasoline, and similar items used in connection with operating your car to and from work. In doing so, you convert personal nondeductible expenses into excludable income.

For example, if it has been costing you $100 a month to commute in the past, you have had to earn $138.89 (at the 28 percent tax bracket) in order to have the funds to pay for your commute. With a carpool arrangement in which your expenses are reimbursed, it costs you nothing. The establishment of a carpool, therefore, gives you an extra $138.89 in after-tax disposable income.

27   Damages (Sec. 104)

Damages received in settlement of a lawsuit or awarded by a court were normally excluded from income under the return of capital doctrine. Theoretically, damages awarded for personal wrong committed against you (for instance, breach of promise to marry, invasion of privacy, libel, slander, alienation of affection) replace the personal capital destroyed by these wrongful acts.[5] Defamation awards were also excludable.[6] Amounts received as damages for personal injury were excludable under both this doctrine and specific congressional mandate.[7] However, damages received as a substitute for income are generally taxable, since they represent a restoration of lost wages or profits that would have been taxable upon receipt.

Back pay and liquidated damages recovered under the Age Discrimination in Employment Act were not excludable from income.[8] These rules were modified by the Small Business Job Protection Act of 1996.

Under *prior law,* gross income did not include any damages received (whether by suit or agreement and whether as lump sums or as periodic payments) on account of personal injury or sickness. The exclusion from gross income of damages received on account of personal injury or sickness specifically did not apply to punitive damages received in connection with a case not involving physical injury or sickness. Courts differed as to whether the exclusion applied to punitive damages received in connection with a case involving a physical injury

---

5. Rev. Rul. 74-77, 1971-1 CB 33.
6. *Threlkeld,* 87 T.C. No. 76.
7. Internal Revenue Section 104(a) (2).
8. *Comm. v. Schleier,* US Sup Ct, No. 94-500, 6/14/95.

or physical sickness. Certain states provided that, in the case of claims under a wrongful death statute, only punitive damages may be awarded.

Courts have interpreted the exclusion from gross income of damages received on account of personal injury or sickness broadly in some cases to cover awards for personal injury that do not relate to a physical injury or sickness. For example, some courts have held that the exclusion applies to damages in cases involving certain forms of employment discrimination and injury to reputation where there is no physical injury or sickness. The damages received in these cases generally consist of back pay and other awards intended to compensate the claimant for lost wages or lost profits. The Supreme Court held that damages received based on a claim under the Age Discrimination in Employment Act could not be excluded from income.

CURRENT LAW

The 1996 law provides that the exclusion from gross income does not apply to any *punitive* damages received on account of personal injury or sickness whether or not related to a physical injury or physical sickness. Prior law continues to apply to punitive damages received in a wrongful death action if the applicable state law (as in effect on September 13, 1995 without regard to subsequent modification) provides, or has been construed to provide by a court decision issued on or before such date, that only punitive damages may be awarded in a wrongful death action.

The 1996 law also provides that the exclusion from gross income *only* applies to damages received on account of personal physical injury or physical sickness. If an action has its origin in a physical injury or physical sickness, then all damages (other than punitive damages) that flow therefrom are treated as payments received on account of physical injury or physical sickness whether or not the recipient of the damage is the injured party. For example, damages (other than punitive damages) received by an individual on account of a claim for loss of consortium due to the physical injury or physical sickness of such individual's spouse are and will be excludable from gross income. In Private Letter Ruling 200410022, the IRS defined "personal physical injuries" as "direct, unwanted or uninvited physical contacts resulting in observable body harms such as bruises or cuts." In addition, damages (other than punitive damages) received on account of a wrongful death continue to be excludable from taxable income as under prior law.

The 1996 law specifically provides that emotional distress is not considered a physical injury or physical sickness. Thus, the exclusion from gross income does not apply to any damages received (other than for medical expenses as discussed below) based on a claim of employment discrimination or injury to reputation accompanied by a claim of emotional distress. Because all damages received on account of physical injury or physical sickness are excludable from gross income, the exclusion from gross income applies to any damages received based on a claim of emotional distress that is attributable to a physical injury or physical sickness. In addition, the exclusion from gross income also applies to the amount of damages received that is not in excess of the amount paid for medical care attributable to emotional stress in other cases. (See REG - 127270-06).

The above provisions generally are effective with respect to amounts received after the date of enactment (August 20, 1996). The provisions do not apply to amounts received under a written binding agreement, court decree, or mediation award in effect on or issued on or before September 13, 1995.

Amounts received to compensate for damages to property or to the goodwill of a business are also excludable up to the amount of the adjusted basis of the assets. Only receipts in excess of this basis will be taxable. For example, if your car, which cost you $500, is completely destroyed in an accident and you receive $600 as compensation for damages, the first $500 is nontaxable as a return of your capital; you include in your gross income only the $100 excess over your basis.

The difference between the taxable and excludable nature of alternative damages awarded provides an opportunity for sophisticated tax planning. For example, in arranging an out-of-court settlement of a suit involving personal injury and loss of income, you should be aware that damages from personal injury suits are excluded from income but the proportion representing loss of income is fully taxable (unless the income loss is a direct result of injury or sickness). Therefore, negotiate for a maximum allocation to the personal injury portion of the settlement.

In fact, it may be more advantageous to take less, totally, if the tax-free portion is increased. Assume you are in the 28 percent bracket and are offered $10,000 for personal injury and $20,000 for loss of income. That leaves you with $24,400 after taxes. A settlement of $20,000 for personal injury and $7,500 for loss of income would give you $25,400, or $1,000 more after taxes. At the same time, it saves the payer $2,500. In such a case, everybody wins—except the Internal Revenue Service.

SPECIAL NOTE

In 2006 the U.S. Court of Appeals for the D.C. Circuit held "unconstitutional" the tax on damages for loss of reputation and mental distress (*Murphy vs IRS*). The case was appealed and reversed.

Tax and Reporting Treatment of Judgment/Settlement Payments to Employees

Payment Character	Income Taxable?	Wages (FICA and ITW)?	Reporting Requirement
Back pay (other than lost wages received on account of personal physical injury or physical sickness)	Yes	Yes[1]	W-2
Front pay	Yes[2]	Yes	W-2
Dismissal/severance pay	Yes	Yes	W-2
Compensatory or consequential damages paid on account of personal physical injuries or physical sickness	Generally, no	No	None
Compensatory damages not paid on account of personal physical injuries or physical sickness (e.g., emotional distress)	Generally, yes	No	1099-MISC, Box 3
Consequential damages not paid on account of personal physical injuries or physical sickness	Yes	No	1099-MISC, Box 3
Punitive/liquidated damages	Yes	No	1099-MISC, Box 3
Interest	Yes	No	1099-INT, Box 1 (if $600 or more)
Costs	Yes	No	1099-MISC, Box 3
Medical expenses	Generally, no	No	None
Overtime	Yes	Yes	W-2
Restoration of benefits: health premiums, TSP employee and employer contributions, and retirement contributions	To be determined	To be determined	To be determined
Taxes—employee income tax or employee portion of FICA	Yes	Yes. See Publication 15-A	W-2
Travel—if requirements of § 62(c) (accountable plan) are met	No	No	No
Travel—if requirements of § 62(c) are not met	Yes	Yes	W-2

[1] If the case is in the 8th Circuit and involves an illegal refusal to hire, contact CC:TEGE:EOEG:ET2 for guidance.

[2] If the case is in the 5th Circuit, contact CC:TEGE:EOEG:ET2 for guidance.

Tax and Reporting Treatment of Attorneys' Fees
Total Employer Payment Made Jointly to Attorney and Employee:

Nature of Payment	Income Taxable to Employee?	Reporting to Employee	Reporting to Attorney
Court award designating attorneys' fees[1]	Yes—attorneys' fees generally taxable to employee.	Attorneys' fees reportable in Box 3 of 1099-MISC (not W-2). Treas. Reg. § 1.6041-1(f)(1) and (2).	Box 14 of 1099-MISC in the amount of the check payable jointly to employee and attorney. Treas. Reg. § 1.6045-5(a), and (f) Ex. 1.
Court award without designation of attorneys' fees	Yes—attorneys' fees generally taxable to employee.	The total award is reportable, as appropriate (on 1099-MISC or W-2).	Box 14 of 1099-MISC in the amount of the the check payable jointly to employee and attorney Treas. Reg. § 1.6045-5(a), and (f) Ex. 1.
Settlement payment	Yes—attorneys' fees generally taxable to employee.	To be determined, based on the nature of the action. If wages, reportable on W-2. If not wages, reportable in Box 3 of 1099-MISC.	Box 14 of 1099-MISC in the amount of the check payable jointly to employee and attorney Treas. Reg. § 1.6045-5(a), and (f) Ex. 1.

[1] Workers' rights statutes, such as Title VII, generally include fee-shifting provisions.

Separate Employer Payments to Employee and to Attorney for Attorneys' Fees:

Nature of Payment	Income Taxable to Employee?	Reporting to Employee	Reporting to Attorney
Court award designating attorneys' fees[1]	Yes—attorneys' fees generally taxable to employee.	Attorneys' fees reportable in Box 3 of 1099-MISC (not W-2) even though paid separately to attorney. Treas. Reg. § 1.6041-1(f) (1) and (2).	Box 14 of 1099-MISC to attorney in the amount of check payable to attorney. Treas. Reg. § 1.6045-5(a), and (f) Ex. 3.
Court award without designation of attorneys' fees	Yes—attorneys' fees generally taxable to employee.	The total award is reportable, as appropriate (on 1099-MISC or W-2) even though attorneys' fees paid separately to attorney. Treas. Reg. § 1.6041-1(f)(1) and (2).	Box 14 of 1099-MISC to attorney in the amount of check payable to attorney. Treas. Reg. § 1.6045-5(a), and (f) Ex. 3.
Settlement payment	Yes—attorneys' fees generally taxable to employee.	To be determined, based on the nature of the action. If wages, reportable on W-2. If not wages, reportable in Box 3 of 1099-MISC.	Box 14 of 1099-MISC to attorney in the amount of check payable to attorney. Treas. Reg. § 1.6045-5(a), and (f) Ex. 3.

[1] Workers' rights statutes, such as Title VII, generally include fee-shifting provisions.

Total Employer Payment to Employee:

Nature of Payment	Income Taxable to Employee?	Reporting to Employee	Reporting to Attorney
Court award designating attorneys' fees[1]	Yes—attorneys' fees generally taxable to employee.	Attorneys' fees reportable in Box 3 of 1099-MISC (not W-2). Treas. Reg. § 1.6041-1 (f)(1) and (2).	None. See, e.g., Treas. Reg. § 1.6045-5(a), (d)(4), and (f) Ex. 4.
Court award without designation of attorneys' fees	Yes—attorneys' fees generally taxable to employee.	The total award is reportable, as appropriate (on 1099-and MISC or W-2).	None. See, e.g., Treas. Reg. § 1.6045-5(a), (d)(4), (f) Ex. 4.
Settlement payment	Yes—attorneys' fees generally taxable to employee.	To be determined, based on the nature of the action. If wages, reportable on W-2. If not wages, reportable in Box 3 of 1099-MISC.	None. See, e.g., Treas. Reg. § 1.6045-5(a), (d)(4), and (f) Ex. 4.

[1] Workers' rights statutes, such as Title VII, generally include fee-shifting provisions.

Total Employer Payment to Attorney:

Nature of Payment	Income Taxable to Employee?	Reporting to Employee	Reporting to Attorney
Court award under fee-shifting statute designated as attorneys' fees[1]	Yes—attorneys' fees generally taxable to employee.	Attorneys' fees reportable in Box 3 of 1099-MISC (not W-2). Treas. Reg. § 1.6041-1(f)(1) and (2).	Total amount of check reported on 1099-MISC, Box 14. Treas. Reg. § 1.6045-5(a) and (d)(4).
Court award without designation of attorneys' fees	Yes—attorneys' fees generally taxable to employee.	The total award is reportable, as appropriate (on 1099 or W-2).	Total amount of check reported on 1099-MISC, Box 14. Treas. Reg. § 1.6045-5(a) and (d)(4).
Settlement payment	Yes—attorneys' fees generally taxable to employee.	To be determined, based on the nature of the action. If wages, reportable on W-2. If not wages, reportable in Box 3 of 1099-MISC.	Total amount of check reported on 1099-MISC, Box 14. Treas. Reg. § 1.6045-5(a) and (d)(4).

[1] Workers' rights statutes, such as Title VII, generally include fee-shifting provisions.

28   Divorce and Separation Arrangements (Sec. 71)

Prior to July 18, 1984, alimony and support payments were taxable to the recipient spouse only if:

a) the payments qualified as periodic payments *and*

b) the payments were received under a decree of divorce or separate maintenance; *or*

c) the payments were received under a written separation agreement (provided the husband and wife were not living together and did not file a joint return).[9]

Alimony and support payments were termed periodic payments when no fixed total sum was established or when the cessation of payments was contingent upon the occurrence of some event, such as the death or remarriage of the divorced spouse or change in economic status of either spouse.

If you are the recipient spouse, you should be aware that lump-sum settlements are not taxed. Furthermore, where a fixed total sum is set and is payable in installments, the income is not taxable unless the sum was payable over a period of more than 10 years.

For arrangements prior to 1984, if a lump-sum settlement was payable in installments of more than 10 years, payments in each year up to 10 percent of the principal sum qualify as periodic payments and will be taxable to you. Ordinary periodic payments are taxable when received, whether received in advance or arrears. Under this same rule, the 10 percent limitation applied to advance payments but not to delinquent installment payments. For example, if under a decree of divorce you were to receive a total payment of $13,000 in 13 annual installments, each payment regularly received would be taxable as a periodic alimony payment. But if your spouse became delinquent in one year and paid $2,000 in the following year, the $2,000 was taxable when received. However, if your spouse paid $1,000 as a regular annual payment and paid an additional $1,000 in advance, the taxable amount would be only $1,300 (10 percent of the principal sum).

CURRENT LAW

The Tax Reform Act of 1984 made several significant changes in domestic relations taxation. Under prior law, gain generally was recognized on transfers of

---

9. A married couple living in the same house are not separated and living apart as a *matter of law.* See *Hertsch,* T. C. Memo 1982-109 Par. 57,684; also see *Washington,* 77 T.C. No. 44; but for a contrary decision in the 8th Circuit, see *Sydnes* 78-2 U.S.T.C. Par. 9487, 42 AFTR 2d 78-5143.

property in exchange for the release of marital claims. The Reform Act provides that transfers of property between spouses that are incident to divorce will generally be nontaxable, carryover basis transactions. This means that your spouse, who takes property from you incident to divorce, will have the same basis in that property that you had.

This provision of the Act applies to transfers after the date of the enactment (July 18, 1984), but not to transfers pursuant to instruments in effect on that date unless both parties elect to have the provisions apply. You and your spouse may, in addition, elect to have the provisions apply just to all transfers after December 31, 1983.

Moreover, the rules for taxation of *alimony* have been changed significantly for agreements executed after 1984. The section on alimony starting on page 141 details these provisions.

If the alimony is taxable to the recipient under the above rules, that same amount can be used by the payer as a deduction from adjusted gross income, even if you do not itemize deductions. Child-support payments are never deductible nor are they ever included in the gross income of the recipient. The amount of child support included in the payments should be clearly designated as such by the decree or written separation agreement. Note, however, that a payment, even one clearly delineated as alimony, will not be considered or treated as alimony if the payment is reduced (a) on the happening of a contingency relating to a child of the payer or (b) at a time that can clearly be associated with such a contingency. For this purpose, a contingency relates to a child of the payer if it depends upon any event relating to that child, regardless of whether such event is certain or likely to occur. Events that relate to a child of the payer include the following: the child's attaining a specified age or income level, dying, marrying, leaving school, leaving the spouse's household, or gaining employment.

There are two situations in which payments that would otherwise qualify as alimony or separate maintenance payments will be treated as arising out of a contingency relating to a child of the payer. The first situation is when the payments are to be reduced not more than 6 months before or after the date that the child is to attain the age of 18, 21, or local age of majority. The second situation is when the payments are to be reduced on two or more occasions that occur not more than 1 year before or after a different child of the payer spouse attains a certain age between the ages of 18 and 24, inclusive. The certain age referred to in the preceding sentence must be the same for each child, but need not be a whole number of years.

The presumption in the two situations that payments are to be reduced at a time clearly associated with the happening of a contingency relating to a child of the payer may be rebutted by showing that the time at which the payments are to be reduced was determined independently of any contingencies relating to the children of the payer. The presumption in the first situation will be rebutted conclusively if the reduction is a complete cessation of alimony or separate maintenance payments during the sixth post-separation year or upon the expiration of a 72-month period. The presumption may also be rebutted in other circumstances, for example, by showing that alimony payments are to be made for a period customarily provided in the local jurisdiction, such as a period equal to one-half of the duration of the marriage.

For example, assume husband and wife are divorced on July 1, 2010, when their children—daughter (born July 15, 1995) and son (born September 23, 1997)—are 14 and 12, respectively. Under the divorce decree, husband is to make alimony payments to wife of $2,000 per month. Such payments are to be reduced to $1,500 per month on January 1, 2016, and to $1,000 per month on January 1, 2020. On January 1, 2016, the date of the first reduction in payments, daughter will be 20 years, 5 months, and 17 days old. On January 1, 2020, the date of the second reduction in payments, son will be 22 years, 3 months, and 9 days old. Each of the reductions in payments is to occur not more than 1 year before or after a different child of husband attains the age of 21 years and 4 months. Actually, the reductions are to occur not more than 1 year before or after daughter and son attain any of the ages of 21 years, 3 months, and 9 days through 21 years, 5 months, and 17 days. Accordingly, the reductions will be presumed to clearly be associated with the happening of the contingency relating to daughter and son. Unless this presumption is rebutted, payments under the divorce decree equal to the sum of the reductions ($1,000 per month) will be treated as fixed for the support of the children of husband and therefore will not qualify as alimony or separate maintenance payments.

Where payments constituting both alimony and child support are made but constitute less than the required amount each year, the payments are considered first to cover child support, with any excess deemed to be alimony.

The excludability of lump-sum alimony and child-support payments provides another avenue for sophisticated tax planning and negotiation. Remember, if the alimony payments are excludable, they are not deductible to the payer. The person making the alimony payments would clearly favor a divorce settlement that includes provisions for deductible alimony payments. On the other hand, the recipient would prefer that the payments do not qualify as includable income. If the payer is in a higher tax bracket than the recipient, both parties may benefit, after taxes, by increasing the payments and constructing them so that they qualify after taxes as "periodic."

For example, assume a husband and wife with no children are in the process of reaching a divorce agreement. If the wife is in a 15 percent tax bracket and the husband is in a 28 percent tax bracket, then $10,000 shifted from property settlement to alimony would produce a net savings of $1,300 [$10,000 × (28 percent minus 15 percent)]. Here again, the husband could pay the wife's taxes and share the $1,300 net savings, and both parties would still be ahead on an after-tax basis.

The same kind of planning can be used with child support. If the recipient is in a higher bracket than the payer, it is a good idea to negotiate for an increase in the amount designated as child support (excludable/nondeductible) in exchange for a reduction in periodic alimony payments (includable/deductible). If the payer is in a higher bracket, increase the amount of includable/deductible alimony in exchange for a reduction in child support.

29 Life Insurance (Sec. 101)

Life insurance proceeds paid to you because of the death of the insured are not taxable unless the policy was purchased by you or transferred to you for a price. This is true even if the proceeds are paid under an accident or health insurance policy or an endowment contract.

If the death benefits are paid to you in a lump sum rather than at regular intervals, they are included in your gross income only if they are more than the amount originally specified as payable at the time of the insured person's death. If the benefit payable at death was not specified, you include the benefit payments in income when they are more than the present value of the payments at the time of death.

If you receive life insurance proceeds in regular installments, you may exclude part of each installment from your income. To determine the excludable part, you must divide the amount held by the insurance company (generally, the total lump sum, the principal, payable at the death of the insured party) by the number of installments that are to be paid. Anything over this excludable part must be included as interest income.

There was one special exception: If insurance proceeds were payable to you after the death of your spouse, and you received the proceeds in installments, you could have excluded up to $1,000 a year of the interest included in the installments in addition to the part of each installment that was excludable as a recovery of the lump sum payable at death. Even if you remarried, you could have continued to take the exclusion. This provision, however, was repealed by the Tax Reform Act of 1986, effective for deaths occurring after the date of enactment (October 22, 1986).

Under current law, if you leave the proceeds from life insurance on deposit with an insurance company under an agreement to pay interest only, the interest paid to you is taxable.

The Health Insurance Portability and Accountability Act of 1996 amended the above rules.

The new law generally excludes "qualified accelerated death benefits" from income. If a contract meets the definition of a life insurance contract, gross income does not include insurance proceeds that are paid pursuant to the contract by reason of the death of the insured. However, recently many chronically or terminally ill individuals with short life expectancies have sold or assigned their life insurance policies to qualified viatical-settlement providers. These companies typically buy policies from people with life-threatening illnesses for a percentage of the policy's face value. Under prior law, recipients of viatical payments would owe federal income taxes on those payments. The new law excludes these payments from income effective for amounts received after December 31, 1996.

There is an exception to the general rule that life insurance proceeds are excluded from income. This exception is applicable to a life insurance contract that has been transferred for a fee to another individual, who assumes ownership rights. Upon receipt of the proceeds, that individual must include as income the difference between the proceeds and the amount he or she paid for the contract, plus any premiums paid. For example, assume person A owns an insurance policy in the face amount of $10,000 upon the life of person B and subsequently sells the policy to you for $2,000. When B dies, you receive the proceeds of $10,000. The amount that you can exclude from gross income is limited to $2,000 plus any premiums you paid after the transfer.

There are, however, four exceptions to this rule. These are transfers to:

A partner of the insured
A partnership in which the insured is a partner
A corporation in which the insured is an officer or shareholder
A transferee whose basis in the policy is determined by reference to the transferor's basis

This last item translates into a basic exception for policies that are transferred as part of a tax-free exchange—for example, a transfer of insurance policies to a corporation by its controlling shareholders in exchange for the corporation's stock or securities.

One technique that has been suggested in order to qualify for the previous second exception is the creation of a partnership between shareholders wherein that partnership would lease equipment to the co-owned corporation. Such a structure would avoid the transfer-for-value limitation that would normally be held to transfers between shareholders. In this case, the transfer is not merely between shareholders but between partners.

30   Qualified State Tuition (§529) Programs

Current law provides tax-exempt status to "Qualified State Tuition Programs." These are programs established by a state or a state agency under which you can (1) purchase tuition credits or certificates for the payment of education expenses or (2) make contributions into an account established to pay qualified education expenses, such as tuition, books, and fees, and for 2009 and 2010 only, computer technology.

The interest or other earnings from such accounts comes out federal and state tax-free! Several states (e.g., New York) have programs where you don't even have to go to school in that state to qualify. All 50 states either have, or are developing, such a program. Following are some of the best. Don't miss this tax-advantaged way to finance your kid's college expenses.

Or, you can get really creative. Name yourself as beneficiary of a Section 529 account and save money for a 2- or 3-year sabbatical—tax-free as long as it involves education at an eligible institution! Not only can you use the money for books and tuition, but you can even pay for your apartment up to the amount specified in school guidelines.

Call toll-free at 877-277-6496 or check www.collegesavings.org or www.savingforcollege.com for more information.

As an alternative, check out the *Independent 529 Plan*. It lets you lock in current tuition rates at more than 200 private colleges.

It works like this. Suppose you contribute $10,000. Assume that's 50 percent of one year's tuition at school "x." When you or your child enrolls, you've got 50 percent of one year's tuition paid.

The deals vary per college. But the money invested grows tax free. If you don't go, you get a refund, plus or minus two percentage points each year, depending on how your investments fared.

Get details and enroll at www.independent529plan.org or 888-718-7878 (see LTR. RUL. 200311034).

State 529 Plans

Alabama	The Higher Education 529 Fund	866-529-2228	www.alabama529.com
Alaska	University of Alaska College Savings Plan	800-478-0003	www.uacollegesavings.com
	T. Rowe Price College Savings Plan	800-369-3641	www.price529.com
	John Hancock Freedom 529	866-626-8529	www.johnhancock-freedom529.com
Arizona	Fidelity Arizona College Savings Plan	800-544-1262	www.fidelity.com/arizona
	Arizona Family College Savings Program	602-258-2435	www.az529.gov
Arkansas	GIFT College Investing Plan	800-857-7301	www.thegiftplan.uii.upromise.com
California	ScholarShare Advisor College Savings Plan	800-544-9999	www.advisor.fidelity.com
Colorado	Stable Value Plus College Savings Plan	800-448-2424	www.collegeinvest.org
	Direct Porfolio Savings Plan	800-997-4295	www.collegeinvest.org
	Scholars Choice College Savings Plan	888-572-4652	www.collegeinvest.org
Connecticut	Connecticut Higher Education Trust	888-799-2438	www.aboutchet.org
Delaware	Delaware College Investment Plan	800-544-1655	www.fidelity.com/delaware
District of Columbia	DC College Savings Plan	800-987-4859	www.dccollegesavings.com
Georgia	Georgia Higher Education Savings Plan	877-424-4377	www.gacollegesavings.com

Hawaii	TuitionEDGE	866-529-3343	www.tutitionedge.org
Idaho	Ideal Idaho College Savings Program	866-433-2533	www.idsaves.org
Illinois	Bright Directions College Savings Program	866-722-7283	www.brightdirections.com
	Bright Start	877-432-7444	www.brightstartsavings.com
Indiana	Indiana College Choice 529 Investment Plan	866-400-7526	www.collegechoiceplan.com
Iowa	College Savings Iowa	888-672-9116	www.collegesavingsiowa.com
Kansas	Schwab 529 College Savings Plan	888-903-3863	www.schwab.com/529
	Learning Quest 529 Education Savings Program	800-579-2203	www.learningquestsavings.com
Kentucky	Kentucky Education Savings Plan Trust	877-598-7878	www.kysaves.com
Louisiana	START Savings Program	800-259-5626	www.startsavings.la.gov
Maine	NextGen College Investing Plan	877-463-9436	www.nextgenplan.com
Maryland	Maryland College Investment Plan	888-463-4723	www.collegesavingsmd.org
Massachusetts	U.Fund College Investment Plan	800-544-2776	www.fidelity.com/ufund
Michigan	Michigan Education Savings Plan	877-861-6377	www.misaves.org
Minnesota	Minnesota College Savings Plan	877-338-4646	www.mnsaves.com
Mississippi	Affordable College Savings Program	800-486-3670	www.collegesavingsms.org
Missouri	Missouri's 529 College Savings Plan	888-414-6618	www.missourimost.s.upromise.com

(continues)

Montana	Pacific Funds 529 College Savings Plan	800-722-2333	www.pacificlife.com
Nebraska	State Farm College Savings Plan	800-321-7520	www.statefarm.com
	AIM College Savings Plan	877-246-7526	www.aimvestments.com
	TD Ameritrade 529 College Savings Plan	877-408-4644	www.tdameritrade.com
	College Savings Plan of Nebraska	888-993-3746	www.planforcollegenow.com
Nevada	The Upromise College Fund	800-857-7305	www.uii.s.upromise.com
	Vanguard 529 College Savings Plan	866-734-4530	www.vanguard.com
New Hampshire	Fidelity Advisor 529 Plan	800-544-9999	www.advisor.fidelity.com
	UNIQUE College Investing Plan	800-544-1914	www.fidelity.com/unique
New Jersey	NJBEST College Savings Plan	877-465-2378	www.njbest.com
	Franklin Templeton 529 College Savings Plan	800-818-4030	www.franklintempleton.com
New Mexico	The Education Plan	877-337-5268	www.theeducationplan.com
	Scholar's Edge	866-529-7283	www.scholarsedge529.com
New York	New York's 529 College Savings Program	877-697-2837	www.nysaves.uii.upromise.com
North Carolina	National College Savings Program	800-600-3453	www.nc529.org
North Dakota	College SAVE	866-728-3529	www.collegesave4u.com
Ohio	College Advantage, A 529 Savings Plan	800-233-6734	www.collegeadvantage.com
Oklahoma	Oklahoma 529 College Savings Program	877-654-7284	www.okforsavings.org

Oregon	OppenheimerFunds 529 Plan	888-876-7529	www.opp529.com
	MFS 529 Savings Plan	866-637-7526	www.mfs.com
	Oregon College Savings Plan	866-722-8464	www.oregoncollegesavings.com
Pennsylvania	Pennsylvania College Savings Program	800-294-6195	www.pa529direct.s.upromise.com
	Pennsylvania 529 Direct Investment Plan	800-294-6195	www.pa529direct.com
	Pennsylvania 529 Guaranted Savings Plans	800-440-4000	www.tapfacts.com
Rhode Island	CollegeBoundfund	888-324-5057	www.collegeboundfund.com
South Carolina	Future Scholar 529 College Savings Plan	888-244-5674	www.futurescholar.com
South Dakota	CollegeAccess 529	866-529-7462	www.collegeaccess529.com
Tennessee	Tennessee's BEST Savings Plan	888-486-2378	www.tnbest.org
Texas	Tomorrow's College Investment Plan	800-445-4723	www.enterprise529.com
Utah	Utah Educational Savings Plan	800-418-2551	www.uesp.org
Vermont	Vermont Higher Education Investment Plan	800-637-5860	www.services.vsac.org
Virginia	Virginia Education Savings Trust	888-567-0540	www.virginia529.com
West Virginia	SMART529 College Savings Program	866-574-3542	www.smart529.com
Wisconsin	Tomorrow's Scholar	866-677-6933	www.tomorrowsscholar.com
	EdVest	888-338-3789	www.edvest.com

Source: August 2007 *Investment Advisor*.

When It Makes Sense to Switch

Should you cash out your child's custodial account pay the long-term capital gains tax bill and put the money in a state sponsored 529 college savings plan? Yes—if you have enough time to earn back the tax payment. Find the number of years before college on the table below then go down a line. A switch makes sense if your custodial account has had any gain up to the percentage shown.

Years to college	1	2	3	4	5	6	7	8+
Maximum gain (%)	30.6	50.8	64.4	75.5	84.0	91.9	99.2	Any amount

Assume the 529 contributions receive an annual state tax deduction of up to $2,500 and the 529 levies 0.3% more in fees than the custodial account.

Source: Data: T. Rowe Price Associates Inc.

Interest in Learning
A look at the different college savings plans available

	Tax Breaks	Contribution Limit	Income Restrictions	Federal Financial Aid Impact	Flexibility of Funds' Use
529 College Savings Plan	Qualified distributions tax-free. (Some states may also offer tax breaks.)	Up to total of about $300,000 for some plans; may pay gift taxes if more than $14,000 a year. Can donate up to $70,000 at one time.	None	Considered parent's assets, assessed up to 5.6%.	Tuition, fees, room, board, and graduate school.

Interest in Learning
A look at the different college savings plans available *(continued)*

	Tax Breaks	Contribution Limit	Income Restrictions	Federal Financial Aid Impact	Flexibility of Funds' Use
529 State Prepaid Plan	Qualified distributions tax-free. (Some states may also offer tax breaks.)	Maximum varies by state, but plans cover, in general, up to five years of college costs.	None	Considered student resource: Reduces aid eligibility dollar for dollar.	For most plans, tuition, fees, room, and board, books, and for 2009 and 2010, computers and Internet access.
Independent 529 Plan	Qualified distributions tax-free.	Up to five years' tuition at the group's most expensive college (currently over $137,000).	None	Considered student resource: Reduces aid eligibility dollar for dollar.	Tuition fees. room and board, and as of 2009, computers and Internet access.
Coverdell Education Savings Account	Qualified distributions tax-free.	Up to $2,000 a year.	For single filers, $95,000–$110,000; for joint filers, $190,000–$220,000.	Considered student's assets, assessed at 35%.	Postsecondary costs; K–12 costs, some computers.

(continues)

Interest in Learning
A look at the different college savings plans available *(continued)*

	Tax Breaks	Contribution Limit	Income Restrictions	Federal Financial Aid Impact	Flexibility of Funds' Use
Custodial Accounts	For kids age 19 or older* earnings taxed at child's rate; under 19, earnings less than $1,000 are tax-free.	No total maximum, but may pay gift taxes if more than $14,000 a year.	None	Considered student's assets, assessed at 35%.	Anything that benefits the minor.
Savings Bonds	Interest earned is tax-free if used for qualified higher education purposes.	Annual limit of $20,000 per owner as of 2008.	For 2013, for single filers, $74,700–$89,700; for joint filers, $112,050–$142,050	Considered parent's assets, assessed up to 5.6%.	Tuition and mandatory fees.
Taxable Accounts	Up to 15% tax on capital gains and dividend income.	Unlimited	None	Considered parent's assets, assessed up to 5.6%.	Unlimited

*As of 2008, it's under age 19, or, if a full-time student, under age 24.

Source: The Wall Street Journal.

How Does the 529 College Savings Plan Compare?

	529 plans	UGMA/ UTMA	Coverdell Educational IRA	EE bonds	Prepaid QSTP	Regular investment account
Tax Deferral	Tax exempt	No (earnings taxed at beneficiary's rate)	Tax exempt until 1-1-11 sunset	Tax-exempt income	Varies by state	No
Maximum Annual Contribution	Up to $70,000 per child gift tax-free	None	$2000* per child under 18 per year	$20,000 per person	Varies by state	None
Maximum Income to Qualify	No limits	No limits	Phases out for single filers at $95,000 to $110,000; for joint filers at $190,000 to $220,000	Phases out for single filers at $74,700 to $89,700; for joint filers at $112,050 to $142,050	Varies by state	No limits
Who Controls Disbursement of Assets	Parent, guardian, or other donor	Custodian until child reaches 18, the child afterward	Parent or guardian	Registered owner	Parent or guardian	Registered owner
Ability to Transfer	In most instances, can be transferred to another member of the same family without penalty, including first cousins as of January 1, 2002	Not permitted	Can be transferred to another member of the same family without penalty	Can be transferred without penalty	Most plans require that the beneficiary is a resident of the offering state	Transfer is considered an asset sale and may trigger capital gains tax liabilities
Estate Planning Features	Assets are transferred out of the donor's estate, yet the donor retains control	Assets are transferred out of the estate	Limited	None	Assets are transferred out of the estate	None
Freedom to Choose Colleges	Can be used for any accredited post-secondary school in the U.S.	No restrictions	Can be used for any qualified educational expense. Must be used before beneficiary is age 30†	No restrictions	Usually restricted to participating schools, can only cover tuition and fees	No restrictions
Early Withdrawal	Earnings are taxed at donor's regular rate, plus a 10% penalty applies	None	Entire withdrawal taxed at donor's rate plus a 10% penalty	None	Fees or penalties vary by state. Typically, the donor gets principal back, plus a modest return	None
Investments Available	Fund or funds	Any legal security or valuable item	Any legal security	EE bonds	Government guarantee	Any legal security
Professional Management/ Asset Allocation	Yes	No	No	No	Yes	No

*$500 prior to January 1, 2002.
†As of January 1, 2002, the age limit does not apply to special needs students, and money can be used for elementary and secondary school expenses.

31   Your Home—The Mother of All Tax Shelters!

Want to invest in a tax shelter that puts a roof over your head? There are more tax advantages and exclusions with respect to your home than any other investment. It's the American way—mom, apple pie, and owning your own home. Let's look at all the deductions and benefits you get when you pay homage to the mortgage gods and go into more debt than your parents earned in their lifetimes.

TAXES

First, you get to deduct all the real property taxes you pay. That includes all state or local taxes for the general welfare. It does not count any trash or garbage collection fees, or homeowner association charges specifically stated and billed.

If you are escrowing for the taxes, you get the deduction when your bank makes the payment, not when you escrow with the bank. Even if you are a tenant shareholder in a co-op, you get to deduct your share of any property taxes paid.

There is no limit on the number of properties on which you can deduct taxes paid. If you have 10 homes, you can deduct the taxes on all 10.

Even if you took the standard deduction, you could have added to that amount $500 ($1,000 on a joint return) for taxes paid on your principal residence for 2008 and 2009.

INTEREST

Uncle Sam wants to put you in a home. Sorry, that does not sound right. How about Uncle Sam wants to put you in a house? We all know a house is not a home. In any case, our government wants to subsidize your home purchase. It does that by making your interest payments deductible.

Interest paid on the purchase of your principal residence is deductible. You can even finance the buy of additional land adjacent to your home and deduct the interest as qualified residence interest. You can also deduct the interest you pay to buy a second residence or vacation home.

There is a cap of one million dollars of acquisition indebtedness on which you can take a personal interest deduction. If you plan on spending more than $1 million for your house, call me and we will work something out.

You can also deduct the interest on as much as $100,000 worth of home equity debt. As long as the house has the equity and the debt is secured by that equity, the IRS does not care what you do with the borrowed money. You can use it for whatever you want, including vacations, or a party to celebrate your newfound deductions.

If you are in the 28 percent bracket, that means that $100 in interest paid only takes $72 out of your pocket. Uncle Sam pays the other $28 in income taxes foregone. Not a bad deal!

GAIN EXCLUSION

Here is where the IRS "gave up the farm." The deal on this one is so good it makes my eyes glaze over (a.k.a. the MEGO effect).

Forget about having to roll over your gain into a new home. Forget about the $125,000 gain exclusion if you are age 55 or older. Both are now ancient history and no longer good tax law.

Here is the new rule . . . good no matter how old you are. If the property was your principal residence for any 2 of the 5 years prior to sale, you can exclude $250,000 in *gain* ($500,000 on a joint return)!

If you qualify under the 2 out of 5 rule, you normally sign an affidavit at settlement. If the house sold for less than $250,000/$500,000, the sale amount is not even reported to the IRS because you have no tax liability on that sale.

This is not a one-time exclusion. You do not have to buy a new house. You can even rent and you can get another full exclusion every 2 years, or whenever you qualify. But, if you have a $250,000/$500,000 gain every 2 years, I want to meet your real estate agent!

The full $500,000 exclusion will potentially be allowed even if the sale is within two years of the death of a spouse.

You can even get a *partial* exclusion based on the time of use and ownership. But you only get the partial exclusion if the sale is because of:

a) a change in place of employment, or

b) health reasons, or

c) unforeseen circumstances.

The partial exclusion is based on the maximum exclusion, not on the basis of your actual realized profit. So, say you bought a home for $250,000 and sold it for a $25,000 profit after only 1 year because of a job change.

Because the sale was covered by a change in employment, you get a partial exclusion. It was your principal residence for 1 year out of 2, so 50 percent of the maximum exclusion, up to $125,000 in gain, is excluded. Since that is more than the $25,000 gain, no tax is due on the sale. You exclude half the maximum allowed, not half the $25,000 in gain. That is a major tax break. Not many properties are going to appreciate more than $125,000/$250,000 in 1 year.

The key is to qualify for the partial exclusion if possible. "Change in employment" covers anyone who lives in the household. They don't even have to be an owner of the property. The "change in employment" must be the *primary* reason for the move. There's a "safe harbor" which assumes that it was the primary reason if your new job is at least 50 miles farther from the residence sold than where you used to work.

If you do not meet the "safe harbor," all is not lost. You will just have to prove (if you are audited) that it was the primary reason for the move based on the facts and circumstances of your case.

Health reasons include advanced age-related infirmities, the need to move to care for a family member, or to obtain or provide medical or personal care for a qualified individual suffering from a disease, illness, or injury.

Unforeseen circumstances is where the IRS really became consumer friendly. Safe harbors here include divorce, death, multiple births from the same pregnancy, and even a change in employment or self-employment status that results in your inability to pay the costs and living expenses of your household. So, if your income goes down, or even if your spouse or other co-owner's income goes down, you can qualify for a partial or even a full exclusion.

Other unforeseen circumstances include an unexpected pregnancy (PLR 143156-04, PLR 200652041, 12/29/06) where unmarried taxpayers ended their relationship, sale of the property due to undisclosed noise from a nearby airport (PLR 200702032), where the owner married a new spouse with adolescent children had bought a new house with additional bedrooms (PLR 200725018), and even where you have a second child born after the purchase (PLR 200745011) or marry someone with children requiring a larger house (PLR 200826024).

Unforseen circumstances even includes a response to a criminal attack and the need to provide for the healthcare of a qualified individual.

And, even if you don't meet one of these "safe harbors," you might still qualify on the basis of your specific facts and circumstances.

Divorced or seperated spouses each can exclude up to $250,000 if *either one* uses the home for the qualifying period. That helps the spouse who has left the home. But, to qualify, there must be a court decree giving use to the other spouse.

However, for homes sold after the signing of the American Jobs Creation Act of 2004, if the house sold was acquired via a like kind swap and the home was sold within 5 years of the exchange, *no* gain will be excluded.

The Housing and Economic Recovery Act of 2008 changed the rules again. Prior to the Act, if a second home became a principal residence, after 2 years the owner could sell it and exclude up to $250,000 in gain from income—or up to $500,000 for couples filing jointly. Now, gain from the sale of a principal residence home will no longer be excluded from gross income for periods that the home was not used as the principal residence ("nonqualifying use"). This new income inclusion rule applies to home sales after December 31, 2008, and is based only on nonqualified use periods that begin on or after January 1, 2009. A period of absence (for example, vacations) generally counts as qualifying use if it occurs after the home was used as the principal residence.

The amount of gain allocated to periods of nonqualified use is the amount of gain multiplied by a fraction, the numerator of which is the aggregate period of nonqualified use during which the property was owned by the taxpayer and the denominator of which is the period the taxpayer owned the property. Remember the "nonqualified use" for this computation does not include any use prior to 2009.

Say you bought a house on January 1, 2010, for $400,000 and rent it for 2 years, taking $20,000 in depreciation. On January 1, 2012, you move in as your principal residence.

You move out on January 1, 2014, and sell it for $700,000 on January 1, 2015.

The rental period (2010–2011) is nonqualifying use. All use post-December 31, 2011, qualifies, including 2014 when you moved out. You owned the property a total of 5 years (2010, 2011, 2012, 2013, 2014). Forty percent of the gain (2 years out of 5 owned) or $128,000 is taxable. The $20,000 gain attributable to depreciation is recaptured at rates as high as 25 percent. Up to $192,000 in gain can still be excluded.

HOME OFFICES

Here's where, in my opinion, the IRS actually crossed the line. But it was in favor of the taxpayer, so I'm not going to complain. Let's assume you use 20 percent of your house as a home office. In the past, when you sold your house, 20 percent of the gain wouldn't qualify for the exclusion because that 20 percent wasn't used as a "residence." It was used exclusively as your office.

New Rule—The IRS doesn't care! Even if you used your home 90 percent for business, as a home office, you can now exclude as much as 100 percent of your gain, up to the $250,000/$500,000 limit!

You're only going to be subject to tax on the gain to the extent of depreciation taken on the building since May 7, 1997.

Wow! That means that, if you qualify, there's no reason not to claim a home office.

I guess Dorothy was right in *The Wizard of Oz* . . . "There's no place like home!"

32 Disabled Veteran Payments

Payments under the Department of Veterans Affairs Compensated Work Therapy program are tax-free. Disabled veterans who paid tax on these benefits should file an amended return if they qualify under the statute of limitations.

33 Exclusion of Income for Volunteer Firefighters and Emergency Medical Responders

For tax years beginning after 2007 and before 2011, gross income did not include:

- Rebates or reductions of property or income taxes provided by a state or local government for providing services as a member of a qualified emergency response organization (defined below). Any such rebate or reduction reduces the amount of the income tax deduction for such taxes.

- Qualified payments made by a state or local government for providing services as a member of a qualified emergency response organization. The exclusion is limited to $30 multiplied by the number of months the member performs such services. A charitable deduction for expenses paid by the member in connection with performing such services must be reduced by any payment excluded from income.

A qualified volunteer emergency response organization is any volunteer organization organized and operated to provide firefighting or emergency medical services for persons in a state or local jurisdiction and required by written agreement with that state or local jurisdiction to furnish such services.

34 Unemployment Benefits

For 2009 only, The American Recovery and Reinvestment Act of 2009 made the first $2,400 in unemployment benefits received, per recipient, tax-free.

35 Homeowner Security

Afraid of losing your job and putting your home at risk? The federal government has a new Homeowner Affordability and Stability Plan to help

struggling homeowners modify their mortgages in order to avoid foreclosure. Under the plan, you can modify your loan and, if timely payments are
received on the modified loan, can qualify for "pay for performance success payments" reducing the balance on your mortgage loan. Those who
qualify can get principal reductions of up to $1,000 per year for up to
5 years. Best of all, these payments are tax-free!

36 Reimbursed Costs to Parents of Children with Disabilities

If a school district cannot provide adequate education for a child with disabilities, federal l   aw requires that it must reimburse the parents for the
costs of special education. Since the district is required to provide free education, such reimbursements are not taxable to either the parents or the
child.

37 Wrongful Conviction and Incarceration

Compensation received from a state for wrongful conviction or incarcera-
tion that caused sickness, injuries, and related damages is now tax free
(CCA 201045023).

38 Restitution Payments

Restitution payments under the Trafficking Victims Protection Act of 2000
are excluded from income. This law requires that a defendant convicted of
a human trafficking offense make payments to the victim to compensate for
costs for medical services, physical and occupational therapy or rehabilitation, transportation, temporary housing, child care expenses, lost income,
attorneys' fees and other costs, as well as other losses the victim suffers as a
proximate result of the offense.

39 Frequent Flier Miles

The IRS will continue to pass on taxing these miles even if earned on a business trip and used personally. But the IRS takes a different position on premiums awarded for opening a bank account or toasters given as incentives
in the past. Such "incentives," even if given in the form of miles, are taxable.

40 Hurricane Sandy

Gross income does not include any amount received as a "qualified disaster relief payment," even cash or benefits from an employer to an employee, state program aid, or relief from a charitable organization. Such payments cover reasonable medical, temporary housing, and transportation expenses.

41 Cancellation of Indebtedness

Up to $2 million in cancellation of indebtedness income on your principal residence escapes taxation through 2013.

F Schedule of Excludable Items

Accident and health insurance premiums paid by your employer

Accident and health proceeds (under insurance purchased by you or under an employee-supported plan) not attributable to a previous medical expense deduction

Annuities (cost excluded over life expectancies)

Awards for noncompetitive achievements (if contributed)

Bequests and devises

Carpool receipts for transportation of fellow employees

Child-support payments received

Contributions paid by your employer to accident and health plans and to sickness and disability funds under sick-benefit laws

Damages for physical personal injuries or sickness

Dependent care, employer-provided services

Disability payments other than for loss of wages

Disability payments under employer-financed accident and health plans

Endowment policy proceeds until cost is recovered

Fellowship and scholarship grants (limited)

Frequent flier miles

Gain on sale of personal residence

Gifts

Group term life insurance premiums—if coverage is $50,000 or less or if employees' contribution premiums exceed the cost of coverage over $50,000

Health insurance proceeds not attributable to medical expense deductions
  in prior years
Inheritances
Interest on bonds of the state, city, or other political subdivision
Life insurance proceeds paid on the death of the insured under the terms
  of the contract, unless paid to a transferee
Medical care payments under employer-financed accident and health plans
Merchandise distributed to employees on holidays
Nobel Prize, Pulitzer Prize, and similar awards (if contributed)
Principal residences—up to $500,000
Qualified State Tuition (§529) Plans
Railroad passes to employees and their families
Restitution payments
Sickness and injury benefits equivalent to workers' compensation
Social Security and disability benefits (limited)
Supper money paid by employer
Tuition paid by employer (limited)
Unemployment benefits up to $2,400 for 2009 only
Viatical payments
Welfare payments

CHAPTER 5

Credits— Dollar-for-Dollar Tax Reductions

"Taxing is an easy business."

EDMUND BURKE
Thoughts on the Cause of the Present Discontent
1770

"It will be of little avail to the people that the laws are made by men of their own choice if the laws be so voluminous that they cannot be read, or so incoherent that they cannot be understood."

The Federalist Papers

"Thousands of pages of pet rocks that have nothing to do with the national interest."

Former SENATOR SAM NUNN *of Georgia*
On the tax code

A *credit* is a dollar-for-dollar reduction in your tax; it is the best kind of expense to have. If you are in the 28 percent tax bracket, a deduction of $100 saves you $28.00 in tax, but a credit of $100 saves you $100 in tax. A credit, therefore, is a payment that counts in full as an offset to your tax liability. Because every dollar of credit is really an additional dollar in your pocket, it is imperative that you recognize those situations where credits are available and that you always claim them on your tax return. A lost or forgotten credit is money thrown away in tax dollars.

There are several areas in which potential credits are available. I shall examine each in turn and discuss the ways you can best take advantage of them. But first I want to detail two significant cash-saving techniques: estimating taxes and withholding exemptions.

A   Estimated Tax and Withholding Exemptions

Significant savings can be realized by minimizing the amount of estimated tax payments or of taxes withheld from your income before they are actually due. You must pay estimated tax if your estimated total tax liability is more than $1,000 and you meet certain conditions (see below), but you still can minimize these payments. You should pay as little estimated tax as possible and therefore have the use and availability of these tax funds for as long as legally possible.

You need to pay estimated tax if your estimated net tax liability is more than $1,000.

Estimated tax normally is paid in quarterly installments. You need *not file* a declaration of estimated tax after 1982 but payments must still be made. There is a penalty, which cannot be deducted as interest, of about 3 percent (this rate changes every 3 months) per year for underpaying the estimated tax—unless the total of all payments ("including withholding") made by the due date of each quarter is at least as much as the smallest of the following figures:

- The amount that you would have paid if the estimated tax were the same as the previous year's tax liability, provided the preceding taxable year was a year of 12 months and you filed a return.

- The amount you would have paid if the estimated tax were 90 percent of the tax on your income up to the month in which the installment date falls. For this purpose, the income is *annualized* (computed at an annual rate), based upon taxable income before exemptions, if deductions are itemized, and the alternative minimum tax if applicable.

The first exception is most advantageous when your current year's income is greater than that of the prior year. The last exception is most useful if the greater part of income is received in the later part of the year. In all cases the objective is to pay no more now than is required. Remember, while you may have to pay the tax on April 15, you will have had the use of the money and the interest earned on it during that interim period.

The rules were modified for those with an adjusted gross income in excess of $150,000 when the prior year's estimated tax safe harbor was changed to 100 percent for 1998, 105 percent for 1999, 108.6 percent for 2000, 110 percent for 2001, 112 percent for 2002, and 110 percent for 2003 through 2013.

For 2009 only, the safe harbor was reduced to 90 percent if

a) Your 2008 adjusted gross income was less than $500,000, and

b) More than 50 percent of your 2008 gross income was from a small business with an average of fewer than 500 employees during that year.

This same pay-as-you-go aspect of the federal income tax system requires your employers to withhold income tax on compensation (salaries, wages, tips) paid to you as their employee. The amount of tax withheld by your employer depends upon the amount of salary or wages paid to you and the information you furnish on the W-4 form (the Employee's Withholding Allowance Certificate) that you file with your employer. If you had no income tax liability for the past year and expect to have no tax liability for the current year, you may claim exemption from withholding of income tax. If you are exempt, your employer will not withhold federal income tax from your wages. To claim exemption from withholding, you still must give your employer a completed W-4 form. On it you need to write "exempt" and no withholding will be taken from your wages.

The money-saving technique recommended here is the same as that with the estimated tax. The objective is to minimize the amount of withholding taken out of each paycheck so that you will have the use and interest on the money until the final tax payment is due. For 2013 returns, there is no penalty on underwithholding as long as the total amount withheld for the year is equal to either 90 percent of your final tax liability or 100/110 percent of your last year's tax liability, whichever is smaller.

Unfortunately, most Americans do not underwithhold; they actually *overwithhold.* While the Internal Revenue Service eventually returns all excess funds, the taxpayer loses the interest that the money would have generated during the time that it is in the hands of the government. This is no insignificant loss, especially when one considers that the average 2012 overwithholding was $2,651 per refund. That's a lot of interest-free money!

How then can you eliminate overwithholding—even better, how can you begin underwithholding? The first step is to get a W-4 form from your employer and see how many allowances you are currently claiming. Each allowance that you claim will reduce the amount that is withheld from your income.

Allowances are available for the following:

- You get an automatic allowance for each exemption you can claim on your tax return—for yourself, your spouse, and your dependents.

- You get a special withholding allowance if you are single and have only one employer, or if you are married and have only one employer and your spouse is not employed.

- You get additional withholding allowances for the estimated tax credits you expect to take. If you expect to take the earned income credit, credit for child and dependent care expenses, or credit for the elderly, these credits may lower your tax and therefore make you eligible for additional allowances.

- You get additional withholding allowances for employee business expenses, moving expenses, and if you qualify for the additional standard deduction for the aged or the blind.

- You get additional withholding allowances for estimated net losses from your business or profession, from capital losses, from losses on rental property, and from losses from farming expenses.

- You can get a special withholding allowance for potential contributions to an IRA.

- You can get additional withholding allowances if you expect to itemize your deductions and/or pay alimony during the year. (Section 3402 [F])

You can use creative accounting especially in these last areas. The key is expected, not actual, deductions, contributions, and losses. Additional allowances can always be claimed under the *expectation* of making charitable contributions, incurring higher medical expenses, or borrowing money and incurring an increase in interest expense. Additional withholding allowances are permitted for anticipated tax credits as well. But be careful not to go overboard: If your total withholdings equal 100/110 percent of last year's taxes or

90 percent of this year's taxes, you are immune from any penalties or interest (see page 100). Under Reg. Sec. 31. 3420 (i)-2, employers must accede to an employee's request that withholding exemptions be increased. Note that as of 2005, if you have more than 10 withholding exemptions, your employer *no longer* must notify the IRS of the fact.

The advantages of reducing your withholdings can be significant. For example, if in 2013, one additional allowance claimed reduces the withholding taken from your salary by about $325 per month ($3,900 ÷ 12 = $325). That adds up to $3,900 a year. With five additional allowances, you have the use and interest on $19,500 every year.

You may file a new W-4 form at any time if you wish to change your withholding allowances for any reason. This gives you yet another opportunity for tax savings. Some sophisticated, tax-knowledgeable individuals significantly underwithhold on their income for the first 11 months of the year, file amended W-4 forms, and then significantly overwithhold in the final taxable month. A cooperative employer may even withhold your full final month's wages so that your total yearly withholding meets the 90 percent or 100 percent tests detailed above and you can avoid the penalty for underwithholding. In the meantime, you have had the use of and interest on the underwithheld amount. Sadly, the Internal Revenue Service does not pay any interest on any amount overwithheld. In effect, overwithholding is nothing more than granting an interest-free loan to the Internal Revenue Service. Better that the interest is in your pocket.

B Credits

The remainder of this chapter discusses specific credits that can be taken to reduce your taxes due. Please take advantage of them.

42 The Earned Income Credit (Sec. 32)

Certain eligible low-income workers are entitled to claim a refundable credit on their income tax returns. The amount of the credit an eligible individual may claim depends upon whether the individual has one, more than one, or no qualifying children and is determined by multiplying the credit rate by the taxpayer's earned income up to an earned income amount. The maximum amount of the credit is the product of the credit rate and the earned income amount. For taxpayers with earned income (or adjusted gross income [AGI], if greater) in excess of the beginning of the phaseout range, the maximum credit amount is reduced by the phase-out rate multiplied by the amount of earned income (or AGI, if greater) in excess of the beginning of the phase-out range. For taxpayers with earned income (or AGI, if greater) in excess of the end of the phase-out range, no credit is allowed.

The parameters for the credit depend upon the number of qualifying children the individual claims. For 2013, the joint return parameters are given in the following table:

	Three or More Qualifying Children	Two Qualifying Children	One Qualifying Child	No Qualifying Children
Credit rate (in percent)	45.00	40.00	34.00	7.65
Earned income amount	$13,430	$13,430	$9,560	$6,370
Maximum credit	$6,044	$5,372	$3,250	$487
Phase-out begins*	$22,870	$22,870	$22,870	$13,310
Phase-out rate (in percent)	21.06	21.06	15.98	7.65
Phase-out ends*	$51,567	$48,378	$43,210	$19,680

*Married filing jointly.

For 2013, the refundable credit for families with three more children is 45 percent of $13,430, for a maximum of $6,044.

For years after 2001, the credit rates and the phase-out rates will be the same as in the preceding table. The earned income amount and the beginning of the phase-out range are indexed for inflation; because the end of the phaseout range depends on those amounts as well as the phase-out rate and the credit rate, the end of the phase-out range will also increase if there is inflation.

In order to claim the credit, an individual must either have a qualifying child or meet other requirements. A qualifying child must meet a relationship test, an age test, an identification test, and a residence test. In order to claim the credit without a qualifying child, an individual must not be a dependent and must be over age 24 and under age 65.

To satisfy the identification test, individuals must include on their tax return the name and age of each qualifying child. Individuals must also provide a taxpayer identification number (TIN) for all qualifying children. An individual's TIN is generally that individual's Social Security number.

The Personal Responsibility and Work Opportunity Reconciliation Act of 1996 amended the above rules.

Individuals are not eligible for the credit if they do not include their taxpayer identification number and their spouse's taxpayer identification number on their tax return. If an individual fails to provide a correct taxpayer identification number, such an omission will be treated as a mathematical or clerical error under the new law and the taxpayer must be given an explanation of the asserted error and a period of 60 days to request that the IRS abate its assessment.

A second change relates to the disqualified income test for the earned income credit itself. Under prior law, an individual would not be eligible for the earned income credit if the aggregate amount of "disqualified income" of that taxpayer for the taxable year exceeded $2,350. This threshold was not indexed. Disqualified income was the sum of:

1. Interest (taxable and tax exempt)

2. Dividends

3. Net rent and royalty income

Under the new law, the following items are added to the definition of disqualified income: Capital gain net income and net passive income that is not self-employment income.

Moreover, the disqualified investment income threshold above which an individual is not eligible for the credit was reduced from $2,350 to $2,200 and that threshold is indexed for inflation after 1996 ($3,300 for 2013).

In addition, the 1996 law modified the definition of adjusted gross income used for phasing out the earned income credit by disregarding certain losses. The losses disregarded are:

1. Net capital losses

2. Net losses from trusts and estates

3. Net losses from nonbusiness rents and royalties

4. 50 percent of the net losses from businesses, computed separately with respect to sole proprietorships (other than in farming), sole proprietorships in farming, and other businesses.

For purposes of (4) above, amounts attributable to a business that consist of the performance of services by the taxpayer as an employee are not taken into account.

The Tax Relief Act of 1997 made several modifications to the earned income credit rule. It added compliance provisions, denied eligibility for prior acts of recklessness, required recertification where the credit was denied in the past, and created a due diligence requirement for paid preparers.

For the purpose of the EIC phase-out, you must now include in adjusted gross income any nontaxable distribution of IRAs, pensions, annuities, and tax-exempt interest, and an addback of 75 percent of business losses. However, the 1997 law provides that workfare payments do *not* qualify as earned income for purposes of the earned income credit.

The Internal Revenue Service (IRS) is required to provide notice to taxpayers with qualifying children who receive a refund on account of the EITC that the credit may be available on an advance payment basis. To prevent taxpayers from incurring an unexpectedly large tax liability due to receipt of the EITC on an advance payment basis, the amount of advance payment allowable in a taxable year is limited to 60 percent of the maximum credit available to a taxpayer with one qualifying child.

The earned income credit represents dollars in your pocket, but it must be claimed to be received. In effect, it is a form of negative income tax—that is, a refundable credit for taxpayers who do not even have a tax liability.

43 Excess Social Security Tax

If you work for two or more employers during the tax year, too much Social Security tax may be withheld from your wages. You may claim this excess amount as a credit against your income tax. The tax consists of two parts: (1) old-age, survivor, and disability insurance (OASDI) and (2) Medicare hospital insurance (HI). For 2013 the rate on OASDI is 6.20 percent (12.4 percent if self-employed), and on HI it is 1.45 percent (2.90 percent if self-employed). Starting 2013, there is a 0.9 percent Medicare surtax for those with *earned* income of more than $200,000 ($250,000 on a joint return) on the excess over these amounts. For 2011 and 2012 only, the employee part of your OASDI tax was cut by 2 percent with potential savings of as much as $2,136 (2 percent of $106,800) and $2,202 (2 percent of $110,100).

Your Social Security tax obligation is computed each year by applying a fixed rate to your wages. There is, however, a maximum wage base* (which is subject to change) to which this tax may be applied. For example, in 2013, all wages in excess of $113,700 will not be subject to OASDI Social Security tax. There is no

---

*The maximum in 1937 was $3,000, with a 1% rate, creating a maximum $30 tax!

cap on HI. Therefore, if you work for two employers, earning $113,700 from each, both employers will take the maximum OASDI (6.2 percent × $113,700, or $7,049.40) from your wages. But because you are only liable for a maximum payment of $7,049.40, you can have a credit against your income tax for the additional $7,049.40 subtracted from your wages. This is money you should get back. Even if you owe no taxes, excess Social Security payments will be refunded to you.

44   The Child and Dependent Care Credit

Congress has attempted to ease the tax burden of those citizens who must pay for dependent care while earning a living by allowing a child care credit. If, in order to work, you incur expenses in connection with the care of certain dependents, you are permitted a credit for those expenses. This credit, unlike the earned income credit or excess Social Security payments, cannot reduce your tax liability below zero—that is, it is not refundable.

To qualify for this credit:

1. Your child and dependent care expenses must be incurred to allow you to work, full-time or part-time, whether for others or in your own business or partnership. "Work" even includes actively looking for work. Furthermore, your spouse is considered to have worked if he or she:

    a) was a full-time student for five months during the tax year; *or*

    b) is physically or mentally unable to function without supervision or aid.

    This rule applies to only one spouse for any one month.

2. You must have income from work during the year. Unpaid volunteer work or work for a nominal salary does not qualify.

3. You must maintain a home in which you and one or more qualifying persons live. This means that you (and your spouse, if you are married) pay more than half the cost of maintaining your principal residence. If you are married, you and your spouse must live together.

Upkeep expenses normally include property taxes, mortgage interest, rent, utility charges, home repairs, insurance on the home, and food costs. Excluded from upkeep are payments for clothing, education, medical treatment, vacations, life insurance, transportation, mortgage principal, or the purchase, improvement, or replacement of property. For example, the cost of replacing a water heater is not considered upkeep, but the cost of repairing a water heater can be included.

A qualifying person is:

a) Your qualifying child who is your dependent and who was under age 13 when the care was provided,

b) Your spouse who was not physically or mentally able to care for himself or herself and lived with you for more than half the year, or

c) A person who was not physically or mentally able to care for himself or herself, lived with you for more than half the year, and either:

  i. Was your dependent, or

  ii. Would have been your dependent except that:

    (*a*) He or she received gross income of $3,900 or more,

    (*b*) He or she filed a joint return, or

    (*c*) You, or your spouse if filing jointly, could be claimed as a dependent on someone else's 2013 return.

Dependent defined. A dependent is a person, other than you or your spouse, for whom you can claim an exemption. To be your dependent, a person must be your qualifying child (or your qualifying relative).

Qualifying child defined. To be your qualifying child, a child must live with you for more than half the year and meet other requirements.

The physical or mental incapacity must be disabling: People who are not able to dress, clean, or feed themselves because of physical or mental problems or who require constant attention to prevent them from injuring themselves or others qualify.

Qualification is determined on a daily basis when the disability lasts for less than a calendar month. For example, if a dependent or spouse for whom you paid work-related expenses no longer qualifies on September 16, you may include in your computation all work-related expenses through September 15.

CHILD CARE CREDITS FOR CHILDREN OF DIVORCED OR SEPARATED PARENTS

Expenses for the care of children of divorced or separated parents are also allowed for the child care credit under certain conditions. If you are divorced, legally separated under a decree of divorce or separate maintenance, or separated under a written separation agreement, and you have custody of your child for a longer time during the calendar year than the other parent, your child qualifies if certain conditions are met.

To qualify, *all* these criteria must be met:

1. The child must be under age 13 or unable to care for himself or herself.

2. The child must be in the custody of one or both of the parents for more than half the year.

3. One or both of the parents must provide more than half of the child's support during the year.

4. You must normally file a joint return if you are married. If you are legally separated from your spouse under a decree of divorce or separate maintenance, you are not considered married and can file for the child care credit. The credit may be claimed on a separate return. If you are still married and want to file a separate return, you will not be considered married if:

    a) your home is the home of a qualifying person for more than half the tax year; *and*

    b) you pay more than half the cost of keeping up your home for the tax year; *and*

    c) your spouse does not live in your home for the last 6 months of the year.

5. You must pay someone other than your spouse or a person you can claim as a dependent for the child's care. You may count payments made to relatives who are not your dependents, even if they live in your home.

Only work-related expenses qualify for the child or dependent care credit, and your expenses must be for the well-being and protection of a qualifying person. Expenses are considered to be work-related if they allow you (and your spouse, if married) to work, not if you incur them while you are working. However, whether the purpose of the expenses is to allow you to work depends upon the facts. Work-related expenses may include the following:

HOME EXPENSES

This covers the cost of ordinary services done in and around your home that are necessary to maintain the well-being and protection of a qualifying person. The services of a housekeeper, maid, or cook usually are considered necessary to run your home if performed at least partly for the benefit of the qualifying person. Payments for the services of a chauffeur or gardener are not included. The expense of food, clothing, education, or entertainment for the qualifying person is not included.

CHILD CARE EXPENSES

These expenses are not limited to services performed in your home. You may include expenses for nursery school or day care for preschool children, or even summer camp (*ZOLTAN* 79 T.C. 1982) if these expenses allow you to work. The Revenue Act of 1987 excludes overnight camp expenses, but summer day camp expenses are still allowable. That's even for special camps for the study of computer science, theater, or soccer and camps that improve reading or study skills. Amounts you pay for food, clothing, or schooling are not child care expenses. However, if a nursery school or day care center provides these as part of its service, the entire cost is treated as child care. Schooling in the first grade or higher is not treated as part of child care. Neither is the cost of getting your child to and from the center, whether by bus, subway, taxi, or private car, unless the cost is included in the tuition and is not billed separately (IRS Letter Ruling 8303037). Half-day, but not full-day, kindergarten can qualify.

DISABLED SPOUSE OR DEPENDENT CARE EXPENSES

Expenditures for out-of-home, noninstitutional care of a disabled spouse or dependent who regularly spends at least 8 hours a day in your home are eligible for the credit. Under prior law, services outside the home qualified only if they involved the care of a child under 13 years of age.

Meals and lodging provided for housekeepers may be added to your child care expenses, and also any added expenses for lodging your housekeeper. For example, if you have moved to an apartment with an extra bedroom for a housekeeper, you may include the added rent and utility expenses for this bedroom.

The *child care credit*, whether for married, divorced, or separated parents, provides a significant opportunity for effective tax planning. For example, if you have an elderly parent whom you wish to help support, money that you give for food may result in a gift tax liability for you. But if you have this parent babysit for your children so that you can work, not only will you avoid a potential gift tax penalty on the money you pay that parent, but you will also receive an income tax credit. Furthermore, if that parent eats at your home while providing child care services, you will receive a tax credit for the value of the food eaten—and the value of that food will *not* be taxable income to your parent.

For example, assume you have your mother provide child care to your son so that you may work, and your mother eats $100 worth of food per week. Even if you pay her nothing in dollars, her income tax is unaffected, your gift tax is unaffected, but your income tax will be reduced by a $20–$35 credit for each week she qualifies.

There are limits on the amount of work-related expenses you may use to figure your credit. These are the earned income limit and the dollar limit.

1. *The earned income limit.* If you are single at the end of your tax year, the amount of work-related expenses that you may use to figure your credit may not be more than your earned income for the tax year. If you are married at the end of your tax year, the amount of work-related expenses may not be more than your earned income or the earned income of your spouse, whichever is *less.*

   If you are married and, for any month, your spouse is either a full-time student or not able to provide self-maintenance, your spouse is considered to have an earned income of $200 a month (if there is one qualifying person in your home) or $400 a month (if there are two or more qualifying persons in your home). That disabled spouse is counted as a qualifying person, along with a dependent child. This rule applies to only one spouse for any one month.

   Earned income is all wages, salaries, tips, other employee compensation, fees for professional services, and net earnings from self-employment. It is reduced by any net loss in earnings from self-employment. It does not include pensions, annuities, or payments for your services that were distributions of earnings and profits, other than a reasonable amount for your work for a corporation. In addition, it does not include amounts received under accident or health plans that are not included in your gross income.

2. *The dollar limit.* Prior to 2003, the child and dependent care credit was computed on a three-tier basis. First, if you had an adjusted gross income of $10,000 or less, you were entitled to a credit equal to 30 percent of your work-related expenses. Then, the credit was reduced by one percentage point for each $2,000 of adjusted gross income (or fraction thereof) above $10,000. Finally, if you had an adjusted gross income of over $28,000, the credit was equal to 20 percent of the work-related expenses you paid during your tax year.

The maximum amount of work-related expenses to which you could apply the credit was $2,400 for one qualifying child or dependent, or $4,800 if more than one was involved. Thus, the maximum credit for one qualifying individual ranged from $720, if your income was below $10,000 ($2,400 × .30), to $480 if your income exceeded $28,000 ($2,400 × .20). Similarly, the maximum credit for two or more qualified individuals ranged from $1,440 to $960.

These figures were yearly limits. You used the $2,400 limit if you had one qualifying person at *any time* during the year. You used $4,800 if you had more than one at *any time* during the year. It was not based on the length of time during the year that your dependent qualified. However, include only the expenses you had for a qualifying person *during the time the person is qualified.* For example, if your child turned 13 in April, you were eligible for the entire $2,400 limit, but only the expenses you had before your child's 13th birthday can be used. If you had expenses of less than $2,400 during that time, only the smaller amount could be used.

The Family Support Act of 1988 amended previous rules. For tax years beginning after 1988, a child of the taxpayer is a qualified individual only if the child is under age 13 (rather than 15, as under prior law). Moreover, the dollar amount of expenses eligible for the credit is reduced, dollar for dollar, by the amount of expenses excludable under a dependent care assistance program provided by an employer. In addition, effective for returns whose due date is after 1989, the taxpayer must identify with name, address, and taxpayer identification number (Social Security number) each person or each institution providing the child care.

Effective January 1, 2003, the Tax Relief Act of 2001 increased the maximum credit to 35 percent and the reduction in the credit amount (phasedown) will begin at adjusted gross income of $15,000 rather than $10,000. The *minimum* 20 percent credit was applied to taxpayers with adjusted gross incomes over $43,000.

The amount of qualified expenses is increased from $2,400 to $3,000 per child. With two children, you can then get a maximum credit of $6,000 × 35 percent, or $2,100, or a minimum credit of $6,000 × 20 percent, or $1,200.

The following example shows you how the child care credit is computed. Assume you are a widow and that you maintain a home for yourself and your two preschool children, whom you claim as dependents. You had an earned income of $44,000 for the year and you incurred work-related expenses of $4,000 (for a housekeeper to care for your children in your home) and $2,200 (for child care at a nursery school).

Your credit is computed as follows:

1. In-home child care expenses	$4,000
2. Plus outside child care expenses	+2,200
3. Total work-related expenses	$6,200
4. Maximum allowable expenses for two qualifying children	6,000
5. Multiply by credit rate	× .20
6. Amount of credit	$1,200

Alternatively, for 2013 assume you are married and have two children. You have an earned income of $44,000, and your spouse was a full-time student from January 2 through May 31 only. If you paid a housekeeper $450 a month from January 2 to May 31 (a total of $2,250) to look after your children, prepare meals, and do housework as time allowed, your credit was figured in this way:

1. Total work-related expenses	$ 2,250
2. Your earned income	44,000
3. Income considered earned by your spouse($500*/month for 5 months) ($2,500 limited to $2,250)	
4. Multiply by credit rate	× .20
5. Allowable credit	$ 450

Remember: Work-related expenses cannot exceed either the $3,000 (for one child)/$6,000 (for two or more) limit *or* your own or your spouse's earned income, and you must use the smaller earned income in your computations.

The 2001 law also created, as of January 1, 2002, a credit to employers of 25 percent of qualified expenses for employee child care and 10 percent for qualified expenses for child care resources and referral services. The maximum annual credit is capped at $150,000.

45 Credit for the Elderly or Permanently and Totally Disabled

To compensate for tax exclusions offered to recipients of Social Security benefits, this tax credit is offered to those taxpayers who are not covered by Social Security and spend their retirement years living off past savings and investments. In this way, the credit attempts to help place all elderly taxpayers on a par.

Prior law provided that individuals aged 65 or over, or under 65 with income from a public retirement system, were eligible for a credit equal to 15 percent of the base amount. *Beginning in 1984,* the law increased the base amounts and limits the credit for those under age 65 to individuals with a permanent and total disability who received disability income from public or private employers on account of that disability. You are considered permanently and totally disabled if (1) you are not able to engage in any "substantial gainful activity" because of your

---

*$250 for one child, scheduled to drop to $400/$200 after 2012.

physical or mental condition, and (2) your condition has lasted or can be expected to last continuously for 12 months or more, or lead to your death.

"Substantial gainful activity" usually refers to paid work that requires the performance of significant duties over a reasonable period of time. Nonproductive make-work activities will not be treated as "substantial gainful activity." However, if you work full-time or part-time at your employer's convenience for at least the minimum wage, you will usually be treated as engaging in substantial gainful activity. If you do a type of work as a volunteer that is generally done for pay, you may be considered to have a gainful activity even though you receive no "gain."

Disability income is the total taxable amount you are paid under your employer's accident or health plan or pension plan for the time you are absent from work because of your disability and that is included in your income as wages (or payments in lieu of wages). For purposes of the credit, disability income does not include any amount you receive from your employer's pension plan after you reach your employer's mandatory retirement age.

If you are claiming disability, you must have a physician certify that you are permanently and totally disabled and you must attach that certification to your return. If the certification states your condition will not improve, you will not have to file certifications in subsequent years. The change in base amounts is as follows:

Description	Prior Law	Current Law
Married with one spouse eligible or unmarried	$2,500	$5,000
Married, joint return, both spouses eligible	$3,750	$7,500
Married, filing separately	$1,875	$3,750

These base amounts *are reduced,* however, by the following:

• Pensions or annuities received under Social Security, Railroad Retirement, and certain other pensions, disability benefits received, and annuities otherwise excluded from gross income; *and*

• One-half of adjusted gross income over:
  $ 7,500—single return
  $10,000—married, joint return
  $ 5,000—married, separate return

In the case of an individual under age 65, the base amount is limited in any event to the amount of his or her disability income. Note that under the Social Security Amendments in 1983, for a married disabled individual filing jointly, one spouse eligible, all disability income will be taxable and no tax credit will be available if adjusted gross income is $20,000 or more.

There are few tax-planning strategies that can be employed with the retirement income credit except to note its existence and the fact that it must be claimed to be received. Any failure to recognize or to claim it represents little more than cutting a hole in your wallet and allowing your tax dollars to float freely in the wind.

C Special Credits

In the past, Congress provided a number of tax incentives to encourage employment or investment in research.

46 Work Opportunity Credit (Formerly Targeted Jobs Tax Credit) (Sec. 51)

The targeted jobs tax credit was available to employers on an elective basis for hiring individuals from several targeted groups. The targeted groups consist of individuals who are either recipients of payments under means-tested transfer programs, economically disadvantaged, or disabled. Included are "high-risk" youths, qualified veterans, and families receiving food stamps, and, as of 2009, unemployed veterans and disconnected youth—those between the ages of 16 and 25 who have not worked or gone to school in the past 6 months.

The credit generally was equal to 40 percent of up to $6,000 of qualified first-year wages paid to a member of a targeted group.

The Small Business Job Protection Act of 1996 amended the above rules.

It replaced the targeted jobs credit with a "work opportunity tax credit." The new credit was available on an elective basis for employers hiring individuals from one or more of now nine targeted groups. The credit generally was equal to 40 percent of qualified first-year wages up to $6,000 ($12,000 for qualified veterans). The maximum credit was $2,400. For employees who work at least 120 but less than 400 hours, the credit falls to 25 percent of the first $6,000, or a maximum of $1,500.

No credit was allowed for wages paid unless the eligible individual was employed by the employer for at least 120 hours in the first year of employment. The credit applied to employees who started work after September 30, 1996 and before January 1, 2008. The credit did not apply to wages paid to a relative, dependent, or prior employee.

The Work Opportunity Tax Credit (WOTC) was extend through 2011. While the WOTC sunset at the end of 2011, Congress passed a new Returning Heroes Tax Credit and Wounded Warriors Tax Credit for the hiring of military veterans after November 21, 2011 through December 31, 2012. It was extended again by the Tax Relief Act of 2012 through December 31, 2013. The credit may be as much as $9,600 per qualified veteran.

The Tax Relief and Health Care Act of 2006 combined this credit with the Welfare to Work Credit below for employees who start work after December 31, 2006.

47   Welfare to Work Credit (Sec. 51)

This was a credit of 35 percent of the first $10,000 of eligible wages paid to recipients of long-term family assistance in the first year of employment and 50 percent of the first $10,000 of eligible wages paid in the second year. The maximum credit was $8,500 per qualified employee. This credit has been combined with the work opportunity credit above. Use Form 5884, Work Opportunity Credit, to claim a credit for an employee who begins work for an employer after December 31, 2006.

48   Research Tax Credit (Sec. 41)

A research tax credit equal to 20 percent of the amount by which a taxpayer's qualified research expenditures for a taxable year exceeds its base amount for that year is allowed.

The 20 percent research tax credit also applied to the *excess* of (1) 100 percent of corporate cash expenditures (including grants or contributions) paid for basic research conducted by universities (and certain nonprofit scientific research organizations) *over* (2) the sum of (a) the greater of two minimum basic research floors and (b) an amount reflecting any decrease in nonresearch giving to universities by the corporation as compared to such giving during a fixed base period, as adjusted for inflation. This separate credit computation was commonly referred to as "the university basic research credit."

49 Orphan Drug Tax Credit

Prior to January 1, 1995, a 50 percent nonrefundable tax credit was allowed for qualified clinical testing expenses incurred in testing of certain drugs for rare diseases or conditions generally referred to as "orphan drugs." The Small Business Job Protection Act of 1996 extended the orphan drug tax credit for 11 months, i.e., for the period July 1, 1996 through May 31, 1997. The Tax Relief Act of 1997 extended it permanently.

50 Adoption Assistance

OLD LAW

Prior law did not provide a tax credit for adoption expenses nor did it provide an exclusion from gross income for employer-provided adoption assistance. The Federal Adoption Assistance Program provides financial assistance for the adoption of certain special needs children. Specifically, the program provides assistance for adoption expenses for those special needs children receiving federally assisted adoption assistance payments as well as special needs children in private and state funded programs. The maximum federal reimbursement is $1,000 per special needs child. Reimbursable expenses include those nonrecurring costs directly associated with the adoption process such as legal costs, social services review, and transportation costs.

The Small Business Job Protection Act of 1996 provided taxpayers with a maximum nonrefundable credit against income tax liability of $5,000 per child ($6,000 in the case of special needs adoptions) paid or incurred by the taxpayer. Any unused adoption credit may be carried forward by the taxpayer for up to five years. Qualified adoption expenses are reasonable and necessary adoption fees, court costs, attorney's fees, and other expenses that are directly related to the legal adoption of an "eligible child."

In the case of an international adoption, the credit is not available unless the adoption is finalized. Credits for domestic adoptions are earned when the expenses are paid—even if the adoption failed. An "eligible child" is an individual (1) who has not attained age 18 as of the time of the adoption, or (2) who is physically or mentally incapable of caring for himself or herself. No credit is allowed for expenses incurred (1) in violation of state or federal law, (2) in carrying out any surrogate parenting arrangement, or (3) in connection with the adoption of a child of the taxpayer's spouse. The credit was phased out ratably for taxpayers with modified adjusted gross income above $75,000 and is fully phased out at $115,000 of modified adjusted gross income.

Note that the credit for non–special needs adoptions was not available for expenses paid or incurred after December 31, 2001. Moreover, special needs foreign adoptions were limited to a maximum credit of $5,000 (rather than $6,000) for qualified adoption expenses until December 31, 2001, at which time the credit for special needs foreign adoptions was also repealed. The credit for special needs domestic adoptions ($6,000) was permanent.

With respect to the exclusion from income, a maximum exclusion of $5,000 ($6,000 in the case of special needs adoptions) was available for specified certain adoption expenses provided by an employer. The limit was a per-child limit, not an annual limitation. The exclusion was phased out ratably for taxpayers with modified adjusted gross income above $75,000 and was fully phased out at $115,000 of modified adjusted gross income. No credit was allowed for adoption expenses paid or reimbursed under an adoption assistance program.

Note that the exclusion was not available for expenses paid or incurred after December 31, 2001 and that special needs foreign adoptions are limited to a maximum exclusion of $5,000 (rather than $6,000) for qualified adoption expenses.

CURRENT LAW

Effective as of January 1, 2002, the Tax Relief Act of 2001 modified the preceding rules.

The 2001 law permanently extended the adoption credit for children other than special needs children. The maximum credit was increased to $10,000* per eligible child, including special needs children. A $10,000* credit is provided in the year a special needs adoption is finalized, whether you have qualified adoption expenses or not. The beginning point of the income phaseout range was increased to $150,000† of modified adjusted gross income. The adoption credit is allowed against the alternative minimum tax permanently. The credit was refundable for 2010 and 2011.

The 2001 law permanently extended the exclusion from income for employer-provided adoption assistance. The maximum exclusion was increased to $10,000* per eligible child, including special needs children. In the case of a special needs adoption, the exclusion is provided, whether you have qualified adoption expenses or not. The beginning point of the income phase-out range was increased to $150,000† of modified adjusted gross income. The 2001 law generally is effective for taxable years beginning after December 31, 2001. The provisions that extend the tax credit and exclusion from income for special needs adoptions, whether you have qualified adoption expenses or not, are effective for taxable years beginning after December 31, 2002.

51   Hope Scholarship Credit

The Tax Relief Act of 1997 created this new *per-child* credit for qualified tuition and fees paid during the *first 2* years of post-secondary or certificate education after 1997. Room and board do not qualify.

The credit was equal to:

100% of the first $1,200 in tuition and fees	$1,200
50% of the next $1,200 in tuition and fees	600
for a maximum Hope Credit of	$1,800

---

*$12,970 for 2013
†$194,580 – $234,580 for 2013.

This credit was phased out for 2012 between adjusted gross income of $80,000–$90,000 for singles and $160,000–$180,000 for joint returns. For all intents and purposes, this credit was replaced by the new American Opportunity Education tax credit for 2009 through 2017.

52 American Opportunity Tax Credit

For 2009 through 2017, the American Recovery and Reinvestment Act of 2009 and several extensions provide taxpayers with an "American Opportunity" tax credit of up to $2,500 of the cost of tuition and related expenses paid during the taxable year. You will receive a tax credit based on 100 percent of the first $2,000 of tuition and related expenses (including course materials and books) paid during the taxable year and 25 percent of the next $2,000 of tuition and related expenses paid during the taxable year. Forty percent of the credit will be refundable. This tax credit is subject to a phase-out for taxpayers with adjusted gross income of $80,000–$90,000 ($160,000–$180,000 for married couples filing jointly).

This credit is available for each of the four years of college. Graduate students are not eligible.

The credit can't be claimed against the following sources:

a) 529 plans

b) Tax-free scholarships

c) Pells grants

d) Coverdell education savings account (ESA)

e) Employer-provided education assistance

f) Military educational assistance

g) Any other tax-free educational assistance

Only one of these credits/deductions can be selected per student:

a) The $2,500 American Opportunity Education tax credit

b) The $2,000 Lifetime Learning tax credit

c) The $4,000 above-the-line deduction

Since 40 percent of the credit is refundable, you can get as much as $1,000 from the IRS even if you have no tax liability.

The American Opportunity Education tax credit is the best of these three because it is a higher credit than the Lifetime Learning tax credit and a $4,000 deduction provides at most $1,400 in relief in the 35 percent bracket.

53   Lifetime Learning Credit

The Tax Relief Act of 1997 created this *per-family* credit for tuition and fees up to $5,000 ($10,000 after December 31, 2001) for undergraduate OR *graduate* level and professional degree courses paid after June 30, 1998. Room and board do not qualify.

The maximum credit is now 20 percent of up to $10,000 of qualified tuition and fees or $2,000. It is a per-family, not per-child (as is the Hope Scholarship Credit), credit. The phase-out is $53,000–$63,000 ($107,000–$127,000 for a joint return).

54   Child Tax Credit

Present law provides a $1,000 tax credit for each qualifying child under the age of 17. Your child becomes 17 on the anniversary of his or her date of birth (Rev. Rul. 2003-72). A qualifying child is one you claim as a dependent. The credit may be partially refundable using Form 8812 even if you only have one child.

The credit is phased out on a joint return earning more than $110,000 and for singles earning more than $75,000. For every $1,000 or part thereof earned, the credit is reduced by $50. For a joint return earning more than $129,000, the credit would have been eliminated completely.

The 2001 Tax Relief Act made the child credit refundable to the extent of 10 percent of your earned income in excess of $10,000 for calendar years 2001–2004. The percentage was increased to 15 percent for calendar years 2005 and thereafter. The $10,000 amount is indexed for inflation beginning in 2002 and was lowered to $8,500 by the Emergency Economic Stabilization Act of 2008. Families with three or more children are allowed a refundable credit for the amount by which your Social Security taxes exceed your earned income credit (the present-law rule), if that amount is greater than the refundable credit based (before the law changed) on your earned income in excess of $12,050 for 2009. The American Recovery and Reinvestment Act of 2009 reduced the threshold to the excess over $3,000. The law provides that the refundable portion of the child credit does not constitute income and shall not be treated as resources for purposes of determining eligibility or the amount or nature of benefits or assistance under any federal program or any state or local program financed with federal funds.

The 2001 law provided that the refundable child tax credit will no longer be reduced by the amount of the alternative minimum tax. In addition, the 2001 law allows the child tax credit to the extent of the full amount of your regular income tax and alternative minimum tax.

55 Disability Credits

This credit was created in 1990 specifically for businesses with gross revenues of $1,000,000 or less, or 30 or fewer full-time employees. The credit is intended to cover Americans with Disabilities Act (ADA)–related business access costs. Anything that helps access or communication is covered, including:

- Provision of readers for customers or employees with visual disabilities

- Provision of sign language interpreters

- Purchase of adaptive equipment

- Production of accessible formats of printed materials (i.e., Braille, large print, audiotape, computer diskette)

- Removal of architectural barriers in facilities or vehicles (alterations must comply with applicable accessibility standards)

- Fees for consulting services (under certain circumstances)

- Provision for access to the Internet for those with disabilities

The credit can't be used for new construction, only for adapting existing facilities. The first $250 doesn't count.

The credit is 50 percent of eligible expenditures per year, worth a maximum expenditure of $10,250. Therefore, the maximum annual credit is $5,000.

56   Health Insurance Credit

On August 6, 2002, President Bush signed a trade bill that gave you a health insurance subsidy if you lost your job "as a result of shifts in imports or exports, or because . . . companies shift production overseas."

You'd get a 65 percent subsidy in the form of an advanceable, refundable tax credit to cover the costs of maintaining your health insurance.

57   Saver's Credit

In order to stimulate savings, Congress gives you a credit of 50 percent on the first $2,000 you sock away in a traditional or Roth IRA or 401(k). So if you contribute $2,000, you'll get a $1,000 credit. That's in addition to the minimum $200 that the $2,000 deduction will save you in taxes (at the 10 percent bracket).

Unfortunately, to get the *50 percent credit,* your adjusted gross income can't be more than $17,750. If you then subtract a $3,900 personal exemption and a $6,100 standard deduction, your taxable income is capped at $7,750. The maximum *tax* on that is $775, not the $1,000 promised by Congress.

On a joint return, the numbers limit the credit to $1,460, rather than the promised $2,000. It's not available for those under age 18 or full-time students or dependents claimed on another tax return.

The saver's credit rate is based on your adjusted gross income for the taxable year for which the credit is claimed, as follows:

Adjusted Gross Income			
Married Filing Jointly	Head of Household	All Other Filers	Credit
$0–$35,500	$0–$26,625	$0–$17,750	50% of contribution
$35,501–$38,500	$26,626–$28,875	$17,751–$19,250	20% of contribution
$38,501–$59,000	$28,876–$44,250	$19,251–$29,500	10% of contribution
Over $59,000	Over $44,250	Over $29,500	Credit not available

Want to push the envelope? Make a $4,000 contribution December 31 into a Roth IRA for 2012 and then take a distribution in January for 2013. Only the income during that period would be taxed and you can get a credit as much as $2,000. But you can only do this once.

Additional information can be obtained toll-free from the IRS at 877-829-5500.

58 Small Employer Credit

The Tax Relief Act of 2001 created a new, nonrefundable income tax credit if you have a small business that adopts a defined benefit or defined contribution plan [including a 401(k) plan], a SIMPLE plan, or a SEP. The credit is 50 percent of the first $1,000 of administrative and retirement-education expenses incurred for the plan for each of the first three years the plan is in existence. Expenses offset by the credit may not be claimed a deduction for those expenses.

The credit may be claimed by an employer that did not employ more than 100 employees with compensation in excess of $5,000 in the preceding year. To qualify for the credit, the employer's plan must cover at least one nonhighly compensated employee [IRC Sec. 45E]. The credit may be claimed for costs paid or incurred in tax years after December 31, 2001, with respect to plans established after that date.

59   Electric Vehicle Credit

Use form 8834 to get a refundable credit of 10 percent of the cost of a qualified electric vehicle that was placed in service after June 30, 1993, and before 2012. The maximum credit was $4,000 per qualified electric vehicle. The portion of the cost of a qualified electric vehicle that was expensed under code Sec. 179 is ineligible for the credit.

The credit applies to a motor vehicle powered primarily by an electric motor drawing current from rechargeable batteries, fuel cells, or other portable sources of electric current. The original use of the vehicle must commence with the taxpayer. For vehicles placed in service in 2004 through 2006, the credit is reduced 25 percent each year. The basis of a qualified electric vehicle is reduced by the amount of the credit allowed.

The credit was extended with a $2,500 maximum for vehicles purchased after February 17, 2009, and before 2012. See pages 131–132 for current vehicle credits.

The Energy Tax Incentive Act of 2005 added several new credits including:

60   Credit for Residential Energy Efficient Property

You can take a 30 percent nonrefundable credit for the cost of *solar* systems to heat air or water, but not pools or hot tubs. It also covers small wind, fuel cell, and geothermal heat pump property. This credit is good for second homes as well as primary residences. You can get 30 percent on a new home furnace and another 30 percent on a water heater. The dollar cap was $2,000 for *each* system and this credit was good only for 2006 through 2008.

The 2008 Energy Improvement and Extension Act extended these credits for 8 years, through 2016. And except for fuel cell property (which remains subject to a maximum credit of $500 per half-kilowatt), the American Reinvestment and Recovery Act (ARRA) repealed the dollar caps that had applied to these renewable energy items. ARRA also repealed the limitation on "subsidized energy financing," including assistance provided under a federal, state, or local program designed to promote energy production or conservation.

This credit is nonrefundable and the depreciable basis of the property is reduced by the amount of the credit.

Heating stoves that use renewable biomass fuel—wood, pellets, plants—now qualify for the tax credit.

Business can get a separate 30 percent credit for renewable energy property such as solar heating systems and for fuel cells used to generate electricity. As of January 1, 2009, the $4,000 limit on the 30 percent tax credit for small wind energy property and the limitaion on property financed by subsidized energy financing was repealed.

61   Energy Saving Home Improvement Credit

This 10 percent credit applied to the cost of skylights, outside doors, windows, pigmented roofs, and high-efficiency furnaces, water heaters, and central air conditioners installed in a *primary home* in 2006 and 2007. The top credit was $500, with no more than $200 attributable to windows. Check out www.energytaxincentives.org for details. Claim the credit on Form 5695.

The American Recovery and Reinvestment Act of 2009 increased the energy tax credit for homeowners who make energy-efficient improvements to their existing homes. The 2009 law increased the credit rate to 30 percent of the cost of all qualifying improvements and raises the maximum credit limit to $1,500 for improvements placed in service in 2009 and 2010. For 2011, the credit was cut to 10 percent up to $500 (reduced by any credit claimed since 2006) with a cap of $50 to $300 on fans, furnaces, hot water heaters, heat pumps, and central air-conditioning and a $200 cap on windows.

The credit applies to improvements such as adding insulation, energy-efficient exterior windows, and energy-efficient heating and air-conditioning systems. While there is a bill currently in Congress to change the rule, the credit does not count the labor costs for installation.

A similar credit was available for 2007 but was not available in 2008. You should be aware that the standards in the new law are higher than the standards for the credit that was available in 2007 for products that qualify as "energy efficient" for purposes of this tax credit. The IRS will issue guidelines that will allow manufacturers to certify that their products meet these new standards.

Until the guidelines are released, you generally may continue to rely on manufacturers' certifications that were provided under the old guidelines. For exterior windows and skylights, you may continue to rely on Energy Star labels in determining whether property purchased before June 1, 2009, qualifies for the credit.

What Is Included in the Energy Saving Tax Credit?

Tax Credit: 10 percent of cost up to $500 or a specific amount from $50–$300

Expires: December 31, 2013

Details: Must be an existing home and your principal residence. New construction and rentals **do not** qualify.

Biomass stoves

Heating, ventilating, air conditioning (HVAC)

Insulation

Roofs (Metal & Asphalt)

Water heaters (nonsolar)

Windows and doors

Tax Credit: 30 percent of cost with no upper limit

Expires: December 31, 2016

Details: Existing homes and new construction qualify. Both principal residences and second homes qualify. Rentals **do not** qualify.

Geothermal heat pumps

Small wind turbines (residential)

Solar energy systems

Tax Credit: Credit details: 30 percent of the cost, up to $500 per .5 kW of power capacity

Expires: December 31, 2016

Details: Existing homes and new construction qualify. Must be your principal residence. Rentals and second homes **do not** qualify.

62 Hybrid Vehicles Credit

For cars bought in 2006 through 2014, you can get a *conservation credit* of between $250 and $1,000 and an additional *fuel economy* credit of between $400 and $2,400, based on estimated lifetime fuel savings and on overall fuel economy. Claim the credit on Form 8910.

The fuel economy credit is based on the following efficiency gains over model year 2002 baselines.

- 125%–149%: $400
- 150%–174%: $800
- 175%–199%: $1,200
- 200%–224%: $1,600
- 225%–249%: $2,000
- 250%+: $2,400

How it's calculated   The conservation credit increases the fuel economy credit based on the following lifetime fuel savings:

- 1,200%–1,799 gal: $250
- 1,800%–2,399 gal: $500
- 2,400%–2,999 gal: $750
- 3,000 gal+: $1,000

Heavy-duty hybrid vehicles are subject to the following incremental cost limitations:

- <14,001 GVWR: $7,500
- 14,001–26,000 GVWR: $15,000
- 26,001+ GVWR: $30,000

Qualifying criteria   To qualify for the credits, the vehicles must meet at least Bin 5 standards if they are up to 6,000 lb GVWR, or Bin 8 standards if the vehicles are 6,001 lb-8,500 lb GVWR.

But don't wait too long. The credit will phase out quickly. The phase-out period is triggered when an auto manufacturer sells its 60,000th hybrid vehicle. That's the total per manufacturer, not 60,000 per model. Once the cap is reached, the phase-out starts at the beginning of the second subsequent calendar quarter.

For the next two quarters, buyers can claim only half the credit.

In the 6 months after that . . . 25 percent of the full credit. So if Honda's cap was reached say, in August 2010, buyers of Honda hybrids would get 100 percent of the credit through December 31, 50 percent for those purchased in January 2011 through June 2011 and 25 percent for any bought in the remainder of the year. After that, zero.

63 Telephone Tax Refund

If you paid a long distance telephone tax, you got a refund on your 2006 tax return. You could have claimed either the tax you paid or a standard refund amount of $30 if you claim one exemption, $40 if you claim two, $50 for three, and $60 for four or more.

64 First-Time Home Buyer Credit

The Housing and Economic Recovery Act of 2008 gave first-time home buyers a refundable tax credit of 10 percent of the purchase price, up to $7,500 ($3,750 for married people filing separately). The credit began to phase out at the $150,000 adjusted gross income level for joint filers ($75,000 for other filers) and was not available for joint filers with income above $170,000 ($95,000 for other filers). It also was not available to nonresident aliens, those who qualified for a similar District of Columbia credit, or those whose financing came from tax-exempt mortgage revenue bonds. The credit was effective for homes purchased on or after April 9, 2008, and before July 1, 2009. But this credit must be paid back, in equal installments for 15 years. So if you got the full $7,500, you'd pay an additional "tax" of $500 each year. Payments start 2 years after the year in which the residence is purchased or earlier, if you sell the house or if it is no longer your principal residence. You qualify as a "first-time home buyer" if neither you nor your spouse had any ownership interest in a principal residence during the 3-year period before the new home is purchased. The best news: is that if you die, you don't have to pay back the credit.

The American Recovery and Reinvestment Act of 2009 changed the rules for those buying a principal residence after January 1, 2009, and before December 1, 2009. It increased the credit to $8,000 and eliminated the obligation to repay (unless the house was sold within 3 years of purchase).

The phase-out to qualify remained the same. You still could not buy from a relative, and multiple buyers could allocate the credit in any "reasonable" way. Whether or not you qualified was determined on the date of closing. So, if you qualified and closed and then married someone who didn't qualify, you still got the credit. If you purchased in 2010, you could have amended your 2009 return and would have received the credit refund before filing your 2010 return in 2011. This provision not only got your money faster, but it allowed you to qualify on the basis of 2009 income if your 2010 income was too high. A copy of your settlement sheet attached to the amended return proved your eligiblity.

If you bought in 2008 and financed with tax-exempt mortgage revenue bonds, you didn't qualify. This restriction was removed for post-2008 purchases.

This credit was extended again to include contracts signed by April 30, 2010, which closed by September 30, 2010. Also added was a credit of up to $6,500 for new buyers who owned a principal residence for at least 5 consecutive years of the 8-year period ending on the date of the new purchases. File Form 5405 to claim this credit.

These new rules raised the income limits for purchases after November 6, 2009. You got the full credit with income up to $125,000 ($225,000 on a joint return) phasing out at $145,000 ($245,000 on a joint return).

Dependents were no longer eligible nor was a home costing more than $800,000. The buyer must be at least age 18 on the day of closing. Members of the armed forces and certain federal employees serving outside the United States for at least 90 days during 2009 and 2010 had an extra year to buy and qualify.

65 "Making Work Pay" Tax Credit

This provision of the American Recovery and Reinvestment Act of 2009 cut taxes for more than 95 percent of working families in the United States. For 2009 and 2010, the provision provided a *refundable* tax credit of up to $400 for working individuals and $800 for working families. This refundable tax credit was calculated at a rate of 6.2 percent of earned income, and phased out for taxpayers with adjusted gross income in excess of $75,000 ($150,000 for married couples filing jointly). You could receive this benefit through a reduction in the amount of income tax that was withheld from your paycheck, or through claiming the credit on your tax return using Schedule M. Amend your return if you missed it!

Phase-out

Unmarried taxpayer (maximum credit)

MAGI	Credit before Phase-out	Credit after Phase-out
$75,000	$400	$400
$80,000	$400	$300
$85,000	$400	$200
$90,000	$400	$100
$95,000	$400	$0

Married taxpayer (maximum credit)

MAGI	Credit before Phase-out	Credit after Phase-out
$150,000	$800	$800
$160,000	$800	$600
$170,000	$800	$400
$180,000	$800	$200
$190,000	$800	$0

If you had no other earned income but were receiving Social Security, SSI, or railroad retirement or veteran disability compensation benefits, your credit was $250. A retired federal employee also qualified for the $250 credit ($500 on a joint return if both spouses are eligible). Both the Social Security and retired government employee benefits were one-shot deals, while the regular "making work pay" credit was available in both 2009 and 2010.

For 2011, this credit was not available, but the loss was offset by a one-year 2 percent reduction in employee (and self-employed) Social Security payroll taxes, extended into 2012, but for the employee side only.

The American Recovery and Reinvestment Act of 2009 added the following new energy credits.

66 Plug-in Electric *Drive* Vehicle Credit (Sec. 1141)

The 2009 law modified the 10 percent credit for qualified plug-in electric drive vehicles purchased or leased after December 31, 2009. To qualify, vehicles must be newly purchased or leased, have four or more wheels, have a gross vehicle weight rating of less than 14,000 pounds, and draw propulsion using a battery with at least 4 kilowatt hours that can be recharged from an external source of electricity. The minimum amount of the credit for qualified plug-in electric drive vehicles is $2,500, and the credit tops out at $7,500, depending on the battery capacity. The full amount of the credit will be reduced with respect to a manufacturer's vehicles after the manufacturer has sold at least 200,000 vehicles. Only one credit per vehicle. Note, this credit is based on energy savings rather than cost.

67 Plug-in Electric Vehicle Credit (Sec. 1142)

The 2009 law also created a special tax credit for two types of plug-in vehicles—certain low-speed electric vehicles and two- or three-wheeled vehicles. The amount of the credit is 10 percent of the cost of the vehicle, up to a maximum credit of $2,500 for purchases made after February 17, 2009, and through 2013 (extended by subsequent laws). To qualify, a vehicle must be either a low- speed vehicle propelled by an electric motor that draws electricity from a battery with a capacity of 4 kilowatt hours or more or be a two- or three-wheeled vehicle propelled by an electric motor that draws electricity from a battery with the capacity of 2.5 kilowatt hours. A taxpayer may not claim this credit if the plug-in electric *drive* vehicle credit is allowable. Only one credit per vehicle. Note, this credit is based on cost.

68 Conversion Kits (Sec. 1143)

The 2009 law also provided a tax credit for plug-in electric drive conversion kits. The credit is equal to 10 percent of the cost of converting a vehicle to a qualified plug-in electric drive motor vehicle and placed in service after February 17, 2009. The maximum amount of the credit is $4,000. The credit does not apply to conversions made after December 31, 2011. A taxpayer may claim this credit even if the taxpayer claimed a hybrid vehicle credit for the same vehicle in an earlier year. Claim the credit on Form 8910.

69 Treatment of Alternative Motor Vehicle Credit as a Personal Credit Allowed against AMT (Sec. 1144)

Starting in 2009, the 2009 law allows the alternative motor vehicle credit, including the tax credit for purchasing hybrid vehicles, to be applied against the alternative minimum tax. Prior to the 2009 law, the alternative motor vehicle credit could not be used to offset the AMT. This means that the credit could not be taken if a taxpayer owed AMT or was reduced for some taxpayers who did not owe AMT.

70 Small Business Health Insurance Credit

Many small businesses and tax-exempt organizations that provide health insurance coverage to their employees now qualify for a special tax credit.

This is designed to encourage small business employers to offer health insurance coverage for the first time or maintain coverage they already have. In general, the credit is available to small business employers that pay at least half the cost of single coverage for their employees.

The maximum credit is 35 percent of premiums paid by eligible small business employers and 25 percent of premiums paid by eligible employers that are tax-exempt organizations. In 2014, this maximum credit increases to 50 percent of premiums paid by eligible small business employers and 35 percent of premiums paid by eligible employers that are tax-exempt organizations.

The credit is specifically targeted to help small businesses and tax-exempt organizations that primarily employ low- and moderate-income workers. It is generally available to employers that have fewer than 25 full-time equivalent (FTE) employees and that are paying wages averaging less than $50,000 per employee per year. Because the eligibility formula is based in part on the number of FTEs, not the number of employees, many businesses will qualify even if they employ more than 25 individual workers.

The maximum credit goes to smaller business employers—those with 10 or fewer FTEs—paying annual average wages of $25,000 or less.

71 Foreign Tax Credit

You can get a credit for foreign income taxes you pay. If the amount totals not more than $300 ($600 on a joint return), you do *not* have to file Form 1116 to claim the credit.

CHAPTER 6

"Above the Line" Deductions

"Take it off. Take it all off. . . ."

GYPSY ROSE LEE

INCOME TAX RATES

Year	Maximum Individual Rate	Year	Maximum Individual Rate
1914	7%	1990	28/33%
1916	15	1991	31
1917	67	1992	31
1918	77	1993	36/39.6
1920	65	1994	36/39.6
1921	50	1995	39.6
1924	40	1996	39.6
1926	25	1997	39.6
1934	63	1998	39.6
1936	79	1999	39.6
1941	81	2000	39.6
1942	88	2001	39.1
1944	94	2002	38.6
1945	91	2003	35
1951	92	2004	35
1954	91	2005	35
1964	77	2006	35
1970	70	2007	35
1981	50	2008	35
1987	38.5	2009	35
1988	28/33	2010	35
1989	28/33	2011	35
		2012	35
		2013	44.3*

*39.6% + 0.9% additional payroll tax on *earned* income + 3.8% additional payroll tax on *unearned* income.

Our tax system is founded on a multistep computation. You begin with gross income. This is all income, all accession to wealth, clearly realized, over which you have dominion, less those items defined earlier as tax exclusions. From gross income you then subtract a certain category of expenses called by tax practitioners *adjustments* or *above the line deductions*. A deduction is a reduction of your taxable income—the income base on which your tax is imposed. *Above the line deductions* include trade and business deductions, alimony, moving expenses, student-loan interest, self-employment, tuition tax deduction, IRA, Keogh, and SEP deductions, certain education expenses, the deduction for contributions to a health savings account, and employee business expenses of performing artists.

Gross income less adjustments (*above the line deductions*) gives your adjusted gross income. From adjusted gross income, you then subtract the greater of your itemized deductions (*below the line deductions*) or your standard deduction. The standard deduction is basically similar to the old zero bracket amount. It is different from the zero bracket amount in that it is a deduction from adjusted gross income and not a tax bracket.

Unlike pre-1987 law, if you itemize your deductions you will not be required to reduce your itemized deductions by the amount of the standard deduction (zero bracket amount). Instead, you will deduct 100 percent of your itemized deductions and not take the standard deduction. Therefore, you will only itemize deductions if they exceed the amount of your standard deduction.

For 2012 and 2013 the standard deduction amounts are as follows:

	2012	2013
Married taxpayers filing jointly	$11,900	$12,200
Heads of households	8,700	8,950
Single taxpayers	5,950	6,100
Married taxpayers filing separately	5,950	6,100

For 2008 and 2009, those who don't itemize could add real estate taxes paid up to $500 ($1,000 on joint returns) plus the motor vehicle sales tax deduction to their standard deduction.

Prior to 1987, an additional personal exemption was available if you were 65 or older or blind. For 2013 tax returns, a taxpayer is deemed to be 65 or older if his or her 65th birthday falls on January 1, 2014, or earlier*; one is legally blind if one's central visual acuity does not exceed 20/200 in the better eye with

---

*For dependency exemptions, the child care credit, the adoption credit, and the child tax credit, you don't get older until your actual birthdate.

corrective lenses, or if the diameter of one's visual field subtends an angle of 20 degrees or less. This additional personal exemption has been replaced by an increased standard deduction called *the additional amount.* If you or your spouse qualified for the age or blindness exemptions under prior law, you will qualify for these additional amounts. The additional amounts are as follows:

1. $1,500 for individuals who are single or head of household

2. $1,200 each for all other taxpayers

These additional amounts, if available, will be added to the regular standard deduction and treated in the same way as the standard deduction. However, any taxpayer who is the dependent of another taxpayer for purposes of the dependency exemption will have a limited standard deduction. Such a taxpayer's standard deduction will be the greater of either $1,000 or that individual's earned income plus $350 up to the amount of the regular standard deduction.

Your tax computation continues with a subtraction for your personal exemptions, leaving a figure called your taxable income. Your tax is based on your taxable income. For the taxable year 2013, the amount of the personal exemption is $3,900. For taxable years beginning in a calendar year after 1989, there is an inflation adjustment to the exemption amount. This inflation adjustment will be based on the consumer price index for all urban consumers issued by the U.S. Department of Labor.

In summary, the process appears as follows:

Gross Income
– Adjustments ("above the line" deductions)
_____

Adjusted Gross Income
– Itemized ("below the line") Deductions or Standard Deduction
_____

(Subtotal)
– Personal Exemptions
_____

Taxable Income

To reduce your tax you must reduce your taxable income. One of the most important things to do, therefore, is to recognize and claim all available deductions. The chart that follows shows the value of every dollar of deductions in terms of dollars saved for each taxpayer classification.

Dollar Values of Deductions Claimed, 2013

Single			Married Filing Joint Returns and Qualifying Widows and Widowers			Married Filing Separate Returns			Head of Household		
Taxable Income Over	But Not Over	Value of Each Dollar of Deductions	Taxable Income Over	But Not Over	Value of Each Dollar of Deductions	Taxable Income Over	But Not Over	Value of Each Dollar of Deductions	Taxable Income Over	But Not Over	Value of Each Dollar of Deductions
$0	$8,925	10¢	$0	$17,850	10¢	$0	$8,925	10¢	$0	$12,750	10¢
$8,925	$36,250	15¢	$17,850	$72,500	15¢	$8,925	$36,250	15¢	$12,750	$48,600	15¢
$36,250	$87,850	25¢	$72,500	$146,400	25¢	$36,250	$73,200	25¢	$48,600	$125,450	25¢
$87,850	$183,250	28¢	$146,400	$223,050	28¢	$73,200	$111,525	28¢	$125,450	$203,150	28¢
$183,250	$398,350	33¢	$223,050	$398,356	33¢	$111,525	$199,175	33¢	$203,150	$398,350	33¢
$398,350	$400,000	35¢	$398,350	$450,000	35¢	$199,175	$225,000	35¢	$398,350	$425,000	35¢
$400,000		39.6¢	$450,000		39.6¢	$225,000		39.6¢	$425,000		39.6¢

Note that the higher your taxable income, the more valuable the dollar amount of deductions. This is the result of our progressive tax structure. I will use this structure later to show you how you could reduce your taxes by shifting income from the 35 percent bracket (where you keep only 65¢ from each additional dollar you earn) to the 10 percent bracket (where you keep 90¢ from each additional dollar you earn). But first you must recognize and understand the concept of tax-deductible expenses. To do that, you must understand the basic difference between deductions *for* adjusted gross income (above the line deductions) and deductions *from* adjusted gross income (below the line deductions).

A Deductions for Adjusted Gross Income

There are several categories of deductions for adjusted gross income that you must be aware of to minimize your taxes. We will take each in turn:

72 Trade and Business Deductions

All "ordinary and necessary expenses," paid or incurred by you during your taxable year in carrying on any trade or business are allowed as above the line deductions.

Here it is very important to understand that the words "ordinary and necessary" are words of art. For an expense to be deductible, it need not be absolutely necessary in the sense that you cannot conduct your trade without incurring such an expense. The courts have interpreted the words "ordinary and necessary" to mean "reasonable and customary," and this interpretation has been accepted by the Internal Revenue Service. Therefore, any expenses that you might incur in your business that are reasonable and customary for that business, even if not in any sense necessary, are deductible.

This provides you with an excellent opportunity to convert what would normally be nondeductible personal expenses into deductible business expenses. For example, assume that you have your own trade or business in New York and want to take a vacation in Miami. Alternatively, you could live in Miami and want to vacation in California. Almost all businesses have professional associations or trade groups who conduct seminars or hold meetings in resort areas. If you could schedule your vacation in these areas at the same time as the professional meeting and attend that professional meeting, your travel expenses, subject to the limits discussed in Chapter 9, would be converted from personal expenses into allowable, deductible business expenses. While attendance at these conventions or trade shows might not be necessary to your business, it would be reasonable and customary. Later in the book I will discuss more of these extensive tax advantages for those who own their own businesses.

73   Employee Business Expenses of Actors and Other Performing Artists

Employee business expenses of actors and other performing artists are deductible in arriving at adjusted gross income. In order to qualify, the performing artist must have performed services in the performing arts as an employee for at least two employers during the year. For this purpose, a nominal employer (i.e., one from whom less than $200 was received for the performance of such services during the year) is excluded.

Moreover, the allowable expenses in connection with the performance of the services must be more than 10 percent of the taxpayer's gross income from the services, and the individual's adjusted gross income for the year, before deducting these expenses, cannot be more than $16,000.

A performing artist who is married at the end of the taxable year must file a joint return with his/her spouse to qualify for the above the line deduction unless both husband and wife live apart at all times during the year. In the case of a joint return, the two-employer requirement as well as the requirement that the expenses be more than 10 percent of gross income are applied separately with respect to each spouse. However, the $16,000 adjusted gross income test is applied to the combined adjusted gross income of both spouses. In effect, such performing artists are allowed the deductions as if they were independent contractors rather than employees.

Such deductions would be allowable above the line and would include all ordinary and necessary expenses incurred by you during your taxable year. These expenses are detailed in the section on Miscellaneous Trade and Business Deductions of Employees on page 303.

74 Employee Business Expenses

Under prior rules, if an employer reimbursed an employee (1) for expenses of the employee in connection with the performance of services as an employee and (2) pursuant to a "reimbursement or other expense allowance arrangement," the amount reimbursed generally was includable in the employee's gross income and is deductible in full by the employee as an adjustment to gross income. On the other hand, unreimbursed employee business expenses can be deducted only as miscellaneous itemized deductions and thus are subject to the 2 percent adjusted gross income floor on such deductions.

In Rev. Rul. 77-350, the Internal Revenue Service held that, in certain circumstances, an employee could claim an above the line deduction for certain expenses incurred pursuant to "nonaccountable plans." Congress became concerned that the 2 percent floor could be circumvented by restructuring the form of an employee's compensation so that the salary amount is decreased but the employee receives an equivalent nonaccountable expense allowance.

Effective for tax years beginning after 1988, employee business expenses paid or incurred under nonaccountable plans are deductible by an employee *only* as an itemized deduction subject to the 2 percent floor. These are arrangements under which the employee is *not* required to substantiate the expenses covered by the arrangement to the person providing the reimbursement, or the employee has the right to retain amounts in excess of the substantiated expenses covered under the arrangement. Otherwise allowable employee business expenses are deductible above the line as reimbursed expenses *only* if they were incurred pursuant to a reimbursement or other expense allowance arrangement that *requires* the employee to substantiate expenses covered by the arrangement to the person providing the reimbursement. The expense must be business-connected, and any excess payment must be returned to the employer. Such "*accountable*" plans yield no income to the employee, and a deduction to the employer. An employee who receives a per diem or other fixed allowance from an employer will be considered as substantiating the amount of expenses covered by the arrangement up to amounts that have been specified by the IRS.

75 Alimony

Certain payments that constitute "alimony" may be taken as above the line deductions by the payer. Such alimony payments may be made from husband to wife or from wife to husband. For illustration purposes, I will refer to payments coming from husband to wife.

The Internal Revenue Service tax code provides that periodic payments received by a wife in discharge of her husband's obligation of support arising out of the marital or family relationship are deductible if any one of the following situations is true:

1. The payments are made in discharge of a legal obligation incurred under a court order, decree of divorce, or legal separation, where the spouses are either divorced or legally separated.

2. The payments are made under a written separation agreement where the spouses are separated, living apart, *and* do not file a joint return.

3. The payments are made under a court order or decree for the spouse's support or maintenance where the spouses are separated, living apart, *and* do not file a joint return.

PRE-TAX REFORM ACT OF 1984 LAW

Such payments were deductible by the husband and would therefore also be included in the wife's income. If any of the payments were fixed, in terms of a total amount of money or of payment for the support of minor children, they would not be deemed alimony and were neither taxed to the wife nor deductible by the husband. Prior to the Tax Reform Act of 1984, to qualify as child support payments rather than periodic alimony, the amounts must have been designated specifically as child support and not left to determination by inference or conjecture. Any amounts paid will be applied first to child support if such amounts are less than the total required to be paid. To be child support, though, the payments must be used for the support of minor children of the payer, the age of majority to be determined by applicable state law.

Periodic alimony payments will be deductible by the payer as an above the line deduction for adjusted gross income. In order to be deductible, the payments must be periodic rather than installment payments of a principal sum. Whether the payments are made at regular intervals is irrelevant; the key is whether they are periodic or principal sum payments, and the distinction between these two is whether there is a total amount to be paid that can be computed with certainty. If this is the case, the payments are *not* periodic. If the payments are contingent on death, remarriage of the wife, or a change in the economic status of either spouse, they *are* deemed to be periodic. This contingency may be a result of the decree or the separation agreement, or may be imposed by local law.

There is an exception to this general rule: If the principal amount payable under the terms of the divorce or separation decree is to be paid over more than 10 years from the date of the decree, then the payments *will* be considered periodic, but only the portion that equals 10 percent of the principal amount. For example, in a settlement of $300,000 to be paid over 15 years, with a first payment of $40,000, the recipient must include as gross income $30,000; the remainder is excludable. This limitation does not apply to late payments, but it does apply to advance payments. Late payments are treated as if they were made on time, and since both parties are deemed to be cash-basis taxpayers, these payments will be deductible when paid.

A payer may establish a trust or use an existing trust to discharge an obligation created by the decree of separation or divorce. All periodic payments from this kind of trust will be taxable to the recipient. Payments made by the trust will not be deductible by the payer, but an amount of the trust income that is equal to what is paid to the recipient will be excludable from the payer's gross income. An equal inclusion and deduction therefore result.

Other payments may or may not be deductible as periodic alimony. Payments for medical or dental insurance or direct medical or dental expenses for the spouse, even though made at irregular intervals, would be periodic. If the parties hold property jointly, any payments made that equal the recipient's interest in the property will be deductible by the payer—except where there is a right of survivorship. In that case, the payer will get a deduction only if the recipient is personally liable on the underlying debt or realizes an ascertainable increase in the value of the property that would be received as a survivor. No payments that are allocatable to the payer's interest in the property can be deducted by the payer or included in the recipient's income.

If the recipient resides in the home, utility expenses and repairs will be deductible regardless of ownership because the recipient is receiving a direct economic benefit. Capital expenditures must be capitalized rather than deducted. Periodic payments of life insurance premiums will also constitute deductible alimony payments if the recipient receives an economic benefit and is the absolute owner. Premium payments are not deductible if the policy is merely a security device, or if the recipient interest is contingent upon not remarrying or upon surviving the payer or the children who are the primary beneficiaries of the policy. In these cases, no present economic benefit to the recipient is ascertainable.

Property settlements, moreover, will not constitute periodic alimony. The intent of the parties, as determined by all of the facts and circumstances, will be the controlling factor here, rather than the label used. Property settlements *not* made out of the marital or family obligation of support will therefore be neither deductible nor includable. You should be aware, though, that if appreciated property is transferred in exchange for your spouse's inchoate marital rights, you will realize a gain equal to the full fair market value of the property less your cost or other basis. The character of the gain will be determined by the nature of the property you transfer. The spouse receiving the property will have a stepped-up basis and realize no gain. The amount realized there is deemed to be equal to what is exchanged.

If the property exchanged has depreciated in value, *never* make the transfer until the marriage has been dissolved. Otherwise, the loss will not be recognized. An alternative route to avoid this tax trap would be to sell the property to a third party and give the proceeds to your spouse. Be aware, though, that the rules do *not* apply in a community property state where all divisions are considered to be partitions of jointly owned property. There, taxable income will not be realized unless the division is clearly unequal in value.

POST–TAX REFORM ACT OF 1984 LAW

The Tax Reform Act of 1984 made significant changes both to the alimony rules and to property transfers incident to a divorce. With reference to property transfers incident to a divorce, the transfer will be treated in the same manner as a gift and therefore no capital gain or loss will be recognized for tax purposes. This rule applies to all transfers made after the date of enactment of the Act, or if both parties elect, to both transfers made between December 31, 1983 and the date of enactment as well as to transfers made after the date of enactment pursuant to instruments in effect before that date.

With reference to the rules governing alimony, the 1984 Act requires that alimony be paid in cash and terminate at the death of the payee spouse, that the parties may not be members of the same household at the time the payment is made, and that no amount will be deductible as alimony to the extent the payment is contingent on the status of a child (for example, if the payment terminates when a child marries, dies, or reaches maturity). Furthermore, under the 1984 Act, if payments in any year exceed $10,000, no part of such payments will be deductible unless the agreement provides that the payments be made for at least 6 years (unless the spouse dies or the payee spouse remarries), and a decline in excess of $10,000 in payments between any two successive years will cause a recapture of the excess amount. The effective date of the rules was January 1, 1985 for divorce or separation agreements executed on or after that date. The provisions apply to divorce or separation agreements executed before January 1, 1985 but modified on or after such date if the modification expressly provides that these provisions will apply.

The Tax Reform Act of 1986, however, amended the 6-year rule. Under the new law, amounts that are considered "excess alimony payments" will be included in taxable income of the payer in the *third* postseparation year. This inclusion will eliminate the benefit of the previous deduction for such payments. The payee will also be permitted a deduction corresponding to the amount includable in the payer's income in that third year.

Excess alimony payments are determined as follows:

- For the first postseparation year the excess alimony payment is that amount that exceeds the average of alimony payments in the second and third years plus $15,000. The excess alimony payment for the second year is that amount that exceeds the payment in the third year by more than $15,000. For example, a divorce agreement provides that the husband will pay his former wife alimony over a 3-year period as follows:

1st year	$35,000
2nd year	10,000
3rd year	20,000

- To calculate the excess alimony payment for the first year, the average of the second- and third-year payments must be computed. This average is $15,000 ([$10,000 + $20,000] ÷ 2). The excess alimony payment for the first year is therefore $5,000 ($35,000 − [$15,000 + $15,000]). In the third year the husband will have to include the $5,000 excess alimony payment in income, and the ex-wife will receive a corresponding deduction of $5,000.

The formula is as follows:

$$\text{Excess payments} = \text{alimony paid in 1st year} - \left[\$15,000 + \frac{\text{alimony paid in 2nd year} - \text{excess payments in 2nd year} + \text{alimony paid in 3rd year}}{2} \right]$$

- To complete the computation, the second-year excess amount must be determined first.

  The excess payment for the second postseparation year is the excess of the second-year alimony paid over the sum of third-year alimony paid plus $15,000; i.e.,

$$\begin{matrix} \text{Excess} \\ \text{payment} \end{matrix} = \begin{matrix} \text{alimony paid} \\ \text{in 2nd year} \end{matrix} - \left(\begin{matrix} \text{alimony paid} \\ \text{in 3rd year} \end{matrix} + \$15,000 \right)$$

- If alimony consists of one payment of $30,000 in the first postseparation year, and no alimony is paid thereafter, the amount recaptured is $15,000:

$$\$30,000 - \left[\$15,000 + \frac{(0-0)+0}{2} \right]$$

- If alimony paid in the first postseparation year is $50,000, in the second is $25,000, and in the third is zero, the second-year excess payment is $10,000:

$$\$25,000 - (0 + \$15,000)$$

- The first-year excess payment is $27,500:

$$\$50,000 - \left[\$15,000 + \frac{(\$25,000 - \$10,000) + 0}{2} \right]$$

- The recapture amount is $37,500, the sum of the first- and second-year excess payments. If $25,000 had also been paid in the third year, the recapture amount would be $10,000, the amount of the first-year excess payment, as there is no second-year excess payment:

$$\$50,000 - \left[\$15,000 + \frac{(\$25,000 - 0) + \$25,000}{2} \right]$$

The objective is to allow alimony payments as deductible if they are made in as few as 3 years. However, if the first payment is made in December of year 1, the second in January of year 2, and the third in January of year 3, the alimony will be deductible even though the payments are in fact spread over only 13 or 14 months.

Moreover, recapture is not required if alimony ceases when death or remarriage occurs before the end of the third postseparation year. Payments under temporary support agreements are also excluded from the recapture rules. In addition, the 1986 Act clarified that payments will not be disqualified from being treated as alimony simply because the divorce or separation agreement does not specifically state that the payments will terminate at the death of the recipient and, finally, that payments contingent on the fluctuating earnings of a business or property or from employment will also not result in recapture, if the obligation to pay extends for at least 3 years. These 1986 amendments apply to divorce or separation instruments executed after December 31, 1986, and divorce or separation instruments executed before that date if modified on or after such date to expressly state that the new provisions will apply.

The Tax Reform Act of 1984 also changed the rules with respect to which divorced parent receives the dependency exemption for a child. Beginning in 1985, the custodial parent is entitled to the exemption unless:

a) the custodial parent releases the exemption for the year, by written declaration on Form 8332, to the noncustodial parent. This form must be signed by the custodial parent and attached to the noncustodial parent's return, *or*

b) a decree of divorce or separate maintenance or a written agreement was executed before 1985, under which the custodial parent released the exemption to the noncustodial parent. In this event, the noncustodial parent can claim the exemption if he or she provides at least $600 annually for the child's support. However, the parties can expressly modify the document to render this exception inapplicable, *or*

c) a multiple support agreement is in effect.

Note also that under the 1984 Act, support by a remarried parent's new spouse is considered support furnished by that parent, and children of divorced parents are treated as *both* parents' dependents for medical deduction purposes. Hence, a parent can deduct medical expenses paid for a child even though the other parent gets the dependency exemption for that child.

Furthermore, a custodial parent who releases a dependency exemption will be considered as retaining that exemption when determining marital and head of household status, the earned income credit, and the child and dependent care credit. If otherwise eligible, such a parent could still qualify for unmarried and head of household status and those credits. For example, to claim head of household status, an individual must maintain a household as his or her home, which is also the principal place of abode for more than half a year for:

1. Any person whom you can claim as a dependent. But do not include:

    a) Your qualifying child whom you claim as your dependent because of the rule for *Children of divorced or separated parents* (see below).

    b) Any person who is your dependent only because he or she lived with you for all of 2013 or

    c) Any person you claimed as a dependent under a multiple support agreement.

2. Your unmarried qualifying child who is not your dependent.

3. Your married qualifying child who is not your dependent only because you can be claimed as a dependent on someone else's 2013 return.

4. Your child who, even though you are the custodial parent, is neither your dependent nor your qualifying child because of the rule for *Children of divorced or separated parents.*

Temporary absences by you or the other person for special circumstances, such as school, vacation, business, medical care, military service, or detention in a juvenile facility, count as time lived in the home.

The status is also available, as before, if a household is maintained for a taxpayer's dependent parents for a full year. The parent does not have to live with you.

The Working Families Tax Relief Act of 2004 modified some rules. A *noncustodial* parent may claim the exemption if awarded it under a decree of divorce or separate maintenance or under a written separation agreement. As of 2005, The Working Families Tax Relief Act of 2004 allows a written release to shift the dependency exemption. The shift should be documented in then formal divorce or separation paperwork. Form 8332 should be signed by the custodial parent and attached to the return of the noncustodial parent claiming the exemption.

In Rev. Proc. 2008–48, the IRS ruled that a child of divorced or separated parents or of parents living apart would be qualified as a "dependent" of both parents for purposes of employee fringe benefits, including medical. expense reimbursement, accident and health plans, the deductibility of medical expenses, and distributions from medical savings accounts and health savings accounts to pay medical expenses.

Several additional tax planning strategies present themselves based upon the rules. If a separation rather than a divorce is desired, you should be aware that while a *decree* of separate maintenance will prevent the filing of a joint return, mere physical separation will not. Physical separation, though, combined with a written separation agreement, will make any periodic payments "alimony," and deductible as such. Therefore, your first tax consideration must be to weigh the benefits of a joint return against an alimony deduction. Depending upon the marginal tax brackets of each party, a limited amount of shifting the tax burden may also occur here. Trade-offs, in terms of higher receipts in exchange for the filing of a joint return, may also be made by sophisticated and aware taxpayers.

You must carefully consider the character of any payments to be made—that is, whether they are for child support or alimony. Child support is neither includable nor deductible. Here again a certain amount of tax shifting is possible.

If any payment for child support is not specifically designated as such, it potentially may be taxed or deducted as alimony. If the recipient is in a lower tax bracket than the payer, any increase in "alimony" from child support will be taxable at a lower marginal rate and deductible at the payer's higher marginal rate. Because of this tax savings, the payer can afford to pay a larger amount of "child support," enough to offset the recipient's increased tax burden, plus a little more.

For example, assume that a husband-payer has a marginal tax bracket of 28 percent and his recipient-wife has a marginal tax bracket of 15 percent. The husband plans to pay periodic alimony of $10,000 and child support of $10,000 per year. The wife has agreed. This agreement would cost the husband $17,200 per year:

Child support (no deduction)	$10,000
Alimony [$10,000 × (1 − .28)]	+7,200
	$17,200

The wife would keep $18,500 per year:

Child support (no inclusion)	$10,000
Alimony [$10,000 × (1 − .15)]	+8,500
	$18,500

If the husband converted the whole $20,000 to alimony, it would cost him only $14,400:

$$\text{Alimony } [\$20,000 \times (1 - .28)] = \$14,400$$

He therefore would save $2,800 over the original agreement. The wife would now have:

$$\text{Alimony } [\$20,000 \times (1 - .85)] = \$17,000$$

which is a loss of $1,500. But this loss could be offset by the $2,800 saved by the husband. All he would have to do is increase the alimony payments to $22,500:

$$\text{Cost to husband } [\$22,500 \times (1 - .28)] = \$16,200$$
$$\text{Wife keeps } [\$22,500 \times (1 - .15)] = \$19,125$$

The result of this plan is that the husband would save $1,000 ($17,200 − $16,200) over the first plan. The wife's position would also be better—by $625 ($19,125 − $18,500)!

Another tax planning strategy involves post-1984 separations. If a husband transfers stock that has appreciated in value from $10,000 to $100,000, the 1984 law relieves him of the tax on the gain and gives it to his wife instead. This presents another alternative strategy for shifting income from a high bracket taxpayer (husband) to a lower bracket taxpayer (wife). To offset this incidence of taxation, the recipient wife should again negotiate an increased payout to absorb, or reduce, the husband's net tax savings on the transfer of appreciated, rather than nonappreciated, property.

76   Interest on Qualified Education Loans

Interest paid on qualified education loans was deductible above the line for payments made during the first 60 months in which payments are required. After December 31, 2001, the 60-month limit is eliminated.

The maximum amount of this deduction was $1,000 for 1998, $1,500 for 1999, $2,000 for the year 2000, and is $2,500 for tax years 2001 and after.

The deduction is phased out for taxpayers with modified adjusted gross income between $60,000 and $75,000 for single filers, and between $125,000 and $155,000 for joint returns.

You must be legally obligated to make the payments (sign the note) and you can't be claimed as a dependent if you want to qualify for this deduction.

77   Retirement Plan Payments

As you get older, it is important that you carefully provide for sufficient retirement funds. The same consideration must also be given to sheltering current income from the painful bite of our progressive tax system. The above the line deduction for retirement plan payments allows you to satisfy both of these needs.

If you are self-employed, which includes being an owner or a partner of an unincorporated business, you may provide for your retirement by setting up either a Keogh plan (H.R. 10 Plan), an individual 401(k) plan, or an Individual Retirement Plan, as described below. Under the Self-Employed Individual's Tax Retirement Act of 1962 (also called the Keogh Act and H.R. 10), you are permitted to put a portion of your yearly earned income, on a tax-deferred basis, into a fund that can earn tax-free income until it starts paying out at retirement.

You are eligible for an individual retirement account (IRA) if you or your spouse are employed, self-employed, or even covered by a corporate pension plan. You may have an IRA in addition to a Keogh plan. But, there will be limits as to what you can deduct.

Under both a traditional IRA and a Keogh plan, a portion of your income is sheltered from current taxation; there is no tax on the earnings of the fund until postretirement distribution; there is no tax on income contributed to the fund until post-retirement distribution; and qualified contributions made by employers to provide employees with retirement benefits are deductible by the employers. Keogh plans, individual 401(k)s, and IRAs allow the self-employed owner of a business to shelter current earned income and allow that income to accumulate and earn currently nontaxable income until postretirement distribution.

The primary difference between a Keogh plan and an IRA is the amount of earnings that may be sheltered. Under an IRA, as much as 100 percent of compensation—up to a normal limit of $5,500 a year—may be put aside, and that amount, subject to the limits detailed below, is deductible. If you have a nonemployed spouse, both of you are age 50 or older, and your modified adjusted gross income is under $115,000, the potential contribution maximum increases to $13,000. With a Keogh plan, the contribution limits are 25[1] percent of earned income or $51,000 for 2013, whichever is less. Defined benefit plans allowed an amount computed to yield a maximum annual benefit of $205,000 for 2013. A special type of IRA called a Simplified Pension Plan will also allow contributions—the lesser of $51,000 or 25 percent for 2013 of earned income. The major constraint for both the Simplified Pension Plan and the Keogh plan is that in both cases the owner (considered an employee as well under certain plans) may be forced to make contributions for other employees as well; however, these contributions will be deductible. The ultimate decision as to whether to establish an IRA or Keogh plan or both should be made on the basis of which has the greatest cash savings after tax.

If you are an employer, you may set up an Individual Retirement Account for yourself without setting up a similar one for your employees. With a Keogh plan you must cover your employees.

IRA PLAN[2]

There are several advantages to an IRA. An IRA allows the owner of a business to shelter personal earned income for retirement *without* the requirement to

---

1. For owner-employees only, this is 25 percent of income after the Keogh deduction. This really equals about 20 percent of pre-Keogh earned income. The actual number is a multistep calculation (see worksheet). I will be using the 20 percent figure as an estimate for examples and discussion.
2. Note that for tax years beginning after 1997, the Tax Relief Act of 1997 created new IRAs and modified the phase-out rules for old IRAs.

For a Single Profit Sharing Plan or a Single Money Purchase Plan

Use this worksheet to calculate your annual Keogh contribution if you have a single Profit Sharing or Money Purchase Plan.

		Example	Yourself
1.	**Net Business Profits** (From Schedule C, C-EZ, or K-1)	$250,000	____
2.	**Deduction for Self-Employment Tax** (From IRS Form 1040)	$9,969	____
3.	**Adjusted Net Business Profits** (Subtract Line 2 from Line 1)	$240,031	____
4.	**Actual Contribution Percentage (expressed as a decimal)** (Desired contribution percentage of earned income—for Money Purchase Plan, 3–25%; for Profit Sharing Plan, 0–25%)	.25	____
5.	**Contribution Factor** (Add 1.00 to Line 4)	1.25	____
6.	**Adjusted Earned Income** (Divide Line 3 by Line 5)	$192,025	____
7.	**Maximum Earned Income** (Enter $255,000 for 2013)	$255,000	____
8.	**Final Earned Income** (The lesser of Line 6 and Line 7)	$192,025	____
9.	**Preliminary Contribution Amount** (Multiply Line 4 by Line 8, round down to closest dollar)	$48,006	____
10.	**Maximum Dollar Contribution Amount** (Enter $51,000)	$51,000	____
11.	**Contribution Amount** (The lesser of Line 9 and Line 10)	$48,006	____

make contributions for employees. As a taxpayer eligible for an IRA, you would be allowed to contribute for a nonemployed spouse and the contribution maximum would increase ($2,000 each for years after 1996, increased to $3,000 each in 2002, $4,000 each in 2005, and to $5,500 each in 2008 and after, plus a $500 catch-up contribution [$1,000 for 2006 and after] if you're age 50 or older). The purpose of this is to provide retirement income for nonemployed homemakers. Contributions are deposited into separate accounts for you and your nonemployed spouse or into one account with subaccounts for each. No one account, however, may have attributed to it more than $5,500 in contributions per year. In case of divorce, the homemaker keeps his or her share of the money. Of course, if both spouses are employed and are eligible, each can set aside 100 percent of earnings, up to $5,500 each year, in separate IRAs.

The tax deduction for the IRA contribution is available as an above the line deduction. Taxes on both contributions to and earnings of the account may be deferred until the funds are withdrawn as retirement benefits. At that time you may be in a lower tax bracket than previously and may qualify for retirement income credits. At age 65 you are entitled to the additional standard deduction (now called "additional amounts"). So during the period you receive your IRA funds, you may be paying a smaller percentage of your income for taxes than you did in earlier years. Benefits from IRA plans can be drawn without penalty anytime after reaching age 59½. Distribution normally begins no later than April 1 in the year following the year you attain age 70½. This rule was modified by the Small Business Protection Act of 1996.

The 1996 law modified the rule that requires all participants in qualified plans to commence distributions by age 70½ without regard to whether the participant is still employed by the employer. Under the 1996 law, distributions are generally required to begin by April 1 of the calendar year following the later of the calendar year in which the employee attains age 70½ *or* the calendar year in which the employee retires. However, in the case of a 5 percent owner of the employer, distributions are required to begin at no later than April 1 of the calendar year following the year in which the 5 percent owner attains age 70½.

In addition, in the case of an employee (other than a 5 percent owner) who retires in a calendar year after attaining age 70½, the 1996 law requires the employee's accrued benefit to be actuarially increased to take into account the period after age 70½ in which the employee was not receiving benefits under the plan. Thus, under the 1996 law, the employee's accrued benefit is required to reflect the value of benefits that the employee would have received if the employee had retired at age 70½ and had begun receiving benefits at that time. However, this actuarial adjustment rule does not apply in the case of a defined contribution plan.

Earnings eligible for IRA contributions include wages, salaries, or professional fees and other amounts received for personal services actually rendered, including (but not limited to) commissions paid to sales personnel, compensation for services on the basis of a percentage of profits, commissions on insurance premiums, tips, and bonuses. Retroactive to 2004, even tax exempt combat pay now qualifies. All contributions must be made in cash. No deductions are allowable for contributions of property other than cash.

If you receive payment from an IRA before you reach age 59½ or before you become disabled, the payment will normally be considered a premature distribution. That amount received is included in your gross income in the tax year of receipt. In addition, your income tax liability for that year will be increased by an amount equal to 10 percent of the premature distribution includable in gross income. This penalty can be avoided by withdrawing substantially equal annual amounts over your life expectancy, until age 59½ or for five years, whichever comes later. For example, if you are 58, you must make withdrawals through age 63. However, if you are age 45, you must continue making withdrawals through age 59½. Once you finish making the *required withdrawals* they may be modified or stopped.

As discussed previously, amounts withdrawn from an individual retirement account (IRA) are includable in income (except to the extent of any non-deductible contributions). In addition, a 10 percent additional tax applies to withdrawals from IRAs made before age 59½ and unless the withdrawal is made on account of death or disability or is made in the form of annuity payments.

A similar additional tax applies to early withdrawals from employer-sponsored tax qualified pension plans. However, the 10 percent additional tax does not apply to withdrawals from such plans to the extent used for medical expenses that exceed 7.5 percent of adjusted gross income.

The Small Business Job Protection Act of 1996 extended the exception to the 10 percent tax for medical expenses in excess of 7.5 percent of adjusted gross income to withdrawals from IRAs. In addition, it provides that the 10 percent additional tax does not apply to withdrawals for medical insurance (without regard to the 7.5 percent of adjusted gross income) if the individual (including a self-employed individual) has received unemployment compensation under federal or state law for at least 12 weeks, and the withdrawal is made in the year such unemployment compensation is received or the following year. If a self-employed individual is not eligible for unemployment compensation under applicable law, he or she is treated as having received unemployment compensation for at least 12 weeks if the individual would have received unemployment compensation but for the fact the individual was self-employed. You also avoid 10 percent penalty if you're age 55 or older and are "separated from service"—fancy legal talk for "lost your job."

The Taxpayer Relief Act of 1997 extended the exception to the 10 percent penalty to *first time home purchases* and *qualified higher education expenses.*

A first-time home buyer is an individual (and/or spouse) who has had no present ownership interest in a primary residence during the 2-year period ending on the date of acquisition (see following) of the principal residence. A first-time home buyer under these rules does not necessarily mean a person buying a home for the first time. For example, individuals could be buying their fifth home yet qualify as "first-time" home buyers if they have had no ownership interest in a primary residence for the past two years. *Both* spouses must qualify, and, if so, *both* may withdraw $10,000 from each IRA.

A date of acquisition is the date when a binding contract to purchase a principal residence is executed or the date when construction or reconstruction of a principal residence begins.

Qualified acquisition cost is the cost of acquiring, constructing, or reconstructing a residence.

The amount withdrawn for the purchase of a principal residence is required to be used within 120 days of the date of withdrawal. You are limited to a $10,000 lifetime withdrawal. Even though withdrawals made from traditional IRAs for first-time home purchases are penalty-free, they may be subject to regular income taxes. (Withdrawals from a Roth IRA, discussed in the following, can be both penalty *and* tax-free if the 5-year requirement is met.)

The 1997 tax law also allows you to make penalty-free withdrawals from traditional IRAs for higher education expenses, such as tuition at an eligible postsecondary education institution, room and board, fees, books, supplies, and equipment required for enrollment or attendance. Expenses for graduate-level courses also are covered. You can use your IRA distribution to pay for these expenses incurred by you, your spouse, your children, your spouse's children, your grandchildren, or your spouse's grandchildren. Please note that this type of withdrawal is not an income-tax-free distribution.

SUMMARY OF PREMATURE DISTRIBUTION RULES

Many taxpayers mistakenly fail to pay the additional 10 percent tax due on premature distributions. Premature distributions (sometimes called early withdrawals or early distributions) are subject to an additional 10 percent tax. The definition of premature distributions are amounts that are withdrawn from traditional individual retirement accounts (IRAs) or annuities before the individual reaches the age of 59½.

In certain circumstances, the additional penalty tax does not apply to premature distributions from an IRA or annuity even though they are made prior to reaching the age of 59½.

There are exceptions for:

- Effective only through December 31, 2007, those in the military, including the Reserve and National Guard, who were on active duty for at least 180 days after September 11, 2001.

- Certain unemployed individuals to pay health insurance premiums. To qualify, you must receive unemployment benefits for 12 consecutive weeks and tap the IRA either in the year that the benefits are paid or in the following year. The 10 percent penalty won't apply even if the medical premiums are paid before the withdrawal is made from the IRA (*Davis*, TC Summ. Op. 2009-61).

Note that the distributions are still subject to income tax, except in the case of a Roth IRA. Contributions from Roth IRAs usually can be withdrawn free of tax.

- Certain medical expenses (beginning after December 31, 1996)
- Disability
- Death
- Annuity distributions
- Qualified higher education expenses (beginning after December 31, 1997)
- Qualified first-time home buyer (beginning after December 31, 1997 $10,000 lifetime limitation)
- IRS levy on IRA (beginning after December 31, 1999)

The additional tax is equal to 10 percent of the premature distribution that must be included in gross income. The tax is in addition to any regular income tax that is due. It does not include tax-free rollovers. For more information regarding the additional 10 percent tax, see Publication 590, Individual Retirement Account Arrangements (IRAs) including Roth IRAs and Education IRAs.

Taxable distributions from an individual retirement account are taxed as ordinary income regardless of their source. They are not eligible for capital gains treatment or the special averaging rules that apply to lump-sum distribution from qualified employer plans (which were available only through December 31, 1999).

Under *old* minimum distribution rules, if you died before receiving the entire interest on your individual retirement account, the remaining interest had to be distributed to your beneficiary within 5 years after death, or be applied to purchase an immediate annuity for the beneficiary payable over the life or for a period not exceeding the life expectancy of that beneficiary. Any annuity contracts so purchased had to be distributed immediately to the beneficiary. A spousal beneficiary may roll the distribution into his or her own IRA account.

Exception to 10% Additional Tax

Type of Distribution	401(k) and Other Qualified Retirement Plans	IRA/SEP, SIMPLE IRA and SARSEP Plans	Internal Revenue Code
After participant/IRA owner reaches age 59½	Yes	Yes	§72(t)(2)(A)(i)
After *death* of the participant/IRA owner	Yes	Yes	§72(t)(2)(A)(ii)
Total and permanent *disability* of the participant/IRA owner	Yes	Yes	§72(t)(2)(A)(iii)
Series of substantially equal payments	Yes	Yes	§72(t)(2)(A)(iv)
Separation from service during or after year employee reaches age 55 (age 50 for public safety employees)	Yes	No	§§72(t)(2)(A)(v) and 72(t)(10)
Dividend pass through from an ESOP	Yes	N/A	§72(t)(2)(A)(vi)
Because of an IRS levy of the plan	Yes	Yes	§72(t)(2)(A)(vii)
Amount of your *unreimbursed medical expenses* (> 7.5% AGI)	Yes	Yes	§72(t)(2)(B)
To an alternate payee under a *Qualified Domestic Relations Order*	Yes	No	§72(t)(2)(C)
Payment of health insurance premiums made while unemployed	No	Yes	§72(t)(2)(D)
Qualified higher education expenses	No	Yes	§72(t)(2)(E)
Qualified first-time homebuyers up to $10,000	No	Yes	§72(t)(2)(F)
Certain distributions to qualified military reservists called to active duty	Yes	Yes	§72(t)(2)(G)
Corrective distributions (and associated earnings) of excess deferrals, excess contributions, and excess aggregate contributions made timely	Yes	N/A	§§401(k)(8)(D), 401(m)(7), and 402(g)(2)(C)
Excess IRA contributions if withdrawn by extended due date of return	N/A	Yes	§408(d)(4)
Earning on *excess IRA* contributions distributed	N/A	No	§408(d)(4)
Permissive *withdrawals* from a plan with auto enrollment features	Yes	Yes for SIMPLE IRAs and SARSEPs	§414(w)(1)(B)
Rollovers	Yes	Yes	§§402(c), 403(a)(4), 403(b)(8), 408(d)(3), and 408A(d)(3)(A)

Governmental 457(b) distributions are not subject to the 10% additional tax except for distributions attributable to rollovers from another type of plan or IRA.

NEW MINIMUM DISTRIBUTION RULES

On January 11, 2001, the Internal Revenue Service proposed regulations (REG-130477-00, REG-130481-00) to simplify the minimum distribution rules for qualified plans and individual retirement accounts.

The rules would:

- Provide a uniform table to determine lifetime required minimum distributions regardless of age
- Permit a beneficiary to be determined up to the end of the year following an employee's death
- Allow life expectancy at the time of death to be taken into account in the calculation of postdeath minimum distributions.

The IRS said the regulations would affect qualified plans, individual retirement plans, tax code Sec. 457 plans, tax code Sec. 403(b) annuity contracts, custodial accounts, and retirement income accounts. The rules would be permissable for determining required minimum distributions for calendar years beginning on or after January 1, 2001, and must be used for distributions after December 31, 2001. However, they could *not* be used for calculating 2000 distributions deferred and made during the 3-month grace period—ending April 1, 2001—available to IRA owners who turned 70½ during 2000.

The regulations provide a uniform distribution period for all employees of the same age, calculated by the minimum distribution incidental benefit divisor table. The MDIB table—based on the joint life expectancies of an individual and a survivor 10 years younger at each age beginning at 70—would allow employees to determine their required minimum distribution each year based only on current age and current account balance, IRS said.

There are now only two calculation choices to be made:

1. **Uniform Distribution Table, Recalculated Life Expectancy.** This method will be used by all IRA owners with one exception, as noted in No. 2. IRA owners will obtain their life expectancy factor from the Uniform Distribution Table. The Uniform Distribution Table [referred to in IRS Publication 590 as the Table for Determining Applicable Divisor for MDIB (Minimum Distribution Incidental Benefit)] assumes that RMDs are based on the lives of an IRA owner and a beneficiary who is 10 years younger than the IRA owner. The IRA owner will refer back to the Uniform (MDIB) Distribution Table each calendar year and use the factor that appears next to the IRA owner's age on his or her birthday during that year. This method

should be used whether an individual or a nonliving entity (such as a charity, trust, or estate) is named as the primary beneficiary of the IRA account.

2. **Joint Life Expectancy, Recalculating Both Life Expectancies.** This is the one exception to the Uniform Distribution Table rule in No. 1: If an IRA owner has named his or her spouse as the *sole primary beneficiary for the entire calendar year and the spouse is more than 10 years younger than the IRA owner,* the IRA owner can choose to use the Joint Life Expectancy Tables. The IRA owner refers back to the Joint Life Expectancy Tables each calendar year and uses the factor that appears at the intersection of the ages of the IRA owner and younger spouse as of their birthdays in that year.

The amount of the Required Minimum Distribution (RMD) is determined by taking the IRA account balance as of the end of the prior year (December 31 value), and then dividing it by the life expectancy factor for that year.

December 31 prior-year balance/life expectancy factor = RMD

The minimum distribution rules were waived for 2009, but returned for 2010 and after.

CALCULATING IRA REQUIRED MINIMUM DISTRIBUTIONS

Use the following table to compute your required minimum distribution. Take the account balance on December 31 of the previous year and divide it by the figure next to your age. If a spouse beneficiary is more than 10 years younger than you are, use the joint-life-and-last-survivor table in IRS Pub. 590.

BENEFICIARY RULES

You no longer have to name a beneficiary for your account by April 1 of the year after you reach age 70½. Failing to do so used to trigger a demand that the IRA be paid out over your relatively brief single-life expectancy. Now, you'll use the uniform life expectancy table even if you don't name a beneficiary. You can name—and change—your beneficiaries at any time, without worrying that a post-70½ switch will speed up required withdrawals.

In most cases, after your death, your beneficiary will use his or her own life expectancy (as shown in Publication 590 and Publication 590 Sup) to figure distributions.

If there are multiple beneficiaries to a single account, the payout is based on the oldest beneficiary's life expectancy. To expand the payout time, you

IRA REQUIRED MINIMUM DISTRIBUTIONS

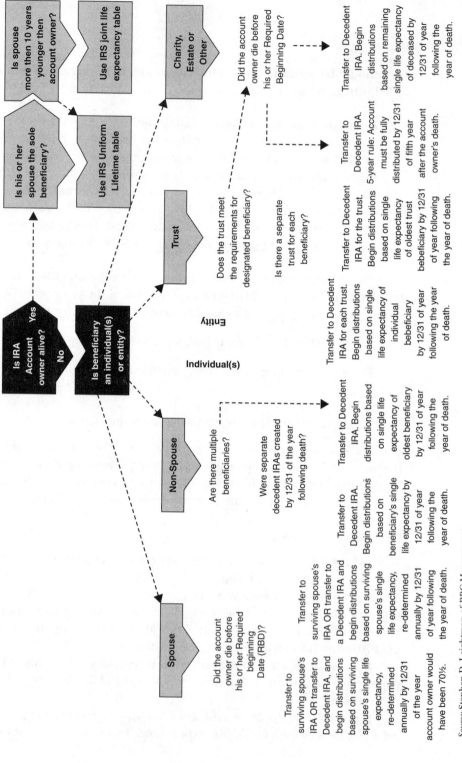

Source: Stephen D. Leightman of RBC Management

Uniform Distribution Table

This table is the new life expectancy table to be used by all IRA owners to calculate lifetime distributions (unless your beneficiary is your spouse who is more than 10 years younger than you). In that case, you would not use this table, you would use the actual joint life expectancy of you and your spouse based on the regular joint life expectancy table. The Uniform Distribution Table is never used by IRA beneficiaries to compute required distributions on their inherited IRAs.

Age	Distribution Period	Age	Distribution Period	Age	Distribution Period	Age	Distribution Period Life Expectancy
70	27.4	81	17.9	92	10.2	103	5.2
71	26.5	82	17.1	93	9.6	104	4.9
72	25.6	83	16.3	94	9.1	105	4.5
73	24.7	84	15.5	95	8.6	106	4.2
74	23.8	85	14.8	96	8.1	107	3.9
75	22.9	86	14.1	97	7.6	108	3.7
76	22.0	87	13.4	98	7.1	109	3.4
77	21.2	88	12.7	99	6.7	110	3.1
78	20.3	89	12.0	100	6.3	111	2.9
79	19.5	90	11.4	101	5.9	112	2.6
80	18.7	91	10.8	102	5.5	113	2.4
						114	2.1
						115 & over	1.9

Single Life Expectancy Table for Inherited IRAs

(to be used for calculating post-death required distributions to beneficiaries)

Designated beneficiaries use this single life expectancy table based on their age in the year after the IRA owner's death. That factor is reduced by one for each succeeding distribution year. Spouse beneficiaries who do not elect to roll the IRA over or treat it as their own, also use the single life table, but they can recalculate each year.

Age	Life Expectancy	Age	Life Expectancy	Age	Life Expectancy	Age	Life Expectancy
10	72.8	29	54.3	48	36.0	67	19.4
11	71.8	30	53.3	49	35.1	68	18.6
12	70.8	31	52.4	50	34.2	69	17.8
13	69.9	32	51.4	51	33.3	70	17.0
14	68.9	33	50.4	52	32.3	71	16.3
15	67.9	34	49.4	53	31.4	72	15.5
16	66.9	35	48.5	54	30.5	73	14.8
17	66.0	36	47.5	55	29.6	74	14.1
18	65.0	37	46.5	56	28.7	75	13.4
19	64.0	38	45.6	57	27.9	76	12.7
20	63.0	39	44.6	58	27.0	77	12.1
21	62.1	40	43.6	59	26.1	78	11.4
22	61.1	41	42.7	60	25.2	79	10.8
23	60.1	42	41.7	61	24.4	80	10.2
24	59.1	43	40.7	62	23.5	81	9.7
25	58.2	44	39.8	63	22.7	82	9.1
26	57.2	45	38.8	64	21.8	83	8.6
27	56.2	46	37.9	65	21.0	84	8.1
28	55.3	47	37.0	66	20.2	85	7.6

*partial table – full table can be found in IRS Publication 590 – www.IRS.gov

might consider multiple accounts with a single beneficiary for each. This method gives your heirs the longest possible period of tax deferral and is best guaranteed by naming a designated beneficiary on your IRA.

Forced lump-sum distributions are gone. Under the new rules, your heirs will never face the tax consequences of being forced to empty the IRA in a single year.

If you die *after* required distributions begin and *without a designated beneficiary,* the distribution period for your heirs will generally be your remaining life expectancy at the end of the year after your death.

If you die *before* mandatory payouts begin and *without a designated beneficiary,* at worst the IRS will allow your heirs up to 5 years to withdraw the money and pay taxes.

A beneficiary who is a surviving spouse can roll over the dollars into his or her own IRA. This allows the spouse to use the uniform Distribution Table and to name beneficiaries that can further extend the payout life of the account.

Under the new RMD rules, non-spousal beneficiaries (e.g., a child) can "stretch" out payments over his or her own life expectancy as well! This results in longer tax defined compounding inside the IRA and much greater family wealth creation.

An excellent MDR calculation can be found at Professor Stephen A. Leimberg's www.Leimbergservices.com.

Also see the following Websites for more details:

- www.ataxplan.com

- www.irahelp.com

- www.stretchira.com

BENEFICIARY DISTRIBUTION OPTIONS

	BENEFICIARY	**DISTRIBUTION OPTIONS**
Death Before Required Beginning Date	**Spouse**	1. Transfer or roll to own IRA. • RMDs must begin at 70½. 2. Decedent IRA—Distributions are required to begin by 12/31 of the year the account owner would have been 70½. • Distributions are based on the single life expectancy of the surviving spouse, redetermined annually. • No 10% penalty. 3. Lump Sum Distribution.
	Non-Spouse— Designated Beneficiary	1. Decedent IRA—Annual distributions must begin by 12/31 of the year following the year of the account owner's death. • Separate beneficiary accounts are established.

BENEFICIARY DISTRIBUTION OPTIONS *(continued)*

	BENEFICIARY	DISTRIBUTION OPTIONS
Death After Required Beginning Date		• Distributions are based on the single life expectancy of the beneficiary, reduced by one for each subsequent year. 2. Five-year death rule. • Discretionary payouts until 12/31 of fifth year after the account owner's death. Account must be fully paid out by this date.
	Non-Spouse—No Designated Beneficiary	1. Five-year death rule. • Discretionary payouts until 12/31 of fifth year after the account owner's death. Account must be fully paid out by this date.
	Spouse	1. Transfer or roll to own IRA. • RMDs must begin at 70½. 2. Decedent IRA—Annual distributions must begin by 12/31 of the year following the year of the account owner's death. • Distributions are based on the single life expectancy of the surviving spouse, redetermined annually. • No 10% penalty. 3. Lump Sum Distribution.
	Non-Spouse— Designated Beneficiary	1. Decedent IRA—Annual distributions must begin by 12/31 of the year following the year of the account owner's death. • Separate beneficiary accounts are established. • Distributions are based on the single life expectancy of the beneficiary, reduced by one for each subsequent year or the hypothetical remaining life expectancy of the deceased account owner, whichever is longer. 2. Five-year death rule. • Discretionary payouts until 12/31 of fifth year after the account owner's death. Account must be fully paid out by this date.
	Non-Spouse—No Designated Beneficiary	1. Decedent IRA—Annual distributions must begin by 12/31 of the year following the year of the account owner's death. • Distributions are based on hypothetical remaining life expectancy of the deceased account owner, reduced by one for each subsequent year.

Source: Stephen D. Leightman RBC Wealth Management

You can call the IRS toll-free at 1(877)-829-5500 if you have a question on retirement plans.

CONTRIBUTIONS

Tax-deductible contributions to an IRA must be made through:

a) an individual retirement account at a bank, federally insured credit union, or savings and loan association, or with certain applicants, any of whom, under temporary regulations, may act as a trustee or custodian;

b) an individual retirement annuity of a life insurance company;

c) individual retirement bonds purchased from the U.S. government; *or*

d) a trust account established by an employer or employee association.

The following transactions with IRA money are prohibited by law:

1. You cannot borrow money from your IRA.
2. You cannot use money in an IRA as collateral for a loan.
3. You cannot transfer property to an IRA in exchange for money.
4. You can put only cash into an IRA. For example, you cannot put stock that you currently own into an IRA account. You must sell the stock first, put the cash from that sale into your IRA, and then purchase the stock again if you want to have that stock in the IRA account.

While not specifically prohibited, note that an IRA investment in a limited partnership interest where business income is passed through would trigger an IRA tax on "unrelated business income" (IRS Letter Ruling 9703026). Any debt-financed property inside a qualified plan will trigger this unrelated business tax (UBT).

You can, however, invest your IRA funds in real estate—from raw land to rental property. While you can't manage the property, your trustee can hire a third party to do so. Moreover, the property must remain in the IRA trust until distribution at retirement and the property can't be mortgaged. Based on *Swanson v. Commissioner*, 106 T.C. 76 (1996), some advisors suggest forming a limited liability company wherein the IRA accountholder is named the manager of the LLC. The accountholder instructs the IRA custodian to deposit the IRA assets into the newly formed LLC. If you want real estate in your IRA, check out Steve Berman and Jay Suttenberg at the Laurel Group, 856-857-2859, www.realestate4IRA.com, or see independent IRA custodians, independent IRA administrators, and IRA advisors www.sterling-trust.com or call toll-free 1-800-955-3434.

Other custodians who take IRAs with unconventional assets, such as real estate or business interests, include:

Fiserv Investment Support Services (recent rollup of Lincoln Trust, First Trust, Resources Trust, Retirement Accounts): 800-525-2124, www.fiserviss.com

Pensco Trust: 415-274-5600, www.pensco.com

Millennium Trust: 800-258-7878, www.mtrustcompany.com

Quads: 800-435-7024, www.quadsweb.com

Trust Administration Services: 800-455-9472, www.trustlynk.com

Moreover, you should note that any stock in an IRA account that is sold loses the capital gains treatment. This means that when you withdraw your money from the IRA, gains cannot be offset by capital losses.

ELIGIBILITY

Starting with 1987, the Tax Reform Act of 1986 made substantial changes in IRA eligibility. Under the prior law, IRA deduction is retained for returns of taxpayers who meet *either* of the following requirements:

1. The taxpayer is not an active participant in certain specified retirement arrangements for any part of the plan year ending with or within the taxpayer's tax year. Active participation status is determined without regard to whether a taxpayer has a vested right to any benefits under a plan and may depend upon the type of plan in which an individual participates or is eligible to participate. For example, for defined benefit plans, a person who is not excluded under the plan's eligibility provisions for any part of the plan year ending with or within the taxpayer's tax year is an active participant. Therefore, even if you elect not to participate in a plan or fail to make an employee contribution required to accrue a benefit attributable to employer contributions, you nevertheless are an active participant in the plan. For defined contribution plans, a taxpayer is an active participant if employer or employee contributions or forfeitures are required to be allocated to his account for a plan year ending with or within the taxpayer's tax year. According to the IRS, a taxpayer may be an active participant even if a required contribution for the plan year is not actually made. However, unlike defined benefit plans, an individual who does not meet the hours of service requirements of a defined contribution plan is not considered an active participant unless contributions or forfeitures have been allocated to her account. For a married individual filing a joint return, neither the individual taxpayer nor the taxpayer's spouse may be an active participant. Moreover, retirement arrangements not only include traditional qualified plans, annuity plans, and trusts, but also include simplified employee pensions and 401(k) plans. For 401(k) plans however, you are usually not an "actual participant" until pay-ins are made to the plan.

2. The taxpayer has adjusted gross income that does not exceed the "applicable dollar amount." For a married couple filing jointly, combined income may not exceed the applicable dollar amount. The applicable dollar amount *was*

(a) $25,000 for an individual, (b) $40,000 for a married couple filing a joint return, and (c) $0 for a married couple filing separately.

$$\frac{\$10,000 - \text{excess adjusted gross income}}{\$10,000} \times \begin{array}{c}\text{the maximum permissible} \\ \text{dollar deduction defined} \\ \text{as the lesser of 100} \\ \text{percent of compensation} \\ \text{or } \$2,000 \ (\$2,250 \text{ for} \\ \text{spousal IRAs})\end{array} = \begin{array}{c}\text{adjusted dollar} \\ \text{deduction limit}\end{array}$$

Active participants whose adjusted gross incomes exceed the applicable dollar amount by no more than $10,000 are still entitled to deduct IRA contributions, but only in a reduced amount calculated according to the following formula provided by the IRS:

Note that for this purpose, adjusted gross income includes Social Security benefits and passive income or losses, but not IRA contributions.

For example, assume in 1997 that you and your spouse earned $25,000 and $20,000 in adjusted gross income (total $45,000) and that your spouse was a participant in a qualified pension plan. Your maximum permissible dollar deduction would have been $4,000 ($2,000 for you and $2,000 for your spouse). Your maximum deductible IRA, however, would be computed as follows:

Maximum IRA	$4,000
Less: Phase-out over $40,000	
$\dfrac{(\$45,000 - 40,000) \times \$4,000}{\$10,000}$ =	$2,000
Tax-deductible IRA	$2,000

Your maximum tax-deductible IRA would therefore be only $2,000. Taxpayers not above the phaseout maximum are permitted a minimum IRA deduction of $200. Moreover, prior to the Tax Reform Act of 1986, a spousal IRA of $250 was allowed only if the spouse had no compensation. Under current law, an individual may elect to be treated as if he or she had no compensation for the taxable year. This means, for an otherwise qualifying couple, the annual deduction contribution has increased from $2,000 to $2,250 ($4,000 for years after 1996, becoming $6,000 for 2002 and $8,000 for 2005, and $10,000 for 2008 through 2012, and $11,000 for 2013 and after).

The Taxpayer Relief Act of 1997 changed the rules again. We now have three kinds of IRAs. The first is the current deductible IRA. The 1997 law raised the phase-out income limits on these front-loaded IRAs for those covered by a qualified plan. Under prior law, if your modified adjusted income (for a joint return) was between $40,000 and $50,000, your IRA deduction was reduced and then eliminated (the limits were $25,000–$35,000 for single filers). These phaseout amounts were raised by $10,000 for couples and $5,000 for singles in 1998, and by $1,000 per year through 2002; in 2003 they increased to $40,000 for single filers and $60,000 for joint filers, and by $5,000 per year thereafter. At the end of that time the phase-out limits would have doubled. The phase-out will then be from $80,000–$100,000 for joint returns, and $50,000–$60,000 for single filers. Moreover, the law allows a nonworking spouse to contribute a fully deductible $5,000, even if the other spouse participates in a qualified retirement plan, with a phase-out of $178,000–$188,000 in 2013. The following table summarizes the changes in phase-out rules:

	Joint (in thousands)	Single (in thousands)
1997	$40–50	$25–35
1998	50–60	30–40
1999	51–61	31–41
2000	52–62	32–42
2001	53–63	33–43
2002	54–64	34–44
2003	60–70	40–50
2004	65–75	45–55
2005	70–80	50–60
2006	75–85	50–60
2007	83–103	52–62
2008	85–105	53–63
2009	89–109	55–65
2010	89–109	56–66
2011	90–110	56–66
2012	92–112	58–68
2013	95–115	59–69

ROTH IRA

The second kind of IRA is the *Roth IRA*. Here, contributions will not be deductible but, if the IRA is held for at least 5 years (the 5-year period starts on the first day of the year for which a contribution is made or in which the first conversion contribution is made) and the account holder is at least 59½ years old, then all withdrawals will be tax-free! Moreover, more people will be eligible to fund these accounts. The 2013 income limits phased out at from $112,000–$127,000 for single taxpayers and from $178,000–$188,000 for couples. However, the combined contributions to these two types of accounts are limited to $5,500 per year for each taxpayer. You could roll a regular IRA into a Roth IRA account but some taxes would be assessed upon the rollover. These taxes were spread over 4 years, if done in 1998, to minimize the impact of the change. I think it was a reasonable toll charge to avoid all future taxes on the account. After 1998, the 4-year spread is not available. Whether you should convert to a Roth is a function of your age and the expected return on the account. The older you are, the less advantageous the conversion becomes. See page 203 for current conversion opportunities.

More than two dozen financial services companies offer Roth IRAs for minors. Here are some examples:

- **American Century Investments:** 800-345-2021
- **Franklin Templeton Investments:** 800-632-2301
- **Strong Financial:** 800-368-1030
- **T. Rowe Price:** 800-638-5660
- **Vanguard Group:** 800-662-7447

Note that distributions from Roth IRAs that are not qualified distributions are generally treated as a recovery of basis first, and then as taxable distributions.

Roth 401(k) and Roth 403(b) distributions that are not qualified distributions are treated differently—they are generally taxed on a pro rata basis.

The Tax Increase Protection and Reconciliation Act of 2005, passed in 2006, eliminated the income limits on conversions of traditional IRAs to a Roth for years starting January 1, 2010. But, you did not have to wait till then. You could have contributed to nondeductible IRAs before 2010 if your income was too high. Then, convert those dollars to a Roth. You pay tax only on the gain, and that tax is spread over 2 years, 2011 and 2012 if you converted in 2010.

The new rule on *after-tax* contributions is much more liberal than the one that governs a conversion from a traditional IRA to a Roth IRA. In that case, the tax-free portion of the rollover is determined by the ratio of nondeductible pay-ins to the total amount in all of your IRAs. So if your $60,000 IRA contains $6,000 in nondeductible contributions and you convert that $6,000 to a Roth IRA, just $600, or one-tenth of the converted amount, would escape income tax. The remaining $5,400 would be taxed at your regular income tax rate. But under the new rules for after-tax money in 401(k)s and 403(b)s and 457 plans, the full $6,000 would escape taxes. Plus, there is no limit on how much you may convert.

What if you convert an IRA to a Roth and the value goes down? Consider using separate Roth IRAs for different asset classes. For the ones that go down in value, you can escape tax on the higher value by recharacterization to a traditional IRA before the due date of the return (plus extensions—normally until October 15). Then, if you want, you can reconvert to a Roth at the new lower value, at a lower tax cost.

For more information about firms that offer Roths, try the Investment Company Institute's Website, at www.ici.org.

COVERDELL EDUCATION IRAs

The 1997 law created a new *Education IRA*, also called *Education Savings Accounts.* As of July 26, 2001, they are called *Coverdell Education Accounts.* Contributions could be made of up to $500 per child under age 18 into an Education IRA, with a *then* income limit of from between $95,000–$110,000 for singles and $150,000–$160,000 for couples. These IRAs are *nondeductible,* but the earnings are tax-free. There is no penalty if they are used for educational purposes (including tuition, fees, room and board), regardless of your age. Any unused portion of an Education IRA can be rolled over to another child but, if the children do not attend college, the amounts must be paid out when the last child turns 30. Even if you don't qualify because of income limits, your parents may qualify to set up an account for their grandchildren. With an Education IRA, the donor doesn't even have to be related to the beneficiary!

The preceding rules were modified by the Tax Relief Act of 2001.

The 2001 law increased the annual limit on contributions to Coverdell Education Accounts from $500 to $2,000. The law expanded the definition of qualified education expenses that may be paid tax-free from an education IRA to include elementary and secondary school expenses. The law increased the phaseout range for married taxpayers filing a joint return so that it is twice the range for single taxpayers. Thus, the phaseout range for married taxpayers filing a joint return is $190,000 to $220,000 of modified adjusted gross income. However, you don't need *earned income* to contribute to an education IRA. If you make too much, gift the dollars to your child and have the child make the contribution.

The 2001 law provided that various age limitations do not apply to special needs beneficiaries.

The 2001 law clarified that corporations and other entities (including tax-exempt organizations) are permitted to make contributions to education IRAs, regardless of the income of the corporation or entity during the year of the contribution.

The 2001 law allows you to claim a HOPE credit or Lifetime Learning credit for a taxable year and to exclude from gross income amounts distributed (both the contributions and the earnings portions) from a Coverdell

2013 Options At-a-Glance

Provision	Traditional IRA	Roth IRA
Eligibility Requirements	Contributions can be made through an individual's 69½ year as long as that individual, or their spouse, has earned income.	Contributions can be made at any age as long as the contributor, or their spouse, has earned income and your modified-adjusted gross income (MAGI) does not exceed (for 2013): **Full** **Partial Contribution** **Not Eligible Contrib.** **Single Filers** up to $111,999 $112,000–$126,999 $127,000 or more **Joint Filers** up to $178,999 $178,000–$187,999 $188,000 or more **Married, Filing Separately** up to $9,999 Not eligible $10,000 or more
Maximum Contribution Limits	• For 2013, the maximum contribution limit is $5,500. • In 2013 an individual age 50 or older may contribute an additional $1,000. • Annual total contribution limit between Traditional IRA and Roth IRA in 2012, is $5,500 (or $6,500 if age 50 or over).	Same as Traditional IRA, subject to restrictions on MAGI as noted in Eligibility Requirements above.
Contribution Deadline	Tax Filing Deadline not including extensions (generally April 15).	Tax Filing Deadline not including extensions (generally April 15).
Key Tax Advantage	Tax-deferred growth. Contribution may be tax deductible.	Federally tax-free growth.

Deductibility of Contributions	**Yes, subject to retirement plan participation and MAGI limits:**
	Single filer, retirement plan participant with MAGI of:
	                    2013
	Fully Deductible $59,000 or less
	Partially Deductible $59,001–$68,999
	Nondeductible $69,000 or more
	Single filer, no retirement plan participation:
	Fully deductible
	Married, filing separately, retirement plan participant with MAGI of:
	                    2013
	Partially Deductible $0–$10,000
	Married, filing a joint return, retirement plan participant with MAGI of:
	                    2013
	Fully Deductible $95,000 or less
	Partially Deductible $95,001–$114,999
	Nondeductible $115,000 or more
		All contributions are nondeductible.

Provision	Traditional IRA	Roth IRA
	Joint filer, no retirement plan participation (but spouse is participant) with MAGI of:	
	2013	
	Fully Deductible $177,999 or less	
	Partially Deductible $178,000–$187,999	
	Nondeductible $188,000 or more	
	Joint filer, neither spouse is a retirement plan participant:	
	Fully deductible	
Required Distributions	Minimum distributions must begin by Required Beginning Date which is April 1 following 70½ year.	No minimum distributions required at any age.
Taxation of Distributions	• Taxes are deferred until distributions are made. All earnings and deductible contributions are taxed as ordinary income upon withdrawal. • If nondeductible contributions have been made each withdrawal is taxed proportionately. You use IRS Form 8606 to calculate your tax-free portion. Non-taxable distributions are also not subject to the 10% premature penalty.	**Qualifying Distributions** are tax and penalty free if your initial contribution to your Roth IRA was made at least five years ago and one of the following exceptions apply: • Attainment of age 59½ or older • Disability • Qualified first time home purchase • Distribution is made to an account beneficiary (lifetime limit of $10,000) **Non-Qualified Distributions** • *Annual contributions* can be withdrawn tax and penalty free at any time. • Distributions from a *conversion amount* must satisfy a five-year investment period to avoid the 10% penalty, unless an exception applies. The conversion amount is not subject to taxation. • Distributions from *earnings* will be taxed as ordinary income unless they are a qualifying distribution. They also will be subject to the 10% penalty unless an exception applies. The exceptions are the same as those for Traditional IRAs.
Exceptions to 10% Premature Penalty	Distributions taken on or after age 59½ or on account of: • Death • Substantially Equal Periodic Payments • Disability • Medical expenses in excess of 7½% AGI • Higher education expenses • Involuntary distributions due to an IRS levy • Insurance premiums paid by certain unemployed individuals • Qualified acquisition costs of a first time home buyer (lifetime limit of $10,000)	Distributions taken on or after age 59½ or on account of: • Death • Substantially Equal Periodic Payments • Disability • Medical expenses in excess of 7½% AGI • Higher education expenses • Involuntary distributions due to an IRS levy • Insurance premiums paid by certain unemployed individuals • Qualified acquisition costs of a first time home buyer (lifetime limit of $10,000)

Death Distributions	Regardless of when the owner dies:
	 • Spouse can transfer directly to own IRA.
	 • If beneficiary is non-spouse living person or qualifying trust:
	   ♦ Generally, distributions must commence by 12/31 of the year following the year of death over the single declining life expectancy of the designated beneficiary; or;
	   ♦ Exception: the 5-year rule.
		Regardless of when the owner dies:
		 • Spouse can transfer directly to own IRA.
		 • If beneficiary is non-spouse living person or qualifying trust:
		   ♦ Generally, distributions must commence by 12/31 of the year following the year of death over the single declining life expectancy of the designated beneficiary; or;
		   ♦ Exception: the 5-year rule.

(continues)

2013 Options At-a-Glance *(continued)*

Provision	Traditional IRA	Roth IRA
Conversions	• Conversion from Traditional IRA, Simple IRA, SEP IRA or qualified plan to Roth IRA is allowed regardless of income. • The amount converted is taxed as ordinary income, but no 10% penalty applies.	• Conversion from Traditional IRA, Simple IRA,[1] SEP IRA or qualified plan to Roth IRA is allowed regardless of income. • The amount converted is taxed as ordinary income, but no 10% penalty applies.
Transfers	• Assets can be transferred to another Trustee/Custodian. • A transfer may not be made between a Traditional IRA and a Roth IRA (however, a distribution from a Traditional IRA and subsequent conversion to a Roth IRA may be made).	• Assets can be transferred to another Trustee/Custodian. • A transfer may not be made between a Traditional IRA and a Roth IRA (however, a distribution from a Traditional IRA and subsequent conversion to a Roth IRA may be made).
Rollovers	• Traditional IRA, SEP IRA, SARSEP or Simple IRA1 to Traditional IRA • With Triggering Event • Qualified Plan to Traditional IRA • 403(b) Plan to Traditional IRA • Governmental Thrift Savings Plan to Traditional IRA • Governmental 457(b) to Traditional IRA	• Roth IRA to Roth IRA

[1]Simple IRA rollovers and conversions to non-Simple IRA accounts are not allowed in the first two years of participation

2013 Retirement Plan Options At-a-Glance

Feature	SEP	SIMPLE IRA	Money Purchase	Profit Sharing	Safe Harbor 401(k)	401(k)	Defined Benefit
Eligible Employer	Any Employer	Employers who, on any day during the preceding year, have 100 or fewer employees earning $5,000 or more in compensation. No other plan may be maintained at the same time.	Any Employer	Any Employer	Any Employer	Any Employer	Any Employer
Establishment Deadline	Employer tax filing deadline, including extensions.	October 1 current year.	Last day of employer's taxable year.	Last day of employer's. taxable year	New plans must be established 3 months prior to plan year-end. Existing plans must be amended by 1st day of plan year.	Last day of employer's taxable year.	Last day of employer's taxable year.
Eligible Employees	May be less restrictive, but cannot exclude those who exceed: • 21 years of age • Employed 3 of the last 5 years • $550 annual income Requires 100% participation of eligible employees.	Employees who receive $5,000 in compensation in *any* two preceding years *and* are expected to receive $5,000 in the current year are eligible. These requirements may be less restrictive.	May be less restrictive, but cannot exclude those who exceed: • 21 years of age • Completion of one year of service. (1,000 hours in 12 months.) May be 2 years if 100% immediate vesting.	May be less restrictive, but cannot exclude those who exceed: • 21 years of age • Completion of one year of service. (1,000 hours in 12 months.) May be 2 years if 100% immediate vesting.	May be less restrictive, but cannot exclude those who exceed: • 21 years of age • Completion of one year of service. (1,000 hours in 12 months.) May be 2 years for employer contribution if 100% immediate vesting.	May be less restrictive, but cannot exclude those who exceed: • 21 years of age • Completion of one year of service. (1,000 hours in 12 months.) May be 2 years for employer contributions if 100% immediate vesting.	May be less restrictive, but cannot exclude those who exceed: • 21 years of age • Completion of one year of service. May be 2 years if 100% immediate vesting. • 1,000 hours of service per year.
Contribution Limits Employers	Employer's discretion up to 25% of employee's compensation with a maximum of $51,000 for 2013. Contributions may continue beyond age 70½.	Employer must make matching contributions up to 3% of employee compensation or contribute 2% of total eligible employee compensation. Total employer contribution may not exceed $12,000 per year for 2013.	As specified in plan. Up to 25% of eligible payroll with a maximum of $51,000 for 2013. Contributions may continue beyond age 70½.	Employer's discretion up to 25% of eligible payroll. Maximum allocation per employee is $51,000 for 2013. Contributions may continue beyond age 70½.	Employer must make dollar-for-dollar matching contributions up to 3% of employee compensation or contribute 3% of total eligible employee compensation. Additional discretionary profit-sharing contributions allowed. Total employer contributions may not exceed 25% of eligible payroll.	Employer's discretion up to 25% of eligible payroll. Can be made as a matching or a profit-sharing contribution may continue beyond age 70½.	Actuarially computed based on age, compensation and years of service. Maximum benefit at age 65 is $205,000 for 2013 or 100% of highest 3 years salary.
Deadline for Employer Contribution	Employer tax filing deadline, including extensions.	Employer tax filing deadline, including extensions.	Employer tax filing deadline, including extensions.	Employer tax filing deadline, including extensions.	Employer tax filing deadline, including extensions.	Employer tax filing deadline, including extensions.	Employer tax filing deadline, including extensions.

(continues)

Feature	SEP	SIMPLE IRA	Money Purchase	Profit Sharing	Safe Harbor 401(k)	401(k)	Defined Benefit
Contributions Limits of Employee	Employee can contribute a traditional IRA contribution of up to $5,500, 2013 limit, $6,500 for 2013 if 50 or older, to their SEP account in addition to the employer's SEP contribution.	Employees can defer up to $12,000 per year for 2013 or 100% of compensation, whichever is less. Employees who are 50 or older can defer an additional $2,500 in 2013.	N/A	N/A	Employees can defer up to $17,500 for 2013. Employees who are 50 and older can defer an additional $5,500 in 2013. Employee and employer contributions per employee cannot exceed $51,000 for 2013.	Employees can defer up to $17,500 for 2013. Employees who are 50 and older can defer an additional $5,500 in 2013. Employee and employer contributions per employee cannot exceed $51,000 for 2013.	N/A
Deductions and Deferrals	Deduction for employer. Tax-deferred for employee.	Employer contributions deductible to employer. Tax-deferred for employee. Employee contributions are pre-tax and tax-deferred.	Deduction for employer. Tax-deferred for employee.	Deduction for employer. Tax-deferred for employee.	Employer contributions deductible to employer. Tax-deferred for employee. Employee contributions are pre-tax and tax-deferred.	Employer contributions deductible to employer. Tax-deferred for employee. Employee contributions are pre-tax and tax-deferred.	Deduction for employer. Tax-deferred for employee.
Vesting	100% vested immediately	100% vested immediately.	Several permissible vesting schedules.	Several permissible vesting schedules.	100% vested immediately on Safe Harbor contributions. Vesting schedule allowed on non-safe harbor profit sharing contributions.	Several permissible vesting schedules.	Several permissible vesting schedules.
Loan Provisions[1]	None	None	Yes	Yes	Yes	Yes	Yes
Testing	Generally not subject to top-heavy testing	No testing	Subject to top-heavy testing.	Subject to top-heavy testing.	Plan will pass 401(k) ADP and ACP tests if Safe Harbor rules are followed and will also meet top-heavy test requirements.	Subject to ADP, ACP, and top-heavy testing.	Yes
Distributions	Same as IRA. 10% premature distribution penalty may apply. Must begin distributions at age 70½. In-service distributions allowed.	10% premature distribution penalty may apply; penalty is increased to 25% during first 2 years. Must begin distributions at age 70½. In-service distributions allowed.	10% premature penalties may apply. Must begin distributions at age 70½ unless still employed.[2] In-service distributions not allowed.	10% premature distribution penalties may apply. Must begin distributions at age 70½ unless still employed.[2] In-service distributions available if plan document allows.	10% premature distribution penalties may apply. Must begin distributions at age 70½ unless still employed.[2] In-service distributions available if plan document allows.	10% premature distribution penalties may apply. Must begin distributions at age 70½ unless still employed.[2] In-service distributions available if plan document allows.	10% premature distribution penalties may apply. Must begin distributions at age 70½ unless still employed.[2] In-service distributions not allowed.

[1] Loan Limits: maximum of 50% of vested balance up to $50,000. Payments must be made at least quarterly with level amortization.
[2] Owners of 3% or more of a company must start distributions at age 70½.

The 2013 Chart: Retirement Plan Options for a SELF-EMPLOYED INDIVIDUAL with No Employees At-a-Glance

Feature	SEP	SIMPLE IRA	Owner-Only 401(k)	Defined Benefit Pension
Key Advantage	Easy to set up and maintain.	Salary reduction plan with less administration.	Often allows for larger contribution than a SEP or SIMPLE IRA.	Highest contribution allowed by IRS
Establishment Deadline	Business' tax-filing deadline, including extensions.	October 1 of current year.	Last day of business' taxable year.	Last day of business' taxable year.
Contribution Limits	Flexible contributions up to 25% of compensation with a maximum of $51,000 for 2013.	*Two sources of contributions*—Salary deferrals up to $12,000 per year, 2013 limit, or 100% of compensation, whichever is less. Individuals who are 50 or older can defer an additional $2,500 for 2013. Must make matching contribution up to 3% of compensation (maximum of $12,000 in 2013) or contribute 2% of compensation.	*Two sources of contributions*—Flexible contributions up to 25% of compensation. Salary deferrals up to $17,500 per year (2013). Individuals who are 50 or older can defer an additional $5,500 in 2013. Total contribution cannot exceed $50,000	Actuarially computed based on factors such as compensation, age, and years of service. Maximum benefit at age 65 is $205,000 for 2013 or 100% of the average highest 3 years of salary.
Employer Deduction/ Contribution Deadlines	Business' tax-filing deadline including extensions	If business is incorporated, salary deferrals must be made through payroll withholding. Deferrals must be deposited into a Simple IRA no later than the last day of the month following the month they were withheld. If business is sole proprietor or partnership salary deferrals must be made by business' tax-filing deadline, including extensions. Deadline for employer matching or non-elective contribution is business' tax-filing deadline, including extensions.	If business is incorporated, salary deferrals must be made through payroll withholding. Deferrals must be deposited to the plan as soon as administratively feasible. If business is sole proprietor or partnership salary deferrals must be made by business' tax-filing deadline, including extensions. Deadline for employer contributions is business' tax-filing deadline, including extensions.	Business' tax-filing deadline, including extensions. Quarterly deposits of plan contributions are required. However, to avoid a funding deficiency excise tax of 10% of the under funded amount a contribution must be made no later than 8 months after the close of the plan year.
Funding Requirements	Flexible	Flexible	Flexible but requires consistent funding.	Annual minimum funding requirements.
Catch-up Provisions	None	Yes	Yes	None
Administrative Responsibilities	Minimal, no employer tax filings.	Minimal, no employer tax filings.	Some administrative requirements – tracking of contributions, loans. IRS 5500 - EZ filing required when plan assets exceed $250,000 and annually thereafter.	Administrator required for contribution calculation, tracking of contributions, loans. IRS 5500-EZ filing required when plan assets exceed $250,000 and annually thereafter.
Distributions	Withdrawals permitted anytime subject to ordinary income taxes, 10% premature distribution penalty may apply.	Withdrawals permitted any time subject to ordinary income taxes, 10% premature distribution penalty may apply; penalty is increased to 25% during first two years.	Permitted after a specified event occurs (e.g. retirement, plan termination etc.). Distributions subject to ordinary income taxes. In-service distributions may be allowed. 10% premature distribution penalty may apply.	Payments of benefits or distribution permitted after a specified event occur (e.g., retirement, plan termination etc.). Distributions subject to ordinary income taxes. In-service distributions are not allowed. 10% premature distribution penalty may apply.
Loan Provisions[1]	No	No	Available	

[1]Loan Limits: maximum of 50% of vested balance up to $50,000. Payments must be made at least quarterly with level amortization. Please note, the plan document must be drafted to allow loans.

2012/2013 Dollar Limitations for Retirements Plans

Account Types		2012 Limit	2013 Limit
IRA	Traditional and Roth IRA Contribution Limit	$5,000	$5,500
	Catch-Up Limit for individuals age 50 and older	$1,000	$1,000
SIMPLE IRA	Elective Deferral Limit	$11,500	$12,000
	Catch-Up Limit for individuals age 50 and older	$2,500	$2,500
SEP IRA	Maximum SEP Contribution	$50,000	$51,000
	SEP Compensation Exclusion	$550	$550
401(k), SARSEP, 403(b) and 457(b)	Elective Deferral Limit	$17,000	$17,500
	Catch-up Limit for individuals age 50 and older	$5,500	$5,500
Profit Sharing, 401(k) and Money Purchase Pension	Defined Contribution Limit (415(c) limit)	$50,000	$51,000
Profit Sharing, 401(k), SEP and Money Purchase Pension	Employee Annual Compensation Limit	$250,000	$255,000
401(k), SARSEP, 403(b) and 457(b)	Highly Compensated Employee (no requirement for 5% owner)	$115,000	$115,000
Profit Sharing, 401(k) and Money Purchase Pension	Top-heavy Plan Key Employee Compensation Limit	$165,000	$165,000
Defined Benefit	Defined Benefit Limit	$200,000	$205,000
Social Security	Social Security Taxable Wage Base	$110,100	$113,700
	Maximum Earnings for Individuals under Normal Retirement Age before Social Security Benefits are reduced. One dollar in benefits will be withheld for every $2 in earnings above the limit.	$14,640	$15,120

Retirement Planning 2012/2013 Key Numbers

While an increasing number of retirement plan and IRA limits are indexed for inflation each year, most of the limits eligible for a cost-of-living adjustment (COLA) did not adjust upward. Some of the key numbers for 2013 are listed below, with the corresponding limit for 2012.

Elective Deferral Limits	2012	2013
401(k) plans, 403(b) plans, 457(b) plans, and SAR-SEPs[1] (includes Roth contributions)	Lesser of $17,000 or 100% of participant's compensation	Lesser of $17,500 or 100% of participant's compensation
SIMPLE 401(k) plans and SIMPLE IRA plans[1]	Lesser of $11,500 or 100% of participant's compensation	Lesser of $12,000 or 100% of participant's compensation

IRA Contribution Limits	2012	2013
Traditional IRAs	Lesser of $5,000 or 100% of earned income	Lesser of $5,500 or 100% of earned income
Roth IRAs	Lesser of $5,000 or 100% of earned income	Lesser of $5,500 or 100% of earned income

Retirement Planning 2012/2013 Key Numbers (*continued*)

Additional "catch-up" limits (individuals age 50 or older)	2012	2013
401(k) plans, 403(b) plans, 457(b) plans, and SAR-SEPs[2]	$5,500	$5,500
SIMPLE 401(k) plans and SIMPLE IRA plans	$2,500	$2,500
IRAs (traditional and Roth)	$1,000	$1,000

Defined Benefit Plan Annual Benefit Limits	2012	2013
Annual benefit limit per participant	Lesser of $200,000 or 100% of average compensation for highest three consecutive years	Lesser of $205,000 or 100% of average compensation for highest three consecutive years

Defined Contribution Plan Limits (qualified plans, 403(b) plans, and SEP plans)	2012	2013
Annual addition limit per participant (employer contributions; employee pretax, after-tax, and Roth contributions; and forfeitures)	Lesser of $50,000 or 100% (25% for SEP) of participant's compensation	Lesser of $51,000 or 100% (25% for SEP) of participant's compensation

Retirement Plan Compensation limits	2012	2013
Maximum compensation per participant that can be used to calculate tax-deductible employer contribution (qualified plans and SEPs)	$250,000	$255,000
Compensation threshold used to determine a highly compensated employee	$115,000 (when 2012 is the look-back year)	$115,000 (when 2013 is the look-back year)
Compensation threshold used to determine a key employee in a top-heavy plan	$1 for more-than-5% owners $165,000 for officers $150,000 for more-than-1% owners	$1 for more-than-5% owners $165,000 for officers $150,000 for more-than-1% owners

(continues)

Retirement Planning 2012/2013 Key Numbers (*continued*)

Retirement Plan Compensation limits	2012	2013
Compensation threshold used to determine a qualifying employee under a SIMPLE plan	$5,000	$5,000
Compensation threshold used to determine a qualifying employee under a SEP plan	$550	$550

Income Phase-out Range for Determining Deductibility of Traditional IRA Contributions for Taxpayers:	2012	2013
1.Covered by an employer-sponsored plan and filing as:		
Single/Head of household	$58,000–$68,000	$59,000–$69,000
Married filing jointly	$92,000–$112,000	$95,000–$115,000
Married filing separately	$0–$10,000	$0–$10,000
2. Not covered by an employer-sponsored retirement plan, but filing joint return with a spouse who is covered by a plan	$173,000–$183,000	$178,000–$188,000

Income Phase-out Range for Determining Ability to Fund a Roth IRA for Taxpayers Filing as:	2012	2013
Single/Head of household	$110,000–$125,000	$112,000–$127,000
Married filing jointly	$173,000–$183,000	$178,000–$188,000
Married filing separately	$0–$10,000	$0–$10,000

[1] Must aggregate employee deferrals to all 401(k), 403(b), SAR-SEP, and SIMPLE plans of all employers; 457(b) contributions are not aggregated. For SAR-SEPs, the percentage limit is 25% of compensation reduced by elective deferrals (effectively a 20% maximum contribution).

[2] Special catch-up limits may also apply to 403(b) and 457(b) plan participants.

Education Account on behalf of the same student, as long as the distribution is not used for the same educational expenses for which a credit was claimed.

The 2001 law repealed the excise tax on contributions made by any person to a Coverdell Education Account on behalf of a beneficiary during any taxable year in which any contributions are made by anyone to a qualified state tuition program on behalf of the same beneficiary.

The 2001 law allows a rollover of unused Coverdell Education Account funds to other family members, provided that they are under age 30, without penalty. If you invest $2,000 a year at 7 percent into a Coverdell Education Account for 18 years, you will have $36,758 in tax-free income and a total account valued at $72,758.

The provisions modifying Coverdell Education Accounts are effective for taxable years beginning after December 31, 2001.

For Bankruptcy filings after October 16, 2005, creditors cannot touch pay-ins to state tuition plans or Coverdell Education Accounts that are made more than 720 days before the bankruptcy filing date. The exclusion falls to $5,000 for pay-ins made more than 365 days but less than 721 days before the filing date, and to zero for any pay-ins made within 365 days.

The tables from Steve Leightman of RBC Wealth Management on pages 170–178 compare the various kinds of IRAs and other retirement plans. The table on page 181 details the rules for the Roth IRA.

Since 1987, *nondeductible* contributions to an IRA may be made up to the maximum deduction, reduced by any deductible contributions. Therefore, even if your contribution deduction is reduced under the adjusted gross income limitation, you can contribute the difference without deducting it. The earnings on such contributions are not taxed until distribution. Any nondeductible contribution must be indicated on your tax return for the contribution year.

If nondeductible contributions are made, withdrawals from IRAs must be divided between taxable and nontaxable segments. The Tax Reform Act of 1986 used an averaging approach to accomplish this task. For purposes of the computations, all of a taxpayer's IRAs are considered to be one single IRA and all withdrawals made during the year are added together and considered as one withdrawal. The percentage of an IRA withdrawal treated as a return of a nondeductible contribution, and therefore not taxable, is represented by a ratio whose numerator is the sum of all nondeductible contributions made to any of the taxpayer's IRAs and whose denominator is the sum of the balances in the taxpayer's IRAs at the end of the tax year plus withdrawals made during the year.

How Your Money Could Grow

◆ $500 invested today and each year thereafter for
   a newborn child

◆ Grows for 17 years at 8% with no taxes due

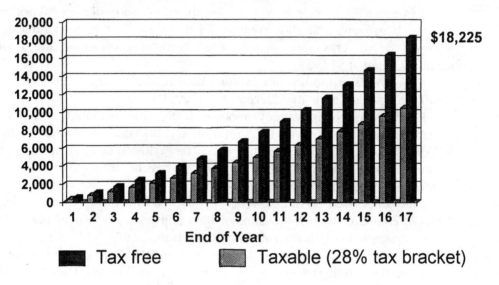

End of Year

■ Tax free   ▨ Taxable (28% tax bracket)

Tables 3 to 6, on pages 182–183, developed by Jerrold J. Stern of the Graduate School of Business, Indiana University, show break-even points at various tax and interest rates for deductible IRA contributions and nondeductible IRA contributions. Note that the tables include a 10 percent penalty on withdrawals prior to age 59½. Where the taxable percentage of the principal is zero, the tables assume that tax and penalty are paid only on the interest earned, and that the principal contribution (for example, $5,500) withdrawn is received tax-free.

Remember that if a taxpayer and spouse have 2013 joint income in excess of $95,000 and if even only one spouse is covered by a retirement plan, joint return deductions for payments to individual retirement accounts are phased out for the covered employee. But if the modified adjusted gross income limits are met ($178,000–$188,000), the noncovered spouse may make deductible contributions (see pages 167 and 184).

Roth IRA

CONTRIBUTIONS	**Maximum**	$5,500 per year of W-2 or Schedule C earnings (contributions allowed after age 70½). Contributions amount is limited if AGI is between: • $112,000 and $127,000 for individual returns • $178,000 and $188,000 for joint returns $5,500 maximum combined contribution into Roth IRA or traditional IRA per individual, per year.
	Provisions above AGI limits	Cannot participate if AGI exceeds stated limits (see "Maximum" subsection).
	Tax deductibility	Contributions are not tax deductible.
ACCUMULATIONS	**Interest, dividends, and capital gains**	Grow tax-deferred and distributed income tax-free as long as you abide by withdrawal rules (see "Distributions" section).
	Suitable investments	CDs; common and preferred stocks; unit investment trusts; government, corporate, and mortgage-backed bonds; mutual funds; private money managers.
DISTRIBUTIONS	**When allowed**	May withdraw up to original contribution amount at any time (may not apply to converted balances)
	Taxation	Withdrawal of earnings after age 59½ are income tax-free as long as investments have been in the account for 5 consecutive years. Before age 59½ and meeting the 5-consecutive-year requirement, earnings may be withdrawn income tax-free if one of the following qualifications is met: • Death. • Disability. • First-time home purchase up to $10,000 (once-in-a-lifetime use).
	When penalty applies	10% IRS penalty (in addition to ordinary income tax rates) applies to investment earnings withdrawn before reaching age 59½ regardless of the 5-year investment period (unless certain exceptions apply as described below or withdrawal qualifies as "special purpose," also described below).
	Exceptions to 10% IRS Penalty	• First-time home purchase up to $10,000 (once-in-a-lifetime use). • Qualified higher education expenses. • Death. • Disability. • Substantially equal payments (annuitization). • Medical expenses exceeding 7.5% of AGI. • Health insurance premiums when receiving unemployment compensation for longer than 12 months.
	Mandatory distributions	No required minimum payments at any time.
ROLLOVERS/CONVERSIONS	**Qualifications**	Taxpayers may roll over a Roth IRA to another Roth IRA without incurring income or penalty taxes. Rollovers must follow the 60-day rules.

**TABLE 3.   Years before Break-Even:
Deductible IRA Contributions**

Interest	Marginal Tax Rates		
Rates	15%	28%	33%
4%	22	14	13
6	15	10	9
8	12	8	7
10	10	6	6
12	8	5	5

**TABLE 4.   Years before Break-Even:
Nondeductible IRA Contributions, Taxable
Percentage of Principal = 0%**

Interest	Marginal Tax Rates		
Rates	15%	28%	33%
4%	37	26	24
6	25	18	17
8	20	14	13
10	16	11	11
12	14	10	9

**TABLE 5.   Years before Break-Even:
Nondeductible IRA Contributions, Taxable
Percentage of Principal = 100%**

Interest	Marginal Tax Rates		
Rates	15%	28%	33%
4%	50	45	44
6	34	30	30
8	26	23	23
10	21	19	19
12	18	16	16

TABLE 6. Years before Break-Even: Nondeductible IRA Contributions, Taxable Percentage of Principal = 50%

Interest Rates	Marginal Tax Rates		
	15%	28%	33%
4%	45	38	38
6	31	26	26
8	24	20	20
10	19	17	16
12	17	14	14

Calculating Deductibility of Your Traditional IRA Contribution*

	2013	
	Single	Joint
AGI limit	$69,000	$115,000
Your modified AGI	– _____	– _____
AGI limit less your modified AGI	_____	_____
Divide remainder by†	$10,000	$10,000
Percentage of your contribution eligible	_____%	_____%
Multiply by $5,500	× $5,500	× $5,500
Amount you can deduct	$_____	_____

Calculating Eligibility for a Roth IRA Contribution*

	2013	
	Single	Joint
AGI limit	$127,000	$188,000
Your modified AGI	– _____	– _____
AGI limit less your modified AGI	_____	_____
Divide remainder by†	$15,000	$10,000
Percentage of your contribution eligible	_____%	_____%
Multiply by $5,500	× $5,500	× $5,500
Amount you can contribute	$_____	_____

*Maximum combined contribution may not exceed $5,500 per individual, per year.
†These numbers are determined by the range between minimum and maximum AGI for partially deductible contributions to the traditional IRA and for eligible contributions to the Roth IRA.

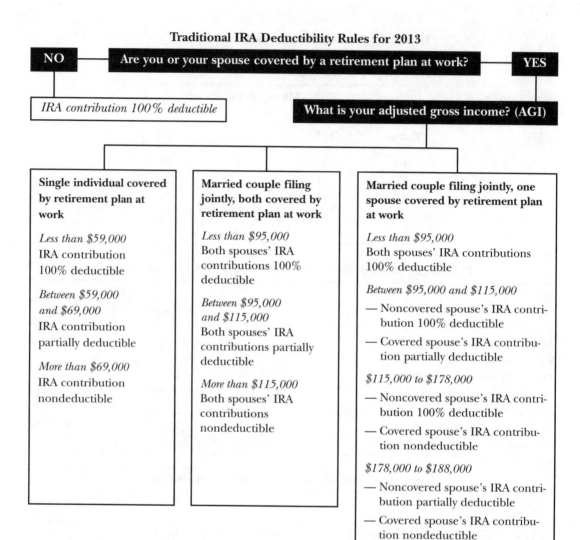

Traditional IRA Deductibility Rules for 2013

NO — Are you or your spouse covered by a retirement plan at work? — **YES**

IRA contribution 100% deductible

What is your adjusted gross income? (AGI)

Single individual covered by retirement plan at work

Less than $59,000
IRA contribution
100% deductible

Between $59,000 and $69,000
IRA contribution
partially deductible

More than $69,000
IRA contribution
nondeductible

Married couple filing jointly, both covered by retirement plan at work

Less than $95,000
Both spouses' IRA
contributions 100%
deductible

Between $95,000 and $115,000
Both spouses' IRA
contributions partially
deductible

More than $115,000
Both spouses' IRA
contributions
nondeductible

Married couple filing jointly, one spouse covered by retirement plan at work

Less than $95,000
Both spouses' IRA contributions
100% deductible

Between $95,000 and $115,000
— Noncovered spouse's IRA contribution 100% deductible
— Covered spouse's IRA contribution partially deductible

$115,000 to $178,000
— Noncovered spouse's IRA contribution 100% deductible
— Covered spouse's IRA contribution nondeductible

$178,000 to $188,000
— Noncovered spouse's IRA contribution partially deductible
— Covered spouse's IRA contribution nondeductible

More than $188,000
— Both spouse's IRA contributions nondeductible

Certain investments are off limits to IRA holders. They include investments in collectibles, such as rare books; rugs; artworks; metals, such as gold, silver, and platinum; antiques; stamps; coins; alcoholic beverages; and any other forms of tangible personal property. In addition, life insurance, as opposed to annuities offered by life insurance companies, is also off limits to IRA investors. Under the Tax Reform Act of 1986, however, you may invest in gold and silver coins issued by the United States. This provision is effective for coins acquired after 1986.

The deadline for making contributions to an IRA is April 15, the date for filing the taxpayer's return. Taxpayers who establish an individual retirement account or annuity are required to file Form 5239, Return for Individual Retirement Savings Arrangements, with their income tax return if they owe IRA penalty taxes (for instance, on excess contributions, premature distributions, or the failure to distribute at age 70½).

In Private Ruling 8527082 the IRS affirmed that you may deduct interest paid on money borrowed to put into an IRA. Note, however, that the Tax Reform Act of 1986 makes interest potentially nondeductible as "consumer interest" (although, I would argue that it was investment interest, but as long as the Roth yields tax-free income, the deduction would still be lost). Moreover, the IRS has ruled that the separate payment by an IRA beneficiary or trustee of administration fees for the IRA will not reduce the amount the beneficiary would otherwise be entitled to treat as a deductible contribution to the IRA, and is deductible as an expense incurred for the production or collection of income (Rev. Rul. 84-146). However, no separate deduction is allowed for brokers' commissions paid by IRAs or even qualified plans. Brokers' commissions are not recurring administrator or overhead expenses, such as trustee or actuary fees, incurred in connection with the maintenance of the trust or plan. Brokers' commissions rather are intrinsic to the value of a trust's assets—buying commissions are a part of the cost of the securities purchased and selling commissions are an offset against the sales price. Therefore, the Internal Revenue Service has ruled that contributions to reimburse for brokers' commissions are not deductible (Rev. Rul. 86-142, 1986-48 I.R.B. 4).

TAX-FREE CHARITABLE CONTRIBUTIONS FROM IRAs

The Pension Protection Act of 2006 allowed taxpayers age 70½ or older to exclude from gross income otherwise taxable distributions ("qualified charitable distributions," or QCDs) from their IRA that were paid directly to a qualified charity. Taxpayers were able to exclude up to $100,000 in both 2006 and 2007.

The law was extended through 2009 by the Emergency Economic Stabilization Act of 2008, extended again, through 2011, by the Tax Relief, Unemployment Insurance Reauthorization, and Job Creation Act of 2010 (the Tax Relief Act), and again by the Tax Relief Act of 2012 through 2013.

You must be 70½ or older in order to make QCDs. You direct your IRA trustee to make a distribution directly from your IRA (other than SEP and SIMPLE IRAs) to a qualified charity. The distribution must be one that would otherwise be taxable to you. You can exclude up to $100,000 of QCDs from your gross income. If you file a joint return, your spouse can exclude an additional $100,000 of QCDs. You don't get to deduct QCDs as a charitable contribution on your federal income tax return—that would be double dipping.

QCDs count toward satisfying any required minimum distributions (RMDs) that you would otherwise have had to receive from your IRA, just as if you had received an actual distribution from the plan. However, distributions that you actually receive from your IRA (including RMDs) that you subsequently transfer to a charity cannot qualify as QCDs.

SIMPLIFIED EMPLOYEE PENSION PLANS

Under a normal IRA, your deduction is limited to the lesser of 100 percent of earned income or $5,500 ($11,000 in the case of spousal IRAs) for contributions made. Under the Simplified Pension Plan, the exclusion limitation for all contributions to this type of IRA is now the lesser of $51,000 or 25 percent of compensation. In the case of a self-employed individual or owner-employee in a noncorporate plan, "compensation" is defined to mean net earnings from self-employment, less excludable contributions to the plan made on his or her own behalf. This effectively reduces the self-employed maximum contribution percentage from 25 to 20 percent. Moreover, if an employer maintains another qualified plan, the maximum amount that can be contributed to that plan for any employee is reduced by all amounts contributed to the SEP. There is a 25/20 percent limitation on deductible contributions to more than one qualified plan [Internal Revenue Code Section 404(h)(3)].

The intent of this type of plan is to establish a simpler mechanism by which employers can make employer-deductible contributions to provide employees with retirement benefits. It offers the owner-employee the opportunity to increase the maximum contributions that may be made to a personal plan, but it does so at the cost of requiring contributions for certain other employees as well.

Contributions made to an SEP by the employer or by a self-employed individual are deposited into individual IRAs in the name of the plan member. Employer contributions to an SEP are not includable in an employee's gross income. The employer contribution must be a specified percentage of the employee's total compensation up to $255,000 for 2013, and the same percentage rate must be used for all employees. That rate may be specified in the plan or set by the employer annually by a written resolution. Unlike profit-sharing plans, an SEP does not require employers to make recurring contributions to the plan to remain qualified.

The five requirements for the establishment of a Simplified Pension Plan are as follows:

1. The IRA must be maintained solely by the individual employee. This means that all employees, including the owner as an employee, must maintain their own individual IRA accounts.

2. Employer contributions must be made pursuant to a written allocation formula.

3. The program must provide for contributions for each employee who has attained age 21, has performed services for the employer during any part of three of the immediately preceding 5 calendar years, and receives compensation of at least $550 during the current year (indexed). Employees under collective bargaining agreements and nonresident aliens may be excluded; part-time employees, however, must be covered.

4. Employer contributions must not discriminate in favor of officers, shareholders, or highly compensated employees. Generally, discrimination will not exist if the contributions bear a uniform relationship to the first $255,000 for 2013 of each employee's total compensation. Employer contributions may be reduced by the amount of the employer's share of the Social Security tax.

5. No limitations may be imposed by the employer on the employee's right of withdrawal.

Unlike the Keogh plan, an SEP can be set up after the end of the calendar year so long as the contribution is made by April 15 of the year following (*plus extensions*). Moreover, there are no annual reporting requirements for SEPs, so long as each individual who participates in the plan receives a copy of the plan agreement and a written document from the employer each year informing that individual of the amount of contributions made on his or her behalf by the employer. An employer can create an SEP by using an unmodified Model Form (Form 5305-SEP), which is available from the Internal Revenue Service. An employer who follows the instructions on this two-page form will automatically satisfy IRS reporting and disclosure requirements.

Additional advantages of an SEP include the following:

- Low start-up costs compared to the cost of establishing regular pension or profit-sharing plans

- No need to pay contributions to the SEP every year (similar to a profit-sharing Keogh)

- Portability of benefits—that is, participants who end their employment can take their benefits with them in the form of individual retirement accounts

- Low administrative costs

- Reduced fiduciary responsibility, because participants choose their own vehicle when they establish an IRA

SARSEP

A salary reduction SEP, known as a SARSEP, was available for firms with 25 or fewer workers. Under a SARSEP, each worker chose how much he or she wanted to set aside through regular payroll deductions. The 2013 maximum is $17,500.

With a SARSEP, 50 percent of all eligible employees must participate and no more than 60 percent of contributions can be made by highly compensated employees. If a firm fails the latter test, called the *top-heavy rule,* the IRS will require the firm to contribute a minimum of 3 percent of salary into employee accounts.

The amounts put into a SARSEP are not currently taxed and therefore you will get tax-free compounding on your investment until the money is withdrawn.

Under SARSEPs, which are not qualified plans, employees could elect to have contributions made to the SARSEP or to receive the contributions in cash. The amount that an employee elected to have contributed to the SARSEP was not currently included in income. Under the Small Business Job Protection Act of 1996, SARSEPs are repealed for years beginning after December 31, 1996, unless the SARSEP was established before January 1, 1997.

Consequently, an employee is not permitted to establish a SARSEP after December 31, 1996. SARSEPs established before January 1, 1997 can continue to receive contributions under prior law rules, and new employees of the employer who are hired after December 31, 1996 can participate in the SARSEP in accordance with such rules.

PLANNING WITH IRAs

As noted, the deadline for making IRA contributions is April 15, but what if you don't have the necessary cash at the moment? One possible solution to this problem is to use an old IRA for the funds required for the current IRA contribution.

There are no immediate tax consequences when an individual withdraws part or all of his or her interest in an IRA and within 60 days deposits the amount withdrawn into another IRA. Therefore, if you have an IRA account established in an earlier year, you can withdraw $5,500 from it and use it for your subsequent year's contribution. So long as the deposit is completed within 60 days, there is no problem.

Question: Where do you get the money to cover your original withdrawal? *Solution:* It is hoped that you get it with the refund you will get from your tax return as filed with the additional IRA deduction. *Worst case theory:* If you cannot find the $5,500 to cover within the 60-day period, then you are still entitled to the deduction for the current contribution year, but you have to include the $5,500 withdrawn (with penalty) on your next year's tax return.

Rather than wait for the last minute, you should make your IRA contribution as early as possible. When you delay, you lose not only the tax-free interest for the year but the interest that would have been compounded on it in future years.

The table below lists how much you lose by making a contribution at the last minute. It assumes that *only* $2,000 is placed annually into an IRA earning 10 percent interest, and it shows the interest forfeited after a given number of years when the contributions are regularly made as late as possible (April 15), as opposed to as early as possible (on January 1 of the preceding year).

Number of Years	Interest Lost
5	$ 1,500
10	$ 4,000
15	$ 8,000
20	$ 14,000
30	$ 41,000
40	$112,000

In 1985, the Internal Revenue Service ruled that a jobless widow could add to her own IRA for the year her husband died. The decedent had created a spousal IRA for his unemployed wife in 1982 and 1983. He died on February 23, 1984, after earning over $2,250 but before adding to either IRA for that year. The taxpayer's spouse earned no wages in 1984 but wanted to make and deduct a $2,000 payment from the decedent's 1984 income to her spousal IRA for 1984. In Private Ruling 8527083, the Internal Revenue Service said that she could so long as she had no earned income of her own, filed a joint return, and showed that no 1984 payment was made to the decedent's IRA.

SIMPLE RETIREMENT PLANS

The Small Business Job Protection Act of 1996 created a simplified retirement plan for small businesses called the Savings Incentive Match Plan for Employees (SIMPLE) Retirement Plan. A SIMPLE plan can be adopted by employers who employ 100 or fewer employees with at least $5,000 in compensation for the current and any 2 preceding years. Employers who no longer qualify are given a 2-year grace period to continue to maintain the plan. A SIMPLE plan can be either an IRA for each employee or part of a qualified cash or deferred arrangement (401(k)) plan. If established in IRA form, a SIMPLE plan is not subject to the nondiscrimination rules generally applicable to qualified plans (including the top-heavy rules) and simplified reporting requirements apply. Within limits, contributions to a SIMPLE plan are not taxable until withdrawn.

A SIMPLE plan can also be adopted as part of a 401(k) plan. In that case, the plan does not have to satisfy the special nondiscrimination tests applicable to 401(k) plans and is not subjected to the top-heavy rules. The other qualified plan rules continue to apply.

A SIMPLE retirement plan allows employees to make elective contributions to an IRA or 401(k). Employee contributions have to be expressed as a percentage of the employee's compensation and cannot exceed $12,000 for 2013. Employer matching can yield as much as $24,000 per year into your SIMPLE account.

All contributions to an employee's SIMPLE account have to be fully vested. Contributions to a SIMPLE account generally are deductible by the employer. Early withdrawals from a SIMPLE account generally are subject to the 10 percent early withdrawal tax applicable to IRAs. However, withdrawals of a contribution during the 2-year period beginning on the date the employee first participated in the SIMPLE plan are subject to a 25 percent early withdrawal tax, rather than 10 percent. The provisions relating to SIMPLE plans are effective for years beginning after December 31, 1996.

KEOGH PLAN

The alternative to an IRA or IRA/SEP is the Keogh plan. Since 1962, self-employed individuals and their employees have been eligible to receive qualified retirement benefits under what is known as an H.R. 10 or Keogh plan. These qualified pension, annuity, profit-sharing, or bond purchase plans must meet the following qualifications:

1. They must be in writing.

2. They must be effective within the tax year for which a qualification is sought.

3. They must be established by an owner for the benefit of employees or their beneficiaries. Self-employed individuals will be treated as employees under these plans.

4. They must be funded plans (that is, a trust or custodial account, an insured plan, or a bond purchase plan).

5. They must benefit a stipulated percentage of employees, or alternatively, the owner may establish a classification of employees that is found by the Internal Revenue Service not to discriminate in favor of highly paid employees.

6. They may not discriminate in favor of highly paid employees for contributions or benefits.

7. In the case of a plan that provides contributions or benefits only for owner-employees, contributions made on behalf of any owner-employee may not exceed the amount deductible by the individual. This means that an owner cannot contribute into a personal plan, in an attempt to defer taxes, an amount in excess of what is deductible for employees.

8. When an owner-employee covered under the plan, alone, or in conjunction with another employee, controls the trade or business for which the plan is established, any transaction between that owner-employee and the trust-forming part of the plan is prohibited. Transactions between the members of the owner-employee's family and the trust are deemed to be transactions between the owner-employee and the trust. Furthermore, even if the owner-employee does not control the trade or business, a transaction between the trust and that owner-employee is prohibited.

   Generally, a disqualified person who engages in a prohibited transaction by contributing property to the trust is subject to a 5 percent excise tax on the amount involved in the transaction. An additional tax of 100 percent of the amount involved is imposed if the prohibited transaction is not corrected within 90 days from the mailing of a notice of deficiency.

9. A plan that covers an owner-employee must also cover all employees age 21 or older (whether or not U.S. citizens) of the trade or business who have completed two or more years of service. A year of service is a 12-month period, beginning on the date of hire, during which an employee has provided at least 500 hours of service (1,000 hours if it is the first year the employee qualifies). In addition, the employees' rights to contributions in their behalf must be 100 percent vested when the contributions are made.

   If eligibility to participate is shortened to one year, employees can be made to wait for a longer time before being able to leave with benefits. A plan can be set up so that an employee with fewer than 5 years of plan participation is not entitled to any benefit whatsoever. This relieves an employer from the expense of paying retirement benefits to all but true long-term employees. Note, however, that if the plan is "top-heavy"—if more than 60 percent of the benefits are for the owners, officers, and more highly paid employees—plan participants' benefits must vest immediately, or 20 percent after two years and 20 percent thereafter, with full vesting after 6 years [Section 416 (b)(1)].

   The following employees are not required to be covered under a self-employed retirement plan, even though they have completed one or more years of service:

   • Employees included in a unit covered by a collective bargaining agreement, if there is evidence that retirement benefits were subject to good faith bargaining between employee representatives and the employer.

   • Nonresident alien employees who do not have earned income from a U.S. source.

10. If the employer is a partnership, each partner is considered the employee of that partnership. The partners must mutually consent to the establishment of the plan, which means that one partner cannot establish a plan for individual services to that partnership. But each owner-employee can decide whether to be covered under the plan, so a partner who is an owner-employee can agree to the plan and still not participate in it.

Under a Keogh plan, both the maximum contribution permitted on behalf of owner-employees and the deduction allowed self-employed individuals is limited to:

a) 25 percent of the earned income from the trade or business for which the plan is established, limited to

b) $51,000 for 2013

Note that a Keogh plan may be structured either as a *money-purchase pension* plan or as a *profit-sharing* plan, or as a combination of both. An owner-employer must reduce his or her compensation base by the contribution made. Under old law this effectively translated into a limit for *profit-sharing* plan-based deductions of 13.0435 percent and a limit for *money-purchase pension* or combination *money-purchase pension/profit-sharing* deductions of 20 percent of earned income.

With a money-purchase pension plan, the employer is locked into making the contributions every year, unless granted a limited reprieve. Contributions can be the lesser of 25 percent of compensation or $51,000. Note that the 25 percent figure is reduced to 20 percent for an owner-employer making contributions for himself or herself.

The *profit-sharing* plan is the simplest type of defined contribution plan. Contributions can be discretionary with respect to both amounts and whether they are made at all. Deductible contributions for nonowner-employers were as much as 15 percent of compensation, up to the maximum each year for each participant.

Combination plans used to typically contribute a fixed 10 percent each year to the money-purchase plan, and, if the cash is available, up to 15 percent to the profit-sharing plan. Note that plan contributions can be reduced to account for an employer's contribution to Social Security made on an employee's behalf. This is known as Social Security integration. Note, however, that if a plan is top-heavy, a minimum 3 percent annual contribution must be made for nonkey employees, and the employer must fund a benefit of at least 2 percent of compensation per year of service for the first 10 years of service. These requirements limit the cost savings sought by Social Security integration.

As of 2002, the Tax Relief Act of 2001 increases the maximum *profit-sharing* contribution to 25 percent. This should eliminate or at least minimize the use of money-purchase plans or combination plans when a fixed minimum contribution is required.

The contribution maximums were computed under what is known as a *defined contribution plan*, in which the limits are delineated on the basis of how much may be contributed. A self-employed individual may choose instead to establish what is known as a *defined benefit plan*, in which the limits are based on payable benefits. This type of plan permits a self-employed individual to state the retirement benefits desired and contribute amounts necessary to provide those benefits. In addition, a defined benefit plan permits yearly contributions to a plan without regard to profits. For 2013, the maximum annual defined benefit amount is increased to $205,000.

Warning! Everyone will tell you that you have until the due date of your return, plus extensions, to make your Keogh contributions. That is what the tax law says, and extensions are allowed up to October 15.

But, these plans are considered "qualified pension plans" under ERISA. That law requires contributions by September 15. If you contribute after that, it doesn't qualify.

The solution? Use a defined contribution profit-sharing plan. Such plans now allow the maximum 25 percent contribution rate and are not subject to the earlier funding date requirement. That allows funding up to October 15 again.

INDIVIDUAL 401(k)

The 2001 tax cut created a new individual 401(k) for businesses in which you and your spouse are the only employees. A 401(k) is simply a profit-sharing plan that allows employee elective deferrals.

The plan must be established by year-end, the contributions are all discretionary each year, and they vest in full immediately.

Big advantage—you can borrow up to 50 percent of your account balance, with a maximum loan of $50,000. You can't borrow from an IRA.

For 2013, the maximum contribution is the sum of A, B, and C below:

A. Employer contribution—up to 25 percent of compensation
B. Salary deferral contribution—up to $17,500
C. If you're age 50 or older, a catch-up contribution of $5,500

A plus B cannot exceed $51,000 or 100 percent of compensation.

If you have no other employees, hire your spouse. Pay your spouse $1,000 per month as reasonable compensation. Give her a $5,500 Christmas bonus. Your spouse can elect to defer $17,500 into the 401(k).

Your family has a $17,500 investment, you have a $17,500 deduction, and your spouse has an additional *zero* in taxable income. Sounds like a great deal to me!

ROTH 401(k)

As of January 1, 2006, we now also have Roth 401(k)s. The standard 401(k) limits apply, with a $17,500 maximum (plus an additional $5,500 catch up) for 2013.

You get no deduction, but qualified distributions come out tax-free.

Pay-ins are subject to the nondiscrimination rules. But there are *no income limitations* (unlike the $178,000–$188,000 adjusted gross income limit for traditional Roth accounts). This is a fantastic investment opportunity for the well-to-do to increase their wealth on a *tax-free* basis.

DB(k) PLANS

A DB(k) plan is a combination of a defined contribution 401(k) plan and a defined benefit plan. It's available only to small business employers, those with at least 2 but no more than 500 employees. The defined benefit is equal to at least 1 percent of final average pay for each year of service up to 20 years. Employees are automatically enrolled in the 401(k) portion with 4 percent of compensation contributed unless the employee opts otherwise. The employer must match at least half the 4 percent.

DB(k)s have minimal paperwork and are exempt from "top heavy" rules, which is an inducement to highly paid employees.

CASH BALANCE PLANS

A cash balance plan is a defined benefit plan that defines the benefit in terms that are more characteristic of a defined contribution plan. In other words, a cash balance plan defines the promised benefit in terms of a stated account balance.

In a typical cash balance plan, your account is credited each year with a "pay credit" (such as 5 percent of compensation from your employer) and an "interest credit" (either a fixed rate or a variable rate that is linked to an index such as the 1-year Treasury bill rate). Increases and decreases in the value of the plan's investments do not directly affect the benefit amounts promised. Thus, the investment risks and rewards on plan assets are borne solely by the employer.

When you become entitled to receive benefits under a cash balance plan, the benefits that are received are defined in terms of an account balance. For example, assume that you have an account balance of $100,000 when you reach age 65. If you decide to retire at that time, you would have the right to an annuity. Such an annuity might be approximately $10,000 per year for life. In many cash balance plans, however, you could instead choose (with consent from your spouse) to take a lump-sum benefit equal to the $100,000 account balance.

In addition to generally permitting you to take your benefit as a lump-sum benefit at retirement, cash balance plans often permit you, if vested, to choose (with consent from your spouse) to receive your accrued benefit in a lump sum if you terminate employment prior to retirement age. Traditional defined benefit pension plans do not offer this feature as frequently. If you receive a lump-sum distribution, that distribution generally can be rolled over into an IRA or to another employer's plan if that plan accepts rollovers.

Cash balance plans are defined benefit plans. In contrast, 403(b) and 401(k) plans are a type of defined contribution plan. There are four major differences between typical cash balance plans and defined contribution plans.

(a) Participation. Participation in typical cash balance plans generally does not depend on the workers, contributing part of their compensation to the plan; however, participation in a 403(b) or 401(k) plan does depend, in whole or in part, on an employees choosing to make a contribution to the plan.

(b) Investment risks. The investments of cash balance plans are managed by the employer or an investment manager appointed by the employer. The employer bears the risks and rewards of the investments. Increases and decreases in the value of the plan's investments do not directly affect the benefit amounts promised to participants. By contrast, 403(b) or 401(k) plans often permit participants to direct their own investments within certain categories. Under 401(k) plans, participants bear the risks and rewards of investment choices.

(c) Life annuities. Unlike many 401(k) plans, cash balance plans are required to offer employees the ability to receive their benefits in the form of lifetime annuities.

(d) Federal guaranty. Since they are defined benefit plans, the benefits promised by cash balance plans are usually insured by a federal agency, the Pension Benefit Guaranty Corporation (PBGC). If a defined benefit plan is terminated with insufficient funds to pay all promised benefits, the PBGC has authority to assume trusteeship of the plan and to begin to pay pension benefits up to the limits set by law. Defined contribution plans are not insured by the PBGC.

The Tax Relief Act of 2001 made significant changes to the retirement rules. These changes are detailed in Chapter 12. However, some changes require additional review and are discussed in the following paragraphs.

VESTING SCHEDULES

Under prior law, a plan was not a qualified plan unless benefits vested at least as rapidly as under one of the minimum vesting schedules.

1. A plan satisfied the first schedule if a participant acquired a nonforfeitable right to 100 percent of the accrued benefit from *employer contributions* after completing 5 years of service.

2. A plan satisfied the second schedule if at least 20 percent of accrued benefits vested after 3 years, 40 percent after 4 years of service, 60 percent after 5 years, 80 percent after 6 years, and 100 percent after 7 years of service.

Faster Vesting. Under current law, faster vesting schedules apply to employer matching contributions. The contributions will be required to vest at least as rapidly as under one of the following two alternative schedules:

1. A plan satisfies the first schedule if 100 percent of employer matching contributions vest after 3 years of service.

2. A plan satisfies the second schedule if matching contributions vest at the rate of 20 percent each year starting with the participant's second year of service. The contributions will be 100 percent vested after 6 years of service.

The new vesting schedule generally applies to contributions for plan years beginning after December 31, 2001. In applying the new vesting schedule, service before the effective date is taken into account.

CREDITOR PROTECTION

Any IRA money can now be rolled over into a qualified plan. If you get deep in debt, this may save your retirement dollars. Although many states do not insulate IRA accounts from creditors, most qualified money is subject to ERISA and is therefore exempt from creditors' claims, even if you declare bankruptcy.[*]

The Bankruptcy Act of 2005 insulated up to $1,000,000[†] (not counting rollovers) of IRA money from creditors in a bankruptcy action. This covers traditional plus Roth IRAs.[‡] See www.wealthdefense.com/irachart.htm for individual state IRA insulation.

---

[*]Creditor protection covered all plans with two or more employees, exclusive of the proprietor and his/her spouse.
[†]$1,245,475 for 2013.
[‡]If filing for bankruptcy, you must have funded the account at least 2 years prior to filing.

NEW RETIREMENT PLAN PROTECTIONS

Type of Plan	Exemption
Single business owner/business owner and spouse (such as Keogh plan and single-owner corporate plan)	Unlimited
Contributory IRA (funded with annual contributions, as opposed to rollovers from qualified plans)	$1 million (Indexed)*
Rollover IRA	Unlimited
Roth IRA	$1 million (Indexed)* if a contributory IRA; unlimited if a rollover IRA was converted to a Roth
SEP-IRA	Unlimited
Simple	Unlimited

*$1,245,475 for 2013.

MINIMUM DISTRIBUTION

If you're not a 5 percent holder of an interest in the business, and you continue to work, you are not subject to the minimum distribution rules when you reach age 70½. If the money was held in an IRA, you would be subject to those rules.

All required regular distributions from IRAs and qualified plans were suspended for 2009. The suspension did not apply to defined benefit plans or deferred 2008 withdrawals. It was only for 2009.

LOANS

As of January 1, 2002, retirement plan loans can be made to sole proprietors, partners, and shareholders of an S corporation. The loans must be made from a qualified plan (IRA loans are still prohibited), and the plan must allow, or be amended to allow, such loans.

BENEFITS OF RETIREMENT PLANS

It is almost always financially superior to adopt either an individual retirement account or a qualified pension plan rather than have no plan at all. Both the IRA and the Keogh plan allow you to shelter current earnings and allow those earnings to appreciate without making that appreciation currently taxable. There may be an extraordinary situation in which having no plan would be superior. Such a situation would exist if the after-tax cash remaining from funds not invested in an IRA or Keogh plan could be invested in a project whose yield would exceed, after taxes, both the amount that could be earned on the qualified retirement investment and the amount initially lost in taxes. Remember, all income that comes out of retirement accounts is taxed at your highest marginal bracket. The maximum tax rate on nonqualified long-term gains for 2013 is capped at 20 percent.

Assume you could put $1,000 in an individual retirement account that would yield 5 percent interest, or $50 a year. For simplicity, assume that your present tax bracket is 20 percent, so that if you do not adopt the individual retirement account, you would have only $800 to invest. But this $800 could be invested in a project yielding 25 percent, or $200 a year. After taxes (at 20 percent) the project would allow you to keep $160 a year. At the end of 2 years you would therefore have, after taxes, $800 + $160 + $160 = $1,120. (The example has been simplified by excluding compound interest on the investment yield.) Under the IRA, you would have only $1,000 + $50 + $50 = $1,100, and that $1,100 would be taxable at a later date, when withdrawn from the individual retirement account. In this case, the decision not to adopt any plan would clearly be superior.

To evaluate a Keogh plan compared to an IRA, you must consider the following questions:

1. How much money can you afford to surrender the present use of? If not over $5,500 ($11,000 if you have an unemployed spouse), choose an IRA.

2. What will be the tax savings on your contributions to each plan?

3. Must you make contributions for your employees?

4. What will be the after-tax cost of those contributions?

5. Compare the net after-tax savings from an individual retirement account a Keogh plan.

For example, assume you are in the 31 percent bracket* and are making $200,000 a year. You plan to retire in 10 years. You can adopt a Keogh plan,

---

*Federal plus state (deductible).

yielding 5 percent. Under the Keogh plan, assume you contribute $15,000 at the end of each year.

Under the Keogh plan, you would contribute $150,000 plus earnings on these contributions, for a total untaxed accumulation of $188,668. You would defer $58,487 in taxes.

But with a Keogh plan qualified employees must also be covered. If you have qualified employees, you would have to contribute 7.5 percent of their earnings (as you contribute 7.5 percent of your own earnings) each year. If you have one qualified employee earning $20,000, you would have to contribute an additional $1,500 per year ($20,000 × 7.5 percent), or $15,000 over the 10-year period. If you have four qualified employees, the contributions would rise to $60,000.

But you are in the 31 percent bracket. Therefore, this would involve an after-tax cost to you of only $41,400. But remember, Keogh saving is merely a tax *deferral*, not a savings. Therefore, the real question is whether the $41,400 after-tax outflow can be justified by a deferral of the taxes of $58,487!

Under the Keogh plan you would accumulate $188,668. If you expected to be in the 15 percent bracket after you retire, the difference between your marginal tax today and your post-retirement marginal tax would be .16 (31 percent – 15 percent).[3] Therefore, your true net savings on the Keogh plan would be the difference in your tax bracket (.16) times the accumulations under the Keogh plan ($188,668), or a net savings of the present value of $30,187. Thus the determining question is whether the present value of $30,187 is greater than the present value of the after-tax outflow for the contributions you would have to make for your employees.

With a single employee, the cash outflow cost would be the present value of 31 percent of $15,000, or the present value of $4,650. Here the net savings of $30,187 would be greater than the incremental cost of $4,650, and therefore the Keogh adoption would still be superior. If there were four employees, the decision model would compare the present value of $30,187 with the present value of 69 percent of $15,000 × 4, or $41,400. Here the IRA would be financially superior.

Keogh accounts, like all ERISA qualified plans, are exempt from creditor attacks. IRA accounts vary in creditor protection. (As noted above, IRAs up to $1 million are now protected from creditors in a bankruptcy.) See www.mosessinger.com/resources/protecting.shtml to check your state.

---

3. The numbers have been simplified for purposes of this example. You would not be in the 15 percent bracket with a lump-sum distribution of $188,668.

(Exemption for annuities and life insurance can be found at www. mosessinger.com/resources/creditprotec.shtml.)

Finally, you must consider whether the employee Keogh contributions would merely replace alternative additional compensation that would be paid to the employee in any case. If so, then the Keogh penalty for employee payments must be reduced by this amount.

DISTRIBUTIONS

On July 3, 1992 former President Bush signed the Unemployment Compensation Amendments Act of 1992 primarily to extend unemployment benefits. Nevertheless, you need to be aware of several significant changes to the pension rules relating to rollovers and withholding on distributions from such qualified plans as profit sharing, money purchase, 401(k), defined benefit, and tax-sheltered annuities [403(b) plans]. *The new rules do not apply to IRAs.*

These provisions affect all qualified plans that make lump-sum distributions or allow in-service withdrawals. The changes are effective for distributions made after Dec. 31, 1992 (except for a delayed effective date for certain tax-sheltered annuities of state and local governments). The new provisions include:

- *Optional Direct Transfer of Distribution.* A participant has 60 days to roll over an eligible distribution from a qualified plan to an IRA or another qualified plan to avoid current taxation. At the time of the distribution, the participant may elect to have federal income taxes withheld or not.

  The 1992 legislation requires a qualified plan sponsor to provide participants who are eligible to receive a rollover distribution the option of making a direct transfer to an IRA or a new employer's qualified plan. However, a qualified plan is not required to accept transfers.

  Even though the participant does not actually receive the money, such a direct trustee-to-trustee transfer is considered a distribution under the current law. Therefore, the spousal consent rules, if applicable, and other beneficiary protection rules will continue to apply.

- *Withholding on Nonperiodic Distributions.* To encourage plan participants to use this direct transfer option, the 1992 law imposes a *mandatory* 20 percent income tax withholding on any amount distributed to the participant. If a participant wants to avoid withholding on the distribution, the participant needs to instruct the employer to transfer the amount directly to another retirement plan or an IRA. Plan participants can no longer elect out of this withholding.

- *Partial Distribution Rules Repealed.* The 1992 Act also changed the situations in which partial distributions can be rolled into an IRA. Under prior law, partial distributions can only be rolled over when:
  - the distribution represents 50 percent or more of the balance to the credit of the employee;
  - the distribution is not one of a series of periodic payments;
  - the distribution is made because of death, disability, or separation from service;
  - the employee elects rollover treatment.

The 1992 rules allow *any part* of the taxable portion of a qualified plan distribution to be rolled over to an IRA, qualified annuity, or another qualified plan unless the distribution is:

- one of a series of substantially equal periodic payments made over the life expectancy (or joint life expectancies) of the participant and the designated beneficiary;
- one of a series of substantially equal periodic payments made for a specified period of 10 years or more;
- required as a result of the mandatory distribution rules at age 70½ under Section 401(a)(9) of the IRS code;
- after-tax employee contributions, which are not eligible for rollover.

Note that to qualify for a direct rollover, you must be alive at the time of the actual asset rollover (PLR 200204038).

TRADITIONAL V. ROTH IRA

Which should *you* use? That depends on the benefits you want to get and your current and projected tax brackets.

The younger you are, the better the Roth IRA appears. If you start early, the Roth allows more years of tax-free accumulations. The younger you are, presumably, the better the chances you are in a lower bracket, therefore reducing the benefit of its deduction with the traditional IRA.

Alternatively, if you are older and in a higher bracket, the better the traditional IRA looks. Additional elements that must be examined or projected are the yields you expect to earn, whether you want to make contributions after age 70½, and the marginal bracket you expect to be in when the dollars are withdrawn.

There are no simple answers. Every brokerage account out there has computer programs that will find you an "answer" based on your assumptions. I have even found different answers with the same input, depending on when the computer assumes the money is invested. Pen your own numbers and relax— your decision is between the better of two strategies, both of which are winners!

CONVERTING A TRADITIONAL IRA TO A ROTH IRA

Should you convert your traditional IRA into a Roth IRA and change from *tax deferral* to *tax-free* accumulations? The answer here also depends on a number of factors.

You can roll all or part of a traditional IRA into a Roth IRA at any time, even if you have started to take withdrawals. However, when you do, you owe income tax on the money you move. If you made the rollover in 2010, you spread that extra income, and tax, over 2 years—2011 and 2012. But the tax rate then may be higher.

Your first consideration should be where you get the money to pay the tax on the rollover. It can't come from the regular IRA or there will be a premature distribution with a penalty because those dollars are not going into the Roth.

Once you have funded your rollover, the considerations are the same as between a traditional and Roth IRA—your age and years to retirement, your bracket now and at retirement, do you want to contribute after age 70½, and will this impact on the taxability of your Social Security. (Traditional IRAs require annual distributions which could increase the taxability of your Social Security receipts. You *don't* have to ever take money out of your Roth although your beneficiaries are subject to minimum distribution rules.) The big difference here is the immediate reduction of your wealth from taxes paid on the rollover, reducing your liquidity for future investments. Again, all of the major brokerage and mutual fund houses offer computer programs which will give you an "answer," based on the assumptions you input.

COMPANY STOCK ROLLOVERS

"Never" roll over *company stock* in your 401(k) into an IRA. If you do, all distributions will be ordinary income.

If you place the stock into a regular brokerage account instead, you will be taxed, at ordinary income rates at *only* the cost-basis of that stock. That's the value when your employer put the stock in your account.

The difference between the cost-basis and the market value of the stock at the time of distribution, called the net unrealized appreciation (NUA), isn't taxed until you sell the stock, and, at that time, at a rate no greater than the 15 percent maximum long-term capital gains rate.

How much "company stock" you want to keep in your retirement savings is another issue.

78   Self-Employment Tax

Beginning in 1990, if you had income from self-employment and you owe self-employment tax, you may deduct one-half of that tax above the line. Note that this deduction reduces your income base for Keogh and SEP deductions as previously discussed.

79   Health Insurance Deduction for Self-Employeds

The deduction for health insurance of self-employed individuals is 100 percent since 2003. This special deduction for health insurance is not subject to the floor of 7.5 percent of adjusted gross income for medical expense deductions.

Certain limitations apply to this new health insurance deduction. No deduction is allowed to the extent that health insurance payments exceed your earned income for the taxable year. Nor is any deduction allowed for any month for which you are eligible to participate in a subsidized accident-and-health plan provided by an organization that employs (whether on a full- or part-time basis) either you or your spouse. Moreover, no deduction is allowed unless you provide coverage under one or more accident or health plans for all of your employees, should you have any. Those plans must also satisfy nondiscrimination rules.

This deduction is available even though you do not itemize your deductions. This deduction did reduce your earnings for the computation of self-employment tax as of the Small Business Jobs Act of 2010, but only for 2010. In addition, it is available for partnerships and S corporation owners (Rev. Rul. 91-26).

80 Moving Expenses

Moving expenses incurred if you change job locations or if you start a new job are generally deductible if you meet certain requirements. For moves made after 1993, your new job location must be at least 50 miles from your former job location, you must make your move within 1 year from the date you start your new job, and you must work full-time for a specified period of time. For moves in 1994 or after, expenses are above the line deductions. (Pre-1994, the mileage was 30 miles and the expenses were itemized deductions.)

You may take a moving expense deduction, subject to dollar limits explained later, for the following expenses:

- Travel for yourself and family to your new job location, including lodging but not meals.

- Moving your household goods and personal items.

- House-hunting trips before you move (pre-1994 only).

- Temporary living expenses at the new location (pre-1994 only).

- Expenses incurred in disposing of your former home and acquiring your new one (pre-1994 only).

You may qualify for such deductions whether you are self-employed or an employee. These expenses, though, must be in connection with starting work at a new job location. You will be able to deduct your moving expenses if you meet the requirements of certain tests.

THE DISTANCE TEST

You may now deduct your moving expenses if your new principal job location is at least 50 miles farther from your former home than was your former principal job location. In addition, the distance from your new home to your new job location must not be longer than the distance from your old home to the new job location. Your home is your primary residence; it may be a house, apartment, condominium, houseboat, housetrailer, or similar dwelling. It does not include other homes owned or kept up by you or members of your family, or a seasonal home (such as a beach cottage).

The distance between two points is measured by the shortest of the most commonly traveled routes between the points. If your old job was 3 miles from your former home, your new job must be at least 53 miles from that home. If you did not have an old job location, your new job location must be at least 50 miles from your former home.

For example, assume your old job was 3 miles from your former home. Your new job is 55 miles from that home. You qualify because the difference (52 miles) is over the minimum of 50 miles. Your new home may be less than 50 miles from your former home, but it must be at least as close to your new job as your former home. If so, you have met the distance test. See the chart below for an example of how you qualify even if the distance between old and new homes is less than 50 miles.

Your principal job location is usually the place where you do most of your work and spend most of your time. A new principal job location is a new place where you will work on a permanent or indefinite basis rather than on a temporary basis. However, you may have a principal job location even if there is no one place where you spend a substantial part of your work and time. In this case, use the distance to the place where your work is centered—for example, where you report for work or otherwise have the "base" for your work.

If you work for a number of employers on a short-term basis, or get work under a union hall system (such as in construction and the building trades), use the distance between your home and the union hall.

		55 miles				
Old Job	3 miles ————	Old Home	49 miles ————	New Home	6 miles ————	New Job

New Job to Old Home	=	55 miles	Old Home to New Job	=	55 miles
Old Home to Old Job	=	−3 miles	New Home to New Job	=	6 miles
Qualifying distance	=	52 miles	New Home is at least as close to new job as Old Home to new job		

TIME TEST

To deduct your moving expenses you also must meet one of the following time tests:

1. If you are an employee, you must work full-time at least 39 weeks during the 12-month period following your arrival in the general area of your new job location. You do not have to work for one employer for the 39 weeks; you do not even have to work 39 weeks in a row. But you must work full-time within the same general commuting area. Whether you are employed full-time depends upon the custom for your type of work. For example, a schoolteacher on a 12-month contract who teaches on a full-time basis for more than six months is considered a full-time employee for the entire 12 months. Any week that you work full-time is used to satisfy the 39 week full-time work test. If the work is seasonal, you are considered to be working full-time during the off-season weeks if your contract or agreement covers an off-season of less than 6 months. You are considered to be working during any week you are temporarily absent from work because of illness, strikes, natural disasters, or the like. You are also considered to be a full-time employee during any week you are absent from work for leave or for vacation that is provided for in your work contract or agreement.

2. If you are self-employed, you must work full-time for at least 39 weeks during the first 12 months and a total of 78 weeks during the 24 months after your arrival in the area of your new job location. Whether you perform services full-time during any one week depends upon the custom of your type of work in your area.

Despite these restrictions, you may deduct your moving expenses even if you have not met the time test by the time your return is due. You may do this if you *expect* to work for 39 weeks by the end of the next year, or for 78 weeks by the end of the second year. Furthermore, you do not have to meet the time test at all if any one of the following situations applies:

- You are in the armed forces and your move is due to a permanent change of stations.

- You move to the United States because you retire or are the survivor of a person who dies while living and working outside the United States.

- Your job ends because of disability, transfer for the employer's benefit, or layoff other than for willful misconduct. The time test does not have to be met in case of your death. If you are transferred, you are expected to meet the test at the time you start the job.

THE START OF WORK TEST

In general you must have moving expenses within 1 year from the time you first report to your job or business at the new location, and the move must be in connection with the start of work at the new location. If you do not move within 1 year, the expenses are ordinarily not deductible unless you can show that certain circumstances prevented the move within that time period. For example, if your family moved more than a year after you started work at the new location in order to allow your child to complete junior high school in the same school, your allowable moving expenses are deductible.

A move is considered closely related to the start of work if:

a) you are required to live at the new location as a condition of employment; *or*

b) you will spend less time or money commuting from the new home to the new job.

It is important that you understand and recognize all of the possible expenses that are deductible under this category. You can deduct expenses of moving your possessions, traveling to your new home, looking for a new home (pre-1994), living temporarily in a new area (pre-1994), selling and buying a home (pre-1994), or settling and signing a lease (pre-1994).

If you use your car to take yourself, your family, or your things to your new home, or for house hunting, you figure your expenses in either of two ways:

1. You may deduct your actual expenses such as gas, oil, and repairs (but not depreciation) for the use of your car, if you keep an accurate record of each expense.

2. You may deduct 24¢ a mile for 2013 instead of the actual costs if you can prove the mileage traveled. You may deduct parking fees and tolls you pay in moving no matter which way you figure your expenses.

Not only may you deduct the expenses of moving your own possessions, but you may also deduct the costs for transporting the possessions of the members of your household. This includes the actual cost of transportation or hauling from your former home to your new one. The cost of packing and crating, in-transit storage, and insurance is included. Expenses of storing and insuring household goods and personal effects are in-transit expenses if incurred within 30 consecutive days after your things are moved from your former home and before they are delivered at your new one.

Prior to 1994, moving expenses also included the cost of transportation, lodging for yourself and members of your household while traveling to your new home, and 80 percent of the cost of meals while moving. This included expenses for the day you arrive, and any meals and lodging expenses incurred in your old neighborhood within one day after your former home becomes uninhabitable because your furniture has been moved out. You could deduct expenses for only one trip to your new home for yourself and each member of your household. However, all members do not have to travel together.

Prior to 1994, deductions were allowed as well for premove house-hunting expenses. House-hunting expenses include the cost of transportation, meals, and lodging for yourself and members of your household while traveling to and from the area of your new job and while you are there. You could deduct these expenses only if you begin your trip *after* you get the job in the new area and if you go primarily to look for a new place to live. Your house hunting did not have to be successful to qualify for this deduction. You and members of your household could travel separately. Furthermore, you were not limited in the number of trips you or members of your household may take.

Prior to 1994, you also could deduct the cost of temporary living expenses. These expenses include not only the cost of lodging in the area of your new job but the cost of meals as well.

HOME SALE, PURCHASE, OR LEASE EXPENSES

In addition, pre-1994, home sale, purchase, and lease expenses also were deductible. You therefore could deduct the costs of selling your home or settling your lease in the former area and buying or leasing a home in the new area.

When you sold or exchanged a home, you could deduct real estate commissions, attorney's fees, title fees, escrow fees, points or loan placement charges you were required to pay, state transfer taxes, and similar expenses connected to the sale or exchange. You could not, however, deduct the cost of physical improvements intended to improve the condition or appearance of your former home. When you bought your new home, you could again deduct attorney's fees, escrow fees, appraisal fees, title fees, points and loan placement charges that did not represent payment or prepayment of interest, and similar expenses connected to the purchase. When you lease a new home, you cannot deduct payments or prepayments of rent.

There are certain dollar limits that you must remember. Deductions for the costs of moving household goods and traveling to your new home are not limited to any amount. For premove travel, meals, and lodging expenses, temporary living expenses, and home sale, purchase, or lease expenses, you could not deduct more than $3,000. Deductions for house-hunting trip costs and temporary living expenses together could not be more than $1,500.

If you are a homeowner, you should have claimed the costs of premove house-hunting expenses and temporary living expenses before you claimed the costs of selling and buying your home as moving expenses. However, within the dollar limits you may choose to deduct any combination of these expenses. If you have expenses from selling or buying a home that you cannot deduct as moving expenses because of the $3,000 limit, you should use these expenses to reduce the gain on the sale of your former home or to increase the basis of your new home.

The following items cannot be deducted as moving expenses:

Home improvements to help sell your home
Loss on the sale of your home
Mortgage penalties
Losses from the disposing of memberships and clubs
Any part of the purchase price of your new home
Real estate taxes
Car tax for the state you move to
Driver's license for the state you move to
Refitting carpets and draperies
New security deposits on a new lease
Security deposits on an old lease because the vacated space needed cleaning or redecorating when the lease ended

However, you may deduct a security deposit that you give up if the lease is broken as a result of the move.

CURRENT LAW

The Omnibus Budget Reconciliation Act of 1993 made several substantial changes in the moving expense deduction—effective for expenses incurred after December 31, 1993. As of 1994, the Act excludes from the definition of moving expenses: (1) the costs related to the sale of (or settlement of an unexpired lease on) the old residence, and the purchase of (or acquisition of a lease on) the new residence in the general location of the new job and (2) the costs of meals consumed while traveling and while living in temporary quarters near the new job. It also contains the following additional modifications:

1. The cost of premove house-hunting trips is excluded from the definition of moving expenses.

2. The cost of temporary living expenses for up to 30 days in the general location of the new job is excluded from the definition of moving expenses.

3. The mileage limit is increased from 35 miles to 50 miles.

4. Moving expenses not paid or reimbursed by the taxpayer's employer are allowable as a deduction in calculating adjusted gross income.

5. Moving expenses paid or reimbursed by the taxpayer's employer are excludable from gross income. *Moving expenses* are now defined as the reasonable costs of

   a) moving household goods and personal effects from the former residence to the new residence; and

   b) traveling (including lodging during the period of travel) from the former residence to the new place of residence.

   Moving expenses do not include any expenses for meals.

EMPLOYER-PAID MOVING EXPENSES

Moving expenses are excludable from gross income and wages for income and employment tax purposes to the extent paid for by the taxpayer's employer (whether directly or through reimbursement). Moving expenses are not excludable if the taxpayer actually deducted the expenses in a prior taxable year. The 1993 law intends that the employer treat moving expenses as excludable unless it has actual knowledge that the employee deducted the expenses in a prior year. The employer has no obligation to determine whether the individual deducted the expenses. Rules similar to the rules relating to accountable plans will apply to reimbursed expenses.

MOVING EXPENSES NOT PAID FOR BY THE EMPLOYER

Moving expenses are deductible in computing adjusted gross income to the extent not paid for by the taxpayer's employer (whether directly or through reimbursement). Allowing such a deduction will treat taxpayers whose expenses are not paid for by their employer in a comparable manner to taxpayers whose moving expenses are paid for by their employer.

TAX STRATEGIES

The availability of the moving expense deduction allows you several very sophisticated tax planning strategies.

One strategic tax move may come about if you are considering retirement and a move to a different—warmer—climate. If you make the move in connection with a change in employment and satisfy the 39-week work requirement, you get a deduction for your moving expenses. The tax effect of this deduction will, in effect, increase your compensation for the 39 weeks of work and perhaps make it worthwhile to postpone your actual retirement. Note that included in the definition of moving expenses are all of your "personal effects." See, for example, *John R. Fogg*, 89 T.C. No. 27 (decided in 1988), wherein a marine officer's moving expense deduction included the cost of moving his boat.

You should recognize that the deductibility of your moving expenses is in effect a tax subsidy of those expenses. So, for example, if you think it may be too expensive to hire a moving company, your decision to save money by moving your household goods yourself may be modified by considering the tax effect of the deduction for moving expenses. Moving company charges of $3,000 actually would represent a cash outflow of only $2,160 if you are single and have taxable income over the $85,650 level ($3,000 × .28 = $840 in tax savings).

81   Clean Fuel Vehicles

If you were the original owner, you could have gotten a deduction of up to $2,000 of the cost of a clean fuel vehicle. That's a vehicle that uses a significant source of energy other than gasoline.

You got the $2,000 deduction if the car was placed in service in 2004 or 2005. Now, you'll use the Hybrid Vehicles Credits found on pages 127–128.

You got the deduction for the year you started driving the car. The IRS has validated *hybrid cars* for this deduction. A hybrid combines an electric motor with a gas-fueled internal combustion engine. (See the Ford Escape, the Toyota Prius and Highlander, and Honda's Insight and Hybrid Civic, among others.) U.S. automakers will focus on sport utility vehicles and pickup trucks rather than passenger cars. If you qualified, the IRS contributed to the cost of your new car. You took the deduction on Line 33 of your Form 1040 by writing in "clean fuel."

82 Deduction for Qualified Higher Education Expenses— Tuition and Fees

The 2001 Tax Act created an above-the-line deduction for qualified higher education expenses you pay. Qualified higher education expenses are defined in the same manner as for purposes of the HOPE credit. Room and board do *not* count.

In 2002 and 2003, if you had an adjusted gross income that did not exceed $65,000 ($130,000 in the case of married couples filing joint returns) you were entitled to a maximum deduction of $3,000 per year. Taxpayers with adjusted gross income above these thresholds didn't get the deduction. Since 2004, taxpayers with adjusted gross income that did not exceed $65,000 ($130,000 in the case of married taxpayers filing joint returns) were entitled to a maximum deduction of $4,000 and taxpayers with adjusted gross income that does not exceed $80,000 ($160,000 in the case of married taxpayers filing joint returns) were entitled to a maximum deduction of $2,000. This deduction was allowable through 2009 and was renewed by Congress through 2013.

The tuition and fees deduction of up to $4,000 is available to help parents and students pay for postsecondary education. Below are 10 important facts about this deduction every student and parent should know.

1. You do not have to itemize to take the tuition and fees deduction. You claim a tuition and fees deduction by completing Form 8917 and submitting it with your Form 1040 or Form 1040A.

2. You may be able to claim qualified tuition and fees expenses as either an adjustment to income, a Hope, American Opportunity, or Lifetime Learning credit, or, if applicable, as a business expense.

3. You cannot take the tuition and fees deduction on your income tax return if your filing status is married and you're filing separately.

4. You cannot take the deduction if you are claimed, or can be claimed, as a dependent on someone else's return.

5. The deduction is reduced or eliminated if your modified adjusted gross income exceeds certain limits, based on your filing status (see above).

6. You cannot claim the tuition and fees deduction if you or anyone else claims the Hope, American Opportunity, or Lifetime Learning credit for the same student in the same year.

7. If the educational expenses are also allowable as a business expense, the tuition and fees deduction may be claimed in conjunction with a business expense deduction, but the same expenses cannot be deducted twice.

8. You cannot claim a deduction or credit based on expenses paid with tax-free scholarship, fellowship, grant, or education savings account funds such as a Coverdell education savings account, tax-free savings bond interest, or employer-provided education assistance.

9. The same rule applies to expenses you pay with a tax-exempt distribution from a qualified tuition plan except that you can deduct qualified expenses you pay only with that part of the distribution that is a return of your contribution to the plan.

10. IRS Publication 970, Tax Benefits for Education, can help eligible parents and students understand the special rules that apply and decide which tax break to claim. The publication is available at IRS.gov or by calling 800-TAX-FORM (800-829-3676).

83 Legal Fees

Fees and court costs you pay to your attorney on settlements or awards for *unlawful discrimination*—sex, race, or age—after the signing of the American Jobs Creation Act of 2004 on October 22, are now allowed as above the line deductions. These deductions are not subject to the alternative minimum tax, nor to the 2 percent floor on miscellaneous itemized deductions.

84   Classroom Materials

From January 1, 2002, through 2013, you get an above the line deduction of up to $250 annually for expenses paid for books, supplies, computer equipment, and supplementary materials if you're an eligible educator. An eligible educator is a kindergarten through grade 12 teacher, aide, instructor, counselor, or principal in a school for at least 900 hours during the school year.

85   Medical Savings Accounts (Archer Medical Savings Accounts)

Under law prior to the Health Insurance Portability and Accountability Act of 1996, self-employed individuals were entitled to deduct 30 percent of the amount paid for health insurance for the self-employed individual and his or her spouse or dependents. (It's now 100 percent.) Any individual who itemized tax deductions could deduct unreimbursed medical expenses (including expenses for medical insurance) paid during the year to the extent that the total of such expenses exceeded 7.5 percent of the individual's adjusted gross income. Prior law did not contain any special rules for medical savings accounts.

A medical savings account (MSA) is a trust or custodial account created exclusively for the benefit of the account holder and is subject to rules similar to those applicable to individual retirement accounts. Within limits, contributions to a medical savings account are deductible if made by an eligible individual and are excludable if made by an employer of an eligible individual. Moreover, earnings on amounts in a medical savings account are not currently taxable and distributions from a medical savings account for medical expenses will also not be taxable.

Since 1997, medical savings accounts have been available to employees covered under an employer-sponsored high-deductible plan of a small employer and to self-employed individuals. An employer is a small employer if it employed on an average no more than 50 employees during either the preceding or second preceding year. In order for an employee of an eligible employer to be eligible to make medical savings account contributions (or to have the employer contributions made on his or her behalf), the employee must not be covered under any other health plan. In the case of an employee, contributions can be made to a medical savings account either by the individual or by the individual's employer. However, an individual is not eligible to make contributions to a medical savings account for a year if any employer contributions are made to a medical savings account on behalf of the individual for the year.

Similarly, in order to be eligible to make contributions to a medical savings account, a self-employed individual must be covered under a high-deductible health plan and no other health plan is allowed (except certain permitted coverages). With both self-employed individuals and employees, medical savings accounts are allowable if the taxpayer has another health plan that provides *only* certain limited permitted coverage for accidents, disability, dental care, vision care, or long-term care. This coverage may be by insurance or otherwise and permitted insurance includes: (1) Medicare supplemental insurance; (2) insurance if substantially all of the coverage provided under such insurance relates to (a) liabilities incurred under Workers' Compensation Law, (b) tort liabilities, (c) liabilities relating to ownership and use of property (e.g., auto insurance), or (d) such other similar liabilities as the Secretary of the Treasury may prescribe by regulations; (3) insurance for a specified disease or illness; and (4) insurance that provides a fixed payment for hospitalization.

Individual contributions to a medical savings account are deductible (within limits) above the line. In addition, employer contributions are excludable within the same limits.

In the case of a self-employed individual, the deduction cannot exceed your earned income from the trade or business with respect to which the high-deductible plan is established. In the case of an employee, the deduction cannot exceed your compensation attributable to the employer sponsoring the high-deductible plan in which you are enrolled.

The maximum annual contribution that can be made to a medical savings account for a year is 65 percent of the deductible under the high-deductible plan in the case of individual coverage and 75 percent of the deductible in the case of family coverage. No other dollar limits on the maximum contribution apply. The annual contribution limit is the sum of the limits determined separately for each month, based upon the individual's status and health plan coverage as of the first day of the month.

A high-deductible plan for 2013 is a health plan with an annual deductible of at least $2,150 and no more than $3,200 in the case of individual coverage and at least $4,300 and no more than $6,450 in the case of family coverage.

In addition, the maximum out-of-pocket expenses with respect to allowed cost (including the deductible) must be no more than $4,300 in the case of individual coverage and no more than $7,850 in the case of family coverage. Since 1999, these dollar amounts have been indexed for inflation in $50 increments based on the Consumer Price Index.

Earnings on amounts in a medical savings account are not currently included in income, and distributions from a medical savings account for the medical expenses of an individual and his or her spouse or dependents generally are excludable from income.

The medical savings account plan was a trial plan. The number of taxpayers benefiting annually from a medical savings account contribution is limited to a threshold level (generally, 750,000 taxpayers). If it is determined in a year that the threshold level has been exceeded then, in general, for succeeding years during the four-year pilot period, 1997–2000, only those individuals who (1) made a medical savings account contribution or had an employer medical savings account contribution for the year or a preceding year or (2) are employed by a participating employer, would be eligible for a medical savings account contribution.

If you have a medical savings account, you attach Form 8853 to your tax return. During 1997–2000, the Department of the Treasury evaluated medical savings account participation and the reduction in federal revenues due to such participation and made reports of such evaluations to Congress. As a result, Congress has voted to expand MSAs.

Few Archer MSAs will be set up after 2005. The reason—Health Savings Accounts. (See IRS Announcement 2007-44.)

86 Health Savings Accounts

I love it! Tax deductible when going in. *And* no tax when you take it out! You can't get much better than that.

I'm talking about the new Health Savings Accounts (HSAs) that were created as part of the Medicare Act of 2003.

The concept is easy. Congress wants to put you in charge of your own health costs. So, if you buy their special ticket, you'll be able to set up a magical account. You'll put money into that account and be able to deduct it. There's no tax while the money is held by the account. And, if you take the dollars out for the right reasons, there's no tax ever.

Technically, it's a bit more complicated. Let's start with the special ticket.

In order to qualify to open a Health Savings Account, you have to be covered by a high-deductible health plan. It must be your only health plan. (There are some exceptions—e.g., workers' compensation, coverage under an auto policy, etc.)

A high-deductible health plan is one with an annual-deductible of not less than $1,250 for 2013 and 2014 for individual coverage and not less than $2,500 for 2013 and 2014 for family coverage. That means you pay for the routine medical visits, tests, eyeglasses, and the like. Remember, the bigger the deductible, the smaller the premium you have to pay.

In addition, the sum of the annual deductible and other out of pocket expenses required to be paid under the plan can't exceed $6,250 for 2013 (6,350 for 2014) for individual coverage, and $12,500 for 2013 ($12,700 for 2014) for family coverage.

Can your employer offer a high-deductible plan? Sure. In fact, many supporters of the concept expect large employers to offer the option before long.

If you've got this special ticket, what does it let you do? If you have a high-deductible health plan, you can now set up your own Health Savings Account.

Where do you get the money? How about from the premiums you saved by switching to a *high-deductible* health plan!?

Technically, the HSA is a trust. You can now (2014) contribute to that trust and *take a tax deduction of* $3,300 ($6,550 with family coverage).

If you're age 55 or older, you can make additional deductible contributions. For 2013 and 2014, it's an extra $1,000.

You can pretty much invest the money any way you want, similar to an IRA. In fact, IRA funds can now be rolled over into an HSA, saving the tax and any 10 percent penalty.

You can dip into this pot at any time. Any dollars used for medical expenses come out tax-free. You can use the HSA for routine doctor visits, lab tests, eyeglasses, dental care, or even cosmetic surgery. Anything left over at the end of the year rolls back into the pot. So, if you're young and healthy, you could built up a nice pot of cash in case of major medical problems years later.

You can't use your HSA to buy health insurance. But, payments for long-term care insurance count. You can also use the money for temporary health insurance while you're unemployed and collecting unemployment, or for COBRA continuation insurance.

If you withdraw for nonmedical purposes, you pay tax, plus a 20 percent penalty (10 percent before 2011), on the nonqualified amount.

Similar accounts, the Archer Medical Savings Accounts, have been around for a while. But, the Archer MSAs were limited to small businesses and the self-employed. They were also temporary and scheduled to potentially terminate after a trial period. That really didn't encourage insurance companies to develop the appropriate policies on a mass basis. The Health Savings Accounts are designed to be permanent and can be used by anybody!

HSAs can be offered to employees as part of a cafeteria plan. Contributions can be made by both employers and employees. Whoever puts the dollars in, gets the deduction. You can contribute to an HSA even if your spouse is covered with insurance, so long as you are not covered by the policy (Rev. Rul. 2005-25).

You can even fund your HSA with a transfer from your IRA. It's a one time transfer. See IRS Notice 2008-51 for details.

Here's how the numbers might work. A 38-year-old couple with two children could buy a health policy with a $5,950 deductible for $250 a month, or $3,000 a year. A plan with a $500 deductible would cost $600 a month, or $7,200 a year.

With the $3,000 plan, they save $4,200 in premiums. That $4,200 can be used to fund an HSA and would be fully deductible.

Now, you're in charge. First you've got the tax savings. In the 35 percent bracket, that's an additional $1,470 in your pocket. But even more importantly, you now have control over your own medical expenditures. For a $10 co-payment, it was easy to visit the doctor. But, now it's *your* money that's being spent. That should help put a break on runaway health costs.

If you're young, healthy, or wealthy, this is a deal you don't want to pass up. I know of no other vehicle where you get a deduction with a deposit and no tax with a withdrawal. That's my kind of tax shelter!

87   Sales Tax Deduction on Motor Vehicles

Taxpayers who bought a new car or several other types of motor vehicles in 2009 may have been entitled to a special tax deduction when they filed their 2009 federal tax returns. The tax break is part of the American Recovery and Reinvestment Act of 2009.

Here are seven things you should know about this old deduction:

1. State and local sales taxes paid on up to $49,500 of the purchase price of qualifying vehicles were deductible.

2. Qualified motor vehicles generally included new (not used) cars, light trucks, motor homes, and motorcycles.

3. Purchases must have occurred after February 16, 2009, and before January 1, 2010.

4. This is an above-the-line deduction and can be taken regardless of whether or not you itemize other deductions on your tax return.

5. Taxpayers will claim this deduction when filing their 2009 federal income tax return. File an amended return, Form 1040X, if you missed it.

6. The amount of the deduction was phased out for taxpayers whose modified adjusted gross income was between $125,000 and $135,000 for individual filers and between $250,000 and $260,000 for joint filers.

Note that there was no separate line to take this deduction. It was added to your standard deduction (like the extra deduction for real estate taxes paid) using Schedule L.

If your state doesn't have a sales or excise tax, you could have deducted other fees or taxes imposed by the state or local government based on the vehicle's sales price or a per-unit fee.

PLAN COMPARISON

	Flexible Spending Account	Health Savings Account	Health Reimbursement Arrangement
Initial Legislator or Regulation	Revenue active 1978	Medicare active 2003	U.S. Department of the Treasury Revenue Ruling 2002
Date Effective	January 1, 1979	January 1, 1997	June 26, 2002
Eligibility	All employees except self-employed	All employers	All employers
Qualified Medical Expenses	Unreimbursed medical care expense as defined by Internal Revenue Code, Section 213	Any qualified medical expense permitted under tax law	Unreimbursed medical expenses as defined by the Internal Revenue Code 213
Nonqualified Medical Expenses	Expenses not under Internal Revenue Code 213 Health insurance premiums under a continuation or coverage arrangement Health insurance premiums when receiving unemployment compensation	Expenses not under Internal Revenue Code 213	Expenses not under Internal Revenue Code 213
Must Be Covered by Health Insurance Plan	No	Yes, a high-deductible health plan	No
Contributor	Employee, employer or both	Employee, employer or both	Employer
Contribution Limits	No statutory limits. Limits may be set by employer.	Up to the amount of the high-deductible health plan but no more than $3,250 for self-coverage and $6,450 for family coverage	No statutory limit. Limit may be set by employer.
Funds Carried Over to Next Year	March 15	Yes	Yes
Portability	Account cannot be maintained if employee is no longer working for the employer. Continued access to unused account balance if the employee is no longer working for the employer	Completely portable	At employer's discretion

Source: Benefits Selling, October 2005.

	Health Savings Accounts (HSAs)	Medical Savings Accounts (MSAs)
Contribution source	Individual (or by a family member on behalf of the individual) and/or employer	Either individual or employer (not both)
Tax-deductible contribution	Up to 100 percent of deductible with a maximum cap determined by the Internal Revenue Service each year: Single coverage: $3,250 Family coverage: $6,450	Single: 65 percent of deductible Family: 75 percent of deductible
Deductible ranges	For 2013: minimums = $1,250 for single; $2,500 for family	For 2013: $2,150–$3,200 for single; $4,300–$6,450 for family
Maximum out of pocket*	For 2013: maximums = $6,250 for single; $12,500 for family	For 2013: maximums = $4,300 for single; $7,850 for family
Who is eligible?	Individual or employer of any size that has established a qualified high-deductible health plan (HDHP); individual must be below Medicare eligibility age (65), not covered by any non-HDHP, and not listed as a dependent on another's tax return	Self-employed and small employers (under 50 employees); individuals must be covered by a qualified HDHP
Is there a "catch-up" contribution provision for older workers?	Individuals between the ages of 55 and 65 may contribute an additional $1,000.	No
Effective date	Must be established on or after January 1, 2005.	Must have been established by December 31, 2003, and before January 1, 2006; rollovers into an HSA are allowed.
Do employers need to make comparable contributions?	Yes, but under HSA legislation both employers and employees can contribute.	Yes

* Includes deductible and any expenses incurred once deductible is met.

Source: MSA Bank (HAS Bank).

CHAPTER 7

"Below the Line" Deductions

"I am proud to be paying taxes in the United States. The only thing is—I could be just as proud for half the money."

ARTHUR GODFREY

"About 510,000 taxpayers who claimed tax standard deductions on their 1998 income tax returns would have saved an average $610 by itemizing their deductions."

General Accounting Office April 13, 2001

"About 948,000 taxpayers in the year 1998 failed to itemize their deductions, even though they qualified to do so, resulting in a $473 million overpayment in taxes."

General Accounting Office April 11, 2002

"Our tax system is complicated and unfair, and it must be eliminated."

RICHARD K. ARMEY (R-Tex.) Former Majority Leader of the House of Representatives and

BILL ARCHER (R-Tex.) Former Chairman of the House Ways & Means Committee

"Congress has a lot of respect for logic—they use it so sparingly."

JEFF SCHNEPPER

Your itemize deductions only if they exceed the amount of your standard deduction.

For 2013, the standard deduction amounts are as follows:

If your filing status is:	2013
Single	$ 6,100
Married, filing jointly, or a qualifying widow or widower	$12,200
Married, filing separately	$ 6,100
Head of household	$ 8,950

For 2008 and 2009, nonitemizers could have deducted up to $500 ($1,000 for joint returns) for real estate taxes paid, plus, for 2009, your standard deduction was also increased by the new sales tax deduction on motor vehicles discussed on page 219.

The minimum income levels for filing a tax return in 2013 are:

Single	$10,000
Single, age 65 or older	$11,500
Married, filing jointly	$20,000
Married, filing jointly, one spouse age 65 or older	$21,200
Married, filing jointly, both spouses age 65 or older	$22,400

In addition, the personal tax exemption is $3,900 for 2013 and the added standard deduction for the aged or blind is $1,200 each on a joint return and $1,500 for a single for 2013.

A The Importance of Filing Status

Your filing status is determined on the last day of each year. This affords you another opportunity for sophisticated tax planning. The rates for married individuals, filing either jointly *or* separately, are much lower than those for single, unmarried taxpayers. For example, for 2013, on taxable income of $87,850, a single person pays a marginal tax rate of 28 percent and a total tax of $17,891. On the other hand, a married taxpayer with a spouse who has no income would pay a marginal rate of only 25 percent and a total tax of $13,820. If you are planning a New Year's wedding, advancing it only a few days to Christmas would therefore save you $4,071—enough to pay for your honeymoon.

Alternatively, if both married partners work, there is, in effect, a tax on the marriage. In 2013, two individuals earning $87,850 in taxable income would each pay $17,891 in taxes for a total outlay of $35,782. If they got married before the year-end, their total income would be $175,700, and they would have filed either a joint return or a return as married, filing separately—either way mandating a total tax payment of $36,662, $790 more than what they would have paid had they remained unmarried!

Marriage Penalties and Bonuses on Income Tax

An April 1999 Treasury Department study shows that nearly as many couples receive a "marriage bonus" as pay a "marriage penalty." In many cases, the average bonus is greater than the average penalty.

1999 Adjusted Gross Income	Percent of Couples Penalized	Average Penalty	Percent of Couples Who Get a Bonus	Average Bonus	Percent Getting Neither
$0–15,000	7.4%	$302	33.4%	$418	59.2%
$15,001–30,000	40.2%	$607	49.5%	$528	10.3%
$30,001–40,000	52.5%	$792	45.7%	$662	1.8%
$40,001–50,000	57.3%	$578	40.0%	$952	2.7%
$50,001–60,000	48.8%	$535	44.3%	$1,299	6.9%
$60,001–75,000	50.6%	$798	41.4%	$1,537	8.0%
$75,001–100,000	64.9%	$1,384	34.4%	$1,960	0.7%
$100,001–200,000	65.0%	$1,926	34.9%	$2,580	0.1%
$200,001 and more	48.5%	$5,688	50.0%	$3,428	1.5%

Source: Treasury Department.

Same-sex couples can now file jointly if your state recognized a union of two people of the same sex as a legal marriage. If you marry in a state that recognizes same-sex marriages and move to one that does not, you still file your federal return as married. In 2010, the IRS required same-sex couples in California (the ruling should cover Nevada and Washington as well), where community property rules govern, to combine their income and each report half of it on their separate tax returns. If the state recognizes same-sex marriages, individual returns should be prohibited.

The extraordinary penalty on marriage is the result of previous congressional actions that attempted to correct apparent inequities in the old tax structure. Prior to 1948, husbands and wives in community property states could each claim half of their household income for tax purposes even if only one of them actually earned all of the income. The law of the individual state attributed half of the income ("property") to the other spouse. For example, if only the husband worked, earning $30,000, both he and his wife would have reported $15,000 in income. Given our progressive tax rate, where each additional dollar earned is taxed at a higher rate, this was a substantial advantage. In 1948, the federal income tax code was amended to allow this benefit to all married taxpayers—including those in non–community property states. This was done by doubling the income brackets for married taxpayers associated with each rate. For example, if the first $500 of income was taxed at 11 percent for a single person, the first $1,000 of income for married couples would have also been taxed at 11 percent.

While those who were married rejoiced, single taxpayers making the same income as married couples were subject to much higher tax rates. In 1970, for example, single taxpayers could have been liable for as much as 42 percent more in taxes than a married couple earning an equivalent income. In response to this harsh inequity, Congress in 1971 changed the rates for single taxpayers to reduce this differential to a 20 percent maximum. The Tax Reform Act of 1986 reduced the differential even further. However, according to the Congressional Budget Office, 21 million couples filing jointly in 1996 suffered the marriage penalty averaging around $1,400 each! According to Senator Hutchison of Texas, that $1,400 marriage penalty number was still valid in March of 1999.

In the past, the tax penalty on marriage when both husband and wife work was compounded by the standard deduction. The Jobs and Growth Tax Relief Reconciliation Act of 2003 remedied this by making the standard deduction for joint returns twice that offered to singles. It also increased the standard deduction for married filing separately to the same as singles.

In addition, high-income earners who married also lost write-offs for personal exemptions faster than their single counterparts. The 2013 exemption of $3,900 is phased out for singles with taxable incomes above $250,000, but the phase-out for a married couple startes at $300,000, about 60 percent of the income amount for two single persons.

Marriage may also wipe out potential IRA deductions. If two taxpayers with incomes of $59,000 each marry and both are covered by an employer plan, neither could write off an IRA contribution. They would lose $11,000 in deductions and pay as much as $2,750 more in total tax.

Because your marital status for the entire year is based upon your status as of December 31, many individuals have been advised to fly to a Caribbean divorce haven, such as the Dominican Republic, for a quickie divorce before the year ends and to remarry in January. The tax savings can often more than offset the cost of legal fees and the Caribbean "vacation."

The Internal Revenue Service has reacted to this situation, declaring: "If you obtain a foreign divorce for the sole purpose of enabling you and your spouse to qualify as unmarried individuals eligible to file separate returns, and if you then remarry each other early in the next tax year, you and your spouse must file as married individuals."

This response has been tested in the Tax Court with interesting results. The Tax Court has ruled that it will not recognize such quickie divorces solely on the basis of the fact that the state in which the taxpayers are domiciled will not recognize such divorces. (The Fourth Circuit Court of Appeals ruled in 1981 that there may be a sham even if your state does recognize the divorce [668 F 2d. 1238]. This ruling is not universally accepted—see *Wake Forest Law Review,* Volume 18, pages 881–901, 1982.) But many states *do* recognize such divorces; by implication, therefore, if you reside in such a state, a quickie divorce and a remarriage could save you substantial tax dollars. Your divorce, though, must be real, with significant economic consequences—for example, loss of rights under a will— and not merely a sham. (See *Felt Estate v. Commissioner,* T.C. Memo 1987-465, September 16, 1987, in which a divorce decree obtained by a husband in the Dominican Republic was recognized for federal income tax purposes.)

In cases where divorces or legal separations would be either impractical or unwanted, you could at least make a substantial initial tax savings by postponing your original Christmas wedding until New Year's. This several days' wait may be worth several thousand tax dollars.

Can same-sex couples now file joint federal income tax returns? They can now! The Defense of Marriage Act has been held unconstitutional by the Supreme Court. Legally married same-sex couples should file amended refund claims for all open tax years if they would benefit taxwise from joint filing. More than joint filing is affected. Gifts between same-sex spouses now get the unlimited gift tax marital deduction. Bequests to surviving spouses are not subject to estate tax, and the survivor is entitled to use any unused estate tax exemption of the deceased spouse. And employer-provided health coverage for same-sex spouses is tax-free.

Being single may also be an advantage in qualifying for excess itemized deductions. For example, assume your spouse has total below the line deductions of $12,200. As you are married and don't exceed the amount of the joint standard deduction, none of these deductions give you any tax benefits.

Filing separately may sometimes help, but a husband and wife filing separate returns must use the same method of claiming deductions: If one itemizes, the other must itemize as well. This could result in a situation in which one spouse who itemizes has an allowable itemized deduction in excess of the standard deduction by, say, $4,000, but the other spouse who has no itemized deductions would have no "below the line" deductions.

In July 2000, the IRS ruled (S.C.A. 200030023) that (1) if a married individual files a separate return with head of household status and elects to itemize deductions, and if the other spouse continues to file as a married individual filing a separate return, then that other spouse is not eligible for the full standard deduction, but (2) if the other spouse who files as married filing separately elects to itemize deductions, then the spouse who files a separate return with head of household status may still use the full standard deduction available for head of household status.

Married filing separately may be profitable if the spouse who has itemized deductions is in a higher tax bracket. For example, if one is in the 28 percent bracket and the other is in the 15 percent bracket, the first would save $1,120 ($4,000 × .28) at a cost to the second of only $915 (married filing separately standard deduction of $6,100 × .15), or a net gain of $205.

However, this advantage may be dissipated by the greater advantage of the married tax schedule over the potentially more costly schedule for married filing separately. For example, filing jointly, a husband with a taxable income of $136,400 and a wife with $10,000 would pay $28,458 in taxes on a total income of $146,400. Filing separately, the husband would owe $33,169 and the wife $1,054, a total of $34,223 and a net *loss* of $5,765! Note that as the rates are condensed, the potential net loss is reduced.

The usual instance in which filing separately is advantageous is when substantial excess itemized deductions can be picked up. For example, as you will see later, medical expenses must be reduced by 10 percent* of your adjusted gross income before they can be included in your itemized deduction computation. Assume one spouse has $6,000 in medical expenses and an adjusted gross income of $10,000, while the other spouse has no medical expenses and an adjusted gross income of $50,000. Filing separately would require a reduction of only $1,000 (10 percent of $10,000) rather than $6,000 (10 percent of $60,000)—a net additional itemized deduction of $5,000. In this case, depending upon the other itemized deductions and specific credits available to each spouse, it might pay to file separately. In any case, if you are married and both parties earn income, it is always to your advantage to prepare your return each way to see which provides the lower tax.

---

*7.5% if you're age 65 or older.

B Tax Planning with Itemized Deductions

There are a number of general strategies that should be implemented when planning for your itemized deductions. The most important of these is the timing of your deductions. Many deductions can be shifted from one year to the next.

You might want to implement such shifting if your itemized deductions are close to the standard deduction amount. Your aim should be to bunch your deductions for expenses so that they exceed the full value of your standard deduction amount. For example, assume that you have itemized deductions of $12,200 each year, of which $3,000 can be accelerated or deferred. With a standard deduction amount of $12,200, none of these deductions would be allowed as excess. What you do, therefore, is to time the expenses you can control so as to itemize deductions of $15,200 in the alternate years ($12,200 + $3,000). This strategy allows you an extra deduction of $3,000 every second year, and if you are in the 28 percent bracket, it saves you $840 in taxes each time.

For you to be able to claim all of your available itemized deductions and to time them appropriately, we must examine and dissect each one in turn.

88 Medical Expenses

You may deduct certain medical and dental expenses not only for yourself but for your spouse and your dependents as well. Medical expenses are payments that you make for the diagnosis, cure, relief, treatment, or prevention of disease. They also include payments for treatment affecting any part or function of the body. Expenses for transportation for needed medical care are included in medical expenses. Payments for insurance that provide medical care for you, your spouse, and your dependents are also included in medical expenses.

The following list shows those items that are generally deductible as medical expenses:

- Fees for doctors, surgeons, dentists, ophthalmologists, optometrists, chiropractors, osteopaths, chiropodists, podiatrists, psychiatrists, psychologists, and Christian Science practitioners.
- Fees for hospital services, therapy, nursing services (including nurses' meals while on duty), ambulance hire, and laboratory, surgical, obstetrics, diagnostic, dental, and X-ray services.
- Meals and lodging provided by a hospital during medical treatment, and meals and lodging provided by a center during treatment for alcoholism or drug addiction.

- Medical and hospital insurance premiums.
- Special equipment such as motorized wheelchairs, hand controls on a car, and special telephones for the deaf.
- Special items, including false teeth, artificial limbs, eyeglasses, hearing aids, bandages, crutches, and guide dogs for the blind or deaf.
- Transportation for needed medical care.
- Insulin and prescription medicines and drugs, including special foods and drinks your doctor prescribes specifically for the treatment of an illness, and pills, birth control items, and vitamins and iron *your doctor prescribes.* Imported prescription drugs are *not* deductible because the importation of foreign drugs is against the law.
- Expenses for diagnostic tests are allowed even if you exhibit no symptoms or sickness (Rev. Rul. 2007-72). This includes electronic scans, pregnancy tests, and physical exams.
- Under certain conditions, medical deductions may be allowed for boarding school expenses. In Letter Ruling 8447014, the IRS ruled that a psychiatrically oriented boarding school is a special school. Thus, the taxpayer was able to deduct, as a medical expense, tuition as well as transportation expenses to and from the school. In Info 2004-0090, the IRS allowed private school tuition as a medical expense when a doctor recommended special education to correct a medical condition.
- The cost of special school programs for children with Attention Deficit Hyperactivity Disorder (PLR 9852015).
- The cost of programs and prescriptions to help you stop smoking (but not over the counter patches and gums) (Rev. Pub. 99-28).
- Radical keratotomy surgery to correct vision is deductible (Ltr. Rul. 9625049) but, so far, even medically prescribed marijuana, even in a state where it is legal, is not (Rev. Rul. 97-9).
- While drugs (except insulin) must be prescribed the cost of needles to inject them does not (see INFO 2005-0008).
- Health club membership fees incurred primarily for the purpose of preventing or alleviating obesity (IRS information letter 2002-0077).
- Nursing home expenses if the principal purpose is the availability of medical care (IRS INFO 2002-0169).
- Weight loss to treat a *specific disease*, but not for appearance or general health (see Rev. Rul. 79-151). Weight loss programs, but not the cost of diet foods, would also qualify (see Rev. Rul. 2002-19).

- The cost of a *prescribed* special diet to the extent that it exceeds the cost of a regular diet (see INFO 2001—0075, 0085, 0086, and 0088).

- The cost of cayenne pepper to treat Raynaud's disease (see INFO 2001-0297).

- Expenses related to obtaining a donated egg for fertilization (PLR 200318017) including egg donor fee, agency fee, insurance and legal fees.

- Breast reconstruction surgery after a mastectomy (Rev. Rul. 2003-57).

- Vision correction surgery (Rev. Rul. 2003-57).

- Egg donor fees and related legal expenses (see INFO 2005-0102), but not the cost of using a surrogate mother (see INFO 2004-0187).

- Tuition costs for kids with learning problems who need special education (PLR 200704001, PLR 200729019, and Ltr. Rul. 200521003).

- Lactation equipment such as breast pumps (Announcement 2011-14).

- The cost of a caregiver for a dementia patient or anyone unable to perform two of the six activities of daily living: eating, toileting, transferring (general mobility), bathing, dressing, and continence.

- Acupuncture (INFO 2011-45).

Amounts paid to whiten teeth discolored as a result of age were *not* allowed as medical expenses.

Costs for male to female gender reassignment surgery were also not allowed (C.C.A. 200603025) according to the IRS. But the tax court in the 2010 *O'Donnabhain* case allowed medical deductions for sex reassignment surgery and hormone therapy. The IRS agreed in AOD no. 2011-03.

In Rev. Rul. 2003-58, the IRS ruled that non-prescription drugs, even if recommended by a doctor, are not allowed as medical expenses. But, in IR 2003-108, the IRS announced that over the counter drugs *would* be covered by Health Care Flexible Spending Accounts (Rev. Rul. 2003-102). Effective for expenses incurred in 2011, the Pension Protection Act requires distributions from health saving accounts, Archer medical savings accounts, and flexible spending accounts *only* for prescribed drugs or insulin. They also ruled in Rev. Rul. 2003-43 that debit cards can be used for Health Reimbursement Arrangements.

Medical expenses paid for a surrogate mother and unborn child also do not qualify (Info 2002-0291) unless this surrogate qualifies as your dependent.

Payments for prostitutes and pornography, which are *not* a part of prescribed sex therapy, were also denied as medical expenses to attorney William Halby by the Tax Court in 2010. Lesson learned? Get a prescription from your doctor first!

There are certain limitations on the amount you may deduct. As of 2013, you may deduct only that part of your medical and dental expenses that is more than 10 percent* of your adjusted gross income. Drug expenses, which include *only* prescription drugs and insulin, are included in this 10 percent pool.

As of 1983, the separate deduction for one-half of medical insurance premiums up to $150 was eliminated. All medical insurance premiums are now included in the 10 percent pool.

Medical care includes a wide array of services. It includes payments for a legal abortion as well as payments for an operation legally performed to make a person unable to have children. It no longer includes payments for purely cosmetic surgery, such as a face-lift, but does cover charges for medical care that are included in the tuition fee of a college or private school, as long as the breakdown of the charges is included in the bill given by the school.

Payments for acupuncture and payments to a treatment center for drug addicts or alcoholics, including meals and lodging provided by the center during the treatment, are also deductible. So too are payments for surgical, hospital, laboratory, and transportation expenses by an actual or possible donor of a kidney or other body organ.

Wages for an attendant who provides nursing services and any out-of-pocket amounts you pay for the attendant's meals are also deductible. Divide the food expense among the household members to find the cost of the attendant's food. If you had to pay additional out-of-pocket amounts for household upkeep because of the attendant, this extra amount you paid is deductible as well. This includes items such as extra rent you paid because you moved to a larger apartment to provide space for the attendant, or the extra cost of utilities for the attendant. If the attendant also provided personal and household services, costs for these must be separated from costs for the nursing, since only the amount spent for nursing services is allowable as a deduction. Remember, though, that even the part of the Social Security (FICA) tax you pay for a worker who provides medical care is deductible.

You may also deduct payments for psychiatric care mainly for relieving a mental illness or defect. You may include the cost of supporting a mentally ill dependent at a specially equipped medical center where the dependent receives medical care, as well as your transportation expenses for regular visits that are recommended as part of that dependent's treatment.

MEDICAL INSURANCE PREMIUMS

Medical insurance premiums are deductible within the limits described earlier. The premiums you pay for medical insurance are for medical care, whether the insurance company pays the provider of the care (hospital, doctor, etc.) directly or reimburses you for payments you've made. Medical insurance premiums you pay may be included in your medical expenses if the premiums are for:

---

*Still 7.5% if you are age 65 or older.

a) policies that pay for hospitalization, surgical fees, and other medical expenses;

b) policies that pay only for prescription drugs;

c) policies that replace lost or damaged contact lenses;

d) the medical part in policies that provide more than one type of payment, if the medical charge is reasonable and is stated separately in the insurance contract or is given to you in a separate statement;

e) membership in an association furnishing cooperative, "free choice" medical service, or group hospitalization clinical care;

f) Medicare B, supplementary medical insurance for the aged (check the information you receive from the Social Security Administration to find out your premium rate and the amount of your deduction);

g) Medicare A, the part of Social Security that covers basic Medicare (you may deduct premiums you voluntarily pay for Medicare A coverage if you are 65 or older and are not entitled to Social Security benefits; Medicare A premiums are not deductible if they are paid as part of your Social Security tax); *or*

h) prepaid insurance premiums you pay before you are 65 for medical care coverage—for yourself, your spouse, or dependents—after you are 65. These are deductible when paid if they are paid in equal installments yearly or more often. The payments must be made for 10 years or more; if paid until you reach 65, the payments must be made for a minimum of 5 years.

You may not deduct premiums paid for life insurance policies or for policies providing repayment for loss of earnings or for the accidental loss of limb, life, sight, etc. Nor can you deduct premiums for a policy that guarantees a specified amount each week (for a specified number of weeks) if you are hospitalized for sickness or injury.

LONG-TERM CARE INSURANCE AND SERVICES

Prior to 1996, the Internal Revenue Code did not provide explicit rules relating to the tax treatment of long-term care insurance contracts or long-term care services. Beginning in 1997, the Health Insurance Portability and Accountability Act of 1996 provides that qualified long-term care insurance premiums will count toward itemized medical expenses and, to the extent that such expenses exceed 10 percent of adjusted gross income, a tax deduction will be available.

There is a cap on the amount of premium that can be applied to the medical expense deduction. See below.

For taxable years beginning after 1997, these dollar limits have been indexed for increases in the medical care component of the Consumer Price Index. Moreover, long-term care insurance premiums will now qualify for the self-employed health insurance deduction (100 percent in 2003 and thereafter).

Under the Pension Protection Act of 2006, as of January 1, 2010, there's no federal tax on the proceeds of an annuity if those proceeds are used to pay for long-term care coverage.

HOSPITAL MEALS AND LODGING

Meals and lodging are also deductible if they are furnished by a hospital or similar institution as a necessary part of medical care and if the main reason for your being in the hospital is to receive that medical care. The cost of your meals or lodging while you are away from home for medical treatment, or for the relief of a specific condition, however, is not deductible if you are not at a hospital or similar institution, even if the trip is made on the advice of your doctor. Under the Tax Reform Act of 1984, a deduction of up to $50 per day per individual for lodging expenses, but not for meals, for the patient and certain accompanying individuals away from home to receive outpatient care at hospitals or certain outpatient clinics is allowed. For example, treatment in an outpatient clinic, such as the Mayo Clinic, that provides substantially similar services to those provided by a hospital would qualify. Moreover, although food costs are not deductible, presumably if they are included in the cost of the lodging, no allocation is necessary and the full cost will be deductible subject to the $50 per day per person limit. (See Letter Ruling 8516025.)

Long-Term Care Deduction Caps

Attained Age at the End of the Tax Year	2013 Maximum Deduction
Not more than 40	$360
More than 40 but not more than 50	$680
More than 50 but not more than 60	$1,360
More than 60 but not more than 70	$3,640
More than 70	$4,550

Alternatively, if an individual is in a nursing home or a home for the aged because of a physical condition, and the main reason for being there is to get medical care, the entire cost, including meals *and* lodging, may be included as a deductible medical expense.

TRANSPORTATION EXPENSES

Transportation payments necessary for medical care also qualify as a deductible medical expense. Assume that you have been ill with a bad heart condition and you live in an area that has extremely cold winters, which makes your condition worse. Your doctor advises you to spend the winter in a warmer place, and you and your family spend the winter in a rented house in Florida. The trip is made for a specific medical reason, and although none of your expenses for food and lodging while on your way to Florida or during your stay there are deductible, your share of the transportation expenses between your home and Florida *is* deductible.

Transportation expenses include the following:

- Amounts paid for bus, taxi, train, or plane fare, or for ambulance hire.

- Out-of-pocket expenses for your car, such as gas and oil. You may not deduct any part of general repair or maintenance expenses. If you do not wish to deduct your actual expenses, you may use the 2013 *standard rate* of 24¢ a mile for each mile you use your car for medical reasons, and add to that any parking fees and tolls that you pay.

- Transportation expenses of a parent who must accompany a child needing medical care.

- Transportation expenses of a nurse familiar with injections, medications, and other treatments required by a patient who is traveling to get medical care but cannot travel alone.

CARE FOR THE HANDICAPPED

Special care may be needed for handicapped individuals. You may include the following payments for this care in your deductible medical expenses:

1. Payments to a special school for mentally or physically handicapped individuals, if the main reason for going is the school's means for relieving the handicap. The cost of sending a blind child to school to learn braille, or a deaf child to learn lip reading, is a medical expense. If you pay for remedial language training to correct a condition caused by a birth defect of the brain, you may deduct these payments as medical expenses.

   Tuition or tutoring expenses you pay on your doctor's advice for a child who has severe learning disabilities caused by a nervous system disorder are also medical expenses. So too are the costs of meals, lodging, and ordinary education supplied by the special school, but only if the main reason for the child's attendance is the availability of medical care.

2. The cost of keeping a mentally retarded individual, at the advice of a psychiatrist, in a specially chosen home that is not the home of a relative; for example, a "halfway" house to help in the adjustment from life in a mental hospital to community living.

3. Payments to a nonprofessional individual for giving "patterning" exercises (coordinated physical manipulation of the individual's limbs to imitate crawling and other normal movements) to a mentally challenged child.

4. Advance payments to a private institution for the lifetime care, treatment, and training of your physically and mentally handicapped dependent in the event that you die or become unable to care for your dependent. The payments must be required as a condition for the institution's future acceptance of your dependent and cannot be refundable.

5. Expenses paid for the care of your invalid spouse in your home. Only amounts spent for care to relieve your spouse's illness are deductible. The cost of household services, such as cooking and cleaning, is not deductible as a medical expense but may be eligible for the credit for household and dependent care expenses.

6. The cost and upkeep of service dogs for those with either mental or physical handicaps.

SPECIAL MEDICAL EQUIPMENT

Moreover, you may also deduct payments for special items and equipment. This includes payments for:

1. False teeth, artificial limbs, eyeglasses, hearing aids, and crutches, or the cost and care of guide dogs for the blind and deaf. Such expenses are medical, not business, even if you use the dog in carrying on your business.

2. The part of the cost of braille books and magazines that is more than the price for regular books and magazines.

3. The cost and repair of special telephone equipment that enables a deaf person to communicate over a regular telephone.

4. Amounts paid for oxygen equipment and oxygen to relieve problems in breathing due to a medical condition.

5. The cost of special attachments, such as a motorized wheelchair or autoette or special hand controls that are installed in a car for the use of a physically handicapped driver.

6. The amount you pay for a special design of a car to hold a wheelchair, as well as the cost of operating and keeping up an autoette or wheelchair used mainly for the relief of sickness or disability.

7. The cost of removing lead-based paints from walls, woodwork, etc., in your home to prevent a child who has lead poisoning (or who has had lead poisoning) from eating the paint. This must be on the advice of a doctor, and it must be determined that the paint contains lead. The areas covered with lead-based paint have to be in poor repair (peeling or cracking) or within the child's reach. The cost of painting the scraped area is not a deductible medical expense.

Payments for special equipment installed in a home, or similar improvements made for medical reasons, may be deductible even if they are capital improvements. If these expenses are for permanent improvements that increase the value of the property, only the amount in excess of the increase in value may be deducted as a medical expense. For example, assume you have a heart ailment, and on your doctor's advice you install an elevator in your home so that you will not need to climb stairs. The elevator costs $1,000. According to competent appraisals, the elevator increases the value of your home by $700. The $300 difference is a medical expense. If the elevator did not increase the value of your home, the whole cost would have been a medical expense.

If a capital expense qualifies as a medical expense, any amount paid for operation or upkeep also qualifies as a medical expense, as long as the medical reason for the capital expense still exists. These expenses are deductible even if none or only part of the original expense was deductible.

Amounts paid by a handicapped individual to buy and install special plumbing fixtures in a rented house are also deductible medical expenses. For example, assume you are handicapped with arthritis and a bad heart condition. You cannot climb stairs or get into a bathtub. On your doctor's advice, you install a bathroom with a shower stall on the first floor of your two-story rented house. The landlord does not pay any of the cost of buying or installing the special plumbing and does not lower your rent. The whole amount you pay for this bathroom is a deductible medical expense. A medical expense deduction is also available for the cost of special equipment used to display subtitles on the television set of a hearing impaired individual (Rev. Rul. 80-340).

In 1987, the IRS released a list of 13 such deductible home improvements. If these improvements are made to accommodate yourself or a family member with a physical handicap, they count in full toward the 10 percent deduction floor (Rev. Rul. Section 7-106, I.R.B. 1987-43).

The improvements on the IRS list are the following:

1. Constructing entrance or exit ramps to the home
2. Widening doorways and entrances or exits to the home
3. Widening or otherwise modifying halls and interior doorways
4. Installing railings, support bars, or other modifications to bathrooms
5. Lowering or making other modifications to kitchen cabinets and equipment
6. Altering the location of or otherwise modifying electrical outlets and fixtures
7. Installing porch lifts or other forms of lifts (this does not include elevators, as they may increase the value of the home)
8. Modifying fire alarms, smoke detectors, and other warning systems
9. Modifying stairs
10. Adding handrails and grab bars, whether or not in bathrooms
11. Modifying hardware on doors
12. Modifying areas in front of entrance and exit doorways
13. Grading of ground to provide access to the home

Note that just because an improvement is not on the list, this does not necessarily mean that such an improvement is not a fully deductible expense.

COMPUTING YOUR MEDICAL EXPENSES

Computing your medical expenses is a simple process. Your allowable drugs, your medical insurance premiums, plus all of your other medical expenses, are reduced by 10 percent of your adjusted gross income. Taxpayers 65 or older are subject to a 7.5 percent limitation.

If you and your spouse live in a community property state and file separate returns, any amount you paid for medical expenses out of community funds is divided equally. Each of you may deduct half of the expenses. If medical expenses are paid out of the separate funds of one spouse, only the spouse who paid the medical expenses may deduct them.

If you and your spouse do not live in a community property state and you file separate returns, each of you may deduct only the medical expenses you actually paid. Any medical expenses paid out of a joint checking account in which you and your spouse have the same interest are considered to have been paid equally by each of you, unless you can show otherwise. Furthermore, you must reduce your total medical expenses for the year by the total reimbursements (repayments) you receive from insurance or other sources for those expenses during the year. This includes payments you receive from Medicare A and Medicare B. The reimbursement may be paid directly to you or to the doctor or hospital.

The actual computation of your medical expense deduction can be demonstrated by the following example. Assume you and your spouse paid the following medical expenses:

a) $595.60 for hospital insurance, $80.40 for medical and surgical insurance, $125 for allowable medicines and drugs, $238 for hospital bills, $39 for doctor bills, and $20 for transportation;

b) $2,000 for doctors and $75 for medicines and allowable drugs for your spouse's dependent mother;

c) $350 for doctors and $100 for medicines for your sister, whom you claim as your dependent.

The hospital and doctor expenses cited have already been reduced by repayment from your insurance company. Your adjusted gross income is $20,000. The deductible amount is computed as follows:

Medicines and drugs	
You and spouse	$ 125.00
Spouse's mother	75.00
Sister	+100.00
Total medicines and drugs	$ 300.00
Insurance:	
Hospitalization	$ 595.60
Medical and surgical	+ 80.40
Total insurance	$ 676.00
Other medical expenses:	
You and spouse (doctors)	$ 39.00
Spouse's mother (doctors)	2,000.00
Sister (doctors)	350.00
You and spouse (hosp.)	238.00
Transportation	+ 20.00
	$ 2,647.00
Total medical expenses [medicine plus insurance plus other expenses ($300.00 + 676.00 + 2,647.00)]	$3,623.00
Minus 10 percent exclusion ($20,000 × .10)	–2,000.00
Total deduction	$1,623.00

Not only must you reduce your total medical expenses by the total reimbursements you have received from insurance and other sources for those expenses, but if you receive payment under an accident insurance contract, you must also reduce your medical expenses by that part of the payment set aside for hospitalization and medical care. However, you need not reduce medical expenses by any repayments you have received for loss of earnings or damages for personal injury. But you must also reduce medical expenses by that amount received in settlement of a damage suit for personal injuries that has been set aside for future medical expenses. Medical expenses paid this year and in future years because of these injuries must be reduced until the amount received in settlement has been completely used. Any amount you pay after that may be deductible.

Even if you fail to file a claim under an insurance policy that would have covered your medical expenses, those expenses that you pay are still deductible (*Weaver*, TCM 1984-634).

If you are reimbursed for medical expenses you deducted in an earlier year, you must report as income the amount of the reimbursement that is equal to or less than the amount you previously deducted as medical expenses. For example, assume you had an adjusted gross income in year A of $10,000, and during that year you paid medical insurance premiums of $300 and incurred medical expenses of $800. No amount was included for medicine and drugs. You deducted $100, figured as follows:

Medical expenses	$ 800
Plus insurance	+300
Total medical expenses	$1,100
Minus 10 percent of adjusted gross income	1,000
Total deduction	$ 100

In year B you collected $50 under your insurance policy as reimbursement for part of your year A medical expenses. If you had collected in year A, your deduction for medical expenses would have been only $50, figured as follows:

Medical expenses	$ 800
Plus insurance	+300
Total medical expenses	$1,100
Minus insurance reimbursements	−50
Balance	$ 1,050
Minus 10 percent of adjusted gross income	−1,000
Total deduction	$ 50

Since the $50 reimbursement is less than the $100 deduction, you should include $50 in income in year B.

If you did not deduct a medical expense in the year you paid it, either because you did not itemize deductions or because your medical expenses were not more than the 10 percent limitation, you should not include in income the reimbursement for this expense that you received in a later year. For example, assume in year C you paid $150 for medical insurance premiums and $400 for medical expenses, but you could not deduct the $550 because it was under the 10 percent limitation. If in year D you were reimbursed for any of the $400 medical expenses, you would also not include the reimbursement in your gross income because you received no tax benefit for it in the earlier year.

There are a number of sophisticated tax planning strategies that you can utilize when claiming medical expense deductions. First, you must recognize that these expenses are deductible only in the year that they are paid. If you charge medical expenses to your credit card, these expenses are deducted in the year the charge is made—it does not matter when you paid the amount charged. But expenses for eyeglasses, dental work, hearing aids, elective surgery, and year-end doctor visits can often be juggled as to the year in which they are actually paid. Since these medical expenses must exceed 10 percent of your adjusted gross income before you can begin taking deductions, it may pay to bunch expenses in one year if that will get you over the hump. You currently cannot deduct a mere prepayment of a possible future bill, however. There must be an actual bill or at least an actual scheduling of services.

Medical expense shifting can be demonstrated by the following example. Assume your adjusted gross income is $30,000. Late this year your doctor bills you $2,000. Your other medical expenses amount to only $250. If you can, pay in January of next year. You will get no deduction in this year, anyway (10 percent of $30,000 is $3,000), so deferring the expense until next year will give you another chance of exceeding the 10 percent floor.

Alternatively, if you have already met your 10 percent floor, you should accelerate the payment of your medical expenses. Payments in December of this year will reduce your taxes and increase your cash balance, and the potential earnings on it, for all of next year. If you wait till January to make the payment, the deduction and its attendant tax benefit will be deferred for an additional year (even assuming that you meet the percent limit in the second year).

For example, assume you have exceeded the standard deduction amount and the 10 percent floor for deducting medical expenses. Further assume that in mid-December you have a $1,000 doctor bill due in 30 days. If you are in the 28 percent bracket and pay the bill in December, you save $280 in taxes, *and* you have an additional $280 on which you can earn interest throughout the next tax year. If you wait until January to make the payment, you will lose the interest on the saved $280 in taxes and may lose the deduction completely if you cannot both pass the percent floor test and exceed your standard deduction amount for excess itemized deductions. The solution in this case, clearly, is to make the payment on December 31.

Effective in 2013, the old 7.5 percent threshold has increased to 10 percent. This increase is delayed until 2018 if you or your spouse has attained age 65 before the close of the tax year.

TAX STRATEGIES

Sophisticated tax planning also involves knowing how to structure your personal deductions so that they qualify as allowable medical expenses. Many expenditures that do not readily appear to be deductible are allowable as medical expenses. For example, elastic stockings qualify as medical expenses if needed by an infirm or elderly person. In one case, the cost of a sacroiliac belt prescribed by a doctor was deductible, as was the cost of high blood pressure medication and a blood sugar test. In another instance, a deduction was allowed for a device installed to add fluoride to a home water supply at a controlled rate; it was represented that fluoride is a chemical that strengthens the dental enamel as the teeth grow, making them more resistant to decay, and that the only purpose of the installation and use of the device was to prevent tooth decay. Travel to Alcoholics Anonymous meetings, based on medical advice, is a deductible medical expense (Rev. Rul. 63-273).

Deductions have been allowed for extraordinary forms of medical equipment. For example, the costs of oxygen equipment and oxygen to alleviate breathing difficulty *and* of a reclining chair recommended by a doctor for a person with a cardiac condition have qualified as medical deductions. So, too, have special mattresses and certain thicknesses of plywood boards prescribed for an individual who had arthritis of the spine. In one instance, a wig purchased to avoid mental upset to a patient who had lost her hair was deductible!

Super medical deductions can be obtained if your doctor can find an ailment in yourself, your spouse, or your dependents that would require you to have a whirlpool for baths, or central air conditioning to provide you or your dependents with pure, dehumidified air. Even the expense of a swimming pool may be deducted if it is installed because of a physician's recommendation and if that facility in any way alleviates your physical condition (see *Cherry*, TCM 1983-470 and Rev. Rul. 63-273, 1963-2 C.B. 112). If such a swimming pool is used for a specific medical purpose—for example, to provide hydrotherapy—then not only is a deduction allowed for the installation, but a deduction is also allowed for the cost of upkeep, including chemicals, cleaning, water, and utilities. Note, though, that the installation is a capital expenditure and therefore only the excess cost over the added value to your property is deductible. (See Rev. Rul. 83-33 and Letter Ruling 822-1128 and 832-6095.)

One of my own favorite medical deductions is the cost of an overseas trip for medical or dental work. For example, it has been established that the cost of extensive dental work is far less expensive in Europe than in the United States. Therefore, even adding the transportation costs to go to an overseas dentist, your total cash outlay is lower than having such work performed locally. On this basis, such transportation costs have been allowed as deductible medical expenses. One woman consulted three different dermatologists in the United States, but none was able to improve her skin condition. Finally, she was treated successfully as an outpatient in a foreign country. The IRS agreed that her expenses were deductible (Letter Ruling 812-6044).

In 1991, the Tax Court let Alex L. and Earlene Polyak of Trenton, Michigan, deduct $1,124 for 1984 transportation to Palm Beach Gardens as essential to her care for heart and lung ailments and arthritis. Her doctors advised her to winter in warmer climates.

You potentially can write off your child's private school tuition as a medical expense. The IRS, in a private ruling, found that one family's dyslexic children required special education that could be deemed medical care.

Take these steps to ensure your deduction:

- Make sure the school offers special education aimed at helping the student overcome a diagnosed handicap. The school should have staff available to design a curriculum aimed at your child's particular handicap, and that should be why the child attends that school.

- Get the school to write a statement about its program.

- Remember that as a legitimate medical expense, it's still not deductible until it exceeds 10 percent of your adjusted gross income. Given the cost of most private schools today, that won't be a problem.

Furthermore, amounts paid for "medical care" may be deductible even if they are for purposes that do not have the sanction of the medical profession or even if the payments are made to persons without medical qualifications. For example, amounts paid to such practitioners as psychotherapists are categorized for tax purposes as fees for medical care, even though those who perform the services may not be licensed, certified, or otherwise qualified to perform these services, and even if certification is required by law. In other words, payments to unlicensed practitioners are deductible if the type and quality of their services are not illegal and if such services may be deemed to fall within the parameters of medical care. In fact, in IRS Letter Ruling 8442018, the Internal Revenue Service allowed as a deductible medical expense electrolysis performed by a nonlicensed technician as "medical care." Remember, *medical care* means any amounts paid for the diagnosis, cure, mitigation, treatment, or prevention of disease or for the purpose of affecting any structure or function of the body. (In Rev. Rul. 82-111, the IRS had ruled that hair removal through electrolysis performed by a state licensed technician was deductible as a medical expense.)

Note that, effective for tax years beginning after December 31, 1990, expenses for unnecessary cosmetic surgery are no longer deductible as medical care expenses, except when the surgery is necessary to correct a deformity due directly to a congenital abnormality, a personal injury resulting from an accident or trauma, or a disfiguring disease.

The law further defines cosmetic surgery as any procedure that is directed at improving the patient's appearance and does not meaningfully promote the proper function of the body or prevent or treat illness or disease.

The definition of cosmetic surgery is quite broad and seems to bar the deductibility of many procedures that are not strictly surgical. Orthodontic work should qualify, but other dental procedures may be considered strictly cosmetic.

A second category of below the line deductions is the taxes that you pay during your tax year. Such taxes fall under three classifications, which will be discussed separately.

89   Income Taxes

You may deduct some state and local income taxes, including taxes on interest income that is exempt from federal income tax. You may not deduct state and local taxes on any other exempt income. For example, the part of state income tax on a cost-of-living allowance that is exempt from federal income tax is not deductible.

State and local taxes are those imposed by the 50 states or any of their political subdivisions (such as a county or city) and by the District of Columbia. You may deduct state, local, or foreign income taxes withheld from your salary, as well as estimated payments made under a pay-as-you-go plan of a state or local government. You also may deduct payments made on taxes due but not paid in an earlier year in the year they were actually withheld or paid. In sum, to be deductible the tax must be paid during your tax year. You may deduct only those taxes paid during the calendar year for which you file a return.

If you receive a refund of these taxes in a later year, you must include the return as income in the year you receive it. This would include refunds resulting from taxes that were overwithheld, not figured correctly, or figured again as a result of an amended return. If you did not itemize your deductions in a previous year, you do not have to include the refunds. Furthermore, the amount included in your income is limited to the tax benefit you received in the earlier years. For example, assume you deducted $500 in taxes and received a refund of $100; your total itemized deductions exceeded your standard deduction amount by only $50. The only tax benefit you received, therefore, was the $50 excess itemized deduction. On this basis you need only include $50 of the refund in your income for the subsequent year.

You also may deduct amounts required to be withheld from your wages for certain state disability benefit funds that provide against loss of wages. These payments to the disability fund are deductible as state income taxes. Furthermore, employee contributions to a state fund that provides indemnity coverage for the loss of wages caused by unemployment resulting from business contingencies are also deductible as taxes. Employee contributions to private disability plans, however, are not deductible.

Foreign taxes include those taxes imposed by a foreign country, a U.S. possession, or any of their political subdivisions.

Foreign income taxes that you pay may either be deducted as an itemized deduction or claimed as a credit against your U.S. tax.

SALES TAXES

For 2004 through 2013, *instead* of deducting income taxes, you have the option of deducting state and local sales taxes (including compensating use taxes) instead of state and local income taxes. Use the actual taxes you pay, or see Publication 600 for optional sales tax tables. You can add to the table amounts any sales taxes paid on a motor vehicle (including leased vehicles), aircraft, boat, home, and home building materials.

This is a great deal for those in low or no income tax states such as Texas, Washington, Tennessee, Wyoming, South Dakota, Alaska, Nevada, or Florida.

Any sales tax paid on business items would be allowed on the business schedules rather than as itemized deductions.

90   Real Property Taxes

Real property (real estate) taxes are any state, local, or foreign taxes on real property levied for the general public welfare. Local benefit taxes are deductible if they are for maintenance or repair, or for interest charges related to these benefits. If only a part of the tax is for maintenance, repair, or interest, you must be able to show the amount of that part to claim the deduction. If you cannot determine what part is for maintenance or repair, none of it is deductible.

If you are a tenant shareholder in a cooperative housing corporation, you may deduct the amounts you pay to that corporation that represent your share of the real estate taxes the corporation pays or incurs on the property. If the corporation leases the land and buildings and is required to pay the real estate taxes under the terms of the lease agreement, however, your part of the taxes is not deductible. Moreover, if your landlord increases your rent in the form of a tax surcharge because of increased real estate taxes, you cannot deduct that increase as taxes either.

Real property taxes also do not include trash and garbage collection fees or homeowners association charges you may pay for the recreation, health, safety, and welfare of residents and for maintaining common areas.

If real estate is sold during the tax year, the real estate taxes must be divided between the buyer and seller. These taxes must be divided according to the number of days in the real property tax year (the period to which the imposed tax relates) that each owns the property. The seller pays the taxes up to the date of the sale, and the buyer pays the taxes beginning with the date of the sale, regardless of the lien dates under local law. If you use the cash method and do not deduct taxes until they are paid, and the buyer of your property is personally liable for the tax, you are considered to have paid your portion of the imposed tax at the time of the sale. This permits you to deduct the portion of the tax to the date of sale even though you did not actually pay for it.

For example, assume that your real property tax year is the calendar year, with payment due on August 1. Your tax on your old home, sold May 5, was $300, and your tax on your new home, bought on May 3, was $200. You are considered to have paid a proportionate share of the real estate taxes on the old home even though you did not actually pay them to the taxing authority. On the other hand, you may claim only the proportionate share of the taxes you paid on your new property even though you paid the entire amount.

Because you held the old property for 125 days (January 1 to May 4, the day before the sale), you are entitled to a deduction of 125/365 of $300, or $102.73. You owned the new home for 243 days (May 3 to December 31, including the date of the purchase), so your taxes on the new home are 243/365 of $200, or $133.15. Your real estate tax deduction is therefore $102.73 + $133.15, or $235.88.

If you and your spouse held property jointly, and you file separate returns, each of you may deduct only the taxes each of you paid on the property.

For 2008 and 2009, nonitemizers could have deducted up to $500 ($1,000 on a joint return) for real estate taxes paid as additions to their standard deduction.

91 Personal Property Taxes

Some personal property taxes are also deductible, subject to certain requirements:

1. The tax must be based only on the value of the personal property. For example, assume your state charges a yearly motor vehicle registration tax of 1 percent of value plus 40¢ per hundredweight. You pay $28.60 based on the value ($1,500) and weight (3,400 pounds) of your car. You may deduct $15 as a personal property tax, since it is based on the value. The remaining $13.60, based on the weight, is not deductible.

2. The tax must be charged on a yearly basis, even if it is collected more or less often than once a year.

3. The tax must be charged on personal property. A tax is considered charged on personal property even if it is for the exercise of a privilege. A yearly tax based on value qualifies as a personal property tax although it is called a registration fee—that is, for the privilege of registering motor vehicles or using them on the highways.

92 Interest

Some interest payments qualify as below the line deductions. The type of deduction you may take depends on whether the money was borrowed for personal use, for rental or royalty property, or for your business.

Interest payment on a loan for income-producing rental or royalty property, on a business loan, and on farm business loans are above the line deductions.

Interest of a personal nature, such as home mortgage interest, is a below the line deduction; normally, so is interest paid on margin accounts held with your broker. Interest on these accounts is considered paid when the broker is paid or when the interest becomes available to the broker through your account.

To deduct interest on a debt, you must be legally liable for that debt. No deduction will be allowed for payments you make for someone else if you are not legally liable to make them. Note that the Tax Court has allowed the deduction even if you don't have title but do have "the benefits and burdens of ownership." See *Adams v. Commissioner* T.C. No. 2563-08, T.C. Memo 2010-72 (April 13, 2010). Both the lender and the borrower must intend that the loan be repaid.

For example, assume you make a loan to your son, hoping to be repaid when he is able. If no true debtor-credit relationship is created, he is not legally liable to pay the debt and will not be able to deduct any interest paid. Here he should sign a note and make scheduled repayments to ensure his interest deduction. Alternatively, if you cosign a note for a loan made by a bank to your son, even if your son is a student, and if both you and your son are jointly liable on the note, you may deduct any interest you pay on the loan in the year you pay it.

You must normally pay the interest before you may deduct it. But if you use the accrual method of accounting, you may deduct interest over the period it accrues regardless of when it is paid. To show how this works, suppose you borrow $1,000 in September, *payable in 90 days* at 12 percent interest. In December you make the payment with a new note for $1,030 due the following March. If you use the cash method of accounting, that $30 is not deductible in the year you give the new note, since you do not actually pay the interest. However, if you pay the $30 and give a new note for $1,000, the interest is deductible. If you are on the accrual method, the $30 is deductible in either case. If you pay interest in advance for a period that goes beyond the end of the tax year, you must spread the interest over the tax years to which it belongs. You may deduct in each year only the interest that belongs to that year.

The following items are generally deductible as interest:

Mortgage interest
"Points," if you are a buyer (see explanation that follows)
Interest on a business loan
Installment plan interest (unless consumer interest)
Investment interest

The following items normally are *not* deductible as interest:

"Points," if you are a seller (potentially deductible by *buyer* under Rev. Proc. 94-27)

Service charges

Credit investigation fees

Loan fees

Interest relating to tax-exempt income

Interest paid to carry single-premium life insurance

Premium on a convertible bond

Interest owed to related taxpayers, unless there is an actual debtor-
creditor relationship

Purchaser mortgage insurance (PMI), except for rental properties where
it would be allowed as "insurance."

But, nonrental PMI is deductible (as interest) for 2007 through 2013 *only*.
It was allowed only for insurance issued after 2006, so prior homeowners did
not qualify. This deduction was phased out for joint returns with adjusted gross
income more than $100,000 ($50,000 for singles).

Effective Interest Rates on Mortgages with Points

Stated Rate (%)	Points				
	1	2	3	4	5
Assuming 30-year mortgage held to maturity					
5	5.09	5.18	5.27	5.36	5.46
6	6.09	6.19	6.29	6.29	6.48
7	7.01	7.20	7.30	7.41	7.52
8	8.11	8.21	8.32	8.44	8.55
9	9.22	9.23	9.34	9.46	9.58
10	10.12	10.24	10.37	10.49	10.62
11	11.13	11.26	11.39	11.52	11.66
12	12.13	12.27	12.41	12.55	12.70
Assuming 30-year mortgage paid off in 15th year					
5	5.11	5.22	5.33	5.44	5.56
6	6.11	6.23	6.35	6.46	6.58
7	7.12	7.24	7.36	7.49	7.61
8	8.12	8.21	8.32	8.44	8.55
9	9.13	9.26	9.40	9.53	9.67
10	10.14	10.28	10.42	10.56	10.70
11	11.14	11.29	11.44	11.59	11.74
12	12.15	12.30	12.46	12.61	12.77

(*continues*)

Effective Interest Rates on Mortgages with Points *(continued)*

Assuming 30-year mortgage paid off in 7th year

5	5.18	5.36	5.55	5.73	5.92
6	6.18	6.37	6.56	6.75	6.95
7	7.19	7.38	7.57	7.77	7.97
8	8.19	8.39	8.59	8.79	8.99
9	9.20	9.40	9.61	9.81	10.02
10	10.20	10.41	10.62	10.83	11.05
11	11.21	11.42	11.64	11.86	12.08
12	12.22	12.44	12.66	12.88	13.11

Assuming 30-year mortgage paid off in 3rd year

5	5.37	5.74	6.12	6.50	6.89
6	6.37	6.75	7.13	7.52	7.91
7	7.38	7.76	8.15	8.54	8.93
8	8.38	8.77	9.16	9.56	9.96
9	9.39	9.78	10.18	10.58	10.98
10	10.39	10.79	11.19	11.60	12.01
11	11.40	11.80	12.21	12.62	13.04
12	12.40	12.81	13.22	13.64	14.06

One of the most usual types of personal interest expense is the interest on your mortgage. You may deduct only the interest part of your mortgage payment. If your records do not show the interest paid, get a statement showing that information from the lender who holds your mortgage. If you are a cash method taxpayer, you may deduct the full amount of interest paid during the year. If you are an accrual method taxpayer, you may deduct the amount accrued each year.

A point is equal to 1 percent of the loan amount, so on a $100,000 mortgage each point would cost you $1,000. If you pay off a mortgage over 30 years, each point on a 12 percent loan adds 0.13 percentage points to the interest rate. Thus on a 12 percent loan with four points charged, the effective interest rate is 12.52. On a 14 percent, 30-year loan, each point adds 0.15 percentage points. On a 16 percent loan, it is 0.17 percentage points. Keep in mind that these figures apply only if the mortgage is paid off over the full 30-year term. If you sell the property and pay off the loan sooner, the effective interest is higher, since those extra dollars paid up front are spread over fewer years of borrowing.

The term *points* is sometimes used to describe the charges paid by a borrower. They are also called loan origination fees, maximum loan charges, or premium charges. If the payment of any of these charges is solely for the use of money, then it is considered interest.

In one case, the Tax Court allowed a taxpayer to deduct interest he paid on a mortgage on his residence, even though the title to the home was held in the name of his corporation. The court reasoned that the taxpayer had always treated the home as his own and the mortgage indebtedness therefore was his (*Lang, Jr.*, T.C. Memo 1983-318). In *USLU v. Commissioner,* T.C. Memo 1997–551, 12/16/97, the Tax Court ruled that a person who lived in a house and made all the payments for it could deduct mortgage interest even though legal title and financing was obtained by the person's brother. All the facts established equitable and beneficial ownership of the house. Also see *Odosada,* T.C. Summ. Op. 2012-17 where beneficial ownership was found again.

The amount you pay in points is deductible in full in the year of payment only if it is paid to buy or improve your main home and if the loan is for that home. The charging of points has to be an established business practice in your area. The deduction may not be more than the number of points generally charged in your area. If these conditions are not met, points are treated as prepaid interest. They must be spread over the life of the mortgage and are considered as paid and deductible over that period. Moreover, in IRS Notice 86-68, May 13, 1986, the Internal Revenue Service ruled that points paid on refinancing a home mortgage are not *currently* deductible. Thus, they could only be deducted over the loan period. For example, assume that $2,400 of points is paid in connection with refinancing a mortgage that is to run for another 20 years (i.e., 240 monthly payments remain to be paid). These points are deductible over the term of the loan, $10 per monthly payment. The IRS reaffirmed this position in Rev. Rul. 87-22, as did the Tax Court in 1988. Points paid in a refinancing, therefore, must be amortized over the life of the loan, unless the money is used to improve the home (*Huntsman,* T.C. 1988, reversed), or unless the refinancing is an integral part of the original purchase of the property.

Points charged for specific services by the lender for the borrower's account (such as a lender's appraisal fee, the cost of preparing the mortgage note or deed of trust, settlement fees, or notary fees) are not interest. Points charged in connection with getting a V.A. loan were not interest until 1992, retroactive to 1991. For example, assume you get a loan from a bank to buy your main home. The loan was insured by the Veterans Administration and you pay the bank a loan origination fee. This fee is 1 percent of the amount of the loan and is charged in addition to the maximum rate of interest permitted. The amount of the 1 percent loan origination fee (one point) is now interest and may be deducted.

Alternatively, assume you got a loan of $48,000 to buy a $60,000 home. In addition to interest at the rate of 7 percent, you paid the lender a loan processing fee of $1,440 (three points). None of the fee was for specific services. The charging of points was an established business practice in the area and the number of points was not more than that generally charged in the area. This loan processing fee to purchase a principal residence is interest and is deductible in full in the year of payment. [See Section 461(g)(2) and *Schubel*, 77 T.C. No. 701 (1981).] [See also *Pacific First Federal Savings and Loan Association*, 79 T.C. No. 33 where points were found to be interest where the fee was for the use or forebearance of money and bore no relation to the actual cost to underwrite the loan.] It is best to exchange checks with your bank rather than just reduce the amount received on your mortgage. In the past, unless you formally exchanged checks, the Internal Revenue Service argued a lack of "payment." However, in IRS Notice 90-70, the separate check for points was ruled as unnecessary as long as you provide a down payment, escrow deposit, or other closing funds "at least equal to" the points charged. This means points are now deductible even if the lender finances them if your cost payments are at least equal to the points charged. [See also Rev. Proc. 92-12.]

The term *points* is also used to describe loan placement fees that the seller may have to pay to the lender to arrange financing for the buyer. Prior to 1994, you could *not* deduct these amounts as interest. See Revenue Procedure 94-27 below to see if you may qualify now. (However, these charges are a selling expense that reduces the amount realized by the seller.) Furthermore, if you pay off your mortgage early, you may have to pay a penalty. This amount is deductible as interest, as is any amount you pay as a tenant stockholder in a housing cooperative for the interest on the cooperative's debt, or for points required in the year you became a tenant-stockholder.

In Rev. Proc. 87-15, I.R.B. 1987-14, the Internal Revenue Service set forth the method for determining the amount of points allocable to each tax year during the term of an indebtedness in a situation where points charged to a taxpayer in respect of the indebtedness are required to be deducted over the period of indebtedness. Such points may be deductible on an internal rate of return basis—i.e., considering the time value of money with the bulk of the deduction being taken in the earlier years—or, alternatively, as a matter of administrative convenience, the Internal Revenue Service will allow a taxpayer consistently to allocate the points ratably over the indebtedness. For example, if $3,600 in qualified points were paid on a 30-year (360-month) loan, $10 per payment would be allowed as deductible point interest ($3,600 divided into 360 monthly payments).

Note that the points must be paid at the time the indebtedness is incurred. In *Schubel*, 77 T.C. 701 (1981), the Tax Court held that points withheld by a lender from loan proceeds may not be deducted by a borrower in the year the points are withheld, because the withholding did not constitute payment within that tax year. Note IRS Notice 90-70 discussed above.

The above rules were modified by Revenue Procedure 94-27 and IRS News Release 94-28 wherein it was ruled that home *buyers will* be able to deduct *seller*-paid points on mortgages so long as the purchase price of the home is reduced by the amount of the seller's payment. This rule does not apply to improvement (rather than acquisition) loans or to loans not for your principal residence.

Other payments also constitute interest. When you buy property on the installment plan, you may deduct your interest payments if they are separately stated, or if they can be determined and proved. Finance charges added to your monthly credit card statements also constitute deductible interest, as do one-time charges made on new cash advances and new check and overdraft advances added to your bank credit card account balance. No part of these one-time charges, though, can be a service charge, loan fee, credit investigation fee, or similar charge.

When you buy personal property such as clothing, jewelry, furniture, or appliances on the installment plan using a revolving charge account, there is usually a separately stated finance charge. The total amount of these finance charges was deductible as interest, subject to the consumer interest deduction phase-out discussed below. For example, if you buy a refrigerator for $300 from the American Department Store and charge it to your revolving charge account, there will be no extra charge if you pay the balance within 30 days after you are billed. But if you make installment payments, your account will be charged the finance charge of 1.5 percent on the unpaid balance each month. These finance charges were previously deductible as interest.

Sometimes when you borrow money the interest is subtracted from the face amount of the note and you receive the balance. If you use the cash method, you may deduct the interest only in the year you make payments. Alternatively, if you use the accrual method, you may deduct the interest as it accrues.

For example, assume you sign a note for $1,200 on March 27, agreeing to pay it in 12 equal installments beginning on April 28. The interest is $1,200 × 12 percent = $144 and is subtracted from the face value of the note so that you receive only $1,056. If you use the cash method, the interest is considered to be repaid in 12 installments of $12 each. Your deduction for the first year is $108 ($12 × nine payments). If you miss two payments in the first year and made only seven payments, your deduction is $84. If you use the accrual method, the deduction is determined by prorating interest over the period in which it accrues. You may therefore deduct $108 (9/12 × $144) in the first year and $36 (3/12 × $144) in the following year.

Interest often is "hidden" in other payments, such as in judgments and personal loans. If you make a late payment of taxes, or if you must pay additional taxes at a later date, part of the amount will usually be for interest. This interest is no longer deductible (see personal interest limitations below). Penalties, in addition, are not deductible. Furthermore, you may not deduct interest on any money you borrow to buy tax-exempt securities or to buy a single-premium life insurance endowment or annuity contract. A single-premium contract includes policies on which you pay almost all the premiums within four years from the date you buy the contract; it also includes policies for which you deposit an amount with the insurer for the payment of future premiums. Also, you may not deduct interest on a loan that is used to buy stock if the collateral on the loan is a single-premium annuity contract.

However, according to Rev. Rul. 83-51, the Internal Revenue Service holds that the "contingent interest" portion of a shared appreciation mortgage (SAM) loan used by a cash-basis individual taxpayer to finance the purchase of a personal residence is deductible as interest when paid. The ruling deals with three situations. In each, the taxpayer purchases a home by securing a SAM from a financial institution. The SAM provides for a fixed interest annual rate and "contingent interest" equal to 40 percent of the appreciation in the value of the residence, payable when the SAM terminates. Termination is to occur at the earliest of (1) prepayment of the entire outstanding balance of the SAM, (2) sale of the residence, or (3) 10 years from the SAM loan. The taxpayer also has the option to refinance the mortgage balance and contingent interest due at the prevailing interest rate. The SAM agreement provides that it creates no more than a debtor-creditor relationship.

In the first situation provided for under the ruling, the taxpayer sells the residence at a profit and uses a portion of the sales proceeds to pay the remaining SAM principal balance and the contingent interest. In the second situation, the taxpayer prepays the outstanding principal balance and contingent interest with funds not obtained from the SAM lender. In the third situation, the taxpayer refinances the principal balance and contingent interest due on maturity of the SAM by obtaining a conventional 30-year mortgage from the SAM lender. The Internal

Revenue Service holds that in the first and second situations, the taxpayer can deduct the contingent interest in the year the SAM is paid off, on the grounds that interest, to be deductible, need not be computed at a stated rate. All that is required is that a definitely ascertainable sum be paid for the use of borrowed money pursuant to a loan agreement. In the first and second situations, the contingent interest is ascertainable. In the third situation, however, the taxpayer cannot deduct contingent interest, because merely executing a new note does not constitute payment. But payments on the new note to the extent allocable to the contingent interest will be deductible in the year paid. In all three situations, the taxpayer can deduct the fixed interest when paid.

To ensure that you have a debtor-creditor relationship and that the SAM does not in substance create an equity arrangement, the SAM agreement should provide, in addition to stating that only a debtor-creditor relationship is intended, that:

a) the mortgage secures only the indebtedness;

b) the mortgagor can sell, transfer, improve, and encumber the property without the mortgagee's consent;

c) the mortgagee is not liable for any decrease in the value of the property; *and*

d) the mortgagor is solely responsible to pay real estate taxes, insurance premiums, and other charges relating to ownership.

The following table, from Patrick O'Rourke, CPA, in Washington, DC, summarizes the tax treatment of various line items at a real estate closing:

Closing Statement Deductions

The closing statement to a real estate purchase contains many potential tax deductions. Treatment of closing statement line items differs depending on whether the property is business (rental) property or used for a personal residence.

We have summarized typical tax treatment of major line items of the often used HUD-1 closing statement. However, there may also be certain items that are treated differently depending on your particular situation. There are differences in tax treatment depending on whether the property is used as a personal residence or rented out. A notation of "basis" refers to costs that become part of the total capitalized cost of the property and not currently deductible; however, these costs can be deducted at the time of sale, or earlier via *depreciation* if they relate to rental property.

Purchaser (Borrower) HUD-1 Closing Statement			
HUD-1 Line #	**Closing Statement Description**	**Tax Treatment— Personal Residence**	**Tax Treatment— Rental Property**
101	Contract sales price	Basis—is relevant if property is later sold or rented	Basis—building portion eligible for depreciation
102	Personal property	Basis—is relevant if property is later sold or rented	Basis—eligible for accelerated depreciation
103	Settlement charges	See Lines 700–1305	See Lines 700–1305
104–105	Miscellaneous	Varies	Varies
106	City/town taxes (See Line 210)	Deductible as itemized deduction on Form 1040 Schedule A*	Deductible as rental expense*
107	County taxes (See Line 211)	Deductible as itemized deduction on Form 1040 Schedule A*	Deductible as rental expense*
108	Assessments (See Line 212)	LID assessments are part of basis; other assessments are typically non-deductible	LID assessments are part of basis; other assessments are typically deductible*
109–112	Miscellaneous	Varies	Varies
210	City/town taxes (See Line 106)	* This credit reduces deductible taxes on Line 106	* This credit reduces deductible taxes on Line 106
211	County taxes (See Line 107)	* This credit reduces deductible taxes on Line 107	* This credit reduces deductible taxes on Line 107
212	Assessments (See Line 108)	* This credit reduces assessments on Line 108	* This credit reduces assessments on Line 108
213–216	Miscellaneous	Varies	Varies
700–703	Sales and Realtors' commissions	Basis	Basis

	Purchaser (Borrower) HUD-1 Closing Statement *(continued)*		
HUD-1 Line #	**Closing Statement Description**	**Tax Treatment— Personal Residence**	**Tax Treatment— Rental Property**
801	Loan origination fee	Deductible as itemized deduction ("points") on Form 1040 Schedule A	Amortized over term of mortgage
802	Loan discount	Deductible as itemized deduction ("points") on Form 1040 Schedule A	Amortized over term of mortgage
803	Appraisal fee	Basis	Basis
804	Credit report	Nondeductible	Basis
805	Inspection fee	Basis	Basis
806	Mortgage insurance fee	Nondeductible	Amortized over term of mortgage
807	Assumption fee	Nondeductible	Amortized over term of mortgage
808–811	Miscellaneous	Varies	Varies
901	Prorated interest	Deductible as itemized deduction—this interest is typically included in year-end interest statement (Form 1098)	Deductible as rental expense—this interest is typically included in year-end interest statement (Form 1098)
902	Mortgage insurance	Nondeductible except for 2007 through 2010	Amortized over term of mortgage
903	Hazard insurance	Nondeductible	Deductible as rental expense
904–905	Miscellaneous	Varies	Varies
1001	Hazard insurance	Nondeductible	Reserves—deductible when paid from escrow
1002	Mortgage insurance	Nondeductible	Reserves—amortizable when paid from escrow
1003	City property taxes	Reserves—deductible as itemized deduction when paid from escrow	Reserves—deductible when paid from escrow

(continues)

HUD-1 Line #	Closing Statement Description	Tax Treatment—Personal Residence	Tax Treatment—Rental Property
	Purchaser (Borrower) HUD-1 Closing Statement *(continued)*		
1004	County property taxes	Reserves—deductible as itemized deduction when paid from escrow	Reserves—deductible when paid from escrow
1005	Assessments	Varies	Varies
1006–1008	Miscellaneous	Varies	Varies
1101	Settlement fees	Basis	Basis
1102	Abstract or title search	Basis	Basis
1103	Title examination	Basis	Basis
1104	Title insurance binder	Basis	Basis
1105	Document preparation	Basis	Basis
1106	Notary fees	Basis	Basis
1107	Attorneys' fees	Basis	Typically part of basis; if tenant-related, may be amortized over term of lease(s)
1108–1110	Title insurance	Basis	Basis
1111–1113	Miscellaneous	Varies	Varies
1201	Recording fees	Basis	Basis
1202	City/county tax stamps	Basis	Basis
1203	State tax/stamps	Basis	Basis
1204–1205	Miscellaneous	Varies	Varies
1301	Survey	Basis	Basis
1302	Pest inspection	Basis	Basis
1303–1305	Miscellaneous	Varies	Varies

The above table summarizes tax treatment for *buyers* of properties. For sellers, these costs (including remaining basis) are deducted at the time of sale, with the exception of costs that are specifically noted as nondeductible. Of course, capital gains may not be recognized if the property is a personal residence and you qualify.

LIMITATIONS

There are certain limitations on the amount of interest that you can deduct.

The deduction for investment interest incurred or continued is limited to net investment income to purchase or carry *property held for investment*. Disallowed investment interest can be carried forward indefinitely and allowed to the extent of future net investment income.

Investment income and investment expenses do not include any income or expenses taken into account when computing income or loss from a passive activity, including any interest paid or accrued on debt to acquire or carry an interest in a passive activity. However, it does include portfolio income from passive activities.

DEFINITIONS

Net investment income means the excess of *investment income* over *investment expenses*. Investment income is defined as income from interest, dividends, rents, royalties, short-term capital gains arising from the disposition of investment assets, and certain recapture amounts (but only if the income is not derived from the conduct of a trade or business), except that all gain (not just short-term gain) attributable to the disposition of property held for investment may be included. The Omnibus Budget Reconciliation Act of 1993 complicated the deductibility of investment interest. The Act provides that long-term capital gains qualify as investment income only if the investor volunteers to have them taxed at the same rate as personal income. "Dividends" taxed at the new 5 percent–15 percent rate do not qualify as investment income.

The calculations can get complicated. If you have a long-term gain of $50,000 and $50,000 of investment interest, with no other investment interest, with no other investment income, you could effectively avoid the tax on the gain by opting to treat it as ordinary income. The savings would be (if you were in a 28 percent bracket) 28 percent of $50,000 or $14,000 (or $7,500 if you qualified for the 15 percent maximum capital gains tax).

However, if you expect $50,000 in investment income the next year, and you pay the $14,000 in this year, you could carry the deduction forward and potentially save $17,500 in income tax at the 35 percent rate in the second year—a net 2-year savings of $3,500. *Investment expenses* are deductible expenses (other than interest) directly connected with the production of investment income. Investment expenses should be considered as those allowed after application of the 2 percent floor for miscellaneous itemized deductions (see page 303). In computing the amount of expenses that exceed the 2 percent floor, expenses that are not investment expenses are disallowed before any investment expenses are disallowed.

Property held for investment includes property that produces interest, dividends, annuities, or royalties plus any interest held by a taxpayer in an activity involving the conduct of a trade or business that is not a passive activity and in which the taxpayer does not materially participate. A passive activity is defined as an activity that involves the conduct of a trade or business in which the taxpayer does not materially participate. The only activity excluded from this definition is a working interest in an oil and gas property that a taxpayer holds directly or through an entity that does not limit the liability of the taxpayer with respect to that activity. However, regulations may be issued that could broaden the class of activities that are excluded under the definition of a passive activity, and the class of activities so excluded would thereby be considered property held for investment.

THE DISALLOWANCE OF DEDUCTION FOR PERSONAL INTEREST

Taxpayers other than corporations are no longer allowed to deduct personal interest paid or accrued during the taxable year. Personal interest means any interest other than (1) interest paid or accrued on indebtedness incurred or continued in connection with the conduct of a trade or business, (2) any investment interest, (3) any interest taken into account when computing income or loss from a passive activity of the taxpayer, (4) any qualified residence interest, and (5) interest payable on extensions of time for payment of estate tax on the value of reversionary or remainder interests in property or where an estate consists largely of interests in a closely held business. In other words, virtually all personal or consumer interest (including interest on underpayment or late payment of taxes) that was allowable as a deduction without limit under prior law may no longer be deducted with the exception of qualified residence interest.

The term *qualified residence interest* means any interest that is paid or accrued during the taxable year on indebtedness secured by any property that (at the time such interest is paid or accrued) is a qualified residence of the taxpayer. The term *qualified residence* means the principal residence of the taxpayer and one vacation home.

Note that interest on income tax deficiencies arising from the conduct of a trade or business *is* personal interest (the Tax Court in *Redlark*, 106 T.C. No. 2, 1/11/96, said it *was* deductible as did the District Court in *Allen v. U.S.*, DC ENC, No. 5:96-CV-909-F, 12/1/97, in North Carolina, but it was later reversed by the 4th Cir. Court of Appeals, No. 98-1401 on 4/20/99, while the Eighth Circuit says it *is not, Miller v. U.S.*, No. A3-92-183, 11/5/93, reversed by the Eighth Circuit, No. 94-3225, 9/7/95). However, the Ninth Circuit also reversed *Redlark* on 4/10/98 (CA-9, No. 96-70398) and was supported by *Stecher v. U.S.*, P. Colo., No. 97-WY-1892-AJ, 6/18/98 and *McDonnell v. U.S.*, 6th Cir., No. 98-5383, 5/27/99. In *Robinson v. Commissioner,* T.C. No. 9574-99, 119 T.C. No. 4, on September 5, 2002, the Tax Court agreed that interest on income tax underpayments was *not* deductible. Interest on tax deficiencies of partnerships and S corporations must be taken *below* the line (*True v. U.S.*, No. 91-CV-1004-J, 7/30/93) as opposed to above the line business entity deductions.

Interest on a credit card used to pay your tax is personal interest and therefore not deductible. Also not deductible were any fees paid to the credit card company to charge the tax (SCA-2001-15032). This position was reversed by IR 2009-37 and such fees are now allowed as miscellaneous itemized deductions.

LIMITATION ON THE AMOUNT OF INTEREST DEDUCTIBLE AS QUALIFIED RESIDENCE INTEREST

The amount of interest that may be deducted on a debt secured by a qualified residence is limited in the following manner: Interest is deductible only to the extent that the indebtedness does not exceed the lesser of (1) the fair market value of the qualified residence or (2) the taxpayer's basis in the qualified residence (adjusted only by the cost of any improvements to such residence). However, as of August 16, 1986, if the aggregate amount of outstanding indebtedness secured by a qualified residence exceeded the taxpayer's basis in the property at that time, the amount of indebtedness at that time would substitute for the taxpayer's basis in the qualified residence when determining qualified residence interest.

The limitation on the deductibility of personal interest may encourage many taxpayers to seek other ways of financing consumer purchases. Two immediate methods of converting what would otherwise be nondeductible personal interest into deductible interest are (1) to borrow against marginable securities (or property held for investment) or (2) to borrow against a qualified residence. Each of these techniques presents potential problems.

USING HOME EQUITY

Originally, interest paid on debt secured by a home could be deductible only to the extent that the debt does not exceed the lesser of (1) the fair market value of the home or (2) the taxpayer's adjusted basis in the home (or if the debt secured by the home exceeded the basis on August 16, 1986, that amount of debt).

Many homeowners who have owned their homes for many years or who have acquired new homes in recent years after rolling over gains from the sale of a previous home have relatively low bases in their homes. In addition, they may have debt secured by these homes that already exceeds their bases. Consequently, the opportunity to increase interest-deductible borrowing in many cases may be limited. Even in cases where the potential to tap home equity exists, in many cases it may be unwise to risk the loss of a home to finance consumer purchases since circumstances could evolve that preclude repayment of the debt.

However, taxpayers who have sufficient equity in their homes and untapped borrowing capacity under the qualified residence interest rules may wish to finance new consumer purchases or consolidate consumer loans by increasing qualified residence borrowing.

Some homeowners could consider selling their homes, using the $250,000/$500,000 gain exclusion, and purchasing a new home. The proceeds from the sale of the home could be used to purchase the new home. They would have potential interest-deductible borrowing capacity equal to the cost of their new homes.

The Revenue Act of 1987, signed in December 1987, modified the above rules on home equity indebtedness but introduced further—and more favorable—limitations for home acquisition indebtedness. Indebtedness that was incurred on or before October 13, 1987, and that was secured by a qualified residence on such date or on any date thereafter is classified as acquisition indebtedness. Such debt will not be subject to the new acquisition indebtedness limitation in 1988 or after. Therefore, interest that was associated with indebtedness incurred on or before October 13, 1987, and that exceeded the limitations under the 1986 Tax Reform Act, will not exceed the limitations under the 1987 Act. The related interest will be viewed as qualified residence interest for 1988 and thereafter.

Under the latest rules, the aggregate amount treated as acquisition indebtedness for any period cannot exceed $1,000,000 (or $500,000 in the case of a married individual filing a separate return). Also, refinancing of indebtedness after October 13, 1987, is considered acquisition indebtedness, but only to the extent of the refinanced indebtedness. If a qualified residence is refinanced for more than the existing indebtedness, the excess amount may qualify in total, in part, or not at all as acquisition indebtedness.

Home equity indebtedness is *now* defined as any indebtedness (other than acquisition indebtedness) secured by a qualified residence to the extent that the aggregate amount for any period does not exceed the lesser of (1) $100,000 (or $50,000 for a married individual filing separately), or (2) the fair market value of such qualified residence less the amount of acquisition indebtedness with respect to the residence.

Note that in *Sophy v. Commissioner,* Dec. 58, 965, 138 T.C. No. 8 (2012), the Tax Court held that unmarried co-owners of two personal residences were **not** each allowed to deduct interest on $1.1 million of acquisition and home-equity indebtedness because the debt limitations are *residence based*, rather than *taxpayer based*. Instead, each taxpayer could only deduct a proportionate share of interest paid on a total of $1 million of acquisition indebtedness plus $100,000 of home-equity indebtedness.

Example 1: Assume that you buy a house for $1,000,000 and borrow $800,000 to finance the purchase. You reduce your debt to $600,000 by making payments over several years. You refinance and take out a new mortgage for $700,000. Your acquisition debt will still be $600,000. However, if you used $100,000 to substantially improve your home, the $100,000 would be added to acquisition debt. Alternatively, the interest may qualify as home equity debt.

Example 2: Assume that you bought your home 15 years ago for $50,000. You have completely paid off your mortgage, and the property is now worth $200,000. You take out a $120,000 home loan. You use $110,000 to make additions to the home and $10,000 to buy a car. Interest on the entire loan is deductible: $110,000 of the loan is acquisition debt, and the balance qualifies as home equity debt.

Example 3: Assume that you have an unpaid balance of $90,000 on your home, which is valued at $300,000. You obtain a *second mortgage* of $110,000 and use the proceeds to help your parents buy a home and to buy personal assets. Interest on $100,000 of the new mortgage is deductible as qualified home equity interest. Interest on the $10,000 balance is personal interest.

Note that the 1987 limits on acquisition indebtedness make it very important not to overlook many elements of the cost of a house besides the amount paid to the seller. These would include appraisal fees, title search, transfer taxes, survey fees, bank or lender fees, legal fees, mortgage taxes, brokers' commissions (if paid by the buyer), and other nondeductible closing costs. Note that the cost of the home and improvements does not include painting and routine maintenance and repairs. However, it does include additions to the home and improvement or replacement of equipment that is part of the home. Such improvements include landscaping; resurfacing the driveway; installing a swimming pool; constructing a new roof; finishing an attic or basement; replacing or making a major improvement to heating, air conditioning, or plumbing systems or to a water heater; or adding on a room or garage.

Can you finance the purchase of additional land, adjacent to your home, and deduct the interest as qualified residence interest? In Private Letter Ruling 8940061, the IRS said yes! In the ruling, a family built a home on 15 acres and later bought five more adjacent acres that will be cleared, landscaped, and incorporated into the family compound. The loan to finance the extra land is secured by both the new land and the original 15-acre tract. The family told the IRS it had no plans to separately develop the five acres.

The IRS said that the loan to buy the five acres was purchase debt, and since total purchase debt didn't exceed $1 million, all of the interest paid was deductible in full.

USING DEBT SECURED BY INVESTMENT PROPERTY

The major advantage of borrowing against a home rather than against property held for investment is that qualified residence interest is not subject to the investment interest expense limitation. When borrowing against property held for investment, care must be taken not to generate investment interest expense in excess of net investment income (plus excess amounts allowed under the phase-in rules for investment interest), or the interest deductions will be disallowed in the year paid or incurred. However, any excess may be carried forward indefinitely and deducted in later years when investment income exceeds investment interest expense paid or incurred in that year. Therefore, carryovers of investment interest will still generally be preferable to personal interest, which is no longer deductible.

PASSIVE ACTIVITIES WITH PASSIVE INCOME

Individuals who own passive activities that are earning passive income may wish to increase borrowing against that activity even if they do not wish to finance consumer purchases. The proceeds could be used to acquire investment assets with appreciation potential that could as well be leveraged up to their respective margin limits, thereby creating investment interest deductions to offset the current income from the portfolio.

The interest on debt used to acquire or carry an interest in a passive activity is not subject to the investment interest expense limitation. Such interest is fully deductible against passive income from the passive activity. However, if the interest expense exceeds the passive income from the passive activity, the excess interest will be treated as a passive loss. That loss may be deducted only against passive income from other passive activities or, on disposition of that passive activity, against gains on the disposition, passive income from other passive activities, and any active income or gain of the taxpayer, in that order.

OTHER INTEREST PLANNING TIPS

To the extent that a loan finances an asset used partially for business and partially for personal purposes, it appears that interest would have to be prorated between the two uses.

Example 1: Ms. Agent, an insurance agent, finances a new automobile to be used 75 percent for business and 25 percent for personal purposes. She would treat 75 percent of the interest as deductible business interest and 25 percent as nondeductible consumer interest.

Example 2: In example 1, Ms. Agent was treated as a self-employed individual. If she was an outside salesperson and an employee, rather than a self-employed individual, apparently all the interest she would pay on her automobile loan would be treated as consumer interest and would not be deductible as interest, even if she used the automobile 95 percent of the time in her employer's business. In that case, get an accountable plan reimbursement from your employer—even if you have to reduce your salary to get it!

Under current law, it may be more advantageous to have a business-use vehicle owned by the employer rather than by the employee, even though the employee must include the value of any personal use as compensation income.

The term *residence* as used in the qualified residence interest exception includes, in addition to houses, condominium units and cooperative housing units and any other property that the taxpayer uses for personal purposes as a dwelling unit, which generally includes a mobile home, a motor home, or a boat with living accommodations. A taxpayer who owns a boat that is large enough to live aboard for short periods, a mobile home, or a motor home may be able to treat it as a second residence for purposes of the residential interest deduction. You need to have kitchen and bathroom facilities as well as a place to sleep to qualify.

Taxpayers who are planning to purchase a new home might consider having appliances and various options such as a deck, fencing, and landscaping installed by the builder and included in the sales price. The interest on these items would then qualify as fully deductible residential interest. Otherwise the interest will be treated as nondeductible consumer financing and will be deductible only to the extent permitted under the phase-in rule.

The use of interest-free and other below-market-rate loans is affected by the interest deduction limitation. An individual borrower's imputed interest deduction will no longer fully offset the imputed interest income. Both borrowers and lenders who are party to employment-related or gift-type interest-free loans should reconsider whether these types of arrangements are still suitable.

Taxpayers with excess investment interest expense should consider recognizing capital gains by selling property held for investment.

There are a number of tax strategies that you should employ in planning your interest deductions. First, you must consider the timing of your actual interest payments in relation to both exceeding your standard deduction amount and determining your subsequent year's income. This technique has been discussed in detail under medical expenses and taxes. Second, you must recognize that unlike many other forms of expenditure, interest expenses need not be reasonable to be deducted. If you borrow money at an exorbitant rate, that interest is deductible regardless of what it has been labeled in order to circumvent a state law on maximum percentages.

Interest is also deductible if paid to a related party for a bona fide indebtedness. This means that if you actually have a legal debtor-creditor relationship with your spouse, for example, you may deduct interest paid to that spouse. In fact, parents may legitimately deduct interest paid on money borrowed from their minor children as long as there is an effective debtor-creditor relationship. This means that you sign a note, arrange for a repayment schedule, and meet that repayment schedule. Substantial savings can be accrued by paying legitimate interest to a child in a lower tax bracket. For example, assume that you paid $2,000 in interest to your dependent child (who has no other income) and you are in the 28 percent bracket. The first $1,000 of that interest is not taxable to the child because of the standard deduction. Therefore, the child pays only $100 on the interest received ($1,000 × 10 percent). But if you are in the 28 percent bracket, you saved $560 in taxes—a net savings of $460!

STUDENT LOAN INTEREST DEDUCTION

The Tax Relief Act of 1997 provided a new *above the line* deduction of up to $1,000 for any interest on any qualified education loan in 1998, $1,500 in 1999, $2,000 in 2000, and up to $2,500 per year in 2001 and thereafter during the first 60 months in which interest payments are required. This deduction begins to phase out at a modified adjusted gross income level of $60,000 to $75,000 for joint filers and $40,000 to $55,000 for all others. These limits are also indexed for inflation.

The Tax Relief Act of 2001 eliminated the 60-month limitation, and increased the phaseout to between $100,000 and $130,000 for joint returns and between $50,000 and $65,000 for single returns, both as of January 1, 2002.*

A qualified education loan is a loan used to pay the costs of attendance at an eligible educational institution for a student enrolled at least half-time in a program leading to a degree, certificate, or other recognized educational credential. The student must be the taxpayer, the taxpayer's spouse, or the taxpayer's dependent at the time the loan was taken.

93 Mortgage Insurance

Private Mortgage Insurance premiums are deductible *only* for 2007 through 2013 and *only* for policies issued after 2006. If you prepaid, the insurance was treated as interest and deducted over the shorter of the term of the loan or 84 months.

This deduction phases out for joint filers with adjusted gross income between $100,000 and $110,000 ($50,000–$55,000 for singles).

This is the insurance you pay if your down payment is less than 20 percent. If your equity is 20 percent or more, notify your lender to eliminate this additional cost.

94 Charitable Contributions

A charitable contribution is a gift to a qualified charitable organization. (To be deemed as making a gift, the taxpayer must have "donative intent"—that is, a detached and disinterested generosity. There must be no *quid pro quo* expected or received. That's why payments for religious education don't count.) The tax law allows charitable contributions to reduce taxable income, and therefore the actual cost of the donation will be reduced by your tax savings. As your income tax bracket increases, the real cost of your charitable gift will therefore decrease, making contributions more attractive for those in the higher brackets.

Regardless of the accounting method you use, contributions are usually deducted in the year in which they are paid. A contribution is paid when you unconditionally deliver or mail your gift to the recipient or to a designated

---

*For 2013, the numbers are $125,000–$155,000 for joint returns and $60,000–$75,000 for singles.

agent or when you make a completed gift of property. A contribution made by a credit card is deductible immediately even if payment to the credit card company is made in a different year.

You can obtain an itemized deduction for your charitable contributions, but these deductions are limited to a maximum of 50 percent of your adjusted gross income for the year. These contributions may consist of gifts to public charities and certain private foundations.* If the 50 percent limit is not exhausted, you can deduct contributions to other entities subject to a more restrictive constraint of 20 percent of your adjusted gross income.†

Appreciated capital gain property generally is further subjected to an additional 30 percent limit. These limits will be detailed in the analysis under planning considerations.

Charitable contributions can take numerous forms. Though cash and property are the main ones, there are others that must be considered. Unreimbursed costs incurred for charity contributions, dues, admission charges, and other payments may be deductible, but not if they are made in exchange for benefits or property you receive. The amount deductible is usually the property's fair market value, yet for gifts of appreciated property this value may be reduced under special rules. Cancelled checks and receipts offer the best proof to the contributor. When a charitable deduction is taken you must be able to state the name of each charity and the amount and date of each gift. The *charitable mileage deduction* is 14¢/mile for 2013.

PLANNING CONSIDERATIONS

Qualified Donees

You can deduct charitable contributions only if they are made to or for the use of a "qualified donee." No charitable contribution deduction is allowed for gifts to other kinds of organizations, even if those organizations are exempt from U.S. income tax.

---

*The following types of foundations qualify: 1. private operating foundations; 2. all other private foundations that distribute all their contributions to public charities within $2\frac{1}{2}$ months after the year-end; and 3. pooled community foundations.

†The Tax Reform Act of 1984 increased the limits on contributions to tax-exempt private *nonoperating* foundations from 20 percent to 30 percent of adjusted gross income, for gifts of cash or ordinary income property. It also provided that excess post-1984 contributions can be carried forward for 5 years. The Act, in addition, provided a deduction at full fair market value for contributions of up to 10 percent of the stock of a corporation to a private *nonoperating* foundation, provided the stock is publicly traded and is long-term capital gain property. These provisions are effective for contributions made after the enactment of the Act.

Organizations that provide sellar funded down-payment assistance to home buyers do *not* qualify as tax exempt charities (Rev. Rul. 2006-27).

The gift must be made directly to an organization to qualify for the deduction. However, in the case of *Rockefeller,* 76 T.C. 178 (1981), the court held that unreimbursed expenses incurred in rendering services to a qualified charitable organization constituted deductible contributions made "to" the charitable organization. The IRS has acquiesced in this decision (Rev. Rul. 84-61, I.R.B. 1984-17). No deduction to an individual or individuals is allowed by the IRS unless that individual or group is acting as an agent for a qualified organization. This rule is necessary because there is no guarantee that the money given to an individual will be forwarded to the charity. Payments to individual ministers have been disqualified as charitable contributions when there was no evidence that the money ever went to the minister's religious organization.

The Treasury Department publishes IRS Publication 78, which lists the organizations to which contributions are deductible, identifies each by type, and states their corresponding limit of deductibility. This list is updated annually. Three cumulative supplements listing only new additions are published every quarter. A list informing the public of organizations that no longer qualify as charitable organizations is published monthly.

Deductions are allowed for contributions given to or for the use of the following qualified organizations:

1. A state or possession of the United States, or the District of Columbia, if the contribution or gift is made for public purposes only.

2. A corporation, trust, or community chest, fund, or foundation if created in the United States and organized and operated exclusively for religious, charitable, scientific, literary, or educational purposes, or to foster national or international amateur sports competition (but not to help provide athletic equipment or facilities), or for the prevention of cruelty to children or animals. No part of the net earnings can benefit any private shareholder or individual. The organization must not be disqualified for tax exemption due to influencing legislation, and must not take part in any political campaign.

3. A post or organization of war veterans, if organized in the United States and if no part of the net earnings benefits any private shareholders or individual. Any dues, fees, or assessments paid by members of these organizations do not qualify for deductions.

4. A domestic or fraternal society, order, or association, operating under the lodge system, if the gift is to be used exclusively for religious, charitable, scientific, literary, or educational purposes, or to foster national or international amateur sports competition, or for the prevention of cruelty to children or animals. Dues to offset sickness or burial costs are deductible.

5. A nonprofit cemetery company whose funds are totally devoted to the continuous upkeep of the cemetery.

You can only deduct contributions to charities created or organized in the United States. But qualifying domestic charities that support foreign charities may be deductible, depending on specific circumstances (INFO 2009-0026).

If an organization qualifies as a church for tax purposes, it need not be required to seek exemption and has no filing requirements. Since Congress did not define the term *church,* the common meaning and usage of the term have been applied. In making this decision, the IRS utilizes the following 13 characteristics of a church:

> A distinct legal existence
> A recognized creed and form of worship
> A definite and distinct ecclesiastical government
> A formal code of doctrine and discipline
> A distinct religious history
> A membership not associated with any other church or denomination
> A complete organization of ordained ministers chosen after completing
>   prescribed courses of study
> Literature of its own
> Established places of worship
> Regular congregations
> Regular religious services
> Sunday schools for religious education of the young
> Schools to prepare their ministers

Not all of the above characteristics must be satisfied, and no single factor is given controlling weight. By listing these characteristics as a rough outline, the IRS gives guidelines for its determination as to whether an organization may qualify as a "church."

Contributions to foreign governments, charities, and private foundations are disallowed. Gifts to Communist-ruled organizations are also disallowed. The Treasury Department does not allow tax-exempt status for private schools that practice racial discrimination, and any donations to them will not qualify as charitable contributions.

No charity can take part in any political activity. Charity status is lost by an organization if any substantial segment of its activities is devoted to formulating propaganda or otherwise trying to influence legislation. However, an organization (other than a church) may qualify as a charity and still perform some of these activities by keeping its political expenditures to an "insubstantial" part of its activities. Furthermore, donations to needy individuals are not deductible under the law.

ADDITIONAL PLANNING CONSIDERATIONS

Donation Limitations

Only if you contribute more than 20 percent of your adjusted gross income to a qualified charity is it necessary to be knowledgeable about donation limitations. Contributions up to this limit are automatically deductible if you itemize. For those who give more than 20 percent, certain rules apply.

If the contributions are all made to maximum deduction organizations (see the list that follows), the deduction ceiling is 50 percent of the contribution base (except that contributions of appreciated capital gain property are subject to a 30 percent ceiling, unless a special election is made). The contribution base is defined as adjusted gross income computed without regard to any net operating loss carryback to the taxable year.

To qualify for the 50 percent ceiling, the contribution must be made "to" one of the maximum deduction organizations (as opposed to "for the use of" an organization). If the contributions are not "to" 50 percent charities but rather are "for the use of" any charities, the deduction limit is 30 percent. Contributions of appreciated capital gain property to nonoperating foundations are limited to 20 percent. For contributions subject to the 20, 30, and 50 percent limits, the amount not deductible in the contribution year may be deductible in a future year as a carryover.

On a joint return, these limits apply to the aggregate contribution base.

You are allowed a 50 percent ceiling on contributions to any of the following maximum deduction organizations:

1. *Churches.*

2. *Tax-Exempt Educational Organizations.* The educational organization should maintain a regular faculty and curriculum and have a regularly enrolled body of students in attendance at the place where its educational activities are regularly conducted.

An organization set up for the benefit of certain state and municipal colleges and universities can also be included if it is organized and operated exclusively to receive, hold, invest, and administer property and to make expenditures to or for the benefit of an acceptable college or university.

The educational organization must be engaged entirely in educational activities (although noneducational activity incidental to the educational activities is allowable). Tuition payments are not deductible, and contributions made under circumstances where you or those related to you benefit may be examined to see if personal benefit is the purpose of the payment.

3. *Tax-Exempt Hospitals and Certain Medical Research Organizations.* Hospitals, in this case, do not include homes for children or the aged or institutes that provide vocational training for the handicapped. The medical research organization must be engaged primarily and directly in the continuous active conduct of medical research. In addition, it must be committed to spending each contribution received on such active conduct of medical research before January 1 of the fifth calendar year after the date the contribution is made.

4. *A Government Unit* as referred to in the Internal Revenue Code Section 170(c)(1) (such as a state or a political subdivision of a state).

5. *A "Publicly Supported" Organization* (such as a community chest). This type of organization normally receives a substantial part of its support (exclusive of operating income) from a governmental unit or from direct or indirect contributions from the general public.

6. *Certain Private Nonoperating Foundations.* These distribute all contributions they receive to public charities within 2½ months after the foundations' fiscal year-end.

7. *A Privately Operating Foundation.* This type of private foundation is one that pools all of its donations in a common fund. Any substantial contributor (or spouse) can annually direct the foundation as to which public charity shall receive the principal from his or her contribution and the interest from that principal.

8. *Certain Membership Organizations.* Only those in which more than one-third of their support comes from the general public are allowable.

The Public Support Test

To determine whether an organization is "publicly supported," you must apply the public support, or mechanical, test. An organization will be considered to be a publicly supported organization for its current taxable year and for the immediately succeeding taxable year if, for the four taxable years immediately preceding the current taxable year, the total amount of the support the organization received from governmental units, from donations made directly or indirectly by the public, or from a combination of the two equals 33.33 percent or more of the total support of the organization. In addition, contributions made by individuals, trusts, or corporations during the four taxable years may not exceed 2 percent of the organization's total support. The 2 percent limitation does not apply to support from governmental units or from other publicly supported organizations.

The Facts and Circumstances Test

A corporation, trust, or community chest, fund, or foundation that does not qualify as a "publicly supported" organization under the mechanical test may qualify on the basis of the facts and circumstances test. There are several requirements, but only requirements 1 and 2 below must be met on an aggregate basis. However, a substantial number of the remaining ones must also be met in the 4 taxable years preceding the current taxable year.

1. *10 Percent of Support Limitations.* The percent of support "normally" received by an organization from governmental units, from the public, whether direct or indirect, or from a combination of these sources must be substantial. The amount of this support must equal at least 10 percent of the total support.

2. *Attraction of Public Support.* An organization must be so organized and operated as to attract new and additional public or governmental support on a continuous basis. It must maintain a continuous program for canvassing funds from the general public, community, or membership groups involved, or it must carry on other activities to attract support.

3. *Percent of Financial Support.* The percent of public support received will be considered. The higher the percent, the lesser will be the burden of establishing the publicly supported nature of the organization.

4. *Sources of Support.* A large number of different contributors is preferred. In determining what a "representative number of persons" is, consideration

will be given to the type of organization involved, the length of time it has been in existence, and any restrictions it practices.

5. *Representative Governing Body.* The fact that the organization has a governing body that represents the broad interest of the public will also be considered in determining whether an organization is publicly supported.

6. *Availability of Public Facilities for the Benefit of the Public.* Public participation in programs or policies will also be reviewed.

7. *Additional Factors.* Pertinent to membership organizations are answers to the following questions:

a) Is the organization designed to enroll a substantial number of persons in a particular field?

b) Are dues set at fixed rates to be affordable by a broad cross section of the interested public?

c) Are the activities of the organization likely to appeal to persons with a broad range of interests, or do they focus on a particular purpose?

Those factors relevant to each case and the weight given to each factor may change depending upon the nature and function of the organization.

Contributions shall be considered as support from the *general public* only if the total amount of all contributions, direct and indirect, does not exceed 2 percent of the organization's total support for a set period, except as provided by the *exclusion of unusual grants.* The 2 percent limit does not apply to support received from governmental units. (The donation is included in full in the denominator but will only be included in the numerator of such a fraction to the extent that it does not exceed 2 percent of the denominator. Any unusual grants may be excluded entirely from the fraction.) The unusual grant exclusion is generally intended to apply to substantial contributions or bequests from disinterested parties whose contributions or bequests:

a) are attracted by reason of the publicly supported nature of the organization;

b) are in unusual or unexpected amounts; *or*

c) would, by reason of size, adversely affect the status of the organization as normally being publicly supported.

Support does *not* include the following:

- Any amounts received by an organization from the exercise or performance of its functional purpose, which comprises the basis for its exemptions

- Contributions of services for which there is no deduction

Both of the above must be excluded from the numerator and the denominator.

An organization dependent on gross receipts from related activities will not satisfy either the mechanical test or the facts and circumstances test. The condition for public support will also not be met if an insignificant amount of the organization's support comes through governmental units from contributions made directly or indirectly by the general public. Support from a governmental unit includes any amount received from a governmental unit, which covers donations, contributions, and amounts received in connection with an agreement with a governmental unit for either the execution of services or for a governmental research grant. However, such amounts will not count as support from a governmental unit if they are for the performance of the organization's exempt activity, and if the reason for the payment is to enable the organization to offer a facility for the direct benefit of the public, rather than to serve only its members.

To summarize the tests involved in determining whether organizations qualify as publicly supported: The organization must normally receive in excess of 33.33 percent of its support from a governmental unit and from direct and indirect donations from the general public to qualify under the mechanical test; or, alternatively, at least 10 percent of its support must come from governmental units and public donations, and most, if not all, of points 3 through 7 of the facts and circumstances test must apply.

COMMUNITY TRUSTS

Community trusts have been established to invite large donations of a capital or endowment nature for the benefit of a certain community. Each has a governing body consisting of representatives of the community it serves. The contributions are often kept in the form of separate trusts or funds subject to changing degrees of control by the governing body.

A community trust must also meet the mechanical test or be able to attract sources on a continuous basis from the government and public in order to meet the facts and circumstances test. This test will usually be satisfied if the trust attracts a broad range of donors from the community served.

Another point concerning community trusts is the treatment of them as single entities. Any organization that meets the requirements described in points 2 through 5 below will be treated as a single entity; all funds linked with an organization that meets the requirements of point 1 will be considered as component parts of that organization.

1. The organization must be established by a gift, bequest, legacy, devise, or other transfer to a community trust that is considered a single entity, and it may not be subjected by the transferor to any restraints.

2. The organization must be recognized as a community trust, fund, or foundation to support charitable events in the community it serves.

3. All funds of the organization must be subject to common governing instruments.

4. The organization must have a common governing body that administers the fund.

5. Periodic financial reports must be prepared to show that all of the funds held by the community trust are funds of the organization.

A few final words on 50 percent limit contributions: Gifts made "for the use of" public charities or 50 percent limit private foundations do not qualify for the 50 percent limit. You must make the gift "to" a 50 percent charity to qualify for the donation. A charitable gift to a fraternal lodge that then contributes a gift to a 50 percent charity does not qualify for the 50 percent limit. A donation of an *income interest* is considered as made for the use of the recipient organization. Thus, you do not get the 50 percent limit. But a gift of a *remainder interest* is treated as made to the donee charity, thus enabling you to reach the 50 percent ceiling.

LIMITS ON DEDUCTION

There is a 20 percent ceiling on deductions for any contributions of appreciated capital gain property to 30 percent charities—i.e., charitable organizations except those listed previously (e.g., a nonoperating foundation). For years beginning with 1987, the amount of your deduction is limited to your basis. Any excess over the ceiling can be carried over to the 5 succeeding tax years.

For example, assume you have a painting with a basis of $15,000 and a $20,000 fair market value. You have an adjusted gross income of $100,000. You want to contribute the painting to a veterans organization (a nonpublic charity). Your charitable deduction will be $15,000, because your basis does not exceed your ceiling of $20,000 (20 percent of $100,000). There is, however, a special rule for gifts of stock. If you contribute *qualified appreciated stock* to a *private non-operating foundation,* you may take as a charitable deduction, subject to the above 20 percent ceiling limit, the full fair market value of the stock. Qualified appreciated stock is any stock of a corporation that (a) has price quotations readily available from an established securities market and (b) if sold would produce a long-term capital gain. This provision does not apply to the gift of any stock or portion of stock that exceeds 10 percent of the ownership interest in a corporation.

This special rule for stock was in effect through 1994 and was extended by the Small Business Job Protection Act of 1996 for gifts made July 1, 1996 through May 31, 1997, extended in 1997 to June 30, 1998, and made permanent in 1998.

If you give property that, if sold, would result in a long-term capital gain (appreciated capital assets or Section 1231 Property),* and the charity is a 50 percent donee, then you are subject to a 30 percent ceiling. If the contributions of capital gain property exceed 30 percent of your contribution base, the excess amount can qualify for a 5-year carryover. Charitable contributions with 30 percent limitations paid during the taxable year are considered after all other charitable contributions.

Donation of a 30 percent capital gain property is defined as the charitable contribution of a capital asset that, if sold by the donor at its fair market value at the time of the contribution, would result in long-term gain; also, the amount of such a contribution must not be required to be reduced under Section 170(3)(1)(B) (this covers tangible personal property used by a donee in a function unrelated to the basis for its exemptions, and contributed "to" or "for the use of" certain private foundations).

You can make a special election to qualify for the 50 percent adjusted gross income limit on this property. In doing so, the deduction for the contribution is limited to your basis. If the election is made, it applies to all donations of capital gain property made during the year as well as to prior-year carryovers of appreciated capital gain property. The election must be made by the due date of the return and cannot be made on an amended return.

---

*Section 1231 Property is real or personal property used in a trade or business that would normally produce ordinary gains or losses upon sale or exchange. Gains on such property are capital gains and losses are ordinary losses.

For example, assume that you have some stock that you would like to give to a public charity. You have held the stock for a number of years and your adjusted gross income is $100,000. The stock has a basis of $45,000 and a fair market value at the time of the donation of $50,000. If you do not make the 50 percent election, your charitable contribution deduction is limited to $30,000 (30 percent of $100,000) with the remaining $20,000 carried over. If you do make the election, you would get a deduction of the full $45,000 basis. Note that in exchange for getting the full $45,000 in the current year, you lose $5,000 of your deduction.

When making this special election, you are actually exchanging a reduced deduction on each separate contribution of appreciated capital gain property for the more generous 50 percent limit. The election of the 50 percent deduction ceiling is made by attaching to the original return for the election year a statement that the election is being taken. The following guidelines should be used in deciding whether the election should be taken:

1. If your long-term capital gain property contributions to 50 percent charities will not total more than 30 percent of your contribution base, do not make the election.

2. If you give long-term capital gain property in excess of the 30 percent ceiling to 50 percent charities, consider the following factors:

   a) any excess over the 30 percent limit, which can be carried over;

   b) your income for the current year, which should be compared with what you expect to earn in the following years; *and*

   c) the amount of unrealized long-term capital gain included in the value of the property.

Where long-term appreciated property consists of *tangible personal property*, such as works of art, the amount of the deduction *depends upon its use* by the charitable organization. If its use by the charity is unrelated to the charity's exempt function, then the amount of the deduction is limited to your basis.

For example, you own a work of art that you have held for more than one year and then you donate that work to a museum. If the donation is used by the museum for display, it is deemed related to the museum's exempt purpose.

Therefore, if the work of art has a fair market value of $24,000 on the date of donation, that donation gives you a deduction of $24,000.

If the donation is made to a hospital, however, the amount of the deduction is limited to your basis. If the basis of the property is $4,000, then the deduction is limited to $4,000.

CARRYOVERS TO OTHER TAX YEARS

If the amount of contributions to 50 percent organizations made within a taxable year exceeds 50 percent of your contribution base for that year, the excess may be carried over for the next 5 succeeding taxable years. Current contributions must first be considered before any carryover is applied. Contributions that are carried over, plus the current year's contributions, must fall within the 50 percent limit. Five-year carryovers are also available for excess 20 percent and 30 percent contributions.

The charitable contribution deduction must be specially computed when taxpayers with carryovers change their filing status. Note that an unused carryover of a deceased spouse can be used on a return for the year the spouse dies; otherwise it is lost.

ORDER OF DEDUCTIBILITY

The amount that you should deduct in any year is determined in the following order:

1. Gifts for the year to 50 percent charities

2. Carryover of gifts to 50 percent charities from the preceding 5 years, from the earliest year first

3. Gifts for the year to 30 percent charities

4. Carryover of gifts to 30 percent charities from the preceding 5 years, from the earliest year first

5. Gifts that are limited by the 20 percent ceiling

Your total deduction for any year cannot exceed 50 percent of your contribution base for that year and cannot exceed the amount actually contributed currently and in the past. Where 50 percent of your contribution base income exceeds the amount of your gifts, any carryovers from prior years are deductible, in order of time, to the extent of this excess. Any carryovers not used up may be carried forward to later years until exhausted or until the 5-year period for each excess contribution runs out.

Contributions to which the 20 percent limitation would apply should be avoided when gifts are made of 30 percent limit property to 50 percent limit organizations that surpass your 30 percent limit. In this situation, you should consider the special election to reduce the 30 percent limit items and receive the 50 percent ceiling on them. This especially applies if a carryover of such a contribution exists from a prior year. Prior years' deductions are not influenced by this special election.

FORM OF THE GIFT

The deduction for a contribution of property is normally equal to the fair market value of the property at the time the donation is made. For a great program to value your contributions, see itsdeductible.com or try bigwriteoff.com. No gain is normally realized on a charitable contribution of appreciated property. You have an advantage when you contribute appreciated property because you get a deduction for the full fair market value of the property contributed, including both your basis and your unrealized paper profit. You are not taxed on this profit, so in effect you receive a deduction for an amount that you need not report as income.

If the fair market value of the property donated is below its basis, no loss is recognized on this donation. In such a case it would be better to sell the property first, realize the loss for tax purposes, and then make a gift of the proceeds. Using this approach, a deduction is allowed for the entire basis of the property.

The deduction for certain contributions of appreciated property must be reduced in some cases, depending on the type of appreciated property or the character of the donee. The amount of deduction for appreciated property must be reduced below its fair market value by the sum of ordinary income or short-term capital gain that would result if the property were sold at the time of the gift. Both a capital asset held for not more than 12 months and property subject to recapture of depreciation would result in ordinary income. Any appreciation in excess of the recapture amount is handled as a contribution of capital-gain property. The above rule applies regardless of the type of donee. Other examples of property that would result in ordinary income are letters, memoranda, and works of art created by the donor. Note that the Tax Increase

Ordering of Deductions to Charity*

	Deduct All:	Up to This % of Contribution Base
First—	Cash contributions to public charities	50%
Second—	Carryover of prior years' cash contributions to public charities	50%
Third—	Cash contributions to private foundations	30%
Fourth—	Carryover of prior years' cash contributions to private foundations	30%
Fifth—	Capital gain property contributions to public charities	30%
Sixth—	Carryover of prior years' capital-gain property contributions to public charities	30%
Seventh—	Qualified appreciated stock contributions to private foundations	20%
Eighth—	Carryover of prior years' qualified appreciated stock contributions to private foundations	20%

*When contributions reach the indicated percentage, any excess must be carried over to the next year. If contributions in any tier are below the indicated percentage in any taxable year, contributions in the next lower tier may be deducted.

Prevention Act of 2005, enacted in 2006, provided that self created music works now qualify when sold, for capital gain treatment. Under prior law, such sales were taxed as ordinal income.

For example, if an artist contributed a personal piece to a charity, there would be no charitable deduction. This portrait would generate ordinary income if it were sold by the artist at fair market value. Therefore, the deduction would be reduced to zero by the subtraction of this ordinary income component.

Except for "qualified appreciated stock" gifted to a private nonoperating foundation, if appreciated long-term capital gain property is donated to a private foundation that is not a 50 percent limit donee, then its value must be reduced by 100 percent of that long-term capital gain. Your deduction is limited to your basis. The deduction for contributed capital gain property that is tangible personal property is reduced in the same manner as when the use of the property is dissimilar to the donee's exempt status.

You will sometimes sell property to a charity for less than the property's fair market value, intending the "bargain" portion as a charitable contribution. Except in the case of ordinary income property sold for its adjusted basis, the seller may treat the amount of the bargain (fair market value minus purchase price) as a charitable donation for deduction reasons.

The donor usually also realizes taxable gain on the bargain sale; thus you must divide your basis (original cost) in the property between the part of the property sold and the part given. Your gain is determined only by that portion of your total cost that the bargain selling price (amount received) bears to the fair market value. The following formula can be used to calculate the adjusted basis of the property sold:

$$\frac{\text{Selling Price}}{\text{Fair Market Value}} \times \text{Property Basis} = \text{Adjusted Basis}$$

You must allocate this figure to the property sold and determine your taxable gain. For example, assume you have 100 shares of appreciated long-term capital gains stock with a tax basis of $4,000 and a fair market value of $10,000. You want to give $6,000 to the American College and you therefore sell this stock for your basis, or $4,000. Your realized gain is shown on the following page.

The rules for determining basis that apply to bargain sales also apply when mortgaged property is donated and the charity assumes the mortgage. The transfer is treated like a sale, with the purchase cost being the mortgage that the charity agrees to pay. In the case of both bargain sales and mortgaged property, the bargain sale rule does not apply unless the exchange produces a charitable deduction.

Fair market value of stock	$10,000
Minus sale proceeds	−4,000
Charitable contribution	$ 6,000
	$ 4,000
Sale proceeds	
Tax basis in property sold:	

$$\frac{\$\,4,000}{\$10,000} \times \text{basis of } \$4,000$$

Sale price	$ 4,000	
Fair value	$10,000	
		−1,600
Gain realized		$ 2,400

The courts have allowed owners of closely held corporations to withdraw funds from their firms tax-free by means of charitable contributions followed by a redemption: The owner gives stock to charity and at a later date the corporation redeems the stock. The donor is allowed a charitable contribution deduction, even though an understanding exists between the donor and donee that the stock will be redeemed shortly after contribution, where redemption is not required.

The valuation for the gift of stock is the average of the high and low sales price reported on the date of the gift.

EASEMENTS ON BUILDINGS IN HISTORIC DISTRICTS

You cannot claim a deduction for a contribution of an easement on a building in a registered historic district made after July 25, 2006, unless the contributed interest includes restrictions preserving the entire exterior of the building (including front, sides, rear, and height) and prohibiting any change to the exterior of the building inconsistent with its historical character. If you claim a deduction for this type of contribution in a tax year beginning after August 17, 2006, you must include with your return a qualified appraisal, photographs of the building's exterior, and a description of all restrictions on development of the building.

FILING FEE FOR EASEMENTS ON BUILDINGS IN HISTORIC DISTRICTS

A new $500 filing fee must be paid for each qualified conservation contribution after February 12, 2007, that is an easement on a building in a registered historic district, if the claimed deduction is more than $10,000. See Form 8283-V, Payment Voucher for Filing Fee.

ATHLETIC EVENT

In Rev. Rul. 86-63, 1986-1 C.B. 6, the IRS ruled that if you make a contribution to an educational institution where athletic games are regularly sold out in advance and in return receive the right to buy tickets to those games, you cannot take a charitable contribution deduction for the amount contributed. This has been congressionally overruled.

Retroactive to tax years beginning after December 31, 1983, 80 percent of the cost of the right to obtain preferred seating at athletic events of a college or university is deductible. No amount paid for the purchase of tickets, whether paid separately or as part of a lump-sum payment that includes the right to purchase tickets, is deductible as a charitable contribution. The statute of limitations for closed years was waived for years affected by this provision if you filed a refund claim before November 10, 1989.

CONTRIBUTION OF SERVICES

No deduction exists for the contribution of your services. However, unreimbursed expenses incurred during the rendering of free services for a qualified charity are deductible as charitable contributions.

Any cost incurred in traveling from your house to where you served is deductible. *A standard mileage rate* of 14¢ per mile is allowed if you use your car. Or you can choose to deduct your actual unreimbursed expenses for gas and oil. Parking fees and tolls are also deductible. No deduction is given for depreciation, insurance, or repairs on the car. Donating blood is considered the contribution of services and thus no deduction is allowed.

A deduction for reasonable outlays for meals and lodgings is also allowed if incurred while away from home. In addition, deductions have been allowed for the cost of baby-sitting services for children whose parents were performing services for charitable organizations.

UNIFORMS

A deduction is allowed for the cost of uniforms used while performing charitable services as long as the clothing isn't suitable for everyday wear. *Classic examples:* you can write off the cost of Boy Scout or Girl Scout uniforms, Salvation Army uniforms, Santa Claus suits for charitable events, etc.

CONSERVATION EASEMENTS

A conservation easement is a binding agreement between a landowner and a nonprofit group called a land trust that places development restrictions on the property. The reduction in value is deductible in 2013 up to 50 percent of your AGI, with a 15-year carryforward for unused contributions.

LIFE INSURANCE POLICIES AND OTHER DONATIONS

If full rights of ownership are contributed, a gift of a life insurance policy is acceptable as a charitable gift. Any subsequent payments of premiums by the donor will also qualify as charitable contributions. Even a single premium whole life payment for the benefit of a charity would be allowed (PLR 200209020). The amount of the deduction for this type is its fair market value (LTR. RUL. 9147040).

Dues, admission charges, etc., where you receive property or benefits can only be deducted if they exceed the value of the benefits received for them. Amounts paid for raffle tickets, bingo, or similar chance games and losses on games of chance are not deductible charitable contributions.

Where amounts are paid in connection with admission to fund-raising affairs for charity, you must show that a clearly identifiable segment of the payment is a gift, and only this amount will qualify. The same rule applies whether or not the tickets are actually used. If you have no intention of using the tickets, you should give them back and make a gift of the purchase price. Using this approach, you will get the full amount as a deduction.

Donations of less than your entire interest in property are not deductible, but there are certain exceptions to this rule. For example, the transfer of a remainder interest in a personal residence or a farm is deductible. Also, the contribution of an undivided portion of your entire interest in property will qualify for the deduction. But a gift of one week's use of a vacation property to a charity yields no deduction for rental value—it was less than the entire interest.

A charitable remainder gift made during your lifetime is also deductible, based upon the value of the remainder interest. The Internal Revenue Service tax code requires that a fixed percentage be paid to one or more persons for a specified term of years (not to exceed 20) or for the life or lives of the income beneficiaries, with an irrevocable remainder to be paid to the charitable organization. If the remainder interest to the charity is subject to a contingency, it is not deductible. In addition, the value of the gift must be readily determinable.

CHARITABLE REMAINDER TRUSTS

The ability to take a deduction today for a gift of a remainder interest to a charity has led to the creation of charitable remainder trusts. You would contribute appreciated property (stocks, real estate, etc.) to the trust in exchange for an income stream over your lifetime—either a fixed amount each year (an annuity trust) or a given percent of the value of the trust annually (a unitrust).

The value of what is projected to go to the charity at your death (you can use multiple lives) is deductible today!

This value is a function of your age and life expectancy (based on IRS tables), the income stream you are receiving, and the assumed rate of return that the trust is expected to generate (the "applicable federal rate" which is published monthly by the IRS).

The advantages of the CRT are:

1. You and the trust pay no tax on the sale of the appreciated asset.

2. Therefore, you get a potentially much higher income stream during your life.

3. You get an immediate tax deduction even though you keep the income stream.

4. You can use the tax savings from the immediate tax deduction to purchase a life insurance policy to replace the value of the asset that goes to the charity at your death.

5. Structured correctly, life insurance can be removed from your estate. Your heirs after the estate tax may have more wealth go to them from a $500,000 life insurance policy not in your estate, than from $800,000 assets had you not transferred them into the CRT.

PROOF

You are required to provide information in support of all of your deductions; therefore, you should be able to prove all charitable contributions through receipts, canceled checks, etc. If a contribution is made in property other than money, you should state the kind of property contributed, the method used in ascertaining the fair market value of the property at the time the contribution is made, and whether the amount of the contribution is reduced because the property is either ordinary income or capital-gain property.

If you contribute property other than money valued in excess of $500, you must attach Form 8283 to the income tax return with the following information:

a) the name and address of the donee organization;

b) the date of the actual contribution;

c) a description of the property;

d) the manner of acquisition;

e) the fair market value of the property at the contribution time and the method utilized in determining the fair market value; *and*

f) the cost or other basis of the property.

Salvation Army Valuation Guideline

Ladies Clothing

	Low	High
Blouse	$ 2.50	$ 12.00
Bathrobes	2.50	12.00
Boots	2.00	5.00
Bras	1.00	3.00
Bathing Suits	4.00	12.00
Coats	10.00	40.00
Dresses	4.00	19.00
Evening Dresses	10.00	60.00
Fur Hats	7.00	15.00
Fur Coats	25.00	400.00
Foundation Garments	3.00	8.00
Handbags	2.00	20.00
Hats	1.00	8.00
Jackets	4.00	12.00
Nightgowns	4.00	12.00
Pant Suits	6.50	25.00
Socks	.40	1.25
Suits	6.00	25.00
Shoes	2.00	25.00
Skirts	3.00	8.00
Sweaters	3.00	15.00
Slips	1.00	6.00
Slacks	3.50	12.00

Men's Clothing

	Low	High
Jackets	$ 7.50	$ 25.00
Over Coats	15.00	60.00
Pajamas	2.00	8.00
Pants-Shorts	3.50	10.00
Raincoat	5.00	20.00
Suits	15.00	60.00
Slacks	5.00	12.00
Shirts	2.50	12.00
Sweaters	2.50	12.00
Shoes	3.50	25.00
Swim Trunks	2.50	8.00
Tuxedo	10.00	60.00
Undershirts	1.00	3.00
Undershorts	1.00	3.00
Belts Ties	3.00	8.00

Children's Clothing

	Low	High
Blouses	$ 2.00	$ 8.00
Boots	3.00	20.00
Coats	4.50	20.00
Dresses	3.50	12.00
Jackets	3.00	25.00
Jeans	3.50	12.00
Pants	2.50	12.00
Snowsuits	4.00	19.00
Shoes	2.50	8.75
Skirts	1.50	6.00
Sweaters	2.50	8.00
Slacks	2.00	8.00
Shirts	2.00	6.00
Socks	.50	1.50
Underwear	1.00	3.50

Dry Goods

	Low	High
Blankets	$ 2.50	$ 8.00
Bedspreads	3.00	24.00
Chair Covers	15.00	35.00
Curtains	1.50	12.00
Drapes	6.50	40.00
Pillows	2.00	8.00
Sheets	2.00	8.00
Throw Rugs	1.50	12.00
Towels	.50	4.00

Furniture

	Low	High
Complete Sets		
Bedroom Set	$ 250.00	$ 1000.00
Dining Room Set	150.00	900.00
Kitchen Set	35.00	170.00
Bed Complete (dbl)	50.00	170.00
Bed Complete (sgl)	35.00	100.00
Air Conditioner	20.00	90.00
Bar	30.00	75.00
Bar Stools	10.00	20.00
Bed (dbl) Complete	50.00	170.00

Furniture (Continued)

	Low	High
Bed (sgl) Complete	$ 35.00	$ 100.00
Bicycles	15.00	65.00
Chest	25.00	95.00
Clothes Closet	15.00	50.00
China Cabinet	85.00	300.00
Convertible Sofa (w/Mattress)	85.00	300.00
Crib (w/Mattress)	25.00	100.00
Carriage	5.00	100.00
Chair (Upholstered)	25.00	75.00
Coffee Table	15.00	65.00
Dresser w/Mirror	20.00	100.00
Desk	25.00	140.00
Dryer	45.00	90.00
Electric Stove (Wkg)	75.00	150.00
End Tables (2)	10.00	50.00
Figurines (Lg.)	50.00	150.00
Fireplace Set	30.00	90.00
Floor Lamps	7.50	40.00
Folding Beds	20.00	60.00
Gas Stove	50.00	125.00
Heaters	7.50	22.00
High Chair	10.00	50.00
Hi Riser	35.00	75.00
Kitchen Table	25.00	60.00
Kitchen Cabinets	25.00	75.00
Kitchen Chair	2.50	10.00
Mattress (dbl)	35.00	75.00
Mattress (sgl)	15.00	35.00
Organ Console	75.00	200.00
Piano	75.00	200.00
Pictures and Paintings	5.00	200.00
Ping-Pong Table	15.00	40.00
Play Pen	15.00	30.00
Pool Table	20.00	75.00
Record Player (Stereo)	30.00	90.00
Record Player (Components)	30.00	200.00
Rugs	20.00	90.00
Refrigerator (Wkg)	75.00	250.00
Radio	7.50	50.00
Secretary	50.00	140.00
Sofa	35.00	200.00
TV (B/W Wkg)	25.00	60.00
TV (Color Wkg)	75.00	225.00
Trunk	5.00	70.00
Wardrobe	20.00	100.00
Washer (Wkg)	50.00	150.00
Waterbed Frame	15.00	40.00
Waterbed Headboard	30.00	90.00
Waterbed (Complete)	150.00	325.00

Sporting Goods

	Low	High
Bicycles	$ 15.00	$ 65.00
Fishing Rods	5.00	25.00
Ice/Roller Skates	10.00	40.00
Skis	15.00	100.00
Sleds	5.00	20.00
Tennis Rackets	5.00	40.00
Toboggans	15.00	90.00

Miscellaneous

	Low	High
Adding Machine	$ 20.00	$ 75.00
Christmas Trees	15.00	50.00
Broiler Oven	15.00	25.00
Copier	100.00	200.00
Home Computer	150.00	500.00
Mimeograph Machine	100.00	200.00
Mixer	5.00	20.00
Mannequins	25.00	200.00
Mower (Riding)	100.00	250.00
Mower (Auto)	10.00	100.00
Power Edger	5.00	25.00
Rototiller	25.00	90.00
Sewing Machine	15.00	75.00
Snow Blower	50.00	150.00
Telephone Ans. Mach.	25.00	75.00
Typewriter	30.00	35.00
Vacuum Cleaner (Wkg)	20.00	60.00
Wigs	5.00	25.00

Wkg = Working

My favorite valuation source is itsdeductible.com. It's a great way to prove your deductions. Another excellent third-party valuation guideline can be downloaded from www.salarmychicago.org/frames/extd_your_help/donations.htm or check out bigwriteoff.com. For a vast database on charities, see www.guidestar.org.

Expert witnesses are frequently brought in during Tax Court cases to evaluate contributed property. The burden is on the individual to establish the value of the contribution.

An appraisal may be your best method to avoid an audit, especially if the property is difficult to value and a substantial contribution is involved. An added attraction is that the appraiser's fees are also deductible.

For other gifts, have the charity value the gift and send you a receipt. This will establish the proof necessary for a gift and may avoid valuation difficulties. Taking out an insurance policy reflecting the property's value might also be a useful technique for establishing the true value of the property.

Furthermore, for tax years beginning after 1982, IRS Proposed Regulation Section 1.170 A-13 (a) would require an individual taxpayer (or a corporation) making a charitable contribution of money to maintain a cancelled check, a receipt, or other reliable written evidence showing the amount of the charitable contribution, the date contributed, and the name of the donee. In the absence of a cancelled check or receipt, the reliability of the other written evidence will depend on the facts and circumstances of the particular case but, in all events, the burden would be on the taxpayer to establish reliability. Factors indicating that such other written evidence is reliable include, but are not limited to, the contemporaneous nature of the writing evidencing the contribution, the regularity of the taxpayer's recordkeeping procedures, and, in the case of the contribution of a small amount, any other written evidence from the donee charitable organization evidencing receipt of a donation that would not otherwise constitute a receipt.

For charitable contributions of property other than money for which the taxpayer claims a deduction in excess of $500, the taxpayer would be required to maintain additional records regarding the manner of acquisition of the property and the property's cost or other basis if it was held for less than one year prior to the date of contribution. For property held for one year or more preceding the date of contribution, cost or other basis information should be maintained by the taxpayer if it is available.

The Tax Reform Act of 1984 mandated the Internal Revenue Service to issue regulations, by December 31, 1984, which would impose appraisal and information reporting requirements on charitable contributions by individuals, closely held corporations, and personal service corporations. Appraisals will be required for each item with a claim value in excess of $5,000 ($10,000 for privately held stock). Similar items are to be added in determining the dollar threshold. This provision would not apply to publicly traded securities. When the rules apply, the donor must obtain a written appraisal of the property's fair market value from a qualified independent appraiser, and a summary of the appraisal must be attached to the donor's tax return.

If the donee charity sells, exchanges, or otherwise transfers donated property valued in excess of $5,000 within 2 years, the donee must furnish an information report to the IRS, with a copy to the donor. These provisions apply for contributions made after December 31, 1984.

Note that if a taxpayer contributes works of art with an aggregate value of at least $20,000, the taxpayer must attach a complete copy of the signed appraisal. In addition, an eight-by-eleven-inch color photograph, or a color transparency no smaller than four by five inches, must be submitted. For donations made after 1987, the submission of the appraisal is mandatory. It was optional for art donated before 1988.

For this purpose, the definition of art includes paintings, watercolors, prints, drawings, sculptures, ceramics, antique furniture, decorative arts, textiles, carpets, silver, rare manuscripts, historical memorabilia, and other similar objects. It does not include gems, jewelry, or books.

These requirements are intended to assist the IRS Art Advisory Panel, which is composed of art dealers, curators, museum directors, and other experts, in checking the valuation of artwork for tax purposes. An evaluation of $20,000 or more must be referred to the panel.

The Internal Revenue Service said that its Art Advisory Panel accepted just 36 percent of the taxpayer art appraisals it reviewed in 2007, a drop of 2 percent from the 38 percent acceptance rate in 2006, according to the agency's annual summary of the panel's closed-door meetings. Nearly half the artwork donated/gifted was found to be misvalued by the panel in 2010, 51 percent misvalued in 2012.

Taxpayers claimed their artwork was worth nearly $279 million for tax purposes; the panel recommended $94.5 million in adjustments across 131 cases.

The Omnibus Budget Reconciliation Act of 1993 changed the substantiation and disclosure rules for charitable contributions. Effective for years after December 31, 1993, no deduction will be allowed for a separate contribution of $250 or more unless you have written confirmation from the charity. E-mail acknowledgments by the charity are acceptable. A cancelled check alone will not be enough. If the contribution is to a religious organization solely for an intangible religious benefit, written substantiation is still required but the charity need not value that benefit. All other contributions of cash must describe the estimated fair market value of any goods or services given in exchange for that contribution. Charities, however, are not required to value noncash contributions if you, as the taxpayer, are required to obtain from the charity a receipt that describes the donated property.

Moreover, any *quid pro quo* contributions of more than $75 solicited will require the charity to tell you in writing how much is deductible; e.g., a charitable dinner ticket costing $90 for a dinner worth $60 will give you a deduction of $30.

In *Rolfs v. Commissioner of Internal Revenue* (T.C. No. 9377-04, 135 T.C. No. 24, November 4, 2010), a taxpayer donated his house to a fire department tox burn down as part of a training exercise. (See below for details.) The Court disallowed a deduction because the taxpayer received the benefits of the destruction of the house in exchange for the donation. In this case, the value of the demolition was more than the fair market value of the house. Any "quid pro quo" will kill the deduction to the extent of the benefit received.

NEW RECORD KEEPING REQUIREMENTS

As of January 1, 2007 you will need a receipt or cancelled check for all donations. For clothing and household items donated after August 17, 2006, no write off will be allowed unless an item is in good condition or better. If the value of an item is more than $500, a deduction cannot be taken without an appraisal.

An interesting technique exists for obtaining a charitable deduction before a cash outlay. This can be done by establishing an irrevocable banker's letter of credit in favor of the charity. The full amount of the letter of credit will be deductible by you in the year in which it is established, even if the charity does not draw upon the credit until the next year. The charity, however, must have the absolute right to draw down the entire amount of the letter of credit immediately. This technique could present an important planning opportunity when you can reasonably expect that the charity would not draw down the funds immediately. For example, when the letter of credit will finance a construction project, it is reasonable to expect the charity to draw down those funds over the various phases of the construction, rather than immediately.

The tax saved from a charitable donation reduces the cost of donating. As the marginal tax rates increase, the actual cost of donating decreases. The actual cost to a person in the lowest tax bracket (10 percent) for a $1 charitable deduction is 90¢. For a person in the highest tax bracket (35 percent), the actual cost is only 65¢ on the dollar.

BEWARE

Any contributions to a *nonexempt* organization will not be allowed. In *United Cancer Council v. Commissioner,* U.S. T.C., No. 2008-91X, 109 T.C. No. 17, 12/2/97, the court ruled that the charity's use of a professional fundraiser resulted in inurement of the organization's net earnings to the fundraiser and the IRS did not abuse its discretion in *retroactively revoking* the exempt status of the organization. Fortunately, this decision was reversed by the Seventh Circuit on February 10, 1999.

Beware once more: The IRS is currently focusing on "overvalued" contributions of autos. If you take the deduction, be prepared to fully substantiate the value.

AUTOS/BOATS

The American Jobs Creation Act of 2004 changed the rules for contributions of autos and boats of more than $500. Effective as of January 1, 2005, the charity receiving the donated vehicle must tell you the actual price it sold for—and your donation is limited to that amount. The charity must give you a 1099-C within 30 days of the sale. You attach it to your return. This may be far less than the Bluebook value usually deducted. If the auto is used by the charity (e.g. a car used for Meals on Wheels), then you get to deduct the full fair market value.

DON'T GET BURNED

Taxpayers who demolished their lakefront home to make way for the construction of a new home by donating it to the local fire department to conduct fire-fighter training exercises benefited from the home's destruction and cannot claim a charitable deduction, the U.S. Court of Appeals for the Seventh Circuit held February 8, 2012 (*Rolfs v. Commissioner*, 7th Cir., No. 11-2078, 2/8/12).

The value *gifted* was found to be less than the benefit received. The value *gifted* was reduced by the "must destroy" limitation.

"No one disputes that $76,000 worth of home value was lost in the fire," wrote the court. "The disagreement concerns the portion of that value, if any, that was actually transferred to the fire department as a gift. By deciding to destroy the house and then making that demolition a condition of their gift, the taxpayers themselves became responsible for that decrease in value, even if the fire department provided the mechanism to accomplish it. None of the value of the house, as a house, was actually given away."

The solution? Gift the house with no limitations.

95 Casualty Losses

A *casualty* is the damage or destruction of property resulting from an identifiable event that is sudden, unexpected, or unusual in nature. Casualty losses can be used to lower your taxes.

Deductible casualty losses may result from a number of different causes, including but not limited to:

Automobile accidents
Civil disturbances
Drought
Earthquakes
Explosions
Fires
Flood
Freezing rain
Hurricanes
Ice and snow
Lightning

Mine cave-ins
Shipwrecks
Smog
Sonic booms
Storms
Vandalism
Winds and tornadoes

A reduction in your property's value because it is in or near an area that suffered a casualty or that might again suffer a casualty is usually not deductible. A neighbor of O. J. Simpson was denied a deduction for the reduction in value of his property due to its proximity to the murder. However, in *Finkbohner, Jr.,* 86-1 USTC para. 9393, 57 AFTRO 2d 86-1400 (CA-11, 1986), a permanent decline in market value due to buyer resistance was includable in the amount of a casualty loss deduction. There, the court refused to follow the prevailing view in two other circuits that limited the deduction to actual physical loss. In the *Finkbohner* case, the taxpayers' residence was unharmed, but 7 of the 12 houses in the neighborhood had to be razed after a flood. The court ruled that the removal of most of the homes in the neighborhood was a permanent change. The diminished market value reflected more than a fear of future flooding, since the residence was above maximum flood levels. They concluded that the fair market value after the casualty would have to reflect such permanent loss of value. A loss is allowed only for the actual casualty damage to your property.

The partial or complete destruction of property must be the result of an identifiable event that is either sudden, unexpected, or unusual. For example, if your spouse, while washing the dishes, inadvertently knocks a diamond ring that you put in a glass next to the sink down the drain and activates the garbage disposal unit, thus destroying the ring, this unusual event will qualify as a deductible casualty. So, too, will the loss of a diamond ring if your spouse slams the car door on your hand. Both of the events were sudden and unusual, therefore allowing the casualty deduction. However, a loss due to the accidental breakage of articles such as glassware or china under normal conditions is not a casualty loss. Neither is a loss due to damage done by a family pet.

The event must be one that is sudden—that is, swift, not gradual or progressive. If a steadily operating cause from a normal process damages your property, it is not considered a casualty. So, for example, the steady weakening of a building due to normal wind and weather conditions will not qualify as a casualty. On the other hand, the rust and water damage to rugs and drapes caused by the bursting of a water heater will qualify—but not the deterioration and damage to the water heater itself. The IRS has ruled that a decline in the value of a house due to chinese drywall is eligible for casualty loss treatment.

If trees, shrubs, or other plants are damaged or destroyed by a fungus, disease, insects, worms, or similar pests, the loss is not deductible as a casualty loss. However, a sudden, unexpected, or unusual infestation by beetles or other insects may result in a casualty loss. If trees and shrubs are damaged by a storm, flood, or fire, the loss is also a deductible casualty loss.

Normally a loss from an accident to your car is deductible. This is not true, though, if your willful negligence or willful act causes the accident, or if it is caused by the willful act or willful negligence of someone acting for you.

If you do have an accident, you must file a claim with your insurance company. If you do not file the claim, you will not be entitled to a casualty loss deduction for the damage done to your car. Casualty loss deductions are allowed only for losses not compensated for by insurance or otherwise. But "not compensated for" doesn't just mean actual payment. When a collectible insurance claim *can* be filed, a deliberate election not to file will not give rise to a casualty loss deduction. Your loss can be "compensated for."

Yet in a 1981 case the Tax Court allowed a theft loss deduction despite a refusal to make an insurance claim predicated on a fear of increased premiums.* The court concluded that *compensated* did not mean *covered* and that since no *compensation* was received, a deduction could be allowed. This ruling was confirmed in the case of *Dixon F. Miller v. Commissioner* on May 2, 1984; the Sixth Circuit joined the Eleventh Circuit and the Tax Court in taking the above position. The Tax Reform Act of 1986, however, imposed a new precondition on the allowance of casualty losses. Any loss that is covered by insurance is taken into account only if the taxpayer files a timely insurance claim. This new limitation applies only to the extent that the insurance policy would have provided reimbursement if a claim had been filed (IRC § 165[a][4][i]).

For example, if you sustain $800 worth of damage for an insured loss with a $500 deductible, if no claim is made $300 of your loss will not be allowable as a deduction. The $500 balance will count as a loss, subject to the $100 and 10 percent adjusted gross income floors.

You should deduct your casualty loss in the year of occurrence. This timing rule is modified, though, when insurance enters the picture. In such a case, the loss deduction is limited to the part of the damage that is not reimbursed that year. If you deduct a casualty in the year of occurrence and receive insurance reimbursement in a later year, you should not amend the earlier return. Instead, the portion of the reimbursement that exceeds the original estimate of recovery should be taken back into income in the later year.

---

*H.L. Hills, 76 T.C. No. 42.

For example, you suffered a $6,000 deductible loss in 2012 and estimated an insurance recovery of $5,000, and you took a $1,000 casualty loss deduction in that year. In 2013, however, your insurance company pays the full $6,000. What you must do on your 2013 return is include the extra $1,000 as income. Note, though, that you must have received a tax benefit for the casualty loss in 2012. If you did not itemize your deductions in that year, you received no benefit and therefore have no additional taxable income when the insurance company repays the full $6,000 in 2013.

The amount of loss from a casualty that can be deducted is generally the lesser of the following two amounts:

a) the decrease in the fair market value of the property as a result of the casualty; *or*

b) your basis in the property before the casualty.

In the case of business property, if the fair market value of the property immediately before the casualty is less than the adjusted basis, the amount of the adjusted basis is deemed to be the amount of the loss. Alternatively, the loss may be measured by the cost of repairing the damage. In a case of nonbusiness (or personal use) property, the deduction is the amount by which the casualty loss exceeds 10 percent of your adjusted gross income plus $100.

The fair market value must be based on a valid judgment of the selling price of the property at the time of the casualty. An appraisal is the best way to do this. The appraisal should be made by an experienced and reliable appraiser. Several factors are important in evaluating the accuracy of the appraisal:

- The appraiser's familiarity with your property before the casualty

- Sales of comparable properties

- Conditions in the area of the casualty

- The method used in making the appraisal

When available, photographs should be used in making the appraisal and in determining the extent of damage from a casualty. The costs of photographs obtained for this purpose are not a part of the loss but can be taken as a miscellaneous deduction. They are an expense of determining your tax liability. Furthermore, you may deduct as a miscellaneous deduction the amount you must pay for the appraisal itself, since it also is an expense of determining your tax liability.

The cost of cleaning up or making repairs after a casualty may be used as a measure of the decrease in fair market value if:

a) the repairs are necessary to restore the property to its condition before the casualty;

b) the amount spent for repairs is not excessive;

c) the repairs do no more than take care of the damage;

d) the value of the property after the repairs is not, as a result of the repairs, more than the value of the property before the casualty.

The cost of restoring landscaping to its original condition may also be taken as an indication of the decrease in fair market value. You may be able to measure your loss by what is spent on the following:

- Removing destroyed or damaged trees and shrubs, minus any salvage you receive

- Pruning and other measures taken to preserve damaged trees and shrubs

- Replanting that is necessary to restore the property to its approximate value before the casualty

The incidental expenses you have due to a casualty, such as expenses for the treatment of personal injuries, for temporary housing, or for a rental car, are not deductible as casualty losses. Moreover, the cost of protecting your property against a potential casualty is not deductible. For example, you cannot deduct what you spend on insurance or to board up your house against a storm. Expenses like these are only deductible by businesses as business expenses. If you make a permanent improvement to your property to protect it against a casualty, the cost should be added to your basis in the property. An example would be the cost of a dike to prevent flooding.

96 Theft Losses

A *theft* is the unlawful and intentional removal of money or property from its rightful owner. It includes, but is not limited to, larceny, robbery, and embezzlement. If money or property is taken as the result of extortion, kidnapping for ransom, or blackmail, it may also be a theft. The simple disappearance of money or property does not constitute a theft. However, an accidental loss or disappearance of property may qualify as a casualty if it results from an identifiable event that is sudden, unexpected, or unusual in nature. The lost diamond ring in the example given in the previous section constitutes such a deductible casualty.

The amount of loss from a theft that can be deducted is generally the lesser of the following two amounts:

a) the decrease in the fair market value of the property as a result of the theft, *or*

b) your basis in the property before the theft.

The fair market value of property immediately after a theft is considered to be zero. That is, a theft loss deduction is either the full fair market value of the stolen property or its basis, whichever is less. If you get your stolen property back, however, your loss is measured like a casualty loss from vandalism. You must consider the actual fair market value of the property when you get it back in order to compute your loss.

The decrease in the fair market value must be based on a judgment of the actual price you could have asked if your property had been sold. Sentimental value is not a factor in determining the amount of the loss. Any loss from the theft of a family portrait, heirloom, or keepsake must be based on its actual market value apart from any sentiment. An appraisal is the best way to make this judgment. This appraisal must recognize the effect of any general market decline that may occur so that any deduction is limited to the actual loss resulting from deprivation of the property. See the preceding section on casualty losses for more information on appraisals.

The cost of any theft-preventive equipment, such as burglar alarm systems or theft insurance, is not deductible. If a protective device increases the value of your property, however, the cost may be added to your basis.

Investors *cannot* deduct the decline in the value of their stock portfolio as a theft loss, even if due to corporate misconduct (IRS Notice 2204-27). You get the deduction when you sell.

MADOFF DEDUCTION

If you suffered losses as a result of the Bernard L. Madoff "Ponzi" scheme, they are allowable as "investment" theft and are not subject to either the 10 percent or $100/$500 reductions (see below).

DEDUCTION LIMITS

The limits and computations for determining both casualty and theft loss deductions are very similar, so they are now grouped together for ease of discussion.

After you have figured the amount of your casualty or theft loss, you must figure how much of the loss you can deduct. There are three ways that you may adjust the casualty or theft loss before you can deduct it:

1. If you receive insurance or another type of reimbursement for your loss, you must subtract the reimbursement from the amount of the loss before you

figure your deduction. As noted above, if you expect to get a reimbursement but have not yet received payment, you must still subtract the expected reimbursement from the loss. In a business situation, though, the cost of repairs made for business purposes *is* deductible, even if insurance recovery later is likely. The amount of the final recovery that is attributable to previously deductible items will be taxable in the later year.*

2. If the stolen, destroyed, or damaged property was for your own or your family's personal use, you must reduce each loss by an additional $100,† because the first $100 of a casualty or theft loss on personal use property is not deductible. However, if you used the stolen, destroyed, or damaged property in your business or for investment purposes, this $100 limit does not apply.

3. For nonbusiness losses, you must reduce the *total* amount of the losses by 10 percent of your adjusted gross income. This is done after the $100 reduction in adjustment 2 above and after any reimbursement from insurance. Note that under the Tax Reform Act of 1984, for purposes of computing the 10 percent floor, the casualty loss deduction (adjusted gross income) is determined without regard to the application of Section 1231 to gains or losses from involuntary conversions arising from a casualty or theft. Gains and losses from these personal casualties (without regard to the period the property was held) will be netted. If the recognized gains exceed the recognized losses from these transactions, then all such gains and losses will be treated as gains and losses from the sale or exchange of a capital asset, and the losses will not be subject to the 10 percent floor. (The amount of any recognized loss will be subject to the $100 floor before netting.) If the recognized losses exceed the recognized gains, all gains and losses will be ordinary. Losses to the extent of gains will be allowed in full. Losses in excess of gains will be subject to the 10 percent adjusted gross income floor.

For example, assume you have $100,000 of adjusted gross income without regard to casualty gains and losses, $50,000 of such casualty gains, and $40,000 of such casualty losses (after applying the $100 floor) for a taxable year. All your personal casualty gains and losses for that year will be treated as capital gains and losses. The 10 percent floor will not be applicable. Assume, however, that your losses for the year are $70,000 rather than $40,000. The gains and losses will all be treated as ordinary. $60,000 of losses will be allowed as a deduction [$50,000 plus the $10,000 excess of the remaining $20,000 over the $10,000 (10 percent of $100,000) adjusted gross income floor].

---

*R.R. Hensler, Inc. v. Commissioner, T.C. 317 (1979).
†For 2009 casualty losses *only*, the $100 floor increased to $500.

If an insurance company reimburses you for any of your living expenses after you lose the use of your home because of a casualty, the insurance payments are not considered a reimbursement reducing your casualty loss. Any part of these payments that covers normal living expenses that you and your family would have during this period anyway must be reported as income on your tax return, but any insurance payments that cover a temporary increase in your living expenses should *not* be reported as income. The same rule applies if you are denied access to your home by government authorities due to the threat of a casualty. Generally, the amount you do not have to report is the amount of your extra expenses for renting suitable housing and for transportation, food, utilities, and miscellaneous services during the period you are unable to use your home because of the casualty.

For example, assume that as a result of a fire you vacated your apartment and moved to a motel. You normally pay $200 a month rent, but none was charged for the month the apartment was vacated. Your motel rent for this month was $275, but you received only $240 in reimbursement for rental expenses from your insurance company. Part of that reimbursement, $75, covers the difference between your actual rent and your normal rent. You do not have to report this amount as income, but the balance of the reimbursement, $165, must be reported as income.

As mentioned, the first $100 of a casualty or theft loss of personal use property is not deductible. This limit applies *after* all reimbursements have been subtracted. Furthermore, a single $100 limit applies to each individual casualty or theft, no matter how many pieces of property are involved. Generally, events closely related in origin are considered a single casualty or theft, as when your summer home suffers wind damage and flood damage caused by a hurricane. A single casualty may also damage two or more widely separate pieces of property.

Remember, though, that the $100 exclusion does not apply if the loss is on business property, property that earns you rent or royalty income, or other investment property. Furthermore, if a husband and wife each sustain a loss from the same casualty or theft and they file a joint return, only one $100 limit applies. It does not matter whether the property involved is jointly or separately owned. If they file separate returns, however, each is subject to a separate $100 limit for the loss, regardless of whether the property is jointly or separately owned. A husband and wife who file separate returns and have a casualty loss on property they own together may deduct one-half of the loss on each return, or either spouse may claim the entire deduction on a separate return.

COMPUTING THE DEDUCTION

The way to figure a deduction for a casualty or theft loss depends upon the kind of property involved. The rules for personal use property are different from those for business and investment property. The rules for real estate property, such as a house, differ from those for personal property, such as a car or furniture.

In figuring a loss to real estate property that you own for personal use, all improvements, such as buildings and ornamental trees, are considered together. A single loss is figured for the entire property. The amount of the loss is either the decrease in fair market value of the entire property or its adjusted basis, whichever is less. From this amount you must subtract any insurance or other reimbursement you receive or expect to receive. The amount remaining that is more than $100 is your personal casualty loss deduction.

As an example, assume that several years ago you bought a house that you then lived in as your home. You paid $5,000 for the land and $20,000 for the house itself; you also paid $1,000 for landscaping. This year, when your adjusted gross income was $10,000, your home was totally destroyed by fire. Competent appraisers said that before the fire the property as a whole had a fair market value of $36,000 but that its value after the fire was only $6,000. Shortly after the fire, the insurance company paid you $20,000 for the loss. Your casualty loss deduction is figured as follows:

Value of entire property before fire	$36,000
Minus value of entire property after fire	– 6,000
Decrease in value of entire property	$30,000
Basis (cost for entire property)	$26,000
Casualty loss (in this case basis)	$26,000
Minus insurance reimbursement	–20,000
Casualty loss before the $100 limit	6,000
Minus: $100 nondeductible amount	– 100
10% of adjusted gross income	– 1,000
Casualty Loss Deduction	$ 4,900

Personal property is generally any property that is not real estate. If your personal property is stolen or is damaged or destroyed by a casualty, you must figure your loss separately for each individual item of property.

For example, assume a fire in your home damaged an upholstered chair and completely destroyed a rug and an antique table. You do not have fire insurance to cover your loss. The chair cost you $150, and you establish that it had a fair market value of $75 just before the fire and $10 just after the fire. The rug cost you $200 and had a value of $50 just before the fire. You bought the table at an auction for $15 before discovering it was a valuable antique. It was appraised at $350 before the fire.

The loss on the chair is limited to the difference in fair market value before and after the fire, or $65, since that decrease is less than its basis ($150). The loss on the rug is limited to its value of $50 just before the fire, because this amount is also less than its basis ($200). The table, on the other hand, had a value just before the fire that was greater than your basis in it. Your loss on the table, therefore, is its basis, $15. Your total loss from the fire is $130, and after subtracting the $100 limit, your deduction is $30 before the reduction for 10 percent of your adjusted gross income.

When a casualty involves both real and personal property, a single $100 limit applies to the total loss, but you must figure the amount of the loss separately for each type of property, as discussed above. Remember, a loss on business property, property that earns you rent or royalty income, or other investment property is *not* subject to the $100 limit. For business and investment property, you must figure your loss separately for each item that is stolen, damaged, or destroyed. If casualty damage occurs to a building and to trees on the same piece of property, the loss is measured separately for each.

If you have business or investment property that is completely lost because of a casualty or theft, your deductible is your basis in the property minus any salvage value and minus any insurance or other reimbursement that you receive or expect to receive. For example, suppose you owned a building that you rented out, and your basis in it, not including land, was $20,000 before it was completely destroyed by fire. Its fair market value just before the fire was only $15,000.

Since this was investment property and since it was completely destroyed, the deduction is your basis in the building, $20,000, decreased by salvage value and by any insurance or other reimbursement. Fair market value is not considered when figuring your loss, even though it is less than your basis in the building.

If business or investment property is damaged but not completely destroyed in a casualty, the loss is the decrease in value because of the casualty, or your basis in the property, whichever is less. From this amount you must subtract any insurance or other reimbursements you receive or expect to receive.

After you take a casualty or theft loss deduction, you must subtract from your basis in the damaged, destroyed, or stolen property the amount of your deduction and the amount of any reimbursement you receive. The result is a new, lower total for your basis in the property. In some cases, this lower basis will carry over to any property you get to replace the property that is stolen or destroyed.

PROOF OF LOSS

To take a deduction for casualty or theft loss, you must be able to show that there was actually a casualty or theft, and you must be able to support the amount you take as a deduction. For a casualty loss, you should be able to show:

a) the nature of the casualty and when it occurred;

b) that the loss was a direct result of the casualty; *and*

c) that you were the owner of the property; or, if you leased the property from someone else, that you were contractually liable to the owner for the damage.

For a theft, you should be able to show:

a) the date on which you found that the property was missing;

b) that your property *was* stolen; *and*

c) that you were the owner of the property.

To qualify for a theft loss deduction, the taking of your property must be illegal under the laws of the state where it occurred. If a theft loss is not reported promptly to the police, you must offer as a substitute the testimony of anyone who witnessed the event or its aftermath. If records were burglarized, steps must be taken to reconstruct the records by gathering substitutes.

Proof of the amount of a theft loss is difficult in the case of cash, where there is little likelihood that there is any documentation of how much you had on your person or in your home. Deductions will be allowed in full when you have evidence of why you had such a large amount of money with you. One theft loss deduction was allowed because the records showed that the victim was on his way to complete the closing on the acquisition of a house.

You do not have to be virgin-pure to qualify for a theft loss deduction. Even if you were naive or greedy and that naïveté or greed resulted in your being the victim of a theft, you may still receive a deduction for that theft. "Indeed," according to one court, "gullibility or cupidity of the victim is often a crucial factor that enables the swindler to succeed in his fraud."*

For both casualty losses and theft losses you must be able to give evidence supporting the amount you deduct. You should have supporting evidence in the following three areas:

1. *Basis.* The purchase contract or deed can show your original basis (its cost) in real estate. Improvements to the property that increase basis should be supported by checks, receipts, and similar items.

2. *Decrease in Fair Market Value.* Appraisals should be used where possible. Photographs of your property before it was damaged or stolen will be helpful in showing its condition and value before the casualty or theft. Photographs taken

---

Perry A. Nichols et al., T.C. 842 (1965).

after a casualty will be helpful in establishing the condition and value of the property after it was damaged. Photographs showing the condition of the property after it was repaired, restored, or replaced may also be helpful.

3. *Insurance and Other Types of Reimbursement.* Keep records of all you receive or expect to receive.

PLANNING CONSIDERATIONS

Ordinarily, a casualty loss is deductible in the year the event took place. However, the tax code permits a special election to take "disaster area" loss deductions in the year prior to occurrence. To qualify, the President must declare the region a "disaster area" eligible for federal relief under the Disaster Relief Act of 1964. Go to www.fema.gov to see if your area qualifies. Once this is done you can make an irrevocable election to treat the entire disaster loss as having occurred in the prior tax year. This allows you to get an immediate tax benefit for the loss rather than forcing you to wait until the subsequent year to claim it.

For example, assume you suffered a casualty loss in 2013. In order to get the tax benefit for that loss, it would have to be claimed as a deduction from your 2013 taxes, payable in April 2014. But if you elected and qualified for the optional disaster relief provision, you could take the disaster loss deduction on your 2012 return, by filing an amended 2012 return. Alternatively, if your income increased in 2013 and put you in a higher bracket, you could decline to make the election and take the higher valued deduction on your 2013 return.

If you were in a federally declared disaster area, for 2009 nonitemizers could have added their casualty losses to Schedule L as an increase in their standard deduction. Those who itemized could have claimed the deduction without the 10 percent adjusted gross income reduction in Schedule A.

As explained above, expenses to prevent a casualty are not normally deductible as casualty losses. Such expenditures are likely to involve the acquisition of property with an estimated useful life of more than one year. But a tax deduction *can* be claimed if the preventive measures do not add to the value of the property. In one case a plant had sustained cave-ins under its flooring, and further trouble of the same sort was anticipated. The drilling and grouting undertaken to forestall this was a deductible business expense. In another case, an individual used temporary dikes to protect his personal residence as well as his business property from flooding. The dikes were constructed of earth and sand bags and were removed immediately after the floodwater receded. While the cost of constructing and removing the temporary dikes was not allowed as a casualty loss with respect to either the business or the nonbusiness property, the cost of constructing and removing the dikes to protect business property was deductible as an ordinary and necessary business expense. In a third case, an expense that had been incurred to prevent an accident—and *was* held to be a different kind of deduction—was the cost of a vasectomy! The moral here is simple: What you may think of only in terms of a casualty loss expense may qualify as a deduction under a noncasualty classification—for example, as an ordinary and necessary business expense or as a medical expense.

97 Miscellaneous Trade and Business Deductions of Employees

Prior to the Tax Reform Act of 1986, if you were an employee who had travel, entertainment, or gift expenses in connection with your employment, you would be entitled to deduct the amounts you spent in those areas as above the line deductions. For years after December 31, 1986, all trade and business deductions of employees must be taken as miscellaneous itemized deductions. As of January 1, 1987, miscellaneous itemized deductions have been allowable only to the extent that they exceed 2 percent of your adjusted gross income.

This 2 percent floor does not apply to impairment-related work expenses for handicapped employees; to gambling losses to the extent of gambling winnings; and to certain actors who are allowed to report their income and expenses from acting as if they were independent contractors, if they had two or more employers in the acting profession during the tax year, and if the expenses relating to their acting profession exceeded 10 percent of their gross income and their adjusted gross income (before deducting expenses related to acting) did not exceed $16,000. The 2 percent floor does apply to investment advisor fees for trusts and, in Private Ruling 9316003, the IRS ruled that a partner may deduct in full (not subject to the 2 percent rule) any expenses that a partnership agreement requires him to pay.

98 Job Loss Insurance

Premiums paid by employees on job loss insurance policies can be written off as employee business expenses to the extent the cost and other miscellaneous expenses exceed 2 per cent of adjusted gross income. If the employer pays for the coverage, the premiums are a tax-free working-condition fringe benefit. No matter who pays the premiums, benefits are subject to the income tax but not employment taxes.

99 Travel Expenses

If you are an employee, you may deduct as miscellaneous itemized deductions all the ordinary and necessary travel expenses, in excess of reimbursements, that you have in connection with your work.

"Ordinary and necessary" has been translated as "reasonable and customary." Travel expenses are those expenses incurred in traveling away from home for your business, profession, or job. Your tax home, for travel expense purposes, is your principal place of business or employment or your station or post of duty, regardless of where you maintain your family residence. The entire city or general area in which your business or work is located is your tax home.

For example, assume you live with your family in Chicago, but work in Milwaukee. You stay in a Milwaukee hotel and eat in a restaurant during the week and return to Chicago every weekend. You may not deduct any of your expenses for traveling back and forth, or for your meals and lodging in Milwaukee, because Milwaukee is your tax home and the travel over the weekends is not for a business reason.

If you regularly work in two or more separate areas, your principal tax home is the general area where your principal work or business is located. The main factors in determining your principal place of business or work are:

a) the total time ordinarily spent in performing your duties in each area;

b) the degree of your business activity in each area; *and*

c) the relative amount of your income from each area. (See *Bowles,* 85-1 USTC Para. 9244, 55 AFTR 2d, 85-1113 [DC Va. 1984], in which the place of the taxpayers' minor business in terms of income was held to be their tax home, since that was where they spent the majority of their time and effort.)

For example, assume you live in Miami where you have a seasonal job for 8 months and earn $15,000, and you work the remaining 4 months in Cincinnati, also at a seasonal job, and earn $4,000. Miami is your principal place of work because you spend most of your time there and earn most of your income there.

You are considered "away from home" when you are on a *temporary* (rather than indefinite or permanent) job that takes you away from your regular or principal place of business. Temporary employment must be temporary in contemplation, and its termination must be foreseeable at the time of acceptance. (See Rev. Rul. 60-189, 1960-1 C.B. 60, Rev. Rul. 60-314, 1960-2 C.B. 48, and *Flowers,* 326 US 465 [S. Ct., 1946].)

In Rev. Rul. 83-82 the Internal Revenue Service stated that employment is temporary "only if its termination can be foreseen within a reasonably short period of time." Where a taxpayer anticipates employment to last for less than 1 year its status will be determined on the basis of the facts and circumstances. Where the taxpayer anticipates employment of 1 year or more, but less than 2 years, and it in fact falls within this range, there is a rebuttable presumption that the employment is "indefinite." An expected or actual stay of 2 years or longer is considered "indefinite" regardless of other facts and circumstances.

To rebut the 1- to 2-year presumption you must (1) clearly demonstrate by objective factors that you realistically expected that the employment in question would last less than 2 years and that you could then return to your claimed tax home, and (2) show that the claimed tax home is your regular place of abode in a real and substantial sense.

The following three factors may be used to determine if point (2) is met: (1) whether you have used the claimed abode as lodging while working in that vicinity immediately before the claimed temporary employment and you continue to maintain work contacts there; (2) whether your living expenses at the claimed abode are duplicated because of your work away from such abode; and (3) whether you (a) have a family member or members (marital or lineal only) currently residing at the claimed abode or (b) continue to currently use the claimed abode frequently for lodging.

If you satisfy the expectation test and all three of the abode tests the IRS will deem the work assignment temporary. If only two of the three abode tests are met, then all the facts and circumstances will be subject to close scrutiny to determine if the assignment is temporary or indefinite. If only one of the abode tests is met the IRS will regard the assignment as indefinite.

These rules were modified in Notice 93-29, where the IRS ruled that travel expenses paid or incurred in 1993 while away from home for a period or more than *1 year* in pursuit of a trade or business will be *non*deductible even if such period began in 1992. This Notice, pursuant to the Energy Policy Act of 1992, now even more clearly defines the difference between temporary and indefinite. (See also Rev. Rul. 93-86.)

But, in *Senulis*, TC Summ. Op. 2009–97, the court ruled that because a worker reasonably expected that a job's duration would be less than 1 year when he took it, his living expenses (meals, lodging, and travel) were deductible even though the job actually lasted 13 months!

You may also be considered as *traveling* away from home when you work in the same city in which you and your family live. Suppose your family residence is in Pittsburgh, where you work for 12 weeks a year. The remainder of the time you work for the same employer in Baltimore, where you eat in restaurants and sleep at a rooming house. Your salary is the same whether you are in Pittsburgh or Baltimore. Since you spend most of your working time and earn most of your salary in Baltimore, that city is your tax home and you may not deduct any expenses incurred for meals and lodging there. However, when you go to work in Pittsburgh, you are away from your tax home even though you stay at your family home. Therefore, you may deduct the cost of your round trip between Baltimore and Pittsburgh and that part of your family living expenses for meals due to your living in Pittsburgh while working there.

Deductible travel expenses include the following:

Air, rail, and bus fares

Operation and maintenance of your automobile

Taxi fares or other costs of transportation between the airport or station and your hotel, from one customer to another, or from one place of business to another

Transportation from the place where you eat and sleep to your temporary work assignment

Baggage charges and transportation costs for sample and display material

Meals (limited to 50 percent of cost) and lodging when you are away from home on business

Cleaning and laundry expenses

Telephone and telegraph expenses

Public stenographer's fees

Operation and maintenance of house trailers

Tips that are incidental to any of these expenses

Similar expenses incident to qualifying travel

You are considered traveling away from home if your duties require you to be away from the general area of your tax home for a period substantially longer than an ordinary day's work. It is not necessary, however, to work the full time. It is reasonable for you to need and to get some sleep or rest to meet the demands of your work or business. This does *not* mean napping in your car to make sure you qualify for the full period. You need not be away from your tax home for an entire 24 hours or from dusk to dawn so long as your relief from duty (rest period) while you are traveling constitutes a sufficient period of time in which to get necessary sleep or rest.

For example, assume you are a railroad conductor and you leave your home terminal on a regularly scheduled round trip between two cities, returning home 16 hours later. During the run you are released for 6 hours at your turnaround point, where you eat two meals and rent a hotel room to get necessary rest before starting the return trip. You are considered to be away from home for tax travel purposes and may deduct the expenses you incur.

Alternatively, assume you are a truck driver. You leave your terminal and return later the same day. You are released at your turnaround point for 1 hour in order to eat. Since you are not released to obtain necessary sleep and the brief interval of release does not constitute an adequate rest period, you are not away from home.

Here again the opportunity for sophisticated tax planning presents itself. You may deduct all those travel expenses you incur in attending a convention if you can show that your attendance benefits or advances the interest of your own work or business, as distinguished from the business or work of another. If the convention is for political, social, or other purposes unrelated to your business or work, the expenses are not deductible. But the agenda of the convention need not deal specifically with your official duties. It is sufficient if the agenda is related to your duties and responsibilities in such a way that attendance for a business purpose is indicated.

Regardless of whether the primary purpose of your trip is business or pleasure, all expenses incurred at your destination that are properly attributable to your trade or business are deductible. So if you make a trip primarily for business and, while there, you extend your stay for nonbusiness reasons, make a nonbusiness side trip, or engage in other nonbusiness activities, the travel expenses to and from your destination are still deductible. Furthermore, you may even deduct the expenses you paid or incurred in attending *foreign* conventions in a tax year. Here, however, the allowable expenses of attending the foreign convention must be extensively substantiated: You must make a schedule for the part of the total days of the trip devoted to business-related activities and even the number of hours of business activity you attend each day, which will limit the deduction.

No deductions are allowed for any travel expenses, including meals and lodging while away from home, for any expenses generally considered entertainment, amusement, or recreation expenses, including expenses for facilities used in connection with such activities, or for any gift expenses, unless you substantiate certain elements.

For *travel* you must prove *all* of the following elements:

- The amount of each separate expenditure for travel away from home, such as the cost of your transportation or lodging. The daily cost of your breakfast, lunch, and dinner and any incidental elements of such travel may be totaled if they are listed in reasonable categories, such as meals, gasoline and oil, and taxi fares.

- The dates of your departure and return for each trip, and the number of days spent on business away from home.

- The destination or locality of your travel, described by name of city, town, or similar designation.

- The business reason for your travel or the business benefit derived or expected from your travel.

Furthermore, an *employee* who receives reimbursement from an employer for travel expenses is excused from the normal recordkeeping and substantiation requirements if the standard reimbursement and allowance rules are satisfied. Under these rules, reimbursement for actual subsistence or travel away from home—lodgings, meals, and incidentals—(exclusive of transportation to and from the destination) is limited to an amount based on your locality or the maximum per diem rate for U.S. government employees in the locality in which travel is performed. If you elect to use the optional allowance, it must be used in computing the deduction for *all* meal expenses for the year (Rev. Proc. 83-71, 1983-39 I.R.B. 19). (See Rev. Proc. 93-21, Publication 1542, Rev. Proc. 93-50, Rev. Proc. 94-77, Rev. Proc. 96-28, Rev. Proc. 96-64, Rev. Proc. 97-59, Rev. Proc. 98-64, Rev. Proc. 2000-9, Rev. Proc. 2001-47, and Rev. Proc. 2002-63.) These rates will be updated every October 1st, and you can get the latest rates at www.policyworks.gov/perdiem, or you could order a copy of Pub. 1542 from the IRS at 1-800-829-3636. The IRS updates its rates on www.irs.gov/pub/irs-pdf/p1542, or for rates outside the continental United States, including Alaska, Hawaii, Puerto Rico, and foreign countries, see www.state.gov/m/a/als/prdm/2013.

If you are *self-employed,* you can use the per diems *only* for meals. You must substantiate lodging separately.

The Tax Reform Act of 1986 further limited deductions for luxury water travel. Luxury water travel consists of travel by ocean liner, cruise ship, or other form of luxury water transportation. This rule applies, for example, in the case of a taxpayer who has business reasons for traveling from New York City to London and who travels by ocean liner. The deduction allowable for luxury water travel cannot exceed twice the highest amount generally allowable with respect to a day of travel for employees of the executive branch of the federal government while away from home but serving the United States, multiplied by the number of days the taxpayer was engaged in luxury water travel. For example, if during a particular taxable year the applicable federal per diem amount is $75, a taxpayer's deduction for a 6-day trip cannot exceed $900 ($150 per day times 6 days). The applicable per diem amount generally is the highest travel amount applying for an area in the conterminous United States.

Moreover, after the 1986 Reform Act, no deduction is allowed for travel as a form of education. This rule applies when a travel deduction would be allowable only on the ground that the travel itself serves an educational purpose (for example, in the case of a teacher of French who travels to France in order to maintain general familiarity with the French language and culture). This disallowance does not apply, however, when a deduction is claimed with respect to travel that is a necessary adjunct to engaging in an activity that gives rise to a business deduction relating to education. (For example, when a scholar of French literature travels to Paris to do specific library research that cannot be done elsewhere or to take courses that are offered only at the Sorbonne.)

The Tax Reform Act of 1986 also amended the rules on charitable travel. As of January 1, 1987, no deduction will be allowed for transportation and other travel expenses incurred in performing services away from home for a charitable organization (whether paid directly by the individual or indirectly through a contribution to the organization) unless there is no significant element of personal pleasure, recreation, or vacation in the travel away from home.

The Tax Reform Act of 1986 also provided that travel and other costs of attending a convention or seminar for investment purposes (i.e., not for trade or business purposes) are not deductible.

All of the foregoing provisions of the Tax Reform Act of 1986 are applicable for tax years beginning after December 31, 1986.

Note, in addition, that the IRS has ruled in Doc. 9237014 that a deduction *would be allowed* for Saturday travel expenses incurred to take advantage of reduced air fares.

100 Transportation Expenses

Transportation expenses, which must be differentiated from *travel* expenses, sometimes can be deducted. Transportation expenses include the cost of traveling by air, rail, bus, taxi, etc., and the cost of operating and maintaining your car, but *not* the cost of meals and lodging.

Commuting expenses, those expenses incurred between your principal or regular place of work and your home, are not part of deductible transportation expenses. This is true regardless of the distance between your home and your regular place of work or of whether you are employed at different locations on different days within the same city or general area. If you work at two places in a day, however, whether or not for the same employer, you may deduct the expense of getting from one to the other. These expenses are part of your allowable transportation deduction. Furthermore, if you have a temporary or minor assignment beyond the general area of your tax home and return home each evening, you can deduct the expenses of the daily round-trip transportation.

If you use your car in your work, and you use it exclusively for that purpose, you may deduct the entire cost of its operation. Included among the deductible items are the cost of gas, oil, repairs, insurance, depreciation, interest to buy the car, taxes, licenses, garage rents, parking fees, tolls, etc.

If you use your car for both personal and business purposes, you must divide your expenses between business and personal use. For example, if you drive your car 20,000 miles during the year, 8,000 for business and 12,000 for personal use, only 40 percent (8,000 ÷ 20,000) of the cost of operating your car may be claimed as a work expense.

Furthermore, if you lease a car that you use in your business, you may deduct any lease payments that are for your business. You may not deduct any part of the lease payments for commuting or other personal use of the car, and any advance payments must be apportioned over the entire lease period. In addition, you may not deduct any payments you make toward the purchase of a car even if the payments are lease payments. They must be capitalized and recovered through a deduction for depreciation.

Instead of deducting your actual itemized automobile transportation costs, you may deduct a standard mileage rate. You must:

a) own the car;

b) not use the car for hire, for example, as a taxi (prior to 2011 only);

c) not operate a fleet of cars, using more than four at the same time;*

d) not have claimed depreciation using any method other than the straight-line method (equal depreciation over the life of the asset); *and*

e) not have claimed additional first-year depreciation on the car.

Standard Mileage Rates, 2002–2013

2002	36.5¢
2003	36.0¢
2004	37.5¢
2005	40.5¢/48.5¢ (after Sept. 1)
2006	44.5¢
2007	48.5¢
2008	50.5¢/58.5¢ (after July 1)
2009	55.0¢
2010	50.0¢
2011	51.0¢/55.5¢ (after July 1)
2012	55.5¢
2013	56.5¢

*Prior to Rev. Proc. 2003-76, the rule was more than one.

In addition to the standard mileage rate, you can also deduct any tolls, interest, taxes, and parking fees paid. Of the standard rate for 2013, 23¢ a mile constitutes an allowance for depreciation, reducing your basis in the car (Notice 2012-72).

In *Wicker* (TCM 1986-1), a nurse-anesthetist maintained an automobile for travel between her office in the cellar of her home and the hospital where she performed anesthesia services. Although she served as head of the Department of Anesthesiology, no office space was provided to her at the hospital. She practiced exclusively at the hospital. The court found that her home office was her principal place of business and that her travel between her home office and the hospital was, therefore, business travel, rather than commuting. The expenses incurred in such travel were deductible.

If you are reimbursed or receive an allowance for your car expenses, you may use the standard mileage rate to determine the cost of operating your car. However, only the cost so figured that is more than your reimbursement or allowance may be deducted.

If you and your spouse have separate cars, *each* one of you can compute the deduction by claiming 55.5¢ per mile (Rev. Proc. 89-66). You can use the optional mileage rate even if you do not own the vehicle (Section 1.274(d) IT).

Moreover, the Internal Revenue Service has stated that depreciation will be considered to have been allowed for standard mileage property at the following rates per mile:

1980–1981	7.0¢
1982	7.5¢
1983–1985	8.0¢
1986	9.0¢
1987	10.0¢
1988	10.5¢
1989–1991	11.0¢
1992–1993	11.5¢
1994–1999	12.0¢
2000	14.0¢
2001–2002	15.0¢
2003–2004	16.0¢
2005–2006	17.0¢
2007	19.0¢

2008–2009	21.0¢
2010	23.0¢
2011	22.0¢
2012–2013	23.0¢

This per mile rate, according to the IRS, will be the "depreciation" used to adjust the basis of standard mileage property (see Rev. Rul. Proc. 85-49 and 87-49).

Most important, a car you acquire will qualify for the depreciation expense if it is used in your work or business. The deduction for transportation expenses may in effect reduce your net cash outlay for a new car to less than half its cost!

For example, assume you are in the 35 percent bracket and you bought a $12,000 car in 2013 that you used 100 percent for business. You elected to expense and depreciate the first $3,060 of the car's cost. You elected 5-year class recovery life for the car. If you ran the car 30,000 miles in its first year, your net cost for the acquisition of the car can be reduced to almost half of its cost as follows:

Cost of car		$12,000
Minus 2013 election to expense and depreciation		
$3,060 × .35		–1,071
Net cost of car		$10,929
Minus expenses:		
30,000 miles @ 15 mpg =		
2,000 gallons @ $3.75/gal	$7,500	
Repairs, oil, and upkeep	900	
Insurance	1,210	
Garage rent, license, & registration	750	
Tolls, parking, interest on auto loan, etc. ($6/day)	2,190	
Total expense	$12,550	
Tax saving ($12,250 × .35)		–4,288
Final Net Cost ($10,929 – $4,288)		$6,641

Let's still assume that you are in the 35 percent bracket. Let's see what would happen if you run the car only 60,000 miles over the first 5 years. Employing the appropriate tax-saving strategy above, your net cost would be zero!

Cost of car		$12,000
Minus: election to expense		
and depreciation ($12,000 × .35)		−4,200
Net cost of car (end of fifth year)		$7,800
Minus expenses:		
60,000 miles @ 15 mpg =		
4,000 gallons @ $3.75/gal	$15,000	
Repairs, oil, and upkeep	3,285	
Insurance	6,050	
Garage rent, licenses, and registrations	3,750	
Tolls, parking, interest on auto loan		
etc. ($6/day)	+10,950	
Total expenses	$39,035	
Tax savings ($39,035 × .35)		−$13,662
Net cash *saved*		$5,862
After car cost *below* zero		

As the cost of gas goes up, so does your tax savings. But, your net cash flow would be hurt by the increased cost. Also note that this is a generic example. For 2013 you could expense and depreciate as much as $11,160 of the $12,000 cost.

101 Meals and Entertainment Expenses

Not only can you deduct the above travel and transportation expenses, but you can also take as additional miscellaneous deductions certain entertainment expenses. Entertainment expenses may be deducted if you can show that the entertainment of prospects has a direct effect on and can reasonably be expected to increase or maintain earnings or your commissions.

These entertainment expenses must be ordinary and necessary (reasonable and customary) and must be incurred in the course of your work. You may deduct entertainment expenses only if you can show that your employer required or expected you to have such entertainment expenses in connection with your work.

You must prove *all* the following elements for entertainment deductions:

- The amount of each separate expenditure for entertaining, except for incidental items such as taxi fares and telephone calls that may be totaled on a daily basis

- The date the entertainment took place

- The name, address or location, and type of entertainment, such as dinner or theatre, if the information is not apparent in the name or designation of the place

- The reason for the entertainment or the business benefit derived or expected to be gained from entertaining and, except for certain business meals, any business discussion or activity that took place

- The occupation or other information about the person or persons entertained, including the name, title, or other designation sufficient to establish the business relationship to you

Effective January 1, 1987, *entertainment expenses* were allowed only to the extent of 80 percent of what was spent. Exceptions allowing full deductibility include (a) expenses reimbursed by an employer (in which case the employer is subject to the percent rule); (b) traditional employer-paid recreational expenses for employees (e.g., holiday parties); (c) items given as compensation to the recipient that are excludable from income as *de minimis* fringe benefits; (d) items made available to the general public (e.g., as promotional activities); and (e) tickets to certain charitable fund-raising sports events. Ticket costs in excess of face value are not deductible, except with regard to tickets for charitable fund-raising sports events. Moreover, deductions for the rental or other use of a sky box at a sports arena are disallowed, to the extent in excess of the cost of regular tickets, if the box is used by the taxpayer for more than one event. This sky box disallowal of deductibility was subject to a 3-year phase-out starting January 1, 1986.

The Tax Reform Act of 1986 also reduced to 80 percent the amount of deductions otherwise allowable for *business meal expenses,* including meals away from home and meals furnished on an employer's premises to its employees. Exceptions allowing full deductibility include (a) employee meal expenses reimbursed by the employer (in which case the employer is subject to the percent rule); (b) employer-furnished meals that are excludable from the employee's income as *de minimis* fringes (including subsidized eating facilities); (c) meals taxed to employees as compensation; and (d) items sold to the public (such as the cost of food to restaurants) or furnished the public as samples or for promotion. Moreover, the meals, to be deductible at all, must be directly related to or associated with a business discussion—i.e., "quiet" business meals are no longer deductible.

The Omnibus Budget Reconciliation Act of 1993, effective for years beginning after December 31, 1993, reduced the 80 percent deduction to 50 percent. The Act also eliminated, after December 31, 1993, all deductions for club dues, including airline and hotel clubs. Club meals may still be deducted if they satisfy the above standards for deductibility.

102 Gifts

You may deduct ordinary and necessary (reasonable and customary) expenses for business gifts made directly or indirectly to any individual. The total value of business gifts to any one individual during the tax year cannot be more than $25. If a gift is not intended for the eventual personal use or benefit of a particular individual or a limited class of individuals, the gift is not considered to be made to an individual.

A gift to the spouse or child of an individual with whom you are doing business is a gift to that individual. However, if one spouse has an independent bona fide business connection with you, such a gift generally will not be considered a gift to the other spouse unless it is intended for that spouse's eventual use or benefit.

An item costing $4 or less on which your name is clearly and permanently imprinted and which is one of a number of identical items distributed by you is not subject to the $25 rule. This includes such items as pens, desk sets, plastic bags, and cases. In addition, incidental costs, such as jewelry engraving or packaging, insuring, and mailing or other delivery costs, are not generally included in determining the cost of a gift for the $25 rule.

A related cost will be considered incidental only if it does not add substantial value to the gift. For example, although the cost of gift wrapping will be considered an incidental cost, the purchase of an ornamental basket for packaging fruit will not be considered an incidental cost of packaging if the basket has a value that is substantial in relation to the value of the fruit.

Furthermore, it must be remembered that we are dealing here with gift, entertainment, travel, and transportation expenses of *employees*. Any of these expenses incurred by employers may be deductible for adjusted gross income as trade or business deductions.

You must prove *all* the following to be allowed a deduction for business gifts:

- The cost
- The date of the gift
- A description of the gift
- The reason for giving the gift or any business benefit derived or expected to be gained from giving it
- The name, title, occupation, or other information about the person receiving the gift, or some other designation sufficient to establish the business relationship to you

KEEP PROOF OF EXPENSES

Substantiation of travel, meals, entertainment, and business gift expenses should be kept in an account book, diary, statement of expense, or similar record, supported by adequate documentary evidence that together can support each element of an expenditure. For example, entries on a desk calendar, not supported by evidence, are not proper proof. The simple rule here, therefore, is to keep receipts and records. For example, if you take a business associate out to dinner, simply jot the associate's name and the general topic of discussion on the back of the receipt given to you by the restaurant.

Note that under DOC 9805007, faxed or e-mailed documents qualify as documentary evidence for meal and entertainment substantiation.

In the area of such deductions there is no such thing as too much documentation. If these deductions are questioned by the Internal Revenue Service, the only things an audit agent will look for are receipts. Therefore, *always* remember to get a receipt, note the cost of the expenditure, the person to whom it relates, and your business relationship. A total of 30 seconds of effort may guarantee you $100 of unquestioned deductions. If your 2013 taxable income is more than $87,850, you're in the 28% bracket and that 30 seconds of effort would have saved you $28 in taxes—that's the equivalent of $3,360 an hour—even more than most tax attorneys make!

103 Reimbursable Employee Business Expenses

Normally, when reimbursement is available to an employee for a business expense incurred, if the employee does not obtain that reimbursement, no deduction is allowed [*Podems*, 24 T.C. 21 (1955)]. However, in *Kessler* (TCM 1985-254), the court ruled that if a taxpayer can establish that reimbursement, though nominally available, is unavailable as a practical matter, then out-of-pocket business expenses should be allowable as a deduction. (See also *Jetty*, TCM 1982-378.) The Tax Court's position was reinforced and supported by the Internal Revenue Service in Action on Decision 1986-011, on January 8, 1986, wherein a recommendation was made that the IRS acquiesce in *Kessler.*

104 Educational Expenses

Educational expenses incurred to maintain or improve your skills in your current position are deductible as a miscellaneous itemized expense. In a private letter ruling (PLR 8706048), the IRS held that a financial consultant may deduct the cost of obtaining a Master of Science degree in financial planning. The taxpayer was a financial consultant and the degree was sought in order to maintain and improve the taxpayer's financial planning skills. If the education will qualify you for a new trade or business or is a minimum requirement for your current job, that education expense is not deductible. In the private letter ruling the Internal Revenue Service held that a master's degree in financial planning was not a minimum requirement for the taxpayer's job as a financial consultant and did not qualify the taxpayer for a new trade or business. Therefore, the taxpayer's expenses for tuition and books incurred in obtaining the degree in financial planning were deductible as ordinary and necessary expenses.

As a general rule, however, if you earn a degree that makes you eligible for a new trade or business, there is no deduction for tuition. The real key is your intent at the time you take the course. For example, in one case, after 23 years in the accounting field, a CPA attended law school at night. He took all the tax courses he could at law school, intending to improve himself as an accountant. He did not intend to go into the practice of law and in fact did not. His purpose was not to obtain a new position or advancement in position. His only intent was to improve his skills as an accountant. The expense of going to law school in this case was deductible (*Berry*, T.C. Memo 1971-110). In *Singleton-Clarke*, T.C. Summ. Op. 2009-182, the court allowed a $15,000 MBA tuition deduction for a registered nurse. She met the criteria.

105 Limit on Itemized Deductions

Under the Omnibus Reconciliation Act of 1990 (OBRA), a new limit was put on itemized deductions. For regular tax purposes, the new law establishes a floor that you must exceed before your itemized expenses are deductible. The 2009 floor for all taxpayers, regardless of filing status (except married filing separate, where it was 1 percent* in excess of $83,400), was 1 percent of the amount of your adjusted gross income (AGI) exceeding $166,800 (indexed for inflation).† Medical expenses, casualty and theft losses, and investment interest expenses were not subject to the floor, and the deduction cannot reduce by more than 80 percent your otherwise allowable deductions.

Example: If your 2009 AGI was $266,800, you must knock $1,000 ($100,000 × 1 percent) off the bottom line of your Schedule A. So each thousand dollars of excess income lops off $2.80 of tax benefits in the 28 percent bracket or $3.50 in the 35 percent bracket.

However, the slicer would not cut your itemized deductions by more than 80 percent (and does not apply at all when computing AMT). Better yet, the 80 percent stopper did not include deductions for medical expenses, investment interest, and casualty or gambling losses.

Note that this reduction applied after the other deduction limits, e.g., 10 percent medical and 2 percent miscellaneous.

There was no reduction for 2010, 2011, or 2012. In 2013, the limits return as per below:

Phase-out Threshold	2013
Married filing jointly	$300,000
Head of household	$275,000
Unmarried	$250,000
Married filing separately	$150,000

Your total itemized deductions are reduced by 3 percent of the excess of your AGI over the above numbers. You can't lose more than 80 percent of your total. Medical expenses, investment interest, casualty losses, and all other gambling losses are exempt from this cutback.

This cutback adds up to 1.19 percent to your marginal rate.

---

* The 1 percent figure for 2008 and 2009 was 2 percent for 2007.
† $166,800 for 2009, $83,400 if married but filing separately.

C Schedules of Deductions

106 Medical Deductions

Abortion
Acupuncture
Advances for lifetime care
Ambulance hire
Apartment rent
Artificial teeth or limbs
Autoette wheelchair
Automobile expenses
Birth control pills
Braille books and magazines
Capital expenditures in excess of
    property's increased value
Central air conditioning
Clarinet lessons
Commutation costs
Computer medical data bank
Contact lens insurance
Cosmetic surgery (limited)
Crutches
Dental care
Diagnostic services
Drug or alcohol therapy centers
Education aids
Elastic stockings
Employee medical plans
Eyeglasses
Guide dogs
Guide for blind individual
Handrails

Hearing aids and component parts
Hospital care
Invalid spouse
Iron lung
Kidney transplants
Laetrile
Last illness expenses
Lip reading
Massages
Mattresses and boards
Meals and lodging if part of
    hospital or treatment charge
Meat diet
Medical insurance premiums
Medical transportation
Medical travel
Medicare B
Medicinal liquors, if prescribed
Medicines and drugs
Nonlocal medical transportation
    costs
Nurse's transportation expenses
Nursing homes and homes for the
    aged
Nursing services
Operations affecting childbearing
Operations and treatments in
    general
Organic foods

Outdoor elevator
Oxygen and oxygen equipment
Paint removal
Patterning exercises
Physician's fees
Prepaid medical insurance
Prosthetic devices
Psychiatric or psychoanalytic care
Reclining chair
Remedial reading
Retirement homes
Salt-free diet
School for the physically or
    mentally handicapped
Sexual therapy
Smoke-ending program, if to
    cure specific disease
Special foods or beverages
Special home for mentally
    retarded

Special plumbing fixtures
Specially designed automobiles
Swimming pool
Telephone equipment
Throat treatment
Transporting patient's relative
Tutoring fees
University medical plan, if charges
    separately stated
Unlicensed practitioners
Vasectomy
Vitamins, if prescribed
Voluntary payments for
    Medicare A
Water fluoridation device
Wheelchair
X-ray treatment

107 Deductible Taxes

Taxes imposed by state, city, and
    possessions of the United States
Auto registration (to the extent
    that it is based on value)
Income (except where claimed as
    credit)
Personal property
Real property
Foreign taxes
Income, war profit, excess profit
    (unless claimed as credit)
Real estate

*If paid or accrued in connection
    with business or for the
    production of income,* you can
    also deduct these taxes:
Federal taxes
    Excise
    Import duties
    Liquor
    Railroad Retirement
        (employers)
    Social security (employers)
    Tobacco
    Unemployment (employers)

State and local taxes
    Admission
    Auto registration
    Beverages
    Cigarettes
    Cosmetics
    Driver's license fees
    Excise
    Liquors
    Mortgage
    Occupancy
    Sales/Use
    Stamp
    Stock transfer
    Tobacco
    Transfer (except estate, inheritance, legacy, succession, and gift taxes)
    Unemployment

108 Charitable Deductions

Aid to evacuees
Artwork contributed by owner
Automobile expenses
Bargain sales to charity
Benefit performances
Book samples
Charitable travel
Church bonds, if donated after purchase
Church building funds
Church dues
Church repairs
Civil Defense volunteer's out-of-pocket expenses
Community chests
Credit card contributions
Delegate's expenses
Domestic fraternal societies
Essays
Excess rent
Eyeglass donations
Films and tape recordings
Foster parent's expenses

Future interest in tangible personal property
Government contributions
Home for elderly
Hospital fees
Installment notes
Insurance policies
Inventory donated
Legal expenses donated
Maintaining student in home
Medical equipment
Membership in art or fine arts association
Music manuscripts
Ordinary income property
Out-of-pocket charitable expenses
Partial interest in property
Patents donated
Promissory notes
Property donated
Rent in excess of fair rental value
Scenic easement
Tickets donated for resale

Uniforms

Unmarried pregnant women programs

Volunteer fire companies

Volunteer income tax assistance

War veterans' organizations

109 Casualty and Theft Loss Deductions

Accidents

Airplane, train, and other transport crashes

Appraisal fees

Automobile damage

Bomb damage

Casualty and theft losses of investment property

Chinese drywall

Cleanup and repair costs

Confiscation by foreign government

Disaster area losses

Driveway breakup

Earthquake or earth slide

Explosion

False representation or pretenses

Fire

Flood

Freeze

Hurricane

Insect and disease damage to trees and shrubs, if sudden

Lightning

Loss of property used partly for rental and partly for personal purposes

"Madoff" thefts

Mine cave-ins

Razing

Shipwrecks

Smog

Snow

Sonic boom

Storms

Swindles

Theft of business property

Theft of personal property

Thin ice

Tornado

Vandalism

Water damage (as from burst water heater)

110 Miscellaneous Deductions

Attorney fees paid by spouse to
    secure taxable alimony
Bad debts
Bar examination fee (amortizable)
Bond premium amortization
Gambling losses (to extent of
    gambling gains)
Job-hunting expenses

Labor union dues and assessments
    for noninsurance purposes
Physician's hospital privilege fee
    (amortizable)
Tax counseling costs
Tax litigation expenses
Tax return preparation
Uncollectible debts
Uncollectible loans

111 Employee Miscellaneous Deductions

Automobile expenses (allocatable
    to business)
    Depreciation
    Garage rent
    Gasoline and oil
    Insurance
    Parking fees
    Repairs for business cars
    State inspection and registration
        fees
    Taxes
    Tolls
    Washing
Briefcase
Christmas gifts to customers
    (limited)
Convention expenses

Dues (except "Club Dues")
    Business association
    Labor unions
    Professional societies
Educational expenses (limited)
Employment agency fees
Entertainment expenses
Fidelity bond costs
Gifts to customers and prospects
    (limited)
Insurance premiums
    Automobile (to extent of
        business use)
    Bonds (fidelity, etc.)
    Malpractice
Job-hunting expenses

Labor unions, initiation fees, dues, fines, assessments for pension funds

Laundry and cleaning while traveling away from home

Legal fees to protect future employment*

Meals or lodging while traveling away from home

Office furnishings†

Outside sales business expenses

Passport fees for business travel

Reimbursed expenses (if reimbursement included in income)

Safety equipment

Subscriptions to professional journals and magazines

Tax return preparation

Technical periodicals

Telephone

Tips

Tools

Transportation expenses

Traveling expenses

Baggage charges

Fares

Laundry and cleaning while away from home

Meals and lodging while away from home

Passport fees, if for business

Sample rooms

Taxis

Telephone and telegraph messages

Tips

Tuition fees

Uniforms not adaptable to general wear

Work clothes

112 Investor Deductions

Investors can deduct expenses incurred to produce or collect income and to conserve, manage, or maintain income-producing property. Anyone who owns securities, rents real estate, or owns other investments should not overlook the typical deductions in the following list.

---

*Renkiewicz, et ux. v. Commissioner, T.C. Memo 2001-1.

†For example, office furnishings bought by an executive with his own funds to maintain his image as a successful district sales manager (Leroy Gillis, T.C. Memo 1973-96).

Accounting fees
Advertising expenses
Alterations and repairs
Attorneys' fees
Auditing expenses
Bad debts
Bookkeeping expenses
Collection of rent costs
Custodian fees
Damages paid for breach of
    contract or lease
Depreciation
    Buildings
    Furniture and fixtures
Exchange of asset losses
Expenses of successfully resisting
    condemnation of property
Fire insurance premiums
Franchise taxes
Heat and light
Interest
Investment counseling costs
Leasehold improvements
Leases
    Amortization of improvements
      by lessee
    Amortization of lease acquisition
      costs
    Rentals paid
    Repairs made by lessee
    Taxes paid by lessee
Legal expenses
License taxes and fees (limited)
Losses (to extent not covered by
    insurance)
    Abandonment of worthless
      interest in real estate
    Bad debts
    Demolition of building

Forced sales
Foreclosure
Forfeitures
Property sales
Property seized by government
Maintenance of property costs
Management expenses
Mortgage foreclosure losses
Moving expenses of machinery
    and equipment
Night protection services
Office rent
Porter and janitor services
Recordkeeping costs
Redecoration costs
Refuse and waste removal expenses
Repairs
Safe-deposit boxes
Salaries
Sales of assets losses
Stationery and supplies
Tax counseling costs
Tax return preparation
Taxes (state)
    General sales (add to basis)
    Gross income
    Income
    License fees (limited)
    Motor fuel
    Personal property
    Real estate
    Stamp
    Stock transfer (adjust basis)
    Transfer of property (except
      estate, inheritance, legacy, gift,
      etc.) (adjust basis)
Traveling expenses
Worthless bonds and stocks

CHAPTER 8

Traditional Tax Shelters

"As a citizen, you have an obligation to the country's tax system, but you also have an obligation to yourself to know your rights under the law and possible tax deductions. And to claim every one of them."

DONALD ALEXANDER,
former commissioner of the Internal
Revenue Service under three presidents

"The tax laws reflect a continuing struggle among contending interests for the privilege of paying the least."

LOUIS EISENSTEIN,
The Ideologies of Taxation

"When Congress talks of tax reform, grab your wallet and run for cover."

Senator STEVE SYMMS of Idaho

The art of sophisticated tax planning requires you to understand the elements of tax-sheltered investments. These investments allow you to offset certain "artificial losses"—noneconomic losses, but losses that are available as deductions under the present tax laws, and not only against the income from those investments but also against your other income from your regular business or professional activity.

Often, tax shelters have been described by the unsophisticated as gimmicks or "loopholes." Nothing could be further from the truth. These laws were adopted by Congress after careful deliberation, with the purpose of serving some major economic or social goal. Therefore, when you utilize these techniques you are not only improving your financial position, but you are also furthering a legitimate national economic goal. For example, the allowance of percentage depletion for oil and other tax provisions for mineral development have been effective incentives to investments in petroleum exploration and discovery. These attractive tax benefits have encouraged other taxpayers to provide the risk capital needed to bring into production many useful sources of oil that would otherwise go untapped. Special tax benefits for equipment leasing and life insurance also serve national economic and social goals.

The Internal Revenue Service, in a manner of speaking, sometimes finds itself involved in a shelter. For example, all of the staff at the regional IRS headquarters in New York are in a shelter. It seems the office building housing the Internal Revenue Service in New York was sold to a tax shelter syndicator.

Among those who have invested in tax shelters are former Attorney General William French Smith and former Internal Revenue Service Commissioner Roscoe Egger, Jr. Clearly, tax shelters are investments that you should consider if appropriate.

THE TAX REFORM ACT OF 1986

The Tax Reform Act of 1986 significantly affected the attractiveness of traditional tax shelters. The 1986 Reform Act effectively limits losses from passive trade or business activities (limited partnership tax shelters, etc.), generally to offset passive income. What this means is that, effectively, tax shelter losses can be used only to offset tax shelter gains. Passive income does not include portfolio income—e.g., dividends on stocks and interest on bonds—or gain from the sale of stocks and bonds, nor does it include income from the rental of property to an entity in which you materially participate. You can't claim passive income from renting personally owned equipment to a partnership you manage. (But see Chapter 9 to learn how to use a trust for your kids to accomplish the same thing.) The following discussion explains the Tax Reform Act and details the remaining potential alternative tax shelter vehicles.

The passive loss rules are sweeping provisions that in general deny any individual, estate, trust, closely held C corporation, or personal service corporation the use of losses or credits generated in "passive activities" to offset other income such as salary, interest, dividends, and active business income. Deductions from passive activities may offset income from passive activities. Credits from passive activities generally are limited to the tax attributable to income from passive activities.

Disallowed losses and credits are carried forward and treated as deductions and credits from passive activities in the next taxable year. Suspended losses from an activity are allowed in full when the taxpayer disposes of his entire interest in the activity in a fully taxable transaction. Suspended credits may not be claimed in full in the year in which the taxpayer disposes of the interest in the passive activity. Rather, they are carried forward until used to offset tax liability from passive income. However, upon a fully taxable disposition of a passive activity, taxpayers may elect to increase the basis of property immediately before the transfer by an amount equal to the portion of any suspended credit that reduced the basis of the property for the taxable year in which the credit arose.

If a closely held C corporation (other than a personal service or S corporation) has "net active income" for any taxable year, the passive activity loss for the taxable year will be allowable as a deduction against net active income. A similar rule applies in the case of any passive activity credit of the taxpayer. The term *net active income* means the taxable income of the taxpayer for the taxable year determined without regard for any income or loss from a passive activity and any *net portfolio income.*

PASSIVE ACTIVITY DEFINED

In general, the term *passive activity* means any activity that involves the conduct of any trade or business and in which the taxpayer does not *materially participate.*

It also includes any rental activity of either real or tangible personal property regardless of whether the individual materially participates. With respect to equipment leasing, short-term rental to various users (where the lessor provides substantial services) is an active business rather than a passive activity.

In general, working interests in any oil or gas property that the taxpayer holds directly or through an entity that does not limit the taxpayer's liability with respect to such interests will be treated as an active trade or business and will not be subject to the passive loss rules.

The passive activity limitations *do not apply* to real estate if you're in the "real property business" that requires substantial activity. Just owning a rental property doesn't put you in the "real property" business. You must spend over 50 percent of your time and at least 750 hours per year to qualify.

MATERIAL PARTICIPATION DEFINED

In general, a taxpayer will be treated as materially participating in an activity only if the taxpayer is involved in the operations of the activity on a regular, continuous, and substantial basis.

All limited partnership interests are treated as not materially participating.

Management decision making by an individual may constitute material participation if such services are substantial and bona fide. For example, when management services are rendered on a full-time basis, and the success of the activity depends on the exercise of an individual's business judgment, such services constitute material participation. The test applies regardless of whether an individual owns an interest in the activity directly or through a pass-through entity such as a general partnership or an S corporation.

Taxpayers who own working interests in oil and gas properties through a limited partnership will be subject to the passive loss rules with respect to that interest. That is notwithstanding the special exclusion for working interests in oil and gas properties.

In 1988, the IRS attempted to clarify the definition of "material participation" and provided special standards for limited partners. A taxpayer who is not a limited partner is a material participant in an activity during the tax year if one of the following tests is met:

1. The taxpayer participates for more than 500 hours.

2. The taxpayer's participation represents substantially all participation in the activity by individuals (including nonowners).

3. The taxpayer participates for more than 100 hours, and no other individual's participation in the activity exceeds that of the taxpayer.

4. The activity is a significant participation activity for the tax year, and the taxpayer's total participation in all significant participation activities for the year exceeds 500 hours.

5. The taxpayer has materially participated in the activity for 5 of the 10 preceding years.

6. The activity is a personal service activity in which the taxpayer has materially participated for any 3 preceding years.

7. In light of the facts and circumstances, the taxpayer participates in the activity on a regular, continuous, and substantial basis. To satisfy this

facts-and-circumstances test, the taxpayer must have at least 100 hours of participation.

Limited partners materially participate in an activity only if they meet one of tests 1, 5, or 6, above.

A significant participation activity is a new concept created by the Internal Revenue Service's temporary regulations. It is any trade or business activity in which the taxpayer has more than 100 hours of participation during the tax year but fails to satisfy all the material participation tests (other than test 4, above, relating to significant participation activities).

This concept is important for taxpayers involved in several trades or businesses, because it allows them to satisfy the material participation test by aggregating hours of participation in different businesses. However, if the taxpayer enjoys *net income* from significant participation activities during the year, that income is considered *nonpassive* and cannot be used to offset losses from other passive activities. If the significant participation activities produce a net loss, the loss is considered *passive* and must be suspended unless there is sufficient income from other passive activities to offset the loss.

NEW TEST FOR LIMITED PARTNERS

Taxpayers will not be treated as limited partners under new Internal Revenue Service rules (REG-109369-10) if they have the right to manage under either a partnership agreement or under state law, an agency official said January 10, 2012.

The right to manage includes the right to bind.

NET PORTFOLIO INCOME

In general, net portfolio income will not be included when determining the income or loss from any passive activity. Net portfolio income means gross income from interest, dividends, annuities, or royalties not derived in the ordinary course of a trade or business less expenses (other than interest) that are clearly and directly allocable to such gross income, less interest expense properly allocable to such gross income, plus gain or less loss attributable to the disposition of property held for investment or producing income such as interest, dividends, or royalties.

Any income, gain, or loss that is attributable to an investment of working capital will not be treated as income or loss from a passive activity.

This provision prevents taxpayers from placing property that would otherwise be producing active portfolio income into an entity that is subject to the passive loss rules, thereby using losses from passive activities to offset active portfolio income.

Income earned for personal services will not be taken into account in computing the income or loss from a passive activity for any taxable year. For example, if a limited partner is paid for performing services for the partnership (whether by way of salary, guaranteed payment, or allocation of partnership income), these payments cannot be sheltered by passive losses from the partnership or from any other passive activity.

TREATMENT OF FORMER PASSIVE ACTIVITIES

If an activity is a former passive activity for any taxable year and has suspended losses or credits from prior years when the activity was passive, the suspended losses may be offset against the income from the activity for the taxable year. Suspended credits allocable to such activity may be offset against the regular tax liability allocable to that activity for the taxable year. Any remaining suspended losses or credits continue to be treated as arising from a passive activity.

It appears that suspended losses and credits from a passive activity may be used to offset active income from the activity in the year in which the activity changes from passive to active and in later years. Any remaining suspended losses or credits will also be allowed as a deduction to income or credit against tax attributable to other passive activities.

If a taxpayer ceases for any taxable year to be a closely held C corporation or personal service corporation, suspended losses and credits will continue to be treated in the same manner as if the taxpayer continued to be a closely held C corporation or personal service corporation, whichever is applicable.

DISPOSITIONS OF ENTIRE INTERESTS IN PASSIVE ACTIVITY

If during the taxable year a taxpayer disposes of his entire interest in any passive activity (or former passive activity) and all gain or loss realized on such disposition is recognized, any suspended losses from the activity are no longer treated as passive activity losses and are allowable as a deduction against the taxpayer's income in the following order:

- Income or gain from the passive activity for the taxable year (including any gain recognized on the disposition)

- Net income or gain for the taxable year from all passive activities

- Any other income or gain

However, if the person acquiring the interest is a related party to the taxpayer, then any suspended losses will not apply against the taxpayer's active income until the taxable year in which such interest is acquired by another person unrelated to the taxpayer. However, such suspended losses may be offset by income from other passive activities of the taxpayer.

To the extent that any loss recognized upon a disposition of an entire interest in a passive activity is a loss from the sale or exchange of a capital asset, the capital loss is limited to the amount of gains from the sale or exchange of capital assets plus $3,000 (in the case of individuals). The limitation on the deductibility of capital losses is applied before the determination of the amount of losses allowable upon the disposition under the passive loss rule.

For example, if a taxpayer has a capital loss of $10,000 upon the disposition of a passive activity that has $5,000 of suspended losses, the $5,000 of suspended losses are allowed, but the capital loss deduction is limited to $3,000 for the year (assuming the taxpayer has no other gains or losses from the sale of capital assets for the year). The remainder of the capital loss from the disposition is carried forward and allowed in accordance with the provisions determining the allowance of such capital losses.

PARTIAL DISPOSITION OF AN INTEREST IN A PASSIVE ACTIVITY

The 1986 law made no provision for the allowance of part or all of the suspended losses and credits attributable to a passive activity when an individual makes a partial or incomplete disposition of an interest in that passive activity. All losses and credits apparently remain suspended until offset by income from the individual's remaining interest in that passive activity or other passive activities, or until the individual completes the disposition of his entire interest in that passive activity.

DISPOSITION AT DEATH

If an interest in an activity is transferred due to the taxpayer's death, suspended losses may be deducted against income to the extent such losses are greater than the excess (if any) of the basis of such property in the hands of the transferee, over the adjusted basis of such property immediately before the death of the taxpayer. Any unused suspended losses as a result of this limitation are not allowed as a deduction for any taxable year.

For example, assume Mother owns rental real estate with a market value of $70,000, an adjusted basis of $50,000, and $25,000 of suspended losses. Mother dies and leaves the property to Daughter. The basis is stepped up to $70,000 in the hands of Daughter. Only $5,000 of the suspended losses are deductible on the income tax return of the estate. The remaining $20,000 of suspended losses (equal to the step-up in basis) is lost forever.

DISPOSITION BY INSTALLMENT SALE

If an individual disposes of an entire interest in an activity in an installment sale, suspended losses are allowed each year based on the ratio of gain recognized each year to the total gain on the sale.

DISPOSITION BY GIFT

If an interest in a passive activity is disposed of by gift, the basis of the interest immediately before the transfer is increased by any suspended passive losses allocable to the interest. Suspended losses that are added to the basis because of the gift of an interest are not allowed as deductions for any taxable year.

Moreover, the specific language of the statute appears to imply that gain on the sale of an interest in a passive activity cannot be offset with passive losses and credits from other passive activities. Only suspended or current year losses and credits from the passive activity may be used to offset gains realized on the disposition of that activity.

For example, an individual has interests in two separate limited partnerships, A and B, which are separate passive activities. Assume the following facts apply:

	A	B
Current year loss	($30,000)	($10,000)
Prior suspended losses	($70,000)	($25,000)

Assume that the individual sells his interest in B for a gain of $40,000. The full amount of the losses from partnership B, $35,000, may offset this gain. However, it appears that none of the current or suspended losses from partnership A may offset the remaining $5,000 gain.

SPECIAL RULE FOR RENTAL REAL ESTATE ACTIVITIES

In the case of rental real estate activities in which an individual actively participates, up to $25,000 of losses (and credits in a deduction-equivalent sense) from all such activities are allowed each year against nonpassive income of the taxpayer. The $25,000 amount that is allowed under this special provision is reduced by 50 percent of the amount by which the taxpayer's adjusted gross income for the taxable year exceeds $100,000. Any losses that this provision disallows in the year incurred and that carry over as suspended passive losses to later years may not be used under the $25,000 allowance in later years.

For example, an individual has $30,000 of net losses from rental real estate activities in which she actively participates. Her adjusted gross income, without regard to the net losses from the rental real estate activity, is $120,000. First, only $25,000 of her net losses are eligible for the special allowance. Second, the amount of the net loss she may deduct against active income (her adjusted gross income before deductions for net losses from rental activities) must be reduced by $.50 for each dollar of adjusted gross income over $100,000, or by $10,000. Therefore, she may deduct $15,000 of these net losses from her adjusted gross income when computing her taxable income. The remaining $15,000 of net losses are carried forward.

The $25,000 allowance is applied by first netting income and loss from all of the taxpayer's rental real estate activities in which he actively participates. If there is net loss for the year from such activities, net passive income (if any) from other activities is then applied against it in determining the amount eligible for the $25,000 allowance.

For example, assume that a taxpayer has $45,000 of losses from a rental real estate activity in which he actively participates. If he also actively participates in another rental real estate activity from which he has $40,000 of passive income, resulting in a $5,000 net loss from rental real estate activities in which he actively participates, then only $5,000 is allowed under the $25,000 allowance for the year.

In the case of rehabilitation and low-income housing credits, the phase-out of the $25,000 allowance does not begin until the adjusted gross income of the taxpayer for the taxable year exceeds $200,000.

In the case of taxable years of an estate ending less than 2 years after the date of the decedent's death, the $25,000 allowance for rental real estate activities applies to all rental real estate activities with respect to which such decedent actively participated before his death.

Married individuals filing separate returns and living apart from their spouses at all times during the taxable year each qualify for half the $25,000 allowance. The phase-out begins for each at $50,000 rather than $100,000 for rental real estate activities other than low-income housing, and at $100,000 rather than $200,000 for low-income housing. If married taxpayers filing separate returns do not live apart from their spouses at *all* times during the taxable year, neither may use the $25,000 allowance for rental real estate activities.

If you are a "real estate professional," you may treat your real estate activities as nonpassive.

RENTAL ACTIVITY

A rental activity is any activity from which gross income is derived primarily from payments for the use of tangible property. In addition, an activity may qualify as a rental activity if the property is held out for rent, even though no rental income is received in a tax year.

There are six exceptions to the general rule. An activity involving the use of tangible property is not a rental activity in any tax year if *any one* of the following situations exists:

1. If the average rental period is 7 days or less, the activity is not considered a rental activity. This exception would exclude many resort properties from the rental category. However, the activity may remain passive if the owner does not materially participate, so the owner must be involved in the day-to-day management or operations of the activity—Treasury Reg. 1.469-5T(f)(2)(ii).

   The passive loss rules are strict for short-term rentals of real estate—average rentals of seven days or less. A couple rented out several property units, and each had rental periods averaging seven days or less. They used the companies that managed the properties to obtain tenants, collect rents, perform maintenance, and the like. They visited occasionally to buy items for the units and make repairs.

   The Taxpayers must materially participate in the units to deduct their losses, the Tax Court says. The easier-to-satisfy active participation test (see below) does not apply in the case of short-term rentals. So to deduct their rental losses, the owners must put in at least 100 or more hours a year on each unit, and their participation must be more than anyone else's. Or they must work over 500 hours on each rental. In this case, the couple did not satisfy either test (*Jende*, TC Summ. Op. 2011–82).

2. If the average rental period is 30 days or less and significant personal services are provided to the customers, the activity is not considered a rental activity.

3. The activity is not treated as a rental activity if extraordinary services are provided to the customers in connection with the use of the property. In order for the services to be "extraordinary," the use of the property by customers must be incidental to the receipt of such services. For example, providing a hospital room to patients would not be considered a rental activity, because the use of the room is incidental to the receipt of medical services.

4. The activity will not be treated as a rental activity if the rental is incidental to nonrental activity. For example:

   a) The property is held to realize gain for appreciation, and the gross rental income is less than 2 percent of the lesser of the unadjusted basis or fair market value of the property. This is the only situation in which rental property will be treated as property held for investment.

b) The property is generally used in a trade or business owned by the individual, and the gross rental income is insubstantial. This exception applies to property that was predominantly used in the trade or business either in the current year or in at least two of the five preceding tax years. The 2 percent test described above is used to test the substantiality of the rental income.

c) If the property is held for sale to customers in the ordinary course of business, the rental of the property will not be rental activity if the property is sold during the year.

d) Lodging rented to an employee for the convenience of the employer is not rental property.

5. If property is customarily made available for nonexclusive use by various customers during specific business hours, the activity is not a rental activity. For example, a golf course where customers either pay daily fees or purchase passes for a longer period is not considered a rental activity regardless of the average period of customer use.

6. If an owner of an interest in a partnership or S corporation provides property to be used in a nonrental activity of the entity, the partner or shareholder is not treated as being engaged in a rental activity if the property is provided in the owner's capacity as a partner or shareholder and no rent is charged.

ACTIVE PARTICIPATION DEFINED

To qualify for the $25,000 allowance for rental real estate activities, an individual must actively participate in the rental activity. Individuals will not be treated as actively participating for any period if, at any time during such period, their ownership interest (including any interest of the individual's spouse) is less than 10 percent (by value) of all interests in such activity. The degree of participation that is required once this 10 percent or more ownership threshold is met is unclear. The Conference Report suggests that the degree of participation required to meet the active participation test is less than the material participation standard.

A limited partnership interest in rental real estate does not meet the active participation requirement (except as described below for rehabilitation and low-income housing credits).

What happens to the $25,000 deduction when you have several rental real estate properties? To the extent that the aggregate loss from several active participation rental real estate activities does not exceed $25,000, the entire loss is deductible. However, where the aggregate net loss exceeds $25,000, the loss must be allocated among activities on a pro rata basis with respect to the losses from each loss activity. For example, if a taxpayer who qualifies for the full $25,000 allowance has $10,000 of losses from one activity and $40,000 of losses from a second activity, then $5,000 is treated as allowed from the first activity and $20,000 is treated as allowed from the second activity.

This allocation is necessary in part because the suspended losses from a specific activity (those that are not deducted) are allowed in full when the taxpayer disposes of his or her interest in that activity.

Note that the IRS does not permit pro rata allocation between pre- and post-October 1986 investments. (See below for the phase-in of disallowance of losses and credits for interests held before October 23, 1986.) Where there were losses from both old (pre-October) activities and new (post-October) activities, the $25,000 allowance is applied to old activities first—that is, without proration. This generally results in a smaller amount of the loss being allowed.

For example, assume that you were an active participant in two rental real estate activities. In 1987, the loss from each was $50,000. One of the activities was acquired before October 23, 1986, and the other after. The following is a comparison of the Internal Revenue Service approach and the pro rata approach:

	IRS		Pro Rata	
	Pre-October 1986	*Post-October 1986*	*Pre-October 1986*	*Post-October 1986*
Loss	$50,000	$50,000	$50,000	$50,000
Allowed under $25,000 rule	$25,000	$0	$12,500	$12,500
Balance subject to 65% phase-in rule	$25,000		$37,500	
65% phase-in	$16,250		$24,375	
Total	**$41,250**		**$49,375**	

Note that the IRS method yielded an allowable loss for 1987 of $41,250 ($25,000 plus $16,250). The pro rata method would permit $49,375 of the loss to be deducted in 1987 ($12,500 plus $12,500 plus $24,375).

The following example shows you how losses are carried forward. Assume that you have invested in three separate passive activities. Activity A is an interest acquired in 1985; Activity B is an interest in a rental activity acquired in 1987; and Activity C is an interest in rental realty acquired in 1987. Also assume that your gross income is under $100,000.

	Activity A	*Activity B*	*Activity C*
	$10,000	($50,000)	($100,000)

1987 results:
Net passive activity loss ($140,000)

Net losses from B and C
  offset against A income:
    B = $10,000 × $50,000/$150,000 = ($3,333)
    C = $10,000 × $100,000/$150,000 = ($6,667)

Net loss from B offset
  against active and portfolio income ($25,000)

Loss carryforward to 1988:
    B = $50,000 – $3,333 – $25,000 = ($21,667)
    C = $100,000 – $6,667 = ($93,333)
    ($115,000)

Assume the following activity in 1988:

	Activity A	*Activity B*	*Activity C*
	$110,000	($20,000)	($40,000)

1988 results:
Net passive activity loss:
    ($60,000 + $115,000 NOL carryover –
    $110,000 income) = ($65,000)

Net losses from B and C
  offset against A income:*
    B = $110,000 × $41,667/175,000 = $26,190
    C = $110,000 × $133,333[†]/175,000 = $83,810
    ($110,000)

Net loss from B offset
  against A income:
    ($21,670 + $20,000 – $26,190) = ($15,480)

Loss carryforward to 1989:

	Activity A	*Activity B*	*Activity C*
	-0-	-0-	($49,520)

*$21,667 + $20,000
[†]$93,333 + $40,000

REHABILITATION AND LOW-INCOME HOUSING CREDITS

In the case of the rehabilitation and low-income housing credits (but not losses), the $25,000 allowance applies on a credit-equivalent basis. This is so regardless of whether the individual claiming the credit actively participates in the rental real estate activity, including participation as a limited partner. After December 31, 1989, investors in low-income housing projects must actively participate to claim the low-income housing credit against the $25,000 allowance. However, if the property is placed in service after December 31, 1989, but before January 1, 1991, an investor will still not have to meet the active participation standard with respect to the low-income housing credit if at least 10 percent of the costs of such property are incurred before January 1, 1989.

The credit equivalent of the $25,000 allowance is $7,000 of passive credits for an individual in the 28 percent tax bracket. However, where a taxpayer has more than $250,000 of adjusted gross income, the taxpayer will generally receive no current benefit from the rehabilitation or low-income housing credit.

PLANNING

The overall effect of the passive activity loss limitation is not to *disallow* the tax benefits of a loss but to *defer* the timing of those benefits until the taxpayer recognizes income from passive activities, or until the taxpayer disposes of the entire interest in a fully taxable transaction. Consequently, the current value of any investment in a passive loss activity, relative to the value of the same investment made under the prior law, is diminished by the time value of the deferred losses.

You will have to plan carefully when evaluating any new tax-sheltered investment opportunity. The economics of the investment will be critical, as it always should have been. "Investment" planning will now be composed of two separate packages of investments: portfolio investments and passive activities.

Prospective investments in rental real estate should be evaluated primarily on their potential economic return, especially by taxpayers whose adjusted gross income exceeds $100,000 (the level at which the $25,000 allowance begins to phase out). However, rental property that qualifies for rehabilitation credits or low-income housing credits may still offer some tax benefits to taxpayers with adjusted gross incomes between $100,000 and $200,000. Income-producing limited partnerships, such as nonleveraged rental real estate, will become a popular vehicle to offset passive losses from other activities. Individuals with passive activity losses and no offsetting passive activity income may find it advantageous to convert income from an active business into passive activity income by reducing the level of involvement in the business. Conversely, individuals with passive activity losses and little or no passive activity income could attempt to convert the passive activity into an activity in which they materially participate. The potential for this would be greatest for passive S corporation shareholders who have invested in a business but who have only marginally participated in its operation.

An alternative avenue of attack would be to attempt to generate passive income from a passive income generator (PIG). One suggestion for creating a controllable passive activity income with which to absorb passive losses is to lease real estate or equipment to a closely held corporation. That rental income will be passive and will offset passive tax-shelter losses. However, if you lease real estate or equipment to a partnership or an S corporation, such rental income, unless paid under a binding lease in effect before February 19, 1988, is recharacterized to active income, which is ineligible to offset tax-sheltered losses. The opportunity to create controllable passive activity income still exists, however, with a rental to a regular or C corporation.

Many taxpayers who actively participate in rental real estate activities may not realize that their effective marginal tax rate for income over $100,000 is considerably higher than 30 percent. The phase-out of the $25,000 allowance for income over $100,000 increased a taxpayer's effective marginal tax rate on income between $100,000 and $150,000 to 42.9 percent in 1988, 46.8 percent in 1989, 47.85 percent in 1990, and over 49 percent in 1991 and later years.

The following example computes the effective marginal tax rate resulting from the passive loss limitation by comparing two situations that are identical except for an additional income of $20,000 in 1988.

Example: In 1988, Mr. and Mrs. Couple had adjusted gross income of $120,000, not counting $25,000 of losses from rental real estate activities in which Mrs. Couple actively participated. Under the passive loss limitation rules, $19,000 of the real estate losses could be used to offset their other income. (The $120,000 of income phases out $10,000 of the loss that would be allowed under the rental real estate allowance. However, the amount disallowed under the $25,000 allowance phase-out was then subject to the more general passive loss rule under which only 60 percent was disallowed in 1988. Therefore, they were allowed $15,000 of losses under the $25,000 allowance rule and $4,000 under the general passive loss rule.) Consequently, their adjusted gross income was $101,000. After itemized deductions and personal exemptions, their taxable income was $90,000. Their tax liability is $22,237.

Mr. and Mrs. Family has an identical income pattern except for the fact that they had an additional $20,000 of capital gains. Under the $25,000 allowance phase-out rule, only $5,000 of their real estate losses was deductible (the $140,000 of income causes $20,000 to be phased out). Of the remaining $20,000 of loss, the general passive loss rule permitted $8,000 to be deducted ($20,000 reduced by 60 percent). This produced $127,000 of adjusted gross income. With the same itemized deductions and personal exemptions, their taxable income was $116,000, and their tax liability was $30,817.

Summary:	Mr. and Mrs. Family's tax	$30,817
	Mr. and Mrs. Couple's tax	$22,237
	Tax on marginal income	$ 8,580

$$\text{Effective tax rate on marginal income} = \frac{\$\,8,580}{\$20,000} = 42.9\%$$

A Deferral and Leverage

There normally are three elements that make up the typical tax shelter arrangement. One or more of these elements will be found in almost all tax shelters. The first is the *deferral concept,* in which deductions are accelerated in order to reduce the tax liability of an individual in the early years of the transaction instead of matching those deductions against the income that is eventually generated from the investment. This deferral of tax liability from the earlier years to the future years results, in effect, in an interest-free loan by the federal government, repayable when the investment either produces net taxable income, is sold, or is otherwise disposed of.

The other element of a typical tax shelter is *leverage,* in which borrowed funds are used in a taxpayer's investments to pay the expenses for which accelerated deductions are received. Your position is enhanced when the borrowing is on a nonrecourse basis, which means that you are not *personally* liable to repay loans and your personal investment risk is limited to your equity investment. Unfortunately, recent tax laws and Internal Revenue Service rulings have limited the availability of tax shelter investments with a nonrecourse-loan basis.

A third tax shelter element for many investments is the *conversion* of ordinary income to capital gains at the time of the sale or other disposition of the investment. Long-term capital gains are taxed at a *maximum* 15 percent (20 percent for sales prior to May 6, 2003; 23.8 percent in 2013 with the surcharge on unearned income) rate. Conversion occurs when the portion of the gain reflecting the accelerated deductions taken against ordinary income is taxed as a capital gain. If you are in a lower income tax bracket in the later years, you effectively convert the tax rate as well.

The rest of this chapter will discuss several of the traditional tax shelters and examine and analyze their elements, advantages, and disadvantages. I will focus on traditional tax shelter investments—real estate, oil and gas, equipment leasing, etc. In the next chapter, I will unveil those super-sophisticated, nontraditional tax shelters that can bring your effective tax liability down to zero.

113 Real Estate

"It'd take a genius to invest in real estate and pay taxes": House Ways and Means Committee member Fortney H. (Pete) Stark, D-Calif., on the committee's decisions regarding the taxation of real estate, 1986. Of the various forms of investments available to you that involve possible tax incentives, the most widely used is real estate. Historically, real estate has been sold as an investment for income and long-term gain, as well as a hedge against inflation. Real estate can be purchased in the form of shopping centers, warehouse net leases, apartment buildings, residential housing, and even raw land.

In the decade before reform, one of the major reasons for the high degree of tax shelter investment in real estate was that the "at risk" rules introduced by the Tax Reform Act of 1976 did not apply to any partnership in which the principal activity was investing in real estate. The "at risk" rules limited your tax deductions to the amount you invested plus the amount of borrowed funds for which you were personally liable. Real estate tax shelters were exempt from this requirement until January 1, 1987 (Tax Reform Act of 1986).

Prior to 1987, the law provided an at-risk limitation on losses from business and income-producing activities other than real estate and certain active corporate business activities applicable to individuals and to certain closely held corporations. Taxpayers could deduct losses from an activity only to the extent of the amount they had at risk in the activity. The amount at risk is generally the sum of (1) the taxpayer's cash contributions to the activity; (2) the adjusted basis of other property contributed to the activity; and (3) recourse debt (amounts borrowed for use in the activity with respect to which the taxpayer has personal liability or has pledged property not used in the activity). Nonrecourse debt (amounts borrowed for use in the activity for which none of the participants assumes personal liability and which is secured only by the assets of the activity) is not considered an amount at risk in the activity. The amount at risk is generally increased (or decreased) each year by the taxpayer's share of income (or losses and withdrawals) from the activity.

The Tax Reform Act of 1986 applied the at-risk rules to the activity of holding real property, with an exception for *qualified nonrecourse financing*. In general, taxpayers will be considered at risk with respect to their share of any *qualified nonrecourse financing* that is secured by real property used in the activity. The term qualified nonrecourse financing means any financing that is borrowed by the taxpayer (1) with respect to the activity of holding real property; (2) from a *qualified person*, or represents a loan from a federal, state, or local government, or is guaranteed by any federal, state, or local government; (3) except to the extent provided in regulations, with respect to which no person is personally liable for repayment; and (4) which is not convertible debt.

In the case of a partnership, a partner's share of any qualified nonrecourse financing of the partnership will be determined on the basis of the partner's share of liabilities incurred in connection with the financing of the partnership.

Borrowing from a "qualified person" means (1) the loan is taken from an unrelated commercial lender, or is from or guaranteed by certain government entities; (2) the property is acquired from an unrelated person; (3) the lender is unrelated to the seller; (4) the lender or a related person does not receive a fee with respect to the taxpayer's investment in the property; (5) debt is not convertible; and (6) the nonrecourse debt does not exceed 80 percent of the credit base of the property. However, nonrecourse debt acquired from related persons may still be qualified nonrecourse financing if the financing from the related person is "commercially reasonable and on substantially the same terms as loans involving unrelated persons."

An analysis of the nontax advantages of real estate investments follows.

LEVERAGE

Leverage is the use of borrowed funds with the anticipation that the property will increase in value at a rate greater than the cost of borrowing, so that a profit will be realized not only on the investor's own money but also on the use of someone else's money. For example, if you make an investment of $100, putting up $10 in cash and borrowing $90 at an interest rate of 10 percent, at the end of the first year you will have a net cash outflow of $19 (your $10 initial investment plus $9 interest on the $90 borrowed). Assume your property increases in value 20 percent during that same period and then you sell it, paying off your $90 debt. You receive a total of $120; subtract the $99 ($90 in principal plus $9 in interest), and you have a net gain of $21. On your initial cash investment of $10, this represents a 210 percent return. You can often use borrowed capital in a real estate purchase to finance as much as 80 percent of the total cost of the property.

INFLATION HEDGE

The supply of real estate is clearly limited. For this reason, many people believe that investments in well-selected real estate can be expected to at least keep up with inflation, and perhaps even increase in value faster than inflation.

CASH FLOW

In many cases, good income-producing real property will generate a favorable cash flow. This cash flow can be augmented by increased income tax savings due to the shelter aspects of real estate investments.

EQUITY BUILDUP

Income-producing real estate may create increased liquidity. Debt reduction plus inflation may create equity that can be the source of new or additional financing.

ABILITY TO POOL CAPITAL

Syndicates or partnerships enable investors to pool their capital in order to acquire large, select properties they would not be able to buy individually.

DEDUCTIBLE EXPENSES

There are basically five different categories of expenses that are deductible on a real estate deal:

1. *Mortgage interest,* that portion of debt service payments represented by deductible interest costs.

2. *Depreciation,* an accounting adjustment that reflects the theoretical wear and tear and economic obsolescence of the property. Because of this, a portion of the income you receive is considered a return of your capital investment and not subject to tax.

3. *Operating expenses,* which include property management, maintenance, insurance, garbage removal, real estate taxes, common area utilities, etc.

4. *Construction period expenses,* deductible expenses incurred before the building is occupied, such as real estate taxes, interest on the construction loan, etc. These costs are not deductible when incurred, but must be amortized over a period of years.

5. *Fees,* a portion of the purchase price that, frequently, the seller of the property agrees to take as payment for services, resulting in an immediate deduction—for instance, guarantees for "rent up," completion, financing, etc.

Note that you can rent living space to a relative at below the fair market rate and still treat the activity as a business entitling you to deduct depreciation, utilities, insurance, and other business expenses. The Tax Court has validated this reduced rate despite a tax code requirement that relatives be charged a "fair" rent. This is because there is less risk involved in renting to a relative than to a stranger, so the relative is entitled to a discount. In one case, the court suggested that a discount of 20 percent would be reasonable (*Lee Bindseil,* T.C. Memo 1983-411).

The tax advantage of real estate results from the possibility that your deductible expenses for tax purposes may exceed your cash outflow. Only operating expenses and mortgage interest are paid in cash from property operations. As a result, your taxable income—for instance, your rental income from the property minus the expenses listed above—does not reflect the cash flow from property operations. Your true cash flow, therefore, is your taxable income or loss plus construction period expenses and fees and depreciation minus mortgage principal payments. Construction period expenses and fees are those costs normally paid when incurred from the limited partner capital contribution or from the mortgage proceeds (but not from property operations). Depreciation is, of course, not a cash expense but rather a bookkeeping entry. Mortgage principal payments are not deductible for tax purposes because they have been included in your basis of the property and are reflected for tax purposes in your depreciation deductions.

Although land itself cannot be depreciated, many land improvements may be. In Rev. Rul. 65-256, 1965-2 C.B. 52, the Internal Revenue Service ruled that the excavating, grading, and removal costs "directly associated" with the construction of buildings and paved roadways are depreciable. Such directly associated costs have included:

1. Grading and graveling of a private road to provide customers with access to a store and warehouse

2. Plank road and filling in and grading of swampland on which a new lumberyard was constructed

3. Expenditures for slag and for grading and building up swampland to make a level racetrack and to create roads and parking space for customers

4. A tunnel constructed under a public road between two business buildings used by a taxpayer

5. The cost of sidewalks, gutters, and drains constructed on a taxpayer's private property in a mill village

Although real estate must now be depreciated over either 27.5 years (for residential) or 39 years (31.5 years for property placed in service before May 14, 1993 unless placed in service before January 1, 1994 and there was either a binding contract or construction started before May 13, 1993), taxpayers can write off *land improvements* over just 15 years, using 200 percent declining-balance depreciation.

The following computations show a hypothetical tax income statement loss and its conversion into a cash flow gain:

Tax Income Statement		
Rental Income		$500
Less:		
operating expenses	$150	
mortgage interest	250	
construction period expenses	80	
fees	25	
depreciation	+175	
	$680	
		−680
Tax Income (loss)		($180)

Cash Flow

Tax Income (loss)		($180)
Add back:		
construction period expenses	$ 80	
fees	25	
depreciation	+175	
	$280	
		$100
Minus mortgage principal payments		– 25
Cash Flow from Property Operations		$ 75

At a 28 percent marginal tax bracket you would save $50.40 in taxes and have a positive total cash flow of $125.40 ($50.40 + $75).

Moreover, the normal real estate tax shelter is usually structured so that any actual cash losses in the first years will be provided, or paid for, by the limited partners' capital contribution or the proceeds of the mortgage itself. This item is referred to as "rent-up loss"—the operating deficit during the period before the property is fully rented.

SUMMARY OF BENEFITS

As the preceding statements indicate, there are a number of benefits achieved from real estate tax shelter investing. The bottom line of the tax income statement shows your taxable loss. Multiply this figure by your tax bracket to determine your tax savings.

The cash flow statement represents the cash distributions you will be paid from the property's operations. Add to this the cash in pocket from the above tax savings and that yields your net cash increase in wealth.

An additional benefit that investing in real estate tax shelters will yield is equity buildup. This is the amount of the mortgage principal that you are paying off each year. Even if the property value merely remains flat with no appreciation, your equity interest in that property will increase each year by the principal payoff.

The final benefit from such an investment is the potential appreciation in the property itself. Building costs are rising with inflation, so it is likely that in 10 years the replacement cost of real estate will be much higher than construction costs today. If a property is well located and well maintained, its cash flow should expand over the years and its value should increase.

Before investing in a shelter you must recognize that real estate projects fall into three major categories:

Commercial
Residential
Government-supported housing

REHABILITATION—CERTIFIED HISTORICAL CREDITS

Each category of investment has its own rules and deduction limits for tax purposes. For example, rehabilitation costs on low-income housing and certified historic structures can still qualify for investment tax credits. For a building in service before 1936 (other than a certified historic structure), the credit is 10 percent; for a certified residential or commercial historic structure, the credit increases to 20 percent! This means that you get the equivalent of one-fifth off your rehabilitation expenses. If you use the rehabilitation credit, however, you must use straight-line depreciation, reduce the base by the full amount of its credit, and make a substantial rehabilitation of the building. This means that the qualifying expenditures of the tax year and the preceding tax year must exceed the adjusted basis of the property or $5,000, whichever is larger. For rehabilitations completed in phases, the 24-month measuring period is extended to 60 months. In addition, to qualify for the credit one of the following three tests must be met:

a) at least 50 percent of the external walls are retained as external walls;

b) at least 75 percent of the external walls are retained as either external or internal walls; *and*

c) at least 75 percent of the internal structural framework is retained in place.

Under government-sponsored housing, you can deduct construction loan interest and taxes immediately; with other real estate you must amortize them over 4 years. Furthermore, an owner of a subsidized housing project may defer any taxes due on the sale of the project if it is sold to a tenant cooperative and the proceeds reinvested in another subsidized housing project within 1 year.

The new rehabilitation credit may be used to offset tax on up to $25,000 of nonpassive income, regardless of whether the individual actively participates, subject to a phase-out between $200,000 and $250,000 of adjusted gross income.

Parties interested in obtaining further information on historic preservation opportunities and procedures should contact the various agencies and organizations listed below.

Copies of historic preservation standards and guidelines set forth by the government for certifying historic structures and a current list of state historic preservation offices are available by writing to the following address:

Tax Reform Act
Office of Archaeology and Historic Preservation
Department of the Interior
Washington, DC 20240

The following is the address of the historic preservation agency that administers the Department of the Interior's preservation tax incentive program:

Historic Preservation Tax Incentives
Archaeology and Historic Preservation
National Park Service
Washington, DC 20240

The following regional offices of the National Park Service review certification applications:

Regional Office	States Administered for Tax Certification Purposes
Mid-Atlantic 143 South Third Street Philadelphia, PA 19106 (215)597-7013	Connecticut, Delaware, District of Columbia, Maine, Maryland, Massachusetts, New Hampshire, New Jersey, New York, Pennsylvania, Rhode Island, Vermont, Virginia, West Virginia
Southeast 75 Spring Street, NW Atlanta, GA 30303 (404)242-2635	Alabama, Florida, Georgia, Kentucky, Mississippi, North Carolina, Puerto Rico, South Carolina, Tennessee

Midwest
Federal Building
200 East Liberty Street
Ann Arbor, MI 48107
(313)378-2035

Illinois, Indiana, Iowa, Kansas,
Michigan, Minnesota, Missouri,
Nebraska, Ohio, Wisconsin

Rocky Mountain
P.O. Box 25287
Denver Federal Center
Denver, CO 80225
(303)234-2915

Colorado, Montana, North Dakota,
South Dakota, Utah, Wyoming

Southwest
5000 Marble Street, NE
Room 211
Albuquerque, NM 87110
(505)474-3514

Arkansas, Louisiana, New Mexico,
Oklahoma, Texas

West
450 Golden Gate Avenue
P.O. Box 36063
San Francisco, CA 94102
(415)556-7741 or 556-7090

Arizona, California, Hawaii, Nevada

Pacific Northwest
Westin Building, Room 1920
2110 Sixth Avenue
Seattle, WA 98121
(206)399-0791

Idaho, Oregon, Washington

Alaska
1011 East Tudor Street
Suite 297
Anchorage, AK 99503
(907)277-1666

Alaska

The National Trust for Historic Preservation, a private, nonprofit membership organization, provides advice on preservation issues and techniques. For more information on membership, write:

National Trust for Historic Preservation
1785 Massachusetts Avenue, NW
Washington, DC 20036

The regional offices of the National Trust are as follows:

Regional Office	States and Territories Administered
Northeast 100 Franklin Street, 7th Floor Boston, MA 02110 (617)223-7754	Connecticut, Maine, Massachusetts, New Hampshire, New York, Rhode Island, Vermont
Mid-Atlantic 1600 H Street, NW Washington, DC 20006 (202)673-4203	Delaware, District of Columbia, Maryland, New Jersey, Pennsylvania, Puerto Rico, Virgin Islands, Virginia, West Virginia
South 456 King Street Charleston, SC 29403 (803)724-4711	Alabama, Arkansas, Florida, Georgia, Kentucky, Louisiana, Mississippi, North Carolina, South Carolina, Tennessee

Regional Office	States and Territories Administered
Midwest 407 South Dearborn Street Number 710 Chicago, IL 60605 (312)353-3419 or 353-3424	Illinois, Indiana, Iowa, Michigan, Minnesota, Missouri, North Dakota, Ohio, South Dakota, Wisconsin
Southwest/Plains 210 Colcord Building Oklahoma City, OK 73102 (405)231-5126	Colorado, Kansas, Nebraska, New Mexico, Oklahoma, Texas
West 681 Market Street, Number 859 San Francisco, CA 94105 (415)556-2707	Alaska, Arizona, California, Guam, Hawaii, Idaho, Micronesia, Montana, Nevada, Oregon, Utah, Washington, Wyoming

The combination of first-year accelerated depreciation and heavy start-up costs may produce tax deductions exceeding the size of your initial cash investment when 80 percent of the cost of that investment is financed with borrowings. What that means is that if you are in the 28 percent bracket, your net initial cash outlay may be reduced to zero! However, with any tax shelter, as with any investment, *never* invest just on the basis of tax deductions alone. You must always consider the total expected cash flow from the property. The advantages of a real estate tax shelter are that the risks are normally minimal and the total cash flow is normally augmented in the early years by substantial tax savings. Furthermore, a good shelter should be structured to give you substantial cash rental income that is either minimally taxed or not taxed at all due to offsetting depreciation expense deductions even in the middle years. These depreciation deductions are pencil transactions that do not involve any real cash outflow, and they arise out of basis created by borrowed money. In effect, with a properly structured transaction you get to eat your cake and keep it too.

LOW-INCOME HOUSING CREDITS

The Tax Reform Act of 1986 created a new low-income housing credit. This housing credit is claimed annually over a 10-year period with percentages set so that over that 10-year period, the credits will equal a present value of 70 percent of the basis of a new building which is not federally subsidized and 30 percent of the basis of an existing building or federally subsidized new building. The credit applies only to expenditures on the low-income units, and rehabilitation expenditures will qualify for the credit only if they exceed $2,000 per unit.

A building will qualify for the credit if either at least 20 percent of the units are occupied by individuals with incomes of 60 percent or less of area median income, or if at least 40 percent of the units are occupied by individuals with incomes of 50 percent or less of area median income. Furthermore, the rent charged to tenants may not exceed 30 percent of the applicable qualified income, which will vary depending on family size.

If a building is placed in service in 1987, the credit percentages are 9 percent annually over 10 years (that equates to the 70 percent present value credit), and/or 4 percent over 10 years (that equates to the 30 percent present value credit).

If a building is placed in service after 1987, the credit percentages will be adjusted monthly by the Treasury to reflect the present values of 70 percent and 30 percent at the time the building is placed in service. In a project consisting of two or more buildings placed in service in different months, a separate credit percentage may apply to each building.

One additional word on real estate tax shelters. The Senate Report on the Tax Reform Act of 1986 (S. Rep. at 742) states that hotel and motel properties ("transient rentals") are not considered to be rental activities, and thus are not per se designated as passive. Consequently, if a real estate investor holds hotel and motel property either through a general partnership interest or ownership in an S Corporation, and if that investor actively manages the property, it may be possible to have these properties designated as active businesses. In this case, the investor would be able to utilize losses from the property to offset other income. In order to qualify as an active manager, you must "materially participate" in the running of the hotel business. You should attempt to do each of the following:

1. Make frequent visits to the hotel for on-site inspections and consultations with the firm managing your condo.

2. Regularly establish room rental rates.

3. Set up and review hiring and other personnel policies.

4. Review and approve periodic financial reports.

5. Participate in budgeting operating costs and establishing capital expenditures.

6. Establish the need and level of financial resources.

7. Select the bank depository for rental proceeds and reserves.

8. Assist in off-site business promotion activities.

Alternatively, if the hotel or motel is producing taxable income, holding such property through a limited partnership interest would characterize the income generated therefrom as passive. By eliminating hotel or motel properties from the rental income classification, the Tax Reform Act presents a unique planning opportunity with respect to such properties. Such ownership gives you, the investor, the opportunity to classify the activities as either active or passive, depending upon which planning approach you choose to undertake.

Watch out for fees in many limited partnership deals. A typical limited partnership will pay 7 to 10 percent of equity in sales commissions; 1 to 3 percent or more of the equity raised for legal, accounting, and paperwork expenses; and up to 15 percent of the equity for organization and mortgage finding fees. Later, sponsors may take 5 to 6 percent of the cash flow in property management fees. After the property is sold, 3 to 6 percent of the sales price may go for commissions, and an additional 10 to 33 percent of any profit on the sale may go to the sponsors. Clearly, the greater the front-end fee, the less money is left to invest in property. According to Arnold G. Rudoff, who analyzes partnerships for the accounting firm of Price Waterhouse in San Francisco, real estate front-end fees should be under 20 percent.

According to a survey by the accounting firm of Coopers & Lybrand, privately offered real estate partnership transactions showed the following fees and structure:

	Typical	Range
Partnership participation		
Cash flow	10%	1–10%
Tax benefits	10%	1–10%
Refinancing/disposition (subordinated)	20%	15–30%
Initial fees (as % of equity raised)		
Sales commission	8%	6–10%
Acquisition and ancillary fees	30%	15–60%
Operating period (as % of revenues)		
Property management	4%	3–6%
Partnership management	Modest	Modest
Reimbursable expenses	Modest	Modest
Disposition fees		
Real estate commission	3%	Competitive
Participation in residual value	20%	15–30%

Reprinted with permission of Coopers & Lybrand © March 1985 Coopers & Lybrand (USA)

One measure of the fairness of offering terms is how the various fees relate to the North American Securities Administrators Association (NASAA) guidelines. These guidelines appear in the next section.

114 Fees in Public Real Estate Partnerships

Front-end fees include sales commissions for the broker/dealer, offering and organization costs, and property acquisition fees paid to the general partner and unaffiliated third parties. The NASAA front-end fee standard is 20 percent of limited partner capital contributions for unleveraged properties, 28.1 percent for 50 percent leveraged properties, and 33 percent for 80 percent leveraged properties.

Operational phase fees are typically paid to the general partner from cash flow (earnings) of the real estate as compensation for management of the day-to-day operation of the partnership and the properties. NASAA approves "property management fees" equal to 6 percent of gross revenues for residential properties and 3 percent of gross revenues for commercial properties, plus a "promotional" interest of 10 percent of annual cash flow (if the liquidation phase fee from net proceeds, explained below, is limited to 15 percent).

Liquidation phase fees are payable to the general partner upon resale or refinancing of the properties. These fees consist of a real estate commission and a percentage of the net proceeds from the sale or refinancing of the property. Normally, these fees are subordinated (not paid to the general partner) until the return of the limited partners' investment, plus a minimum return. NASAA approves a real estate commission to all parties, not to exceed 3 percent. The promotional or incentive fee is limited to 15 percent if the sponsor also received 10 percent of annual cash flow, or 25 percent otherwise. The real estate commission and the appreciation percentage are "subordinated" to the return of limited partner capital, plus a minimum return of 6 percent per annum on initial capital reduced by periodic cash distributions.

115 Oil and Gas

Petroleum and gas are important sources of energy throughout the world. Accordingly, Congress has determined that certain types of investments in oil and gas are deductible. Former Attorney General Smith invested in an oil and gas partnership. An investment in an oil and gas program is probably your most advantageous single-year tax-advantaged investment if the economics are viable.

The tax advantage in an oil and gas deal is the ability to deduct, as a current expense, the investments in capital expenditures known as intangible drilling and developing costs, or IDCs. The income tax regulations define *intangibles* as any cost incurred that has no salvage value and is "incident to and necessary for the drilling of wells and the preparation of wells for the production of oil and gas." This definition includes the hours worked by the drilling crew and the cost of the installation of tangible equipment placed *in the well,* although the cost of such equipment must be capitalized and recovered through depreciation. Expressly excluded from classification as *intangibles* are expenditures incurred in connection with equipment, facilities, or structures (including installation charges) that are not incident to or necessary for the drilling of oil or gas wells but are used in operations after the oil or gas is produced (for instance, structures for storing and treating oil or gas).

Essentially, then, nearly all costs of drilling and completing a well, except for the bare cost of the lease, the cost of tangible equipment and labor, and the geological and geophysical costs incurred prior to the selection of a drill site, are deductible in the year incurred. Without this special break accorded to intangible drilling and development costs, you would be unable to deduct them until drilling was either abandoned or the product was actually being extracted from the wells.

In the first year you are able immediately to deduct 70 percent to 80 percent of productive-well costs as intangible expenses, and 100 percent of dry well costs. In many public tax shelter programs, you pay for only intangible costs and can therefore immediately deduct up to 100 percent of the amount you invest.

There is a catch: with gas and oil deals the Internal Revenue Service will not permit deductions in excess of your personal cash investment, or "at risk" basis. In the past, however, it did permit the year-end deduction of all the intangible costs of wells even if those wells were not actually to be drilled until the following year. (Thus promoters of oil and gas shelters tried to "front load" deductions in the initial year of the shelter by prepayment of intangible costs.) In all other tax shelters, legislation has ruled out retroactive allocations of losses for year-end investments; it also no longer allows immediate deductions for many expenses that are incurred prior to actual operations—for example, cattle feeding programs—unless there is a clear business purpose. And on St. Patrick's Day, 1980, the Internal Revenue Service asserted that prepaid intangible drilling costs *also* must be disallowed as a deduction in the year paid—unless the taxpayer can demonstrate the existence of some commercial exigency making it advisable to prepay the costs.*

In an Eighth Circuit 1984 Court of Appeals Case (*Keller*, 84-1 USTC Par. 9194, 53 AFTR2d 84-663), the Court found that prepayments for intangible costs served no business purpose and materially distorted the taxpayer's income. The taxpayer's deduction, therefore, was deferred until the subsequent year.

The Keller case, however, did not involve a "turnkey" contract. In fact, the Court found that with a "turnkey" contract, where the amounts expended could not be refunded, a prepayment would be deductible in the year paid. This was a validation of the general rule that intangible drilling and development costs under a "turnkey" agreement were deductible in the year paid (*Ruth*, T.C. Memo 1983-586).

Furthermore, the Tax Reform Act of 1984 provided that "tax shelters" (other than forming syndicates), whether on the cash or accrual method, will not be able to deduct prepaid expenses until both economic performance occurs and the expenses actually paid are incurred. A deduction, however, will

*Rev. Rul. 80-71, I.R.B. 1980-11, 7.

be allowed for prepaid expenses where economic performance occurs after the end of the year under the following conditions:

a) Economic performance occurs within 90 days after the end of the taxable year;

b) the deduction is limited to the cash investment made by the person (i.e., not paid for with any recourse or nonrecourse liabilities); *and*

c) the requirements of present laws are met.

For purposes of this exception in the case of intangible drilling expenses, economic performance occurs when the well is "spudded." If oil and gas prepayments do not meet the requirements of the 90-day exception, economic performance will occur as the drilling services are provided. If drilling is commenced in the year of prepayment (and the above exception is not met), only that portion of the intangible drilling cost attributable to drilling prior to the end of the year will be deductible in that year. This provision applies for prepayments made after March 31, 1984, and enhances the potential significance of a "turnkey" contract.

Note, in addition, that working interest in any oil or gas property that you hold directly or through an entity that does not limit your liability with respect to such interest will be treated as an active trade or business and will not be subject to the passive loss rules.

TAX SHELTER STRATEGIES

A sophisticated shelter will sustain the current deductibility of an intangible drilling cost prepayment by the following techniques:

- The prepayment requirements should be set forth in the contract.

- The contract should set forth the particular well to be drilled and provide for a definite commencement date.

- If it is a co-owner situation, the same prepayment requirement should be imposed on other co-owners.

- The contract should be with the actual driller, if possible, and not with an intermediary.

- There should be a business benefit to be derived from the prepayment requirement (that is, the price might be lower if the driller is paid in advance).

- The contract should be binding on the driller.

- Prepayment should not be more than a reasonable estimate of the amount to come due to the driller.

- The payments should actually be made prior to the end of the year, and the driller's access to the funds should not be restricted (that is, payment into an escrow account may not constitute a valid prepayment).

Additional tax shelter is still available through your ability to take 200 percent declining-balance depreciation on the remaining 20 to 30 percent of the costs of the wells (capitalized costs). A statutory depletion deduction (one that is provided by law), which is 15 percent of your gross income from the well before expenses, also is available.

After the development of the property and the drilling are completed, the program will begin to receive cash from oil or gas sales, if any successful wells are drilled. If receipts exceed operating and overhead costs as well as depletion and depreciation, you will have taxable income.

The depletion allowance you are allowed to claim is the *greater* of cost depletion or percentage depletion.

COST DEPLETION

Cost depletion is computed by dividing the estimated total units (barrels of oil or thousand cubic feet of gas) recoverable from the property into its adjusted tax basis in order to obtain the per-unit depletion allowance, and then multiplying the per-unit depletion allowance by the number of units sold during the year. Cost depletion is then compared to percentage depletion on a property-by-property basis to determine the amount to be deducted.

PERCENTAGE DEPLETION

Percentage depletion for up to 1,000 barrels of average daily production of oil or 6 million cubic feet of domestic natural gas is allowed to "independent producers and royalty owners" at the rate of 15 percent of gross revenue. This depletion allowance is limited to 50 percent of the net income from the property. The allowance calculated is further limited to 65 percent of your taxable income (prior to taking the depletion allowance). The 65 percent limitation and average daily production limitation are calculated at the individual investor or partner level.

Both cost and percentage depletion are computed separately for *each* property in which you have an interest. Percentage depletion at the applicable statutory rate is computed on *gross* income from the property before deductions of any kind, including production or windfall profit taxes, operating expenses, or depreciation. Accordingly, the benefit obtained is significantly more than the statutory rate as a percentage of net (taxable) income.

The Supreme Court has ruled, in *Commissioner v. Engle et ux.*, S. Ct. Docket 82-599, that lessors of interests in mineral deposits are entitled to percentage depreciation allowances on any bonus or advanced royalties whether or not there is actual production of the underlying mineral in the year of payment. Production, therefore, has been found not to be a prerequisite for claiming percentage depletion deductions on lease bonus and advanced royalty income.

Percentage depletion is almost always larger than cost depletion. For example, if a well is drilled on a lease that cost $2,000 and yields an estimated 100,000 barrels of recoverable reserves, the rate of cost depletion for that property would be 2¢ per barrel of oil produced. This is far less than percentage depletion at the applicable rate. Fifteen percent of the gross income of oil selling at $85 per barrel is $12.75. The net impact of the depreciation and depletion deductions is that, with normal operating expenses, from about a quarter to a third of your income from the well is tax-free.

Oil and gas drilling tax shelter programs break down into three types:

1. *Wildcatting,* also known as exploratory drilling, which involves drilling operations in search of a yet-undiscovered pool of oil or gas, or with the hope of greatly extending the limits of a pool already developed. It is an attempt to find new fields where the probability of success for an individual well may be 10 percent and the chances of "proving," or discovering, a big field are about 1 percent to 2 percent.

2. *Development drilling,* which involves drilling an additional well to a reservoir that supports an already-producing well on a lease or on an offset lease that is usually close to or adjacent to the producing well. Development wells can have success rates of from 75 percent to 100 percent, but real fortunes are made only by "proving" a big field and selling or developing it.

3. *Balanced or combination programs,* which involve both exploratory and development drilling, therefore promising up-side potential with limited downside risk. Unfortunately, most balanced programs combine wildcatting's delayed significant cash flow (3 years can be common) with a development program's low multiple cash return (on average, 2.5 × the cash investment).

Unlike most investments, investments in oil and gas exploration may result in a complete loss. Industry statistics reflect that about 1 out of 10 wildcat wells is productive and that many of the productive wells do not have sufficient reserves to cover the drilling, equipping, and operating costs of the wildcat venture. Approximately 1 out of 200 wildcat wells discovers a medium-size field, and only 1 out of 1,000 discovers a large field. As indicated by the statistics, investments in oil and gas exploration should be spread over a sufficient number of prospects to provide you with a reasonable expectation of a return on your investment.

If you are interested in entering the oil business, there are several ways to participate, including the following:

- Participation with an oil operator on a selective basis for fractional interest in a number of oil and gas prospects

- Participation with several different oil operators for a fractional interest in selected oil and gas prospects

- Investments in a limited partnership with one or more oil and gas prospects

- Various combinations of these

NONTAX CONSIDERATIONS

In addition to the tax considerations discussed above, you must examine the following nontax considerations if you want to get involved with oil and gas.

Management

Management in the oil business is of primary importance. The ability to operate an oil and gas investment program successfully consists basically of two skills: technical expertise and administrative competence. The organization must have the technical expertise to assemble prospects, select drilling sites, supervise the drilling and completion of wells, operate productive wells, and market the output. The competence of the technical staff is extremely difficult to evaluate on a short-run basis, since entirely new prospects are assembled and drilled each year.

Program Size

There is no optimum program size. However, the size of the technical and administrative staffs will dictate certain minimum and maximum projects that can be undertaken. The program should have enough capital to drill a sufficient number of prospects for a reasonable spread of the risks; also, a minimum amount of capital must be raised to be used for administrative costs associated with offering the program and other administrative matters.

The area in which operations will be conducted is also important. A $5 million program that will explore an area where the average well costs $400,000 could offer a satisfactory spread of risk. A $5 million program exploring in areas where the average well costs $1.5 million may *not* offer an adequate spread. The geographic area in which the technical staff has expertise should also be considered. A technical staff with operating experience in Colorado and Wyoming may not be qualified to conduct operations in Texas and Louisiana.

Past Performance

One of the most important nontax considerations that you must examine is the drilling company's past record of performance. You should measure and compare the net future revenues from proven oil and gas reserves in relation to limited partner capital contributions. Use only proven reserves, not what are called probable or possible reserves. Examine the price escalation figures and use only formulas provided by an independent reserve engineering firm.

Do not focus on past performance success ratios or cash distribution tables. The success ratio is the percent of all wells drilled that are completed as producing wells. A better success ratio does not necessarily mean a better economic result. For example, drilling in the Appalachian Basin (Ohio and West Virginia) should be successful 90 percent of the time, while drilling in Louisiana may be successful only perhaps 30 percent or 40 percent of the time. Why then should you invest in a project that drills in Louisiana? The answer is more abundant reserves and a potentially greater return on investment.

The cash distribution tables show the cash actually paid out to the investor. These can be deceiving in that some types of wells pay (or produce) over 50 percent of all that they will ever pay out in the first 2 years of their productive life; after the first 4 years, they do not produce any significant revenues. Other types of wells produce a lower percentage in their earlier life but continue to produce for as long as 20 to 30 years.

Management Costs

An additional nontax risk of oil and gas deals is the overpricing of the leases so that various parties in the promotional and marketing chain can realize this compensation from the initial capital invested. As compensation, the general partner and/or operator may receive up to 25 percent of the revenues earned by the limited partners after paying oil and gas royalties to the land owner and other promotional interests. In addition, there is usually a first-year management fee of about 5 percent of the amount of the investment.

Generally, you should expect to hold your interest in the well for its life-time. Your investment is a capital asset and if sold should produce capital gains. But if the well is sold, then a portion of the intangible drilling costs deducted during the developmental phase of the shelter may be "recaptured" and treated as ordinary income, as may some of the depreciation taken. Many public programs offer buy-back provisions after 2 or 3 years of operation, but generally you will receive a better return if you wait 5 to 7 years. With a successful shelter, you might well be advised to retain your interest in the shelter, collect the cash flow from the sale of the oil, and shelter this income with percentage depletion. It is not normally recommended that you buy the interest of an original investor as a tax shelter. This is because although percentage depletion is available to investors who are in a successful oil deal during the developmental phase, an investor who purchases the interest of the original investor in the deal is purchasing a "proven property" and therefore is not entitled to percentage depletion deductions.

Compensation

If you are interested in involving yourself as an active developer of oil and gas properties, you should note that compensation paid in oil rights potentially can be tax-free. In Letter Ruling 813-7006, the Internal Revenue Service held that a consultant who contributed only services to the pool of capital, acquiring in return an interest in the minerals (oil) in place, is not required to include that interest in his income. The same reasoning has been extended to accountants, lawyers, geologists, petroleum engineers, and lease brokers who receive an interest in an oil or gas drilling venture in return for services rendered. The contributors are not viewed as performing services for compensation but are viewed as acquiring capital interests through making a contribution to the pool of capital that is necessary for development (see Rev. Rul. 77-176, 1977-1 C.B. 78, and G.C.M. 22730, 1941-1 C.B. 214, but see Rev. Rul. 83-46, where overriding royalty interest to a corporate promoter, an attorney, and an employee were found to be includable in gross income at fair market value immediately. See also Rev. Proc. 93-27, 6/9/93, where a partnership profit interest received for services was not a taxable event).

STRUCTURING A SUCCESSFUL OIL OR GAS TAX SHELTER

Assume that you are in the 43 percent bracket, including not only federal taxes but state and local income taxes as well. You invest $50,000 in an oil program in which 80 percent of your investment is deductible as intangible drilling costs.

The remaining 20 percent is depreciated and deducted on a 10-year straight-line basis. Assume in addition that the well produces a lifetime total income of only $50,000.

First Year

IDC deduction (80% of $50,000)	$40,000
Plus depreciation deduction (1/10 of 20% of $50,000)	+ 1,000
	41,000
First-year net cost [$50,000 – ($41,000 × .43)]	$32,370

Subsequent Years' Total

Total income		$50,000
Depletion sheltered (15% × $50,000)	$ 7,500	
Plus depreciation		
(9/10 of 20% of $50,000)	+ 9,000	
Nontaxable cash income	$16,500	
Plus after-tax cash from taxable income		
[$33,500 – (.43 × $33,500)]	+19,095	
After-tax return		$35,595
Minus first-year net cost		–32,370
Net Cash Return		$ 3,225

Note that while no allowance for discounting future income to present value is made in the above analysis, if your oil or gas investment returns a total income at least equal to your initial cash investment, it will be at least marginally successful. Any excess return over your initial investment will substantially multiply your yield on that investment, especially on an after-tax basis.

SELF-EMPLOYMENT TAX TECHNIQUES

The Tax Reform Act of 1986 has made purchasing a working interest in oil and gas wells a popular technique by allowing a working interest owner to escape the passive loss rules and claim drilling costs against other income, such as salaries, interest, or dividends. An interesting opportunity has recently been created with respect to self-employment tax on oil and gas income. The IRS has taken the position that a working interest constitutes a trade or business for purposes of the self-employment (Social Security) tax. It is irrelevant whether operations were conducted by the working interest owner or by a third party. In that case, the IRS viewed the third-party operator as acting as the agent for the owner (Rev. Rul. 58-166). The position of the Internal Revenue Service, therefore, was that any income from a working interest in a gas or oil well constituted self-employment income. Such income or such losses were therefore added or subtracted if the taxpayer was not over the Social Security maximum with compensation from other employment and the like. Such income, however, would qualify for a Keogh contribution.

In *Howard W. Hendrickson,* T.C. Memo 1987-566, November 12, 1987, the Tax Court ruled that a salesman who had no experience in the oil and gas industry and who purchased a 21.875 percent interest in a gas well, as well as similar interest in two other wells, was not in the trade or business of producing oil and gas and therefore was not subject to self-employment tax.

These conflicting opinions allow you the following choice. If you are under the Social Security maximum and have losses from a working interest in a gas or oil well, the IRS position should be adopted to further reduce your potential self-employment taxes. However, if you have gains from a working interest and are not at the Social Security maximum, and *if you fit within the parameters* of the *Hendrickson* case, you should adopt the position of the Tax Court and not increase your self-employment income for Social Security tax purposes. [Note that the Tax Court, in *Cokes,* 91 T.C. 222 (1988) and *Perry,* T.C. Memo 1994-215, came to a conclusion in opposition to *Hendrickson.* The facts in those cases, however, were different.]

116 Equipment Leasing

Leasing, as a method of financing capital assets for industry, has grown tremendously in recent years and can be a good tax shelter. According to the National Association of Securities Dealers, equipment leasing deals have been the fastest growing category of direct placement programs (tax shelters). Capital assets frequently financed by leasing include computers, airplanes, railroad rolling stock, ships, pollution control equipment, and industrial machinery.

A lease contract allows the lessee to use the equipment for a specified length of time in return for periodic rental payments. While a variety of lease contracts have been developed, such contracts will normally be classified either as finance (full-payout) leases or as operating (non-full-payout) leases.

Finance leases provide the lessor with recovery of the cost and a reasonable profit from rentals and tax benefits over the original noncancelable lease term. These leases may be leveraged or nonleveraged. A leveraged lease is one in which the lessor has financed a significant portion (typically up to 80 percent) of the equipment purchased from third-party lenders. In the case of a non-leveraged lease, the lessor provides 100 percent of the equipment cost, either entirely through equity or by a combination of equity and recourse debt (a debt on which you are personally liable). Finance leases are almost invariably net leases—that is, the lessee is obligated to pay for most of the expenses, such as maintenance and property taxes associated with the equipment and insurance.

Operating leases do not provide the lessor with a return of cost over the initial noncancelable lease term. In order to realize a profit, lessors rely on their ability to sell or re-lease the equipment profitably at the end of the initial lease term. An operating lease may or may not be a net lease. It is not unusual for lessors writing operating leases to provide other services, such as maintenance and repair, along with the equipment.

The typical format of an equipment leasing transaction includes the following:

- Purchase of the equipment by a limited partnership (or direct ownership by the investor) for a cash down payment plus financing (either recourse or nonrecourse) for the balance of the purchase price.

- The equipment is then typically leased as either a full-payout finance lease or an operating lease.

- The lease may grant an option to purchase the equipment at a specified price at its fair market value.

- The lease may contain renewal options.

NONTAX CONSIDERATIONS

As an investor-owner, you must be aware of several nontax considerations. First, with a normal financing lease, you are in effect making a loan to the lessee of the purchase price of the equipment. Under an equipment leasing deal, you normally will have a greater economic return than you could realize on a conventional loan transaction.

Alternatively, since you are the owner of the equipment, you must take the risk of technological improvements—for instance, the obsolescence of the equipment. This risk can be modified by leasing on what is known as a "hell and high water" basis. Under such an arrangement, the lessee is obligated to make lease payments whether or not continued use of the equipment is desired. In effect, you are shifting the risk of obsolescence to the lessee. But as a result of that shift, you will receive reduced lease payments.

In addition, you must face a credit risk. Will the lessee be financially able to meet the lease payments? If not, your cash flow will be terminated and you will have to find another lessee.

There is also an interest risk. You as a lessor are essentially extending credit throughout the lease term at a fixed rate, while at the same time you may obtain your funds at variable rates—usually from banks at the prime rate or higher. In addition, your total annual debt service cost can be quite a bit higher than the interest charge alone because of the repayment of principal. If the interest rates on your borrowing increase, they can completely eliminate your return. When the cost of debt service exceeds the cash flow from the property, you have what is known as "negative leverage." Under these circumstances, your only real alternative is to repay the debt.

Finally, the residual value risk must be considered. Will the property be worth the anticipated amount at the end of the lease term? If not, your return could be significantly reduced.

There are also some nontax considerations for the lessee. Normally, the lessee will be making lease rental payments in amounts less than the direct purchase price of the equipment, even if paid on an installment basis.

In many cases, the lessee is cash poor or has limited borrowing capacity, and an equipment leasing arrangement reduces short-term cash outlay. In some cases, equipment leasing tax shelters may be structured in a sale leaseback format: The lessee originally owns the equipment but sells it to meet an immediate cash need. Under the terms of sale, the lessee turns around and leases the equipment from the buyer-lessor. Such a transaction will immediately augment the lessee's short-term cash position.

TAX BENEFITS

The key tax benefit that results from equipment leasing is deferral, which is a means of postponing a tax liability until a later and more convenient time. In years when your tax liability is high, you can invest in an equipment leasing program. You deduct a large amount of depreciation in the first year, along with miscellaneous front-end expenses and interest on the borrowed capital. After the first 3 to 5 years, the lease will begin generating taxable income because depreciation and interest will have been reduced. Be aware, though, that there may not be any cash income paid to you because of the debt service payments due on the borrowed money. However, you should note that by the time you start receiving taxable income prior to sufficient tax-flow generation, you will have had the use and yield on the considerable tax savings for a significant period of time.

DEPRECIATION

The deferral advantage of equipment leasing discussed above comes mainly from depreciation. The accelerated depreciation rate is 200 percent of straight-line depreciation. Furthermore, what is known as "the half-year convention" is automatically imputed in the ACRS depreciation tables. The half-year convention allows a person who puts equipment into service anytime during the year to depreciate that equipment as though that person had had it for half the entire year. However, the Tax Reform Act of 1986 provides that a mid-quarter convention be applied to all property that is more than 40 percent of all property placed in service by a taxpayer during the last 3 months of the taxable year. This mid-quarter convention treats all property placed in service during any quarter of a taxable year as placed in service on the midpoint of such quarter. Moreover, if the leasing constitutes a trade or business, you now have the option of expensing up to $500,000 (for 2013) in personal property immediately rather than over time through depreciation deductions.

In addition, as an investor, you should recognize that you would normally need a long-term, full-recourse loan to help buy the equipment. Otherwise, the depreciation that you take will quickly exceed your cash basis, and you will not be able to take any further deductions. What this means is that you should be extremely careful in leasing the equipment. Your major risks are residual value and that the lessee will default, so a good equipment leasing program will involve major corporations with superior credit ratings. With such programs, your effective risk is minimal.

SUMMARY OF ADVANTAGES

By taking accelerated depreciation on the equipment over a life shorter than your loan repayment period, you can obtain substantial cash-flow benefits from federal income tax deferrals over the first few years of ownership. The total cash required to be put up is normally only about 20 percent of the cost of the equipment. These funds become available due to the tax deductions resulting from the purchase. Your tax deductions in each of the first few years of the transaction will be a significant multiple of the cash invested in that year. Substantial deductions will also normally be enjoyed for several more years.

You will enjoy an interest-free loan as a result of the transaction. If a reasonable value is attributed to the use of the funds produced by the interest-free loan, you will normally secure a return of your original investment in the equipment even if the equipment has less than the originally anticipated residual value at the end of the lease. An economic return over and above the profits earned on the interest-free loan is normally provided from re-lease revenues generated by the equipment at the end of the initial lease and by full payment of your bank debt.

117 Single-Premium Life Insurance

Prior to the Technical and Miscellaneous Revenue Act of 1988 (TAMRA), single-premium life insurance was one of the last remaining quality tax shelters. With single-premium life insurance, for a single lump sum, which may range from $1,000 to $5 million, a policyholder receives a little insurance protection and a big tax-deferred investment account. Single-premium life insurance offers a tax-free buildup of cash along with life insurance. Unlike universal life, the policy carries just enough insurance to qualify for tax-free status under the Internal Revenue Code. Therefore, more of the premium goes toward earning tax-deferred interest rather than buying insurance.

In fact, some experts have said that the insurance is a "free" bonus, since most single-premium policies quote a net rate of return. There are no fees or up-front commissions. That means that all of your cash immediately starts growing at the full rate quoted.

In the case of single-premium whole life, there was usually a 4 percent minimum guaranteed return. With an investment in single-premium variable life, like other variable products, there are no guaranteed rates of return, but the policyholder can pick his investments and move between alternative investments.

One suggested technique to avoid the limitations on Clifford trusts and the kiddie tax on children under 14 years of age was to purchase a single-premium policy on the life of the parent with a young child as owner and beneficiary. The income can accumulate inside the policy until the child reaches 14 or college age. At that point the child has two options: he can take out the income and be taxed at his own, lower bracket, or he can simply borrow it. Prior to TAMRA, if he borrowed the money, there were no tax consequences. Policyholders can normally borrow against the amount of their initial deposit, in some cases at no interest, and in other cases with interest charges of 2 or 3 percent. They can borrow their accumulated interest typically at a rate equal to what the policy is then currently earning—i.e., at a net zero cost.

If the parent dies, the child receives the death benefit, and because the child is the owner of the policy, it does not go into the parent's estate. If the parent lives, the child is able to pay for his education with pre-tax dollars. The proceeds of the insurance policy are tax-free anyway, the parent has leveraged his investment, and the child's wealth has been magnified by compounding. If the loan is not repaid—it need never be—it is subtracted from the death benefit.

For example, a 35-year-old male pays $25,000 for a single-premium variable life insurance policy. He then can choose his own investment options and switch between different investments. For the $25,000, he would get a death benefit only of approximately $80,000 to $85,000 on a typical policy. While he could possibly buy the same protection for only $100 a year, the life insurance is not the real objective.

Assume the taxpayer is able, through a combination of stocks, bonds, and other investments, to achieve a return of 12 percent a year on the investment portion of his policy. At the end of 15 years, when he is 50 years old, the death benefit would be typically in excess of $230,000 and the policy would have a cash surrender value of $100,000.

If the taxpayer then cashes in the policy, he pays taxes at that time. Alternatively, he could have borrowed over $22,000 tax-free each year for four years to put his child through college. This would bring the death benefit down to between $160,000 and $170,000 with a cash surrender value of approximately $30,000.

If the taxpayer did not touch his policy until he retired at age 65, his 12 percent rate of return would give him a death benefit of approximately $650,000 with a cash surrender value in excess of $400,000. At that time he could cash in his policy and pay tax on the money. Alternatively, he could annuitize part of the policy when he retires by rolling over part of the cash surrender value into an annuity that would pay him income for life, leaving enough money in the policy to keep it in force and provide a tax-free benefit to his spouse. There would be no taxes due on the money rolled over into the annuity.

This would allow the taxpayer to buy a cheaper annuity on his own life only, while he is providing insurance benefits for his spouse.

There are innumerable creative ways of using single-premium life insurance policies. For example, assume, prior to TAMRA, you have $1 million in bank certificates of deposit paying 10 percent and you are in the 33 percent tax bracket. After tax you get $67,000 in earnings. If you were to put the $1 million into a single-premium whole-life policy, also earning 10 percent, it would, in the past, throw off $100,000 in tax-free income through policy loans. Assume, to make the numbers simple, that you are also paying $100,000 in tax-deductible alimony. If you keep your $1 million in a taxable investment, remember you get to keep only $67,000 after tax. Alternatively, if you used your insurance policy $100,000 to pay the alimony, you would have, prior to TAMRA, reduced your tax bill by $33,000 (33 percent of $100,000).

Single-premium life insurance policies are not without their disadvantages. If you cash in your policy, every penny earned inside the policy over however many years you have held it is taxed as ordinary income. In addition, most insurance companies impose a surrender charge in the first few years of the policy, although the charge usually shrinks year by year.

Single-premium life insurance was too good to last in the above form. In order to discourage the purchase of life insurance as a tax shelter investment vehicle, TAMRA altered the federal tax treatment with respect to a class of life insurance contracts that are statutorily defined as "modified endowment contracts." If a contract is a modified endowment contract:

a) amounts received under the contract are treated first as income, and then as recovered basis;

b) loans under the contract (and loans secured by a modified endowment contract) are treated as amounts received under the contract; *and*

c) an additional 10 percent income tax is imposed on certain amounts that are includable in gross income.

Policies entered into before June 21, 1988, have been grandfathered and will not be affected by the TAMRA changes unless they undergo a material change. TAMRA changes the tax treatment of any policy entered into on or after June 21, 1988, in which the aggregate premiums paid during the first 7 years of the contract exceed 7 times the annual net level premium of a 7-paid policy. This is called the "7-pay test."

For example, if the annual net level premium for a $100,000 7-pay policy is $4,500, then any $100,000 policy for the same insured on which the aggregate premiums exceed $4,500 during the first year, $9,000 during the first 2 policy years, $13,500 during the first 3 policy years, $18,000 during the first 4 policy years, $22,500 during the first 5 policy years, $27,000 during the first 6 policy years, or $31,500 during the first 7 years of the policy will be considered and treated as a modified endowment contract.

If the aggregate premiums paid during the first 7 years are less than the aggregate premiums that would have been paid on a level annual premium basis using the net level premium amount ($4,500 a year in this example) for a 7-paid policy for the same insured, the policy will *not* be a modified endowment contract and will receive the same tax treatment previously applicable to all policies.

Under these new rules, single-premium policies have lost their potential for use as a strictly investment-oriented, tax-deferred vehicle. If a policyholder is forced to borrow from a modified endowment contract, he or she will have taxable income for the portion of the loan that represents internal gain on the policy. For example, a policy with a $50,000 single premium that has a $60,000 cash value would have a maximum of $10,000 gain that could be taxed. A policy loan of $15,000 ($10,000 of taxable income plus a $5,000 nontaxable portion) would generate $10,000 of taxable income plus a 10 percent penalty if the policy holder is under age $59\frac{1}{2}$. The penalty is applied only to the taxable portion of the loan. In this case the penalty will be 10 percent of $10,000, or $1,000. If you are in the 28 percent bracket, this loan would cost you a total of $3,800 ($10,000 × 28% plus $1,000 penalty).

Single-premium policies may still be viable and desirable for other reasons. They provide a mechanism to pass assets to others without subjecting them to the costs, delays, and uncertainties of probate. Attacks on or elections against an insured's will are avoided, as are any claims of potential creditors. Such policies also provide a way to fully prefund future debts or pledges with discounted tax-advantaged dollars. Moreover, at death they are still income tax-free and can be arranged to be both estate and inheritance tax-free.

In shopping for single-premium life insurance, the following considerations should be evaluated:

1. Does the life insurance company offering the policy have a rating of A or better from AM Best Corporation, the authoritative source on financial stability in the industry?

2. What is the current net interest being paid on the policy? Does this take into consideration the mortality charge—i.e., has that charge been taken out of the rate that is quoted?

3. Is the net rate guaranteed, and if so for what period of time?

4. Is there any minimum interest rate guaranteed over the life of the policy?

5. Is there a bailout provision under which you can get out of the policy if rates fall below a certain level?

6. What is the surrender charge if you cash in the policy?

7. Does the surrender charge decrease over a period of time?

8. What is the rate at which you can borrow the accumulated interest?

9. What is the rate at which you can borrow against your original premium?

10. Is there a minimum guaranteed death benefit?

11. Can you make additional payments, and if so what are the time and quantity limitations?

118 Cattle Feeding Programs

A cattle feeding program can enable you to spread income earned in one year over a number of years so that it can be taxed at lower rates. There are no capital gains or depreciation opportunities. You buy calves in the spring or early summer and deduct the cost of feeding them for the remainder of the year. When they reach commercial weight the following year, you will sell them and pay ordinary income taxes. You have, in effect, deferred income from one year to the next, unless beef prices have fallen in the interim.

Feeding programs seek to convert grain (or grass) into beef, at the same time offering a short-term tax deferral and an opportunity for substantial profit or loss. If the cost of converting feed to beef is less than the per-pound cost of the beef added, the cattle feeding program results in a profit to you. If the cost of feeding the cattle is more than the price of beef, you lose.

A 1979 IRS ruling made prepaid feed deductions difficult for tax shelter schemes.* Under the prior rule, a prepaid feed expense had to meet three criteria:

1. It could not be on "deposit"—you had to own the feed and bear the economic risk of price fluctuations.

---

*Rev. Rul. 79-229, 1979 C.B. 2.

2. The purchase of the feed had to be for a "valid" business purpose.

3. The deduction could not result in a "material distortion of income."

Under the 1979 rule, these three criteria are retained, but in addition the Internal Revenue Service looks at the substantive purpose behind the transaction. According to the latest ruling, a motive based on the income tax advantages of prepayment is *not* a valid business purpose, and if you lack other motives, your deduction will be disallowed.

Moreover, the Tax Reform Act of 1984 included statutory language to include any arrangement with the principal purpose of tax avoidance within the definition of what constitutes a farm syndicate. According to the Conference Committee Report, "The prepaid expense provisions will apply to individual taxpayers engaged in farming activities with the principal purpose of tax avoidance. The conferees intend that marketed arrangements in which individuals carry on farming activities utilizing the assistance of a common managerial or administrative service may be presumed under certain circumstances to have the principal purpose of tax avoidance. If under such arrangements, taxpayers prepay a substantial portion of their farming expenses with borrowed funds, they should generally be presumed to have a principal purpose of tax avoidance."

The Internal Revenue Service could argue that all feed lot customers are tax shelters because they use the high leverage customary to the industry and feed cattle through a custom feed yard. If so, then the 1984 provisions would effectively limit all deductions for commercial cattle feeders to consumed feed. There would be no allowance of prepayments for feed, seed, fertilizer, or other farm supplies unless the taxpayer were "actively participating in the management." In addition, if the above provisions were to apply, they would preempt and eliminate the 90-day allowance rule on prepayments as contained in Section 461(i). Therefore, if you want to receive the benefits of a cattle feeding program, you must be able to document "active participation," establish a substantial business purpose, and prove that your principal purpose is not tax avoidance, in order to still be eligible to deduct valid prepayments for your farm expenditures.

A typical cattle feeding tax shelter will provide for the purchase of very young calves (or feeders) in the summer or fall. The animals are generally raised in feed yards for which you will be charged a fee in addition to the cost of the feed. The cattle are usually sold the following year, when they reach their commercial weight. If you meet the "valid business purpose" test just described by proper timing of feeder-cattle purchases and sales, you should be able to deduct your expenses in the first year and pick up this amount, plus or minus the profit or loss, in the following year. You should be able to meet the "valid business purpose" test if you can establish a legitimate expectation of higher feed costs in the future—that is, it is cheaper to buy the feed now than to wait—and a legitimate expectation of profit on the ultimate sale of the cattle.

Moreover, under the Tax Reform Act of 1986, farmers using the cash method of accounting will not be allowed to deduct any amount paid for feed, seed, fertilizer, or other supplies prior to the year in which such items are used or consumed to the extent that they exceed 50 percent of expenses for which economic performance has occurred. This provision is effective for prepayments made on or after March 1, 1986. Since most investors in cattle feeding will not have other farm expenses, they will not be entitled to deduct prepaid feed costs. Except for investors in other farming ventures who may have such expenses and who will therefore be entitled to the deduction within the specified limits, cattle feeding as a tax deferral for non-full-time farmers is no longer an effective tax shelter.

119 Cattle Breeding Programs

Cattle breeding programs seek to increase herd size. Prior to ultimate sale, the cattle breeding program offers substantial tax deductions of a long-range deferral nature.

In a cattle breeding program, you might purchase a herd of 50 to 100 cows, which should triple in 3 to 4 years. Over a 5-year period your average annual outlay of cash on a 100-cow herd can be about $12,000. This outlay may be offset by tax deductions of $6,000 a year.

Expenses normally are deducted as incurred. This includes amounts paid for feed, seed, fertilizer, or other similar supplies. The provision that expenses are deducted as incurred normally prevents the allowance of current deductions for prepaid expenses. If use or consumption of the supplies during the taxable year is prevented on account of fire, storm, flood, or other casualty, however, the items may then be taken as an expense in the current period.

The cattle usually are bred in the summer or fall, so the calf crop will be born in warm weather. A calf crop of 75 percent to 95 percent can be expected. After the calves are weaned, the steers are sold and the heifers are retained to build up the breeding herd. The new crop of heifers is generally bred after 2 years. Each year, certain animals are culled from the breeding herd and sold.

After 5 to 7 years, the entire herd is usually sold. You can take depreciation on your breeding cattle, but gain equal to the depreciation taken will be recaptured as ordinary income upon their sale. Depreciation can be taken over a 5-year period using the 200 percent declining-balance method.

Prior to 1986, you were also entitled to the investment tax credit in a breeding operation. That was a credit against your tax bill of 10 percent of the purchase price, not just your investment. For example, if you bought a herd for $20,000 in 1985, putting in $2,000 in cash and borrowing the additional $18,000, you got an investment tax credit of 10 percent of the total $20,000, or $2,000. In effect, therefore, your initial net cash investment was zero. The Tax Reform Act of 1986 eliminated the investment tax credit as of January 1, 1986.

You can get into the breeding business with as little as 10 percent equity. With feeders, you can get in with as little as 5 percent equity. Up to 90 percent or 95 percent of the purchase price can be borrowed from the feedlot operator, the rancher, or a bank. You can therefore heavily leverage your investment, but this leverage must be based upon full-recourse financing.

The economics of breeding and feeding cattle can be seriously affected by the cyclical market price of cattle. Conditions such as increased costs (feed grains and supplies), price controls, reduced consumption due to high beef prices, and large supplies of available fat cattle have, at times, forced many one-way ventures into economic losses.

Diversification into combined feeding and breeding provides for a longer-lasting investment. The yearly cycle of feeding is extended to a period that provides for the building of herds in hope of a rising demand. In both feeding and breeding programs, management compensation is normally 5 percent to 10 percent of the herd value in the first year, and 5 percent to 10 percent of the operating expenses in subsequent years. Both activities are subject to the "at risk" limitation, and you will be personally liable for any loans if you finance your investment to obtain added tax leverage in order to take the full deductions available.

One very real advantage of cattle breeding is the flexibility that it extends to tax planning. Just as you can defer the recognition of income in a cattle feeding program by continuing to reinvest the proceeds of the sale of cattle, you can also pick the date on which you wish to realize the majority of the income from the sale of your breeding herd. Similarly, depreciation of the purchased cattle, the cost of their maintenance, and interest on any debt create additional deductions until the herd is sold. Remember, though, this flexibility, while useful in tax planning, does not ensure that when the herd is eventually sold, it will be sold at a profit. Furthermore, cattle breeding is a long-term investment. You can expect little, if any, cash flow from the breeding venture for a substantial period of time. But the potential gains are there. Prior to 1987, all gain on the raised portion of the herd that had been held for more than 24 months and any gain on purchased animals in excess of prior depreciation would receive long-term capital gain treatment. And throughout the breeding and raising period, you would have been taking ordinary income deductions for your expenses. By eliminating the long-term capital gains deduction, however, the 1986 Reform Act significantly impaired the tax advantage of cattle breeding programs. However, the current tax on long-term capital gains is capped at 23.8 percent. In addition, cattle breeding programs still give you the advantage of tax deferral.

120 Tax Straddles

A commodity tax straddle is designed to defer short-term capital gain into your next year or to convert it into long-term capital gain. Straddling involves a simultaneous purchase and *short sale* (the sale of a security you do not currently own) of two futures contracts—that is, agreements first to buy and then to sell stated amounts of the same commodity at set prices and times in the future.

To offset the short-term capital gain, you straddle a very volatile commodity (such as copper, silver, or pork bellies) near year-end, hoping for significant price movement—up *or* down—before December 31. If prices rise, you cover your short position at a loss; if prices fall, you liquidate the long position. Either way, the short-term capital loss from commodities offsets your short-term capital gain from other sources. After year-end you liquidate the profitable position. This moves your short-term gain into the next year or (depending on how you hold the contract) converts it to a long-term capital gain. According to former IRS Commissioner Jerome Kurtz, the worst that can happen is that you "receive the equivalent of an interest-free loan from the government for the period of deferral." But if the price does not move, or if it turns around before you can liquidate the profitable position, you will have a loss.

Straddles can be used not only with commodities but with government securities, such as treasury bills, bonds, or "Ginnie Maes," or with options on those securities as well. The objective is the same—to create a loss that will reduce your taxable income for one year while you also set the stage to cover that loss with a capital gain in the next year. If the year works out right, you get a current tax benefit and come close to breaking even on the transaction itself.

Prior to 1987 it was possible through straddling to reduce your tax rate by as much as 30 percent. Ordinary income, which was taxed up to 50 percent, was converted into long-term capital gains, which were taxed at a maximum of 20 percent. Moreover, unlike other investments, commodity investments could qualify for long-term capital gain treatment after only 6 (rather than 12) months.

Treasury bills were a favorite vehicle for straddles because, unlike most securities, they are not classified as capital assets. Under tax rules, any gain or loss from the sale of Treasury bills was treated as ordinary income. These bills are sold at a discount of face value and appreciate to *par* (face value) at maturity. Because the bills are such safe collateral, margin requirements on these straddles are low, as little as 3 percent of the bills' face value. The following example shows you how a Treasury bill straddle might have worked.

Assume that on December 17 you sell short $1 million in Treasury bills due December 26, and you buy $1 million in Treasury bills due the following March 26, which you intend to sell on January 2. The March maturity date allows for what is generally considered a reasonable period of market risk. But for purposes of this example, assume that between December 26 and January 2 interest rates are high. The result is that you don't receive the full $1 million face value because the bills due December 26 have 9 days to go until maturity. Assuming a discount of 16.83 percent, the purchase price is $995,793. On the maturity date, you have to cover the sale of borrowed securities. This will cost $1 million, giving you a loss on the transaction of $4,027 for the year.

The $1 million in bills due March 26 that you buy after making the short sale have 99 days to maturity. Assuming a discount of 16.30 percent, the purchase price is $955,175. When you sell those bills on January 2, you collect $962,419, for a gain of $7,244.

After commission costs of approximately $1,200, the net economic gain on the two transactions is $1,837. This gain is reduced by any interest charges on a margin account. In terms of the tax deduction, the straddles saved an investor in the 50 percent bracket (including state, federal, and local taxes) $2,103.50 in taxes for the first year ($4,027 × .50).

Such commodity straddles appear to be no-lose situations. In fact, though, they may turn out to be no-win situations. The Internal Revenue Service views these transactions as "wholly tax motivated and without any real economic substance." Internal Revenue Service staff members who screen and classify returns are being trained to recognize "straddle" returns and are targeting them for audit. According to the IRS, "taxpayers claiming tax benefits from these transactions will face a substantial likelihood of having their return selected for audit and their claims of artificial losses disallowed on examination."

The bottom line on commodity tax straddles is that until they have been court approved as legitimate tax strategies, they should be avoided. The Economic Recovery Tax Act has made this shelter a dead issue by requiring you to "mark to market"—i.e., close all your positions even if they are not sold at year-end. Moreover, the Tax Reform Act of 1986 eliminated the capital gains deduction (the tax on long-term gains is now capped at 23.8 percent. There is little reason, therefore, to use a tax straddle as a tax shelter. Stay away from straddles. There are too many *legal* tax shelters for you to buy into this kind of audit *dis*allowance.

121 Art Reproduction

Art reproduction is another tax shelter that you should forget. Almost all lithograph shelters are going to be disallowed by the Internal Revenue Service. Under a lithograph shelter, you will be asked to purchase a lithograph plate that the artist uses to make a limited number of prints (50 to 500). An estimate of revenues available from sales is used to value the plates, from which investment tax credits and depreciation could be obtained.

In a typical shelter, you would give an artist $30,000 cash, say, plus a promissory note for $170,000 and assume the entire responsibility for marketing the prints. Prior to 1986, you would then seek a 10 percent investment tax credit and a first-year depreciation of 25 percent. At a 50 percent tax rate, you would reduce your tax payments by $43,750 [(200,000 – 10,000) × .25 = $47,500 in depreciation, or a tax savings of $23,750 at a 50 percent rate, plus an additional $20,000 from the 10 percent investment tax credit]. You would therefore be $13,750 ahead. However, the Internal Revenue Service would view the personal promissory note as a sham unless there was a real compulsion to pay it and would argue that the actual investment was only $30,000. In fact, most of these deals are marketed with the assumption that the full risk of the personal promissory note will be paid only out of the proceeds from the sale of the prints. In effect, they are really nothing but shams.

Out of the $30,000 cash paid, $7,500 might go for printing, advertising, and sales; $7,500 to accountants and lawyers; $6,000 to the promoter; and $9,000 to the artist. You must either market the prints yourself or hire the promoter's "marketing" firm to do so for you. In one case, an investor sought to claim depreciation deductions and investment tax credit as a result of the purchase of a lithographic plate "master" and prints made from the "master."* According to the Internal Revenue Service, no depreciation could be claimed because the master was a nondepreciable work of art with a life of less than 3 years. The bottom line on this shelter is: Stay away.

122 Noncash Gift Shelters

This is another that you should avoid unless you are anxious to be part of an audit. The noncash gift shelter works as follows: You are asked to buy property such as books, Bibles, gemstones, etc., that are supposed to appreciate in value. You hold these objects for a period longer than 12 months and then contribute these "investments" to a charity. In return, you will get a charitable contribution deduction equal to the fair market value of the property.

For example, assume that you purchase rare Bibles at a cost of $5,000, and one year later they "appreciate" to a value of $30,000. You then contribute those Bibles to a church, claiming a deduction of their alleged fair market value of $30,000. If you are in the 35 percent bracket, this saves you $10,500 in tax—a $5,500 profit over your cost.

This is another shelter that the Internal Revenue Service considers nothing more than a sham. In one case a taxpayer-investor purchased limited-edition art books at a volume discount and then donated them to charity. The Internal Revenue Service ruled that the investor's activity was tantamount to that of an art dealer and that the investor's charitable deduction had to be reduced by the amount of gain that would not have been long-term capital gain had the investor sold the books.† In other words, the deduction was limited to only the cost basis.

---

*Rev. Rul. 70-432, I.R.B. 1979-53, 20.
†Rev. Rul. 79-419, I.R.B. 1979-52, 9.

Internal Revenue Service auditors have been instructed to look for non-cash gift deductions exceeding $5,000, particularly for deductions of well over the property's cost or basis, and especially if the property was held for less than 2 years. They will consistently challenge any determination of fair market value and try to disallow all of these shelters that they catch.

I question the validity of the Internal Revenue Service's position where it applies to true investments (for instance, gemstones) that may appreciate substantially over a year's period. However, in *Anselmo,* 80 T.C. No. 46, the Tax Court concluded that gems without settings would not be sold at retail, but rather sold to jewelers who would set the gems into rings or other jewelry. Since the jewelers are the consumers of gems, such stones should be valued on the basis of what the jeweler would pay to a *wholesaler* to obtain comparable gems.

Nonetheless, even if your shelter were to be allowed as a matter of law, you would be buying an audit on the question of valuation. The courts have consistently ruled against the taxpayer in these situations. I therefore recommend avoiding these types of shelters.

123 Municipal Bond Swaps

A municipal bond swap is an intriguing tax idea that allows you to maintain your equivalent current investment and yet at the same time take a tax-deductible loss on it. The swap lets you write off current paper losses and keep the advantage of owning municipal bonds as a shelter from federal income taxes, and possibly from state and local taxes as well. When interest rates increase, municipal bonds will normally be traded at substantially less than their face value. To do a swap, you merely sell your devalued bonds. This gives you a tax deduction for the current year. Then you reinvest the proceeds in other municipals of comparable yield and quality.

If you are contemplating any kind of swap, you must be aware of—and *avoid*—the "wash sale": You can deduct the realized loss on your current federal income tax return by selling your devalued bonds any time right up through December 31. But the Internal Revenue Service will call it a wash sale—and disallow the current loss deduction—if you turn around and buy the same bonds, or "substantially identical" ones, without waiting a full 30 days. That's 30 days either before or after the loss sale.

"Substantially identical" has never really been clearly defined. If the issuer is different, there should be absolutely no problem. But if the bonds you are selling and the bonds you are buying are from the same issuer, the farther apart they are in maturity or interest rate the safer you will be. At a minimum, you should look for a five-year difference in maturities, or a spread of at least 50 *basis points* (0.5 percent difference in yields to maturity).

If you hold the original bonds for a year or less, you have a short-term loss, which can be used to offset, dollar for dollar, gains from the sale of other assets. Likewise, long-term losses can be used to offset gains dollar for dollar.

Any loss up to $3,000 that isn't absorbed can be deducted from your ordinary income. Losses in excess of gains plus $3,000 can be carried over to future years.

B How to Analyze a Tax Shelter

The most important part of a tax shelter offering is the prospectus. It summarizes the deal, details the history of the participants, and gives you a lawyer's opinion as to the projected tax consequences. Read it carefully! The summary and introduction in the front of most prospectuses are a good starting point, but make sure that you go beyond them. Look at the section on sources and uses of the proceeds very carefully. This will indicate who gets what and how much of the proceeds are going to the promoters and their affiliates, as opposed to being invested in the main objective of the partnership. Read the tax risks and considerations section equally carefully, as this should explain in detail the various tax considerations that might affect you as an investor.

Choose carefully the lawyer or accountant who will evaluate the deal. An unfamiliar lawyer or accountant who brings a deal to your attention at a social gathering may simply be representing the promoters. Find out whether your lawyer or accountant will be receiving a commission from the promoters if the deal is sold. On the other hand, it could also be unwise to rely on your own lawyer or accountant in evaluating a deal. Lawyers and accountants are prejudiced in the other direction, since if the deal goes sour, they could lose you as a client. They therefore have very little incentive to recommend anything with any risk.

Make sure that the deal evidences an intent to make a profit. If a shelter is based on deductions of interest and depreciation, with only a remote possibility of the receipt of revenues, it stands a greater risk of being disallowed by the Internal Revenue Service. For example, a 1985 shelter that marked up a $10 product to $100, took a 10 percent investment tax credit to make the $10 initial contribution, and then took depreciation on the whole $100 was a high risk and unlikely to be approved if questioned in an audit.

Always invest in a tax shelter on the basis of economic returns. For example, the phase-out rule with respect to actively managed real estate could also produce a devastatingly high marginal tax rate as you approach the phase-out point. For example, assume you have $102,000 of adjusted gross income. You can claim up to $24,000 of losses from actively managed real estate. If you have $104,000 of adjusted gross income, then you claim $23,000 of deductions from such real estate activities. Assume instead that you had $1,000 of such losses from actively managed real estate activities and adjusted gross income of $148,000. Clearly the $1,000 is fully deductible. But, if you get a $2,000 raise, your adjusted gross income would rise to $150,000 and the $1,000 deduction would be disallowed. As a result, an extra $2,000 of gross income would be taxed at an effective rate of 42 percent. There would be a tax of $840 (28 percent of $3,000 increase in taxable income based on the extra $2,000 salary plus the $1,000 loss deduction), when your adjusted gross income rose only $2,000. This $840 increase in taxes on a $2,000 increase in your tax base produces a marginal rate of 42 percent.

Many shelters appear to give high write-offs on the basis of interest expense accrued according to the Rule of 78's. The Rule of 78's computes interest in a manner analogous to the sum of the year's digits methods for depreciation. The interest is ascertained by applying a fraction to the total interest due, the numerator of which is the number of payment periods remaining and the denominator of which is the sum of the periods. In Rev. Rul. 83-84, I.R.B. 1983-23, 12, the IRS ruled that it would no longer recognize interest deductions computed under that rule which exceeded the "economic accrual of interest." An exception was made for short-term consumer loans in Rev. Proc. 83-40, I.R.B. 1983-23, 22.

Determine the actual profit potential—that means measure the potential *after-tax return* against the *after-tax cost*. This allows a comparison of the cost of the tax shelter investment with other alternatives, such as stocks and bonds acquired with after-tax dollars. Make sure that you take into consideration how long it will take to get the yield from the after-tax dollars. For example, a three-to-one return ($3 of cash received for each $1 invested) looks better than a two-to-one return at first, but it will not be better if it takes several years longer to realize the full profit.

Examine the promoter's past history. What kind of track record does the person have? Have past deals been successful? Examine the financial statements of the general partner and evaluate them to ascertain that person's strength and staying power in the face of adversity. What are the sharing arrangements and front-end fees of the general partner? That person's share of revenues should be reasonably related to the services he or she renders to the program. Fees, commissions, and other front-end-loaded charges should be reasonable, too.

Does the program provide for additional assessments? You must be told (a) the maximum amount of additional capital that the general partner can assess for unexpected expenses, (b) when the assessment can be made, (c) the tax consequences of meeting the assessment, and (d) the penalty if you fail to comply.

Carefully examine the forecast figures provided in the prospectus. Review even more carefully the footnotes accompanying the forecast, which explain the assumptions involved in putting that forecast together.

Review your state of mind. Probably the most important consideration that you must ponder before entering into a traditional tax shelter is your own personal tax-comfort level. Many people are not temperamentally suited to invest in projects that increase the possibility that they may be audited. It is important, therefore, for you to decide whether you can live comfortably with this added potential risk.

124 Getting Out of the Tax Shelter

Tax shelters, by definition, are long-term investments. However, there may come a time when you need to get out of the shelter immediately because of pressing cash requirements. There are four major firms that purchase partnership units:

- Liquidity Fund (1900 Powell Street, Emeryville, California 94608; 415-652-1462) buys public and private real estate programs, with the exception of government-subsidized housing partnerships.

- MacKenzie Securities (650 California Street, San Francisco, California 94108; 800-854-8357; in California, 800-821-4252) buys only public and private real estate deals that are at least 3 years old and have current cash flow. The firm won't buy private programs if the investor still owes payments to the sponsors.

- Equity Resources Group (1776 Massachusetts Avenue, Cambridge, Massachusetts 02140; 617-876-4800) deals only in private real estate programs. It turns down programs with more than half the investment unpaid.

- Livon Oil (220 Bush Street, San Francisco, California 94104; 415-781-6427) buys units in public and private oil and gas drilling and income programs. It also won't purchase partnerships from investors who still owe payments to the sponsors.

Other such firms include the following:

- Raymond James Limited Partnership
  Trading Desk
  140 66th Street North
  St. Petersburg, FL 33710
  1-800-237-7591

- National Partnership Exchange
  P.O. Box 578
  Tampa, FL 33601
  1-813-222-0555

- Investors Advantage Corp.
  The Fountains Financial Center
  US 19 North
  Suite 302
  Palm Harbor, FL 33563
  1-800-282-5865

- Partnership Securities Exchange
  1814 Franklin Street
  Suite 820
  Oakland, CA 94612
  1-415-763-5555

- Realty Repurchase, Inc.
  50 California Street
  Suite 1300
  San Francisco, CA 94111
  1-800-233-7357

- Oppenheimer & Bigelow
  489 Fifth Avenue
  New York, NY 10017
  1-800-431-7811

In addition, the Chicago Partnership Board, Inc. (800-272-6273) and the Partnership Exchange (10051 Fifth Street, North, Box 21438, St. Petersburg, Florida 33742; 800-356-2739; in Florida, 800-336-2739) match buyers and sellers of private and public real estate, oil and gas, equipment leasing, and cable TV partnerships.

125 Master Limited Partnerships

A master limited partnership is not a tax shelter. It is merely a vehicle or form in which an investment can be made. A master limited partnership is a large publicly registered limited partnership that is the principal or sole owner of multiple assets or partnerships that themselves may have been structured as tax shelters.

Master limited partnerships can pass through income and losses like traditional limited partnerships but provide investors greater liquidity. Units in numerous master limited partnerships are listed for trading on national securities exchanges, and master limited partnerships generally have the ability to issue additional units in the future.

There are two basic forms of master limited partnerships. The first is the roll-up, in which multiple assets or small limited partnerships are consolidated into a large single master limited partnership. The second is the roll-out, in which the apparent entity, like a corporation, spins off some of its assets into a separate master limited partnership. A third form is known as a roll-in. In this form new assets are put into a master limited partnership with the promise to add additional assets in the future.

Master limited partnerships may be attractive as passive income generators to shelter passive losses from other activities. For example, dividends distributed by real estate investment trusts (REITs) are classified as portfolio income, which cannot be sheltered by passive losses. However, income distributed by real estate master limited partnerships will be treated as passive income.

Another advantage of the master limited partnership is that it can pass through to investors a greater portion of each dollar of operating income than a corporation since the master limited partnership itself is not subject to taxation. Moreover, unlike REITs, a master limited partnership can actively engage in real estate activities, and they are entitled to more favorable depreciation. The master limited partnership structure, however, increases the difficulty of complying with the new partnership allocation rules because of the large number of investors and constant trading of partnership interests.

The Revenue Act of 1987 had a substantial impact on master limited partnerships. Such partnerships, falling under the classification of publicly traded partnerships (PTPs), will be treated as corporations for tax years after 1987. An exception is made, however, for those partnerships whose gross income is predominantly (90 percent or more) "qualifying income." Qualifying income consists of the following:

1. Interest: This category does not include interest derived in the conduct of a financial or insurance business, nor does it include amounts contingent on profits.

2. Dividends.

3. Real property rents: This category generally includes rents from interest in real property, charges for services customarily furnished in connection with the rental of real property, and rental income attributable to personal property in connection with the lease of real property. Amounts contingent on income or profits are not generally treated as rents from real property.

4. Gain from the sale or other disposition of real property.

5. Income or gains from the exploration, development, mining or production, refining, transportation, or marketing of any mineral or natural resource.

6. Any gain from the sale or other disposition of a capital asset or Section 1231 asset held for the production of any type of income described in 1 through 5, above.

7. Income and gains from commodities (other than those held for sale to customers in the ordinary course of business) and futures, options, or forward contracts with respect to other commodities.

Moreover, although the general corporate treatment applies for tax years beginning after 1987, in the case of an "existing partnership" it applies to tax years beginning only after 1997. An existing partnership is any one of the following:

1. A partnership that was publicly traded on or before December 17, 1987.

2. A partnership for which a registration statement was filed with the Securities and Exchange Commission on or before December 17, 1987.

3. A partnership for which an application was filed with a state regulatory commission on or before December 17, 1987, seeking permission to restructure a portion of a corporation as a publicly traded partnership.

These "grandfathered" partnerships have been given the opportunity to remain partnerships by the Tax Relief Act of 1997. The price, however, is a 3.5 percent tax on gross income, or on gross receipts minus cost of goods sold. Those that choose not to pay will be taxed as corporations, and face the 35 percent corporate tax rate. In the case of publicly traded partnerships that are not treated as corporations, the passive loss rules are to be applied separately for the items attributable to each PTP. The net losses of a partner from each PTP are to be suspended at the partner level and carried forward and netted against the partner's share of the nonportfolio income of that PTP in a later year or years. Generally, these losses may not be applied against passive income from other activities. Similarly, a partner's share of the credits is to be suspended, carried forward, and applied against the tax liability of a subsequent year or years attributable to that PTP. Generally, these credits may not be applied against tax liability attributable to other activities. Moreover, a partner's share in the net income of a PTP (both portfolio and business income) will generally not be treated as income from a passive activity; that is, it will generally be treated as portfolio income. However, a partner's share of the net business (nonportfolio) income of a PTP will be treated as passive income for carryover purposes. This means that a partner's share of a PTP's net business income may be offset by any suspended business losses of that PTP carried forward from an earlier year, but a partner's share of portfolio income may not be offset by any other current or carryover losses from other passive activities.

126 Abusive Shelters

In May 2002, the General Accounting Office reported that offshore and abusive tax shelters cost the Treasury an estimated $25 billion to $45 billion in lost revenue each year. Those are the tax shelters that Yale professor Michael J. Graetz defines as "a deal done by very smart people that, absent tax considerations, would be very stupid."

The IRS is now targeting all forms of abusive shelters. *Stay away!* I've discussed and suggested avoiding those kinds of investments. The Health Care and Education Reconciliation Act passed on March 30, 2010, makes it easier to stay away from "bad" shelters. Now you have to prove that any transaction had a substantial nontax business purpose and that it leads to a meaningful change in economic position.

Acting Assistant Attorney General John A. Di Cicco said it best, "Those who promote tax fraud schemes will be investigated, prosecuted, and convicted, and they will also face substantial prison sentences."

A strict liability penalty of as much as 40 percent, will be applied to under-statements arising out of undisclosed transactions, reduced to 20 percent for disclosed transactions. But don't let that stop you from investing in the economically based and completely legal structures explained earlier.

CHAPTER 9

Super Tax Shelters

"When more of the people's sustenance is exacted through the form of taxation than is necessary to meet the just obligations of government. . ., such exaction becomes ruthless extortion and a violation of the fundamental principles of a free government."

GROVER CLEVELAND
Second Annual Message
December 1886

"As to the astuteness of taxpayers in ordering their affairs so as to minimize taxes, it has been said that the very meaning of a line in the law is that you intentionally may go as close to it as you can if you do not pass it."

Superior Oil Co. v. Mississippi, 280 U.S. 390, 395–96

"This is so because nobody owes any public duty to pay more than the law demands; taxes are enforced exactions, not voluntary contributions."

J. FRANKFURTER,
Atlantic Coast Line v. Phillips, 322 U.S. 168, 172–73 (1947)

"Only feeble minds are paralyzed by facts."

ARTHUR C. CLARKE
Science fiction author

This is the chapter that alone is worth more than a hundred times the cost of this book. Each of the following shelters is completely legal and has been sold to sophisticated taxpayers for thousands of dollars. These shelters have been worth the cost—they have saved those taxpayers many multiples of their acquisition price in taxes not paid. Each of these supershelters will be presented, explained, and structured in detail. Study them well. They will show you how legally and painlessly to reduce your own taxes to zero.

A Family Shifts

The first rule of income taxation is that a tax liability for personal service income may not be avoided by the earner of that income by assignment or other transfer before the income is realized. If you perform services that earn monetary reward, that income will be taxed to you. The second law of income taxation, however, is that income earned from *property* belongs to the owner of that property. Therefore, the first key to reducing your taxes is to transfer income-producing property to a family member in a lower bracket. If you make a bona fide transfer of income-producing property that you own, you have effectively shifted all future income from that property. After the transfer, the future income and all income tax due on that income will belong to the new owner in the lower tax bracket.

Part of your solution to the problem of reducing your tax, therefore, is to get your current income taxed to lower-bracketed family members. This strategy is based on the premise that a family is an economic and social unit and that it is immaterial to the welfare of the family as a whole which member derives income or owns property. From a tax perspective, however, it is extremely material.

For example, assume you are in the 28 percent bracket and transfer $1,000 of annual income to your son so that it is taxable to him instead of to you. Immediately you save $280 in taxes. Furthermore, the whole $1,000 will come tax-free to a child who has no other income, even if the $1,000 represents unearned income (for instance, interest, dividends, or rents). Moreover, not only can the savings be multiplied by the number of children involved, but if your son is under age 19 or is a full-time student under age 24, you can still claim the personal exemption for him on your tax return as long as you supply more than one-half of his total support.

The shift does not have to be made to a child. Suppose you are supporting a parent out of your current income. You might save an enormous amount of taxes if you could transfer some of that income so that the tax would be shifted from you directly to your lower-bracketed parent. For 2013, your parents, if over age 65, get personal exemptions of $3,900 × 2 and a standard deduction of $12,200 + ($1,200 × 2). Thus, if you are paying $22,400 a year of your after-tax income to your parents, you could save $6,272 a year in taxes if you are in the 28 percent bracket. Such a shift of income can be accomplished through a direct gift of income-producing property or by using one of a number of trusts that will be examined later in this chapter.

The standard deduction now permits the tax-free transfer of $1,000 of investment income to a child or other member of your family who has no other income. Alternatively, if the child is of sufficient age to work, that child can earn up to $11,100 ($6,000 standard deduction plus $5,000 IRA*) a year in income and still pay zero taxes. Remember, however, that the objective is not necessarily that the family member pay zero taxes, but rather that the taxes paid be less than what you would pay if the income were taxed directly to you. For example, even if that family member is in the 10 percent bracket, a shift of $1,000 in income from you in the 28 percent bracket would result in a net savings of $180.

There are a number of ways to effect an income shift within the family. Remember, when transactions among family members are genuine, they must be given full legal effect for tax purposes.

Note, however, that the Tax Reform Act of 1986 limited the availability of certain income-shifting techniques to children under age 14, increased to under age 18 as of January 2006. In 2007, Congress upped the age limit to as high as under age 24.

NEW RULES

For 2007:

The Tax Increase Prevention and Reconciliation Act of 2006 expanded the kiddie tax to children under age 18 who earn more than $1,700 in interest, dividends, capital gains, and other unearned income.

The first $850 ($900 for 2008, $950 for 2009 through 2012), 1,000 for 2013 is taxed at a zero rate, with the next $850 ($900 for 2008, $950 for 2009 through 2012, 1,000 for 2013) taxed at the child's rate, currently 10 percent (as low as zero percent for long-term capital gains). Any unearned income in excess of $1,700 ($1,800 for 2008, $1,900 for 2009 through 2012, 2,000 for 2013) will be taxed at the parents' highest marginal rate, as much as 35 percent.

It gets worse.

For 2008 and after:

The Small Business and Work Opportunity Act, signed into law May 25, 2007, changed the rules again.

If your child is under age 19, he or she is subject to the kiddie tax, *unless* his or her earned income is more than half his or her support.

---

*Many companies, including Merrill Lynch, Charles Schwab, and TD Waterhouse, will establish IRA accounts for children. However, at this age, a nondeductible Roth IRA may be preferable.

If your child is a full-time student, *unless* his or her earned income is more than half his or her support, the kiddie tax applies up to age 24. A child is generally considered a full-time student if he or she attends school full-time for at least five months during the year.

At age 24, the child would be taxed at his or her own rate. For 2013, that would subject the first $8,925 to a 10 percent rate and the next $27,325 to a 15 percent hit. Long-term capital gains and qualified dividends would be taxed as low as 0 (zero) percent for income up to $36,250.

The kiddie tax will apply only if:

a) the child is not married and does not file a joint return; *and*
b) at least one of the child's parents is alive at year-end.

The child's age is determined by his or her age on December 31. Note that the kiddie tax only applies to unearned income. Earned income from a job or self-employment is exempt from the kiddie tax.

The tax payable by the child on net unearned income is essentially the additional amount of tax that the parent would have had to pay if the net unearned income of the child were included in the parent's taxable income.

If parents have two or more children with unearned income to be taxed at the parent's marginal tax rate, all of the children's applicable unearned income will be added together and the tax calculated. The tax is then allocated to each child based on the child's pro rata share of unearned income.

The intent of the law is to create three stages:

1. There will be no tax on the first $1,000 of unearned income because of the child's standard deduction. The standard deduction for a dependent in 2013 is the greater of $1,000 in *unearned* income or the sum of $300 plus any *earned* income, with a total of $6,100.

2. The next $1,000 of unearned income will be taxed to the child at the child's bracket.

3. Unearned income in excess of the first $2,000 will be taxed to the child at the appropriate parent's rate.

The term *unearned income* means income from sources *other* than wages, salaries, professional fees, and other amounts received as compensation for personal services actually rendered.

The parent whose taxable income will be taken into account is the custodial parent of the child in the case of unmarried parents. In the case of parents who are married but filing separately, the individual with the greater taxable income will be the parent whose taxable income is used in these calculations.

The parent of a child subject to the kiddie tax receiving unearned income is required to provide that child with the parent's taxpayer identification number (TIN). That number (typically the parent's Social Security number) must be included in the child's tax return.

Upon written request a parent's return must be disclosed to the child or the child's legal representative to the extent necessary for the child's return to be properly filed.

PLANNING SUGGESTIONS

Note that the so-called *kiddie tax* rules discussed above apply regardless of who gave the children the income-producing property. They apply even if the cash or other property generating the income was transferred prior to 1987. So income from existing custodial accounts and income distributed from existing nongrantor trusts may be taxable to children at the parent's rates regardless of when the account or trust was created.

It may appear that the advantage of shifting income was eliminated by the reduction in bracket spreads (until 1987 the spread from the top bracket of 50 percent to the bottom bracket of 11 percent was 39 percentage points, but now the spread is from 39.6 percent to 10 percent, a 29.6 percentage point difference). But this is an oversimplification. Once a child becomes 19, all earned and unearned income is potentially taxed at the child's rate. So dropping $10,000 a year of income from the 39.6 percent bracket to the 10 percent bracket will save 29.6 percent per year of the amount of income shifted. In 10 years that amounts to $29,600 in tax savings!

If a child can be claimed as a dependent on a parent's return, the child may not take a personal exemption. Furthermore, the child's standard deduction is limited to the greater of (a) $1,000, or (b) the sum of $300 and the child's earned income (limited to a maximum of that year's standard deduction). This will force more parents than ever to file tax returns for their children (children with more than $1,000 of unearned income will have to file income tax returns), those returns will be more complicated than ever (and therefore the cost of filing the returns will be increased), and the taxes payable by children will rise precipitously.

127 Unearned Income of Minor Children

Beginning in 1989, the parent whose marginal tax rate would be applied in calculating the tax on the new unearned income of a child subject to the kiddie tax may elect on Form 8814 to include the child's net unearned income on his or her own return. The election can only be made if:

a) the child has gross income only from interest or dividends;

b) such gross income is more than $1,000 and less than $9,500; *and*

c) no estimated tax payments for such year are made in the name and taxpayer identification number of such child, and no amount of tax has been withheld.

If the election is made, the child will not have to file a tax return, and the parent's gross income will be increased by the amount of the child's net income over $2,000. The parents' tax will also normally be increased by $100 (10 percent of the $1,000 that would have been taxed to the child).

There may be two advantages to a parent in directly including a child's income on his or her own return. First, it avoids the filing of an additional return. Second, and perhaps even more important, if the parent is subject to a limit on the amount of investment interest that he or she can deduct, the inclusion of the child's investment income on the parent's return may obviate this interest expense limitation to the extent of additional investment income. However, to the extent that the parent's adjusted gross income is a factor in computing certain itemized deductions—such as the miscellaneous itemized, medical expense, and casualty loss deduction—such inclusion may actually reduce the deductions on the parent's return. You should weigh the administrative savings and the savings on tax preparation fees against any potential additional cost.

There are still many ways to shift both wealth and income and save taxes.

WHAT SHOULD YOU DO NOW?

If your kids are not currently subject to the kiddie tax, but would be next year, you have a small window of opportunity. Give long-term appreciated assets to the kids to sell now. The tax on any gain would fall from your 15/20 percent rate to as low as 0 (zero) percent, a 15/20 percent differential in your family pocket.

You can gift as much as $14,000 in securities to each child without even filing a gift tax return. With two kids, and two parents, that's as much as $56,000 that can be transferred gift tax-free. If it is more than that amount, Form 709, the gift tax return, must be filed. But, in addition to the $14,000 annual per donee exclusion, each donor has a lifetime $5.25 million exclusion for 2013. So, even if you do have to file the return, you probably won't be liable for any gift tax.

Consider using a Section 529 plan to invest for your child. If the money is used for qualified college expenses, all income comes out tax-free.

For financial aid purposes 20 percent of the money held in your child's name is considered fair game to pay for his or her tuition. But, only 5.6 percent of money held in a parents' name counts. Even though the 529 plan benefits the child, it is considered an asset of the parents for aid determination.

Also consider converting current UGMA accounts in the child's name to 529 accounts. Under both umbrellas, the hit to financial aid is the same. But, at least with the 529 account, the kiddie tax slam is avoided.

What else can you do?

1. Give a Series EE U.S. Savings Bond that will not mature until after the donee-child is age 19 (24 for full-time students, in all examples below as well). No tax will be payable until the bond is redeemed. At that time the gain will be taxed at the child's relatively lower tax bracket. Remember that this strategy will not work if the child already owns Series EE bonds and is already reporting each year's interest accrual as income. Once the election to report income currently is made, it is irrevocable. But, if the total interest is not more than $1,000 per year, you may want immediate recognition at a zero tax cost!

2. Give growth stocks (or growth stock mutual funds) which pay little or no current dividends. The child will therefore pay no tax currently and can hold the stock until reaching age 19. Upon a sale the child will be taxed at the child's bracket.

3. Give *deep discount* tax-free municipal bonds that mature on or after the child's 19th birthday. The bond interest will be tax-free to the child and the discount (face less cost basis) will be taxed to the child at the child's bracket when the bond is redeemed at maturity.

4. Employ your children. Pay them a reasonable salary for work they actually perform. Remember that the standard deduction for children is the greater of (a) $1,000 or (b) earned income plus $300 in unearned income (up to a 2013 $6,100). You could pay an additional tax-free $5,000 if they open a traditional deductible IRA. Regardless of how much is paid to the child, the business will have a deduction at its tax bracket, and the amount will be taxable to the child at the child's bracket. Alternatively, the child could establish a Roth IRA to shelter income forever.

5. Sell all nonappreciated property (be sure to consider brokerage costs and time value of money) and purchase tax-free municipals for the child.

6. Consider the multiple advantages of a *term of years* charitable remainder trust for children over age 19—so the income will be taxed to the child, but the grantor will receive an immediate income tax deduction.

7. In making gifts to your children consider support obligation cases such as *Braun, Sutliff,* and *Miller.* Parents who can with ease meet the support needs of even an adult college-age child may be considered obligated to provide support. If UGMA (the Uniform Gifts to Minors Act) or 2503(c) trust funds are used to send a child to college, will the parent be taxed? Worse yet, do these cases mean the UGMA custodian (or 2503(c)) trustee violates a fiduciary duty by using such funds to pay for a college education when it's the parent's duty (thus making such funds unavailable for the very purpose for which they were intended)?

   Assuming the support problems addressed above are not applicable, judicious use of a 2503(c) trust (but not a UGMA account) will allow significant income shifting. The trust can accumulate income while the beneficiary is under age 19 and avoid the kiddie tax.

8. Life insurance and annuity policies that stay within statutory guidelines (ask for a written guarantee from the home office) for life insurance should be particularly attractive, assuming *loading* costs are relatively low and/or backended. This includes universal, variable, and traditional whole life of the single-, annual-, and limited-payment types. In the case of the SPWL (Single-Premium Whole Life) the entire single premium paid at purchase starts earning the declared interest rate immediately. The cost of insurance and expenses is recovered by the insurer from the difference between the declared interest rate and the rate the insurer actually earns. If surrendered, any unrecovered expenses are deducted from the policy's cash values. The owner can obtain cash values at any time by (1) surrender (gain over cost is taxable) or (2) loan (loan interest is probably nondeductible). But note the limitations and new penalties imposed by TAMRA in 1988. Interest is charged at about the same rate credited on borrowed sums and is free of current tax. Earnings compound free of current taxation. Unlike tax-free municipal bonds there is no market risk, and SPWL is highly liquid. A parent can purchase the product on his or her own life which makes college education for the children more likely, and the parent does not have to give up control or make a gift.

9. Concentrate on gift and estate tax savings devices such as the annual exclusion. Parents should consider gifting $14,000–$28,000 a year of non-income-producing assets to a minor's trust or custodial account, which could be converted into income-producing assets slowly after the child turns age 19. The fund can become self-liquidating and exhaust itself by the time the child finishes college/graduate school.

10. If the parent's return shows a loss, will the child's return be affected by it? The Code is silent.

11. The custodial parent is often the mother who may have less income (and therefore be in a lower tax bracket) than the father. But what about the logistics of tax-return disclosure where the father is filing returns and paying tax for the children? Suppose he doesn't want her to know how much he's put aside for the kids and she doesn't want to reveal her income or her new husband's income. Furthermore, the filing father cannot prepare the children's returns until the mother prepares her returns. What about multiple children from multiple marriages? Split custody?

12. We still have limited shifting of income to children under the age of 19 with the 2013 $1,000 minimum standard deduction and the special rule taxing the first $1,000 of unearned income at the child's marginal tax rate. Assuming that the parent is in the highest marginal tax rate (39.6 percent), the first $1,000 of income shifted to the child would result in $396 of tax savings ($1,000 × .396), and the next $1,000 of transferred income would result in $296 of tax savings [$1,000 × (.396 − .10)] for a total of $692.

Over a period of years, the tax savings generated by shifting $2,000 of income to the child can be significant. For example, if the annual tax savings were invested at 8 percent for a 18-year period, the total tax savings and interest would be $25,915. Furthermore, the one-time gift necessary to generate the $2,000 of unearned income would closely approximate the $28,000 annual gift tax exclusion for both parents, so that little, if any, of their estate tax exclusion is used.

The above limitations apply only to the shifting of unearned income—e.g., interest, dividends, rents, etc. For those shifts discussed later in this chapter, assume that whenever there is a reference to shifting unearned income to children, those children are not under age 18. The following techniques can be used to shift income to lower-income members of your family.

128 Outright Gifts

A gift of income-producing property to members of your family is perhaps the most common method of splitting income to gain a tax advantage. The simplest way to transfer money, tax-free, is by gifts in relatively small lumps. You can give an annual gift of $14,000 per person to any number of family members—$28,000 if the gift is made jointly with a spouse—without incurring any gift liability. In order to qualify for the $14,000 or the $28,000 exclusion in the year the gift is made, it must be a gift of a *present interest* (current benefit). A gift tax return is required for any gifts in excess of these amounts to any recipient in any year if the gift is one of a present interest. A gift tax return is required for a gift of any amount if it is of a future interest. A gift is a completed transfer of the entire legal and beneficial interest in the property given.

For a gift to your spouse, there is now an unlimited gift tax marital deduction. If the family members to whom you wish to give gifts are adults, then normally there are no problems. This is *not* true if the objects of your income shifting are minor children, who lack full legal capacity. In consequence, legal difficulties are often encountered in connection with their ability to manage and dispose of the property that they acquire. Furthermore, they normally lack full maturity and it is often less desirable from a practical standpoint to give them control over property.

Certain types of property are more suited than others to practical ownership by minors. Securities that require no management control can be put in the name of a minor when there is no desire to dispose of them before majority. If there is such a desire, the securities should be in bearer form or registered in the name of an adult nominee who may dispose of them at the direction of the minor. Under such circumstances you should file a Form 1087 putting the Internal Revenue Service on notice as to the true ownership of the stock. Alternatively, savings bonds may be purchased and registered in the sole name of a minor and may be redeemed at the option of the minor or a parent.

Cash is the simplest thing to give to a minor. It may be kept in a savings account by the parent in trust for the child. If you want to give cash to a family member but must sell appreciated stock to do so, it is normally cheaper to give your family member the securities and *then* have them sold. Any gain realized will be taxed at the lower marginal tax bracket rate of that person if he or she is 14 or older.

It is very important to note that under no circumstances should funds transferred to a minor be used to satisfy a parent's legal obligation of support (see *Sutliff v. Sutliff,* 489 A.2d 764 [Super. Ct. PA 1985], subsequently invalidated by a later ruling by the Pennsylvania Supreme Court, and *Braun v. Commissioner,* T.C. Memo 1984-285). If funds are so used, the income will be taxed to the parent!

GUARDIANS

Many of the practical and legal difficulties inherent in dealing with minors can be alleviated either by having a guardian appointed for the minor or by creating a trust for the benefit of the minor. A guardian must be appointed by the state court having jurisdiction over such matters. There is normally little difficulty in securing the appointment on the petition, with the consent of both parents. Once appointed, the guardian usually becomes responsible to the appointing court for the proper and faithful performance of any duties. The judiciary standards governing a guardian's investment powers are those set by state law. A guardian is not allowed a choice or discretion beyond standards that are usually quite conservative. There are, however, a number of problems in using a guardian. The guardian is usually required by state law to furnish a bond for the faithful performance of duties. If sureties are required on the bond, the guardian is further restricted by the supervision exercised by the sureties. Furthermore, the guardian may be required to get court approval and certification that any actions—for instance, a sale of securities—are in the best interest of the ward.

Each state has its own standards and requirements detailing the duties and responsibilities of a guardian. For example, some statutes require that annual or periodic accounts be presented for approval by the courts. On the other hand, many of these provisions are often disregarded in a parent-guardian situation where harmony prevails within the family. This is because, as a practical matter, the courts usually do not take any action except on a complaint of a party in interest.

TRUSTS

Many of the technical and legal difficulties of guardianship can be eliminated through the use of a trust for the benefit of the minor. The standards governing the investment and management powers of the trustee may be as broad or narrow as the creator of the trust desires. If the trust that is created comes into being during your lifetime (*inter vivos* trust), that trust usually is under no direct court supervision. Furthermore, if you should so provide, no bond will be required by the trustee for faithful performance of duties and no court approval will be necessary for the disposal of trust assets in the usual course of the trustee's administration of that trust. Furthermore, while it is usually preferable to have an independent trustee, it is legally permissible for you as a parent to act as trustee.

You should be aware, however, that there are certain limits and dangers in the use of the trust for income shifting:

1. The income must not be "applied or distributed for the support or maintenance of a beneficiary (other than the grantor's spouse) whom the grantor is legally obligated to support or maintain." You have the legal obligation to support your minor children. If the income or principal of

a trust you create is used to discharge this obligation, it is regarded as your income and taxable to you. The solution here is to use the funds for non-support purposes. For example, in most states a college education would not constitute a legal obligation that would fall under the umbrella of "support." In the case of *Frederick C. Braun, Jr, et al. v. Commissioner* (T.C Memo 1984-285) however, the Tax Court found that under New Jersey law, financially able parents have the legal obligation to provide their children with a college education. The court therefore ruled that to the extent that income from two trusts was used to pay for tuition, room, and board for Braun's children, the income was taxable to Braun. The solution here would have been to distribute the income directly to the children and have them pay for their own college expenses. Structured that way, the income would not have been taxable to the parents. (See also the Pennsylvania case of *Sutliff v. Sutliff*, 489 A.2d 764, 1986, wherein the Appellate Court held that a parent may not use Uniform Gifts to Minors Act [UGMA] funds for a child's support. The import of this case, which arose out of a divorce situation, is that the court ruled that the parental duty of support may extend to providing a college education, even though the child has attained an age of majority under general state law but not under UGMA. This case was later invalidated by a subsequent ruling by the Pennsylvania Supreme Court. See also *Stone*, T.C. Memo 1987-454, wherein the Tax Court again ruled that trust payments for private school tuition are within a parent's legal support obligation; thus, such payments are taxable to the grantor/parent instead of the minor trust beneficiary. *Stone* involved only the payment of private school tuition to minor beneficiaries, thus avoiding the more difficult question of the support obligation in regard to payments of college expenses for adult children. These cases follow the analysis in *Braun* with reference to a college education constituting parental support, and its solution should be approached in the same manner—i.e., distributing the income directly to the children and having them pay for their own education expenses.)

2. The trust must *not* be set up so that it could be considered to be carrying on a business or as having sufficient attributes of a corporation to make it taxable as a corporation by the federal government. An ordinary, valid, and legal trust is not an association taxed as a corporation.

3. The property contributed to the trust by gift must not be deemed a gift of a future interest. If it is, the gift will not be entitled to the benefits of the annual exclusion for gift tax purposes. A gift to a minor, in trust or

otherwise, will *not* be considered a gift of a future interest (and the annual exclusion will be available) if:

a) the property and income may be used for the benefit of the minor; *and*

b) any amount not so used will pass to the minor at age 21, or to that person's estate, or to any testamentary appointee in the event of an early death. A gift of an income interest that meets this test is considered a present interest.

4. The trust must be irrevocable or, if the transfers to the trust were made prior to March 2, 1986, irrevocable for at least 10 years, and you as a grantor cannot retain powers that, in the eyes of the tax law, constitute a beneficial interest in the property.[1] I will examine these 10-year trusts under the section on Clifford Trusts.

To simplify the procedures for making gifts to minors of securities and other specified property, all states have enacted what is known as the Uniform Gift to Minors Act. The effect of this act is to permit such gifts to be made through a custodian, and to permit a subsequent transfer without the appointment of a guardian or the creation of a trust. Under the Act, securities can be transferred to minors by registering them in the donor's name, in the name of an adult member of the minor's family, or in the guardian's name, as *custodian* for the minor, and delivering the securities to the custodian. If the donor is the custodian, registration constitutes delivery. Securities in bearer form can be given by delivery to an adult member of the minor's family (other than the donor) or to the guardian as custodian for the minor, together with the deed in statutory form.

The custodian gets the managerial power a guardian would have, and the minor gets absolute legal title to the securities. The custodian can sell and reinvest, and can collect income and accumulate it or apply it for the minor's benefit. When the minor reaches the age of majority (21 or, in some states, 18), the custodian must turn over the securities and any accumulated income. If the minor dies before then, the securities and the income are part of the estate. Remember, however, that any income from the transfer that is used to discharge, in whole or in part, the legal obligation to support and maintain a minor is *pro tanto* taxable to the person who made the transfer. Furthermore, you should note that if you are the donor and name yourself as custodian of the securities or succeed to custodianship, your death before the minor reaches the age of majority will throw the securities into your estate.

---

1. Internal Revenue Code, Section 676.

129 Clifford Trusts

Prior to March 2, 1986, as an alternative to a completed gift, you could have considered the creation of a temporary trust commonly known as a Clifford Trust. Clifford or temporary trusts to shift taxable income from a high-bracket taxpayer to a low-bracket taxpayer were extensively used in the past.

The Tax Reform Act of 1986 effectively eliminated the use of Clifford Trusts. Except for transfers made prior to March 2, 1986—with another exception under which the 10-year rule of prior law would continue to apply to certain trusts created pursuant to certain binding property settlements entered into before March 1, 1986—Clifford Trusts are taxed as grantor trusts as of January 1, 1987. That means that the income of the trust is taxed at *your* higher marginal tax bracket.

130 Interest-Free Loans

Because of the limits imposed on the transfer of funds to a Clifford Trust free of gift tax, an alternative planning strategy was devised. As an alternative or a supplement to transferring funds to a Clifford Trust, you could have made an unlimited interest-free loan to your lower-bracketed family member.

Unfortunately, the use of interest-free loans as a method to allocate income to lower-bracketed taxpayers was effectively eliminated by the Tax Reform Act of 1984. Under that Act, foregone interest on a loan is treated as a gift from the lender to the borrower and is subject to the gift tax. Moreover, the lender (parent) is deemed to have interest income if the loan is more than $100,000. For loans from a corporation to a shareholder, the interest element is treated as if a dividend includable in income was paid by the corporation to the shareholder. A loan to a person providing services results in the foregone interest being treated as compensation.

131 The Schnepper Shelter: Gift Leasebacks

An alternative technique used to increase income-shifting potential is the gift-leaseback transaction. In the typical situation, the taxpayer, usually a professional such as a doctor, attorney, accountant, or even a shareholder in a closely held corporation, establishes a trust for any children. Then business property, such as an office building, furniture, equipment, autos, trucks, or machinery, is transferred to the trust, which agrees to lease it back to the taxpayer. The lease payments are then deductible by the high-bracketed taxpayer and reported as income by the low-bracketed trust beneficiary.

In effect, the taxpayer has relinquished title in exchange for significant income shifting. There is no depreciation recapture on such transfers,[2] nor should there be any investment credit recapture.[3] In addition, not only is the first $1,000 of the shifted income to each child exempt from tax,[4] but the parent-taxpayer will also continue to be entitled to a personal exemption for each child until each is 19 or as long as each is a full-time student if more than half of each child's total support is received from the parent.[5]

The Tax Court has approved the gift-leaseback technique as a legitimate means of reducing your tax liability. It has developed four requirements that must be satisfied before it will permit a grantor to deduct the lease payments.[6] These requirements are as follows:

1. The grantor must not retain substantially the same control over the property that was held before making the gift. This requirement can be satisfied by appointing an independent trustee. The Tax Court has recognized both commercial banks[7] and personal attorneys[8] as independent trustees. In no case should the grantor-taxpayer become the trustee[9]; neither should the spouse.[10]

---

2. See I.R.C. Section 1245(b)(1) and (3) and Section 1250(d)(1) and (3). Potential recapture is deferred until a subsequent disposition of the property—see *Rainier Companies, Inc. v. Comm.*, 61 T.C. 68 (1973), acq., 1974-1 C.B.2.
3. Reg. Section 1.47-3(g) provides that the recapture provisions will not apply where qualified property is disposed of and, as part of the same transaction, is leased back. The regulation is directed at sales but "disposed of" should incorporate and apply as well to gifts in trust situations.
4. I.R.C. Section 63(b)5.
5. See I.R.C. Section 152, Section 151(e)(1)(B) and Section 151(e)(4).
6. See *Mathews v. Comm.*, 61 T.C. 12 (1973), rev'd, 520 F.2d 323, 75-2 USTC Par. 9734, 36 AFTR2d 75-5965 (CA-5, 1975) *cert. den.* See also *Rosenfeld v. Comm.*, (CA-2, 1983), 51 AFTR 2d 83-1251 (May 2, 1983), and *May v. Comm.*, 76 T.C. 7 (1981) (CA-9, 1984), 53 AFTR 2d 84-626, where a gift leaseback was found valid despite an oral lease!
7. See *Serbousek*, TCM 1977-105.
8. See *Lerner*, 71 T.C. 290 (1978).
9. See *Penn*, 51 T.C. 144 (1968); *Van Zandt*, 40 T.C. 824 (1963), aff'd, 341 F.2d 440, 65-1 USTC Par. 9236, 15 AFTR2d 372 (CA-5, 1965) cert. den.
10. See *Larry Benson*, T.C. 86, for problems created with a spouse trustee. See also *Rosenfeld*, T.C. Memo 1982-263 re: control.

2. The leaseback should normally be in writing and must require payment of a reasonable lease rental. The trustee should have the trust property appraised[11] and find out the lease price of similar property to justify the reasonableness of the lease rental. A payment schedule should be established and adhered to.[12] Moreover, the trustee's powers detailed in the trust instrument should be broad enough to maintain independence. One suggested technique to ensure the court's recognition of the trustee's independence is to make the initial term of the lease less than the term of the trust. In doing so the trustee is forced to exercise independent power to renegotiate renewal agreements.[13]

3. The leaseback (as distinguished from the gift) must have a bona fide business purpose. This requirement can be easily satisfied, since the trust property is business property intended to be used again in the taxpayer's business. Certain circuits of the U.S. district court, however, require a bona fide business purpose for *both* the leaseback *and the gift*. Merely to place trust property beyond the reach of creditors has been held to be insufficient as a business purpose for the gift.[14] One suggested business purpose would be to get managerial expertise in the control and operation of the property.[15] This would be especially effective, for example, if the taxpayer were a doctor, the property an office building, and the trustee an attorney expert in real estate.

4. The taxpayer must not possess a disqualifying "equity" in the property. Once the property is transferred, the taxpayer possesses only a reversionary interest in the trust property. The Tax Court holds that a reversionary interest is not a disqualifying equity, since its enjoyment is realized only after the trust expires.[16] Unfortunately, the Internal Revenue Service does not accept this position.[17] One way to avoid litigation on this matter would be to create a remainder interest that passes to the taxpayer's spouse or children, or to a corporation set up for the purpose, at the termination of the trust.[18]

---

11. Supra, note 13.
12. Supra, note 14.
13. See *Mathews*, supra, note 11, and *Quinlivan*, TCM 1978-70 aff'd 599 F.2d 269, 79-1 USTC Par. 9396, 44 AFTR2d 79-5059 (CA-8, 1979) cert. den.
14. See *Butler*, 65 T.C. 327 (1975).
15. See *Skemp*, 8 T.C. 415 (1947), rev'd, 168 F.2d 598, 48-1 USTC Par. 9300, 36 AFTR 1089 (CA-7, 1948).
16. See *Oaks*, 44 T.C. 524 (1965) and *Serbousek*, supra, note 12.
17. See Rev. Rul. 54-9, 1954-1 C.B. 20.
18. See supra, note 13 and supra, note 10.

Once the gift-leaseback trust is established, the benefits can be substantial. For example, assume a married taxpayer in the 30 percent federal and state tax bracket established a trust for three children by transferring business property valued at $84,000 into the trust. No gift taxes are payable on such a transfer.[19] Assume further that this is property that has been fully depreciated and that therefore no further deductions are available to the taxpayer if the property is retained. The fair rental for such property, though, is $250 per month.

The higher-bracket taxpayer therefore pays lease rentals of $3,000 per year and takes that amount as a business deduction. This saves $900 in taxes.[20] The three children each include $1,000 in their income, less their share of the trustee's management fee. Ignoring that fee for illustrative purposes and assuming no other income, the three children may pay zero taxes and retain $3,000. As a result of a transfer of $3,000, total family wealth has increased by $3,900, for a net increase of $900.[21]

If the property were still subject to depreciation by the original taxpayer, the above benefits would be reduced by the tax savings from depreciation deductions foregone in the transfer. These deductions, though, would be available to the children-beneficiaries. Any maintenance or upkeep expenses incurred for the property can still be deducted by the lessee-taxpayer, if so provided in the lease agreement. Note that in this example the $1,000 retained by each child can be used to pay that child's college expenses.[22] If the trust were not used, to accumulate $3,000 for tuition would require the 30 percent taxpayer to earn an incremental $4,286 in pretax dollars.[23]

Furthermore, if the property that you're contemplating transferring into trusts for your children is subject to a mortgage, you should be aware that the Garn Act lists certain property transfers that should never trigger loan acceleration under a due on sale clause. These exceptions apply to all loans— to loans originated by state chartered institutions and by federal lending institutions, regardless of the date of their origination. Included in these safe harbor transfers is a transfer in which a spouse or *children* of the borrower receive ownership of the property.

Note that the Tax Reform Act of 1986 eliminated the viability of Clifford Trusts for tax savings. The above trust-leaseback technique, however, would still

---

19. Split gift ($14,000 × 2) × 3 = $84,000 exclusion.
20. The lease payments would be deductible as ordinary and necessary business expenses under I.R.C. Section 162—$3,000 × .30 = $900 reduction in taxes at that bracket level.
21. $3,000 retained plus $900 saved in taxes = $3,900.
22. Or any other nonsupport expenses. See supra, note 8.
23. $4,286 at a marginal 30 percent rate leaves $3,000 after taxes.

be viable using an irrevocable trust. All of the other provisions, as discussed above, would apply.

Trust leasebacks have been specifically validated in at least the following 23 states: Alaska, Arizona, Arkansas, California, Delaware, Hawaii, Idaho, Illinois, Indiana, Missouri, Montana, Nebraska, Nevada, New Jersey, New York, North Dakota, Oregon, Pennsylvania, Rhode Island, South Dakota, Vermont, Washington, and Wisconsin.

The IRS will no longer litigate gift-leaseback cases where the lessee is a taxable entity separate from the grantor. This position was announced in an Action on Decision on April 23, 1984. By separate taxable entity, the IRS means a regular corporation, rather than a partnership or a Subchapter S corporation. Two-party gift-leaseback arrangements have been upheld not only by the Tax Court but by the following circuits: the Second (*Rosenfeld,* 706 F. 2d 1277, 83-1 USTC para. 9341 [CA-2, 1983], see *Use of gift leaseback to shift income given substantial boost by new decision,* 12 TL 128 [Sep/Oct 1983]); the Third (*Brown,* 180 F. 2d 926, 50-1 USTC para. 9219; 39 AFTR 155 [CA-3, 1950]); the Seventh (*Skemp,* 168 F. 2d 598, 48-1 USTC para. 9300, 36 AFTR 1089 [CA-7, 1948]); the Eighth (*Quinlivan,* 599 F. 2d 269, 44-2 AFTR 2d 79-5059 [CA-7, 1979]), and the Ninth (*Brooke,* 468 F. 2d 1155, 72-2 USTC para. 9594, 30 AFTR 2d 72-5284 [CA-9, 1972]). However, they have been held invalid in the Fourth and Fifth Circuits (*Perry,* 520 F. 2d 235, 75-2 USTC para. 9629, 36 AFTR 2d 75-5500 [CA-4, 1975], and *Van Zandt,* 341 F. 2d 440, 65-1 USTC para. 9236, 15 AFTR 2d 372 [CA-5, 1965]). In the circuits where gift leasebacks have been held invalid, however, the transactions only involved two parties; i.e., there was no corporation involved, but instead the lessee was the individual grantor.

An interesting twist on this technique has been developed by Schnepper Associates of Cherry Hill, New Jersey. Assume the children in the preceding example are too young for college and that the taxpayer has a current need for the funds being paid out in lease rentals. The Schnepper Shelter directs the taxpayer to make the lease payments and then to borrow back the money at a fair rate of interest.[24] The interest may be fully deductible, depending on what the money is used for.

To use the above example, the taxpayer would make payments of $3,000 and borrow back $3,000 for use in business, paying $300 in interest yearly (10 percent). Each child aged 19 or older would pay approximately an additional $10 in taxes on the interest payments, a total of an additional $30, but the taxpayer would save

---

24. Note that the interest expense need not be limited to the prime rate. In fact, "there is no requirement . . . that deductible interest be ordinary and necessary or even that it be reasonable." *Dorzback v. Collison,* 52-1 USTC Par. 9263, 195 F.2d 69, 72 (3d Cir. 1952). An interest payment as high as 60 percent to the taxpayer's *mother* has been upheld. *Raymond J. Barton,* 38 TCM 934 (1979).

an additional $90 in taxes (30 percent of $300)—a difference of $60 per year or $300 over 5 years. Of course, as its lease rentals increase, so too do tax savings. For 2013, up to $8,925 in taxable income can be taxed to a nonstudent child aged 19 (age 24 for a student) or older at the 10 percent rate, and the next $27,321 would be taxed at 15 percent.

When the children begin college and tuition is due, the taxpayer would then repay the borrowed money, in effect getting a current income tax deduction for future cash payments for the children's tuition. If the taxpayer dies before repayment is made, any remainder value in the trust is included in the estate,[25] but that estate (and therefore any tax due on it) is reduced by any debts owed to the trust—further magnifying the benefits of the Schnepper Shelter.[26]

While the Schnepper Shelter also appears to be contrary to congressional intent to eliminate assignment of income among family members, all of its components have been court tested and accepted. Here again, as long as the trustee is truly independent, the separate entity identity of the trust protects the legality and validity of a properly structured transaction. If such a shelter is to be eliminated, it too must be done through congressional action. Until such action, the Schnepper Shelter is a viable technique that should be considered in your planning to reduce your taxes to zero.

Moreover, the leaseback technique can provide substantial advantages to a taxpayer whose passive losses have been reduced or eliminated by the Tax Reform Act of 1986. For example, let's say a doctor owns a corporation that he does not materially participate in, which needs additional equipment, furniture, etc. Instead of buying that equipment through his or her corporation, the doctor will buy the equipment personally and lease it to the corporation. The lease rental payments made by the corporation would be extensively sheltered by the depreciation taken on this "leased business" equipment. Any net profits over and above the depreciation sheltered cash flow could be sheltered as passive income by the doctor's excess passive losses. By utilizing this technique, the doctor is able to take money out of the corporation at a zero tax cost. The cash flow is sheltered by previously unused passive losses and by the depreciation on the new equipment. Moreover, the corporation is entitled to a tax deduction for the "nontaxable" lease rental payments made to the doctor! This technique only works if the taxpayer doesn't materially participate in the activities of the corporation (Reg. Section 1.469-2(f)(6). Otherwise, the income is considered nonpassive.

---

25. See I.R.C. Section 2033. The value of that reversionary interest is determined by actuarial tables. See *Comm.v. Henry's Estate (Biddle)*, (3 Cir: 1947), 161 F2d 574, 35 AFTR 1252 aff'g 4T.C. 423.
26. See I.R.C. Section 2051; Section 2053 (a)(3) and Section 2053 (a)(4).

Remember that the Tax Reform Act of 1986 effectively eliminates the use of Clifford Trusts as planning devices. Therefore, in order to effectively use the gift-leaseback technique, rather than a Clifford Trust, you should create an irrevocable trust. With an irrevocable trust, the property is transferred to the trust (beneficiaries) irrevocably. Unlike the Clifford Trust, you will not get it back after 10 years. However, if you are leasing back personal property—e.g., business furniture, equipment, etc.—that has been fully depreciated, that equipment would normally be over 15 years old when it would be returned using a Clifford Trust. The value of that equipment then would be minimal. Had you been gift-leasebacking an office building, however, the Tax Reform Act of 1986 forces you to relinquish present and future ownership of an asset with substantial value. If this is a strategy to be employed, the loss of that value is the price that must be paid.

132 The Schnepper Deep Shelter

Another alternative for shifting income to a lower-bracketed family member is to transfer rental property, excluding the building, to a trust for your children and rent the land back from the trust. The donor parent would still get all of the depreciation on the building, and the trust beneficiary children would be taxed on the lease rental income received. That lease rental income, however, would be a deductible investment expense by the parent. In effect, the parent would be paying lease rental income to the children, deducting that rent expense in the higher bracket and having it taxed to the children at the lower bracket. Moreover, this transfer of family wealth could take place without any gift tax consequences. In *Stanley J. Wolfe*, T.C. Memo 1984-446, this arrangement was validated with a sale leaseback of land to an irrevocable 10-year trust. The leaseback had a bona fide business purpose, and the lease payments were determined to be reasonable rent. Here again, the Tax Reform Act of 1986 would require the use of an irrevocable trust if this technique were to be used effectively.

133 Family Partnerships

If you are an individual business owner, the use of a family partnership can play an important role in your income tax planning. By giving or selling an interest in your business to members of your family (particularly to your children), you can decrease your personal income tax payments and thereby increase your family unit's spendable income and capital.

For this arrangement to work, however, the establishment of the partnership must be genuine. This has been simplified by an IRS tax code section that specifically allows you to set up a family partnership by gift or purchase even though the family partners render no services.[27] Therefore, in those cases where capital is a material income-producing factor for the partnership, significant income shifting to lower-bracketed family members can be accomplished through the establishment of family partnerships.

A family partnership can be established in any of the following ways:

- Take into the partnership any child or relative who can contribute capital.

- Make a gift of a partnership interest to children or other relatives.

- Sell a partnership interest to children or other relatives. This sale can be substantially on credit, to be paid out of subsequent partnership income.

- Accept into partnership any child or other relative who can be expected to perform important work in the business on a regular basis.

134 Family Trusts

A family trust should be very carefully differentiated from a family partnership. A family trust is a trust to which you transfer "the exclusive use of your lifetime services and all the currently earned remuneration therefrom."

The problem with family trusts is that they do not work. A basic rule of taxation is that income must be taxed to the person who earned it. The transfer of your lifetime services and the income earned through the performance of those services is simply an assignment of income, and therefore ineffective in shifting the tax burden from you to the trust. *You cannot shift income earned through personal service.* A family trust, therefore, is nothing more than a tax avoidance scheme.[28] Do not, however, confuse a family trust with a trust to which income-earning *property* is transferred. When property is transferred, the income from that property *can* be shifted.

---

27. Section 704(e) of the Internal Revenue Code.
28. *Hailey, Jr.,* 73 T.C. No. 99 (1980).

135 The Schnepper Malagoli Super Shelter

This one is going to get me in *lots* of trouble!

How would you like to take money out of one pocket, deduct it as a business expense, and then put it in your other pocket tax-free? Even better, how would you like to do it completely legal?!

Follow me on this. It's really very simple once you get the basic idea. Let me give you the concept. Here's how it works. . . .

For this technique to work, you need a legitimate business. Assume you have a legitimate business and rent a suite in a hotel for a business meeting. You actually have and can document the meeting as a business event.

Clearly, the rent you pay is an allowable business deduction. Both small and big businesses do this all the time. Nothing new here . . . yet.

The other side of the coin is that the hotel has taxable rental income.

Now, instead of your business renting a suite in a hotel, you rent my home. Once again, if you actually use it for business purposes, and can document the business use, there's no reason why you shouldn't get the same "rental" deduction on your tax return.

The other side of the coin is that I should have rental income, right?

Wrong!

I want you to think Olympics, Super Bowl, and World Series.

Many years ago, Congress recognized that there were going to be situations where someone might rent out his or her home on a short-term basis. Rather than require an allocation of heat, electric, utilities, depreciation, interest, taxes etc. over the short-term rental, Congress actually came up with a reasonable solution.

The short-term landlord gets zero additional deductions for the "rental" expenses. But none of the income is taxable!

The code section—because everyone's going to look it up—is Section 280A (g). It specifically states that if you rent out your home for less than 15 days during the calendar year, none of the income is taxable.

Be careful when you read the code section. The general rule is that you get no deduction with respect to the use of your home for a business.

There are several exceptions, one of which is for the rental of the house. The Internal Revenue Code is full of general rules, exceptions, and exceptions and limitations to the exceptions.

If you're an employee of the business that rents the house, then there's an exception to the exception. You get no deductions for the rental of your house to your employer.

But, we're not talking about the deductions you, as the landlord, are getting for the rental of your house. You're getting none of those deductions anyway. What we're excited about is the deduction your company (the short-term tenant) gets for renting your house. That's not the subject of these limitations. Just the deductions for your expenses as the landlord are denied. And, I'll trade them any day for the tax-free income!

Let's get creative. If you have a regular corporation (the tax pros call it a "C corporation"), the corporation gets the deduction and you get tax-free income rather than taxable dividends or compensation. That's the easy one.

Now, let's assume you have what the tax pros call an "S corporation." That's a corporation that passes through its expenses and income to the owners. It's taxed similar to a partnership.

If your S corporation rents and uses your home for business, then it gets the expense and the deduction is passed through directly to you, reducing your personal income tax liability. And, if you don't rent out the home for more than 14 days, none of the income is taxable to you.

Take it out of one pocket—deduct it—and put it in the other pocket tax-free!

What if you're self-employed? What if you don't have a corporation?

Remember the old Wall Street adage, "Bulls make money; bears make money; pigs get slaughtered." You can push the envelope. But, don't be a pig.

If the house is in your name, that may be the pig position. But, what if the house is in the name of your spouse? Arguably, that should work. Remember, the Internal Revenue Code will exclude the landlord's deductions for the rental of the house. But we're not getting them anyway. We're after the deduction for the tenant and the tax-free income.

Alternatively, if I rent Charley's house, and Charley rents your house, and you rent my house, we're clearly within the four corners of the law.

What arguments can the IRS make? As long as the space is used for business, there should be no issue as to the legitimacy of the deduction. You just have to prove the business use. The tax pros call that the business "nexus."

Prove the business use with specific documentation. If you have a monthly meeting (last time I looked, 12 was less than 15, so monthly meetings should qualify for the tax-free treatment), keep the minutes. Craft the minutes with the reason why you're having the meeting outside your normal business location. The standard reason is so that you're not bothered by the interruptions of your normal business setting.

Prove the reasonableness of the rental charge by getting a letter from a local hotel. If the Four Seasons is charging $500 a day for a suite for a meeting, a note from them should be sufficient substantiation for your $500 a day rental expense. On a monthly basis, that's a $6,000 deduction (saving $2,100 in tax each year) plus $6,000 in tax-free income.

So long as you can substantiate the business connection and the reasonableness of the charge, the deduction should be allowed.

As for the tax-free receipt of the rental income—the Internal Revenue Code clearly states that it's *not* taxable as long as you rent it for less than 15 days during the year. The IRS really has no argument here.

Is this an aggressive strategy? Absolutely! Is it reasonable? Yes, because it's based on the clear meaning in the tax code.

Was this part of the Congressional intent when the Code was drafted? Absolutely not!

But just because Congress didn't think about it when they drafted the law, that doesn't mean it doesn't work under the law that was passed.

Use this technique now to reduce your taxable income. Once it becomes known and used by many, I strongly suspect Congress will move to change the law.

136 Employing Members of the Family

If you are an individual business owner, a simple and effective method of splitting your income with a family member is to employ that family member in your business and pay compensation. The employment must be bona fide and the salary paid must be reasonable in relation to the services rendered. Even a young child can be compensated for the reasonable value of such services as cleaning your office, mailing your letters, or opening your mail. A 1982 tax court decision allowed a $1,200 deduction for a 7-year-old child who performed a variety of services—maintenance and office work—for a mobile-home-park operator.[29] Be aware, however, that wages actually used by your children for their own support can affect your claim for their dependency exemptions. When in doubt, have your children bank their wages, thereby saving the exemption and teaching them the virtue of thrift as well.

If your business is not incorporated, services performed by your child under the age of 18 are excluded from Social Security coverage. (Prior to the Revenue Act of 1987, the exclusion was for a child under the age of 21, and payments to your spouse were also exempt.) This means that you can deduct the value of the

29. See *Eller,* 77 T.C. No. 66. See also *James A. Moriarty,* T.C. Memo 1984-249, where a doctor was allowed to deduct salaries he paid his teenage children for handling business correspondence, insurance forms, etc., and for keeping patient files in order.

services that you pay to your children from your income tax without the added expense of paying Social Security taxes on that compensation. Services performed in the employ of a corporation, however, are not within this exclusion. But all is not lost if you are in a corporate firm. If your spouse is a bona fide employee of your corporation, such tax breaks as Social Security, workmen's compensation, tax-free sick pay, pension or profit-sharing plan benefits, stock option plans, group life insurance, and many others are open to you. According to IRS regulations, services performed in the employ of a partnership are also not within the exclusion unless the requisite family relationship exists between the employee and each of the partners comprising the partnership. Although wages paid to a child under age 18 by an unincorporated business are exempt from Social Security and federal unemployment taxes (up to age 21), wages paid to a parent are exempt from federal unemployment taxes but not from Social Security taxes.

Furthermore, if your spouse works for you, you may be able to deduct all your medical expenses. (If you hire your spouse, make sure that you can substantiate the payments that are made. Keep records or a journal of hours worked, and make payments with a check. No record keeping means no substantiation. No substantiation means no deduction [L.T.R. 8753003].) Normally, the deduction for medical expenses is limited to expenses that exceed 10 percent of your adjusted gross income. If you have your own business, however, you can install a written medical reimbursement plan for your employees. As a sole proprietor, you would not be considered eligible because you do not qualify as a common-law employee. Your spouse, however, would qualify. *You* would qualify as well if the plan included all employees, the dependent children, and the employee's *spouse!* With such a plan, your cost for insurance coverage and for the medical reimbursement plan would be deductible in full as a business expense. (See *Frahm,* T.C. Memo 2007-351.) Payments from the plan, of course, would be tax-free to you and your spouse. To achieve the anticipated tax results, the plan must be a welfare plan for all employees (Rev. Rul. 71-588; see also Doc. 9409006).

In C.C.A. 2005 24001, the IRS ruled that a self-employed individual who is a sole proprietor may deduct the medical care insurance costs of the sole proprietor and his or her family from the earned income of his or her trade or business when the health insurance policy purchased by the sole proprietor is issued in his or her individual name and not in the name of the sole proprietor's trade or business.

HRAs

On June 26, 2002, the IRS established a new Health Reimbursement Arrangement (HRA) that bypasses the complex limitations of Health Flexible Spending

Accounts (FSAs) or cafeteria plans and sets up a simple structure for health cost coverage.

These plans must be funded 100 percent by the employer. The big new advantage is that dollars under these plans don't disappear at the end of the year under the "use it or lose it" FSA rules (under a 2005 ruling, amounts left over in an FSA at year-end may be carried over for 2½ months before they are forfeited). Any unused amounts carried over from year to year or maintained following termination or retirement are excluded from the income of the employee. This new arrangement makes it easy to hire your children and deduct 100 percent of their medical costs—above the line!

The children's work need not be full-time and can even be done during their summer vacations. Furthermore, provided that you continue to furnish more than one-half of your child's support and your child is younger than 19 or is a full-time student under age 24 for part of each of 5 months during the year, you can continue to claim a personal exemption deduction for that child. Remember, a child with earned income in 2013 pays *zero* taxes on the first $6,100 worth of earned income. That means if you are in the 28 percent bracket and pay each of your three children $6,100 for services rendered, their tax is zero, the money remains within the family group, and your tax savings is $5,124! Note that another $5,000 could be paid tax-free to each child if placed in an IRA. That could produce a total tax saving of $9,324 ([$6,100 + $5,000] × 3 × .28).*

Want to push the envelope? Under the new 401(k) rules, you can hire your child and pay up to the 401(k) contributor limit—$17,500 for 2013.

Put the $17,500 in the child's 401(k) individual account and you get:

1. A deduction of $17,500 to the employer parent
2. No current taxation to the child

Now let's change the numbers. Pay $6,100 plus $17,500 or $23,600 in reasonable salary to each of your three children—a total of $70,800—and in the 28 percent bracket, you save $19,824 in income tax. If you're not above the Social Security maximum ($113,700 for 2013), you save an additional 15.3† percent or $10,832 for a total tax savings of $30,656! Even if you're above the Social Security maximum, you'll still save the 2.9 percent Medicare tax for an additional $2,053 in tax savings. Your children pay zero tax!

---

*But normally a nondeductible Roth IRA would be a better way to go for your children. The following companies have Roth IRAs for minor children: American Century Investments (1-800-345-2021), Franklin Templeton Investments (1-800-632-2301), Strong Financial (1-800-368-1030), T. Rowe Price (1-800-638-5560), and Vanguard (1-800-662-7447).
†13.3 percent for 2011 and 2012.

137 Author's Delight

An interesting income allocation technique was made possible by an Internal Revenue Service ruling (Ltr. 8217037). A writer signed a contract with a publisher for royalties based on sales of a completed book. The contractual rights owned were then transferred to trusts for the benefit of minor children.

The IRS ruled that this was not a transfer of income, but rather of income-producing property. As long as the income was not used to meet the support obligations of the parents, such income would be taxed only to the trusts/children! In Letter Ruling 8444073, an author assigned to his child all royalties and interest in his publishing contract within 10 days after completing the book. The IRS again ruled that the author's child, not the author, would be taxed on the book royalties. Be careful, however: If an author assigns less than the entire contract, the IRS could assert the assignment of income doctrine to tax the income [see *Lewis*, 45-2 USTC Para. 9348, 34 AFTR 124 (CA-3, 1945)]. Both the contract and the royalties must be assigned: An assignment of the royalty income alone would not be a complete assignment of all of the author's property.

Note, however, that in IRS Letter Ruling 8444073, the IRS ruled that if the author was required in the contract to make revisions to the book, and no additional compensation were received for such revisions, the royalties would represent, in part, compensation for the author's services and would be taxable to that author. The measure of the compensation would presumably be what the publisher paid someone else to do the revisions. The solution to this problem is to have a separate contract or agreement specifying additional or different compensation for revisions. In addition, note that the rule that expenses incurred by an author in writing a book after 1986 must be capitalized and deducted over the life of the income stream of that book (Section 23[b] of the Tax Reform Act of 1986) has been repealed. The IRS had ruled that an author could deduct 50 percent of those expenses in the first year and 25 percent in each of the subsequent 2 years, in lieu of total income stream capitalization (Notice 88-62, 1988-22 I.R.B.). That ruling is now obsolete.

B Running Your Own Business

One of the important and effective techniques to reduce your taxes to zero is to convert your personal expenses to deductible *business* expenses. In order to do that you must own your own business. This is not complicated, expensive, or difficult to do, and incorporation is *not* needed. I will, however, detail the extensive tax benefits available if a corporate form of business is used.

To be in business, you merely declare yourself to be so. If you want to operate in a noncorporate form under a name different from your own, you can do that as well. In some states, however, if you are operating under an assumed name, you must file what is known as a "DBA" (Doing Business As) form with your local county clerk. Basically, this is merely a statement containing your name, address, and the assumed name under which you are doing business. For example, a form might merely say, "Jeff A. Schnepper is doing business under the name of 'Super Tax Savings Associates'."

Moreover, your business need not make a profit in order for your expenses to be allowable deductions. All you need to do is establish a "profit motive." Under the Internal Revenue Service tax code, a "profit motive" is presumed if you earn any net income in any 3 out of 5 business years (2 out of 7 for horse racing and breeding). In the early loss years you can insist that the Internal Revenue Service defer challenge until the 5-year period is up (Form 5213). Furthermore, in fact, you need *never* have to actually show a profit if you can show a *profit motive* (*Melvin Nickerson*, CA-7, No. 82-1323; see also *Paul Farrell*, T.C. Memo, 1983-542 where farming expenses were held deductible despite 5 straight years of losses. See also *Churchman*, 68 T.C. No. 59, where despite 20 years of losses, the court found a profit objective and allowed deductions of business losses in full, *Frazier*, T.C. Memo 1985-61, *Dennis*, T.C. Memo 2010-216, and *Blackwell v. Commissioner of Internal Revenue*, T.C. No. 29287–09, T.C. Memo 2011-188, August 8, 2011.)

The test for deductibility is whether you have an actual and honest profit *objective*—you need not even have a reasonable expectation of profit (Treasury Regulation Section 1.183-2(a); *Dreicer v. Commissioner*, 78 T.C. 642, 1982). While the Tax Court requires a primary or dominant profit motive (*Lemmen*, 77 T.C. 1326 [1981]), in *Johnson*, 86-2 U.S.T.C. Par. 9705, 58 AFTR 2d 86-5894, the U.S. Claims Court held that having a reasonable chance to make a reasonable profit, apart from tax considerations, would suffice. Although the ultimate question is whether or not you have an intent to make a profit, the determination of your motive is made by reference to objective standards, taking into account all of the facts and circumstances. The facts that will be taken into consideration include the following:

1. The manner in which you carry on the activity

2. The expertise of yourself and your advisors

3. The time and effort expended by you in carrying out this activity

4. The expectation that assets used in your business may appreciate in value

5. Your success in carrying on similar or dissimilar activities

6. Your history of income or losses with respect to the activity

7. The amount of occasional profits, if any, that are earned

8. Your financial status

9. The elements of personal pleasure or recreation ("Suffering has never been made a prerequisite for deductibility."—*Jackson v. Commissioner,* 59 T.C. 312)

The fact that you are employed full-time elsewhere will not bar a finding of your being in a separate trade or business. (See *Watson,* T.C. Memo 1988-29. See also *Riddle,* 205 F.2d 357, 62-2 USTC para. 9261, 10 AFTR 2d 5042 [DC Colo., 1962], wherein a full-time government employee was held to be in the trade or business of a consultant, despite the fact that he couldn't deal with anyone who had a government contract; *Estes,* 69-1 USTC para. 9261, 23 AFTR 2d 69-903 [DC Ala., 1969], wherein another full-time government employee was held to be in the lapidary business, so that his expenses were deductible; and *Christensen,* T.C. Memo 1988-484.)

One effective tax planning strategy, therefore, is to convert your personal hobby into a business. For example, one of my clients raced stock cars as a hobby. When he came to me, I converted that hobby into a business. He had cards and stationery printed. He ran ads looking for a sponsor. He gave his "hobby" the image and appearance of a "business," and he demonstrated a real profit motive. This client had a salary income of $40,000. When his new "business" expenses were deducted, not only did he pay zero taxes, but because he qualified for the earned income credit, the Internal Revenue Service paid him money!

Two years later he was audited on that year's return. The law requires that you prove your business expenses, with receipts, checks, or a log book that is updated daily. Unfortunately, he had not kept a log or any receipts for his expenses for the first year. His expenses, though, were legitimate, and he had receipts for the subsequent 2 years. On the basis of the receipts for the 2 subsequent years not in question, this taxpayer with $40,000 in other income and *no* receipts, after an IRS audit, paid less than $100 in taxes, including interest and penalties! Had he kept receipts for the first year, he would have paid zero.

To be allowable, your business expenses must be:

a) ordinary and necessary;

b) paid or incurred during the taxable year; *and*

c) connected with the conduct of a trade or business.

"Ordinary and necessary" has been interpreted by the courts and the Internal Revenue Service as "reasonable and customary" and this really depends upon your specific business and the business customs in your locale. In fact, an "ordinary" expense is one that is customary or usual. It need not be customary or usual for you, provided that it is customary or usual for your particular trade, industry, or community. The Supreme Court has held that even a one-time outlay falls within the definition (*Welch v. Helvering*, 290 US 111, 1933). Similarly, the Second Circuit Court of Appeals defined "necessary" as "appropriate" and "helpful," rather than necessarily essential to a taxpayer's business (*Blackmer v. Commissioner*, 70 F.2d 255).

For example, in one case a husband and wife produced, exhibited, and sold their sculptured works. The expenses incurred by them in doing so were held to be ordinary and necessary business expenses.[30] In another case, a breeder and raiser of bird dogs tried to develop an outstanding dog so that he could reap profits from sales and stud fees. Some years were profitable and some showed losses, yet all of the business expenses were found to be deductible.[31] In a third, a coal miner operated a kennel for bird dogs. Despite the fact that he sustained 11 years of losses, there was sufficient evidence of an ever-present profit motive for all of his expenses to be allowed as deductible.[32] In fact, in *Donald C. Kimbrough*, T.C. Memo 1988-185, a high school teacher's golfing activity was engaged in "for profit," resulting in his losses being allowed as deductible expenses. In *Harrison*, T.C. Memo 1996-509, the Tax Court found a profit motive and allowed gold-hunting expenses as deductible. In the 2003 case of *William Whitehurst*, the Tax Court validated bowling with a profit motive as a business and allowed his deductions. In 2005, in *Morrissey et ux vs. Commissioner*, T.C. Summ. OP. 2005-86, losses from drag racing activities were allowed as business expenses.

Owning your own business, therefore, affords you the opportunity to convert a great many of your personal expenses into allowable business deductions. The rest of the section will detail some of the most important reservoirs of deductible expenses.

138 Your Home

Probably the most significant conversion of a personal expense into a business expense occurs when you use your home for your business. (This can apply to

---

30. *Road*, 184 F. Supp. 791.
31. *Sloan*, T.C. Memo 1956-36.
32. *Sasso*, T.C. Memo 1961-216.

a primary *or* secondary business.) To be deductible, these home business expenses must be allowable under the Internal Revenue Service tax code.

The code states that no deduction for any business expenses attributable to an at-home office will be allowable unless these expenses are attributable to a portion of the home used "exclusively and on a regular basis" as:

a) the principal place of business; *or*

b) a place of business that is used by patients, clients, or customers in meeting or dealing with you in the normal course of your business.

Watch out for "exclusive." IRS auditors may question the amount you use your office computer for "business as opposed to investment." Is it 90 percent–10 percent or 50 percent–50 percent. The question is a trap! If you say anything less than 100 percent, you have failed the "exclusive" test and lose all your home office deductions. (Basic rule of thumb—never represent yourself at your own audit. You don't know what *not* to say and can never plead ignorance to a difficult question.)

While the Code requires that any office at home constitutes your principal place of business, this does not mean that it must be your *single* principal place of business, where all of your businesses are considered together. The test according to the courts is "whether with respect to a particular business conducted by a taxpayer, the home office [is] his principal place for conducting that business." Also, your home office can qualify if it is the principal place of your first *or* second business. (See *Jones,* TCM 1984-544 and *Green,* TCM 1989-599.)

There have been many rulings on this important question. In *Drucker et al. v. Commissioner,* 52 AFTR 2d 83-5804, for example, the Second Circuit Court of Appeals allowed concert musicians home office deductions for the business use of their apartments because they spent most practice time at home and their employers did not provide the musicians with space for the essential task of private practice.

In *Weissman v. Commissioner,* 84-4031, December 20, 1984, the U.S. Court of Appeals for the Second Circuit ruled that a college professor may deduct the expenses of maintaining a home office used exclusively to do most of the research and writing expected of him as a condition of retaining his teaching position. The Court found that the college professor's principal place of business was not necessarily the college at which he teaches any more than a musician's principal place of business is necessarily the concert hall at which he performs. However, the Tax Court, in *Neville Bardsley Dudley et ux.,* T.C. Memo 1987-607, ruled that a full-time business professor at the downtown campus of Wayne County Community College in Detroit was provided office space at the

college, was not required to maintain an office in his home, and had no substantial out-of-classroom responsibilities such as research and publication. The
Court concluded that Dudley's deduction for home office expenses was legitimate only if his home office was indeed the principal place of business. It was
not, so Dudley was denied his deduction.

In *John Meiers et ux. v. Commissioner,* No. 85-1209 (Seventh Cir., January 14,
1986), the Seventh Circuit found that the "principal place of business" must be
determined by looking at both hours worked and functions performed. The
Court found that the Meierses, who each day spent an hour in the laundromat
and two hours at their home office devoted exclusively to administrative work on
behalf of the laundry, were entitled to the claimed deductions for the home
office. This was another reversal of the Tax Court's "focal point" test. Under that
test, the principal place of business has been held to be that place where goods
and services are provided to customers or clients or where income is produced.

The 9th Circuit Court of Appeals, in *Pomarantz v. Commissioner,* No. 87-
7151, decided on November 7, 1988, that a physician's principal place of business was the hospital where he spent more of his time and treated patients, not
his home where he studied medical journals and kept records of patients but
treated no patients; therefore, no home office deduction was allowable. Here
the court chose not to adopt a specific standard, but found that under any
of these tests, the hospital, rather than the home, was the doctor's principal
place of business. The doctor consistently spent more time on duty at the hospital than at home. The court found the essence of his profession to be the
hands-on treatment of patients, which he did only at the hospital, never at
home. Finally, the court found that the doctor had generated income only by
seeing patients at the hospital, not by studying or writing at home.

In another example, the taxpayer was a dermatologist, and the hospital was
his principal place of business. But he also owned and managed 6 rental units,
and he had set aside a room in his residence used exclusively for managing that
activity. The court found that in this case the managing of rental property was a
trade or business and that his home office expenses *were* deductible.[33] This decision was codified in PL 97-119 on December 28, 1981, when President Reagan
signed into law an act specifically allowing a deduction for business use of a
home for activities other than a taxpayer's primary occupation. (The Black Lung
Benefits Revenue Act of 1981 [including other tax provisions adopted], Public
Law No. 97-119, Section 113(c), 95 Stat. 1642 [1980].) Furthermore, these
changes were made retroactive to years beginning after 1975. Moreover, on
November 19, 1982, the Court of Claims ruled that investment activities can

---

33. *Edwin R. Curphey,* T.C. 61.

constitute a trade or business and therefore allowed home office deductions for taxpayers who managed large investment portfolios full-time (*Moller,* 82-2 USTC Par. 9694, 51 AFTR 2d 83-369). Unfortunately, on November 18, 1983 the Claims Court was overruled by the Federal Circuit Court of Appeals (721 F. 2d 810).

In *Anthony J. Ditunno* [80 T.C. No. 12 (February 7, 1983)], the Tax Court overruled prior precedent and provided a new definition and set of criteria for determining whether a taxpayer is engaged in a trade or business for tax purposes. The Court broadened the meaning of the phrase "trade or business" by replacing the previous "goods and services" test with a "facts and circumstances" test which requires a subjective determination to be made in each instance by "an examination of all the facts involved in each case." Despite a Second Circuit Court of Appeals decision to return to the "goods and services" test in *Gajewski,* 84-1 U.S.C. Par. 9116, 53, AFTR 2d 84-386 (CA-2, 1983), and the *Estate of Dan B. Cole,* No. 83-1601 (6th Circuit, October 23, 1984), where the Appeals Court ruled that one must hold oneself out to others as a provider of goods or services to be in a trade or business, the Tax Court has reaffirmed its "facts and circumstances" test in *Robert P. Groetzinger v. Commissioner,* 82 T.C. No. 61 (May 24, 1983) where it ruled that Groetzinger's trade or business under the Code was gambling. However, on May 23, 1985, the Tax Court revised its decision and deferred to the Second Circuit when it ruled that Gajewski was not in a trade or business (*Gajewski,* 84 T.C. No. 63). *Groetzinger,* however, *was* affirmed by the 7th Circuit Court of Appeals on August 21, 1985 (No. 84-2507). These conflicting decisions were resolved when the Supreme Court, on February 24, 1987, again affirmed *Groetzinger* (480 U.S. 23, 28 (1987)], ruling that the taxpayer, who made gambling his full-time livelihood "with continuity and regularity," was in a trade or business. See also *Linda M. Myers v. Commissioner,* T.C. Summary Opinion 2007–194 (November 19, 2007), *Michael Ferguson v. Commissioner,* T.C. Summary Opinion 2007–30 (February 28, 2007), *Merkin v. Commissioner,* T.C. Memo 2008–146 (June 5, 2008), and *Crawford v. Commissioner,* T.C. No. 10413-08, T.C. Memo 2010-54 (March 22, 2010) where the facts failed to support the taxpayer. But the taxpayer won in *Le,* T.C. Summary Opinion 2010–94 and *Mayo,* 136 T.C. No. 4, 2011.

Furthermore, in *Morley v. Commissioner,* No. 40685-84, 87 T.C. No. 69, decided on November 19, 1986, the court ruled that a taxpayer's purchase, for the first time, of property that he intends to resell, followed promptly by bona fide efforts to resell the property, constituted a trade or business. Here, even the single purchase of a parcel of real estate, with the requisite intent, constituted a trade or business.

In 1982, the Tax Court ruled that an employee who was required by his employer to take frequent after-office-hours telephone calls from clients could deduct the cost of maintaining his at-home office used exclusively and regularly for that purpose. The Tax Court agreed with the Internal Revenue Service that the taxpayer had failed to prove it was "his principal place of business." But a majority of the Court, siding with the taxpayer, held that his office met the alternative test "as a place of business in which patients, clients, or customers meet or deal with the taxpayer in the normal course of the taxpayer's business." The significance of this decision is that the Court found no requirement "that such meetings or dealings are limited to physical encounters."[34] This decision, however, was reversed upon appeal to the Ninth Circuit on May 31, 1983, and the reversal was affirmed by the Tax Court in *Frankel*, 82 T.C. No. 26 on February 28, 1984. But in the case of *Feldman v. Commissioner,* 14126-82, 84 T.C. No. 1, on January 8, 1985, the Court allowed a taxpayer the costs of maintaining space in his home that he *leased* to his corporate employer for his use as a home office. Here Feldman maintained an office in his home that was rented to his employer for his own use. The employer, of which the taxpayer was a shareholder and director, paid $5,400 designated as rent to Feldman in 1979. The taxpayer reported the rental income and deducted his costs of maintaining the leased space, which he calculated as 15 percent of his home. The Court found, to the extent that the payments were reasonable, that they constituted rent and that the costs of producing that rental income may be deducted. By using the rental strategem, the taxpayer was able to create an allowable home office without "physical encounters." (But see below under depreciation for 1986 Tax Reform Act limits.) Moreover, in Rev. Rul. 86-148, the IRS allowed a deduction for a monthly fee to a security service for a home office used as a dental practice.

In *Soliman*, 94 T.C. No. 3 (March 27, 1990), the Tax Court changed the rules again. An anesthesiologist spent approximately 30 percent of his work time at his home office. He kept office equipment there, as well as a telephone, insurance and patient records, and his medical library. He never saw patients at his home, however. For a deduction, Section 280A(c)(1)(A) requires a portion of the home to be used exclusively and regularly as the principal place of a trade or business. Under the "focal point" test previously used by the Tax Court, a home office is a principal place of business if that is where goods and services are provided to customers and revenues are generated. Noting that the test had been questioned by the Second, Seventh, and Ninth Circuits, the Tax Court now states that "where a taxpayer's occupation requires essential organizational and management activities that are distinct from those that generate income, the place where the business is managed can be the principal place of business." The court also concluded that such an administrative location of the business need not be where the taxpayer spends most of his work time. The time spent there need only be substantial and the activities conducted there must be essential to the business as

---

34. *John W. Green,* 78 T.C. No. 30.

a whole. The focal point test is now replaced by a "facts and circumstances" test—as per the wisdom of *Soliman*. This was affirmed in *Kahaku*, TCM 1990-34.

Unfortunately, *Soliman* was reversed by the U.S. Supreme Court No. 91-998 (January 12, 1993), which ruled that a home office must achieve preeminence in a comparative analysis of the various locations of your trade or business in order for that office to be your "principal place of business." Two primary factors must be examined:

1. The relative importance of the activities performed at each business location; *and*

2. the amount of time spent at each location.

In Rev. Rul. 94-24, the IRS ruled that a comparison of the relative importance of the activities performed at each location depends on characteristics of each business, and if the business requires a taxpayer to meet with clients or to deliver goods or services to clients, the place where the contact occurs must be given great weight in determining where the most important activities of the business are done.

The IRS also said in the ruling that time spent on business at home must be compared to time spent on business at other locations and that the time test becomes more important if the relative importance test provides no definitive answer to the principal place of business.

The revenue ruling also holds that the relative importance test will be applied first to determine whether an office in the home is the taxpayer's principal place of business and if no definitive answer is reached, the IRS will apply the time test. In some cases, the application of both tests may result in a finding that there is no principal place of business.

The IRS provided four examples of how they would apply the ruling—a self-employed author who uses a home office to write, a self-employed retailer of costume jewelry, a self-employed plumber, and a teacher who grades papers at home.

In the example concerning the self-employed author, who spent approximately 30 to 35 hours per week in the home office to write, and 10 to 15 hours a week at other locations conducting research or meeting with publishers or attending promotional events, the IRS said that the essence of the author's home office is the principal place of business and the author can deduct expenses for the business use of the home, the IRS concluded.

The IRS said a self-employed plumber who works 40 hours at customer locations and spends 10 hours per week at a home office talking with customers on the telephone, deciding what supplies to order, and reviewing the books, could not deduct expenses for the business use of the home.

Even though the plumber employs a nonrelated, part-time employee in the home office to schedule appointments, order supplies, and keep books, the essence of the plumber's business requires the plumber to work at the homes or offices of customers and the fact that the plumber has an employee working in the home office does not alter the result, the IRS said.

In the case of the jewelry retailer, the most important activity of the business—sales to customers—is conducted at a number of locations, including craft shows and consignment shops. In this case, the amount of time spent at each location assumes particular significance, the IRS said. Because the retailer spent more time per week in the home office, expenses for business use of the home are deductible.

In the case of the teacher, the IRS said the principal place of business is clearly the school, and although work done at home is essential and time-consuming, expenses cannot be deducted for business use of the home.

Purely administrative or billing activities alone would not normally be determinative. In *Crawford v. Commissioner*, No. 1380-90, T.C. Memo 1993-192, April 29, 1993, the Tax Court applied the *Soliman* test to deny a home office deduction to a doctor who did follow-up patient work at home and who worked as an independent contractor for several Dallas hospitals.

Current rules. The Tax Relief Act of 1997 reversed *Soliman* for tax years beginning after December 31, 1998. *Now* home offices will be allowed for purely administrative or management activities if you have no other fixed place of business for those activities.

On April 17, 2001, the Ninth Circuit joined U.S. Second Circuit in allowing a concert and recording musician a home office deduction for a portion of her apartment used exclusively for practice (*Popov v. Commissioner*, 9th Cir., No. 99-70749).

Note that in *Lynn Crawford*, T.C. Memo 1993-192, the Tax Court ruled that the IRS could not add penalties to your tax bill when it disallows a home office deduction that was supported by the Tax Court's decision at the time it was taken.

Another option is available to qualify space for a home office deduction—if that space is used as a storage unit. The Small Business Job Protection Act of 1996 clarified that the special rule contained in prior law, Section 280A(c)(2), permits deductions for expenses relating to a storage unit in a taxpayer's home regularly used for inventory or product samples (or both) of the taxpayer's trade or business of selling products at retail or wholesale provided that the home is the sole fixed location of such trade or business. Such deductions will now be allowed for business expenses related to a space within a home that are used on a regular (*even if not exclusive*) basis as a storage unit.

Unfortunately, however, the Tax Reform Act of 1986 provided that when an *employee* leases a portion of his home to his employer, no net losses would be allowable. Get around this by making the home office a condition of your employment and have your employer reimburse you for expenses under an "accountable plan" (see page 436).

The following expenses for your home office will be allowable:

1. *Depreciation on Your Office Furniture and Equipment.* This would include any desks, chairs, couches, lamps, etc., that you put into your office. In *Liddle*, No. 94-7733, 9/8/95, a professional musician was allowed depreciation on his violin. Moreover, in *Zeidler*, T.C. Memo 1996-157, the court ruled that a computer used in a home office for business was deductible even without records of usage. Don't be a tax case—keep records.

2. *Depreciation on Your "Office Building."* If your home is owned, you can depreciate the portion of the acquisition cost and improvements allocatable to your home office. Note that in *Weightman*, T.C. Memo 1981-301, the Tax Court held that a taxpayer need not have an entire room as an office but could set aside an area for exclusive business use. Therefore, one part of a room could be used for personal reasons without affecting the deduction for the business use of another part of the room.

3. *Rent.* If your home is rented, you can deduct an allocatable portion of that rent for your home office.

4. *Homeowner's Insurance.* If you own your home, an allocatable portion of your homeowner's insurance is deductible.

5. *Electric Utilities.* An allocatable portion of your electric bill for providing current and light to your home office is also deductible.

6. *Heating and Air Conditioning.* An allocatable portion for heating your home office in winter or air conditioning your home office in summer would also be an allowable, ordinary, and necessary business expense. In addition, if you put in an air conditioner that does not become a structural part of the building—a window or portable air conditioner—that air conditioner's cost can be recovered through depreciation or expenses under Section 179.

7. *Lawn Care and Landscaping.* "In *Hefti* (T.C. Memo 1988–22), the Tax Court even permitted a deduction for an allocable share of lawn care and landscaping expenses where the taxpayer "had clients visiting on a regular basis and the appearance of the residence and the grounds would be of significance" to the taxpayer's business operations.

8. *Phone.* The use of your home phone would also normally be an ordinary and necessary business expense. You can either deduct an allocatable portion of your regular phone bill or insert a separate line exclusively for the use of your "business." Even part of the basic charge for a home phone, when used for business, was deductible (*Robert H. Lee,* T.C. Memo 1960-58)

until January 1, 1989. Thereafter, deductible costs for business use of a phone at home are still allowable for:

a) Long-distance calls

b) Equipment rental

c) Call waiting

d) Call forwarding

e) Charges for a second phone line

Moreover, you should determine whether basic local service includes charges for local message units. If not, then a proportionate part of these would also be deductible.

The following example demonstrates the available tax advantage of having a home office: Assume that you have a five-room home costing $150,000, with $50,000 allocatable to land and $100,000 allocatable to the building. The home has a 39-year recovery life, because the "office space" is not *residential* rental space. You purchase $20,000 in furniture with a 7-year recovery life for your one-room home office and incur the following total costs over the year:

	Allowable Deductions
Heat and air conditioning ($2,400 × 1/5) =	$ 480
Electricity ($1,200 × 1/5) =	240
Second phone (50 percent business) ($1,200 × 1/2) =	600
Depreciation on furniture:*	
Election to expense	19,000
First year depreciation	
[($20,000 – $19,000) × .1428]	143
Depreciation on home (39 years)	
[(100,000 ÷ 5) × .02461]	492
Total Deductions	$20,955
Tax savings in the 28 percent bracket	$ 5,867

Under IRS regulations, these "indirect" deductions are allowable only if they do not exceed the amount of gross income derived from the use of your home for your trade or business reduced by the deductions that are allowed without regard to their connection with your trade or business—that is, interest

---

* Depreciation on furniture and equipment is a "direct" expense, allowable without the home office limitations.

and taxes. Note that in addition to the expenses deducted above for your home office, you can also deduct an allocatable portion of the interest on your mortgage and your home taxes. These deductions are allowable as "above the line" business deductions even if you do not qualify to itemize your deductions.

The limitation on home office deductions can be shown by the following example. Assume the same deductions as in the previous case, but in addition, assume that you pay $3,000 in real estate taxes and $10,000 in mortgage interest. Furthermore assume that you have gross revenue of $22,000 from your "business." Your deductions are limited as follows:

Gross revenue (income)	$ 22,000
Minus direct expenses (furniture depreciation)	–19,143
Minus allocatable portion of interest in taxes	
[1/5 × ($10,000 + $3,000)]	–2,600
Limit on remaining expenses	$ 257
Remaining expenses (from above)	$ 1812
Deductible expenses (lesser of actual expenses or limit)	$ 257

The $1,555 is carried forward as a deduction to offset income in the subsequent year.

Several additional factors should be noted. First, the Internal Revenue Service instructions talk about gross income, not gross revenue. They are equivalent. I am talking here about total inflow of dollars before *any* expenses. Second, with such high expenses in relation to income, you should elect straight-line depreciation over an extended life period. Third, note that even though your home office expenses are limited, there is no limitation on other expenses—for instance, travel, entertainment, supplies, etc.—for your business. Note that these examples do not contain *all* of the possible home office deductions. Anything that relates to your home office per se would be a potential deduction. For example, add any allocatable water charges, sewer charges, repairs, depreciation on such improvements as painting, aluminum siding, etc. In Rev. Rul. 86-148, the IRS allowed a deduction of a proportionate share of the monthly fee for a home security system, as well as depreciation deductions on that system, to a homeowner who used one-sixth of his house as office space. Your deductions are limited only by your imagination and your ability to relate your expenditures to your business.

Although the above limitations on home office deductions are contained in the Internal Revenue Service regulations, in the Tax Court case of *Scott v. Commissioner,* No. 18916-82, 84 T.C. No. 45, decided on April 15, 1985, Judge Simpson and the Court ruled that those regulations were invalid.

According to the Judge, Section 280A(c)(5) limits the deductions allocable to the use of a home office to the gross income derived from such use. For purposes of this limitation, "gross income is not reduced by the other deductions attributable to the . . . businesses carried on in the building." What this means is that in the above example, the deductions would be limited not to $257, but to the gross revenue of $22,000 (allowable, of course, to the actual remaining expenses incurred). While *Scott* was specifically overruled by the Tax Reform Act of 1986 for years after 1986, the Internal Revenue Service National Office has held that it would apply for open years prior to 1987 (TAM 8640001).

If you fear taxable recapture of depreciation upon sale of your house note that in Rev. Rul. 82-26 (February 8, 1982) the IRS ruled that the *prior* business use of a residence would not require the recognition of gain when the residence is sold. The IRS looked to the use of the residence at the time of the sale (Rev. Rul. 59-72). Thus, if the entire house was used as the principal residence in the year of sale, the entire gain on the sale would have been eligible for tax-deferral, regardless of prior use. [See IRC Sections 1234 and 1250(d)(7)(A).] Unfortunately, the Tax Reform Act of 1997 now requires the recapture of any depreciation taken after May 7, 1997, upon sale, and this depreciation may be taxed up to a 25 percent rate. However, you still have the time value of the tax savings. Moreover, while any depreciation will be recaptured to the extent of the gain, real appreciation recognized on the sale can *now* be sheltered by the $250,000/$500,000 exclusion if you qualify. See page 66.

In Rev. Proc. 2005–14, the IRS validated the combination of the $250,000/$500,000 home sale exclusion with a like kind swap. First you apply the gain exclusion to the primary home. Then the tax-free swap rules can exclude gain on the business portion—including depreciation after May 6, 1997, which would be otherwise taxed. To qualify, you'd need a new home office in the new home.

SIMPLE OPTION

In Rev. Proc. 2013, the IRS announced a new simplified, optional method of claiming a home office deduction. Under the new procedure, a significantly simplified form is used. The new optional deduction is limited to $1,500 per year based on $5 per square foot for up to 300 square feet. Homeowners using the new option will not be able to depreciate the portion of their home used in a trade or business. However, they will be able to claim allowable mortgage interest, real estate taxes, and casualty losses on the home as itemized deductions on Schedule A of Form 1040. The new option is available beginning with year 2013 return.

Simplified Option	Regular Method
Deduction for home office use of a portion of a residence allowed only if that portion is exclusively used on a **regular basis** for business purposes	Same
Allowable square footage of home use for business (not to exceed 300 square feet)	Percentage of home used for business
Standard $5 per square foot used to determine home business deduction	Actual expenses determined and records maintained
Home-related itemized deductions claimed in full on Schedule A	Home-related itemized deductions apportioned between Schedule A and business schedule (Sch. C or Sch. F)
No depreciation deduction	Depreciation deduction for portion of home used for business
No recapture of depreciation upon sale of home	Recapture of depreciation on gain upon sale of home
Deduction cannot exceed gross income from business use of home less business expenses	Same
Amount in excess of gross income limitation may **not** be carried over	Amount in excess of gross income limitation may be carried over
Loss carryover from use of regular method in prior year may not be claimed	Loss carryover from use of regular method in prior year may be claimed if gross income test is met in current year

To prove a home office, photograph it, have it on your business cards and stationery, and keep a log of whom you see, when you use the office, and what you work on.

In addition, travel expenses between your home office and job sites are deductible. For example, one taxpayer operated a home-repair business using his home as a business headquarters where he received inquiries for possible contracting services. He claimed a deduction for the expenses of traveling between his home and job sites. The deduction was allowable because his home was the sole fixed location of his business and was essential to his business operations (*Adams*, TCM 1982-223). In fact, in *Carl F. Worden*, T.C. Memo 1981-366, a home office had the effect of converting a personal residence into a job site.

In that case, the Tax Court found that the insurance salesman's home was his place of business. Therefore, *all* his travel costs were allowable as business deductions. See also 76 T.C. No. 72, *Wisconsin Psychiatric Services, Limited,* where Wess R. Vogt, a psychiatrist, established that his home office was his principal office and therefore that trips to and from his home were business trips and not nondeductible commuting expenses; *Wicker,* TCM 1986-1, wherein the court ruled that a home office that was the principal place of business for a nurse-anesthesiologist enables her to deduct the costs of going from there to the hospital where she was associated and where she practiced exclusively, but without office space; and *Ronald Carey,* SD, OH, No. C-3-80-422, where a salesman who worked out of his home was able to deduct the cost of his daily sales trips because the salesman's home was his principal place of work.

In *Walker v. Comm.,* No. 20919-19, 101 T.C. No. 36, 12/13/93, the court applied Revenue Ruling 90-23 and held that a self-employed taxpayer could deduct truck expenses paid for traveling to various locations in a national forest where he worked as a logger. It found that his residence was a "regular place of business" and that transportation expenses between a "regular place of business" and a "temporary work location" were deductible. The advance in *Walker* was that the residence did *not* qualify as a home office—such as the principal place of business under *Soliman.*

In Revenue Ruling 94-37, the IRS ruled that *Walker* would be followed only if one of two other conditions apply.

Under the first condition, if the taxpayer has one or more regular work locations away from the taxpayer's residence, the taxpayer may deduct daily transportation expenses incurred in going between the taxpayer's residence and a *temporary* work location in the same trade or business, regardless of the distance.

Under the second condition, if the taxpayer's residence is the taxpayer's principal place of business, the taxpayer may deduct daily transportation expenses incurred in going between the residence and another work location in the same trade or business, regardless of whether the other work location is *regular or temporary* and regardless of the distance.

In 1999, the IRS modified the rule again. Issued January 15, 1999, Revenue Ruling 99-7 now provides three exceptions to the general rule that transportation expenses between a residence and a place of business or employment are not deductible. Now you *can* deduct:

a) expenses incurred in going from your residence and a temporary work location outside the metropolitan area where you live and normally work;

b) expenses incurred going between your residence and a temporary work location in the same trade or business in which you have one or more regular work locations away from this residence; *and*

c) expenses incurred going between your home office (principal place of business) and another work location in the same trade or business, regardless of the distance or whether the work location is regular or temporary.

A work location is "temporary" if employment there is realistically expected to last—and does in fact last—for 1 year or less. But, in *Senulis*, T.C. Summ. Op. 2009–97, the taxpayer who took on a 9-month project that actually lasted 13 months was allowed to deduct away-from-home expenses—meals, lodging, and travel. The worker "reasonably" expected that the job's duration would be less than a year when he took it.

Note that if you file a separate income tax from your spouse, an additional income-shifting opportunity is available. In Rev. Rul. 74-209, the Internal Revenue Service ruled that rent paid by a husband to his wife for the use of the jointly owned Wisconsin real estate that the husband used in his business is deductible as a business expense on the husband's separate income tax return. For this strategy to be successful, you should compare the net results on a joint return to those on separate returns. It is a technique that should be considered where appropriate.

Moreover, additional tax savings can be found if you have a home office that requires a secretary or a receptionist to be present at all times during business hours and the only person available is a member of your family. In the previous section we discussed the advantages of employing members of your family in your business as an income-shifting device. In this case, any member of your family, including your spouse, can reap enormous tax-saving advantages. The tax code excludes from gross income the value of any meals furnished to an employee by the employer for the convenience of the employer if the meals are furnished on the business premises of the employer.[35] If your spouse, for example, is required as your employee to be on your business premises—that is, your home office—as a receptionist, telephone operator, etc., then any meals (for instance, lunch) provided are not compensation that your spouse would include in gross income, but they are a *deductible* business expense to you! By structuring your first or second business in this manner, you can effectively and *legally* deduct the cost of your spouse's or children's lunches. Your spouse must truly be employed and required to be on business premises during lunchtime or the deduction will not be allowed (*Weidmann*, 89-1 USTC ¶9197 [DC N.Y. 1989]). Given the price of food today, this is an enormous benefit that can result in substantial tax savings. Moreover, no Social Security payments are due on such lunches. At $5 per lunch, five times a week for 50 weeks, your total deductible expense would be $1,250. In the 28 percent bracket, this saves you $350 in taxes!

---

35. Section 119 of the Internal Revenue Code.

139 Your Car

Automobile expenses incurred in your business travel are deductible either as a travel expense (if away from home on business) or as a transportation expense (even if you are not away from home). Remember, transportation expenses are not normally deductible unless they are incurred in a business or investment situation. To get the deduction here, there must be a direct connection between the use of the car and your trade or business or some income-producing activity—for instance, to check on your investments. If you have one car that you use both for personal and for business use, only the portion of your car expenses directly attributable to business use is deductible.

In allocating your car expenses between business and personal use, there are a number of methods that you can use. One simple method is known as the mileage cost basis. Using this method, you multiply your business mileage by a standard mileage rate that the IRS allows in lieu of the operating and fixed costs of your car, along with parking fees, interest, taxes, and tolls.

Standard Mileage Rates

2008	50.5¢ January–June/58.5¢ July–December
2009	55.0¢
2010	50.0¢
2011	51.0¢ January–June/55.5¢ July–December
2012	55.5¢
2013	56.5¢

So, for example, if you drive your car 24,000 business miles over the year, you will deduct 24,000 × .565 for a total of $13,560. In addition to this $13,560 deduction, you will be allowed all of your expenses for parking fees, interest, taxes, and tolls.

As an alternative to the standard mileage cost basis, you can use the mileage percentage basis. Under the mileage percentage method, you simply divide your business mileage by your total mileage and take that percentage of your total expenses as a deduction.

Included in such auto expenses, when using the mileage percentage method, are not only your parking fees and tolls (at 100 percent) but also depreciation on your car, interest, taxes, registration and license fees, and gas, oil, and repair expenses. Given the cost of gasoline, it would probably be to your advantage to keep receipts and records of your actual expenditures. Whereas the Internal Revenue Service allows you a deduction of 56.5¢ per mile under the mileage cost basis, studies by auto-renting firms have established that actual mileage costs may be two to three times greater than that allowance.

There is a special tax planning strategy that you can use if you have two cars in your family. Assume that you have been using one car exclusively for business and the other exclusively for personal family use and that you put 36,000 miles each year on your business car and only 12,000 miles a year on your family car. Normally you can deduct only the costs of using the business car. Now, suppose you switched the use of each car every 6 months. The combined mileage of both cars in the original example is 48,000 miles per year. By rotating your cars equally between business and family use, each car will be driven 24,000 miles a year, 75 percent of which will be business miles (36 ÷ 48). Therefore, 75 percent of your depreciation and other costs on *each* car will be deductible. This can be a lot more than simply deducting all of the costs on one car and nothing on the other.

A taxpayer cannot normally deduct commuting expenses. However, if you have a regular place of business, you *can* deduct daily transportation expenses from your *home* and a *temporary* work location (Rev. Rul. 90-23, 1990-11 I.R.B. Rev. Rul. 94-37, and Rev. Rul. 99-7).

What is a temporary place of business? For purposes of determining whether daily transportation expenses are deductible business expenses or nondeductible commuting expenses, a regular place of business is any location at which the taxpayer works or performs services on a regular basis, and a temporary place of business is any location at which the taxpayer performs services on an *irregular or short-term* (i.e., generally a matter of days or weeks) basis. A taxpayer may be considered as working or performing services at a particular location on a regular basis whether or not the taxpayer works or performs services at that location every week or on a set schedule. For example, daily transportation expenses incurred by a doctor in going between the doctor's residence and one or more offices, clinics, or hospitals at which the doctor works or performs services on a regular basis are nondeductible commuting expenses. However, daily transportation expenses incurred by the doctor in going between a clinic and a hospital or between the doctor's residence and a temporary work location are deductible business expenses.

Under this rule, a doctor's expense of travel from home to a patient's home for a house call is deductible.

An executive or salesperson may make calls on customers or clients. If these visits are on an infrequent basis, the client's office would be a temporary place of business. The cost of travel from home to client's office is deductible.

The rule is not limited to prospective application. Thus, it applies retroactively to open years (see also Rev. Rul. 99-7 discussed above).

If the taxpayer is an employee, the deduction for these expenses can only be claimed as a miscellaneous itemized deduction. As such, it is subject to the 2 percent of adjusted gross income floor on such deductions.

The IRS warns that if an audit shows a clear pattern of abuse by the taxpayer in claiming a business expense deduction for daily transportation expenses paid or incurred in going between the taxpayer's residence and asserted temporary work locations without proof of a valid business purpose, the IRS will disallow any deduction for those expenses and impose appropriate penalties.

Employer reimbursement. In some cases, an employer may reimburse an employee for otherwise deductible daily transportation expenses. The IRS says that the employee doesn't have to include such reimbursement if it is paid under an *accountable plan,* i.e., one that (a) requires the employee to substantiate expenses covered by the arrangement to the person providing the reimbursement, and (b) requires the employee to return any amount above the substantiated expenses. Reimbursement that is paid under a nonaccountable plan must be included by the employee in gross income. In turn, the employee can deduct the deductible daily transportation expenses as a miscellaneous itemized deduction.

Employer reporting. An employer is not required to report on the employee's Form W-2, or to withhold payroll taxes on, amounts paid as a reimbursement or other expense allowance for daily transportation expenses that are paid under an accountable place. However, reporting and withholding are required for amounts paid as reimbursement or other expense allowance for daily transportation amounts that are paid under a nonaccountable plan.

140 Meals and Entertainment

Wouldn't it be great to have the Internal Revenue Service pay part of the cost of your meals and entertainment? When you have your own business, you can have the Internal Revenue Service split the bills for these expenses with you.

In order to deduct any expenses for travel, entertainment, gifts, or listed property, you must have a receipt or other documentary evidence for any lodging expenditure of $75 or more. For expenditures incurred prior to October 1, 1995, the $75 amount was $25. (Internal Revenue Service Notice 95-50, issued September 29, 1995.)

Any expenses for food and drink furnished under circumstances of a type generally considered conducive to a business discussion, and when a business discussion is held, are deductible business expenses. Therefore, the custom of entertaining business clients or potential business clients with food and drink in restaurants and hotels will be deductible if they meet the requirements of an ordinary and necessary expense. When you go out with friends or relatives for a meal or drink, do you ever pick up their check? If they are or *could be* potential clients or customers for your business, and if you discussed business with them, then that expense would be deductible. Alternatively, if they are in business and they pay your expenses for meals at a restaurant, those expenses would be deductible for them.

Note that under the Tax Reform Act of 1986, no deduction is allowed with respect to entertainment, amusement, or recreation unless the taxpayer establishes that the item was directly related to or, in the case of an item directly preceding or following a substantial and bona fide business discussion, that such item was associated with the active conduct of the taxpayer's trade or business and that meals are now included as entertainment expenses for this purpose. A meal expenditure is associated with the active conduct of a trade or business if the taxpayer establishes a clear business purpose in making the expenditure. The meal must directly follow or precede a substantial and bona fide business discussion. The directly follow or precede standard is satisfied if the meal occurs on the same day as the business discussion.

The directly related test is satisfied if any one of the following four tests is satisfied:

1. The taxpayer had more than a general expectation of deriving some business benefit; the taxpayer actively engaged in a business meeting, negotiation, or other bona fide business transaction; the principal character or aspect of the meal was the active conduct of the taxpayer's business; and the expenditure was allocable to the taxpayer and persons with whom the taxpayer engaged in the active conduct of business.

2. The expenditure occurred in a clear business setting, directly in furtherance of the taxpayer's trade or business.

3. The expenditure was made directly or indirectly for the benefit of an individual (other than an employee), and if such expenditure was in the nature of compensation for services rendered or paid as a prize or award, that is required to be included in gross income.

4. The expenditure was made with respect to a facility used by the taxpayer for the furnishing of food or beverages in an atmosphere conducive to business discussion.

However, even if one of the four directly related tests is satisfied, expenditures will not be directly related to the active conduct of a trade or business if incurred under circumstances where there is little or no possibility of engaging in the active conduct of a trade or business.

You should have receipts specifying the name of the restaurant, the amount, and the date. The relationship of your guest to your business activity should also be noted. Recognize, however, that no actual business need come from the meeting so long as you discuss business at the restaurant. In this area be careful not to simply alternate days in which you and your friend pick up the check. Any "regular" exchange of meal checks, if caught by the Internal Revenue Service, will be disallowed as a sham in an audit and subject you to fraud penalties.

Moreover, not only can you deduct meals, but you can also deduct business entertainment expenses. Amounts spent for business entertainment, amusement, or recreation will be allowable if you can show that the expense was:

a) for entertainment directly preceding or following a substantial bona fide business discussion (including business meetings at a convention that was associated with your trade or business); *or*

b) directly related to the active conduct of your trade or business.

Examples of entertainment, amusement, or recreation include entertaining guests at nightclubs, theaters, football games, prizefights, and on hunting, fishing, and vacation trips. In *Detko v. Commissioner,* No. 14790-81, T.C. Memo 1987-99, February 18, 1987, an anesthesiologist was found to be entitled to deductions for entertainment expenses and depreciation in connection with a fishing boat on which he entertained doctors who were his referral source!

In applying the "directly related" or "associated with" tests, remember these points:

1. The entertaining must be to further your trade or business. So, for example, if you entertain at a time when you already have more business than you can possibly handle, your deduction will be disallowed.

2. Expenses that violate public policy or local law—for instance, providing "call girls" for clients or serving liquor where it is against local law—will not be deductible.

3. Entertainment, amusement, or recreation expenses that are considered lavish or extravagant under the circumstances will be deductible *only* up to a reasonable amount. What a "reasonable amount" is depends upon all of the facts and circumstances; given today's business and entertainment climate, it would be very difficult to exceed a "reasonable amount."

The Tax Reform Act of 1986 limited deductions for most meals and entertainment to 80 percent of cost. After December 31, 1993, the limit fell to 50 percent. Moreover, expenditures qualify as business meals or business entertainment only if business is actually discussed. Business transportation (airfare, taxis, etc.) remains fully deductible, but travel to *investment* seminars or *investment* conventions is not. The chart below summarizes these rules.

Type of Expense	Deductible
Lunch with customer/client; business before, during, or after the meal	50%
No business discussed	None
Cab fare to restaurant	100%
Air fare to Philadelphia to call on customer/client	100%
Lodging in Philadelphia	100%
Meals in Philadelphia (alone)	50%
Meals with customer/client; no business discussed:	
a. Your meal	50%
b. Customer's/client's meal	None
Air fare to New York for dentist to attend dental convention	100%
Meals in New York	50%
Air fare to Dallas for investment seminar	None
Lodging in Dallas	None
Tickets to ball game for taxpayer and customer/client; business discussed	50%
Taxi fare to game	100%
Food and drink at game	50%
Complimentary theater tickets for customer/client; taxpayer *not* present (note possible deduction as a gift)	None
Lunch at service organization as member	50%
Tickets to charity golf tournament run by volunteers	100%
Greens fees, carts, food and beverages consumed while hosting customer/client; business discussed	50%

Note that some meal and entertainment expenses remain fully deductible:

- expenses treated by the employer as compensation to an employee (the 50 percent reduction applies at the employee level if the employee claims the deduction);

- expenses reimbursed under an "accountable plan" (fully deductible to the person receiving the reimbursement, *if* reported in income with the deduction applying to the person making the reimbursement);

- expenses incurred for recreational or social activities provided by the employer for the benefit of its employees (e.g., holiday parties, summer outings, etc.);

- expenses for goods, services, and facilities made available by the taxpayer to the general public, such as promotional tickets or customer samples;

- food or beverage expenses excludable under the "de minimis fringe benefit" rules; *and*

- expenses related to the ticket package costs for sporting events arranged primarily for the purpose of charitable fund-raising.

For years after December, 31, 1997 the business meal deduction will be increased by 5 percent every other year to 80 percent *for persons subject to the federal hours of service limitation.*

With entertainment as well as with meals, your expenses must be substantiated. You should have a receipt detailing the amount paid, the client you entertained, the business relationship, the date, and the place. The deductions for meals and entertainment allow you substantial opportunities to convert your personal expenditures into allowable business deductions. Do not fail to claim them and do not fail to keep them because of lack of adequate substantiation. In the 28 percent tax bracket, $100 worth of football tickets costs you $72. No matter how much money you are making, it would be worth $28 in tax savings to spend thirty seconds noting the name of your business client on the back of the ticket stub. That's the same as earning, tax-free, $3,360 an hour!

141 Travel and Vacation

There is no law prohibiting you from combining a business trip and a vacation. The Internal Revenue Service concedes that you are entitled to a deduction for attending a business convention. While such attendance must benefit or advance your business to be a deductible expense, there is no reason why such a convention cannot coincide with your vacation. If a business purpose can be established, the expenses of your spouse may also be deductible (Rev. Rul. 56-168; see also *Bank of Stockton*, TCM 1977-24). Note, however, that such business conventions or seminars must relate to your specific business. For example, in IRS Letter Ruling 8451027 and Rev. Rul. 84-113, 1984-31 I.R.B. 5, the Internal Revenue Service ruled that investment seminars in resort locations and a financial planning seminar dealing with general planning strategies were not deductible because they did not relate specifically to the taxpayer's activities.

The Omnibus Budget Reconciliation Act of 1993, effective after December 31, 1993, denies a deduction for travel expenses paid or incurred with respect to a spouse, dependent, or other individual accompanying a person on business travel, unless (1) the spouse, dependent, or other individual accompanying the person is a bona fide employee of the person paying or reimbursing the expenses, (2) the travel of the spouse, dependent, or other individual is for a bona fide business purpose, and (3) the expenses of the spouse, dependent, or other individual would otherwise be deductible. The denial of the deduction does not apply to expenses that would otherwise qualify as deductible moving expenses.

WITHIN THE UNITED STATES

If the business-vacation trip is within the United States, the transportation expenses will be deductible only if the trip is primarily for business. If the trip is primarily for pleasure, no transportation expenses can be taken as a deduction. This means that you have to establish a primary business motive for making the trip—for instance, a convention located in that city, or a client or potential client that you want to see at that location. It would be advisable under such a situation to write to this person and receive in return a letter requesting you to visit her or him to discuss business matters. The amount of time that you spend on business as opposed to pleasure will be a factor in answering the "primarily" question. For example, if you spend 5 days conducting business and 3 days sightseeing and seeing shows, the trip will be deemed primarily for business (5 days vs. 3 days) and the transportation will be deductible. Alternatively, if you conducted business for 2 days and vacationed the remaining 6, the trip will most likely be found primarily personal, and no transportation expenses will be allowed.

Even if the trip is found to be primarily personal, any expenses incurred at the destination that are properly allocatable to business—meals, lodging, and incidental expenses during your "business days"—will be deductible.

OUTSIDE THE UNITED STATES

If the business-vacation trip is outside the United States, Canada, certain other Caribbean countries,[36] Mexico, and the Pacific Islands Trust Territories, special rules apply. If you were out of the country for 7 days or less, or if less than 25 percent of the time was for personal purposes, no allocation of transportation expenses need be made. Furthermore, no allocation is required if you had no substantial control over the trip arrangements and if the desire for a vacation was not a major factor in taking the trip. Alternatively, if the trip was primarily for pleasure, none of the transportation expenses will be deductible. In all other cases, all travel expenses must be allocated between business and personal expenses, and days devoted to travel are considered business days.

For example, assume that you took a trip from New York to London primarily for business purposes. You were away from home from July 20 through July 29 and spent 3 days vacationing and 7 days conducting business (including 2 travel days). Your fare was $500 and your meals and lodging amounted to $75 per day. You can deduct 70 percent of your transportation expenses (7 days out of 10) and $75 per day for 7 business days, as you were away from home for more than 7 days and more than 25 percent of your time was devoted to personal purposes.

If you find your trip is subject to the allocation rule, there is a planning strategy to maximize your tax deductions. When booking your flight, arrange for a stopover within the United States at the point closest to your destination. That way, the portion of the trip between your home and the stopover point will be fully deductible. You will have to allocate only the cost of the remainder of the trip.

---

36. The Caribbean Basin Initiative (CBI) was enacted on August 5, 1983, authorizing preferential tax measures for Caribbean Basin countries and territories. The Act allows deductions for business expenses incurred while attending conventions and meetings in a designated Caribbean Basin beneficiary country, if that country enters into an agreement with the United States to provide for the exchange of certain tax information. The following countries have been eligible and qualify for the benefits of the CBI: Antigua and Barbuda, Aruba, the Bahamas, Barbados, Belize, Bermuda, Costa Rica, Dominica, the Dominican Republic, El Salvador, Grenada, Guatemala, Haiti, Honduras, Jamaica, Montserrat, the Netherlands Antilles, Panama, St. Christopher-Nevis, St. Vincent, and Trinidad and Tobago. As of 2007, the countries that remain eligible but have not yet qualified for the benefits of the CBI are Anguilla, The British Virgin Islands, the Cayman Islands, Guyana, Nicaragua, St. Lucia, Surinam, and the Turks and Caicos Islands (see Rev. Rul. 2007-28). Updates to the list of qualifying countries can be obtained by calling 1-202-287-4851.

For example, assume that you live in New York and will be attending a 3-day business convention in the Bahamas that will be followed by a 6-day vacation. If you fly directly to the Bahamas from New York, only one-third of the cost of your round-trip flight is deductible (3 business days out of 9 days total). However, if you fly from New York to Miami, conduct business in Miami, then take another flight to the Bahamas, the entire cost of the trip from New York to Miami would be deductible—as well as one-third of the cost of the trip from Miami to the Bahamas and back.

FOREIGN CONVENTIONS

No deduction will be allowed for expenses attributable to a foreign convention/vacation unless it is "reasonable for the convention to be held outside North America." "North America" means the countries below and on the next page including the Pacific Islands Trust Territories. Under Rev. Rul. 94-56*, 1994-36 I.R.B. 10, for purposes of claiming deductions for expenses incurred in connection with a convention, seminar, or similar meeting, the following areas are included in the "North American Area":

1. the 50 states of the United States and the District of Columbia;

2. the possessions of the United States, which for this purpose are American Samoa, Baker Island, the Commonwealth of Puerto Rico, the Commonwealth of the Northern Mariana Islands, Guam, Howland Island, Jarvis Island, Johnston Island, Kingman Reef, the Midway Islands, Palmyra, the United States Virgin Islands, Wake Island, and other United States islands, cays, and reefs not part of any of the 50 states or the District of Columbia;

3. Canada;

4. Mexico;

5. the Trust Territory of the Pacific Islands (that is, Palau);

6. the Republic of the Marshall Islands; *and*

7. the Federated States of Micronesia;

---

* Updated by Rev. Rul. 2003-109.

Country	Deduction Allowed for Expenses Incurred in Attending a Convention That Began After
8. Barbados	November 2, 1984
9. Bermuda	December 1, 1988
10. Costa Rica	February 11, 1991
11. Dominica	May 7, 1988
12. Dominican Republic	October 11, 1989
13. Grenada	July 12, 1987
14. Guyana	August 26, 1992
15. Honduras	October 10, 1991
16. Jamaica	December 17, 1986
17. St. Lucia	April 21, 1991 but not after April 4, 2007
18. Trinidad and Tobago	February 8, 1990
19. Antigua and Barbuda	February 9, 2003
20. Netherland Antilles	March 21, 2007
21. Aruba	September 12, 2004
22. Bahamas	December 31, 2005

In other words, there is no deduction if it is more reasonable to have the convention within rather than outside of North America. Three factors must be considered in determining the reasonableness of the convention location:

1. The purpose of the meeting and the activities taking place at the meeting
2. The purpose and activities of the sponsoring organization or groups
3. The residence of the active members of the sponsoring organization or groups and places where other meetings of the sponsors have been or will be held

CRUISE CONVENTIONS

In addition, there is no limit on the number of foreign conventions/vacations that yield deductible expenses, but no deductions will be allowed for conventions, seminars, or other meetings held on cruise ships, except if:

a) the convention or meeting is directly related to your trade or business;

b) the cruise ship is U.S. registered; *and*

c) all ports of call are located in the U.S. or its possessions. Only the following ports qualify as possessions: The U.S. Virgin Islands (St. Thomas, St. John, St. Croix), American Samoa, Guam, the North Mariana Islands, and Puerto Rico.

Even under these circumstances, the maximum deduction is $2,000 for each taxpayer (Highway Revenue Act of 1982) and you must attach two written statements to your return. The first statement, signed by you, must include information as to the number of days that were devoted to scheduled business activities, a program of the scheduled business activities, and such other information as may be required by regulations. The other statement, signed by a representative of the sponsoring organization, must include a schedule of the business activities each day, the number of hours you attended such scheduled activities, and such other information as may be required by regulations. Business seminars on cruise ships that are U.S. registered are now being offered by United States Line and American Hawaii Cruises (to Hawaii) and Delta Line Cruises (on the Ohio and Mississippi Rivers). In addition, American Cruise Lines and the Clipper Cruise Line, which operates a variety of voyages in intercoastal waters from New England to Florida, are also operating under the seminar restrictions.

WATER TRANSPORTATION

Note that the Tax Reform Act of 1986 limits the deduction for expenses incurred for transportation by water to twice the highest federal government per diem allowance (for employees traveling away from home but serving in the United States) times the number of days in transit. These rates are changed annually and are found in Publication 1542 available free from the IRS. In addition, according to Notice 87-23, the now 50 percent limitation on meals and entertainment is applied prior to the above maximum per diem limitations. If meal expenses are not separately stated, the amount deductible under the luxury water or travel limitation is not subject to the 50 percent rule.

Ship travel, however, can be an asset on a combined business-vacation trip. Days spent in transit count as business days in the allocation formula. For example, assume a 2-day business meeting in London followed by a 2-week British vacation. If you fly (1 day each way), only 22 percent of your travel excluding transportation is deductible—2 business days plus 2 days of travel out of a total of 18 days away. But if you sail (5 days each way), 46 percent is deductible—2 business days plus 10 days of travel out of a total 26 days away.

Remember, the key to being able to deduct your vacation as a business expense is prior planning. Make sure that you can substantiate your business purpose for the trip and your expenses. Properly planned and substantiated expenses will allow you to deduct the cost of your transportation, food, meals, lodging, entertainment, cleaning, etc. I have found that perhaps the easiest way to maintain a substantiation record is to keep a diary or account book of such expenses. Combined with appropriate receipts, such a diary will help reduce your taxes to zero.

142 Gifts

Ordinary and necessary expenses for business gifts you make directly or indirectly to any individual will be allowed as deductible expenses. However, the total value of business gifts during the tax year to any one individual cannot be more than $25, and in addition, gifts from a husband and wife are treated as coming from one donor in applying this limitation. Incidental costs, such as packaging, mailing or other delivery, and insuring the gifts, are not included in this limitation.

The following items are not subject to the $25 limitation:

1. Items of a clear advertising nature that cost $4 or less

   a) on which your name is permanently printed; *or*

   b) which are among a number of identical items generally distributed by you.

2. Signs, display racks, or other promotional material given by you as a producer or wholesaler to a retailer for use on the business premises of the retailer

3. Employee awards

Here again you must provide substantiation for your expenses in order to make them allowable. While the price of allowance is increased record keeping, the benefit now is that gifts to friends, relatives, etc., who are or may become business clients or associates have been converted from nondeductible personal expenses to allowable income tax deductions. Every time you convert a personal expense to a deductible business expense you take one more step on the road to reducing your taxes to zero.

143 Advertising

The Tax Court allowed the sponsor of an amateur basketball team to deduct the costs of the team as an advertising expense. The taxpayer used the team sponsorship as the main form of advertising for his rental housing and commodity brokerage businesses. Before games, the taxpayer would meet with customers to discuss business. The Court said that, while there was an element of personal satisfaction, the team sponsorship promoted the taxpayer's business at low cost. *James C. Bower,* T.C. Memo 1990-16.

144 Deductible Clothes

The costs of buying and maintaining a uniform are deductible business expenses only if the uniform is (1) specifically required to be worn as a condition of employment and (2) is not adaptable for general or continued use. Uniforms that can be worn as ordinary clothing don't meet this second test and can't be considered ordinary and necessary business expenses.

Uniforms worn by police officers, fire fighters, nurses, bus drivers and railway workers have been held to meet this two-part test [Rev. Rul. 70-474, C.B. 1970-2, 34], as have commercial fishermen's protective clothing [Rev. Rul. 55-235, C.B. 1955-1, 274]. But work clothing worn by painters (white shirts, caps, bib overalls, and work shoes) did not qualify, even though the clothing was required by a union [Rev. Rul. 57-143, C.B. 1957-1,89].

Note, however, that ordering clothes imprinted with the name of your business may be deductible as *advertising*.

145 Creative Deductions—Busting the IRS

In Green Bay, Wisconsin, a stripper got a tax deduction for surgically enlarged breasts. Then she put her deductions on display and called it a victory for all exotic dancers.

"It is simply a stage prop we are carrying around to make money," Cynthia Hess said before appearing at the Bamboo Room.

Hess, otherwise known as "Chesty Love," and her husband, Reginald R. Hess of Fort Wayne, Ind., claimed a $2,088 deduction on the implants that enlarged her bust size to 56FF.

The Internal Revenue Service turned it down.

But Hess found an ally in Special Trial Judge Joan Seitz Pate, who ruled that the breasts did increase her income, and at 10 pounds each, were so cumbersome that she couldn't derive personal benefit from them.

146 Medical Premiums

Section 162(m), added by the Tax Reform Act of 1986, permits self-employed individuals to deduct a percentage of their health insurance premiums (including Medicare payments). For 1998, the percentage was 45 percent; it increased to 60 percent in 1999, went to 70 percent in 2002, and is 100 percent in 2003 and after. The amount of this deduction is limited to your self-employment income and is not available on a month-by-month basis, if you or your spouse is eligible to participate in any subsidized health plan maintained by any employer of either you or your spouse. The deduction is also not available unless the premium is paid under a nondiscriminatory health plan. The premium paid is an "above the line" deduction. That means that it is deductible even if you do not itemize your deductions.

147 Borrowing from Your Company

If your own business is in a corporate form, you have a special opportunity for tax savings. This opportunity is the supersophisticated technique of borrowing from your own corporation or from your corporate pension plan. This can be done as long as the loan bears a reasonable rate of interest—that is, the prime rate, give or take a percentage point.

This extraordinary technique allows you to borrow money, pay yourself interest, deduct the interest you pay (see Chapter 7 for limitations), and receive the same interest tax-free. It normally is done by having a qualified profit-sharing or pension plan make a loan to you as one of its participants. This technique was approved by the Internal Revenue Service for a qualified plan even with *single* participant.[37]

This technique will be approved by the Internal Revenue Service for a qualified plan that has a loan provision *if* the loan:

a) is available to all participants and beneficiaries on an equal basis;

b) is not made available to highly compensated office employees, officers, or shareholders in a percentage amount greater than that available to other employees;

c) is made in accordance with specific provisions regarding such loans set forth in the plan;

d) bears a reasonable rate of interest; *and*

e) is adequately secured.

The vested portion of your account (for a profit-sharing or money purchase plan) can be used as security for the loan. Moreover, loans from such plans can exceed the vested amount in your account without the plan's risking disqualification as long as:

- The loans are adequately secured by other than the nonvested portion of the plan.

- The loans bear a reasonable interest rate.

- The loans are repaid within a specified period of time.

- The loan payments are made on a level basis, at least quarterly.

Loan security for a defined benefit pension plan can be provided up to an amount equal to the actuarial equivalent, or present value, of your accrued benefit. Furthermore, the arrangement must be an actual loan. There must be evidence that a true debtor-creditor relationship exists; otherwise the "loan" will be labeled by the Internal Revenue Service as an "advance distribution," making such funds taxable income to you.

The Tax Equity and Fiscal Responsibility Act of 1982 restricts borrowing against the vested benefits of your plan. Effective with respect to loans made after August 13, 1982, the law allows loans up to the lesser of $50,000 or 50 percent

---

37. Letter Ruling 800-8059.

of the value of your vested employee benefit, but not less than $10,000. Additionally, the loan must be repaid within 5 years. But a loan used to acquire, construct, or rehabilitate your personal residence or the residence of a member of your family would not be subject to the 5-year repayment rule.

The extraordinary savings from this technique can be demonstrated by the following example:

Your vested share in a profit-sharing plan	$100,000
Amount borrowed to purchase a home	$50,000
Interest rate	20%
Tax-free interest you pay into the plan	$10,000
Amount deducted	$10,000
Tax savings at 28 percent tax bracket	$2,800
New value of your profit-sharing plan	$60,000

In effect, you pay yourself $10,000 and, by virtue of your tax deduction, come out ahead by $2,800!

The Tax Reform Act of 1986 eliminated this benefit for key employee loans made after December 31, 1986. Effective for loans made after that date, the top loan is limited to $50,000 less the outstanding loan balance of plan loans on the date of the loan *and* less the excess of the highest outstanding loan balance from the plan during the 1-year period ending on the day before the date of the loan over the outstanding loan balance of plan loans on the date of the loan. For example, assume you have a balance of $150,000 in your profit-sharing plan and have never made any loans from the plan. On January 1, 2013, you borrow $35,000. On May 1, 2013, the loan balance is $30,000. On November 1, 2013, the loan balance is $25,000. At that time you would like to borrow an additional amount without having to include it in income. The maximum amount you may borrow on that date is $15,000 ($50,000 − $25,000 − [$35,000 − $25,000]).

Moreover, the former 5-year repayment period has been tightened. Effective for loans made after December 31, 1986, the 5-year period may be extended only in the case of a loan made to purchase the principal residence of the plan participant. The extension of the 5-year period is not permitted in the case of refinancing a principal residence. In addition, the repayment of loans made after December 31, 1986, must be made in level payments. The use of balloon payment arrangements is no longer permitted. Such payments must be made no less frequently than quarterly.

Finally, no interest is deductible for any post-1986 loan to a key employee. This means that even if you use the funds to purchase a principal residence, if you are a key employee, no interest will be deductible, even though all interest would have been fully deductible had you secured normal financing of the home.

A key employee was defined as a plan participant who at any time during the plan year or the preceding 4 plan years was (1) an officer of the company, (2) an employee owning one of the 10 largest interests in the company, (3) a 5 percent owner of the company, or (4) a 1 percent owner of the company earning more than $150,000 per year (IRC § 416)(i)(1)(A).

The Tax Relief Act of 2001 redefined a *key employee* as (1) an officer with compensation in the prior year of more than $130,000,[38] (2) a more than 5 percent owner, or (3) a more than 1 percent owner with prior-year compensation of more than $150,000.

Note also the limitations on the deduction of interest discussed on page 259.

148 Miscellaneous Corporate Advantages

There are a number of other miscellaneous tax saving strategies that owning your own company in a corporate form will allow you. They include the following:

1. The corporation can purchase for you $50,000 of group term life insurance with tax-deductible dollars. Term life insurance in excess of $50,000 is also available at a negligible after-tax cost to you. For example, assume that you are 39 years old and the corporation purchases $100,000 in term life insurance for you. The premium would be 100 percent deductible to the corporation, and you would have to report only $54 per year of additional income. In the 28 percent bracket, this would cost only an additional $15.12.

2. The corporation can accumulate dividend income or other income at the low rate of 15 percent on the first $50,000. Furthermore, the corporation can receive dividend income and exclude from taxation 80 percent[39] of those dividends, reducing its effective tax rate to 3 percent (15% × 20% = 3%).

---

38. $165,000 for 2013.
39. Seventy percent if the corporation does not own at least 20 percent of the dividend-paying corporation. In order to qualify for the dividends-received deduction, the stocks must have been held by the corporation for at least 46 days. The holding period is 91 days for cumulative preferred stock in arrears for more than 366 days. Borrowing to purchase equities by corporate investors will reduce the amount of the dividends-received deduction.

3. IRA plans absolutely prohibit owner-employees from borrowing money from the plan. But all plan participants *may* borrow their money from a corporate retirement plan. The advantages of such a provision have already been detailed.

   Remember, the interest earned on such loans will not be taxed to either the corporation or the plan and may be deductible by you on your personal income tax return. In the process, it will increase the amount of money accumulating tax-free in the plan, as well as your total financial wealth.

4. Prior to the Tax Reform Act of 1984, a current deduction for future college costs could have been allowed. The corporation could have set up an educational benefit plan in which a trust was established to which the corporation contributed funds to provide a given amount per year for each employee's child enrolled in an accredited college or university, without regard for financial need or academic achievement. In the case of *Greensboro Pathology Associates,* Federal Circuit, December 15, 1982, the Court ruled that the contributions to the trust were deductible when made by the corporation and only taxable income to the employees when the money was withdrawn. This can be a significant deferral tax advantage if the children are relatively young. In such a situation, the company can receive its deductions several years before the employees must pick up the income.

   In determining that this was a welfare plan rather than a plan of deferred compensation wherein the corporate deduction would have been deferred until the employee recognized the income, the court looked at the following questions:

   a) Is the plan concerned with the employees' well-being?

   b) Are the benefits based on the earnings of the employees?

   c) Are benefits based on the length of service?

   d) Are benefits available to all employees?

   e) Are benefits really a substitute for salaries?

   f) Does the plan serve its stated purpose, or is it a sham?

   g) Does the employer lose control of the funds contributed?

   h) Can the funds revert to the company or its shareholders?

   i) Is the plan administered by someone independent of the company?

The court said that if items b and c were present, there was a strong presumption that the plan was a form of deferred compensation—no deduction allowed until funds were distributed. It also said that item d, availability to all employees, was essential if the plan was to qualify for current deductions.

The passage of the Tax Reform Act of 1984 appears, however, to effectively overrule the *Greensboro* case as to the immediate deductibility of plan contributions. The Tax Reform Act of 1984 provides that contributions to a funded welfare benefit plan will not be deductible under Section 162 but will now be governed by new Section 419. Section 419 provides that a contribution made to a funded welfare plan will be deductible in the year of contribution only to the extent that it would have been allowable as a deduction if the employer had paid the benefits directly and the employer used the cash-basis method of accounting. In essence, unless the plan is distributing benefits, no immediate deduction is allowable for fund contributions by the employer. Section 419, however, does provide for a carryover of contributions in excess of deductibility to the succeeding taxable year. Moreover, these new rules on plan contribution deductions apply not only to formal welfare benefit plans but to any method of employer contributions having the effect of a plan.

5. A final advantage of the corporate form of business is the elimination of the danger of vicarious liability that exists in a professional partnership. For example, assume that Dr. Smith and Dr. Jones operate as a partnership. Dr. Jones is on a vacation on the day that her partner, Dr. Smith, creates a potential malpractice problem in the operating room. Under the vicarious liability rules that apply to partnerships, Dr. Jones is just as responsible for the malpractice as is Dr. Smith, who is directly involved. In a corporate setting, Dr. Smith and the corporation are liable. Dr. Jones is personally off the hook.

CHAPTER 10

Investment Planning to Save Taxes

"If Patrick Henry thought that taxation without representation was bad, he should see how bad it is with representation."

OLD FARMER'S ALMANAC

"There's nothing more dangerous than the U.S. Congress with an idea."

E. PATRICK MCGUIRE of the Conference Board,
Opening a Conference Examining Tax Incentives

"The alternative minimum tax is a 'perfect example' of a lack of common sense in the tax code. . . ."

NINA OLSON,
National Taxpayer Advocate

The first key to investment planning for 2013 tax purposes is finding out the ever-changing status of the capital gains tax on sales of capital assets. Capital assets include such things as stock, securities, real estate held as an investment, and most properties held for personal purposes. In fact, all property except the following is included under the umbrella of capital assets:

- Stock in trade, inventory, and other property held primarily for sale to customers in the ordinary course of business

- Depreciable property used in a trade or business and real property used in a trade or business

- Accounts and notes receivable acquired in the ordinary course of a trade or business for services rendered or from the sale of stock in trade, inventory, or other property held for sale to customers

- A copyright or a literary, or artistic composition (not musical) held by a person whose personal efforts created it, or held by a taxpayer whose basis is determined by reference to the creator's basis (e.g., by gift)

- A letter or memorandum or similar property held by a person for whom the property was prepared or produced, or held by a taxpayer whose basis is determined by reference to the first person's basis (e.g., by gift)

- Obligations of the federal or a state government or one of its political subdivisions that are issued on a discount basis and payable without interest at a fixed maturity date not exceeding one year from the date of issue

- Free U.S. government publications

- If you go after your investment advisor and get a settlement for recovery or long-term capital losses, that portion of the award is treated as long-term capital gain PLR 200724012.

OLD LAW

Prior to 1987, an individual could deduct from gross income 60 percent of *net long-term capital gain* (the excess of net long-term capital gain over any net short-term capital loss), leaving only 40 percent taxable. Since the maximum regular income tax rate was 50 percent, the deduction meant that net capital gain was taxed at a maximum rate of 20 percent (50 percent × 40 percent).

Capital losses were allowed in full against capital gains. Capital losses were also allowed against up to $3,000 of ordinary income; however, only one-half of the excess of long-term capital loss over net short-term capital gain was allowed for this purpose. Unused capital losses could be carried forward indefinitely.

The Tax Reform Act of 1986 repealed the net long-term capital gain deduction. However, the maximum rate on long-term capital gains of individuals was made 28 percent.

The 1986 law did not change the character of gain as ordinary or capital, or as long- or short-term capital gain. Capital losses are allowed in full against capital gain, as under prior law.

Capital-loss treatment also was changed by the 1986 law. Capital losses continue to be fully offset by capital gains. The overall deduction limit of $3,000 per year (against ordinary income) still applies. Losses over that amount can be carried over to future years. Short-term capital losses continue to be fully deductible against ordinary income, up to this $3,000 limit. Long-term capital losses also continue to be fully deductible against up to $3,000 of ordinary income. Beginning in 1987, both short-term and long-term capital-loss carry-forwards can be used to offset ordinary income on a dollar-for-dollar basis up to a $3,000 limit.

Note that the difference between long-term and short-term capital gains and losses still exists under current law. A gain from the sale or exchange of an asset acquired after December 31, 1987, will not be treated as long-term capital gain unless you held it for more than 1 year. The holding period was more than 6 months for assets acquired after June 22, 1984, and before January 1, 1988. Recognize that the longer holding period still has an impact, beyond the maximum rate, in that it affects charitable contributions of certain property. For example, a deduction normally cannot exceed 50 percent of your adjusted gross income. The equivalent limit for contributions to a private nonoperating foundation is 30 percent. For contributions of long-term capital gain property, however, the limit is 30 percent of the contribution base, or 20 percent if the contribution is made to a private nonoperating foundation.

Capital gain property includes only property that would have produced long-term capital gain if it had been sold at the time of the contribution. With the longer holding period, it would be that much longer before assets acquired after 1987 fall into that definition and within the lower percentage limits.

Moreover, the otherwise allowable deduction for a charitable contribution of property has to be reduced by the amount of gain that would not be long-term capital gain if the contributed property has been sold at the time of the contribution. That covers the amount of hypothetical gain that would have been recaptured in an actual sale (e.g., depreciation). However, it also covers all the hypothetical gain on an asset acquired after 1987 and not held for more than 1 year. Thus, the deduction for contributions of such post-1987 capital gain property would be limited to the property's adjusted basis.

In post-1986 tax years, if the sale of the property would have produced long-term gain, the difference between the allowable deduction for the contributed property and its adjusted basis was a preference item for alternative minimum tax purposes. The rule did not apply, however, to contributions of tangible personal property beginning in 1991 and all property, real, personal, and intangible, after December 31, 1992.

The Tax Relief Act of 1997 changed the above rules. Retroactive to May 7, 1997, the law cut the top capital gains tax rate from 28 percent to 20 percent for investments (excluding collectibles such as art, stamps, or coins which will retain a maximum 28 percent rate) held for at least 18 months (12 months if the investment was sold before July 29, 1997). The top rate dropped further to 18 percent for assets purchased after 2000 and held for 5 years or longer. Gains on real estate, to the extent of Section 1250 depreciation recapture, will be taxed at a maximum 25 percent rate. Capital assets held for more than 12 months but less than 18 months retained the maximum 28 percent rate.

For those in the lower brackets, the rate would fall to as low as 10 percent on investments held more than 18 months. That rate would drop to 8 percent for assets held for 5 years or longer regardless of when the asset was acquired.

The 1998 Reform Act changed the rules again. As of January 1, 1998, the long-term holding period is again 12 months!

The impact of the change? Enormous! The difference between short-term and long-term gains was then the difference between 38.6 percent and as low as 18 percent, which was 20.6 percent. On a $100,000 gain, that was $20,600 in your pocket.

CURRENT LAW

The 2003 Tax Act cut the long-term capital gains rates again. The maximum capital gains rate for long-term sales on or after May 6, 2003 is 15 percent. For those in the 10 or 15 percent bracket, the rate has been slashed to 5 percent! For 2008 and after that rate goes to ZERO!

The American Taxpayer Relief Act of 2012 raised the maximum long-term capital gains rate to 20 percent for those in the 39.6 percent tax bracket. Joint returns with *taxable* income of more than $450,000 ($400,000 for singles) will pay this extra 5 percent. The actual top rate is 23.8 percent. That includes 3.8 percent 2013 surtax on unearned income discussed below.

The rate reduction hurts tax-deferred investments. All payments out of retirement plans (except for Roth IRA plans discussed in Chapter 6) are taxed at ordinary income rates. The advantage of tax deferral disappears when you could have paid a 0–20 percent capital gains tax and end up paying ordinary income tax at the 39.4 percent rate. If you are close to retirement and expect to remain in the higher brackets, tax deferral may even work against you.

3.8 PERCENT MEDICARE SURTAX ON INVESTING INCOME

The Patient Protection and Affordable Care Act imposes a 3.8 percent surtax on investment income starting in 2013. It hits those in the top (39.6 percent) bracket. You will use new Form 8960 to report this tax.

The tax is 3.8 percent of the lessor of

1. Net investment income, or

2. The amount by which your modified adjusted gross income exceeds the $200,000/$250,000 thresholds.

Net investment income includes interest, dividends, royalties, rents, net gains from the disposition of property (capital gains), and nonqualified annuities. Qualified annuities, pensions, IRA distributions, and alimony are specifically exempt from the tax.

The tax also applies to passive income, which is income from a trade or business that is a passive activity under Code Sec. 469. An activity is passive if it involves the conduct of a trade or business in which you do not materially participate. Very generally, material participation exists if you are involved in the operations of the activity on a *regular, continuous*, and *substantial* basis. Accordingly, if you materially participate in the entity's business, the tax on net investment income does not apply to income from the entity. If you do not materially participate, the income is characterized as passive and may be subject to the tax. You must put in 750 hours per year to "materially participate."

How to minimize the impact? See if you can qualify as a "real estate professional" by putting in 750 hours on your rental activity. Any net rental income won't count. Consider a charitable remainder trust (see pages 285–286). The gain on the sale would be exempt and the 3.8 percent tax on that gain would go away. Time your income to fall under the thresholds. Use installment sales, tax-free income, and deferred income to avoid the surtax hit. Note that the tax applies to any gain on the sale of a second home, and any gain *in excess* of the potential $500,000 exclusion on the sale of your principal residence.

Also consider direct IRA donations to a charity (if you qualify) or charitable contributions of appreciated property. Let's keep that adjusted gross income down!

The following tax planning strategies and techniques are suggested to optimize the advantages of favored capital gains rates at the end of the year:

Planning Year-End Securities Transactions

Results to Date	Unrealized Portfolio Gains and Losses	Possible Action to Be Taken Before Year-End
Short-term	Losses and gains	Cover short-term gain by taking losses. Take additional loss to offset ordinary income.
Short-term gain only	No losses	Taxwise, nothing need be done.
Short-term loss	Gains only	Generally no advantage to realizing additional gains, except gains can be realized tax-free to extent of losses.
Long-term gain	Losses and gains	Cover long-term gain by taking losses. Take additional losses to offset ordinary income.
Long-term gain	Gains only	Taxwise, nothing need be done.
Long-term loss	Gains only	Generally nothing further need be done. Long-term loss will offset ordinary income. Remainder will carry forward. Opportunity exists to realize gains at no tax cost to extent of losses.
Long-term loss	Losses only	Nothing need be done.
None	Losses and gains	Generally no advantage to realizing gains except to extent of losses. Consider taking loss to offset ordinary income.

149 Short Sales

In a short sale, you contract to sell stock that you do not own or intend to make available for delivery upon sale. The securities are borrowed for delivery to the buyer. The sale must eventually be covered by the purchase of the securities in the market or by the delivery of securities owned at the time of the short sale. The taxable event occurs when the securities are delivered to the lender (usually your brokerage firm) by the seller to close the short sale.

Whether capital gain or loss on a short sale is long- or short-term will generally be determined by how long the seller held the stock used to close the short sale. However, special rules exist regarding short sales where substantially identical property is held by the short seller at the time of the short sale. These rules prevent the conversion of a short-term gain into a long-term gain or the conversion of a long-term loss into a short-term loss.

The definition of substantially identical is a question of fact. Securities of different corporations are not substantially identical. However, a convertibility feature or an impending reorganization under which such securities will be exchanged for one another could lead to a different conclusion. Bonds of different issuers, or with a difference in maturity of at least 20 percent, or a difference in coupon of at least 30 percent would not be substantially identical.

A short sale could have been used to defer the recognition of a capital gain into the next taxable year. For example, an investor selling "short against the box" will lock in the selling price but can defer recognition of the gain until the position is closed, which can be in the next taxable year. Here you are selling short securities that you already own to lock in gain but defer recognition.

Unfortunately, the Tax Relief Act of 1997 closed this area of tax planning. Generally, for all short sales made after June 8, 1997, such sales are considered "constructive sales" and are taxable in the year made.

The Internal Revenue Service issued a revenue ruling concerning the tax treatment of "short sales." It clarified the timing of gains or losses. Timing is critical when doing year-end tax planning and in determining the holding period of the stock for gain or loss purposes. Two common scenarios were addressed.

In the first, the taxpayer directs his broker to borrow shares in January of year 1. On December 31, the broker is directed to purchase shares (which have increased in value) to close the position. The shares are delivered on January 4 of year 2. The IRS ruled that the sale is not complete until the shares are delivered in year 2. Accordingly, the loss is realized in year 2.

In the second, the facts are the same, but the stock has decreased in value and the short sale results in a gain. The taxpayer is considered as having entered into a constructive sale position and realized a gain in year 1.

150 Broad-Based Index Options and Regulated Futures Contracts (RFCs)

Broad-based index options and RFCs are subject to special rules. Those open at year-end must be marked to market, and unrealized gains and losses are taxed as if the position had been closed at year-end. Under these special rules, 60 percent of the capital gain or loss is treated as long-term and 40 percent is treated as short-term, irrespective of the actual holding period.

151 Wash Sales

The wash sale rule applies only to losses. A wash sale occurs when an investor who sells a security at a loss purchases (or acquires an option to purchase) securities that are substantially identical to those sold within the 61-day period, beginning 30 days before the sale and ending 30 days after the sale.

A current deduction is denied for losses realized under those circumstances. Instead, the disallowed loss is added to the basis of the substantially identical securities acquired. The holding period of the securities sold at a loss is added to the holding period of the newly acquired securities.

A wash sale may be avoided by purchasing an equivalent amount of the same security, holding both lots for 31 days, and then selling the original security at a loss. Alternatively, you could reinvest in securities that are not substantially identical, such as those of another company in the same industry.

Rev. Rul. 2008-5 applies the wash sale limitation even if you have your IRA purchase the identical stock.

152 Premiums on Taxable and Tax-Exempt Bonds

At your option, the premium on a taxable bond may be amortized and deducted each year (with a corresponding reduction in cost basis) over the remaining life of the bond.

Otherwise, upon sale or maturity, the premium may result in a capital loss that would be deductible at that time. For bonds acquired before October 23, 1986, the amortized amount of premium is considered a miscellaneous itemized deduction not subject to the 2 percent floor. For bonds acquired after October 22, 1986, and before 1988, the deduction for amortized bond premium is treated as interest expense, subject to the investment interest expense limitations.

However, effective for bonds acquired after 1987 or, if elected, for obligations acquired after October 22, 1986, amortizable bond premium is treated as an offset to interest income on the bond rather than as a separate interest deduction (and therefore not subject to investment interest expense limitations).

On tax-exempt bonds, the premium must be amortized over the life of the bond or to the earliest call date. The premium cannot be deducted because it is an expense of earning tax-exempt interest. The basis of the tax-exempt bond is reduced by the amount of premium attributable to the period for which the bond is held. If the bond is held to maturity, no capital loss will result from the purchase of a tax-exempt bond at a premium.

153 Original Issue Discount (OID)—Taxable Bonds

OID interest on government bonds issued after July 1, 1982, and on corporate bonds issued after May 28, 1969, accrues and must be reported annually for tax purposes even though it is not payable until sale or maturity of the instrument. For corporate bonds issued before July 2, 1982, OID is computed on a straight-line monthly accrual basis. For corporate and government bonds issued after July 1, 1982, OID is computed on a constant-interest-rate method based on the original issue price and yield-to-maturity.

154 Original Issue Discount (OID)—Tax-Exempt Bonds

Tax-exempt OID is calculated under two different methods, depending on when the bond was issued. OID on a tax-free municipal bond is treated as tax-exempt interest income and is not included in taxable income. However, calculating OID on tax-exempt bonds is necessary for purposes of adjusting basis in order to determine whether there is a capital gain or loss on sale or redemption prior to maturity and for determining whether Social Security benefits are taxable.

For tax-exempt OID securities issued prior to September 4, 1982, or acquired prior to March 2, 1984, OID is calculated on a straight-line basis. For tax-exempt OID securities issued after September 3, 1982, and acquired after March 1, 1984, OID is calculated under the constant-rate method.

155 Market Discount

A market discount occurs when you buy a bond in the secondary market for a price *below* a certain value. For most bonds, that value is par (usually $1,000). In the case of original issue discount (OID) bonds (e.g., zero coupon bonds), the measuring stick is the bond's current "accreted" value. This is the increased value of the bond due to the pro rata accretion of the discount while you hold the bond. If an old bond is bought for less than its accreted value, it becomes a market discount bond. The discount, therefore, is normally the difference between acquisition price and par or accreted value.

In the past, when market discount bonds were sold, called, or matured, the excess of the redemption or sales price over the purchase price was treated as capital gain rather than ordinary income. Market discount bonds *purchased after* April 30, 1993 will now have the difference taxed as ordinary income.

156 Municipal Bond Swaps

Municipal bond swaps are transactions in which municipal bonds in a given portfolio are sold and the proceeds of the sale are then used to purchase other municipal bonds of like quality, coupon, par value, and yield.

Traditionally, this "tax swap" is the favorite method among individual investors to reduce their tax liabilities. Municipal bond market prices characteristically move up or down uniformly. Therefore, in most cases, if your bonds have depreciated in value, all other issues have as well, because interest rates have risen. The result is that by effectuating a swap, you merely establish paper losses for tax purposes. Your capital loss is the difference between your adjusted cost (or book value) and the current selling price of the bonds. The proceeds of a sale can be used to purchase other bonds, which should differ from those sold in coupon, maturity, or issuer. In most cases, tax swapping can be accomplished with a small adjustment (extension) of maturity to overcome market spreads.

Correctly done, a timely tax swap can provide you with the following benefits:

- Equal or greater income from your investments

- Equivalent quality and/or maturity in bond portfolios

- Continued participation in a favored security, or realizing tax losses that reduce your tax

- Meaningful tax savings to offset both capital gains taken in your current year and up to $3,000 of other income, by using capital losses realized through the tax swap

The mechanics of a tax swap are relatively simple. If you want to establish a capital loss for tax purposes, sell a bond for less than you paid for it. If at the same time you want to maintain your portfolio, buy a similar bond. There is no actual loss. At maturity the bond pays its face amount. If you buy one bond at $900 and sell it at $850, and then buy another at $850 and hold it to $1,000 maturity, you still make the $100 difference between your original purchase price and maturity; the intermediate sale and purchase do not matter. If you have a portfolio of bonds, therefore, you should contact your broker at year-end to arrange for an appropriate tax saving swap. If structured correctly, whether you do it with municipal bonds or with regular bonds, you should be a tax winner.

157 Employee Options—Nonqualified

Another investment tax saving strategy involves the handling of employee stock options. The grant of a nonqualified stock option results in no compensation to you as an employee. But exercising your option does result in compensation, measured by the difference between the option price and the fair market value at the time of the exercise.

For example, the *grant* of an option to buy 1,000 shares at $20 per share when the market value is $25 per share results in no income to you. If you *exercise* the option later when the market value is $40, you will recognize compensation income of $20,000 ($40,000 – $20,000). This taxable income plus the cash investment necessary to exercise the option are the major disadvantages of non-qualified stock options. In order to exercise the option in the above example, you must raise $26,000 in cash—$20,000 to buy the stock and as much as $6,000 to pay the tax in the 30 percent bracket.

The Internal Revenue Service has ruled that if full or partial payment for stock acquired upon exercise of a nonqualified stock option is made by transferring identical shares in the employer company, it will not result in any gain to you on the shares used to pay for the stock option.[1] The following example shows how you can take advantage of this ruling. Assume you own 1,000 shares of stock of your employer, acquired for $10 per share. You exercise a nonqualified option to acquire 2,000 shares of identical stock at an option price of $25 per share ($50,000 total). At the time of exercise, the market value of the stock is $50 per share ($100,000 total value).

If your employer agrees, you can pay for the 2,000 new shares by transferring to that employer the 1,000 shares of identical stock you already own. Since the value of the stock surrendered equals the option price, no cash is needed to buy the stock. In this way, you defer recognition of gain on the transfer of the 1,000 old shares, but you enjoy the full appreciated value by converting 1,000 shares of stock into 2,000 shares.

Using this technique, the cash required has been reduced to $15,000, the amount necessary to pay the tax on the $50,000 of compensation in a 30 percent federal and state bracket. Without this technique, you would also need $50,000 more to pay for the stock. Thus, the total cash outlay has been reduced from $65,000 to only $15,000. Of course, a proportionate reduction in the number of shares or the value of the shares would result in a proportionate reduction in the amount of cash that you actually would have to lay out.

158 Incentive Stock Options (Sec. 422A)

The Economic Recovery Tax Act of 1981 provided for a new type of stock option, called an "incentive stock option." No tax consequences result from the grant of an incentive stock option or from the exercise of an incentive stock option by an employee. You, the employee, will be taxed when you sell the stock. Furthermore, you must normally be an employee from the date of granting the option until 3 months before the date of exercise.

---

1. Revenue Ruling 80-244.

In its simplest form, a stock option is the right to buy a company's stock sometime in the future for a fixed priced. An option granted in 2005 to buy stock at $10 a share by 2015 yields a $5-a-share profit if the stock rose to $15 a share by then and the owner exercises the option and sells the stock.

Summary of Incentive Stock Option Features

Typically granted to	Executives; senior management.
Option price	Must be granted at a price that at least equals the stock's market value at the time of the grant.
Taxation	
When granted	None
At exercise	None but the spread between the exercise price and the fair market value may be subject to alternative minimum tax.
After sale of the stock	If you hold your shares for more than one year after exercise, the entire spread between the sale price and your cost basis is characterized as a long-term capital gain and taxed at a maximum of 15%.
	If you hold your shares for less than a year, you "disqualify" your ISO shares, and the difference between the fair market value at the time of exercise and the option price is taxed as ordinary income. The fair market value of the stock at the time of exercise becomes your cost basis, and the difference between the cost basis and the price at which you sell the stock is taxed as a short-term capital gain.
Vesting	May be subject to a graduated or cliff vesting schedule, according to the terms set forth in the option agreement.
Expiration	Typically 10 years following the grant date, as set forth in the option agreement.
Remember	If the gain on the stock granted through an ISO qualifies for special long-term capital gains treatment, the spread between the option price and the stock's fair market value at the time of exercise is a preference item for alternative minimum tax (AMT) purposes. Consult your tax advisor to determine if and how the AMT may affect you.

Summary of Nonqualified Option Features

Typically granted to	All employees.
Option price	May be lower than the value of the stock on the date of the grant, making it instantly "in-the-money."
Taxation	
When granted	None.
At exercise	In the year of the exercise, ordinary income tax is due on the spread between the fair market value of the stock on the date you exercise and the exercise price.
After sale of the stock	In the year of the sale, capital gains tax is due on the difference between your cost basis (the fair market value of the stock on the date you exercise your NSO) and the price at which you sell the stock. If you sell within one year of exercise, the gain will be characterized as short-term.
Vesting	May be subject to a graduated or cliff vesting schedule, according to the terms set forth in the option agreement.
Expiration	Typically 10 years following the grant date, as set forth in the option agreement.
Remember	Your employer must report the income you realize when you exercise your options on your W-2 and withhold income and employment taxes. Usually, you must pay your employer the amount of any withholding along with the exercise cost of your options.

The tax-favored treatment of capital gains adds to the usefulness of incentive stock options for stock-based executive compensation. Moreover, incentive stock options still retain an advantage for an employee over *nonqualified options* (those options that do not qualify under Sec. 422A—for example, an option that is exercisable 11 years after the date it is granted). The recipient of an incentive stock option will continue to avoid regular income tax on the exercise of such an option. However, the *open* spread by which the fair market value of the incentive stock option, at time of option exercise, exceeds the stock's option price is a tax preference under the alternative minimum tax rules.

In contrast, upon *exercise* of a nonqualified option, the excess of the nonqualified option stock's fair market value over the option price is treated as additional compensation and taxed at regular income tax rates. Thus, an employee who exercises a nonqualified option must find the funds to pay tax as well as to pay for the stock.

Example: Assume an executive in the 28 percent tax bracket exercised an *incentive* stock option to acquire stock worth $150 for $100. His total *cost* for the stock ranges from $100 (if he is not subject to the alternative minimum tax) to a maximum of $113 ($100 option price plus 26 percent minimum tax on the $50 spread). In contrast, if the stock was acquired through the exercise of a *nonqualified* option, the cost to the executive to buy the stock would be $114 ($100 option price plus 28 percent tax on the $50 spread).

The employer is not entitled to a deduction for the benefit realized by the executive on an incentive stock option exercise. Since a deduction continues to be available when a nonstatutory option is exercised, nonstatutory options retain the employer's tax advantage over incentive stock options after 1986.

Therefore, incentive stock options continue to provide better tax advantages to employees than nonstatutory options, and since the current corporate tax rates reduce the employer's tax benefits from nonstatutory options, incentive stock options will continue to offer advantages for executive compensation packages.

Under the 1998 Reform Act, when you sell your ISO shares, the entire profit (the spread at exercise plus subsequent appreciation) can qualify for the maximum rate on long-term capital gains. This beneficial deal applies only when you sell the ISO shares more than 2 years after the option grant date (the date you received the option) and more than 12 months after you actually bought the shares by exercising your ISO.

Gains from ISO shares sold more than 2 years after the grant date and more than 12 months—but not more than 18 months—after the exercise date were taxed at a maximum 28% rate in 1997. Now the holding period is back to 12 months.

Example: On January 2, 2012, you received an ISO giving you the right to purchase 100 shares of employer stock for $10 a share. You exercised that right on February 1, 2013, when the market price was $16. Your per-share basis is $10 (exercise price). You sell on February 2, 2014, for $25 a share. The sale date is more than 2 years after the January 2, 2012 grant date and more than 12 months after the February 1, 2013, exercise date. Therefore, your entire $1,500 profit was treated as a long-term capital gain qualifying for the 15 percent rate.

Now what if you meet the above rules but sell your ISO shares at a price that's either below the market value on the exercise date or (even worse) below the exercise price? In this case, your basis in the shares is the exercise price, so when the sale price exceeds that number, you have a gain that qualifies for the maximum rate. If your sale price is below the exercise price, you've got a long-term capital loss.

An interesting twist on the incentive stock option concept is the junior stock plan, which works as follows. The employer corporation issues special "junior" nonvoting common stock, paying dividends. These shares can be exchanged by holders for regular common stock, share for share, at a specified date if the holders meet certain conditions. The junior shares are sold to employee executives at a bargain price—for example, $20 while the regular common is trading at $30. Each executive pays taxes on the original price differential—the $10 price spread. At the end of the term, with the employer common stock trading at, for example, $80, the executives swap the junior stock for the common in a tax-free exchange. On sale of the common stock, the executive has a tax basis of $30—the $20 paid for the junior shares plus the $10 on which he was taxed. Thus he has a gain of $50 per share—$80 less $30—taxed at a maximum percent rate.

This technique adds several breaks not available under normal incentive stock option rules. For example, junior stock lets an executive effectively buy the company's shares at a price far below the market. This allows far easier financing of a purchase of a block of shares.

159 Year-End Stock Sales

The Internal Revenue Service had ruled that gains from stocks sold in a year's last week come under the installment sales law. That allowed you to choose—at leisure—to incur the tax in either the current year or the next. Prior to 1982, a gain on stocks sold through a broker in one year for payment in the next was considered taxable in the payment year; to make it taxable in the year of sale, you had to allow 5 business days for settlement. Under the installment sales law, however, an installment sale is one where any payment is made in a later year. That makes gain taxable in the later year unless you elect not to use the installment method; in that case, the gain is taxable in the sale year. You did not have to make an election to choose the year in which to incur the tax until the due date for your sale-year return, including the automatic 4-month extension. This means that if you expected your income to increase, it may have been advisable for you to recognize the gain earlier, in the lower-bracketed year.

Effective January 1, 1987, taxpayers who sell stock or securities *on an established securities market* are *not* permitted to use the installment method to account for such sales. The trade date is considered the date of tax recognition (see also Rev. Rul. 93-84).

160 Fund Strategies

When a mutual fund sells stock inside the fund, your proportional share of the gain is taxable to you. To minimize this tax, some advisors have recommended either index funds or exchange traded funds (ETF).

Like index funds, ETFs aim to match the performance of a stock market benchmark. But ETFs don't redeem shares or issue new shares depending on the buying and selling of individual investors. Instead, they are traded like regular stock.

That means that the underlying shares of stock never have to be sold in response to a wave of redemptions. Anything that reduces volatility reduces your potential "inside" gain or the investment.

HOLDRS (Holding Company Depository Receipts) aren't technically funds. They are a fixed portfolio of securities which allow an investor to exchange his HOLDRS for the underlying stocks (tax free) and sell the "losing" shares to offset gain elsewhere in his portfolio. They're another arrow in your quiver of tax minimization techniques.

161 Dividends

The 2003 Tax Act changed the rules on the taxation of dividends.

Under prior law, dividends were taxed at a rate as high as 38.6 percent and long-term capital gains were subject to a maximum tax of 20 percent.

The 2003 law reduced those rates substantially. For those in the 15 percent bracket or less (for 2013, singles with taxable incomes of $36,250 or less and couples with taxable income of $72,500 or less), the tax rate on dividends and long-term capital gains had been slashed to only 5 percent. For 2008 and after, the rate changes to ZERO!

Regardless of your income, the maximum rate on dividends has been capped at 15 percent, 20 percent as of 2013, not counting the 3.8 percent surtax.

Great news for the retired and elderly. AARP (American Association of Retired Persons) estimates that 75 percent of dividends paid go to investors over the age of 50.

Be careful, everything called a "dividend" really isn't a "dividend" and won't qualify. A qualifying dividend is a distribution of a corporation's earnings and profits, which has already been taxed to the corporation. Let's look at some examples where there may be some confusion.

1. Mutual funds have, in the past, reported short-term capital gains as "dividends." Both were taxed at ordinary rates rather than at the lower capital gains rates. Now, such distributions must be separated out. That's because short-term capital gains don't qualify for the lower rates.

2. Do you have a margin account with your broker? If so, then you may have a problem. Your broker often lends out securities in such accounts to other investors who sell short using your stock. These borrower investors receive the dividends and they reimburse you for what they receive. You end up with the same dollars but these "payments in lieu of dividends" don't qualify as "dividends" and could be taxable at rates as much as 39.6 percent!

   The rate reduction on dividends is retroactive to January 1, 2003. So, if earlier in the year your broker lent out your securities, and a dividend was paid, that dividend didn't qualify for the lower rate. SURPRISE!

3. Dividends paid by Regulated Investment Companies (RICs) and Real Estate Investment Trusts (REITs) *do* qualify.

4. You just bought a stock and the company declares and pays a dividend. Then you sell the stock. Is your dividend subject to the maximum rate? Maybe!

Here's why: Congress wants you to invest for the long-term. In order to get the lower rate, you needed to have held the stock for 61 days during the 121 day period beginning 60 days before the ex-dividend date. So, if you don't hold the stock a minimum of 61 days, there's no way you're going to qualify for the lower rates. Even if you hold the stock for 61 days, it has to be within that 121 day window to qualify.

Remember, "Simplification" wasn't ever even suggested for the title of this new law!

What to do? (5) Focus on long-term rather than short-term gains. Consider preferred stock and stock that has a high dividend payout, such as utilities. Income investing and focusing on dividends now becomes more attractive.

Companies with lots of free cash become buys. Those are the companies that have the ability to pay more out in tax advantaged dividends. And because they are "buys," they also should generate capital appreciation as more taxpayers seek their tax advantages. This creates a double benefit as both dividends and capital gains are now tax favored.

Municipal bonds and tax shelter investments become less attractive compared with other investments. That's because the tax versus tax free gap has been reduced.

Those in the higher brackets should consider investment leverage. Borrow money at interest rates that are deductible at 35 percent and invest where the return is taxed at only 15 percent.

You can even make out if your yield is *lower* than your cost of money. For example, if you borrow $10,000 at 5 percent your interest is $500. At a 35 percent tax rate, your deduction reduces your net after tax cost to only $325 (65 percent of $500).

If your $10,000 investment only yields 4.5 percent, you have $450 in income. After tax at a maximum 15 percent rate, you have $382.50 left (85 percent of $450). That's $57.50 more in your pocket on an investment that yields less than your cost of money!!!

But there's a trap here. First, you have to itemize your deductions to get the deduction for investment interest. Then, that investment interest deduction is limited to your investment income.

But the law says that dividends that qualify for the 15 percent maximum rate don't qualify as investment income for the investment interest deduction. So, if your only investment income is the dividends, you don't get the deduction for the interest you paid.

In order for this investment leverage to work, you need other investment income (such as interest, rents, etc.) to offset the interest expense. Otherwise, you're borrowing at a higher net marginal cost than your marginal revenue. And you ain't gonna make it up with volume!

6 REASONS WHY DIVIDENDS ARE BETTER THAN CAPITAL GAINS

I'm a financial professional. I've spent a good part of the last three decades practicing tax alchemy—trying to convert ordinary income into capital gains. That's because ordinary income has been taxed at rates as high as 39.6 percent and capital gains as low as zero. That's been a gap of 39.6 percent!

The Tax Relief Act of 2003 blessed dividends with a 15 percent maximum rate (now 20 percent). Even though both are taxed at the same maximum rate, I think dividends are better than capital gains. Here's why:

1. *Keep Your Investment.* You get capital gains when you sell a capital asset. Your capital gain is the excess of what you get over what's technically called your

basis, normally the cost of the asset you sold. You're only taxed on that difference.

If you don't sell the asset, say shares of stock, you don't have any gain. But, if you don't sell the stock, you don't have any additional dollars either. So, to have capital gains, you have to liquidate your position.

That's not true with dividends. You still get to keep your original shares of stock. This is incremental money in addition to your shares of stock. In fact, in many cases, you can use your dividend dollars to buy more shares without a broker's commission on the purchase.

2. *Stock Returns to Predividend Level.* Yes, theoretically the value of the stock should decrease by the dividends paid. But, in the real world, that's not always the case. That allows you to eat a piece of your cake, and keep the whole cake too. Yummy!!

3. *Ask Any Senior Citizen—Regularity Is Good!* Remember, capital gains require you to liquidate your position. It's a one-time cash inflow.

That may not be appropriate in all situations. An investor may be looking for a relatively predictable regular cash flow each year. Baby boomers seeking income-producing investments for retirement cash flow are going to be attracted to dividend-paying securities. Americans over age 65 have equity portfolios with an average yield of 2.6 percent compared to only 0.8 percent for those under 65.

AARP estimates that 75 percent of dividends paid go to investors over the age of 50.

4. *Bunching Is Bad.* Even adjusting for the time value of money, there's a gazango difference between receiving $100,000 in capital gains in a single year, and receiving $10,000 yearly in dividends over 10 years.

While both may be taxed at the same rate, the one-year additional $100,000 could substantially thin your wallet. That's because many deductions and exemptions are reduced and or eliminated as your adjusted gross income (AGI) increases. For example:

- Medical expenses are reduced by 10 percent of AGI.

- Miscellaneous itemized expenses are reduced by 2 percent of AGI.

- Your deduction for student loan interest is eliminated if your modified AGI is $75,000 or more ($155,000 on a joint return).

- Your deduction for IRA contributions is phased out as your modified AGI goes from $59,000 to $69,000 ($95,000 to $115,000 on a joint return).

- Hope and Lifetime Learning credits, the earned income credit, the American Opportunity credit, the first-time home buyers credit, the exclusion of savings bond interest used to pay educational expenses, the adoption assistance exclusion, and even your total itemized deduction are all phased out as your AGI increases.

- As a cherry on the cake, the single-year $100,000 capital gain also increases your exposure to the Alternative Minimum Tax (AMT) by phasing out your AMT exclusion.

5. *Shorter Holding Period.* To qualify for the maximum rate on capital gains, you have to hold the stock for more than one year.

   To qualify for the maximum rate on dividends, your holding period may be as little as 61 days. But, it has to be 61 days during the 121-day period beginning 60 days before the ex-dividend date. That's the date on which, even if you buy the stock and the dividend is paid after your buy, you still don't get the dividend dollars. That's because there wouldn't be enough time after your purchase for the corporation to change its records to show you as the owner

   You must hold the stock during that window, or you don't qualify.

6. *No Broker's Commission.* If you're gonna sell stock, you're gonna pay a commission. That's gonna suck some dollars out of your pocket, even with a low cost on line broker.

   There are no brokers' commissions on dividends. That's more money for you!

162 Tax-Exempt Income

A final word should be said about tax-exempt income. In the investment context, tax-exempt income results primarily from nontaxable interest from municipal securities. The table shown here indicates the equivalent rate of return that fully taxable income, such as rents or taxable interest, would have to yield in order to produce net income equivalent to that produced by various tax-exempt returns at the same tax rates.

Based on federal income tax brackets (also see page 59):

Tax-Exempt/Taxable Yield Equivalents

Tax Bracket	25%	28%	33%	35%
Tax-Exempt Yield	Taxable Yield Equivalents			
1.00%	1.33%	1.39%	1.49%	1.54%
2.00%	2.67%	2.78%	2.99%	3.08%
2.50%	3.33%	3.47%	3.73%	3.85%
3.00%	4.00%	4.17%	4.48%	4.62%
3.50%	4.67%	4.86%	5.22%	5.38%
4.00%	5.33%	5.56%	5.97%	6.15%
4.50%	6.00%	6.25%	6.72%	6.92%
5.00%	6.67%	6.94%	7.46%	7.69%
5.50%	7.33%	7.64%	8.21%	8.46%
6.00%	8.00%	8.33%	8.96%	9.23%
6.50%	8.67%	9.03%	9.70%	10.00%
7.00%	9.33%	9.72%	10.45%	10.77%
7.50%	10.00%	10.42%	11.19%	11.54%
8.00%	10.67%	11.11%	11.94%	12.31%

THE VALUE OF TAX-FREE YIELDS

Munis make the most sense for people whose tax-equivalent yield on a tax-free bond or bond fund would be greater than the yield from a similar taxable alternative. Here are two equations to determine whether the tax-exempt yields are right for you.

For tax-equivalent yields:

$$\frac{\text{Tax-Free Yield}}{(1 - \text{Tax Rate})} = \text{Tax-Equivalent Yield}$$

For combined effective federal/state tax rates (if you're considering buying bonds or funds with bonds issued in your home state):

$$\text{State Rate} \times (1 - \text{Federal} = \text{Effective State Rate})$$

$$\text{Effective State Rate} + \text{Federal Rate} = \text{Combined Effective Federal/State Tax Rate}$$

See www.investinginbonds.com to compute equivalents.

At a 33 percent marginal tax rate, you would need to earn 8.96 percent in taxable interest to have the same after-tax return as 6 percent tax-free.

To find the equivalent taxable income return for a tax-exempt return not given in the table, multiply the tax-exempt return rate by the figure in the 1 percent column next to the applicable tax rate. For example, at a 33 percent tax rate, a taxable investment would have to yield 8.96 percent to produce the same amount of after-tax income that is produced by a tax-exempt investment that yields a 6 percent return (6 percent × 1.49 = 8.96 percent).

To find the tax-free income equivalent to a given taxable income, divide that taxable income by the figure in the 1 percent column next to the given rate. For example, at a 33 percent tax rate, $2,000 in taxable income yields $1,342.28 ($2,000 ÷ 1.49).

Note, in addition, that state taxation of interest income should be taken into consideration in computing total yield. For example, most states do not tax interest on municipal bonds issued within their own state. Thus, a New Jersey tax-free municipal bond held by a New Jersey investor would be exempt both on the federal and on the New Jersey tax return. In many states there is no difference in the state tax treatment of in-state versus out-of-state bonds. The chart below summarizes state bond taxation as of 1993. If appropriate, check the current position of your own state.

States That Tax Their Own and Other States' Bonds

Illinois	Iowa
Oklahoma	Wisconsin

States That Tax Other States' Bonds but Not Their Own

Alabama	Louisiana
Arizona	Maine
Arkansas	Maryland
California	Massachusetts
Colorado	Michigan[§]
Connecticut	Minnesota
Delaware	Mississippi
Georgia[§]	Missouri
Hawaii	Montana
Idaho	Nebraska
Kansas	New Hampshire
Kentucky[§]	New Jersey

New Mexico

New York

North Carolina§

Ohio

Oregon

Pennsylvania

Rhode Island

South Carolina

Tennessee

Vermont

Virginia

West Virginia

States That Do Not Tax Their Own or Other States' Bonds

Alaska[†]

District of Columbia

Florida§

Indiana

Nevada[†]

North Dakota[††]

South Dakota[†]

Texas[†]

Utah

Washington[†]

Wyoming[†]

[†] Alaska, Florida, Nevada, South Dakota, Texas, Washington, and Wyoming do not currently levy an income tax.

[††] North Dakota does not tax its own or other states' bonds when the "piggyback" method is used to compute state income tax liability.

§ These states also subject municipal interest income on out-of-state bonds to state intangibles taxes.

163 Old Prices

You can find stock prices back to 1971 at bigcharts.com if you have the date of purchase.

164 Alternative Minimum Tax for Individuals

Prior to 1987, individuals were subject to an alternative minimum tax (AMT), which was payable, in addition to all other tax liabilities, generally to the extent that it exceeded the individual's regular tax liability. The tax was imposed at a flat rate of 20 percent on alternative minimum taxable income (AMTI) in excess of an exemption amount.

In computing alternative minimum taxable income, adjusted gross income was reduced by AMT itemized deductions (which were a limited subset of the itemized deductions allowable for regular tax purposes).

The AMTI was computed by increasing the adjusted gross income (less allowable AMT itemized deductions) by the items of tax preference, which included the following:

- The dividend exclusion of $100 for a single return and $200 for a joint return

- For all real property and tangible personal property subject to a lease, the excess of accelerated depreciation over straight-line depreciation based upon the property's useful life

- An amount equal to the 60 percent net capital gain deduction for the year, other than gain from the sale of a personal residence

- For certified pollution-control facilities, the excess of 60-month amortization over the depreciation otherwise allowable

- For research and experimentation expenditures that were expensed rather than capitalized, the excess of the deduction claimed over the amount allowable if the expenditure were amortized over a 10-year period

- For mining exploration and development costs (other than intangible drilling costs [IDCs]), the excess of the amount expensed over that allowable if the expenses were amortized over a 10-year period

- For oil and gas IDCs, the amount by which the excess of the amount expensed exceeded the amount allowable if the IDCs were amortized over a 10-year period, and the amount of oil and gas income

- Percentage depletion to the extent in excess of the adjusted basis of the property

- For circulation expenses relating to newspapers, magazines, and other periodicals, the excess of the amount expensed over the amount allowable if amortized ratably over a 3-year period

- For incentive stock options, the excess of the fair market value received through the exercise of the option over the exercise price

For certain preferences, individuals could elect for regular tax purposes to take a deduction ratably over 10 years (3 years in the case of circulation expenses) and thereby avoid an AMT preference.

In general, no refundable credits (such as investment tax credits) were allowed to offset the AMT except the foreign tax credit. Also, for years after 1982 net operating loss deductions were allowed in computing the AMT only to the extent not attributable to tax-preference items.

POST-1986 LAW

The individual alternative minimum tax is retained under the current law, but with significant modifications. The AMT is computed starting with regular taxable income (rather than adjusted gross income, as under prior law), which is determined with certain adjustments. Preference items are then added back to regular taxable income in calculating the AMT. The minimum tax rate was increased by the Revenue Reconciliation Act of 1990 to 21 percent. The exemption amount ($40,000 for married persons filing jointly, $30,000 for singles, and $20,000 for married persons filing separately) was reduced by 25 percent of the amount by which AMTI exceeds $150,000. For married taxpayers filing separately the phase-out will begin at $75,000 and for single taxpayers at $112,500. More important, the AMT became a separate tax computation with its own accelerated cost recovery system, basis, gain or loss computations, etc.

However, to remove an incentive for separate filing by married individuals,

	Exemption	Phase-out Begins At	Phase-out Ends At
Married filing jointly and surviving spouse	$40,000	$150,000	$310,000
Single and unmarried head of household	$30,000	$112,500	$232,500
Married filing separately	$20,000	$ 75,000	$155,000

Congress provided that the maximum exemption phase-out for married individuals filing separately will be the same as for married taxpayers filing jointly. It thus provides that the alternative minimum taxable income (AMTI) of married individuals filing separately is increased by the lesser of (1) 25 percent of AMTI over $155,000 or (2) $20,000. This provision is effective for taxable years ending after November 10, 1988.

Moreover, Congress retroactively provided that personal exemptions are not allowed for AMT purposes. Thus, taxpayers who were subjected to the AMT in 1987 and who did not add back the personal exemption owe additional taxes. The above rules were changed again by the Omnibus Reconciliation Act of 1993, which established a two-tiered graduated rate schedule. A 26 percent rate now applies to the first $175,000 of AMT income in excess of the exemption amount, and a 28 percent rate applies to AMT income more than $175,000 in excess of the exemption amount. For married individuals filing separate returns, the 28 percent rate applies to AMT income more than $87,500 above the exemption.

The exemption amount was increased to $45,000 for joint returns, $33,750 for single taxpayers, and to $22,500 for married individuals filing separate returns, estates, and trusts.

Preference Items and Adjustments

The current law retains most of the prior law preferences, although it modifies the computation of certain items. The items of preference adjustment include the following:

- Accelerated depreciation on real property placed in service after 1986 will be considered a preference item to the extent that it exceeds depreciation computed on a 40-year straight-line basis. For personal property the preference item will be the excess of accelerated depreciation over the depreciation computed using the 150 percent declining-balance method (switching to straight line in the year necessary to maximize the deduction). However, the preference does not apply to property that is expensed under Sec. 179.

- Depreciation with respect to property placed in service prior to 1987 is treated as a preference only to the extent that it constituted a preference under prior law. Also, for property placed in service after 1986 with respect to which the alternative depreciation system is used, no AMT preferences will arise.

  Under the revised AMT, the alternative depreciation system is substituted for the accelerated cost recovery system (ACRS). This system permits *netting*. If the AMT depreciation exceeds the ACRS with respect to real or personal property for that year, the amount of the preference is reduced. Since the AMT uses the alternative depreciation system, separate depreciation basis adjustments must be made for AMT purposes. Therefore, the amount of gain on disposition may differ for AMT and regular tax purposes.

- As under prior law, the rapid amortization for pollution-control facilities, the excess of allowable depletion over the adjusted basis of the property (determined without regard to the depletion deduction), mining exploration and development costs, circulation expenditures, research and development costs, the amount by which the fair market value of a share of stock at the time of exercise of an incentive stock option exceeds the option price, and intangible drilling costs (except that the net income offset is reduced from 100 percent to 65 percent) are all still tax preference items.

The 1986 law also added the following new preference items and adjustments:

- Tax-exempt interest on nongovernmental purpose bonds issued after August 7, 1986. Exceptions are provided for bonds issued on behalf of certain tax-exempt organizations and certain bonds issued before September 1, 1986. However, no exceptions are provided for industrial development bonds.

- For any long-term contract entered into by the taxpayer after March 1, 1986, use of the completed contract is not permitted for AMT purposes. Instead, the taxpayer is required to use the percentage-of-completion method for AMT purposes.

- For dispositions after March 1, 1986, the use of the installment-sale method is not permitted for AMT purposes by dealers and others subject to proportionate disallowance of the installment method (sales of trade or business or rental property when the purchase price exceeds $150,000).

- Charitable contributions of appreciated property. Prior to 1993, a tax preference existed to the extent of the unrealized appreciation of contributed capital gain property. Therefore, for minimum tax purposes, the charitable-contribution deduction was limited to the property's adjusted basis. In calculating the amount of the preference, unrealized gains on appreciated property were offset by unrealized losses. The amount of preference was determined by disregarding any amount that was carried forward to another taxable year for regular tax purposes. This preference was eliminated by the Omnibus Budget Reconciliation Act of 1993.

- Passive activity losses that are allowed under the passive loss phase-in rules must be added back to taxable income in computing the AMT with the following revisions: (1) the amount of losses that otherwise would be added back for the current taxable year is reduced by the amount of the taxpayer's insolvency; (2) in calculating passive losses, minimum tax measurements of items of income and deduction will be used rather than regular tax measurements; and (3) the amount added back is reduced by other items of tax preference to prevent double counting.

Because of these calculations the amount of suspended passive losses relating to a passive activity may differ for AMT and regular tax purposes. However, it appears that after the five-year phase-in of the regular tax passive loss rules, differences should be minimal.

- Passive farm losses from a tax-shelter farming activity are treated like passive activity losses with the revisions discussed immediately above (for passive activity losses) and with the following special provisions: (1) each farm is treated as a separate activity—no netting between farming activities is allowed; (2) the preference applies to personal service corporations; and (3) loss from a disposition of a tax-shelter farm activity shall be allowed for minimum tax purposes and not treated as a loss from a tax-shelter farm activity.

- The standard deduction must be added back to taxable income when computing the AMT.

- Non-AMT itemized deductions used in computing taxable income must be added back in computing the AMT.

- The $100 ($200 joint filing) exclusion for dividends and the net capital gain deduction have both been deleted as items of tax preference because they are no longer applicable for regular tax purposes.

AMT Itemized Deductions

In general, the AMT itemized deductions are the same as under prior law and include the following:

- Theft, casualty, and wagering losses

- Charitable contributions

- Medical expenses, except the floor is 10 percent of adjusted gross income instead of 7.5 percent, as used for regular tax purposes

- Qualified interest expenses (which include interest paid or incurred on debt to acquire, construct, or substantially rehabilitate the taxpayer's principal or qualified dwelling and other investment interest to the extent it does not exceed the taxpayer's qualified net investment income for the taxable year)

- The deduction for estate taxes for recipients of income in respect of decedents

The definition of investment interest is the same as under the current law for regular tax purposes. No AMT deduction is allowed for consumer interest. Disallowed investment interest deductions may be carried forward. Interest paid on a refinanced loan is treated as qualified residence interest if it qualified under the original loan and the amount of the loan was not increased. Also refunds of state and local taxes are not included in alternative minimum taxable income.

Carryover of Tax Credits

As under prior law, nonrefundable credits are not allowed against minimum tax liability. Refundable credits that do not benefit the taxpayer because of the minimum tax can be carried back or forward to other taxable years. The recomputed foreign income tax credit is allowed against AMT.

Minimum Tax Credit

Under prior law minimum tax incurred by a taxpayer in one year had no effect on regular tax liability in other years.

The current law creates a minimum tax credit for prior-year minimum tax liability that may offset regular tax in later years. The AMT tax credit is equal to the excess of the AMT tax liability attributable to *deferral preferences* over the regular tax liability for the year. Deferral preferences are essentially all tax preferences except those relating to percentage depletion, tax-exempt interest, the appreciated-property charitable deduction, and regular tax itemized deductions that are not allowed for AMT purposes. The AMT credit can be carried forward (but not back) indefinitely.

Example: Ms. Fortunate has a regular tax liability of $35,000 after taking into account $15,000 of passive losses attributable to accelerated depreciation deductions on leased equipment that were deductible under the phase-in of the passive loss limitation. Her AMT is $39,000. She must pay tax of $39,000 but has a minimum tax credit to the extent that her AMT was attributable to the accelerated depreciation deferral preferences. The minimum tax credit is $3,150 ($39,000 AMT − $35,850 adjusted net minimum tax).

If Ms. Fortunate has a regular tax liability of $28,000 and an AMT of $26,000 in the next year, $2,000 of the minimum tax credit may be applied in that year. The remaining $1,150 of credit carries forward to the following year and, if necessary, later years.

Net Operating Losses (NOLs)

For AMT purposes a separate computation of NOLs and NOL carryovers will be required. In general, the AMT NOL, which cannot offset more than 90 percent of AMT income, is computed in the same manner as the regular tax NOL, except for two special rules. The items of tax preference arising during the taxable year are added back to taxable income, and only AMT itemized deductions are taken into account.

Example: In year 1 a taxpayer has $10,000 of income and $35,000 of losses, of which $10,000 are preference items. The AMT NOL for year 1 is $10,000.

Regular Tax Elections

Under the new law taxpayers may still elect for regular tax purposes to deduct ratably over 10 years (3 years for circulation expenditures) certain expenditures (IDCs and mining exploration and development expenditures) that are otherwise currently deductible and thus avoid treatment of the items as minimum tax preferences.

CREDITS

Starting in 1998, nonrefundable personal credits (the dependent care credit, the credit for the elderly and disabled, the adoption credit, the child tax credit, the credit for interest on certain mortgages, residential energy efficient property credits, nonbusiness energy property credits, personal use portion of the alternative motor vehicle credit, and the Hope Scholarship and Lifetime Learning credits) are allowed to offset your regular tax in full. These credits can now also reduce your alternative minimum tax.

IMPACT OF THE TAX RELIEF ACTS OF 2001, 2003, AND AFTER

The 2001 law increased the individual alternative minimum tax exemption amount by $2,000 for single taxpayers and by $4,000 for married taxpayers filing joint returns for 2001 through 2004, but only through 2004. No big deal! With the reduction of the marginal rates, more people will be hit by the AMT. Many taxpayers making between $72,000 and $627,000—especially those with large families, big medical bills, or homes in higher-tax states like New York, New Jersey, Connecticut, Massachusetts, Illinois, and California—will see perhaps two-thirds of their Bush income tax cuts taken away by the alternative minimum tax.

About 1.5 million Americans were hit by the AMT in 2001, a number that was then projected to reach 20 million by 2010. In fact, about 23 million taxpayers will be hit by the AMT in 2007.

The 2001 law also allowed the child credit and the adoption credit to be claimed against both the regular tax and the alternative minimum tax on a permanent basis. In addition, the refundable credits will no longer be reduced by a taxpayer's AMT.

In 2003, Congress again voted to reduce, but not eliminate, the AMT. As amended in 2004, for 2003, 2004, and 2005, the AMT exempt increases to $58,000 for joint returns and $40,250 for single taxpayers—up from $49,000 and $35,750.

AMT victims who get hit because of incentive stock options may recoup some or all of their AMT payments through an "AMT Credit." This credit can reduce your regular tax bill to what it would be under the AMT in years when your regular tax bill is higher.

Beginning in 2007 and for each year through 2012, a taxpayer with unre-covered AMT credits more than 3 years old can claim a refundable credit equal to either $5,000 of his old credit or 20% of his old credit, whichever is greater. A taxpayer with old AMT credits of $1 million would get $200,000 back. If he otherwise owed $50,000 in 2007 taxes, the credit would wipe those out, and the IRS would cut him a $150,000 check. In 2008 he'd have $800,000 in old, unused credit left and get another 20 percent—in this case, $160,000—back.

This break phases out for couples with adjusted gross incomes above $239,950 (over $159,950 for singles).

Congress tinkered once more in 2006 and 2007, raising the exemption level to $62,550 for joint returns and $42,500 for single filers in 2006 and to $66,250/$44,350 for 2007 only. For 2008 Congress raised the exception to the $46,200/$69,950. It also increased the 20 percent rate to 50 percent. This is a BIG change! Use Form 8801 to claim your credits.

The following credits are now allowed against the AMT:

1. Child tax credit (up to $1,000 per child)

2. Hope Scholarship education tax credit (up to $1,800) and Lifetime Learning education tax credit (up to $2,000)

3. Child and dependent care tax credit

4. Adoption tax credit

5. Retirement saver's tax credit

6. Tax credit for certain energy-saving equipment installed in your residence

7. Tax credit for elderly and disabled individuals

8. Mortgage tax credit

9. First-time D.C. home buyer tax credit

Another provision in the 2008 law lets you walk away from any unpaid AMT bills that were outstanding on October 3, 2008, if they were caused by your exercising incentive stock options before 2008. You can also walk away from any related interest and penalty charges assessed by the IRS. If you already paid some interest and penalty charges, you can recover them over two years under the new and improved refundable AMT credit rules

Congress increased the exemption amounts yearly, for 2009 and 2010. For 2011, the exemption for singles was $48,450, joint returns get $74,450, and those married and filing separately are limited to $37,225. The table below summarizes 2012 and 2013 changes:

Maximum AMT exemption amount	2012	2013
Married filing jointly or surviving spouse	$ 78,750	$ 80,800
Single or head of household	$ 50,600	$ 51,900
Married filing separately	$ 39,375	$ 40,400

AMT income exemption phaseout threshold	2012	2013
Married filing jointly or surviving spouse	$150,000	$153,900
Single or head of household	$112,500	$115,400
Married filing separately	$ 75,000	$ 76,950

AMT tax rate (26% rate applies to AMTI at or below amount; 28% applies to AMTI above amount)	2012	2013
All taxpayers except married filing separately	$175,000	$179,500
Married filing separately	$ 87,500	$ 89,750

PLANNING CONSIDERATIONS

In general, middle- and high-income individuals will have to pay even more attention to the alternative minimum tax. There are many changes. The AMT rate has been raised from 20 to 24 to as high as 28 percent, and the exemption amounts are phased out as AMT income increases. The passive loss rules apply for AMT purposes, except that the preference is reduced by the amount, if any, of the taxpayer's insolvency. In addition, passive losses are reduced to the extent attributable to tax preference, since those preferences are added in elsewhere.

Tax planning for the AMT will involve many of the techniques applicable under prior law. In years when the AMT is inevitable, a taxpayer's objective should be to *accelerate* income and *defer* deductions. A taxpayer's marginal tax rate while subject to the AMT is as high as 28 percent for all additional income realized until the AMT is used up. The taxpayer's tax rate jumps to the marginal rate for regular tax purposes as soon as the AMT is used. If a taxpayer is subject to the alternative minimum tax, non-AMT itemized deductions provide no tax benefit. Additional alternative minimum tax itemized deductions provide a tax deduction rate only equal to the AMT rate. Additional tax preferences, like non-AMT itemized deductions, provide no benefit when the taxpayer is subject to the AMT.

Methods taxpayers may wish to consider for accelerating income when subject to the AMT include:

- Take prepayments of salary and bonuses.

- Declare and pay corporate dividends from closely held corporations. This may also have a potentially positive effect on the corporation if it has a problem with the accumulated earnings tax.

- Consider redeeming Series EE U.S. savings bonds, or elect to report all the accrued interest on the bonds in the current year.

- Redeem certificates of deposit.

- Make early sales of U.S. T-bills.

- Make early sales of investment certificates.

- Recognize gains on portfolio securities.

- Elect out of the installment method for any installment sales (under Sec. 453(d)).

- Consider converting tax-free municipal investments into taxable investments.

- Sell stocks acquired by incentive stock options (ISOs) within a year after the ISOs are exercised. Under Sec. 422(a)(1) this is a disqualifying transaction that makes the gains taxable as ordinary income (even if the transaction takes place in a taxable year subsequent to the year the ISOs were exercised). In addition, this transaction eliminates the tax preference if the transaction takes place in the same taxable year as the exercise of the options. By so doing, you can possibly zero out the AMT (with no additional tax paid because the regular tax is increased while the AMT is reduced). You can immediately repurchase the stocks and effectively step up the basis in the stock and avoid the tax that would otherwise be realized sometime in the future.

- Withdraw funds from IRAs in some circumstances if subsequent withdrawals are anticipated at tax rates greater than 36–38 percent (26–28 percent AMT plus 10 percent penalty).

Taxpayers may also benefit by deferring deductions, especially non-AMT itemized deductions.

Taxpayers subject to the AMT should also try to capitalize otherwise deductible expenses. For example, they should not expense any part of the cost of a depreciable business asset. They should consider electing 10-year write-offs on any portion of currently deductible expenses that constitute tax preferences (which also eliminates the preference). The items to which this applies are research and experimentation expenditures, mining exploration and development costs, and intangible drilling costs. In addition, magazine circulation expenses may be capitalized and written off over a 3-year period. Taxpayers with research and experimentation expenditures for their own business should consider electing to amortize those expenditures over 60 months or longer. This will both shift deductions out of the current year and reduce AMTI. Taxpayers acquiring new depreciable property should consider electing depreciation under the alternative recovery system, which will defer deductions and reduce AMTI.

You may be hit with the alternative minimum tax even if you don't have one single dollar of tax preferences. For example, assume that you had an adjusted gross income of $150,000. In 1987 you paid $25,000 in state and local income taxes (including your April 1987 payment for your 1986 taxes) and $22,000 in property taxes on raw land you own as an investment. You paid $6,000 in interest on home equity loans you took out to pay college

Alternative Minimum Tax Preference Items Under Prior Law and Current Law

Tax Preferences	Individual		Description of Tax Preference
	Prior Law	Current Law	
Long-term contracts	No	Yes	Income must be calculated on the percentage-of-completion method for new contracts
Certain tax-exempt interest	No	Yes	Interest income on certain private-activity tax-exempt bonds issued after August 7, 1986
Appreciated property charitable deduction	No	Yes prior to 1993	Unrealized appreciation on long-term capital gain property
Passive activity losses	N/A	Yes	Net losses from passive activities
Accelerated depreciation on new property	N/A	Yes	Depreciation for AMT is calculated using the Alternative Depreciation System except that the preference for personal property is based on the 150 percent DB method
Premodified ACRS and pre-ACRS depreciable leased personal property	Yes	Yes	Excess of accelerated over straight-line deductions
Mining exploration and development costs	Yes	Yes	Excess over amount allowable if amortized ratably over 10 years
Circulation expenditures	Yes	Yes	Excess over amount allowable if amortized ratably over 3 years

Alternative Minimum Tax Preference Items Under
Prior Law and Current Law *(continued)*

| | Individual | | |
Tax Preferences	Prior Law	Current Law	Description of Tax Preference
Research and experimental costs	Yes	Yes	Excess over amount allowable if amortized ratably over 10 years
Depletion	Yes	Yes	Excess of depletion over adjusted basis in property
Incentive stock options	Yes	Yes	Excess of fair market value over option price at date of exercise (basis of stock adjustment for AMT)
Dividend exclusion from income	Yes	N/A	Amount of dividends excluded
Capital gains	Yes	N/A	Under present law full LTCG deduction is no longer a preference
Intangible drilling costs	Yes	Yes	Excess over amount allowable if amortized ratably over 120 months over 65% of net income from oil and gas
Pollution-control facilities	Yes	Yes	Excess of amortization over allowable depreciation
Individual itemized deductions	Yes	Yes	Certain itemized deductions not allowed
Alternative tax net operating loss	Yes	Yes	NOLs with certain adjustments
Installment method accounting	No	Yes	Installment method generally not allowed for AMT purposes

expenses for your children and had $8,000 in other itemized deductions, including $2,000 for investment expenses in excess of 2 percent of your adjusted gross income. Assume further that you had absolutely no tax preferences.

Because your itemized deductions for purposes of the alternative minimum tax are not the same as your itemized deductions for your regular tax, your alternative minimum tax was $260 higher than your regular tax. Therefore, you paid an extra $260 in taxes for 1987. As the regular tax rates fell in 1988, however, the chance of being hit with the alternative minimum tax increased, and your potential alternative minimum tax bill got bigger. For example, on these same facts, you would have owed an alternative minimum tax of more than $2,400 in 1988! What this means is that you should watch your itemized deductions as they may, by themselves, subject you to the AMT. Because personal exemptions are not allowed in computing the AMT, you can be hit by it just because you have "too many" children!

165 U.S. Savings Bond Exclusion (Sec. 135)

To help finance qualified higher educational expenses, Congress has created an incentive to purchase U.S. savings bonds. Under prior law, interest that accrues on certain U.S. savings bonds need not be reported until the bond is redeemed, unless you elect to report the increase in redemption value annually.

For years after 1989, you can potentially exclude all or a portion of the interest that accrues on the bond. In order to qualify for the exclusion, you must:

a) purchase a qualified U.S. savings bond;

b) pay qualified higher educational expenses in the year of redemption;

c) not be married and filing separately; *and*

d) not have income over a certain amount.

If your modified adjusted gross income exceeds $60,000 (indexed) in case of a joint return and $40,000 (indexed)[2,3] in all other cases, there is a phase-out of the benefit. For joint filers, the entire benefit was phased out once modified

---

2. $112,050 and $142,050 for 2013.
3. $74,700 and $89,700 for 2013.

adjusted gross income exceeds $95,250. For all other taxpayers, the phase-out was completed at $58,500. There is a proportional phase-out of the benefit for income within the phase-out range. For example, if modified adjusted gross income on a joint return was $80,000, then approximately two-thirds of the total benefits would be phased out.

A qualified U.S. savings bond is any bond issued after 1989 at a discount to an individual who has attained age 24. Bonds acquired in the names of minor children will not qualify for the exclusion. Moreover, the exclusion is not available to the individual who is the owner of a Series EE bond (Series E bonds issued in June 1950 stopped paying interest in June 2010) that was purchased by another individual other than a spouse. The bond should therefore not be purchased by a parent and put in the name of a child or another dependent, even if such a child or dependent is 24 years of age at the time of the purchase. Nor should bonds be bought by a relative, such as a grandparent, and gifted to a parent or child if the exclusion is desired. If you bought "wrong," you can file a reissue form PDF 4000 with the Bureau of Public Debt, Parkersburg, WV 26106-1328 and plead your case. You can get bonds commission-free from Treasury Direct at 1-800-722-2678 or at www.savingsbonds.gov. See also www.investinginbonds.com, www.treasurydirect.gov, and www.treasuryhunt.gov for the current value of your bond.

If you paid for your bonds with a credit card, you could have picked up some frequent flyer mileage or cash back. Not anymore. Uncle Sam will no longer accept credit cards for savings bond purchases.

The Impact of Inflation on Yields

Rate of Inflation	Interest Rate Needed to Break Even in Following Tax Brackets:		
	15%	28%	35%
1%	1.18%	1.39%	1.54%
2%	2.35	2.78	3.08
3%	3.53	4.17	4.62
4%	4.71	5.56	6.15
5%	5.88	6.94	7.69
6%	7.06	8.33	9.23
7%	8.24	9.72	10.77
8%	9.41	11.11	12.31

(continues)

The Impact of Inflation on Yields *(continued)*

Rate of Inflation	Interest Rate Needed to Break Even in Following Tax Brackets:		
	15%	28%	35%
9%	10.59	12.50	13.85
10%	11.76	13.89	15.38
11%	12.94	15.28	16.92
12%	14.12	16.67	18.46
13%	15.29	18.06	20.00
14%	16.47	19.44	21.54
15%	17.65	20.83	23.08

In the past you could buy up to $15,000 worth of EE bonds (purchase price, *not* face value) each year, per owner. That's a $30,000 face value. Starting January 1, 2008, that dropped to $20,000 in face value—$10,000 in paper bonds bought at a bank and another $10,000 in an online Treasury Direct account. Note that there is no direct tracing of the redeemed bond proceeds to the payment of tuition. However, the qualified higher education expense must equal or exceed the redeemed proceeds for the full exclusion to apply. See www.treasurydirect.gov.

The Bureau of the Public Debt announced that as of January 1, 2012, *paper* savings bonds will no longer be sold at financial institutions. But savings bonds, introduced in 1935, are not going away. Series EE and I electronic savings bonds will remain available for purchase in TreasuryDirect accounts. You can also buy up to $5,000 in bonds with your refund by using Form 8888. Persons currently holding paper savings bonds can continue to redeem them at financial institutions. Bonds that have not matured, but were lost, stolen, or destroyed, can be reissued in paper or electronic form.

Now may be a good time to review your bond holdings to ensure they are still earning interest. All Series E bonds have reached final maturity and no longer earn interest. Series EE bonds, first issued in 1980, reach "final maturity" 30 years from the date of issue, meaning bonds purchased in 1980 and 1981 have almost all "expired."

The Treasury has a variety of online tools for evaluating U.S. savings bonds at http://savingsbonds.gov/indiv/tools/tools.htm.

166 Madoff Losses

In Revenue Ruling 2009–9, the IRS ruled that investors who suffered Ponzi scheme losses could claim the losses as investment thefts. The ruling provides that:

- You can claim investment theft losses, which are not subject to the usual tax code limits on personal theft losses that are 10 percent of adjusted gross income plus $100;

- Investment theft losses are deductible in the year in which the fraud is discovered, unless you have a reasonable prospect of recovering the investment assets in a later year;

- You can claim theft loss deductions for the net amount you invested and for the fictitious income that the promoter credited to your investment accounts and that you reported as income before discovering the fraudulent scheme; and

- Investment theft losses that create a net operating loss can be carried back and forward, as prescribed by law, to generate a refund of taxes paid in other taxable years.

- Revenue Procedure 2009–20 allows investors to deduct 95 percent of their "Madoff" investment minus any recoveries from insurance, the Securities Investor Protection Corp., or lawsuits.

CHAPTER 11

Last-Minute Tax Planning

"Potius sero quam numquam." (Better late than never.)

TITUS LIVIUS, 59 B.C.–A.D. 17

"You cannot help the poor by destroying the rich. You cannot lift the wage earner by pulling down the wage payer."

ABRAHAM LINCOLN

While effective tax planning is basically a year-round proposition, certain techniques are still available even if you buy this book during the last week in December. This chapter will explain those last-minute tax strategies that can help you reduce your overall tax burden.

167 Defer Taxes

Certain kinds of investments allow you to postpone paying taxes from the year in which the income is earned to a later year. At that point, you may be in a lower tax bracket, or you will at least have had the use and yield on the tax savings in the interim.

Series EE savings bonds offer this feature, as do deferred annuity contracts. As of April 30, 1997, they pay interest at a rate equal to 90 percent of the 5-year Treasury note rate. Interest on savings bonds is normally not taxed until the bonds are cashed. As with an annuity, you postpone taxes on the interest until the income is actually paid out. Series EE savings bonds sold after May 1, 1995 no longer have a *minimum* guaranteed yield of 4 percent (7.5 percent if purchased between November 1, 1982, and October 31, 1986) even if the bonds are held for at least 5 years. When alternative investments are yielding amounts equal to or less than the Treasury rate, the investment attractiveness of Series EE bonds is magnified even more. The limit on Series EE bonds that can be purchased in the name of one person as of January 1, 2008, is $20,000 face amount (or $10,000 issue price) in any one calendar year.

The interest on Series EE bonds does not accrue daily, but only on two days every year. The interest accrual dates are:

1. The anniversary of the bond's issue date

2. The midpoint between anniversary dates

The interest rate earned changed each May 1 and November 1. Thus, an owner who is considering an exchange or a cashing out of a bond would have done well to do so on or shortly after an interest accrual date.

Series EE Savings Bonds issued on and after May 1, 2005, will earn fixed rates of interest. The fixed rate will apply for the 30-year life of each bond, which includes a 10-year extended maturity period, unless a different rate or rate structure is announced and applied at the start of the extension period.

Rates for new issues will still be adjusted each May 1 and November 1. The Treasury guarantees that a bond's value will double after 20 years, its original maturity. Series EE bonds issued prior to May 1, 2005, will continue to be governed by the terms in effect when they were issued.

A current listing of redemption values for all savings bonds—Form PD 3600—is available free from the Bureau of the Public Debt. Values are shown for 6 months, so an investor who follows a bond across the six columns can figure out the two months of the year in which the value rises.

Meanwhile, two useful one-page listings are available by writing the public affairs office of the U.S. Savings Bonds Division, Department of the Treasury, Washington, D.C. 20226 (202-377-7715). One sheet shows the current guaranteed minimum interest rates for Series EE and E bonds and Savings Notes bought *prior* to May 1, 1995. Holders get the higher of those minimum rates, which range from 4 percent to 8.5 percent, or variable rates that are based on market conditions.

The second sheet, dubbed "Table of Interest Accrual Dates," shows the two months a year in which Series E and EE bonds rise in value.

Savings bond holders can also call their nearest Federal Reserve Bank for savings bond information. Another option is an information service offered by Mr. Pederson, the former Federal Bank of Chicago official. His Savings Bond Informer Inc. in Detroit (313-843-1910) sells computer printouts listing key dates, interest rates, and redemption values for an investor's bonds. The cost for between 26 and 75 bonds: $22.50. Alternatively, if you are on-line, you can get the value of a Series EE bond from www.execpc.com\nmmrsoft or from the Bureau of Public Debt at www.publicdebt.treas.gov/sav/sav.htm.

Taxes are also deferred on income that builds up in Individual Retirement Account, corporate pension, and Keogh plans. Furthermore, as discussed earlier, if you qualify for these plans, you also can deduct from your current income the amount you contribute to your plan each year.

One old tax planning strategy for taxpayers close to retirement was to buy Series EE savings bonds (which stop paying interest after 30 years) today and, when they retire, exchange those bonds for HH bonds, which are available only through such an exchange. This would have allowed you to defer tax on the interest the EE bonds earned before the exchange until you redeem the HH bonds. In the meantime, you will get a check for interest on the HH bonds every 6 months. That interest rate is fixed, however, and is taxable. There is no limit to the dollar amount of HH bonds that may be acquired through the exchange process. It is important though that you compare the after-tax cash flows from the bonds and alternative investments. It may be better to pay the tax and reinvest the net proceeds at a higher yield than the HH bonds for a higher net after- tax cash return.

Unfortunately, as of August 31, 2004, the Treasury no longer issues Series HH bonds. If you buy certain 6-month bank certificates of deposit (CDs) now, you can defer paying part of the tax on the interest until you file your return in the subsequent year. The CD must be the type on which the interest is neither credited to your account nor made available to you without substantial penalty before the maturity date. In addition, an investment in U.S. Treasury bills provides a similar tax benefit. This is because interest on them is not recognized until the bills are redeemed. Note, furthermore, that Treasury bill (also called T-bill) interest is not subject to state or local tax; however, taxable short-term CDs may yield a higher rate of interest.

You also can defer your taxes on fees and compensation. For example, a binding agreement to delay until January the grant of a bonus otherwise payable in December defers taxation on that bonus until the subsequent year. But this agreement must be entered into before the bonus is "constructively received." Deferring fees or service compensation is easy. All you need to do is delay billing until late December. You will not receive payment—therefore, no taxable income either—until the next year.

A final alternative strategy for delaying your tax payments is to delay your receipt of income with an installment sale. You should consider postponing part or all of the profit from a big gain to next year or later. Not only could an installment sale keep this year's tax cost down (you pay tax only on the share of the profit you receive during the year), but it could also allow you to avoid a big bulge in income that could force you into a higher bracket.

168 Accelerate Expenses

You may have a great deal of flexibility in the timing of a number of your expenses. For example, any of your medical expenses not reimbursed are deductible in the year they are paid. An effective tax reducing strategy, therefore, would be to concentrate as many expenses as possible in a year when it appears that the percent medical expense deduction limit will be exceeded. If, at year-end, it is apparent that no deduction will be available, defer payment of medical bills until the following year when the situation may be otherwise. In a year when the deduction is probable, make sure that all medical needs are satisfied and paid for in that year.

For example, eye examinations, new glasses, and dental work may be accelerated by a month or two to permit a deduction; the remaining balance on your children's orthodontic work may be paid immediately in full. Note, however, that a deduction *is* available in the current year for medical needs charged to your credit card before the year-end, even if payment is not actually made until the subsequent year.

Tax payments can also be accelerated. The principal categories here are real estate taxes, personal property taxes, and state and local income taxes. Amounts withheld for income taxes are deductible in the year withheld. If your state or city income tax exceeds your withholding, estimated tax payments are probably required. The last installments of these taxes should be paid before the end of the current year even though they may not be due until the next year. This will accelerate your deduction into the current year. Moreover, prepayments of real estate taxes are deductible in the year paid—if they are not merely advance deposits paid before the tax becomes a liability. Each of these accelerated payments represents a current deduction from your income tax liability. But watch out for the Alternative Minimum Tax (AMT).

Charitable contributions are also susceptible to acceleration. Sometimes it is feasible to make a large contribution in a high-income year in order to satisfy a charitable commitment extending over a number of years. Do not make a contribution on January 1 that you could have made on December 31. Remember, however, that contributions are deductible subject to certain limitations based upon your adjusted gross income. Contributions that exceed these limitations should *not* be made.

Moreover, contributions of appreciated capital gain property, such as securities held over 12 months, will allow you a tax deduction equal to their full market value. Therefore, a gift of appreciated securities has the advantage of a market value deduction without the payment of a tax. Conversely, you should never make charitable donations of securities that have declined in value below cost, since you would forfeit the tax loss. In those situations, it is better to sell the securities, take the tax loss, and contribute the cash proceeds.

169 Accelerate Special Deductions

The election to expense allowance is available for depreciable personal property used in your business and acquired after 1981. This is a deduction against your business income. This accelerated expense is *in addition* to your regular depreciation (on the reduced basis) and is as much as $500,000 for 2013. And, again, it does not matter how late in the year the property is put into service.

170 Dependents and Personal Exemptions

A dependent is someone related to you or a "qualifying relative" who need not be related if he or she is a member of your household for whom you provide more than half the support. You may claim a 2013 dependency exemption of $3,900 for each person who meets *all* exemption tests, with certain exceptions. For example, the gross income test does not apply if your child is a full-time student under age 24 or a nonstudent under age 19 or any age if permanently and totally disabled and if the income of such person is for services performed at a sheltered workshop. Also, special support rules apply to children of divorced parents and to those dependents being claimed under multiple support agreements. Furthermore, whether the dependent is born or dies during the year is irrelevant. If you pass the tests for the portion of the year during which the dependent was alive, you will receive the full $3,900 exemption.

The following tests must be met with respect to the person in question in order to qualify you for a dependency exemption:

1. *Support.* You must furnish over one-half of the total support of the person in the calendar year in which your tax year begins. Support includes amounts spent for food, shelter, clothing, medical and dental care, education, church contributions, child care expenses, wedding apparel and receptions, capital items (a car or a TV set), and the like. It does *not* include the value of services performed for a dependent, or scholarships received by a dependent student. Also, support is what is spent, not what is available. This means that even if your child earns $10,000 and banks $5,000 of it, as long as you contribute $5,001 in support, you have contributed more than one-half.

   Several tax-saving strategies present themselves in this area. A year-end budgeting of support expenditures can produce substantial tax benefits and thus reduce the out-of-pocket cost of supporting a dependent. For example, assume that you are unmarried and live with your mother. By December 1, your mother has spent $4,000 of her nontaxable Social Security payments for her own support and you have contributed $2,000 for her support. During the rest of the year, you provide for all of your mother's support at a cost of $800 and give her a $1,400 television set for her exclusive use in her room. Consequently, you provide more than 50 percent of your mother's total support (that is, $4,200 of a total of $8,200) for this year. Thus, you can claim the $3,900 dependency exemption for your mother.

When two or more persons furnish the support of a dependent, one of the contributing group is entitled to take the deduction for the dependent if:

a) no one person contributes more than half of the dependent's support;

b) each member of the group, were it not for the support test, would be entitled to claim the individual as a dependent;

c) the one claiming the deduction gives more than 10 percent of the dependent's support; *and*

d) every other person who gives more than 10 percent of the dependent's support files a written relinquishment of the claim to the exemption in the same calendar year.

2. *Relationship of Dependent.* The person supported must be your relative or a "qualifying relative," which includes a nonrelated member of your household. Your relatives include your children, grandchildren, great-grandchildren, and step-children; foster children; brothers, sisters, half-brothers, half-sisters, step-brothers, and step-sisters; parents, grandparents, great-grandparents, step-mother, and step-father; nephews, nieces, uncles, and aunts; and sons-in-law, daughters-in-law, fathers-in-law, mothers-in-law, brothers-in-law, and sisters-in-law. A legally adopted child or one placed with you for adoption is considered a child by blood. Furthermore, on a joint return, this condition is satisfied if the qualifying relationship exists between the person claimed as a dependent and either you *or* your spouse.

If a person is not one of your relatives, that person may qualify as a dependent if he or she is a member of your household. A member of your household is one who, during your entire tax year, or during part of it, uses your home as the principal dwelling. By tax magic, a member of your household may now qualify as your "Qualifying Relative."

But it must not be an illegal relationship. In states with statutes forbidding sexual relations between unmarried people (and there have been a bunch, including Florida, Michigan, Virginia, North Carolina, Idaho, Mississippi, North Dakota, and West Virginia), the IRS could disallow exemptions for live-ins. Residents of those states who claim such exemptions were exposed to a fight with the IRS. But, in light of recent Supreme Court decisions, I doubt the IRS would bring the issue to the courts. The IRS clearly won't balk at exemptions claimed by residents of states without such statutes—if, again, they meet the basic requirements.

Dependent Exemption Summary

A.   To claim a dependency *exemption* for a qualifying child, all of the qualifying child dependency tests must be met:
   - Dependent taxpayer test
   - Joint return test
   - Citizenship test
   - Relationship test
   - Age test
   - Residency test
   - Support test

B.   To claim a dependency *exemption* for a qualifying relative, the person must meet the following tests:
   - Dependent taxpayer test
   - Joint return test
   - Citizenship test
   - Not a qualifying child test
   - Member of household or relationship test
   - Gross income test
   - Support test

---

3.   *Dependent's Gross Income.* Your dependent's gross income for the calendar year in which your tax year begins must be less than $3,900. This does not apply to children who are students under age 24 or nonstudents under age 19 and certain income earned by those permanently and totally disabled. A child is a student if, during each of any 5-months of the calendar year in which your tax year begins, he or she (a) is in full-time attendance at an educational institution or (b) is taking a full-time course of institutional or farm training.

   In figuring your dependent's gross income, you exclude any type of exempt income. This includes Social Security benefits, tax-exempt interest, etc. Remember, though, that if your dependent has used these tax-exempt benefits for support, generally the benefits *will be* considered in determining whether the support test has been met.

4.   *Joint Return.* Generally, you will lose an exemption for a married dependent who files a joint return. This rule does not apply, however, if neither the dependent nor his or her spouse is required to file a return but they file a joint return solely to claim a refund of tax withheld. Here you should

examine the advantage to your dependent in terms of tax savings from filing a joint return as opposed to the tax cost to you from losing the exemption. In many cases it would pay for you to compensate your dependent for a tax loss and claim the deduction for the exemption. For example, assume that you are in the 28 percent bracket and that the tax loss to your married dependent from filing a separate as opposed to a joint return is $200. The $3,900 personal exemption would save you $1,092 in taxes in your tax bracket. In this case, it would pay for you to give $200 to your dependent for this "loss." After taxes, you would still be ahead $892.

5. *Citizenship or Residency.* A dependent, to qualify you for an exemption, must be a U.S. citizen or a resident of the United States, Canada, or Mexico at some time during the calendar year in which your tax year begins.

The above rules and tests are used to determine whether your dependent qualifies you for the $3,900 exemption deduction. If you fail the gross income test—that is, your dependent has a gross income of $3,900 or more—but you pass the other four tests, you may have what I call a *nondeductible* dependent. This still affords several significant advantages. For example, a nondeductible dependent could qualify an unmarried taxpayer to use the more advantageous head of household rate schedule; likewise, a married but separated taxpayer with a nondeductible dependent child could also use the more advantageous single taxpayer or head of household rate schedule. Moreover, any payments made by you for a nondeductible dependent's medical expenses can qualify as a medical expense deduction on your return. These rules were modified in 2005 (see below).

For example, assume that your 60-year-old mother and father, who have no taxable income, reside in a nursing home, primarily to obtain medical care. Therefore, the entire cost of their maintenance (including meals and lodging) at the home qualifies as a medical expense. You pay your parents' nursing home bills, totaling $12,400 yearly, and thereby provide over half of their support. Furthermore, assume that you are single, that you have an adjusted gross income of $80,000, and that, after all deductions except those relating to your parents, you are in the 28 percent bracket.

You can now claim a medical expense deduction of $4,400 ($12,400 − 10% of $80,000) and (if they pass the gross income test) a dependency deduction of $3,900 each for your mother and father. In the 28 percent bracket, this will save you $3,416 in taxes [$4,400 + (2 × $3,900)] × .28. Moreover, you can probably reduce your taxes even further because you are now entitled to compute your tax as head of household instead of single taxpayer.

Note, however, that an individual who is eligible to be claimed as a dependent by another is not eligible for his or her own personal exemption. For that reason it becomes very important to examine the potential tax consequences to your parents. The loss of the dependency exemption may cause them to pay taxes in excess of your own tax savings. In all situations, therefore, a comparative analysis should be made to maximize the tax savings to all parties.

The above rules were too simple. So Congress went to work confusing this issue for 2005 and future years. Under the new rules a "qualifying child" does not have to pass the gross income test to be a "dependent" but a "qualified relative" does.

Your potential "dependent" must be either a "qualifying child" or a "qualified relative"—which includes a nonrelated member of your household.

For a qualify relative you need to provide more than half his/her support. But for a qualifying child, the rule is that the child can not provide more than half his/her own support.

171 Phase-out of Exemptions

As part of the 1990 Tax Reform Act, Congress mandated a phase-out of personal exemptions for high income taxpayers. When adjusted gross income (AGI) exceeded the following thresholds, the 1990 law began to reclaim the tax savings from personal exemptions:

- $100,000 for singles (indexed) ($166,800–$289,300 for 2009)

- $150,000 for joint returns (indexed) ($250,200–$372,700 for 2009)

- $75,000 for marrieds filing separately (indexed) ($125,100–$186,350 for 2009)

- $161,150 for head of household ($208,500–$331,000 for 2009)

Every time AGI exceeded the threshold by another $2,500 ($1,250 for marrieds filing separately), 2 percent was cut off the dollar amount of personal exemptions. *Example:* If your AGI exceeded the threshold by $25,000, you lost 20 percent of your personal exemptions ($25,000 ÷ $2,500 =10; 10 × 2% = 20%). At $122,500 ($61,250 for marrieds filing separately) above the threshold, all claimed exemptions were wiped out.

For 2009, even after the phase-out, your minimum exemption amount was $2,433.

This translated into a marginal-rate increase of about one-half of 1 percent for each exemption claimed. Thus, parents of two children with sufficient taxable income might really be paying almost 37 percent. Add the effect of the itemized deduction cap and that marginal rate nears 38 percent.

There was no phase-out of exemptions for 2010, 2011, or 2012. But it is back for 2013 as per below:

Personal Exemption Amount

Amount	2012	2013
Personal exemption amount	$3,800	$ 3,900

Married filing jointly	2012	2013
Phase-out threshold amount	N/A	$300,000
Completed phase-out amount after	N/A	$422,501

Head of household	2012	2013
Phase-out threshold amount	N/A	$275,000
Completed phase-out amount after	N/A	$397,501

Unmarried	2012	2013
Phase-out threshold amount	N/A	$250,000
Completed phase-out amount after	N/A	$372,501

Married filing separately	2012	2013
Phase-out threshold amount	N/A	$150,000
Completed phase-out amount after	N/A	$211,251

The loss of personal exemptions adds as much as 1.05 percent per exemption to our true tax rate. You lose 2 percent for each $2,500 or part above the adjusted gross income threshold amounts.

172 Timing Strategies

We have already discussed timing strategies in terms of accelerating expenses and deferring income. Remember, you can take deductions on items paid for by check in the current year, even if you mail the check on New Year's Eve, as long as there is no impediment to cashing the check in the ordinary course of business in early January. If you mail a check covering a large deductible item in late December, use certified mail so that you will receive a date-stamped receipt as proof that you actually mailed the payment in the earlier year.

Furthermore, wherever possible you should charge deductible items on credit cards. Deductible items charged in the current year on nonspecific store credit cards can be deducted in that year, even if you do not actually pay (or receive) the credit card bill until next year. Credit card charges also provide excellent proof as to the amount and nature of expenses—especially travel and entertainment expenses. (In addition, credit card charges have been known to get lost. Lost credit card charges do not reduce your taxes but do provide you with free goods and services.)

173 Retirement Plans

If you participate in a qualified retirement plan of your employer, you receive a number of tax advantages—especially if you are your own employer. The employer is entitled to deduct payments to the plan immediately. As an employee, you do not have to recognize current income from the contributions; rather, you will be taxed only when you receive distributions from the plan. Since distributions are normally made after you retire and have less taxable income, these distributions may be taxed at lower rates. Moreover, the retirement plan itself is exempt from tax. This means that your earnings will accumulate tax-deferred at a faster rate.

If you are self-employed, you have the option of two basic forms of noncorporate qualified retirement plans, discussed in the next two sections.

174 Individual Retirement Plans (IRAs)

Even if you are covered by an employer retirement plan, and if you do not exceed the appropriate income limits, you may establish an IRA for your own retirement. You are eligible for an IRA deduction even if you have a Keogh, but cannot take both in the same year. The maximum allowable deduction is the lesser of $5,500 ($6,500 if age 50 or older). In order to generate a deduction, the contribution must be made (and the plan established) by the due date (*not including extensions*) for filing your return. According to the IRS national office, you should make the contribution prior to filing the return—i.e., you cannot take the deduction and file on March 1 and make the contribution on April 15.

For married persons, the maximum deduction is computed separately for each individual who has compensation. An eligible individual with a nonemployed spouse may make a deductible contribution to a special joint IRA account in an amount up to $11,000 ($5,500 each) or $5,500 each in his or her own account.

Furthermore, in a 1983 Private Letter Ruling 832-9049 the IRS has held that a separate payment to an IRA for custodian fees does not constitute an excess contribution and such a payment is deductible as an itemized expense under Section 212. Moreover, according to IRS Letter Ruling 843-2109, the amount that you can contribute to an IRA is not diminished by the *separate payment* of brokerage commissions or other fees. Accordingly, the payment of brokerage commissions and other fees, such as administrative and service fees that are separately billed and paid, will not be considered additional contributions to your IRA.

175 H.R. 10 or Keogh Plans

In general, the maximum annual deduction for self-employed retirement plans is the lesser of 20 percent of earned income, less your deduction for half your self-employed payroll tax, before the deduction, or $51,000. (This equates to 25 percent of net earned income after the deduction.) Under certain circumstances, a defined benefit type of self-employed retirement plan may allow a contribution in excess of the usual limits.

Individuals who have part-time self-employment income, such as directors and consultants, are allowed to establish such a plan. Thus, even if you are covered by your employer's qualified retirement plan, you might also establish a Keogh plan with any outside fees or other income that you receive. If your self-employment income is from a business that has employees, they must also be included under the plan.

With a Keogh plan you may deduct contributions made *after* the end of the taxable year, if paid by the due date for filing your return including extensions. The plan must be established before the end of the tax year.

There are substantial tax advantages to either of these plans. You obtain an immediate tax deduction for the contribution; earnings accumulate on the contributions free of current taxes; and when distributed, the plan benefits may be taxed at a lower rate.

A number of considerations are involved in deciding whether to establish a retirement plan and selecting between IRAs and Keogh plans. For example, the amount that may be contributed under a Keogh plan is greater than the amount allowable under an IRA. Alternatively, using an IRA rather than a Keogh plan will allow you to restrict the retirement plan to cover only yourself, which can mean a substantial tax savings if you have a lot of employees. All of these factors must be considered and discussed with your tax advisor.

176 Marital Status

Whether you are single or married can have a substantial impact on your tax bill. Speeding or delaying the ceremony can yield you an enormous one-time tax savings.

In general, marriage will cut taxes only if one spouse works or earns almost all of the income. Alternatively, if both spouses work and earn relatively good salaries, marriage will substantially boost your taxes. This is because holy wedlock will push your combined income into a higher tax bracket.

If you are planning an end of the year/New Year's day wedding, it would be well worth your while to compute your taxes both singly and jointly. You may find that the savings from deferring (or accelerating) your wedding date could be enough to pay for your honeymoon vacation.

In conclusion, recognize that the focus of this chapter has been to reduce your current year's income tax. Due to inflation, any tax liability deferred to a later year will be paid with cheaper dollars. Moreover, a deferral of income to a later year is the equivalent of an interest-free loan because it enables you to use the funds that you would otherwise have to pay toward your tax liability. Be aware, however, that this might not always be the correct planning strategy. If you expect your income to go up substantially in later years, you do not want to bunch more income into those years, because the graduated rates could bring about a greater total aggregate tax liability over the years involved. Furthermore, you should *always* take into consideration the political climate for tax changes. If tax rates are expected to go down in the future, then income deferral and expense acceleration is the right strategy. Alternatively, if rates go in the other direction, you will want to recognize your income now and defer your expenses until later.

177 The Goldinger Deferral

An interesting tax deferral technique was developed by Jay Goldinger in Beverly Hills. He has suggested the acquisition of a one- or two-month bank certificate of deposit by putting up 1.5 percent of the purchase price and borrowing the rest from your broker. The deal is close to a wash. Assume the certificates would pay about 9.25 percent, and the loan would cost 9 percent, including the broker's markup. But by paying the interest on or before December 31, you could deduct the expense from your current year's income. If the certificate of deposit is from a sound bank, your risk is low.

To swing such a deal on a one-month $1 million certificate of deposit, the smallest negotiable denomination, you would need $24,000—a $15,000 down payment and about $9,000 for interest on the loan. In January of the next year, when the certificate matures, you would repay the loan and collect the income on the certificate of deposit. That income would be taxable in the new year, but you would have a $9,000 deduction allowable in the earlier year.

Be aware of the limits on personal and investment interest deductions here. You should have sufficient other investment income to cover the investment interest expense.

Also be aware that the courts have disallowed "straddle" transactions where the primary motivation was to generate tax benefits and not realize profits (*Ewing v. Com*, 91 T.C. 396, 1988). Be careful you document your motive here.

CHAPTER 12

The Economic Growth and Tax Relief Reconciliation Act of 2001

"Our current tax system is an 'abomination.'"

U.S. Treasury Secretary PAUL O'NEILL
in a May 17, 2001, interview with the *Financial Times*.

"Enough is enough folks."

President GEORGE W. BUSH, April 16, 2001

When President Bush signed the Tax Relief Act of 2001, he made changes to 441 sections of the Internal Revenue Code and put into action the biggest tax reductions in two decades, and the first income tax rate cuts since 1986. These changes will be phased in over a 10-year period, and then, as of 2011, they all disappear! As of January 1, 2011, all of the changes are repealed and we go back to prior law.

Since 1986, there have been about 7,000 changes to the federal tax code. In the past 5 years alone, there have been 1,916 changes. We're now faced with a decade of annually changing provisions, all of which "sunset" after December 31, 2010.

It's a recipe for disaster, unless you know the rules. Remember, the changes are spread over a 10-year period. If you move too soon, you may not qualify for the benefits you expect. Don't move without retaining lots of flexibility. Don't forget the hidden time bomb that causes all the changes to expire in 2011. You don't want to be locked in a situation that explodes if covered by the old, rather than new, rules.

This chapter will cover those changes that affect your income tax. You'll be taken through each relevant change, and shown those tax planning opportunities and strategies that are created.

178 Marginal Rate Reductions

A Individual Income Tax Rate Structure

1. NEW 10 PERCENT RATE BRACKET

The 2001 law creates a new 10 percent regular income tax bracket for a part of your taxable income that was taxed at 15 percent, effective for taxable years beginning after December 31, 2000. This 10 percent bracket applies to the first $6,000 of taxable income for single individuals ($7,000 for 2008 and thereafter), $10,000 of taxable income for heads of households, and $12,000 for joint returns ($14,000 for 2008 and thereafter).

The change is retroactive to January 1, 2001, but will come in the form of a check, rather than a bracket change. Personally, I always prefer the check alternative . . . Next year the difference will be reflected directly in a bracket change.

The difference between the new 10 percent and old 15 percent bracket is 5 percent. That's the check you'll be getting as a refund.

For singles, 5 percent of $6,000 creates a refund check of $300. Heads of household will get 5 percent of $10,000, or $500, and joint filers will get 5 percent of $12,000, or $600.

Ex-Treasury Secretary Paul O'Neill revealed in a June 7 statement that the first rebate checks will be mailed in the week of July 23. All taxpayers who timely filed their 2000 tax returns would receive their checks by September 30.

According to the IRS, the rebate checks were mailed on a schedule based on the last two digits of your Social Security number. Those ending with 00 through 09 will go out the first week, those ending with 10 through 19 the second week, and so on.

Because perception trumps the cost of postage, the IRS sent you a letter mid-July confirming the amount of refund you'll get, and when your check will be sent.

"We want to make this process as simple as possible for all taxpayers. These letters should give people all the important details they need," according to IRS Commissioner Charles O. Rossotti. "All you need do is open your mailbox. We'll take care of everything else."

Some people didn't get a check. Those not eligible for the rebate under the law include taxpayers who could have been claimed as a dependent on another person's return, nonresident aliens, and those whose nonrefundable credits exceeded their tax liability. These people were notified by the IRS, with a letter of explanation.

However, according to the Bush Administration, the Treasury Department decided to allow rebates to both nonresident aliens and dependents who file their own returns.

Phase-in of Marginal Income Tax Rate Reductions

Calendar Year	Portion of 15% Rate Reduced to:	28% Rate Reduced to:	31% Rate Reduced to:	36% Rate Reduced to:	39.6% Rate Reduced to:
2001	10	27.5	30.5	35.5	39.1
2002 thru 2003	10	27	30	35	38.6
2004 thru 2005	10	26	29	34	37.6
2006 and later	10	25	28	33	35

According to the IRS, if you didn't have any income tax liability for 2000 but have one for 2001, you'll be able to claim the tax credit on your 2001 return . . . to the extent you're eligible.

If your rebate received is less than the credit amount computed on your 2001 return, you'll be able to claim the rest of the credit when you file your 2001 return. For example, if your taxable income as a single filer in 2000 was only $5,000, you'll only get a check for 5 percent of the $5,000, or $250. But, if you have taxable income of $6,000 or more in 2001, you pick up the $50 difference as a credit against your 2001 tax return.

Amazing, but true according to the IRS. . . . if the opposite is true, and you receive a larger rebate than you should (your 2000 income was higher than your 2001 income, within the targeted bracketed amounts), you can keep the difference! I guess the IRS used up its postage allowance on the letters and it wouldn't be worth their time and cost to bill you for the difference.

But, for some people, there's some rain with the sunshine. Eight states allow their taxpayers to take a deduction on their *state* income tax return for federal income taxes paid. They include Missouri, Iowa, Oklahoma, Louisiana, Oregon, Alabama, North Dakota, and Montana.

If you deducted federal taxes that were refunded to you, then you overdeducted. Normally, to compensate for this overdeduction, the refund, to the extent you received a tax benefit from it, would be included as taxable income on your *state* return for the next year.

While to me, this makes complete sense, it has created a public relations nightmare for the politicians in those states. At least two states, Iowa and Oregon, have proposals to exempt this "special refund" from state taxation.

According to the U.S. Treasury Department, an estimated 91.6 million rebate checks will be issued totaling $39 billion. Enjoy your refunds . . . but remember . . . it always *really* was *your* money.

B Phase-out of Restrictions on Personal Exemptions

You can claim a personal exemption for yourself and each of your dependents. However, the deduction for personal exemptions is phased out if your adjusted gross income exceeds certain dollar thresholds. The thresholds for 2001 were $132,950 for singles, $199,450 for marrieds filing jointly, $166,200 for heads of households, and $99,725 for marrieds filing separately.

Under the phase-out, your total deduction for personal exemption was reduced by 2 percent for each $2,500 of income ($1,250 for marrieds filing separately) in excess of the threshold. So, for example, if your adjusted gross income exceeds the appropriate threshold by $50,000 in 2001, personal exemptions are reduced by 40 percent (or $1,160) each.

For 2001, the point at which your personal exemptions are completely phased out was $255,450 for singles, $321,950 for marrieds filing jointly, $288,700 for heads of households, and $160,975 for married filing separately.

The 2001 law phases out the rest rictions on personal exemptions. Under the conference agreement, the otherwise applicable personal exemption phase-out is reduced by one-third in taxable years beginning in 2006 and 2007, and is reduced by two-thirds in taxable years beginning in 2008 and 2009. The provision is fully effective for taxable years beginning after December 31, 2009.

C Phase-out of Itemized Deductions

If you itemize your deductions, you face a deduction limitation similar to that for personal exemptions. The total amount of otherwise deductible expenses (other than medical expenses, investment interest, and casualty, theft, or wagering losses) is reduced by 3 percent of your adjusted gross income in excess of a threshold amount. In 2001, the threshold is $66,475 for marrieds filing separately and $132,950 for everybody else. So, for example, if your adjusted gross income exceeds the threshold by $100,000, then your itemized deductions are reduced by $3,000. However, there is a ceiling on the reduction of itemized deductions: The otherwise allowable itemized deductions may not be reduced by more than 80 percent.

The 2001 law eliminates the overall limitation on itemized deductions for all taxpayers. The otherwise applicable overall limitation on itemized deductions is reduced by one-third in taxable years beginning in 2006 and 2007, and by two-thirds in taxable years beginning in 2008 and 2009. The overall limitation is eliminated for taxable years beginning after December 31, 2009.

The bottom line . . . rates will go down, therefore, your best strategies are to defer income (which will be taxed at a lower rate) and to accelerate expenses (which will give you a lower benefit in the future years).

Individual Income Tax Rates

Provision	Present Law	2001	2002	2003	2004	2005	2006	2007	2008	2009	2010
Create 10% bracket	NA	10% applied to first $6,000 of taxable income for singles and $12,000 for married couples filing jointly							Raise bracket thresholds to $7,000 and $14,000	Index thresholds for inflation	
Marginal rate reductions	39.6%		38.6%	38.6%	37.6%	37.6%			35%		
	36%		35%	35%	34%	34%			33%		
	31%		30%	30%	29%	29%			28%		
	28%		27%	27%	26%	26%			25%		
	15%						15%				
Repeal "pease" (limitation on itemized deductions)							Limitation reduced by ⅓	Limitation reduced by ⅓	Limitation reduced by ⅔		Repeal
Repeal personal exemption phase-out (PEP)							Phase-out reduced by ⅓	Phase-out reduced by ⅓	Phase-out reduced by ⅔		Repeal

Individual Income Tax Rates Summary:

- Provides benefit of a new 10 percent rate for first $6,000 rate for singles, $10,000 for single parents and $12,000 for married couples in 2001 through a lump-sum refund of up to $300 for single taxpayers, up to $500 for single parents, and up to $600 for married taxpayers.
- Lowers the top tax rate from 39.6 percent to 35 percent and lowers other tax rates to create a new rate structure of: 10 percent, 15 percent, 25 percent, 28 percent, 33 percent, and 35 percent.
- Repeals personal exemption phase-out (PEP) and limit on itemized deductions (Pease) over 5 years, beginning in 2006.

179 Tax Benefits Relating to Children

A Increase and Expand the Child Tax Credit

The new law increases the child tax credit for children under age 17 to $1,000, phased in over 10 years, effective for taxable years beginning after December 31, 2000. The following table shows the increase of the child tax credit.

Increase of the Child Tax Credit

Calendar Year	Credit Amount per Child
2001–2004	$ 600
2005–2008	$ 700
2009	$ 800
2010 and later	$1,000

The new law makes the child credit refundable to the extent of 10 percent of your earned income in excess of $10,000 for calendar years 2001 through 2004. The percentage is increased to 15 percent for calendar years 2005 and thereafter. The $10,000 amount is indexed for inflation beginning in 2002. Families with three or more children are allowed a refundable credit for the amount by which your Social Security taxes exceed your earned income credit (the present-law rule), if that amount is greater than the refundable credit based on your earned income in excess of $10,000. The new law provides that the refundable portion of the child credit does not constitute income and shall not be treated as resources for purposes of determining eligibility or the amount or nature of benefits or assistance under any federal program or any state or local program financed with federal funds.

The new law provides that the refundable child tax credit will no longer be reduced by the amount of the alternative minimum tax. In addition, the new law allows the child tax credit to the extent of the full amount of your regular income tax and alternative minimum tax.

The provision generally is effective for taxable years beginning after December 31, 2000. The provision relating to allowing the child tax credit against alternative minimum tax is effective for taxable years beginning after December 31, 2001.

B Extension and Expansion of Adoption Tax Benefits

The new law permanently extends the adoption credit for children other than special needs children. The maximum credit is increased to $10,000 per eligible child, including special needs children. A $10,000 credit is provided in the year a special needs adoption is finalized, whether you have qualified adoption expenses or not. The beginning point of the income phase-out range is increased to $150,000 of modified adjusted gross income. Finally, the adoption credit is allowed against the alternative minimum tax permanently.

The new law permanently extends the exclusion from income for employer-provided adoption assistance. The maximum exclusion is increased to $10,000 per eligible child, including special needs children. In the case of a special needs adoption, the exclusion is provided, whether you have qualified adoption expenses or not. The beginning point of the income phase-out range is increased to $150,000 of modified adjusted gross income. The new law generally is effective for taxable years beginning after December 31, 2001. The provisions that extend the tax credit and exclusion from income for special needs adoptions, whether you have qualified adoption expenses, are effective for taxable years beginning after December 31, 2002.

C Child Care Credit

As of January 1, 2003, the maximum child or dependent care credit you can get increases from 30 percent to 35 percent, with a maximum single-child expense basis of $3,000, up from $2,400 in 2001. This credit doubles if you have two or more qualifying children/dependents.

180 Marriage Penalty Relief Provisions

A Standard Deduction Marriage Penalty Relief

The new law increases the basic standard deduction for a married couple filing a joint return to twice the basic standard deduction for an unmarried individual filing a single return. This increase is phased in over 5 years beginning in 2005 and would be fully phased in for 2009 and thereafter. The following table shows the standard deduction for married couples filing a joint return as a percentage of the standard deduction for single individuals during the phase-in period.

Phase-in of Increase of Standard Deduction for Married Couples Filing Joint Returns

Calendar Year	Standard Deduction for Joint Returns as Percentage of Standard Deduction for Single Returns
2005	174%
2006	184%
2007	187%
2008	190%
2009 and later	200%

B Expansion of the 15 Percent Rate Bracket for Married Couples Filing Joint Returns

The new law increases the size of the 15 percent regular income tax rate bracket for a married couple filing a joint return to twice the size of the corresponding rate bracket for an unmarried individual filing a single return. The increase is phased in over 4 years, beginning in 2005. The following table shows the increase in the size of the 15 percent bracket during the phase-in period.

Increase in Size of 15 Percent Rate Bracket for Married Couples Filing a Joint Return

Taxable Year	End Point of 15 Percent Rate Bracket for Married Couple Filing Joint Return as Percentage of End Point of 15 Percent Rate Bracket for Unmarried Individuals
2005*	180%
2006	187%
2007	193%
2008 and thereafter	200%

* Amended in 2004 to 200 percent through 2010.

Marriage Penalty Relief

Provision	Present Law	2001	2002	2003	2004	2005	2006	2007	2008	2009	2010
Increase standard deduction for married couples to twice the deduction for singles		Standard Deduction for Married Couples as a Percent of the Standard Deduction for Singles									
	167%					174%*	184%	187%	190%	200%	200%
Increase size of 15% bracket for married couples to twice the size of the 15% bracket for singles		Size of 15% Tax Bracket for Married Couples as a Percent of the Size of the Bracket for Singles									
	167%					180%*	187%	193%	200%	200%	200%

* Amended to 200 percent in 2004 through 2010.

C Marriage Penalty Relief and Simplification Relating to the Earned Income Credit

For married taxpayers who file a joint return, the new law increases the beginning and ending of the earned income credit phase-out by $1,000 in the case of taxable years beginning in 2002 through 2004; by $2,000 in the case of taxable years beginning in 2005 through 2007; and by $3,000 in the case of taxable years beginning after 2007. The $3,000 amount is to be adjusted annually for inflation after 2008.

The new law also simplifies the definition of *earned income* by excluding nontaxable employee compensation from the definition of earned income for earned income credit purposes. The new law repeals the present-law provision that reduces the earned income credit by the amount of your alternative minimum tax.

The new law adopts a simplified definition of a child for purposes of the earned income credit and modifies the present-law tie-breaking rules. The new law also simplifies the calculation of the earned income credit by replacing modified adjusted gross income with adjusted gross income.

In addition, the new law authorizes the IRS, beginning in 2004, to use math error authority to deny the earned income credit if the Federal Case Registry of Child Support Orders indicates that the taxpayer is the noncustodial parent of the child with respect to whom the credit is claimed.

The preceding changes are effective for taxable years beginning after December 31, 2001. The provision to authorize the IRS to use math error authority if the Federal Case Registry of Child Support Orders indicates the taxpayer is the noncustodial parent is effective beginning in 2004.

181 Education Incentives

A Modifications to Education IRAs

The new law increases the annual limit on contributions to education IRAs (now called Coverdell Education Accounts) from $500 to $2,000. The new law expands the definition of qualified education expenses that may be paid tax-free from an education IRA to include elementary and secondary school expenses. The new law increases the phase-out range for married taxpayers filing a joint return so that it is twice the range for single taxpayers. Thus, the phase-out range for married taxpayers filing a joint return is $190,000 to $220,000 of modified adjusted gross income. However, you don't need earned income to contribute to an education IRA. If you make too much, gift the dollars to your child and have him or her make the contribution.

The new law provides that various age limitations do not apply to special needs beneficiaries.

The new law clarifies that corporations and other entities (including tax-exempt organizations) are permitted to make contributions to education IRAs, regardless of the income of the corporation or entity during the year of the contribution.

The new law allows you to claim a HOPE credit or Lifetime Learning credit for a taxable year and to exclude from gross income amounts distributed (both the contributions and the earnings portions) from an education IRA on behalf of the same student as long as the distribution is not used for the same educational expenses for which a credit was claimed.

The new law repeals the excise tax on contributions made by any person to an education IRA on behalf of a beneficiary during any taxable year in which any contributions are made by anyone to a qualified state tuition program on behalf of the same beneficiary.

The new law now allows a rollover of unused education IRA funds to other family members, provided that they are under age 30, without penalty.

The provisions modifying education IRAs are effective for taxable years beginning after December 31, 2001.

B Private Prepaid Tuition Programs; Exclusion from Gross Income of Education Distributions from Qualified Tuition Programs—Section 529 Plans

The new law expands the definition of "qualified tuition program" to include certain prepaid tuition programs established and maintained by one or more eligible educational institutions (which may be private institutions) that satisfy the requirements under section 529 (other than the present-law state sponsorship rule). In the case of a qualified tuition program maintained by one or more private eligible educational institutions, persons are able to purchase tuition credits or certificates on behalf of a designated beneficiary, but would not be able to make contributions to a savings account plan.

The new law modifies the definition of qualified higher education expenses to include expenses of a special needs beneficiary that are necessary in connection with his or her enrollment or attendance at the eligible education institution.

Under the new law, an exclusion from gross income is provided for distributions from qualified tuition programs to the extent that the distribution is used to pay for qualified higher education expenses. Qualified distributions are now tax-free, not just tax-deferred.

The new law also allows you to claim a HOPE credit or Lifetime Learning credit for a taxable year and to exclude from gross income amounts distributed (both the principal and the earnings portions) from a qualified tuition program on behalf of the same student as long as the distribution is not used for the same expenses for which a credit was claimed. Now you can get both!

The new law provides that a transfer of credits (or other amounts) from one qualified tuition program for the benefit of a designated beneficiary to another qualified tuition program for the benefit of the same beneficiary is not considered a distribution. This rollover treatment does not apply to more than one transfer within any 12-month period with respect to the same beneficiary.

The new law eliminates the present-law penalty on distributions not used for higher education expenses and instead applies the same additional tax that applies to education IRAs. The new law provides that assets of qualified tuition plans of private institutions must be held in trust.

The provisions are effective for taxable years beginning after December 31, 2001, except that the exclusion from gross income for certain distributions from a qualified tuition program established and maintained by an entity other than a state (or agency or instrumentality thereof) is effective for taxable years beginning after December 31, 2003.

C Exclusion for Employer-Provided Educational Assistance

The new law extends the exclusion for employer-provided educational assistance to *graduate* education and makes the exclusion (as applied to both undergraduate and graduate education) *permanent,* effective with respect to courses beginning after December 31, 2001. The maximum tax-free benefit of $5,200 was unchanged.

D Modifications to Student Loan Interest Deduction

The new law increases the income phase-out ranges for eligibility for the student loan interest deduction to $50,000 to $65,000 for single taxpayers and to $100,000 to $130,000 for married taxpayers filing joint returns. These income phase-out ranges are adjusted annually for inflation after 2002. The conference agreement *repeals* both the limit on the number of months (60) during which interest paid on a qualified education loan is deductible and the restriction that voluntary payments of interest are not deductible. You can now get the deduction, no matter how long it takes you to pay off the loan. The provision is effective for interest paid on qualified education loans after December 31, 2001.

E Eliminate Tax on Awards Under the National Health Service Corps Scholarship Program and the F. Edward Hebert Armed Forces Health Professions Scholarship and Financial Assistance Program

The new law provides that amounts received by you or a medical, dental, nursing, or physician assistant student, under the NHSC Scholarship Program or the Armed Forces Scholarship Program are eligible for tax-free treatment as qualified scholarships under Sec. 117, without regard to any service obligation. As with other qualified scholarships under section 117, the tax-free treatment does not apply to amounts received by students for regular living expenses, including room and board. The provision is effective for education awards received after December 31, 2001.

F Deduction for Qualified Higher Education Expenses

The new law permits taxpayers an above-the-line deduction for qualified higher education expenses paid by the taxpayer during a taxable year. Qualified higher education expenses are defined in the same manner as for purposes of the HOPE credit.

In 2002 and 2003, taxpayers with adjusted gross income that does not exceed $65,000 ($130,000 in the case of married couples filing joint returns) are entitled to a maximum deduction of $3,000 per year. Taxpayers with adjusted gross income above these thresholds would not be entitled to a deduction. In 2004 and 2005, taxpayers with adjusted gross income that does not exceed $65,000 ($130,000 in the case of married taxpayers filing joint returns) are entitled to a maximum deduction of $4,000 and taxpayers with adjusted gross income that does not exceed $80,000 ($160,000 in the case of married taxpayers filing joint returns) are entitled to a maximum deduction of $2,000.

The provision is effective for taxable years beginning after December 31, 2001.

182 Pension and Individual Retirement Arrangement Provisions

The new law makes extensive changes to the rules relating to individual retirement arrangements (IRAs) and qualified pension plans. Among the changes are the following provisions:

1. Increased contribution limits and catch-up contributions to IRAs

2. Provisions for expanding coverage, including increased contribution and benefit limits for qualified plans, increases in elective deferral limits, and a credit for certain elective deferrals and IRA contributions

3. Provisions to enhance fairness for women, including additional catch-up contributions for individuals over age 50

4. Provisions for increasing portability for plan participants

5. Provisions for strengthening pension security and enforcement

6. Provisions for reducing regulatory burdens

LIMITS AND CATCH-UP PROVISIONS

Under prior law, contributions to a *defined contribution plan* cannot exceed the lesser of compensation or $35,000 (for 2001).

Under a *defined benefit plan,* the maximum annual benefit payable at retirement is generally the lesser of average compensation or $140,000 (for 2001). The dollar limit is adjusted for cost of living in increments.

Compensation Limit. The annual compensation of each participant that may be taken into account for contributions and benefits under a plan is limited to $170,000 (for 2001). The compensation limit is increased for cost-of-living adjustments in $10,000 increments.

New Higher Limits. The 2001 Tax Relief Act provides for across-the-board increases in plan contribution limits.

Defined Contribution Plans. The new law raises the percentage limit on annual additions to compensation and increases the dollar limit to $40,000 for plan years beginning after 2001. The $40,000 amount is indexed in $5,000 increments for inflation occurring after July 1, 2001.

Defined Benefit Plans. For plan years ending after 2001, the new law increases the annual benefit limitation for a benefit plan to $160,000. The benefit limit will be indexed in $5,000 increments for inflation occurring after 2001. The new law defined that the annual benefit limit is decreased if benefits begin before age 62 and increased if benefits begin after 65.

Compensation Limit. The new law increases the limit on compensation that can be taken into account to $200,000 starting in 2002. The $200,000 limit will be indexed in $500 increments.

SECTION 401(K) PLANS

Under current law, the maximum annual amount of elective deferrals that an individual may make to a 401(k) plan is $10,500 (for 2001). This dollar limit is indexed for inflation in $500 increments.

New higher limits. Under the Tax Relief Act, the dollar limit on annual elective deferrals to 401(k) plans will be $11,000 in 2002. For 2003 and later years, the limit will be increased in annual $1,000 increments to $15,000 in 2006. The limit will be indexed in $500 increments after 2006.

	Limits
2002	$11,000
2003	12,000
2004	13,000
2005	14,000
2006	15,000

SIMPLE PLANS

Certain small businesses can establish a simplified retirement plan called the savings incentive match plan (SIMPLE) retirement plan. SIMPLE plans can be adopted by employers that employ 100 or fewer employees who received at least $5,000 in compensation during the preceding year and who do not maintain another sponsored retirement plan. A SIMPLE plan can be either an IRA for each employee or part of a Section 401(k) plan.

A SIMPLE retirement plan allows employees to make elective contributions up to a maximum of $6,500 indexed for inflation in $500 increments.

New Simple Limits

2001	$ 6,500
2002	7,000
2003	8,000
2004	9,000
2005	10,000

Beginning in 2005, the limit will be indexed to inflation in $500 increments.

Other Limit Increases

1. *SARSEP*

2002	$11,000
2001	10,500
2002	11,000
2003	12,000
2004	13,000
2005	14,000
2006	15,000—indexed for inflation thereafter in $500 increments

2. 403(b) annuities

2001	$10,500
2002	11,000
2003	12,000
2004	13,000
2005	14,000
2006	15,000—indexed for inflation thereafter in $500 increments

3. Section 457 plan

2001	$ 8,500
2002	9,000
2003	9,500
2004	10,000
2005	10,500
2006	11,000
2007	12,000
2008	13,000
2009	14,000
2010	15,000—indexed for inflation thereafter in $500 increments

NEW IRA LIMITS

Under prior law, the maximum individual total that could be contributed to a traditional or Roth IRA was $2,000. The new law increases this maximum combined contribution as follows:

2001	$2,000
2002	3,000
2003	3,000
2004	3,000
2005	4,000
2006	4,000
2007	4,000
2008 and later years	5,000 indexed for inflation in $500 increments

CATCH-UP CONTRIBUTIONS

Under the new law, after 2001, if you are age 50 or older, you can make additional catch-up IRA contributions as follows:

Year	Additional Contribution	Total Contribution
2002	$ 500	$3,500
2003	500	3,500
2004	500	3,500
2005	500	4,500
2006	1,000	5,000
2007	1,000	5,000
2008	1,000—indexed for inflation in $500 increments	6,000

OTHER CATCH-UP PROVISIONS

401(k)/457 Plans/SEP/Simple Plans

Under the new law, the otherwise applicable dollar limit on elective deferrals under a Section 401(k) (b) annuity, SEP, SIMPLE, or deferrals under a Section 457 plan for individuals who have attained age 50 by the end of the year is increased.

The additional amount of elective contributions that may be made by an eligible individual participating is the lesser of (1) the applicable dollar amount or (2) the participant's compensation for the year reduced by elective deferrals of the participant for the year. The applicable dollar amount under a Section 401(k), 403(b) annuity, SEP, or Section 457 plan is as follows:

a) $1,000 for 2002.

b) $2,000 for 2003,

c) $3,000 for 2004,

d) $4,000 for 2005, *and*

e) $5,000 for 2006 and thereafter.

The applicable dollar amount under a SIMPLE is as follows:

a) $500 for 2002,

b) $1,000 for 2003,

c) $1,500 for 2004,

d) $2,000 for 2005, *and*

e) $2,500 for 2006 and thereafter.

The $5,000 and $2,500 amounts are adjusted for inflation in $500 increments in 2007 and thereafter.

Catch-up contributions are not subject to any other contribution limits and are not taken into account for contribution limits. So, for example, the catch-up contributions can be made even if they put the total contributed to a defined contribution plan over the new law's $40,000 limit. In addition, catch-up contributions are not subject to the code's nondiscrimination rules. However, a plan will fail the nondiscrimination tests unless the plan allows all individuals participating in the plan to make the same election for catch-up contributions. An employer may make matching contributions with respect to catch-up contributions. Any such matching contributions will be subject to normal applicable rules.

The catch-up provisions are described in the new law as a matter of fairness to women, many of whom presumably were out of the workplace to bear and raise children and had no earned income in some years. But workers of either sex can make catch-up contributions, even if they have worked continuously.

NEW TAX DEFERRED SAVINGS OPPORTUNITIES

Roth 401(k)

In a traditional 401(k), you can save up to $10,500 in before-tax income in 2001, as well as a certain percentage of your salary in after-tax dollars. But when money is withdrawn, taxes are owed on pretax contributions and all investment gains. With a Roth 401(k), contributions will be made with after-tax dollars, but all investment gains will be tax-free and the money does not have to be withdrawn before death.

Workers will be allowed to have both traditional and Roth 401(k) plans, with a combined maximum of $15,000 annually, or $20,000 for people 50 and older after 2005.

The current income limits for a Roth contribution ($160,000 on a joint return, $110,000 for single) do *not* apply for the Roth 401(k).

You will be making after-tax contributions, but all withdrawals will be tax-free, and there are no minimum distributions during your lifetime. If you plan to use the money as a bequest, rather than for retirement, this is the way to go.

Say you contribute $10,000 to a Roth 401(k), live 10 years, then leave the money to a teenage grandchild. At 8 percent annual return, you've given that grandchild over $600,000 in tax-free dollars over his or her projected lifetime.

Section 403(b) Annuities

Under the new law, you can now make elective deferral contributions under Section 403(b) annuity and have those contributions treated as nondeductible Roth contributions as well. The Roth option for both 401(k)s and 403(b) annuities is effective for years after 2005.

New Retirement Tax Credit

The new law creates a temporary, nonrefundable retirement tax credit. You can receive a credit of as much as 50 percent of the amount you save, up to a $1,000 credit on $2,000. You can receive a credit of 10 percent up to 50 percent of what you save, up to $2,000, if you owe income taxes, which this credit can reduce to zero. This credit is available for elective contributions to a Section 401(k) plan, Section 403(b) annuity, SIMPLE, or an SEP; contributions to a traditional or Roth IRA; and voluntary after-tax employee-qualified plans.

The credit is available for tax years after December 31, 2001, and before January 1, 2007 (2002 through 2006).

The credit rates based on adjusted gross income are as follows:

Joint Filers	Heads of Households	All Other Filers	Credit Rate
$0–$30,000	$0–$22,500	$0–$15,000	50 percent
$30,000–$32,500	$22,500–$24,375	$15,000–$16,250	20 percent
$32,500–$50,000	$24,375–$37,500	$16,250–$25,000	10 percent
Over $50,000	Over $37,500	Over $25,000	0 percent

SAVING FOR RETIREMENT

Congress will let Americans save more in tax-favored accounts as part of the new tax-cut bill.

Maximum Any Individual Under 50 Can Save/*Maximum Those 50 and Older Can Save*

	2002	2003	2004	2005	2006	2007	2008
Individual Retirement Accounts	$3,000	$3,000	$3,000	$4,000	$4,000	$4,000	$5,000*
	3,500	*3,500*	*3,500*	*4,500*	*5,000*	*5,000*	*6,000*
SIMPLE Plans†	$7,000	$8,000	$9,000	$10,000	$10,000*	$10,000*	$10,000*
	7,500	*9,000*	*10,500*	*12,500*	*12,500*	*12,500*	*12,500*
401(k), 403(b) and 457 Plans‡	$11,000	$12,000	$13,000	$14,000	$15,000	$15,000*	$15,000*
	12,000	*14,000*	*16,000*	*18,000*	*20,000*	*20,000*	*20,000*
Roth 401(k)	N/A	N/A	N/A	N/A	$15,000	$15,000*	$15,000*
					20,000	*20,000*	*20,000*

*Plus inflation adjustment in $500 increments.

†Simple plans are for enterprises with 100 or fewer workers.

‡Section 403(b) plans are for nonprofits; 457 plans are for governments. In the last 3 years before retirement, workers in 457 plans can save double the limit for those under 50.

Note: The maximum that an employer can contribute annually will rise to $40,000 next year, a 14 percent increase, and will be adjusted for inflation thereafter.

Source: H.R. 1836 as passed by Congress.

PLAN LOANS

Under the new law, shareholder employees of an S corporation and sole pro-prietors can now take loans from their qualified plans after December 31, 2001. The new law does *not* permit loans to IRA owners.

ROLLOVERS

Effective after December 31, 2001, you can now roll over distributions between qualified retirement plans, Section 403(b) annuities, and governmental Section 457 plans. Distributions from an IRA can now be rolled over to employer-sponsored qualified plans, annuities, or a governmental Section 457 plan. This can be important. In many states, IRA dollars can be attached by creditors while ERISA governed qualified plans are secure from attachment under federal law. A rollover from an IRA to a qualified plan insulates those dollars from any potential creditors.

SMALL EMPLOYER TAX CREDIT

The Tax Relief Act creates a new, nonrefundable income tax credit for a small business that adopts a defined benefit or defined contribution plan [including a 401(k) plan], a SIMPLE plan, or a SEP. The credit is 50 percent of the first $1,000 of administrative and retirement-education expenses incurred for the plan for each of the first 3 years the plan is in existence. Expenses offset by the credit may not be claimed a deduction for those expenses.

The credit may be claimed by an employer that did not employ more than 100 employees with compensation in excess of $5,000 in the preceding year. To qualify for the credit, the employer's plan must cover at least one nonhighly compensated employee [IRC Sec. 45E]. The credit may be claimed for costs paid or incurred in tax years after December 31, 2001, with respect to plans established after that date.

USER FEE WAIVERS

The new law waives the user fee (usually $125 to $1,250) for a retirement plan determination letter, provided that there is at least one nonhighly compensated employee participating in the plan. This is effective as of January 1, 2002.

EMPLOYER-PROVIDED RETIREMENT ADVICE

The new law, after December 31, 2001, allows an employer to provide retire-ment planning advice to employees on a tax-free basis. The exclusion does *not* apply to tax preparation, accounting, legal, or brokerage services.

183 AMT Relief

The new law increases the individual alternative minimum tax exemption amount by $2,000 for single taxpayers and $4,000 for married taxpayers filing joint returns for 2001 through 2004—but only through 2004!

No big deal! With the reduction in the marginal rates, more people will be hit by the AMT. Many taxpayers making between $72,000 and $627,000—especially those with large families, big medical bills, or homes in higher-tax states like New York, New Jersey, Connecticut, Massachusetts, Illinois, and California—will see perhaps two-thirds of their Bush income tax cuts taken away by the alternative minimum tax.

About 1.5 million Americans will be hit by the AMT in 2001, a number that was projected to reach 20 million by 2010. Under the new law, that number is expected to balloon to more than 35 million victims of this add-on tax.

However, the new law also allows child credit and the adoption credit to be claimed against both the regular tax and the alternative minimum tax on a permanent basis. In addition, the refundable credits will no longer be reduced by a taxpayer's AMT.

184 Health Insurance for Self-Employed

There has been no change in this area. The new law retains the old schedule of allowance for premiums paid:

2001	60%
2002	70%
2003	100%

185 Income Tax Treatment of Certain Restitution Payments to Holocaust Victims

The new law provides that excludable restitution payments made to an eligible individual (or the individual's heirs or estate) are: (1) excluded from gross income; and (2) not taken into account for any provision of the code that takes into account excludable gross income in computing adjusted gross income (e.g., taxation of Social Security benefits). The provision is effective for amounts received on or after January 1, 2001, with no inference with respect to the income tax treatment of any amount received before January 1, 2000.

186 Estate, Gift, and Generation-Skipping Transfer Tax Provisions

While this is a book about how to pay zero income taxes, I would be remiss if I didn't at least review the basic changes in the gift and estate tax laws.

A Phase-out and Repeal of Estate and Generation-Skipping Transfer Taxes; Increase in Gift Tax Unified Credit Effective Exemption

Under the new law, in 2002, the 5 percent surtax (which phases out the benefit of the graduated rates) and the rates in excess of 50 percent are repealed. In addition, in 2002, the unified credit effective exemption amount (for both estate and gift tax purposes) is increased to $1 million. In 2003, the estate and gift tax rates in excess of 49 percent are repealed. In 2004, the estate and gift tax rates in excess of 48 percent are repealed, and the unified credit effective exemption amount for estate tax purposes is increased to $1.5 million. (The unified credit effective exemption amount for gift tax purposes remains at $1 million as increased in 2002.) In addition, in 2004, the family-owned business deduction is repealed. In 2005, the estate and gift tax rates in excess of 47 percent are repealed. In 2006, the estate and gift tax rates in excess of 46 percent are repealed, and the unified credit effective exemption amount for estate tax purposes is increased to $2 million. In 2007, the estate and gift tax rates in excess of 45 percent are repealed. In 2009, the unified credit effective exemption amount is increased to $3.5 million. In 2010, the estate and generation-skipping transfer taxes are repealed.

From 2002 through 2009, the estate and gift tax rates and unified credit effective exemption amount for estate tax purposes are as shown in the following table:

Estate and Gift Tax Rates and Unified Credit Exemption Amount

Calendar Year	Estate and GST Tax Deathtime Transfer Exemption	Highest Estate and Gift Tax Rates
2002	$1 million	50%
2003	$1 million	49%
2004	$1.5 million	48%
2005	$1.5 million	47%
2006	$2 million	46%
2007	$2 million	45%
2008	$2 million	45%
2009	$3.5 million	45%
2010	N/A (taxes repealed) under the bill (gift tax only)	Top individual rate

In 2010, the estate and generation-skipping transfer taxes are repealed. Also beginning in 2010, the top gift tax rate will be the top individual income tax rate as provided under the bill, and, except as provided in regulations, a transfer to trust will be treated as a taxable gift, unless the trust is treated as wholly owned by the donor or the donor's spouse under the grantor trust provisions of the Code.

After repeal of the estate and generation-skipping transfer taxes, the present-law rules providing for a fair market value (i.e., stepped-up) basis for property acquired from a decedent are repealed. A modified *carryover basis* regime generally takes effect, which provides that recipients of property transferred at the decedent's death will receive a basis equal to the lesser of the adjusted basis of the decedent or the fair market value of the property on the date of the decedent's death (or the alternate valuation date, if elected).

The new law provides that, if certain requirements are met, the executor of the estate may elect to step up the basis of selected property up to $1,300,000 (plus unused capital losses, net operating losses, and certain built-in losses of the decedent). Also, *spousal property* (as defined by the Internal Revenue Code and the Act) acquired by the surviving spouse can obtain an additional step-up in basis of $3 million, for a total of $4,300,000 of new basis.

There are additional taxes and costs associated with the modified carry-over basis rules. When the inherited property is disposed of (i.e., sold), the capital gains tax will have to be paid by the seller, whether it is the decedent's estate, heir, beneficiary, or spouse. This provision also imposes extensive record-keeping of cost basis, and reporting requirements when assets are transferred. Not only does the property owner need to keep records of his or her cost basis during the entire period of ownership, but the onus of recordkeeping could last for generations into the future. In the event professional assistance is used to track the basis or meet the reporting requirements, there will be the added cost of fees for such services.

Under the new law, from 2002 through 2004, the state death tax credit allowable under present law is reduced as follows: in 2002, the state death tax credit is reduced by 25 percent (from present law amounts); in 2003, the state death tax credit is reduced by 50 percent (from present law amounts); and in 2004, the state death tax credit is reduced by 75 percent (from present law amounts). In 2005, the state death tax credit is repealed, after which there will be a deduction for death taxes (e.g., any estate, inheritance, legacy, or succession taxes) actually paid to any state or the District of Columbia, in respect of property included in the gross estate of the decedent. Such state taxes must have been paid and claimed before the later of: (1) 4 years after the filing of the estate tax return; or (2) (a) 60 days after a decision of the U.S. Tax Court determining the estate tax liability becomes final, (b) the expiration of the period of extension to pay estate taxes over time under Section 6166, or (c) the expiration of the period of limitations in which to file a claim for refund or 60 days after a decision of a court in which such refund suit has become final.

The estate and gift rate reductions, increases in the estate tax unified credit exemption equivalent amounts and generation-skipping transfer tax exemption amount, and reductions in and repeal of the state death tax credit are phased in over time, beginning with estates of decedents dying and gifts and generation-skipping transfers after December 31, 2001.

Year	Death Tax Credit
2002	25%
2003	50%
2004	75%
2005	Repealed

B Expand Estate Tax Rule for Conservation Easements

The new law expands availability of qualified conservation easements by eliminating the requirement that the land be located within a certain distance from a metropolitan area, national park, wilderness area, or urban national forest. Thus, under the conference agreement, a qualified conservation easement may be claimed with respect to any land that is located in the United States or its possessions. The provisions are effective for estates of decedents dying after December 31, 2000.

C Modify Generation-Skipping Transfer Tax Rules

The new law makes the following modifications to the generation-skipping transfer tax provisions:

1. Deemed allocation of the generation-skipping transfer tax exemption to lifetime transfers to trusts that are not direct skips
2. Retroactive allocation of the generation-skipping tax exemption
3. Severing of trusts holding property having an inclusion ratio of greater than zero
4. Modification of certain valuation rules
5. Relief from late elections
6. Substantial compliance

The provisions are generally effective after December 31, 2000.

D Availability of Installment Payment Relief

The new law expands the availability of installment payment rules to qualified lending and finance business interests and certain holding company stock. In addition, the conference agreement increases from 15 to 45 the number of partners of a partnership or shareholders in a corporation eligible for installment payments of estate tax. The provisions are effective for decedents dying after December 31, 2001.

Estate Tax Summary

Year	Unified Credit Exemption	Qualified Family-Owned Business Deduction	Top Tax Rate
2001	$675,000*	$675,000*	55%
2002	1,000,000*	675,000*	50%
2003	1,000,000*	675,000*	49%
2004	1,500,000	NA	48%
2005	1,500,000	NA	47%
2006	2,000,000	NA	46%
2007	2,000,000	NA	45%
2008	2,000,000	NA	45%
2009	3,500,000	NA	45%
2010	NA	NA	NA%
2011	1,000,000*	675,000*	55%

*Combined UC exemption and QFOB deduction limited to $1,300,000.

Gift and Estate Tax Table
(Upper Brackets)

| | Value of Estate | | | |
	From	To	Tax on Col. 1	Rate on Excess
2001, 2011 and later	$1,500,000	$2,000,000	$555,800	45%
	2,000,000	2,500,000	780,800	49%
	2,500,000	3,000,000	1,025,800	53%
	3,000,000	10,000,000	1,290,800	55%
	10,000,000	17,184,000	5,140,800	60%
	17,184,000	—	9,451,200	55%
2002	$1,500,000	$2,000,000	$555,800	45%
	2,000,000	2,500,000	780,800	49%
	2,500,000	—	1,025,800	50%
2003	$1,500,000	$2,000,000	$555,800	45%
	2,000,000	—	780,800	49%

Gift and Estate Tax Table *(continued)*
(Upper Brackets)

	Value of Estate From	To	Tax on Col. 1	Rate on Excess
2004	$1,500,000	$2,000,000	$555,800	45%
	2,000,000	—	780,800	48%
2005	$1,500,000	$2,000,000	$555,800	45%
	2,000,000	—	780,800	47%
2006	$1,500,000	$2,000,000	$555,800	45%
	2,000,000	—	780,800	46%
2007 to 2009	$1,500,000	—	$555,800	45%

187 Sunset

To ensure compliance with the Congressional Budget Act of 1974, all provisions of the law generally do not apply for taxable, plan, or limitation years beginning after December 31, 2010. In other words, *none* of the changes remain in effect after 2010 unless Congress reenacts them and the new legislation is signed into law by the President.

Because of this sunset provision, I have de-emphasized planning suggestions beyond next year, because its rules will probably change again before they become effective.

As the new law takes effect, future editions of *How to Pay Zero Taxes* will discuss the best ways to structure your finances to maximize your wealth and minimize your taxes. In the meantime, with the mandated changes each year scheduled to implode in 2011, any long-term planning is reduced to mental masturbation.

Overview of the Economic Growth and Tax Relief Reconciliation Act of 2001

Provision Rates	Present Law	2001	2002	2003	2004	2005	2006	2007	2008	2009	2010
	39.6%	39.1%	38.6%	38.6%	37.6%	37.6%	35% fully effective				
	36.0%	35.5%	35.0%	35.0%	34.0%	34.0%	33% fully effective				
	31.0%	30.5%	30.0%	30.0%	29.0%	29.0%	28% fully effective				
	28.0%	27.5%	27.0%	27.0%	26.0%	26.0%	25% fully effective				
	15.0%	10% for the first $6,000 of income for singles and $12,000 for married couples Remaining portion of 15% bracket unchanged							Raise bracket threshold to $7,000 and $14,000		Index thresholds for inflation	

Provision	Present Law	2001	2002	2003	2004	2005	2006	2007	2008	2009	2010
Marriage Penalty Relief											
Standard Deduction						Gradually increase standard deduction for married couples				Twice single level Fully effective	
15% Bracket						Gradually increase 15% bracket for married				Twice single level Fully effective	
Child Credit	$500		$600			$700				$800	1,000 fully effective
Personal Exemption Limitation Repeal							Phasein period				Repeal
IRA Limit	$2,000		$3,000				$4,000		$5,000	Index $5,000 for inflation	
AMT Exemption	$33,750 Single $45,000 Married		$35,750 Single $49,000 Married				$33,750 Single $45,000 Married				
Estate Tax											
Top Rate	55%		50%	49%	48%	47%	46%	45%			Repeal
Exemption	$675,000		$1 million		$1.5 million		$2 million			$3.5 million	Repeal

CHAPTER 13

The Job Creation and Worker Assistance Act of 2002

"Tax simplification is complicated stuff."

PAM OLSON, Deputy Assistant
Treasury Secretary for Tax Policy

"Another 161 places in the Code that need to be changed."

JEFF A. SCHNEPPER

You didn't think Congress would miss a chance for a new tax law in 2002, did you? This is the 36th of the last 38 years in which we've had a major tax law.

This one, signed by President Bush on March 9, 2002, has several tax provisions you should be aware of.

188 Bonus Depreciation

The new law allows an additional first-year depreciation deduction equal to 30 percent of the adjusted basis of the property. The property must be purchased after September 10, 2001, and before September 11, 2004. It must be placed in service before January 1, 2005.

189 Net Operating Losses

The new law extends the general net operating loss (NOL) carryback period from 2 years to 5 years for NOLs arising out of tax years 2001 and 2002.

190 Classroom Materials

The new law allows, as of January 1, 2002 and before January 1, 2004 (extended in 2004 through 2005—an additional 2 years), an above-the-line deduction of up to $250 annually for expenses paid by an eligible educator for books, supplies, computer equipment, and supplementary materials. An eligible educator is a kindergarten through grade 12 teacher, aide, instructor, counselor, or principal in a school for at least 900 hours during the school year.

Prior to the change, these expenses were miscellaneous itemized employee business expenses that had to exceed the 2 percent floor (2 percent of adjusted gross income).

191 Electric Vehicle Credit

A 10 percent credit is provided for the cost of a qualified electric vehicle, up to a maximum credit of $4,000. The full amount of the credit is available for 2002, but it phases down and out by January 1, 2005.

192 Work Opportunity Tax Credit

The new law extends this credit through December 31, 2003 (extended in 2004 through 2005).

193 Welfare to Work Tax Credit

The new law extends this credit through December 31, 2003 (extended in 2004 through 2005).

194 Archer Medical Savings Account

The new law extends the availability of these medical savings accounts through December 31, 2003.

195 Liberty Zone Benefits

If you're in the area where the Twin Towers were attacked, you get special tax considerations. Your election to expense, normally capped at $24,000 for 2002, is increased by $35,000 for a potential total of as much as $59,000. This is in addition to a 30 percent bonus first-year depreciation for property acquired after September 10, 2001 and before September 11, 2004, as long as the property is placed in service by January 1, 2005.

For example, assume you bought $200,000 in new equipment. The normal cap on expensing is $24,000. But, since your business is in the Liberty Zone, you can expense another $35,000 for a total of $59,000 (scheduled to increase to $60,000 for 2003).

You also now have a bonus depreciation write-off of $42,300 (30 percent of $200,000 minus $59,000). That's a total deduction of $101,300. You then depreciate the remaining $98,700 under normal rules.

The Job Creation and Worker Assistance Act of 2002 only made a few changes to our tax code. But they were important changes that create additional opportunities for you to reduce your taxes to zero!

CHAPTER 14

The Tax Relief Reconciliation Act of 2003

"I don't think you can take the tax system seriously anymore."

CHRISTOPHER S. RIZEK,
former Associate Tax Legislative Counsel

Rep. Jim Saxton (R-N.J.) reported that taxpayers with incomes greater than $200,000 will see their share of the income tax burden increase from 44.8 percent of 45.4 percent, and receive an average 10.8 percent cut in income taxes. Taxpayers with incomes between $30,000 and $40,000 will see a tax reduction of 19.3 percent, reducing their share of taxes from 2.1 to 1.9 percent.

Another year—another tax act! This one made only 50 changes but it shrunk the tax bill of just about every taxpayer. If you're an income investor or a parent of children under age 17, the goodies are so good that you won't be able to wipe that smirk from your face for a week.

Let's get specific. Here are the new rules and how to take advantage of them.

A Rate Reductions

The rates are falling! The rates are falling!! I feel like Paul Revere with *good* news.

Retroactive to January 1, 2003, here are the new marginal income tax rates:

Prior	New
38.6%	35%
35%	33%
30%	28%
27%	25%

In addition, the two lowest brackets—10 percent and 15 percent—have been expanded by the new law. For example, the 10 percent rate will apply to the first $14,000 on a joint return rather than the first $12,000. That's an additional $100 in your pocket right there ($2,000 × the 5 percent difference). For singles, the income level goes from $6,000 to $7,000, a $50 saving ($1,000 × the 5 percent difference).

What do you do? (1) If you're paying estimated tax, recompute and reduce your payments. If you're an employee, the IRS is scheduled to come out with new reduced withholding tables for July 1. You'll be seeing fatter take home paychecks at that point.

But be careful. Remember, the rate reductions are effective as of the beginning of the year, but the adjustment only starts in the second half. That means that if you're going from a 27 percent bracket to a 25 percent rate in the last 6 months, in order for you not to be over withheld, the tables are going to impose a 23 percent rate for those last 6 months. That way, the average is the appropriate 25 percent.

The good news is that you're going to get double the reduction and double the extra money in your paycheck through the end of December. More money to spend and a bigger boost to the economy.

The bad news is that your 23 percent withholding rate jumped back to 25 percent as of January 1, 2004.

B The Marriage Penalty

The new law also attacks the marriage penalty. That's the quirk in our tax code that imposes a higher net tax on many married couples than they would have to pay if they remained single.

The new law increases the standard deduction for married couples to twice that of single filers and widens the 15 percent bracket for joint returns. The new standard deduction is now $9,500, up from $7,950 (for married filing separately, the standard deduction is increased to $4,750, the same as for a single). Income taxed at 15 percent is now capped at $56,800, up from $47,450. That's $9,350 more taxed at 15 percent rather than 25 percent, a 10 percent difference or $935 more in your pocket for this year.

The penalty will still be there. Increasing the standard deduction doesn't help those who itemize. And the income of the second spouse will still *start* to be taxed at the first spouse's highest marginal rate. But your tax hit will be smaller.

What to do? (2) Face the music guys, and prepare to walk down that aisle. Your family friendly Congress has just undercut your argument that getting married would not be financially prudent.

Relax and enjoy it! You were going to get married (or buried) anyway. Now, it just won't cost you as much.

C The Alternative Minimum Tax

After years of talking about it, Congress has finally done something about the AMT.

Under the new law, for 2003 and 2004, the AMT exemption increases to $58,000 for joint returns and $42,250 for unmarried taxpayers, up from $49,000 and $35,750. It was not the complete elimination we were hoping for, but any help is better than none. This one was revisited by Congress in 2004 and was extended through 2005.

What to do? (3) More people are going to be able to escape this tax. So don't fear to incur those preference items that increase your potential exposure. For example, taxes you deduct, investment expenses, and employee business expenses are all items that add to your AMT income. With the higher exemptions, you have a reduced chance of being hit with the AMT.

So, pay your fourth-quarter estimated state income taxes on December 31 rather than in January of the next year. Pay your fourth-quarter real estate tax on December 31 rather than in January/February of the next year. By accelerating the deductions, you get to keep more cash in your pockets now, rather than later.

But do the computations. The higher exemptions decrease your AMT exposure. They don't completely eliminate it.

D Child Tax Credit

This one is so good, I had a moment when I was almost sad. I no longer had adolescent kids. But then I remembered. . . .

Under prior law, you got a $600 per child credit for your children under age 17. A credit is a dollar-for-dollar reduction in your tax. In the 25 percent bracket, a $100 deduction saves you $25. A $100 credit saves you $100.

The new law increases this credit to $1,000 for 2003 and 2004. It shrinks to $700 per child for 2005, 2006, 2007, and 2008. Then, it increases to $800 for 2009 and back to $1,000 for 2010. In 2004, it was amended permanently to be $1,000.

This credit is phased out for couples earning more than $110,000 and singles earning over $75,000 ($55,000 if married filing separately). If you are close to those numbers, see if you can defer income into the next year in order to qualify this year for the increased credit.

What if you get your advanced $400 refund and later fail the income test? Two summers ago, Congress allowed taxpayers to keep advanced refunds. Congress will again decide that the administrative cost will outweigh any out-of-pocket loss and allow you to keep the money.

E Dividends/Capital Gains

Under prior law, dividends were taxed at a rate as high as 38.6 percent and long-term capital gains were subject to a maximum tax of 20 percent.

The new law now reduces those rates substantially. For those in the 15 percent bracket (for 2003, singles with taxable incomes of $28,400 or less and couples with taxable income of $56,800 or less), the tax rate on dividends and long-term capital gains has been slashed to only 5 percent. Dividend reduction is retroactive to January 1, 2003. The capital gains reduction covers all sales after May 5, 2003. Regardless of your income, the maximum rate on dividends and long-term capital gains (on sales after May 5, 2003) has been capped at 15 percent.

Great news for the retired and elderly. AARP estimates that 75 percent of dividends paid go to investors over the age of 50.

What to do? (5) Focus on long-term rather than short-term gains. Consider preferred stock and stock that has a high dividend payout, such as utilities. Income investing and focusing on dividends now becomes more attractive.

Companies with a lot of free cash become buys. Those are the companies that have the ability to pay more out in tax advantaged dividends. And, because they are "buys," they also should generate capital appreciation as more taxpayers seek their tax advantages. This creates a double benefit as both dividends and capital gains are now tax favored.

Municipal bonds and tax shelter investments become less attractive compared with other investments. That's because the tax versus tax-free gap has been reduced.

Those in the higher brackets should consider investment leverage. Borrow money at interest rates that are deductible at 35 percent and invest where the return is taxed at only 15 percent.

You can even make out if your yield is *lower* than your cost of money. For example, if you borrow $1,000 at 5 percent, your interest is $50. At a 35 percent tax rate, your deduction reduces your net after-tax cost to only $35.50 (65 percent of $50).

If your $1,000 investment only yields 4.5 percent, you have $45 in income. After tax at a maximum 15 percent rate, you have $38.25 left (85 percent of $45). That's $5.75 more in your pocket on an investment that yields less than your cost of money!

You can actually win even if your yield is lower than your cost of money. For example, borrow $10,000 at 5 percent and your interest is $500. At a 35 percent tax rate, your deduction reduces your net after-tax cost to only $325 (65 percent of $500).

If your $10,000 is invested at 4.5 percent, you will have $450 in income. Taxed at a 15 percent rate, that leaves you with $382.50 (85 percent of $450). That's $57.50 more than the cost of borrowing the money!

But there's a trap here. First, you have to itemize your deductions to get the deduction for investment interest. Then, that investment interest deduction is limited to your investment income.

But the law says that dividends that qualify for the 15 percent maximum rate do not qualify as investment income for the investment interest deduction. So, if your only investment income is the dividends, you do not get the deduction for the interest you paid.

In order for this investment leverage to work, you need other investment income (such as interest, rents, etc.) to offset the interest expense. Otherwise, you are borrowing at a higher net marginal cost than your marginal revenue. And you ain't gonna make it up with volume!

This is true . . . but everything called a "dividend" really isn't a "dividend" and won't qualify. A qualifying dividend is a distribution of a corporation's earnings and profits, which has already been taxed to the corporation. Let's look at some examples where there may be some confusion.

1. Mutual funds have, in the past, reported short-term capital gains as "dividends." Both were taxed at ordinary rates rather than at the lower capital gains rates. Now, such distributions must be separated out. That's because short-term capital gains don't qualify for the lower 5 percent–15 percent rates.

2. Do you have a margin account with your broker? If so, then you may have a problem. Your broker often lends out securities in such accounts to other investors who sell short using your stock. These borrower investors receive the dividends and they reimburse you for what they receive. You end up with the same dollars but these "payments in lieu of dividends" do not qualify as "dividends" and would be taxable at rates as much as 35 percent!

   The rate reduction on dividends is retroactive to January 1, 2003. So, if earlier in the year your broker lent out your securities and a dividend was paid, that dividend did not qualify for the lower rate. Surprise!

3. You just bought a stock and the company declares and pays a dividend. Then you sell the stock. Is your dividend subject to the maximum 15 percent rate? Maybe!

Here's why: Congress wants you to invest for the long-term. In order to get the lower rate, you needed to have held the stock for more than 60 days during the 120 day period beginning 60 days before the ex-dividend date. So, if you do not hold the stock a minimum of 60 plus days, there's no way you're going to qualify for the lower rates. Even if you hold the stock for more than 60 days, it has to be within that 120 day window to qualify.

F Deduct Your SUV—Election to Expense

The new law has increased your Section 179 election to expense (rather than to depreciate) from $25,000 to $100,000. Headlines have declared this to be an opportunity to buy and completely deduct the cost of a SUV in a single year. But let's look at what's really happening.

Many years ago, Congress passed a law limiting the annual deductions you can take on a "luxury" car that's used for business. A "luxury" car was defined as just about anything that had an engine! Actually, back in 1986, it covered cars costing as little as $11,250. For 2002 tax returns, the vehicle had to cost as little as $15,500 to be impacted.

To avoid covering "real" business vehicles, like trucks, the law was written so that cars with unloaded gross vehicle weight over 6,000 pounds were exempt. In fact, for trucks and vans, the standard was loaded gross vehicle weight—the maximum recommended weight for the vehicle, fuel, passengers, and cargo.

So, *if* your car weighs more than 6,000 pounds, it is not covered by the limitations. It has nothing to do with a special break for SUVs. It's only a weight issue. A sufficiently heavy Rolls Royce would qualify.

If your SUV weighs 6,000 pounds or less, you are covered by the limitations and your maximum first year's deduction for a vehicle used 100 percent for business is capped at $10,710 ($3,060 plus a new bonus depreciation of $7,650).

If the limitations don't apply, your vehicle is considered just like any other piece of business equipment. Just like a new copier, such "equipment" would qualify for the special Section 179 election (if used more than 50 percent for business). That means that, if you used the vehicle 100 percent for business, you could deduct, in the first year, as much as $100,000 in cost!

The rules were changed by the American Jobs Creation Act of 2004 for property placed in service after the enactment on October 22. The provision that allows business owners to deduct up to $100,000 as a business expense (saving as much as $35,000 in taxes) will apply only to vehicles weighing 14,000 pounds or more. This would protect most business-use heavy trucks or vans, such as refrigerated trucks. Anything smaller, including the Ford Excusrion and Hummer, weighing between 6,000 and 14,000 pounds, would be deductible up to $25,000 (for a potential savings of $8,750).

Bonus Depreciation Break. Last year's tax legislation introduced a new first-year bonus depreciation deduction equal to 30 percent of the cost of new (but not used) assets with a normal depreciation recovery period of 20 years or less. The 2003 Act takes the bonus depreciation idea and makes it bigger.

For qualifying assets acquired after May 5, 2003 and before 2005 (and placed in service before 2005, or 2006 for certain assets with long production periods), you can deduct 50 percent of cost in the first year. This break is available regardless of the size of your business. Qualifying assets acquired before May 6th of this year are still eligible for a 30 percent first-year bonus depreciation. Under a sunset rule, however, the bonus depreciation rule will vanish after 2004 unless Congress takes further action.

Extra Bonus Depreciation for Business Autos. If you use a car for business purposes, you should be aware of the unfavorable "luxury auto" depreciation rules. Until now, the maximum first-year depreciation write-off for a new (not used) vehicle placed in service this year was only $7,660. As a result of the new 50 percent bonus depreciation break, you can deduct up to $10,710 worth of first-year depreciation for new (not used) vehicles acquired after May 5 of this year. For new autos acquired this year but before May 6, the maximum first-year depreciation deduction is still only $7,660 (under the 30 percent bonus depreciation rule). For used vehicles placed in service at any time this year, the maximum first-year depreciation deduction remains at only $3,060.

To keep within budget, Congress attached "sunset" provisions to the tax breaks. All will expire over the next few years unless Congress votes to extend them (as may well happen).

The chart below shows how long each break was scheduled to last. The subsequent tax changes in 2004 have modified the phase-out. Congress appears to be anxious to change the rules each year.

Cuts at a Glance

Following are new tax rates for different types of income.

	If Your Rate Was	Your Rate Is Now	Through the End of
Ordinary Income Tax Rates	38.6%	35%	2010
	35%	33%	2010
	30%	28%	2010
	27%	25%	2010
Qualified Dividend Rates	38.6%	15%	2008
	35%	15%	2008
	30%	15%	2008
	27%	15%	2008
	15%	5%	2007[1]
	10%	5%	2007[2]
Long-Term Capital Gains Rates*	20%	15%	2008
	18%	15%	2008
	10%	5%	2007[2]
	8%	5%	2007[3]

* Maximum rate on long-term net gains realized after 5/5/03.

[1] 0% in 2008, 15% in 2009.

[2] 0% in 2008, 10% in 2009.

[3] 0% in 2008, 8% in 2009.

	Sunset Years							
Tax Action	**2003**	**2004**	**2005**	**2006**	**2007**	**2008**	**2009**	**2010**
Rate reductions	•	•	•	•	•	•	•	•
Expanded 10% bracket	•	•						
Marriage penalty relief	•	•						
Lower dividend rates	•	•	•	•	•	•		
Lower capital gains rates	•	•	•	•	•	•		
Increased child credit	•	•						
Alternative minimum tax exemption	•	•						

Source: Joint Committee on Taxation.

Those who don't benefit from the new law include those with low incomes, singles, and those with no kids. But if you're low income and single with no kids, you probably weren't paying a whole lot in tax anyway.

This was also a relatively clean tax bill. There were lots of special benefits proposed for specific companies/industries, but they didn't make the final cut. With this bill at least, the Gucci loafers got stomped!

Also note that many of the above provisions are subject to sunset. That means that after a few years, the provisions will automatically expire. Stay tuned to Congress's next session. The tax wars have only just begun.

Table Summarizing Tax Reduction Provisions of Jobs and Growth Tax Relief Reconciliation Act of 2003

Description	2003	2004	2005	2006	2007	2008	2009	2010	2011
Child Tax Credit	$1,000	$1,000	$700	$700	$700	$700	$800	$1,000	$500
10% Bracket									
—Single filers	$7,000	$7,000[1]	$6,000	$6,000	$6,000	$7,000	$7,000[1]	$7,000[1]	$0
—Joint filers	$14,000	$14,000[1]	$12,000	$12,000	$12,000	$14,000	$14,000[1]	$14,000[1]	$0
Marriage Penalty Relief									
—Standard deduction[2]	200%	200%	174%	184%	187%	190%	200%	200%	?
—15% bracket[2]	200%	200%	180%	187%	193%	200%	200%	200%	?
Income Tax Rates[3]									
—28% rate	25%	25%	25%	25%	25%	25%	25%	25%	28%
—31% rate	28%	28%	28%	28%	28%	28%	28%	28%	31%
—36% rate	33%	33%	33%	33%	33%	33%	33%	33%	36%
—39.6% rate	35%	35%	35%	35%	35%	35%	35%	35%	39.6%
AMT Exemption Amounts									
—Single filers	$40,250	$40,250	$33,750	$33,750	$33,750	$33,750	$33,750	$33,750	$33,750
—Joint filers	$58,000	$58,000	$45,000	$45,000	$45,000	$45,000	$45,000	$45,000	$45,000
First Year Bonus Depreciation Allowable	30%/50%[4]	50%	0%	0%	0%	0%	0%	0%	0%
Section 179									
—Expense amount	$100,000	$100,000[1]	$100,000[1]	$25,000	$25,000	$25,000	$25,000	$25,000	$25,000
—Threshold amount	$400,000	$400,000[1]	$400,000[1]	$200,000	$200,000	$200,000	$200,000	$200,000	$200,000
Long-Term Capital Gain Rates									
—10/15% bracket taxpayers	5%[5]	5%	5%	5%	5%	0%	10% (8%)[6]	10% (8%)[6]	10% (8%)[6]
—Higher bracket taxpayers	15%[5]	15%	15%	15%	15%	15%	20% (18%)[6]	20% (18%)[6]	20% (18%)[6]
Qualifying Dividend Rates									
—10/15% bracket taxpayers	5%	5%	5%	5%	5%	0%	taxed at ordinary income rates		
—Higher bracket taxpayers	15%	15%	15%	15%	15%	15%	taxed at ordinary income rates		

[1] Subject to increase to reflect cost-of-living adjustment.

[2] Year columns indicate amounts applicable to joint filers as a percentage of amounts applicable to single filers.

[3] Rates shown in "Description" column are the rates in effect prior to the Economic Growth and Tax Relief Reconciliation Act of 2001.

[4] 30 percent rate is available for qualified property purchased before May 6, 2003; 50 percent rate is available for purchases of qualified property after May 5, 2003.

[5] The 5 and 15 percent rates apply to gains recognized on or after May 6, 2003. For gains recognized before May 6, 2003, the applicable rates are 10 percent (8 percent for 5-year gain) for lower-bracket (that is, 10 or 15 percent bracket) taxpayers and 20 percent (18 percent 5-year gain) for higher-bracket taxpayers.

[6] Amount in parentheses indicates applicable rate for 5-year gain property.

Source: Tax Practice, June 27, 2003.

CHAPTER 15

Income Averaging and Hurricane Tax Breaks

"Suppose you were an idiot.
And suppose you were a member of Congress....
But then I repeat myself."

MARK TWAIN

The American Jobs Creation Act of 2004 amended the Internal Revenue Code to permit fishermen to average their income over 3 years, similar to taxpayers involved in a farming trade or business.

BACKGROUND INFORMATION

- For taxable years beginning after December 31, 1997, individual taxpayers engaged in a farming business may elect to compute their income tax liability by treating all or a portion of their taxable income from farming as if one-third of it had been earned in each of the prior 3 years. Making this election may give taxpayers a lower tax liability for the current year if their farming income is high in the current year and their taxable income was low in the prior 3 years.

- The American Jobs Creation Act of 2004 amended the code to permit fishermen to average their current income over the prior 3 years, similar to taxpayers involved in a farming business.

DEFINITION OF FISHING BUSINESS

"Fishing business" means the conduct of commercial fishing, which is defined by cross-reference to the Magnuson-Stevens Fishery Conservation and Management Act. The Magnuson-Stevens Act defines "commercial fishing" as fishing in which the fish harvested are intended to or do enter commerce through sale, barter, or trade. More specifically:

- "Fishing" is defined as the catching, taking, or harvesting (activities that result in the killing of fish or the bringing of live fish onboard a vessel) of fish (finfish, mollusks, crustaceans, and all other forms of marine animal and plant life, other than marine mammals and birds); the attempted catching, taking, or harvesting of fish; activities that reasonably can be expected to result in the catching, taking, or harvesting of fish; or operations at sea in support of or in preparation for the catching, taking, or harvesting of fish.

- "Fishing" does not include any scientific research activity conducted by a scientific research vessel.

FARMER AND FISHERMAN INCOME AVERAGING PROVISIONS

An individual engaged in a farming or fishing business may make an income averaging election to compute their current year income tax liability by averaging, over the prior 3-year period (base years), all or a portion of their current year eligible income. The amount a farmer or fisherman may elect to average (referred to as Electable Farm Income, or EFI):

- is the amount of income attributable to farming and fishing;

- does not include gain from the sale or other disposition of land; and

- cannot be more than taxable income, and any EFI from a net capital gain attributable to a farming or fishing business cannot be more than total net capital gain.

It's raining tax breaks!

Hurricane Katrina and the devastation it caused led to several new tax breaks.

The IRS extended filing deadlines for those affected.

The Service also flipped the rules on loans from qualified plans to those who need relief. Normally qualified plans must specifically contain loan provisions. Now the IRS is allowing plans that don't currently provide for loans or hardship provisions to make current distributions and amend their plans later.

Even if you don't reside in the disaster locations, if your books, records, or tax professionals are located in the affected areas, you also can get relief. Identify yourself as a hurricane victim by marking "Hurricane Katrina" in red ink on your tax forms.

Congress also jumped into the act with **The Katrina Emergency Tax Relief Act of 2005.** Here's what it provides:

- A qualified Hurricane Katrina Distribution is one made from a qualified retirement plan or an IRA after August 25, 2005 and before January 1, 2007 to an individual whose principal place of abode on August 28, 2005 is located in the Hurricane Katrina disaster area. Such qualified distributions are capped at $100,000. If your distribution is "qualified," then the 10 percent early withdrawal penalty is waived and any income attributable to the distribution is included in your income ratably over 3 years.

- If you recontribute the money any time within the 3-year period, any such amounts are considered rollovers and are *not* included in your income.

- Hardship distributions from qualified plans or first-time home buyer distributions from an IRA to purchase or construct a home in the Hurricane Katrina disaster area may also qualify as a rollover if recontributed to the plan by February 28, 2006. Such recontributed distributions would not be considered income and would also escape the 10 percent penalty tax. This provision protects taxpayers who took distributions to purchase or construct a home that was **not** acquired because of Hurricane Katrina.

- Loans from qualified plans normally may be made up to $50,000. Loans to qualified individuals can now be made up to $100,000 without tax.

- Qualified plans may now be amended *retroactively* to allow current hardship distributions and loans as per the above provisions. This provision mandates legislatively what the IRS allowed administratively.

- The Work Opportunity Tax Credit of 40 percent of wages up to $6,000 ($2,400) per qualified new worker is now available to employers who hire those who lived in the disaster area and who lost their jobs as a result of the hurricane even if the new job is outside the core disaster area, if hired by December 31, 2005. If the new job is within the disaster area, the job must be started by August 28, 2007, 2 years after the actual hurricane. The credit is limited to employers with not more than 200 employees.

- Individual charitable contributions are normally limited to 50 percent of your adjusted gross income and are subject to an overall itemized deduction limit where you may lose as much as 3 percent of your itemized deductions over a given annual floor. Contributions to Katrina relief are now excluded from both these reductions.

- If you housed a Hurricane Katrina displaced individual free of charge for at least 60 days, you may claim an additional exemption of $500 for each individual—up to $2,000. This displaced individual can't be your spouse or dependent. This additional $500 per individual is not subject to the income based phase-out for personal exemptions and is allowed as a deduction in computing your Alternative Minimum Tax (AMT).

- The standard mileage allowance for charitable use of your car is 14¢ per mile. The new law ups that to 70 percent of the current business allowance for use for Katrina relief. Since September 1, 2005, that's 70 percent of 48.5¢ or 34¢ per mile.

- Normally, if your debt is cancelled, you have income to the extent of debt relief. This provision won't apply to the discharge of nonbusiness debts if you lived in the disaster area and suffered economic loss due to the hurricane.

- Casualty loss deductions must be reduced by $100 per casualty and are allowable only to the extent they exceed 10 percent of your adjusted gross income. Both of these limitations are removed from losses attributed to Hurricane Katrina.

- Gains from involuntary conversions may escape taxation if similar property is acquired within 2 years. The new law extends that period to 5 years.

- Your earned income credit is based on your earned income and how many children you have. The $1,000 child credit is refundable to the extent of 15 percent of your earned income in excess of $11,000 for 2005. (This number is indexed for inflation each year.) The new law allows qualified individuals to elect to calculate their 2005 child care credit and earned income credit based on 2004 rather than 2005 numbers.

- The new law also allows the IRS to make adjustments to the applicable tax laws to ensure that taxpayers don't lose any deduction or credit or experience a change of filing status by reason of temporary relocations caused by Hurricane Katrina.

The IRS has created a Katrina relief page with links to all the new hurricane extensions, deductions, etc. You can get up-to-date information from http://www.irs.gov/newsroom/article/0,,id=148203,00.html.

CHAPTER 16

2006 Tax Reform

*I don't make jokes. I just watch the government
and report the facts.*

WILL ROGERS

We had two major tax acts that went into effect in 2006: the Tax Increase Prevention and Reconciliation Act of 2005 and the Pension Protection Act of 2006.

A The Tax Increase Prevention and Reconciliation Act of 2005

Give these guys a calendar! It was signed into law on May 17, 2006, I guess Republicans really are conservative. They don't change the year until June?!

Once again we have a new tax law. Let's see what this one does!

The winners: Investors, because the 15 percent tax rate on capital gains and dividends remain in place through December 31, 2010. Also, starting in 2010, the current ceiling for Roth IRA conversions is eliminated, the Section 179 election is extended, and musical composers win big.

The losers: Alternative Minimum Tax (AMT) victims who will receive only short-term minimal relief. Families with children earning investment income could be hit with a tax increase.

If you need to compromise your tax liability with the IRS, you will discover the compromise process more expressive. If you work overseas you will find your housing-cost exclusion limited to less than $1,000 per month.

Reduced Tax Rate on Capital Gains and Dividends Extended through 2010: Currently, the maximum tax rate on long-term capital gains (assets held for more than one year before being sold) and corporate dividends is 15 percent. For people in the lowest two tax brackets, the rate is 5 percent through 2007, and then will be 0 percent in 2008. Originally scheduled to rise in 2009, the 15 percent and 0 percent tax rates on long-term capital gains and corporate dividends will now remain in place through 2010.

Income Limitation for Roth Conversions Disappears in 2010: Under the current rules, you can only convert your IRAs to a Roth IRA if your income is less than $100,000. The same threshold of $100,000 applies to single individuals and to married couples alike. Starting in 2010, the income limitation disappears, and anyone can convert their IRAs to a Roth IRA. For 2010 Roth conversions, you'll also have the option to pay the taxes due in one year, or to spread the tax liability over two years starting in 2011.

What to do now? If your income is too high for a current IRA, contribute to a "nondeductible IRA." Then, in 2010, convert to a Roth.

Minimal AMT Relief through 2006: More and more middle income taxpayers are being hit with the Alternative Minimum Tax (AMT) each year. For 2006, the AMT exemption, which reduced the impact of this tax was scheduled to fall from $58,000 to $45,000 for married couples, and from $40,250 to $33,750 for single individuals. This tax act restores the AMT exemption to $62,550 ($42,500 for single taxpayers) for 2006 only.

"Kiddie Tax" Age Increased to 17: Under prior law, any unearned income above a certain threshold earned by a child under the age of 14 was taxed at the parent's tax rate. Now, the Kiddie Tax now applies to children who are 17 or younger and earn more than $1,700 (in 2006) in interest, dividends, capital gains, and other nonwage income.

What to do now? Consider section 529 Plans, Series EE Bonds, Qualified Dividend Stocks, and Stocks for long-term appreciation. How about T-bills for kids almost age 18?

Increased Section 179 Deduction Available through 2009: Small business owners can elect to write off the business equipment they buy instead of depreciating the cost of the asset over its useful life, normally of 5 or 7 years. Effective 2008, the maximum Section 179 deduction was set to drop to $25,000 from its current limit of $108,000 (in 2006). This tax act extends the increased Section 179 limits through 2009.

Capital Gains Treatment for Certain Self-Created Musical Works: At your election, the sale or exchange of musical copyrights or compositions in musical works created by your own efforts, will be treated as a sale or exchange of a capital asset. This process is effective for transactions before January 1, 2011, in taxable years beginning after the date of enactment.

AMT Relief for Personal Tax Credits: Certain nonrefundable personal credits (including dependent care, elderly and disabled, Hope Scholarship and Lifetime Learning credits) are allowed only to the extent that you have regular income tax liability in excess of the tentative minimum tax, which has the effect of disallowing these credits against AMT. Temporary provisions have been enacted which permit these credits to offset the entire regular and AMT liability through the end of 2005. The new law allows the nonrefundable personal tax credits to the full extent of your regular tax and alternative minimum tax for taxable years beginning in 2006.

Offers-in-Compromise Partial Payments: Under the new law, you must make a good faith down payment of 20 percent of any lump sum offer-in-compromise with any application for an offer. For periodic payment offers, you are required to comply with your own payment schedule while the offer is being considered. The provision also provides that an offer is deemed accepted if the IRS does not make a decision with respect to the offer within 2 years from the date that the offer was submitted. Offers from certain low-income taxpayers and offers based on doubt as to liability may be excepted.

Amend Section 911 Housing Exclusion: The new law made changes to the foreign earned income exclusion and housing allowance. The income exclusion is now indexed for inflation starting in 2006 (rather than 2008 under prior law). The base housing amount used in calculating the foreign housing cost exclusion in a taxable year is now 16 percent of the amount of the foreign earned income exclusion limitation (instead of the prior law 16 percent of the grade GS-14, Step 1 amount). Reasonable foreign housing expenses in excess of the base housing amount remain excluded from gross income, but the amount of the exclusion is limited to 30 percent of the taxpayer's foreign earned income exclusion. The Treasury Secretary is given authority to issue regulations or other guidance providing for the adjustment of this 30 percent housing cost limitation based on geographic differences in housing costs relative to housing costs in the United States.

Under prior law, workers could exclude "any reasonable amount" for housing expenses over and above an amount equaling 16 percent of the amount paid to a GS-14 government worker.

TIPRA changed that base amount to 16 percent of the $82,400 exclusion. In addition to that change, Congress cut the housing exclusion to just 30 percent of the total $82,400 benefit.

In effect, overseas workers now will be limited to a maximum housing exclusion of $11,536, for 2006. See IRS Notice 2006-87 for *increased* housing cost exclusion amounts allowed by the IRS for certain locations.

B The Pension Protection Act of 2006

At least they got the year right on this one! It was actually signed on August 17, 2006.

Here's what it gives you:

Tax-Free IRA Distributions to Charities: If you're age 70 ½ or older, for 2006 and 2007,* you can distribute as much as $100,000 directly from your IRA without recognizing any income. You don't get a charitable donation deduction (unless the distribution was from a Roth IRA) but the distribution does count toward your minimum distribution amount.

If you don't get the donation deduction, what's the advantage of this over just taking the money and writing a deductible check directly to the charity? It's simpler. Not everybody qualifies to itemize their deductions. And, if the income was recognized, it would increase your adjusted gross income. That would potentially decrease your medical deductions, your miscellaneous itemized deductions, your exemptions for dependents, and your total itemized deduction allowance. It would also potentially increase the exposure of your Social Security income to tax.

Cash to Charities: Starting in 2007, you're going to need some sort of paperwork to back up even your smallest cash contribution if you expect your deduction to survive an audit. I guess if you throw your change in a Red Cross container in a supermarket, the cashier gives you a receipt?!

Clothing and Household Items to Charities: As of August 18, 2006, deductions for donations of clothing or household items are limited to those items in a good or better condition. If a single item has a value of $500 or more, an appraisal will now be required. The IRS has the authority to deny a deduction for items of minimal value. Former President Clinton once deducted his underwear. His would still count because it would probably exceed "minimal" value as a collector's piece. But, *my* deduction's gone!

Section 529 Plan Distributions: Qualified distributions from a Section 529 Education Plan are currently tax-free. But, the tax exclusion was scheduled to "sunset" or expire after 2010. The exclusion is now permanent, and the cloud that had been shadowing the issue since its original passage is removed.

---

*This provision was extended through 2009 by the Emergency Economic Stabilization Act of 2008.

Annual Form 5500-Z Threshold: The threshold for requiring the filing of the annual Form 555-EZ for one participant retirement plans was $100,000. It's been increased to $250,000. Less paperwork is always good!

Direct Rollovers to a Roth from Non-IRA Accounts: After 2007, if your adjusted gross income is $100,000 or less, you can make a direct rollover to a Roth IRA from any employer-sponsored retirement plan, e.g., a 401(k). Currently, you can only convert money in a traditional IRA to a Roth IRA. So, you'd have to first roll the 401(k) into an IRA, and then roll the IRA account into the Roth account. Combine this with the elimination of the income limitation in 2010 for Roth conversions included in the Tax Increase Prevention and Reconciliation Act of 2005 (passed in 2006), and you have strong incentives to fund your retirement with a Roth account.

Savers Tax Credit Made Permanent: If your income isn't more than $25,000 ($50,000 on a joint return), you can potentially get a Savers Credit of as much as $1,000. That's $1,000 off your tax, not just your income. This credit, scheduled to expire in 2006, has been made permanent, and is now subject to inflation adjustments. Check out Form 8880 at www.irs.gov to see how much you can save.

Direct Deposit of Your Refund into an IRA: Starting this year, you can tell the IRS to directly deposit your refund into as many as three different accounts, including your IRA! Use Form 8888 also available at www.irs.gov.

Retirement Plan Limits: The Economic Growth and Tax Relief Reconciliation Act of 2001 "sunsets" after December 31, 2010. That means that none of the changes remain in effect unless reenacted by Congress. This tax act permanently extends the increased retirement plan limits. That means that the higher contribution limits, e.g., $5,000 in an IRA for 2008 and after ($4,000 for 2006), and $15,000 for a 401(k) ($15,500 for 2007) are here to stay, and both will be indexed for inflation in the future.

401(k) Stretch: As of January 1, 2007, 401(k)s have the same stretch-out flexibility as IRAs. Inherited 401(k)s can now be converted into an inherited IRA for, say, your kids, with the tax deferral going over their own life expectancies, which could be decades. Before the change, if you left your 401(k) to a nonspouse beneficiary, you also bequeathed those heirs a tax headache. Now, a 20-year-old heir gets 63 years to withdraw the fund. You could always take the money sooner, without penalty, but you'd pay the tax.

Penalty-Free Withdrawals: Military reservists called to active duty can receive payments from their IRAs, 401(k) plans, and 403(b) tax sheltered annuities, without having to pay the 10 percent early distribution tax. To qualify, the reservist must be called to active duty for at least 180 days or for an indefinite period. The best part? Eligible reservists activated after September 11, 2001, and before December 31, 2007, qualify for this relief. If you do qualify, and have paid the tax in a prior year, file Form 1040X to get a refund. You can normally amend up to 3 years after the due date of the return. Get the Form 1040X from www.irs.gov.

In addition, payouts from state and local pension plans to public safety employees such as firefighters, police, and EMS technicians who retire after turning age 50 are also exempt from the 10 percent penalty.

C Tax Relief and Health Care Act of 2006

Congress didn't care if the tax forms were already printed. Members played politics until December 9, 2006, and the bill became law on December 20.

Here's what it provided:

EXTENDERS

1. State and local sales tax deduction—extended through 2007

2. Qualified tuition deduction—extended through 2007

3. Educator expense deduction—extended through 2007

4. Research tax credit—extended through 2007

5. The election to include combat pay in earned income for calculating the earned income credit—extended through 2007

6. Contributions to Archer Medical Savings Accounts—extended through 2007.

NEW DEDUCTIONS

1. Mortgage insurance—now deductible for 2007 *only*, for contracts issued in 2007. The deduction phases out notably by 10 percent for each $1,000 by which your adjusted gross income exceeds $100,000 (10 percent for each $500 and $50,000 for singles).

2. Gain on the sale of musical compositions or musical copyrights created by your personal efforts (or received by gift) is now permanently treated as the sale of a capital asset. This provision was set to expire after 2010.

3. The annual deductible limitation of Health Savings Account contributions is repealed. For 2007, HSA contributions can go to $2,850 for single coverage and $5,650 for family coverage, even if the deductible is less than that.

WHISTLE-BLOWERS

Report a tax cheat and now you may get a reward with a floor of 15 percent and a cap of 30 percent of the proceeds collected.

CREDIT FOR PRIOR YEAR MINIMUM TAX

If you have any unused minimum tax credit carryforward from 2003 or earlier years, your minimum tax credit allowable for 2007 is not less than the "AMT refundable credit amount." In addition, a portion of the credit may be refundable in 2007. That means, if the refundable part of the credit is more than your tax, you can get a refund of the difference. To figure the refundable amount of your minimum tax credit, and the AMT refundable credit amount, apply the rules that follow below.

Long-Term Unused Minimum Tax Credit

To figure the refundable amount of your minimum tax credit, you must first determine whether you have any "long-term unused minimum tax credit." Your long-term unused minimum tax credit is the amount of your minimum tax credit carryforward from 2003 (2003 Form 8801, line 26), reduced by the amount of any minimum tax credits you claimed for 2004, 2005, and 2006 (line 25 of your 2004, 2005, and 2006 Forms 8801).

AMT Refundable Credit Amount

After you figure your long-term unused minimum tax credit, you then must figure your "AMT refundable credit amount."

If Your Long-Term Unused Minimum Tax Credit Is . . .	THEN Your AMT Refundable Credit Amount Generally Is . . .
Less than $5,000	Your long-term unused minimum tax credit
At least $5,000, but not more than $25,000	$5,000
More than $25,000	20% of your long-term unused minimum tax credit

The AMT refundable credit amount is reduced if your adjusted gross income (AGI) exceeds certain threshold amounts based on your filing status. The AGI threshold amounts for 2007 are in the table that follows. Your AMT refundable credit amount is reduced by 2 percent (.02) for every $2,500 ($1,250 if your filing status is married filing separately) that your AGI exceeds the threshold amount. Use your 2006 tax return as a guide in figuring your AGI (2006 Form 1040, line 38, or Form 1040NR, line 36) for 2007.

If you are filing Form 2555, 2555-EZ, or 4563, or you are excluding income from sources within Puerto Rico, you must refigure your AGI by adding back any foreign earned income and housing exclusion (2006 Form 2555, line 45, or 2006 Form 2555-EZ, line 18), foreign housing deduction (2006 Form 2555, line 50), income from American Samoa that you are excluding (2006 Form 4563, line 15), and income from Puerto Rico that you are excluding.

For 2007, the AMT refundable credit amount is reduced if your AGI is more than the applicable amount in the second column of the following table and is eliminated if your AGI is more than the applicable amount in the third column.

Filing Status	AGI That Reduces Credit	AGI That Eliminates Credit
Single	$156,400	$278,900
Married filing jointly or qualifying widow(er)	$234,600	$357,100
Married filing separately	$117,300	$178,550
Head of household	$195,500	$318,000

Credit Refundable

The refundable amount of your credit is the amount by which your minimum tax credit for the year exceeds the amount your minimum tax credit would be without regard to the above rules.

Form 8801

To claim the refundable and nonrefundable parts of this credit, use the 2007 Form 8801, Credit for Prior Year Minimum Tax—Individuals, Estates, and Trusts.

CHAPTER 17

Tax Reform, 2007–2008

"Taxation is the art of plucking the chicken so as to get the maximum number of feathers with the minimum amount of squawking."

LOUIS RÉNN from Peter Vico, CPA

"The current tax system is very unstable."

JOHN BUCKLEY
Majority chief tax counsel for the House Ways and Means Committee, November 6, 2007

Congress appears to have an annual need to tinker with the Tax Code. Here's a summary of the major litigation over the last few years:

A The Mortgage Forgiveness Debt Relief Act of 2007

Call me Scrooge! Congress and President Bush handed a $1.153 billion Christmas gift to the American public—much of which will go to the wealthy.

B The New Debt Relief Act

Here's the deal. On December 20, 2007, the president signed H.R. 3648, the Mortgage Forgiveness Debt Relief Act of 2007. This new law excludes from income as much as $2 million in debt relief on a mortgage foreclosure or renegotiation.

Under prior law, if your bank or mortgage company forgave part or all of your debt, that relief was considered taxable income. You had borrowed money and no longer had to pay it back. Borrowed money normally isn't taxable because you have the obligation to pay it back. Now you don't. Since it wasn't a gift, unless you are insolvent, you should have "income."

Under the new law, up to $2 million in debt forgiveness on your primary residence escapes taxation for the years 2007–2012 (extended beyond 2009 in 2008). The original House bill sought permanent relief. But the Senate limited the exclusion to three years. At the signing ceremony at the White House, President Bush applauded the new law. "With this bill, Congress has taken a strong step to address the turbulence in the housing market."

WHY IT'S WRONG

Too bad everybody was so busy playing to the media, that they didn't think about what they were doing. My problem with the law isn't the objective. Debt relief limited to the middle-class taxpayer whose interest rate exploded while the value of his or her house cratered is appropriate. But, that's not where the big money is going.

This law excludes as much as *$2 million* in debt relief. Personally, I know very few people making less than $250,000 a year who qualify for a $2 million mortgage. If you have a $2 million mortgage, you're more likely than not to be in the 35 percent bracket. That's a $700,000 reduction in your taxes—paid for by the rest of us!

For 2007, couples filing joint returns were in the 25 percent bracket with taxable incomes over $63,700. Two million dollars in debt relief at that level is still a half-million dollars. That's more than most teachers make in 5 years, before tax.

If you're smart enough to get a $2 million loan, you should be smart enough to pay it back—or eat the tax when your debt is forgiven. I'd cap the relief at $500,000 (sorry California) and exclude those with adjusted gross incomes over $200,000. At least the forgiven debt reduces the basis in the house. But, if you quality, the $500,000 gain exclusion on the sale is still allowable.

HOW NOT TO REDUCE REAL ESTATE SPECULATION

The new law also extends, for 3 years, through 2010, the deductibility of private mortgage insurance. While I like anything that can be deducted, I must be missing something here.

My understanding of the housing crises is that we want to temper, rather than encourage, real estate speculation. Private mortgage insurance is for those who borrow more than 80 percent of the value of their homes. By making the premiums deductible, the government, with our money, is financing higher leverage and increasing the risk. Isn't that what we're trying *not* to do?

WHAT ELSE IS IN THE NEW ACT

- Surviving spouses get a real estate break. If a surviving spouse sells a personal residence within 2 years of the other spouse's death, the survivor qualifies for the $500,000 gain exclusion. Normally, a single taxpayer would be limited to a gain exclusion of only $250,000. This provision applies only to sales after December 31, 2007. It's projected to cost $67 million over the next 10 years.

- Certain state and local government payments to volunteer firefighters and emergency medical responders are excluded from income. That's projected to reduce tax revenue by $267 million over the next 10 years.

- In an attempt to partially offset these tax breaks, Congress imposed and increased late filing penalties for partnership and S corporation tax returns and increased estimated tax payments by some large corporate taxpayers by 1.5 percent. The partnership penalty jumps from $50 per partner per month for up to 5 months to $85 per partner per month for up to 12 months. The new S corporation penalty is also $85 per shareholder per month for up to 12 months.

Sorry, I really don't care what color crayon they're using. That's not going to cover the cost of our latest federal giveaways.

C The Economic Stimulus Act of 2008

THE REBATE

Under the Economic Stimulus Act of 2008 signed into law on February 13, 2008, more than 130 million American households received economic stimulus payments beginning in May. The only way to get one in 2008 was to file a federal tax return for 2007. This filing requirement also applied to some people who did not normally file, including many low-income people and recipients of Social Security, certain benefits received from the Department of Veterans Affairs, and certain railroad retirement benefits.

The rebate is really an advanced payment of a credit against your 2008 taxes. It has two components; the basic credit and the qualifying child credit.

Eligible individuals are generally entitled to a basic credit equal to the greater of:

- Net income tax liability (generally, total tax liability less nonrefundable tax credits other than the child credit) up to $600 ($1,200 in the case of a joint return)

- $300 ($600 in the case of a joint return) if an individual has either (1) a minimum of $3,000 in earned income, Social Security benefits, and veterans' disability payments; or (2) a net income tax liability of at least $1 and gross income greater than $8,950 for single individuals and married individuals filing separate returns; $17,900 for married individuals filing a joint return; or $11,500 for individuals filing as head of household

If you're eligible for any portion of the basic credit, you may also be eligible for a credit of $300 per qualifying child. In general, you're eligible to claim a $300 credit for each child who:

- Qualifies as your dependent, and

- Is under age 17 (and will not reach age 17 in 2008), and

- Is your son, daughter, stepchild, sibling, stepbrother, stepsister, or a child or grandchild of one of these individuals

The recovery rebate credit is phased out for individuals with higher incomes. Specifically, your total rebate credit (the sum of both the basic credit and any qualifying child credit) is reduced by 5 percent of the amount by which your adjusted gross income (AGI) exceeds $75,000 ($150,000 if you file a joint return with your spouse).

For example, a married couple filing a joint return with two qualifying children is potentially eligible for a total rebate credit of $1,800 ($1,200 basic credit and $300 per qualifying child), assuming their net income tax liability is at least $1,200. If the combined AGI of the couple is $160,000, however, they will be entitled to a credit of only $1,300 (their AGI exceeds $150,000 by $10,000; 5 percent of $10,000 is $500; $1,800 − $500 = $1,300). If the combined AGI of the couple was $186,000, they would be entitled to no rebate credit at all.

Assuming that you're otherwise entitled to the full basic credit, your total rebate credit is limited (or phased out entirely) according to the following AGI ranges:[*]

Table A.   Individuals Who File Married Filing Jointly

Qualifying Children	Phase-out Begins	No Credit After
No Children	$150,000 AGI	$174,000 AGI
1 Child	$150,000 AGI	$180,000 AGI
2 Children	$150,000 AGI	$186,000 AGI
3 Children	$150,000 AGI	$192,000 AGI
4 Children	$150,000 AGI	$198,000 AGI

Table B.   All Other Individuals

Qualifying Children	Phase-out Begins	No Credit After
No Children	$75,000 AGI	$87,000 AGI
1 Child	$75,000 AGI	$93,000 AGI
2 Children	$75,000 AGI	$99,000 AGI
3 Children	$75,000 AGI	$105,000 AGI
4 Children	$75,000 AGI	$111,000 AGI

* Tables provided by Stephen D. Leightman of RBC Wealth Management.

If you don't file for 2007 and qualify, you can get the credit on your 2008 tax return. If you don't qualify in 2008, but you did quality based on 2007 numbers, the IRS will not go after any dollars already sent to you. If your 2008 figures qualify you for a larger credit than you got, the difference can be claimed against your 2008 tax.

INCREASED EXPENSING

- In general, Section 179 provides that, instead of depreciating property, a business with a sufficiently small amount of annual property purchases may choose to expense the cost of the property. For taxable years beginning in 2008, the Economic Stimulus Act increased the Section 179 expensing limit allowing more property to be currently expensed.

- The Economic Stimulus Act increased the maximum Section 179 expense deduction to $250,000 for qualified Section 179 property that is placed in service in tax years that begin in 2008. This is a 95 percent increase from the previous limitation of $128,000.

- The Economic Stimulus Act also increased the total amount of qualifying property a taxpayer could purchase before the Section 179 expensing limit begins to be reduced. Under the new law, the $250,000 deduction amount is reduced only when a business acquires more than $800,000 of qualifying property. Prior to changes made by the Economic Stimulus Act, the reduction began when a business acquired more than $510,000 of qualifying property.

- The new law does not alter the Section 179 expense limit for sport utility vehicles, which remains at $25,000.

SPECIAL DEPRECIATION ALLOWANCE

- The Economic Stimulus Act also provided a 50 percent special depreciation allowance for property acquired and placed in service during 2008. Depreciation is an income tax deduction that allows you to recover the cost or other basis of certain property over several years. It is an annual allowance for the wear and tear, deterioration, or obsolescence of the property.

- Under the new law, you are entitled to depreciate 50 percent of the adjusted basis (after subtracting any section 179 deduction taken on that property) of qualified property during the year the property is placed in service. For example, if you purchased and placed in service in 2008 a single piece of property at a cost of $450,000 that qualified for section 179 expensing and the 50 percent special depreciation allowance, $250,000 of the cost could be immediately expensed (under Section 179), and the remaining $200,000 of adjusted basis would be available for the 50 percent special depreciation allowance. You would also be permitted to take regular depreciation on the remaining $100,000 of adjusted basis during that year. This is similar to the special depreciation allowance that was previously available for certain property placed in service generally before January 1, 2005, often referred to as "bonus depreciation."

- The types of property that qualify for the 50 percent special depreciation allowance included property with a recovery period of 20 years or less, off-the-shelf computer software, water utility property, and qualified leasehold improvement property.

- To qualify for the 50 percent special depreciation allowance, you must meet all of the following tests:

  ○ You must have acquired the property after December 31, 2007, and before January 1, 2009. If a binding contract to acquire the property existed before January 1, 2008, the property does not qualify for the special depreciation allowance.

  ○ The property must be placed in service before January 1, 2009 (before January 1, 2010, for certain transportation property and certain property with a long productions period).

  ○ The original use of the property must begin with you after December 31, 2007. In other words, the property must be "new" property.

- Prior to the enactment of the Economic Stimulus Act, the total depreciation amount (including the Section 179 deduction) a business could deduct for a passenger automobile was $2,960. The Economic Stimulus Act increased this limitation by $8,000. Therefore, the maximum limit is increased to $10,960 for automobiles for which the special bonus depreciation allowance is claimed.

- Prior to the enactment of the Economic Stimulus Act, the total depreciation amount (including the Section 179 deduction) a business could deduct for a truck or van used in a business and first placed in service in 2008 was $3,160. The Economic Stimulus Act increased this limitation by $8,000. The new maximum limit is increased to $11,160 for trucks and vans for which the special bonus depreciation is claimed.

- The Economic Stimulus Act is the most recent legislation that provides depreciation tax benefits. Previously, the Job Creation and Worker Assistance Act of 2002 allowed an additional first-year depreciation deduction equal to 30 percent of the adjusted basis of qualified property for property acquired on or after September 11, 2001, and generally placed in service before January 1, 2005. The Jobs and Growth Tax Relief Reconciliation Act of 2003 provided an additional first-year depreciation deduction equal to 50 percent of the adjusted basis of qualified property for property acquired after May 5, 2003, and generally placed in service before January 1, 2005.

D The Heroes Earnings Assistance and Relief Act of 2008

This act was signed into law on June 17, 2008, as a military tax relief bill. This new law includes the following provisions:

- Soldiers receiving combat pay can have their money counted as income for purposes of the earned income credit.

- Spouses of active duty military personnel can receive economic stimulus payments even if they do not have a Social Security number.

- It makes permanent a provision allowing tax-free withdrawals from IRA accounts for reservists.

- It permits recipients of military death benefit gratuities to roll over the amounts received, tax-free, to a Roth IRA or an educational savings account.

- It increases the penalty for failure to file a return within 60 days of the due date to the lesser of $135 or 100 percent of the amount required to be shown on the returns.

- It allows reservists to tap unused funds from flexible spending accounts (FSAs) without being subject to the "use it or lose it" regulations.

- It provides a tax credit for companies with 50 or fewer employees who pay reservists the difference between their civilian work and the pay they received while on active duty.

E The Housing and Economic Recovery Act of 2008

Remember it's an election year. And the economy is not so hot. So here's what Congess cooked up in July to cushion the cratering of the housing market:

- *First-Time Home Buyer Tax Credit.* The new law gives first-time home buyers a refundable tax credit of 10 percent of the purchase price, up to $7,500 ($3,750 for married people filing separately). The credit begins to phase out at the $150,000 adjusted gross income level for joint filers ($75,000 for other filers) and is not available for joint filers with income above $170,000 ($95,000 for other filers). It's also not available to nonresident aliens, those who qualify for a similar District of Columbia credit, or those whose financing comes from tax-exempt mortgage revenue bonds. The credit is effective for homes purchased on or after April 9, 2008, and before July 1, 2009. But this credit must be paid back, in equal installments for 15 years. So if you get the full $7,500, you'd pay on additional "tax" of $500 each year. Payments start 2 years after the year in which the residence is purchased or earlier, if you sell the house or if it is no longer your principal residence. You qualify as a "first-time home buyer" if neither you nor your spouse had any ownership interest in a principal residence during the 3-year period before the new home is purchased. The best news: If you die, you don't have to pay back the credit.

- *Nonitemizer Property Tax Deduction.* In the past, if you took the standard deduction, you got no tax benefit from the real estate taxes you paid. But, for 2008 and 2009 only, the new law gives nonitemizers a limited deduction for state and local real property taxes by increasing the amount of their standard deduction by the lesser of: (1) the amount of real property taxes paid during the year, or (2) $500 ($1,000 for a married couple filing jointly). That would raise the standard deduction to $5,950 for singles, $11,900 on joint returns, and $8,500 for head of household. If you still have a big mortgage, you're probably itemizing. But if you paid off your mortgage, lost the interest deduction, and now take the standard deduction, put a smile on your face!

OFFSETS

The Housing Act had lots of other benefits for the housing industry, including changes to the low-income housing tax credit, tax-exempt housing bonds, mortgage revenue bonds, REIT reforms, and benefits for military personnel. These mortgages had to be paid for, and here's is how Congess did it:

- *Credit Card Information Reporting.* Under the new law, banks and other processors of merchant payment card transactions (credit and debit cards) will be required to report a merchant's annual gross payment card receipts to the IRS (and to the merchant). The law also requires reporting on third-party network transactions (such as ones used by many online retailers). The new treatment is effective for sales made on or after January 1, 2011. But the law creates an exception from information reporting if the aggregate value of third-party network transactions does not exceed $20,000 for the calendar year or the aggregate number of these transactions does not exceed 200. Congress is looking to close the tax gap. If a merchant refuses to give a tax identification number (TIN), there's a required 28 percent withholding on *gross* payments.

- *Reduced Home Sale Exclusion.* Prior to this act, if a second home became a principal residence, after two years the owner could sell it and exclude up to $250,000 in gain from the income—or up to $500,000 for couples filing jointly. Now, gain from the sale of a principal residence home will no longer be excluded from gross income for periods that the home was not used as the principal residence ("nonqualifying use"). This new income inclusion rule applies to home sales after December 31, 2008, and is based only on non-qualified use periods that begin on or after January 1, 2009. A period of absence, (for example, vacations) generally counts as qualifying use if it occurs after the home was used as the principal residence. The amount of gain allocated to periods of nonqualified use is the amount of gain multiplied by a fraction, the numerator of which is the aggregate period of nonqualified use during which the property was owned by the taxpayer and the denominator of which is the period the taxpayer owned the property. Remember that "nonqualified use" for this computation does not include any use prior to 2009. Say you bought a house on January 1, 2009, for $400,000 and rent it for 2 years, taking $20,000 in depreciation. On January 1, 2011, you move into it and use it as your principal residence. You move out on January 1, 2013, and sell it for $700,000 on January 1, 2014. The rental period

(2009–2010) is nonqualifying use. All use after December 31, 2010, qualifies, including 2013 when you moved out. You owned the property a total of 5 years (2009, 2010, 2011, 2012, and 2013). Forty percent of the gain (2 years out of 5 owned) or $128,000 is taxable. The $20,000 gain attributable to depreciation is recaptured at rates as high as 25 percent. Up to $192,000 in gain can still be excluded.

CHAPTER 18

2009 Tax Changes

*"It's just as important to get it done right
as it is to get it done quickly."*

BRUCE JUSTIN,
Executive Vice President,
U.S. Chamber of Commerce

On February 17, 2009, President Obama signed into law H.R. 1, the American Recovery and Reinvestment Act of 2009 (ARRA). The nearly $800 billion plan seeks to stimulate the economy and address the current financial challenges we face through a combination of $326 billion in tax relief, aid to states and municipalities, and direct federal spending. ARRA includes a wide variety of tax relief provisions for businesses, low- and moderate-income individuals, and families. These are discussed below.

196 "Making Work Pay" Tax Credit

This provision of the American Recovery and Reinvestment Act of 2009 cuts taxes for more than 95 percent of working families in the United States. For 2009 and 2010 the provision provides a *refundable* tax credit of up to $400 for working individuals and $800 for working families. This refundable tax credit is calculated at a rate of 6.2 percent of earned income and will phase out for taxpayers with adjusted gross income in excess of $75,000 ($150,000 for married couples filing jointly). You can receive this benefit through a reduction in the amount of income tax that is withheld from your paycheck or through claiming the credit on your tax return using new Schedule M.

Phase-out

Unmarried taxpayer (maximum credit)

MAGI	Credit before Phase-out	Credit after Phase-out
$75,000	$400	$400
$80,000	$400	$300
$85,000	$400	$200
$90,000	$400	$100
$95,000	$400	$ 0

Married taxpayer (maximum credit)

MAGI	Credit before Phase-out	Credit after Phase-out
$150,000	$800	$800
$160,000	$800	$600
$170,000	$800	$400
$180,000	$800	$200
$190,000	$800	$ 0

If you have no other earned income, but are receiving Social Security, SSI, railroad retirement, or veteran disability compensation benefits, your credit is $250. A retired federal employee also qualifies for the $250 credit ($500 on a joint return if both spouses are eligible). Both Social Security and retired government employee benefits are one-shot deals, while the regular "making work pay" credit is available in both 2009 and 2010.

197 Reducing the COBRA Bite

If you worked for a company that had 20 or more employees, COBRA (Consolidated Omnibus Budget Reconciliation Act) entitles you to continue your health benefits for 18 months after you leave your employer. It's very expensive, though—an average of $1,069 a month for a family plan.

The American Recovery and Reinvestment Act of 2009 provides for a 65 percent subsidy on COBRA and COBRA-comparable state continuation premiums for certain assistance-eligible individuals for up to 9 months. (Note: Comparable COBRA coverage is not defined in ARRA.)

Who Is Eligible for the Subsidy?

With respect to state continuation, assistance-eligible individuals are qualified beneficiaries under COBRA-comparable state continuation who meet the following:

- Had their employment involuntarily terminated between September 1, 2008, and December 31, 2009, and extended to May 31, 2010, by the Temporary Extension Act of 2010;

- Elected continuation coverage of health benefits, as made available under state law, at any time during the period beginning September 1, 2008, and ending December 31, 2009, and extended to May 31, 2010, by the Temporary Extension Act of 2010;

- Have not exhausted their state continuation right as mandated by state law;

- The individuals' modified adjusted gross income is not more than $125,000 (individual filer) or $250,000 (joint filer).

Under ARRA, assistance-eligible individuals are required to pay only 35 percent of the cost of the continuation coverage for a period of 9 months. The premium reduction period will begin with the first coverage period following the enactment of ARRA (generally March 1, 2009).

198 First-Time Home Buyer Credit Expanded

The Housing and Economic Recovery Act of 2008 gives first-time home buyers a refundable tax credit of 10 percent of the purchase price, up to $7,500 ($3,750 for married people filing separately). The credit begins to phase out at the $150,000 adjusted gross income level for joint filers ($75,000 for other filers) and is not available for joint filers with income above $170,000 ($95,000 for other filers). It's also not available to nonresident aliens, those who qualify for a similar District of Columbia credit, or those whose financing comes from tax-exempt mortgage revenue bonds. The credit is effective for homes purchased on or after April 9, 2008, and before July 1, 2009. But this credit must be paid back in equal installments for 15 years. So if you get the full $7,500, you'd pay an additional "tax" of $500 each year. Payments start two years after the year in which the residence is purchased or earlier, if you sell the house or if it is no longer your principal residence. You qualify as a first-time home buyer if neither you nor your spouse had any ownership interest in a principal residence during the 3-year period before the new home was purchased. The best news is this: If you die, you don't have to pay back the credit.

The American Recovery and Reinvestment Act of 2009 changed the rules for those buying a principal residence after January 1, 2009, and before December 1, 2009. It increased the credit to $8,000 and eliminated the obligation to repay (unless the house is sold within 3 years of purchase).

The phase-out to qualify remains the same; you still can't buy from a relative, and multiple buyers can allocate the credit in any "reasonable" way. Whether or not you qualify is determined on the date of closing. So if you qualify and close, and then marry someone who doesn't qualify, you still get the credit. If you purchase in 2009, you can amend your 2008 return and receive the credit refund before filing your 2009 return in 2010. This provision not only gets your money faster, but it allows you to qualify on the basis of 2008 income if your 2009 income is too high.

If you bought in 2008 and financed with tax-exempt mortgage revenue bonds, you didn't qualify. This restriction has been removed for 2009 purchases.

199 American Opportunity Tax Credit

For 2009 and 2010, the American Recovery and Reinvestment Act of 2009 provides taxpayers with a new "American Opportunity" tax credit of up to $2,500 of the cost of tuition and related expenses paid during the taxable year. Under this new tax credit, you will receive a tax credit based on 100 percent of the first $2,000 of tuition and related expenses (*including course materials and books*) paid during the taxable year and 25 percent of the next $2,000 of tuition and related expenses paid during the taxable year. Forty percent of the credit will be refundable. This tax credit is subject to a phase-out for taxpayers with adjusted gross income in excess of $80,000 ($160,000 for married couples filing jointly).

This credit is available for each of the 4 years of college. Graduate students are not eligible.

The credit can't be claimed against the following sources:

a) 529 Plans

b) Tax-free scholarships

c) Pells grants

d) Coverdell education savings account (ESA)

e) Employer-provided education assistance

f) Military education assistance

g) Any other tax-free educational assistance

Only one of the following credits/deductions can be selected per student:

a) The new American Opportunity Education tax credit

b) The existing $2,000 Lifetime Learning tax credit

c) The $4,000 above-the-line deduction

The new American Opportunity Education tax credit is the best of the three because it is a higher credit than the Lifetime Learning tax credit, and a $4,000 deduction at most provides $1,400 in relief in the 35 percent bracket.

200 Energy Credits

ARRA increases the energy tax credit for homeowners who make energy-efficient improvements to their existing homes. The 2009 law increases the credit rate to 30 percent of the cost of all qualifying improvements and raises the maximum credit limit to $1,500 for improvements placed in service in 2009 and 2010.

The credit applies to improvements such as adding insulation, energy-efficient exterior windows, and energy-efficient heating and air-conditioning systems.

A similar credit was available for 2007 but was not available in 2008. You should be aware that the standards in the new law are higher than the standards for the credit that was available in 2007 for products that qualify as energy efficient for purposes of this tax credit. The IRS will issue guidance that will allow manufacturers to certify that their products meet these new standards.

Until the guidance is released, you generally may continue to rely on manufacturers' certifications that were provided under the old guidance. For exterior windows and skylights, you may continue to rely on Energy Star labels in determining whether property purchased before June 1, 2009, qualifies for the credit.

201 Plug-in Electric *Drive* Vehicle Credit (Sec. 1141)

The new law modifies the credit for qualified plug-in electric drive vehicles purchased or leased after December 31, 2009. To qualify, vehicles must be newly purchased or leased, have four or more wheels, have a gross vehicle weight rating of less than 14,000 pounds, and draw propulsion using a battery with at least 4 kilowatt hours that can be recharged from an external source of electricity. The minimum amount of the credit for qualified plug-in electric drive vehicles is $2,500, and the credit tops out at $7,500, depending on the battery capacity. The full amount of the credit will be reduced with respect to a manufacturer's vehicles after the manufacturer has sold at least 200,000 vehicles. Only one credit per vehicle. Note, this credit is based on energy savings rather than cost.

202 Plug-in Electric Vehicle Credit (Sec. 1142)

The new law also creates a special tax credit for two types of plug-in vehicles—certain low-speed electric vehicles and two- or three-wheeled vehicles. The amount of the credit is 10 percent of the cost of the vehicle, up to a maximum credit of $2,500 for purchases made after February 17, 2009, and before January 1, 2012. To qualify, a vehicle must be either a low-speed vehicle propelled by an electric motor that draws electricity from a battery with a capacity of 4 kilowatt hours or more or be a two- or three-wheeled vehicle propelled by an electric motor that draws electricity from a battery with the capacity of 2.5 kilowatt hours. A taxpayer may not claim this credit if the plug-in electric *drive* vehicle credit is allowable. Only one credit per vehicle. Note, this credit is based on cost.

203 Conversion Kits (Sec. 1143)

The new law also provided a tax credit for plugin electric drive conversion kits. The credit is equal to 10 percent of the cost of converting a vehicle to a qualified plug-in electric drive motor vehicle and placed in service after February 17, 2009. The maximum amount of the credit is $4,000. The credit does not apply to conversions made after December 31, 2011. A taxpayer may claim this credit even if the taxpayer claimed a hybrid vehicle credit for the same vehicle in an earlier year.

204 Treatment of Alternative Motor Vehicle Credit as a Personal Credit Allowed against AMT (Sec. 1144)

Starting in 2009, the new law allows the Alternative Motor Vehicle credit, including the tax credit for purchasing hybrid vehicles, to be applied against the Alternative Minimum Tax. Prior to the new law, the Alternative Motor Vehicle credit could not be used to offset the AMT. This means that the credit could not be taken if a taxpayer owed AMT or was reduced for some taxpayers who did not owe AMT.

205 AMT Patch

ARRA ups the AMT exemption to:

	New	Old
Joint/surviving spouse	$70,950	$69,950
Unmarried	46,700	46,200
Married filing separately	35,475	34,975

206 Earned Income Credit

For years 2009 and 2010, ARRA increases the EIT credit percent for families with three or more qualifying children to 45 percent.

For 2009, the credit is 45 percent of $12,570, or a maximum credit of $5,656.50.

207 Child Tax Credit

Part of your child tax credit is refundable. ARRA increases that amount for 2009 and 2010 from 15 percent of the excess over $12,550 to only 15 percent of the excess over $3,000.

For example: You have $15,000 of earned income, three qualifying children, and income taxes of $1,000. Your child credit is $3,000, but because it is generally nonrefundable, only $1,000 is usable in reducing taxes to zero. However, because you have three qualifying children, the earned income formula can trigger up to $1,800 of refundable credit (.15 × $12,000 [$15,000 − $3,000]). Without the change, the refundable portion would be $367.50 (.15 × $2,450 [$15,000 − $12,550]). You increase your refund by $1,432.50 ($1,800 − $367.50).

208 Section 529 Plans

ARRA expands the definition of higher education expenses for 2009 and 2010 to include the purchase of computer technology, equipment,

Internet access, and related services. These expenses are now in addition to tuition, fees, books, supplies, and equipment.

209 Unemployment Benefits

For 2009, the first $2,400 received in unemployment benefits comes to you income tax free.

210 Qualified Transportation Benefits

The monthly exclusion for employer-provided transit and van pool benefits is increased from $120 to the same as the exclusion for employer-provided parking—$230 per month. This is effective for all months beginning on or after February 17, 2009, through December 2010.

211 Estimated Taxes

For 2009 the safe harbor for estimated taxes has been reduced to 90 percent of your 2008 total tax if:

a) Your 2008 adjusted gross income is less than $500,000, and

b) More than 50 percent of your 2008 adjusted gross income was from a small business—one that had an average of fewer than 500 employees in 2008.

212 Motor Vehicle Sales Tax

You have to buy a *new* vehicle that's a passenger car, motorcycle, motor home, or light truck with a gross vehicle weight of not more than 8,500 pounds (except for the motor home); you have to buy it on or after February 17, 2009, through December 31, 2009. This is for your 2009 return only.

If so, the state or local sales tax on the first $49,500 is deductible on Schedule L as an added standard deduction. or as an itemized deduction.

If you elect to itemize and deduct state and local sales taxes rather than income taxes, you get no benefit from this provision.

The IRS and the Treasury have determined that purchases made in states without a sales tax—such as Alaska, Delaware, Hawaii, Montana, New Hampshire, and Oregon—can also qualify for the deduction.

Taxpayers who purchase a new motor vehicle in states that do not have state sales taxes are entitled to deduct other fees or taxes imposed by the state or local government. The fees or taxes that qualify must be assessed on the purchase of the vehicle and must be based on the vehicle's sales price or as a per unit fee. According to the IRS, Congress intended for these fees or taxes to qualify for this special tax deduction.

The amount of the deduction is phased out for taxpayers whose modified adjusted gross income is between $125,000 and $135,000 for individual filers and between $250,000 and $260,000 for joint filers.

Six percent of $49,500 is $2,970. In the 35 percent bracket, that saves you a maximum of $1,039.50, unless your sales tax is more than 6 percent.

213 Business Depreciation

ARRA extended the 50 percent bonus depreciation to apply to property acquired and placed in service through December 31, 2009. This adds another $8,000 to the normal caps for new vehicles.

214 NOL Carrybacks

The rules for net operating losses of corporations, partnerships, or sole proprietors with average annual gross receipts of $15 million or less for each of the immediate 3 years have changed.

Normally, such losses are allowed to be carried back 2 years and then carried forward 20 years.

ARRA allows eligible small businesses to carry back such losses for 3, 4, or 5 years to offset and recover taxes previously paid during those years.

CHAPTER 19

More Tax Changes

"It's all political theater. It's not about legislating anymore. It's all for the next election that's coming up shortly."

Senator OLYMPIA SNOWE (R-Maine)
August 2010, before the Congress
congressional recess

"Today we are creating an IRS where the American taxpayer comes first and customer service is second to none."

Treasury Secretary ROBERT RUBIN and
Commissioner of Internal Revenue
CHARLES O. ROSSOTTI

"In the last decade, taxes have been raised four times explicitly for deficit redution. In the year following each hike, the deficit actually incrreased."

Senator DAN COATS 1993

Congress did manage to pass several tax changes earlier in the year. Here's a summary of the most important new laws and how to use them to keep more money in your pockets.

A   The Hiring Incentives to Restore Employment (HIRE) Act of 2010

The HIRE Act, signed into law on March 18, 2010, contained $18.6 billion in tax provisions including:

- Extension of higher limits for Section 179 small business expending through 2010, allowing small businesses to deduct up to $250,000 (increased by a subsequent tax law) from taxable income, but the value is decreased by the amount by which the cost of qualifying property placed in service exceeds $800,000.

- Payroll tax forgiveness for employers hiring individuals who have been unemployed or worked fewer than 40 hours for at least 60 days, beginning February 3, 2010, and ending December 31, 2010 (consider hiring students who spent time in class rather than working), and an additional income tax credit up to $1,000 for employers, equal to 6.2 percent of paid wages for every new employee retained for 52 weeks. Family members, other relatives, and household employees generally do not qualify for the credit but a spouse may qualify for the 6.2 percent Social Security exemption.

- Expansion of the Build America Bonds program to allow issuers of other qualified tax credit bonds used for construction of schools and energy-related projects to receive refundable credits. The bonds provide a direct subsidy of 65 percent of the interest payment to the bond issuer instead of the bond holder.

To pay for those tax breaks, the new law:

- Imposes a 30 percent withholding penalty on foreign financial institutions that do not agree to disclose their U.S. account holders to the IRS.

- Requires taxpayers to disclose their foreign accounts on their U.S. tax returns.

- Increases the statute of limitations to 6 years for failure to report certain offshore transactions and income.

- Clarifies when a foreign trust is considered to have a U.S. beneficiary.

- Treats substitute dividend and dividend equivalent payments to foreign persons as dividends for purposes of U.S. withholding.

- Delays implementation of a law that would allow for simpler accounting of worldwide interest allocation until 2021.

- Increases corporate estimated tax payments for corporations with at least $1 billion in assets for the third quarters of 2014, 2015, and 2019.

B The Patient Protection and Affordable Care Act

This massive bill, signed into law on March 23, 2010, has provisions effective from 2010–2018. Here's what's scheduled:

2010

- Adoption credit—made refundable and extended through 2011; credit increased to $13,170 for 2010.
- 10 percent excise tax imposed on indoor tanning services effective July 1, 2010.
- Economic substance required for transactions mandated. Now a transaction must have a substantial nontax business purpose creating a meaningful change in economic position to be tax recognized.
- Student debt forgiven for medical professionals working in "underserved" areas escape taxation for years after December 31, 2008.

Many small businesses and tax-exempt organizations that provide health insurance coverage to their employees now qualify for a special tax credit. This is designed to encourage small business employers to offer health insurance coverage for the first time or to maintain coverage they already have. In general, the credit is available to small business employers who pay at least half the cost of single coverage for their employees.

The maximum credit is 35 percent of premiums paid in 2010 by eligible small business employers and 25 percent of premiums paid by eligible employers that are tax-exempt organizations. In 2014, this maximum credit increases to 50 percent of premiums paid by eligible small business employers and 35 percent of premiums paid by eligible employers that are tax-exempt organizations.

The credit is specifically targeted to help small businesses and tax-exempt organizations that primarily employ low- and moderate-income workers. It is generally available to employers who have fewer than 25 full-time equivalent (FTE) employees and who are paying wages averaging less than $50,000 per employee per year. Because the eligibility formula is based in part on the number of FTEs, not the number of employees, many businesses will qualify even if they employ more than 25 individual workers.

The maximum credit goes to smaller business employers—those with 10 or fewer FTEs—paying annual average wages of $25,000 or less.

Eligible small businesses can claim the credit as part of the general business credit starting with the 2010 income tax return they file in 2011. For tax-exempt employers, the IRS will provide further information on how to claim the credit.

2011

- Businesses must report the value of health-care benefits on employees' W-2.

- Money in health savings accounts, flexible spending accounts, and other health reimbursement arrangements can be used only for *prescribed* over-the-counter medicines or face a 20 percent penalty. Solution? Talk to your doctor.

- The 10 percent penalty for nonqualified use of funds from health savings accounts doubles to 20 percent.

2012

- New 1099 reporting mandated for all businesses making payments of over $600 over the course of a year to a corporation.

2013

This is when the major changes take effect:

- A 3.8 percent tax will be imposed on *unearned* (investment) income of individuals with incomes of more than $200,000 ($250,000 for joint filers). This would apply to rents, interest, dividends, royalties, capital gains, and so on and *only* to amounts in excess of those floors. Distributions from retirement accounts would not be taxed as unearned (investment) income nor would life insurance proceeds, municipal bond interest, and veterans benefits count.

The 3.8 percent Medicare surtax won't apply to all home sale profits after 2012. Most gains on sales of primary residences will be exempt. Only the portion of profits that exceeds the $250,000 or $500,000 exclusion will be subject to the tax.

But profits on sales of rental properties and second homes will be hit by the surtax, assuming that the seller's adjusted gross income is large enough.

What should you do? Consider Roth accounts because Roth withdrawals don't increase your income. Also consider installment sales to keep your income below the floors. Life insurance becomes more attractive as you can borrow against it without increasing your income and the proceeds are not subject to the tax.

- The normal 1.45 percent Hospital Insurance (HI) payroll tax on wages or earnings will be increased by 0.90 percent to 2.35 percent for individuals with income of more than $200,000 ($250,000 on a joint return). Again, only the excess over the floor would be subject to the added tax. Employers will still pay only 1.45 percent. Self-employed individuals who pay the additional 0.90 percent will not be able to deduct any part of the increase.

- The floor for claiming medical expenses increases from 7.5 percent of adjusted gross income to 10 percent. For those aged 65 or over the floor stays at 7.5 percent until 2016.

- Contributions to health-care flexible spending accounts limited to $2,500. This cap will be indexed to consumer price inflation beginning in 2014.

2014

- You will be required to have health insurance or face a tax of as much as 2.5 percent of taxable income. Those without coverage pay a tax penalty of the greater of $695 per year up to a maximum of three times that amount ($2,085) per family or 2.5 percent of household income. The penalty will be phased in according to the following schedule: $95 in 2014, $325 in 2015, and $695 in 2016 for the flat fee or 1 percent of taxable income in 2014, 2 percent of taxable income in 2015, and 2.5 percent of taxable income in 2016. Beginning after 2016, the penalty will be increased annually by the cost-of-living adjustment. Exemptions will be granted for financial hardship, religious objections, American Indians, those without coverage for less than 3 months, undocumented immigrants, incarcerated individuals, those for whom the lowest cost plan option exceeds 8 percent of an individual's income, and those with incomes below the tax filing threshold.

- Assess employers with more than 50 employees who do not offer coverage and have at least one full-time employee who receives a premium tax credit of $2,000 per full-time employee, excluding the first 30 employees from the assessment. Employers with more than 50 employees who offer coverage but have at least one full-time employee receiving a premium tax credit will pay the lesser of $3,000 for each employee receiving a premium credit or $2,000 for each full-time employee. Employers with 50 or fewer employees are exempt from any of the above penalties.

- Require employers who offer coverage to their employees to provide a free choice voucher to employees with incomes less than 400 percent of the federal poverty level whose share of the premium exceeds 8 percent but is less than 9.8 percent of their income and who choose to enroll in a plan in the exchange. The voucher amount is equal to what the employer would have paid to provide coverage to the employee under the employer's plan and will be used to offset the premium costs for the plan in which the employee is enrolled. Employers providing free choice vouchers will not be subject to penalties for employees who receive premium credits in the exchange.

2018

- A 40 percent excise tax on high-cost insurance plans goes into effect based on the amount of premium in excess of $10,200 ($27,500 for families). The tax is paid by the insurers or self-insured firms.

According to the tax policy center, 85 percent of the tax burden under the new law will be shouldered by the top 1 percent of taxpayers.

C Small Business Jobs Act of 2010

Signed into law by President Obama on September 27, 2010, the SBJA makes the following changes:

1. The Act extends the additional 50 percent first-year depreciation deduction through 2010. Fifty percent of the basis of the property can be deducted in the first year with the other 50 percent under normal depreciation rules. Let's take an example of a new (used doesn't count) SUV with a loaded weight of over 6,000 pounds costing $50,000 and used 100 percent for business. The first $25,000 is expensed, the maximum for the vehicle. Half the remaining cost of $25,000 ($12,500) is claimed as bonus depreciation. Normal depreciation is 20 percent of the $12,500 balance or $2,500. That's a total first-year deduction of $40,000 on a $50,000 purchase!

   For assets put in use after September 8, 2010, and before January 1, 2012, the bonus depreciation is 100 percent, allowing an immediate expense of assets with a useful life of 20 years or less, including machinery, land improvements, and mixed-purpose farm buildings.

2. Effective for 2010 and 2011, the maximum you can *expense under Section 179* is increased to $500,000. This number is reduced if capital expenditures exceed $2 million.

3. If you're self-employed, your *health insurance costs* have been deducted above the line. Starting 2010, your HI premiums will now also reduce your income subect to self-employment taxes. If your net self-employment income is more than $106,800, that's an additional 15.3 percent saved. So if you pay premiums of $10,000 and are in the 28 percent bracket, you save $2,800 in income taxes and an additional $1,530 in Social Security and Medicare taxes. See Schedule SE for this deduction.

4. The Act *delists cell phones* and other communications devices from "listed property." This removes the strict substantiation of use requirement and the limit on depreciation deductions.

5. The amount of *start up expenses* that can be deducted is increased from $5,000 to $10,000.

6. The Act eliminates 100 percent of both the regular tax and the AMT on the sale of *small business stock* acquired at original issue after September 27, 2010, and before January 1, 2011 provided you hold the stock for at least 5 years.

7. If you pay anybody $600 or more for *rental property services* (e.g., plumbers, painters, etc.), you will now have to file a Form 1099 MISC to report that income paid. (Repealed in 2011.)

8. Small businesses will now be able to *carry back general business credits* up to 5 years (as opposed to only 1) and offset both regular and AMT tax liabilities. A small business is a non–publicly traded corporation, partnership, or sole proprietorship with gross receipts of $50 million or less each year.

9. If your 401(k) offers a *Roth* option, you can now move funds from the regular 401(k) to the Roth so that future earnings will be tax-free. The same rule applies to Section 403(b) and Section 457(b) plans. Such *rollovers* are allowed, but any untaxed money will be subject to tax—but you can defer the tax until 2011 and 2012 if you convert in 2010.

The conversion is optional and your plan must allow it. It must be an eligible rollover distribution, such as resulting from termination, disability, death, or reaching age 59½. Certain distributions, such as the hardship distribution and minimum required distributions, are not eligible rollover distributions and are not eligible for conversion.

This provision is for distributions after September 27, 2010.

D The Tax Relief, Unemployment Insurance Reauthorization, and Job Creation Act of 2010

It was almost mid-December 2010 when Congress finally passed the Tax Relief, Unemployment Insurance Reauthorization, and Job Creation Act of 2010 (2010 Tax Relief Act). It basically said, "never mind." Extending provisions for just 2 years up through 2012, the Act sets up a major issue for the 2012 presidential election and merely postpones final decision making. Here's what's been extended and what's new.

INDIVIDUAL CHANGES

Tax Rates. The 2010 Tax Act extends all individual tax rates at 10, 15, 25, 28, 33, and 35 percent through December 31, 2012.

Capital Gains/Qualified Dividends. The Act also extends the maximum 15 percent rate (0 percent for those in the 10 and 15 percent tax bracket) for long-term capital gains and qualified dividends through December 31, 2012. Dividends from regulated investment companies (RICs), real estate investment trusts (REITs), and other qualified pass-through entities continue to qualify.

Itemized Deduction (Pease) Limitations. The Act repeals this reduction in itemized deductions based on income through December 31, 2012.

Person Exemption Phase-out. Prior to 2010, taxpayers with incomes above a certain level were subject to a reduction in their personal exemptions. The Act extends the repeal of this deduction reduction through December 31, 2012.

Marriage Penalty Relief. Prior legislation reduced the marriage penalty by increasing the basic standard deduction for a married couple to twice that of a single filer. The Act extends this marriage penalty relief through December 31, 2012.

Child Tax Credit. The Act extends the $1,000 child care credit through December 31, 2012. It was scheduled to fall to $500.

Earned Income Credit. The Act extends the enhanced earned income credit through December 31, 2012.

Adoption Credit/Exclusion. Prior legislation increased the dollar limitation for the adoption credit and increased the exclusion for employer-provided assistance to $10,000 increased by another $1,000 by the Patient Protection and Affordable Care Act for 2010 and 2011. The 2010 Act extends the enhancements to the credit and exclusion through December 31, 2012. However, the PPACA is not available after 2010.

Dependent Care Credit. The 2010 Act extends the enhanced dependent care credit through December 31, 2012.

Employer-Provided Child Care. Employers who provide child care facilities have been able to claim a 25 percent tax credit for qualified expenses and a 10 percent tax credit for qualified resource and referral services. The Act extends these credits through December 31, 2012.

Mortgage Insurance Premiums. Under current law, certain qualified mortgage insurance premiums are potentially allowable deductions. The 2010 Act extends this deduction for one year.

American Opportunity Tax Credit. The 2010 Act extends this four-year credit through December 31, 2010.

Educational Assistance Exclusion. The 2010 Act extends this exclusion of up to $5,250 in employer-provided education assistance through December 31, 2012.

Student Loan Interest Deduction. The 2010 Act extends through December 31, 2012, the elimination of the 60-month rule and the expanded income phase-out amount for this potential $2,500 deduction.

Coverdell Education Savings Accounts. Scheduled to fall back to $500, the maximum $2,000 annual contribution has been extended through December 31, 2012.

Annual Extenders. The following individual benefits and deductions have been extended for 2 years, 2010 and 2011. That means Congress will have to revisit them again next year:

- State and local sales tax deduction

- Higher education tuition deduction

- Teacher's $250 above the line classroom expense deduction

- Charitable contribution deduction of appreciated property for conservation purposes.

- Charitable contribution of IRA proceeds. Here the IRS has allowed direct contributions made in January 2011 to count for 2010.

Alternative Minimum Tax. The 2010 Act patches the AMT with higher exemption amounts for 2010 and 2011. Without the changes, an estimated 21 million more taxpayers would be subject to the AMT. The new exemption amounts are:

	2010	2011
Single	$47,450	$48,450
Joint/Surviving Spouse	$72,450	$74,450
Married Filing Separately	$36,225	$37,225

Payroll Tax Cut. This one is new. The 2010 Act cuts the 2011 employee share of the Social Security tax from 6.2 to 4.2 percent. This 2 percent cut can potentially save you as much as $2,136 (2 percent of $106,800). Self-employed individuals will calculate the above the line deduction for employment taxes without regard to the temporary rate reduction.

Transit Benefits. Employer-provided transit benefits (transit passes and vanpool benefits) may be tax-free to employees. For 2010, the ceiling is $230. The 2010 Act extends these benefits for one year, through 2011.

Energy Incentives. The 2010 Act extends energy credits through 2011. But the total maximum $1,500 credit for 2009 and 2010 has been reduced to pre-2009 Recovery Act limits ($500) for 2011.

BUSINESS CHANGES

100 percent Bonus Depreciation. The 2010 Act increases bonus depreciation from 50 percent to 100 percent for qualified investments made after September 8, 2010, and before January 1, 2012. It also makes 50 percent bonus depreciation available for qualified property placed in service after December 31, 2011, and before January 1, 2013.

Code Section 179 Expensing. To encourage business spending, Congress increased the amount that can be expensed and the investment limit to $500,000 and $2 million, respectively, for 2010 and 2011. For 2012, the numbers are $125,000 and $500,000, both indexed for inflation.

Research Tax Credit. This credit was renewed for 2 years, 2010 and 2011.

Work Opportunity Credit. Scheduled to expire after August 31, 2011, the 2010 Act extends this credit through the end of 2011. But, the Act does not extend this credit for unemployed veterans and disconnected youth beyond 2010.

Small Business Stock. The 2010 Act extends the 100 percent exclusion of gain from the sale of qualified small business stock by noncorporate taxpayers to stock acquired before January 1, 2012. The stock must be held for more than 5 years, and the amount excluded is limited to the greater of $10 million or 10 times your basis in the stock.

Business Energy Incentives. These incentives, such as the credits for biodiesel fuel, refined coal facilities, and so forth, have been extended for 2 years.

FEDERAL ESTATE TAX

The 2010 Act revives the Estate Tax for 2011 with a $5 million exclusion and a top marginal bracket of 35 percent. Step-up basis is returned. For those dying in 2010, estates have the option of using the 2010 rules with no tax and a limited step up, or the new 2011 rules with a full step up in basis and the $5 exclusion.

Big Change! The exclusion is now portable between spouses. So if a husband dies and uses up $2 million of his $5 million exclusion, the surviving spouse has an exclusion of $5 million plus the unused $3 million from the husband's estate for a total $8 million exclusion. If the surviving spouse is predeceased by more than one spouse, the exclusion amount available is limited to the lesser of $5 million or the unused exclusion of the last deceased spouse.

Gift Taxes: For gifts made after 2010, the gift tax is reunified with the estate tax with a top gift tax rate of 35 percent and a maximum exclusion amount of $5 million.

Tax Relief Act of 2010: Quick Guide

The Tax Relief, Unemployment Insurance Reauthorization, and Job Creation Act of 2010 was signed into law on December 17, 2010. Here's quick guide to some of the changes.

Tax Rates

	Before Act	After Act
Federal income tax brackets	Five 2011 tax brackets: 15%, 28%, 31%, 36%, 39.6%	Six 2010 tax brackets extended to 2011 and 2012: 10%, 15%, 25%, 28%, 33%, 35%
Maximum tax rate on long-term capital gains	Starting in 2011: 20% (10% for individuals in the 15% tax bracket)[1]	2010 rates extended to 2011 and 2012: 15% (0% for individuals in the 10% or 15% tax brackets)
Tax on qualifying dividends	Taxed as ordinary income starting in 2011	2010 treatment extended to 2011 and 2012: 15% (0% for individuals in the 10% or 15% tax brackets)
Alternative minimum tax (AMT)	Exemption amounts 2010: • $45,000 (married joint) • $33,750 (single) • $22,500 (married separate)	Exemption amounts 2010: • $72,450 (married joint) • $47,450 (single) • $36,225 (married separate) Exemption amounts 2011: • $74,450 (married joint) • $48,450 (single) • $37,225 (married separate)
	Personal tax credits not allowed against AMT beginning in 2010	Personal tax credits allowed against AMT in 2010 and 2011

(continues)

Tax Relief Act of 2010: Quick Guide *(continued)*

Estate Tax

	Before Act	After Act
Top estate tax rate	No estate tax for 2010 (modified carryover basis rules applied), estate tax would return in 2011 with top rate of 55%	Estate tax retroactively reinstated for 2010; top rate of 35% applies to 2010, 2011, and 2012
Estate tax exemption equivalent amount (basic exclusion amount, formerly called applicable exclusion amount)	No estate tax for 2010 (modified carryover basis rules applied), estate tax would return in 2011 with $1 million applicable exclusion amount	$5 million basic exclusion amount applies to 2010, 2011, and 2012[2]; ($5 million amount will be indexed for inflation in 2012)
Portability of exemption amount	N/A	For 2011 and 2012, when one spouse dies, any unused portion of that spouse's estate tax exemption equivalent amount may be transferred to the surviving spouse

Gift and Generation-Skipping Transfer Tax

	Before Act	After Act
Gift tax	For 2010: $1 million lifetime exemption equivalent, top rate of 35% For 2011: $1 million lifetime exemption, top rate of 55%	For 2011 and 2012, there will be a $5 million lifetime exemption equivalent, estate tax rates (top rate of 35%) applies
Generation-skipping transfer tax (GSTT)	No GSTT for 2010, $1 million exemption for 2011 with tax rate of 55%	GSTT exemption amount for 2010, 2011, and 2012 is $5 million; 0% rate applies for 2010; tax rate of 35% applies for 2011 and 2012

Tax Relief Act of 2010: Quick Guide *(continued)*

Business/Self-Employed Individuals

	Before Act	After Act
"Bonus" depreciation	50% additional first-year depreciation allowed for 2010, no bonus depreciation beginning in 2011	100% bonus depreciation for property acquired and placed in service after 9/8/10 and before 1/1/12, 50% bonus depreciation allowed for property acquired and placed in service after 12/31/11 and before 1/1/13
IRC Section 179 expensing	For 2010 and 2011, $500,000 expense limit, reduced by amount by which cost of qualifying property placed in service during the year exceeds $2 million; beginning in 2012, limit would be reduced to $25,000 with $200,000 phase-out threshold	2010 and 2011 unchanged; for 2012, the limit will be set at $125,000, reduced by amount by which cost of qualifying property placed in service during the year exceeds $500,000 ($125,000 and $500,000 amounts indexed for inflation)
Tax credit for research and experimentation expenses	Expired at the end of 2009	Retroactively reinstated for 2010 and extended through 2011
New markets tax credit	Expired at the end of 2009	Retroactively reinstated for 2010 and extended through 2011
Indian employment tax credit	Expired at the end of 2009	Retroactively reinstated for 2010 and extended through 2011

Source: Steve Leightman of RBC Wealth Management.

[1] Slightly lower rates would apply to qualifying property held for 5 or more years.

[2] For individuals who died in 2010, an election can be made to choose the estate tax provisions in effect prior to the Act.

E   American Tax Relief Act of 2012

Finally passed on January 1, 2013 (Congress still can't get the year right), the new law provides for the following:

1. INCOME TAX RATE INCREASE?

Not for you unless you make more than $400,000 ($450,000 for joint returns). If you're part of the 2 percent that may get hit with this extra tax, suck it up! It's only another 4.6 percent and that only applies to the excess over the $400,000 ($450,000). So, a couple making $500,000 would pay an extra $2,300 ($50,000 × 4.6%). The rest of us are still paying under the old Bush rates.

2. PAYROLL TAX INCREASE

Even if your rates stay the same, your check is going to be smaller. Facing a projected shortage in future funds to pay benefits, fiscal fools in Congress had cut the employee half of the Social Security tax from 6.2 percent to 4.0 percent. Those self-employed also enjoyed a 2 percent reduction in their obligation. This payroll tax holiday ended in 2012. For 2013, you'll pay an additional 2 percent on as much as $113,700, or as much as $2,274.

3. DIVIDENDS

Qualified dividends are still taxed at a reduced rate. For those at the $400,000/$450,000 income levels, the top rate was increased from 15 to 20 percent. That's still a lot lower than the 39.6 percent dividend rate originally proposed by the Obama administration. "Qualified dividends" are those held for an extended period. Technically, you start with the ex-dividend date, the date on which the company looks at its books for a list of shareholders who will get the dividend. Go back 60 days and forward 60 days. If you held the stock for any 60 days during that 121 day period, the dividends are "qualified" for the lower rate.

4. CAPITAL GAINS

The top tax on net long-term capital gains also jumped from 15 to 20 percent, but only for those at the $400,000/$450,000 income levels. To qualify as "long term," the asset must have been held for more than 1 year. It must be *more* than 1 year. Exactly 1 year defines your gain as short term, subject to a rate as high as 35 percent, and up to 39.6 percent for those at the $400,000/$450,000 levels.

For those in the 10 or 15 percent tax brackets, both qualified dividends and long-term capital gains continue to be taxed at a *zero* rate.

5. 3.8 PERCENT MEDICARE SURTAX

This wasn't part of the fiscal cliff deal, but you better be aware of it if you earn more than $200,000 ($250,000 for joint filers). To the extent your investment income (interest, dividends, rents, royalties, distribution from nonqualified annuities, income from passive activities, etc.) exceeds these levels, you're hit with an additional 3.8 percent Medicare surtax. So, if you're a single filer with $230,000 in income of which $30,000 is investment income, you're hit with an additional tax of $1,140 ($30,000 × 3.8%). That brings the potential tax on short-term dividends for high-income taxpayers to as much as 43.40 percent (39.6% + 3.9%).

6. PERMANENT AMT FIX

This awfully mean tax is a required alternative minimum tax computation that claws back certain deductions such as taxes paid and miscellaneous itemized deductions, denies you any deductions for personal exemptions, gives you an exemption deduction that disappears as your income increases, and applies a flat 26/28 percent rate on the balance. You pay the higher of the AMT or your regular tax.

The exemption amount was scheduled to fall to $33,750 ($45,000 on joint returns). Had that happened, as much as an additional 100 million taxpayers would have been hit with an AMT created tax increase. The new deal increases the exemption to $50,600 ($78,750 for joint returns) and indexes it for inflation for future years ($51,900 for individuals, $80,750 on joint returns, for 2013).

7. STATE AND LOCAL SALES TAX DEDUCTION

You can elect to deduct state and local sales taxes in lieu of income taxes as an itemized deduction on your Schedule A. This is a great benefit for taxpayers living in states without a state income tax, such as Alaska, New Hampshire, Tennessee, Florida, South Dakota, Washington, Nevada, Texas, and Wyoming.

The new tax deal extends this expired deduction for 2 years, 2012 and 2013.

8. TEACHER'S TAX DEDUCTION

From January 1, 2002, through 2011, you got an above-the-line deduction (you didn't have to itemize to get this) of up to $250 for expenses paid for books, supplies, computer equipment, and supplementary materials if you qualified as an eligible educator. That's a kindergarten through grade 12 teacher, aide, instructor, counselor, or principal in a school for at least 900 hours during the year.

The new tax deal extends this deduction for 2 years, 2012 and 2013.

9. BENEFITS

The new law makes permanent the $5,250 exclusion for employer-provided education assistance for college and graduate school education. It also extends through 2013 the monthly exclusion from income for employer-provided mass transit benefits from $125 to $240, and it makes permanent the $10,000 tax exemption for adoption expenses paid by your employer. Also made permanent was the $10,000 tax credit (a credit is a dollar-for-dollar reduction in your tax) for families that pay for their own adoption expenses.

10. ESTATE TAXES

Scheduled to drop to $1 million, the estate tax exclusion was raised to $5 million with a 40 percent top rate (the top rate for 2012 was 35 percent). Portability of a spouse's unused exclusion amount was made permanent. That means that there is now zero federal estate tax on a married couple unless their combined estate is more than $10 million.

Unless indicated otherwise, all of the above changes are made permanent. Note also that when the law refers to "income" here, it means taxable income, after all deductions.

11. EXTENSIONS

The new deal extends for 5 years the $1,000 child tax credit (which would have dropped to $500), the earned income tax credit, and the $2,500 American Opportunity Tax Credit for college tuition. It also permanently allows a $2,000 contribution to Coverdell Education Accounts, which otherwise would have fallen to $500, and permanently excludes as much as $5,250 in employer-provided education assistance.

The $2 million exclusion of cancellation of indebtedness on your principal residence income was extended through 2013.

The Work Opportunity Tax Credit, the Individual Energy Efficient Residence Improvement Tax Credit ($500 total, $200 for windows and skylights), and the Renewable Resources Tax Credit for facilities that produce energy from wind were all extended through 2013.

The deduction for mortgage insurance premiums as interest and the above-the-line deduction for tuition and fees were both extended through 2013.

It also extends for 2 years (2012 and 2013) the tax-free distribution of direct charitable donations of IRA assets up to $100,000 for taxpayers age 70½ or older. That means such distributions are not even included in income and don't reduce deductions that must exceed a percent of your adjusted gross income to be allowable—e.g., the 10 percent floor for medical expenses and the 2 percent floor for miscellaneous itemized deductions.

12. LIMITATIONS

The new law revives the "Pease" *limitations on itemized deductions* for singles with incomes of $250,000 or more and joint returns showing income of $300,000 or more.

It also restores the *personal exemption phase-out* for individuals with the same income thresholds.

13. BUSINESS PROVISIONS

For 2012 and 2013, Code Section 179 expensing limits were raised to $500,000 with a $2 million investment limit.

The 50 percent bonus depreciation was extended through 2013.

CHAPTER 20

How to Avoid/Survive an IRS Audit

"Where deductions are based on a number of small items not susceptible to complete documentary substantiation, reasonable determinations should be made at the district examination level. Consideration will always be given to the reasonableness of the taxpayer's claimed deductions."

Policy Statement P4-39

"If we don't change our system of collecting taxes, it will break down . . . Our traditional approach cannot sustain an acceptable level of compliance."

IRS Commissioner SHIRLEY PETERSON
to the Annual Meeting of the
New York State Bar Association's Tax Section
(January 31, 1993)

"Citing a survey showing that taxpayers annually spend more than 5 billion hours dealing with the tax system, former IRS Commissioner Fred Goldberg said, "American people have every right to demand a tax system they can live with."

October 10, 1991

"The objective of the Internal Revenue Service is to 'encourage and achieve the highest degree of voluntary compliance with the tax laws and regulations and to maintain the highest degree of public confidence in the integrity and efficiency of the IRS.'"

IRS statement of organization and functions,
39 Fed. Reg. 11,572, 1974

"A taxpaying public that does not understand the law is a taxpaying public that cannot comply with the law."

Former IRS Commissioner LAWRENCE B. GIBBS,
March 2, 1987

"Some agents 'need more training in how to be courteous.'"

Former IRS Commissioner LAWRENCE B. GIBBS,
April 14, 1987

"The examiner has a responsibility to the taxpayer and to the government to determine the correct tax liability and to maintain a fair and impartial attitude in all matters relating to the examination . . . The fair and impartial attitude of an examiner aids in increasing voluntary compliance. An examiner must approach each examination with an objective point of view."

Internal Revenue Manual 4015.3(1)

"The IRS cannot do some of the basic accounting and recordkeeping tasks it expects American taxpayers to do."

GAO, March 1, 1999

". . . You don't have to be nasty to people to collect money."

CHARLES O. ROSSOTTI, IRS Commissioner,
May 17, 2001

"I think the complexity of our Tax Code is the worst problem facing our society. . . . We wouldn't have either evasion or avoidance if we didn't have 10,000 pages of Tax Code it takes a machine to understand."

Treasury Secretary PAUL O'NEILL,
March 14, 2002

"The function of the Internal Revenue Service is to administer the Internal Revenue Code. . . . Administration should be both reasonable and vigorous. It should be conducted with as little delay as possible and with great courtesy and considerateness. It should be reasonable within the bounds of law and sound administration. It should, however, be vigorous in requiring compliance with the law and it should be relentless in its attack on unreal tax devices and fraud." (Rev. Proc. 64-92)

"There is little debate today: The Internal Revenue Code is a Kafkaesque maze of complexity that confounds millions of Americans every single year," says Rep. Steny Hoyer, a Maryland Democrat and the House Democratic Whip. "Our tax

system is an embarrassment that treats many taxpayers unfairly."

July 15, 2004

The IRS needs to do a better job of educating taxpayers and tax preparers. ...

Treasury Inspector General
for Tax Administration,
J. RUSSELL GEORGE
March 15, 2007

Dear Taxpayer:

This is to inform you that we, at the Internal Revenue Service, have lost your file. Unless we find it within thirty (30) days, you will face a $10,000 fine and a jail sentence of not less than five (5) years. Please advise.

IRS TERROR

The letter on the preceding page is, of course, a phony. At least I thought it was a phony until an equivalent letter reached one of my clients. In fact, the Internal Revenue Service has lost about 2 million tax returns or related documents from its files each year, according to an in-house study. It lost over 40,000 documents and $1.2 billion in payments in Pittsburgh alone in 2001—not to mention 2,300 computers and several firearms that somehow disappeared. The checks' in the Bay—in 2005, 30,000 estimated payment to the IRS were dumped into San Francisco Bay after an auto accident. "It's very embarrassing to tell a taxpayer, 'I am disallowing all of your losses,' and then ask them to provide a copy of their return because we can't find their original return," said one IRS employee quoted in an agency study. The report drew on questionnaires, interviews, and a random sample of 15,000 requests for tax documents in 1987. "In most federal record centers, we found Forms W-2 scattered on the floor," it stated. The report estimated that 21 percent of taxpayers who paid the fee for photocopies of tax returns got their money back because the document could not be found within 90 days.

It's not surprising that to most American taxpayers, receiving correspondence from the Internal Revenue Service is on a par with spending three weeks in a dentist's chair or two hours in a locked room with an encyclopedia salesperson. Greetings from the IRS means one thing: the ultimate curse of a civilized society—a tax audit.

The Internal Revenue Service defines an audit as "an impartial review of the taxpayer's return to determine its completeness and accuracy." Former Senator Edward V. Long of Missouri didn't agree. He compared the Internal Revenue Service to a "Gestapo preying upon defenseless citizens." His Senate committee found the audit and investigative techniques of the IRS to include defying court orders, picking locks, stealing records, illegally tapping telephones, intercepting and reading personal mail, using hidden microphones to eavesdrop on the private conversations of taxpayers with their lawyers, employing undercover agents with assumed identities, and using sexual entrapment.

In an April 26, 1982, hearing before the House Ways and Means Subcommittee on Oversight, Representative George Hansen of Idaho alleged the existence of "IRS Hit Lists, Snooping and Spying Operations, political retaliatory audits . . . and arbitrary assessments and seizures for punitive rather than tax collection purposes . . . ." The case against the Internal Revenue Service, however, was presented more strikingly by the alleged victims of Internal Revenue Service brutality, who methodically testified to individual confrontations with the service in great detail, including descriptions of forced detention, physical force, and the use of weapons for intimidation.

One taxpayer's wife, stricken with polio, needed an iron lung to keep her alive. An IRS agent threatened to seize the iron lung unless taxes claimed to be due were immediately forthcoming. The panicked taxpayer paid the claimed deficiency immediately.

IRS terrorists show no fear. In Kansas City, police officer Paul Campbell stopped a speeder and started to write a ticket. The offending driver, after making the usual objections, identified himself as an agent for the Internal Revenue Service. When Officer Campbell continued to write, the agent sneered, "We'll just have to check out your taxes." Soon after Campbell filed his next tax return, he was ordered to report to the Internal Revenue Service for an audit. It took four months of agency interrogations, repeated phone calls, and constant letter writing before the IRS finally admitted that Campbell owed it nothing.

In *Richman,* 78-1 U.S.T.C. Par. 9331, 41 AFTR 2d 78-1072 (DC Ill., 1978), the court was outraged at the lengths to which the IRS went to collect and keep some $5,000 to which, it turned out, it was not entitled. The IRS agents had padlocked the door to the taxpayer's place of business and discussed with the taxpayer the various sources from which he might beg or borrow the money in a conversation "distressingly like those between 'juice loan' debtors and creditors." The court found that the "conduct of the IRS agents was almost beyond belief."

In another case, senator Nancy Kassebaum of Kansas remarked, "They should not be hit with outlandish penalties for failing to memorize the Federal Tax Code." She was talking about a $50 penalty against an 84-year-old Kansas City woman who underpaid her income tax by $0.60! According to the *Washington Post,* on July 11, 1984, one couple was assessed $205 when they were found to be one cent shy after paying taxes of nearly $9,000!

In a 1977 incident, several IRS collection agents bashed in the side window of a Volkswagen owned by a woman in Alaska who owed some taxes, then dragged her from the car and seized it as a payment for the money she owed. A photographer caught the incident on film; otherwise, it would have gotten little national notice.

In March 1989, then Senator, now former Vice President Albert Gore of Tennessee revealed that IRS tax examiners in the Memphis Service Center "have been instructed to remain silent" when they uncover legitimate deductions that taxpayers failed to take. "For example, retirees and those laid off from their jobs who failed to claim withholding on pensions in lump sum distributions are not given credit, even if tax examiners catch the mistakes." The IRS attributed the embarrassment to "procedures used in the information document matching program for tax year 1987." However, it was not explained where those procedures and the policy behind them originated. Moreover, one then-current IRS employee claimed that examiners had been *instructed* to let withholding errors in the IRS's favor go uncorrected.

According to Beryl Abbin, then Director of Federal Tax Services for Arthur Andersen and Company, "On the local IRS level, you have some very bad apples out there—agents who try to push their way and intimidate."

In one study of the Internal Revenue Service, almost half the agents surveyed said they are hesitant to reveal their occupation to people they meet. Their general attitude is, "People don't trust us." Understandably so. As Internal Revenue Service agent Thomas Mennitt so succinctly put it in public testimony, "I violate laws at all times; it's part of my duties."[1] On June 28, 1987, the *Washington Post* reported three instances of the IRS intercepting first-class mail and altering checks that were made out to third parties. These allegations followed an earlier report about a San Francisco man whose $1,300 mortgage check to a bank was intercepted by the IRS in July 1986. The words "Internal Revenue Service" were stamped over the bank's name, and the check was then cashed. According to Ronald Noll of the Pennsylvania Society of Public Accountants, testifying before a House subcommittee in Congress, "The IRS has sunk so low in public opinion that a responsible accountant honestly believes he needs a hood to protect himself from IRS retaliation." IRS agents have been authorized to pose as doctors, lawyers, journalists, and clergy to conduct undercover investigations.

As former senator from Kansas and former Chairman of the Senate Finance Committee, Bob Dole blasted the IRS as an "intrusive" and "oppressive" presence in American life. "We don't need the IRS; we can get rid of the IRS," he vowed. Dole suggested that we abandon what he called "the whole twisted wreck of federal tax law." He decried what he called "KGB-like" audits that allow the government to snoop into a citizen's style of life.

Moreover, despite Internal Revenue Service National Office policy against collection quotas, IRS regional managers continued to instruct their revenue agents to make collections at almost any cost. According to a June 22, 1987, hearing before the Senate Finance Subcommittee on IRS Oversight, there was considerable competition among revenue officers and almost a daily comparison of what they have collected. Management challenged employees to "go out and make seizures . . ." and ". . . intimidation, and [the] abusiveness and harshness . . . is passed down to [the] taxpayers."

Things were no better in 1998. First, the IRS sent out apologies to 20,000 taxpayers for mistakes it made in handling their accounts. Then, the IRS sent

---

1. Jeff A. Schnepper, *Inside IRS* (New York: Stein and Day, 1978), p. 187.

1 million taxpayers tax packages with the wrong bar code, making them unusable because of zip code errors.

Things then got worse. Kenneth L. Steen of Chattanooga, Tennesse expected a refund of $513. Instead, he received a letter from the IRS demanding the payment of $300,000,007.57! An IRS official reported 3,000 people around the nation got similar erroneous notices.

Then things got really bad. The IRS itself issued a detailed report of 12 of the agency's 33 districts.

It found that the IRS had increasingly relied in recent years on numerical goals—such as the dollars that each revenue officer collects or the number of properties seized by a certain office—in enforcing tax laws, and that an obsession with such goals has raised the possibility of overzealous collections.

Though Congress outlawed the use of numerical goals almost two decades ago in 1988, high-profile Senate hearings in 1997 and an IRS report released in December, 1997 showed that the practice remained common.

It was found that more than a third of the IRS front line collection managers were evaluated based on enforcement statistics and that a fourth of all collection officers "feel pressure to achieve enforcement goals and take enforcement actions."

Things *are* getting better. The Treasury Inspector General, in a March 2003 study, concluded that the IRS "is generally compliant" with the restriction on using statistics to evaluate employee performance. In a 2005 study, the Inspector General found the IRS "complying" with legal guidance to evaluate employees on taxpayer treatment, rather than enforcement quotas. A 2007 investigation again found that the IRS continued to be "compliant." A July 27, 2010, TIGTA report concluded that the IRS "had complied well overall" with the evaluation guidelines.

Apparently, no one is immune from foul-ups by the Internal Revenue Service. In the summer of 1987, the Internal Revenue Service acknowledged that it had accidentally placed an erroneous $338.85 lien against then President and Mrs. Reagan. Although the lien was discovered and rescinded, it will remain a permanent entry in the County Court record system where it had been filed.

As the 1998 IRS report and Roth hearings demonstrate, IRS horror stories are not just in the far past. As a 1993 Tax Court decision noted, an IRS agent contacted Chicago businessman Vince Han and his wife to arrange an audit. At the second meeting—at Mr. Han's house—the agent's supervisor arrived on the premises and shouted: "You have to pay $70,000 now—if you don't pay it, you are going to jail!" Actually, Mr. Han owed the government nothing. The IRS auditor didn't bother reading key documents Mr. Han provided and instead merely asserted that Mr. Han "was not an honest taxpayer." It took a 4-year legal struggle for Mr. Han to clear his name and recover some of the heavy legal costs he incurred.

The horror continued. In 2007 an Arkansas federal court found that the "extortionary" conduct of two IRS agents amounted to fraud or malfeasance and penalties against them justified (Barry J. Jewell v. U.S. No. 4:06-CV-684 November 19, 2007).

Fear of the Internal Revenue Service *is* justified. All too often IRS agents are arbitrary, antagonistic, and capricious. According to a study commissioned by the Federal Administrative Conference, the Internal Revenue Service has been found to be "whimsical, inconsistent, unpredictable, and highly personal" in dealing with those caught in its machinery. The study concluded, among other things, that different IRS districts follow different rules and that the same district can be either easy or tough depending upon whether it is ahead or behind its acknowledged "quota" for recoveries.

For example, according to the conference, a New Yorker's chances of being audited averaged 1:39, compared to 1:78 in New Mexico. IRS audit negotiators in Brooklyn averaged 32¢ on the dollar in settling disputes, while those in Baltimore extracted 74¢. In Albany, New York, 6 of every 10 delinquent accounts led to tax seizures, but only 3 of 10 did in New Mexico. The Federal Administrative Conference also found that the higher the deficiency the Internal Revenue Service claimed, the lower the percentage it finally accepted in settlement. The conference suggested that this was due to the ability of rich taxpayers to hire lawyers to argue their cases while poorer taxpayers had no choice but to pay up.

Odds of IRS District Tax Audit 2000 All 1040/10140A Returns Filed by Individuals

Region	District	Average Adjusted Gross Income Reported	Rank	Percent Audited	Rank
	United States	42,917	–	0.20	–
Northeast Region	Brooklyn	46,252	16	0.29	7
Northeast Region	Connecticut-Rhode Island	59,576	2	0.18	16
Northeast Region	Manhattan	66,191	1	0.37	5
Northeast Region	Michigan	48,251	9	0.11	31
Northeast Region	New England	51,448	5	0.16	19
Northeast Region	New Jersey	58,295	3	0.10	33
Northeast Region	Ohio	42,121	27	0.10	32
Northeast Region	Pennsylvania	45,198	17	0.13	29
Northeast Region	Upstate New York	42,394	25	0.14	22
Southeast Region	Delaware-Maryland	50,972	6	0.13	26
Southeast Region	Georgia	44,284	21	0.11	30
Southeast Region	Gulf Coast	36,256	31	0.20	12

(continues)

Odds of IRS District Tax Audit 2000 All 1040/10140A Returns Filed by Individuals
(continued)

Region	District	Average Adjusted Gross Income Reported	Rank	Percent Audited	Rank
Southeast Region	Indiana	43,951	23	0.14	25
Southeast Region	Kentucky-Tennessee	39,342	30	0.13	27
Southeast Region	North Florida	39,923	29	0.14	23
Southeast Region	North-South Carolina	40,472	28	0.16	20
Southeast Region	South Florida	46,562	14	0.23	9
Southeast Region	Virginia-West Virginia	46,308	15	0.13	28
Midstates Region	Arkansas-Oklahoma	35,625	33	0.21	11
Midstates Region	Houston	47,493	10	0.22	10
Midstates Region	Illinois	50,679	7	0.14	24
Midstates Region	Kansas-Missouri	43,231	24	0.16	18
Midstates Region	Midwest	44,540	19	0.19	14
Midstates Region	North Central	47,259	11	0.47	2
Midstates Region	North Texas	44,529	20	0.19	15
Midstates Region	South Texas	36,061	32	0.17	17
Western Region	Central California	50,117	8	0.29	6
Western Region	Los Angeles	44,215	22	0.48	1
Western Region	Northern California	52,650	4	0.41	4
Western Region	Pacific Northwest	46,993	12	0.15	21
Western Region	Rocky Mountain	44,709	18	0.20	13
Western Region	Southern California	46,563	13	0.47	3
Western Region	Southwest	42,180	26	0.29	8

Source: Transactional Records Clearinghouse, Syracuse University.

Average Yield of an IRS Audit

United States	$5,330
IRS Region	
Southwest (SW)	$7,883
North Atlantic (NA)	$7,606
Mid-Atlantic (MA)	$5,013
West (W)	$4,441
Southeast (SE)	$4,401
Midwest (MW)	$3,665
Central (C)	$3,424
States and IRS Districts	
1. Colorado (SW)	$17,614
2. Texas (all) (SW)	$9,780
Austin District	$4,002
Dallas District	$1,665
Houston District	$6,789
3. Alaska (W)	$8,973
4. Maryland[a] (MA)	$7,532
5. Oklahoma (SW)	$7,382
6. Arkansas (SE)	$7,218
7. Florida (all) (SE)	$7,136
Fort Lauderdale District	$8,980
Jacksonville District	$5,826
8. Nevada (W)	$6,566
9. New Jersey (MA)	$6,341
10. Idaho (W)	$6,295
11. New York (all) (NA)	$6,216
Albany District	$3,846
Brooklyn District	$6,216
Buffalo District	$3,846
Manhattan District	$8,414
12. Massachusetts (NA)	$5,642
13. California (all) (W)	$5,608
Laguna Niguel District	$4,735
Los Angeles District	$9,538
Sacramento District	$4,138

(continues)

Average Yield of an IRS Audit *(continued)*

San Francisco District	$3,884
San Jose District	$3,884
14. Oregon (NW)	$5,561
International[b]	$5,391
15. Illinois (all) (MW)	$5,176
Chicago District	$5,590
Springfield District	$3,422
16. Kansas (SW)	$4,825
17. Pennsylvania (all) (MA)	$4,572
Philadelphia District	$5,089
Pittsburgh District	$3,550
18. Utah (SW)	$4,372
19. Michigan (C)	$4,315
20. Arizona (SW)	$4,290
21. Tennessee (SE)	$4,178
22. Wyoming (SW)	$4,154
23. Louisiana (SE)	$4,140
24. New Hampshire (NA)	$3,957
25. Connecticut (MA)	$3,889
26. Hawaii (W)	$3,882
27. Delaware (MA)	$3,756
28. Georgia (SE)	$3,727
29. Kentucky (C)	$3,713
30. Virginia (MA)	$3,640
31. New Mexico (SW)	$3,590
32. Ohio (all) (C)	$3,534
Cincinnati District	$3,057
Cleveland District	$3,765
33. Wisconsin (MW)	$3,382
34. North Carolina (SE)	$3,286
35. South Carolina (SE)	$3,209
36. Washington (NW)	$3,188
37. Indiana (C)	$3,180
38. Maine (NE)	$3,069
39. Iowa (MW)	$3,049

Average Yield of an IRS Audit *(continued)*

40. Rhode Island (NE)	$2,965
41. Minnesota (MW)	$2,949
42. Missouri (MW)	$2,922
43. Nebraska (MW)	$2,728
44. South Dakota (MW)	$2,629
45. Mississippi (SE)	$2,529
46. Alabama (SE)	$2,513
47. West Virginia (SE)	$2,375
48. Montana (MW)	$2,181
49. Vermont (NE)	$2,095
50. North Dakota (MW)	$1,825

Source: Derived from statistics in the 1987 Commissioner's Annual Report.

ªIncludes the District of Columbia.

ᵇReturns filed in Puerto Rico and from abroad.

CONGRESS RESPONDS

In response to these problems, Congress passed a Taxpayer's Bill of Rights in 1988. The creation of Senator David Pryor of Arkansas, it consists of procedural safeguards and penalties to help clarify and ensure the rights and obligations of a taxpayer and the IRS during an audit or appeal, as well as during the refund and collection processes. As then Finance Committee Chairman Lloyd Bentsen put it, the bill's provisions counter the "bully mentality" that many taxpayers perceive behind IRS tax law enforcement. The focus of the bill was to create a more balanced relationship between the tax agency and the citizenry. The details of the bill can be found on page 702 and following. A second Taxpayer Bill of Rights was passed in 1996, and a third in 1998 as part of the Reform Act.

In 1997, the IRS received two additional hits. Responding to reports of unauthorized inspection of tax return information by IRS employees, Congress passed the Taxpayers Browsing Protection Act, which imposes both civil and criminal penalties for the unauthorized inspection of tax returns and return information. Between late 1994 and April 1997, more than 700 IRS employees were punished for improperly accessing agency information.

Moreover, in March 1997, Rep. Bill Archer and Sen. William Roth, the then Chairmen of the House Ways and Means and the Senate Finance Committees, respectively, agreed to investigate allegations that the IRS was conducting politically targeted audits of exempt organizations.

Responding to serious IRS deficiencies, the National Commission on Restructuring the IRS, in a June 25, 1997 report, recommended sweeping changes for the agency.

The key recommendations in the commission's report called for:

- creating a seven-member board of directors for IRS, with five members from the private sector, appointed (and removable) by the president and confirmed by the Senate;

- consolidating congressional oversight of IRS by creating a joint committee of leaders of the multiple committees that now oversee IRS on Capitol Hill;

- stabilizing the IRS' budget for the next 3 years so it can plan for modernization;

- giving IRS and Treasury more flexibility to hire the qualified personnel they need to implement modernization;

- giving IRS more input into the administrability of tax laws before they are enacted; *and*

- requiring IRS to provide taxpayers with compensation for damages incurred as a result of wrongful actions by IRS, among other taxpayer rights provisions.

Many of these issues were addressed again in the 1998 Reform Act. Things *were* changing. On August 5, 1999, the IRS issued T.D. 8830 to establish a balanced measurement system for employees. Specifically, the new rules measure employee performance and implement requirements that all employees be evaluated on the basis of "providing fair and equitable treatment to taxpayers." The use of records of tax enforcement results to evaluate or to impose or suggest goals for any employee of the IRS is barred.

But as then IRS Commissioner Charles O. Rossotti stated in July 1999, "Frankly, we haven't yet succeeded in building an IRS that accomplishes, or is ever capable of accomplishing, our goals at an acceptable level."

Yet things *were* changing in 2000. More than one-fifth of IRS employees, the equivalent of nearly 21,000 people working full-time, were assigned to customer service, up from 12,000 4 years ago by one measure and nearly 18,000 by another. By either measure there were thousands fewer workers available to conduct audits and collect overdue taxes.

The IRS culture was also changing. "Don't aggravate taxpayers—that's what our managers are telling us," the *New York Times* quoted an IRS agent in a December 1999 article. As he spoke six colleagues nodded in agreement and offered similar comments from their bosses.

A revenue agent in Florida said his manager told him: "Don't probe deeply. Just find three or four obvious items and close the case."

An IRS worker in Nashville said anyone there could get a tax case resolved favorably if the taxpayer had enough influence to get a senator or congressman to complain to the IRS. "We just collapse," the 14-year veteran said.

"Please don't call us tax collectors in the newspaper," one longtime revenue officer in New York said. "We don't collect taxes anymore. We aren't allowed to."

The chief of IRS operations, John Dalrymple, said "none of these comments shock me."

The pendulum has now swung in the other direction. Former IRS Commissioner Everson declared enforcement, rather than service, to be the new priority. "The agency will not brook arguments by taxpayers that the IRS is abusing its enforcement powers." "The law is that if you make money, you have to pay taxes."

As the Congressional Research Services noted in an August 23, 2007 report, the proposed IRS budget for fiscal year 2007 "continues a trend, several years in the making, of putting greater stress on enforcement at the expense of the modernization effort and, to a lesser extent, taxpayer service."

They really mean it. In March 2010 *The Week* reported that two dark-suited IRS agents showed up at a California car wash, hand-delivering the owner an unpaid tax bill of 4 cents. Aaron Zeff, of Harv's Metro Car Wash in Sacramento, says the agents were "deadly serious" about the $0.04 bill from 2006, which had accrued $202.31 in late fees and taxes. "It's hilarious," said Zeff, who paid the bill. "I think (the IRS) may have a problem with priorities."

UNDERSTANDING THE SYSTEM

Short of adopting a vow of poverty and hiding in a monastery or joining the ever-growing army of illegal tax evaders, what can you do? The best defense is a good offense. If you know how the service works internally and where it is vulnerable, you can at least better your odds of winning when the tax man calleth.

Making your return indistinguishable from the "average" individual return can lessen your chances of facing an audit. Once you have prepared and signed your return, you mail it to the IRS Regional Service Center for your geographical area. The center checks some of the figures and transfers all information to magnetic tape, which then goes to the IRS computer center in Martinsburg, West Virginia. Here it becomes part of a master file for the Internal Revenue Service's complex automatic data processing system. With the master file, the Internal Revenue Service can locate people who fail to file returns and taxpayers who do not report such income as dividends or bank interest. Each tax return is assigned a document locator number (DLN) by the local Service Center. To better understand the document locator system, let us "decode" a hypothetical DLN: 3414133300134. Working from left to right, the digits indicate the following:

34	=	the IRS district (viz., the Cleveland District)
1	=	the tax class (viz., withholding tax)
41	=	the document code (viz., Form 941)
333	=	the control date (the numeric day of the year remittance was made)
001	=	the block number
34	=	the serial number of the specific DLN

An understanding of the document locator number system can help you better understand the communication process of the Internal Revenue Service.

In addition to printing out notices and letters to advise you of a tax refund due, to request information, or to report actions taken on returns already filed and the status of your account, the system is programmed to check returns for three basic mistakes.

First, all returns are examined for mathematical errors. Mistakes in arithmetic or in transferring figures from one schedule to another—for example, the total of itemized deductions to the Form 1040—result in an immediate correction notice. If the error leads to a tax deficiency, you automatically receive a bill for that amount. If you overpaid, the excess is applied to future taxes, credited, or refunded at your request. You cannot appeal such corrections, but you can ask in writing that they be reviewed. Errors in arithmetic alone rarely lead to a full audit.

The Internal Revenue Service's second computer check also provides for automatic adjustments to your return before any audit is made. This Unallowable Items Program is designed to catch clearly illegal deductions, such as claiming an exemption for a spouse who is filing separately. Under this program, the computer cross-checks reported income against the W-2 forms received from your employer. The dividends and interest reported by banks, brokerage houses, and other financial institutions are cross-checked in over 99 percent of the cases. As a result of this cross-checking, the Internal Revenue Service sends out notices for taxes and interest on overdue taxes or for income or other payments that were not reported. Unfortunately, however, according to the General Accounting Office, about half of the ten million correction notices the IRS issues each year have been "incorrect, unresponsive, unclear, or incomplete." If you get an incorrect notice, follow the appropriate procedures to contest it, or contact your local Problem Resolution office, now known as the Office of the Taxpayer Advocate, at 1-877-777-4778.

Another common mistake picked up by this program is a claim for a deduction that exceeds limits set by the Internal Revenue Service tax code. For example, not all medical expenses may be claimed. You may itemize and write off only those medical expenses that exceed 10 percent of adjusted gross income. The Unallowable Items Program is also likely to catch excessive deductions for charitable contributions or failure to reduce a "casualty loss" by $100, as required by the tax code. When an adjustment is made, you receive a letter allowing you to explain or protest. If you accept the change, you are asked to sign the "correction notice."

Unless the mistakes are extensive, these automatic adjustments do not usually lead to a full audit. However, basic errors like these should be avoided: Anytime your return is made to stand out, *for any reason*, it increases your chances for a full audit, with all the corresponding consequences.

Another IRS program for checking tax returns is the Questionable Items Program. Here, your whole return or a part of it is subjected to a detailed investigation. You are, in effect, being challenged rather than corrected. You must justify each deduction to the last penny, and to the satisfaction of the examining agent.

IRS computer programs use three techniques to decide which returns to review under this program: random selection, "discriminant function" selection, and special target selection.

Your income, claimed deductions, and profession are irrelevant when returns are selected at random. A student earning only $6,000 a year at part-time jobs may be invited to the local IRS office for a tax audit only to find a business executive making $600,000 in the same situation.

Once the return is in the computer, you are at the mercy of the second selection criterion—"discriminant function" *(DIF)* analysis. Based on previous experience, the Internal Revenue Service has created a number of composite hypothetical "taxpayers." These composite "norms" are determined by interviewing a random selection of taxpayers. Unfortunately, this can be a horror for the taxpayer selected as a "norm": The IRS agent asks questions about every single item on the return; the taxpayer has to produce a birth certificate, marriage certificate—the works. Each item is checked, and the results are fed into the computer. In a "discriminant function" analysis, the characteristics of these "average" taxpayers are given different weights and compared to a return selected for audit.

Of the 1.1 million closed books and records audits received in 1992, 1993, and 1994, 59 percent were selected on the basis of "*DIF*" scores.

Average taxpayers were determined by the IRS Taxpayer Compliance Measurement Program (TCMP). One research audit covered 54,000 personal returns for 1988. The IRS planned to TCMP audit about 153,000 returns of all types for 1994 to be picked randomly in 1995 to represent 25 business sectors, 5 personal income groups, and 30 geographic areas. Budget constraints put these audits on hold.

But, they're back, now called National Research Program (NRP) audits. The IRS scheduled these audits for late fall 2002 and 2003. Here's how they set it up:

- 8,000 returns were reviewed without the taxpayers being contacted.

- 9,000 taxpayers got letters asking questions about their returns.

- 30,000 returns were subject to "limited"-scope face-to-face audits.

- 2,000 others were to be subject to the audit from hell, where they'll be required to back up every line on their returns. These audits are technically called *Calibration Audits.*

By summer of 2005, the IRS had selected nearly 90 percent of the returns to be audited. They put the new audit formulas in place in 2006. Your odds of winning the Powerball lottery in 2002 were 1 in 80 million. Your odds of facing an audit from hell were 1 in 65,000. As Kevin McCormally commented, "A grateful nation appreciates your sacrifice."

These NRP audits continue. On June 6, 2007, the IRS announced plans to launch a new study, the first of an ongoing series of annual individual studies using an innovative multi-year rolling methodology. The study started in October 2007 and examined about 13,000 randomly selected tax year 2006 individual returns. Similar sample sizes will be used in subsequent tax years.

An advantage of using this method, which combines results over rolling three-year periods, is that the IRS will be able to make annual updates to compliance estimates and develop more efficient workload plans on an annual basis, after the initial three annual studies. Previous studies started from scratch, drew tax returns from a single tax year, and involved examinations of more than 45,000 taxpayers.

A September 2009 TIGTA report found that examination productivity is improving for individual returns selected by the updated DIF scores.

Let's see how the DIF score works. First, the deductions on the selected returns are added up and weighed for what is called the "discriminant function" score. The computer then recommends audits for significantly differing returns. The computer is also programmed to notice special deviations. For

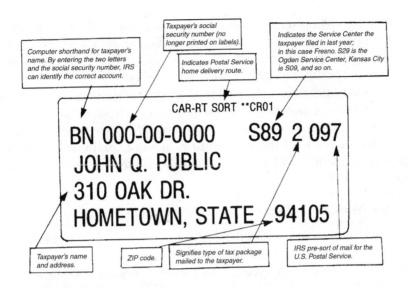

Computer shorthand for taxpayer's name. By entering the two letters and the social security number, IRS can identify the correct account.

Taxpayer's social security number (no longer printed on labels).

Indicates Postal Service home delivery route.

Indicates the Service Center the taxpayer filed in last year; in this case Fresno. S29 is the Ogden Service Center, Kansas City is S09, and so on.

CAR-RT SORT **CR01

BN 000-00-0000   S89 2 097

JOHN Q. PUBLIC

310 OAK DR.

HOMETOWN, STATE 94105

Taxpayer's name and address.

ZIP code.

Signifies type of tax package mailed to the taxpayer.

IRS pre-sort of mail for the U.S. Postal Service.

example, it may recommend an audit if all your deductions turn out to be nicely rounded even numbers. It will also compare your deductions to your job. A person who works as a construction laborer will rarely have a need for a home office deduction. The computer model-match takes into account income level, profession, number of dependents claimed, whether your spouse works, and even your address: A Beverly Hills zip code with a ghetto-level reported income will immediately signal for an audit. According to former IRS Commissioner Roscoe L. Egger, Jr., two-thirds of the audited returns were selected on the basis of the IRS discriminant function formula. The rest were chosen on the basis of tax-avoiding trends, such as abusive tax shelters.

You should also understand the bar-coded envelopes and peel-off labels that come with your returns. Some taxpayers believe that the coding somehow triggers an audit. In fact, the coding simply allows the IRS to process the mail on their automatic sorting machine, which reads the bar codes and separates the mail by type of return (i.e., 1040A, 1040EZ, 1040), thus expediting processing. Uncoded mail must be sorted by hand, which is much more time-consuming and slows up processing, which slows up refunds.

The coded numbers on the preprinted address label affixed to your tax package also speed up processing of returns and expedite refunds. Again, the label coding has no relationship to audits. It assures the IRS that the name is valid and it includes, for each taxpayer, an assigned "check digit"—two characters based on the taxpayer's name. Data transcribers pick up the two-stroke check digit from the label to input tax information to a taxpayer's account. If the label is not used, your full name, and complete address must be input—significantly extending processing time and adding the potential for common errors that delay the issuance of refunds. The illustration above shows the preprinted label and explains the meaning of the various coded symbols. Current labels leave off your Social Security number for privacy reasons.

Most returns are currently field electronically. Your numbers go directly into the IRS computer and are then subject to the same audit criteria.

A single oversized deduction will probably not trigger an immediate audit. For you the name of the game is to match the computer's norm as closely as possible. The table below reveals average deductions claimed on returns filed in 2012 for 2011.

Average Itemized Deductions, Individual Income Tax Returns for 2011

Adjusted Gross Income	Taxable Income	Interest Expense	Taxes Paid Deduction	Charity	Medical Expenses Deducted	Total Itemized Deductions
Under $15,000	$2,734	$7,414	$3,137	$1,443	$8,350	$15,014
$15,000–$29,999	9,461	7,346	3,249	2,127	7,838	15,092
$30,000–$49,999	21,841	7,436	3,988	2,287	6,943	15,422
$50,000–$99,999	47,720	8,768	6,235	2,881	7,375	19,311
$100,000–$199,999	99,561	11,266	10,852	3,889	10,002	26,832
$200,000–$249,999	174,065	15,216	18,083	5,703	16,814	38,814
$250,000 & above	553,805	20,685	47,616	18,490	34,796	88,058

Source: Statistics of Income Internal Revenue Service, Publication 1136

The averages for state and local taxes appear low because they include filers who reside in states that don't have an income tax and elect to deduct sales taxes.

COMPUTER CHAOS

A dual expansion of IRS computer operations was substantially completed in 1985. First, the major equipment replacement program, with a new UNIVAC 1100 System, was made operational in all service centers. This system tripled the capacity and speed of the old equipment. Second, administration of office examinations was computerized and operates from the service centers. As District appointments become available, the computer selected cases by priority and generated both appointments and taxpayer notification letters. These letters detailed the time and place of the examination, the issues to be resolved, what to bring, etc. The system also identified whether the taxpayer has other years under examination and automatically routed the examination to the same agent. In 1994, the IRS spent an additional $689 million to upgrade its computer system. Unfortunately, it still didn't work properly. After spending $8 billion on new computer systems, even a top agency official, in 1997, admitted that the systems "do not work in the real world."

A 7-year program to upgrade and modernize the agency's system at a cost of almost $4 billion received a scathing review from the General Accounting Office. Among the problems: cost overruns, failure to move toward a more efficient system, and continued inability of IRS employees to get current and accurate information on taxpayer returns.

The computer systems and processes did not interact with each other. The result was a problem that may be resolved by one IRS office, but another department showed the issue is still open. The taxpayer thinks the matter is closed . . . but not every IRS office is necessarily in agreement. Steps were taken to develop a centralized system that will allow all existing computers and systems to communicate with each other.

The then Commissioner of Internal Revenue, Charles O. Rossotti, was not an attorney nor an accountant—he was a computer systems expert. Rossotti said that reforming the IRS could take the better part of a decade; the computer modernization program also was likely to extend into the next century.

Moving to the new millennium hasn't helped yet. In April 2000, on technological modernization, Rossotti admitted the IRS still depended on a "very, very old . . . frankly unacceptable system" as the backbone to the administration function. Sometimes, embarrassingly, the IRS has been forced to ask a taxpayer for information it should be able to get but simply cannot find or extricate. This is akin, he said, to a bank not knowing exactly, at any one time, the balance of some of its customers, which is unacceptable.

In May 2001, the IRS project to replace the agency's 1960s database with a comprehensive modern computer framework was delayed again to "ensure its functionality."

It seems to be working better. In 2001 taxpayers who called phone numbers in two IRS publications were referred to adult chat lines—progress?

According to the General Accounts Office (GAO) in January 2003, the IRS's compliance programs, modernization, and financial management continued to be "high risk" activities. By June 2003 things had not improved.

The Internal Revenue Service is facing ongoing challenges and problems in the massive effort to overhaul its antiquated computer systems, the Treasury Inspector General for Tax Administration said in a semiannual report.

"IRS's major modernization projects continue to experience delays, cost increases, management difficulties, and reductions in deliverables," according to the report, which covers October 1, 2002, through March 1, 2003.

In July 2003, the Internal Revenue Service announced the delay of the first phase of the program to modernize its taxpayer master files, the Customer

Account Data Engine (CADE), until the 2004 filing season. The first group of taxpayers, approximately 6 million 1040 EZ filers, was originally scheduled to move to the new system in 2001.

"This most recent setback is a serious matter," said then IRS Commissioner Mark W. Everson.

Everson also announced the IRS has launched an independent review of the program to evaluate its progress and determine whether any changes are needed. Following up on a commitment he made when becoming Commissioner in May 2003, Everson announced the selection of Software Engineering Institute of Carnegie Mellon University to conduct the study and report back to the IRS in 60–90 days.

When fully operational, CADE will be a modern database that will house tax information for more than 200 million individual and business taxpayers. It replaces the antiquated, magnetic tape-based system that came into use 4 decades ago. The system, called the Master File, takes a week to update its records, creating delays in providing accurate account information for taxpayers. When completed, CADE will provide a variety of benefits to taxpayers, such as faster refunds along with daily postings of transactions and updating of accounts.

Or, alternatively, you could always go back to the adult chat lines. . . .

By 2004, things had not gotten a lot better. Then IRS Commissioner Everson conceded that the Business Management System (BMS) "has failed" on the CADE project, the new Master File system, and the new IRS financial systems. The BMS alone had suffered cost overruns of $290 million since 1999.

Moreover, the GAO has found "significant computer security weakness" at the IRS. According to the GAO in a February 2004 report, the IRS has blamed delays on improving its computer system on the costs and resources used to implement the advanced child tax credit payments. Maybe they were too focused on the adult chat lines. . . .

As of July 2005, the GAO concluded that "incremental improvements" had been made, but long-term problems associated with cost overruns and schedule delays remain a concern. In April 2006, the Government Accountability Officer (GAO) concluded that the IRS's ambitious program to modernizing its outdated tax administration and financial systems still lacks adequate policies and procedures to ensure program success.

In an earlier 2005 report, the GAO found that "significant" weaknesses in the security of the IRS information systems continues to threaten the confidentiality, integrity, and availability of key financial and tax data.

In July 2006, the Treasury Inspector General for Tax Administration report found the IRS Business Systems Modernization (BSM) program "faulty" and it concluded that the IRS Customer Account Data Engine (CADE) was "not fully developed to provide a foundation for IRS current and planned modernization systems." The CADE system was designed for managing taxpayer accounts.

In an August 2006 Treasury Inspector General for Tax Administration report, it was revealed that about $318 million in erroneous tax refunds were issued as a result of a computer based foul up that left the IRS without any fraud detection program for the 2006 filing season. Another bad sign.

As of August 2007, things weren't a lot better. Sixty percent of Internal Revenue Service employees were duped into giving control of their passwords to unauthorized callers, according to an inspection report that found lingering problems with computer security years after they were supposed to have been corrected.

Sixty-one of 102 employees telephoned by the Treasury Inspector General for Tax Administration were fooled by undercover inspectors posing as computer support help desk representatives. The inspectors asked for help with correcting a computer problem and requested the employees to provide their user names and temporarily change their passwords to the ones suggested by the inspectors.

The majority of them complied. Only eight of the employees reported the incident to either the audit team, TIGTA's Office of Investigations, or the IRS's own computer security people as they were supposed to do.

As for the CADE project, it still wasn't where it should have been, despite the IRS spending more than $230 million to right it over the last few years. By June 2008 the program was in its 10th year, and $2.5 billion into contract court costs and $310 million in internal expenses. Another $267 million was budgeted for fiscal 2008, and the program still fails to give the appropriate level of service taxpayers expect, according to the TIGTA.

And even what worked needed better supervision. In 2007, Senate Finance Committee Chairman Max Baucas (D-Mont) reported that the IRS's failure to follow procedures put the integrity of the electronic filing program at risk and exposed a greater probability of inaccurate returns, fraud, and identify theft. The TIGTA in 2008 found IRS security controls "inadequate." In 2009, the TIGTA concluded that cost overruns and schedule delays had increased with the IRS's returns system modernization program. In July 2010 the TIGTA found IRS data "at risk" for unauthorized access or disclosure.

As of February 2011, the GAO still found the IRS Business Systems Modernization (BSM) a high-risk area. Progress is slow, and the TIGTA even found that the IRS's Modernized e-File (MeF) system was not performing to expected levels. "Due to recent events at IRS facilities and the potentially expanding role of the IRS, security has replaced modernization as the top challenge facing the IRS," said Treasury Inspector General for Tax Administration J. Russell George, in December 2010.

Good news! In October 2011, the GAO found the Business Systems Modernization "on good track." In fact, in December 2011, the TIGTA upgraded the modernization effort all the way up from "Material Weakness" to "Deficiency." That's after spending nearly $20 billion on information technology over the last decade. I for one feel so much better!

2012 was a much better year. The IRS Oversight Board took note of milestones achieved by the IRS in fiscal 2012 in a number of key areas, such as technology, enforcement and issue resolution. Most notable was the successful launch of the Customer Account Data Engine 2, or CADE 2, in January 2012, allowing the IRS to migrate from a weekly to a daily processing cycle for individual taxpayer accounts.

AUDIT HOT BUTTONS

After these computers have "graded" income tax returns to determine their "audit worthiness," the returns with the highest scores are screened by humans. The following characteristics are what these human screeners look for:

- Insufficient income to support claimed deductions
- Refunds out of line with gross income and exemptions
- Possibility of unreported income
- Profit from business or profession below the "norm"
- Investment yield or profits below the interest income that would have been earned if the funds had been deposited in savings accounts

Other Internal Revenue Service guidelines used in choosing returns to be audited include:

- Comparative size of the item—a questionable expense item of $5,000 when expenses total $25,000 would be significant; however, if total expenses were $250,000, the item ordinarily would not be significant.

- Absolute size of the item—despite the comparability factor, size itself may be significant. For example, a $60,000 item may be significant even though it represents a small percentage of taxable income.

- Inherent character of the item—although the amount of an item may be insignificant, the *nature* of the item may be significant. For example, airplane expenses claimed by a carpenter may be significant.

- Evidence of intent to mislead—this may include missing, misleading, or incomplete schedules, or showing an item incorrectly on the return.

- Beneficial effect of the manner in which an item is reported—expenses claimed on a business schedule rather than claimed as itemized deductions may be significant.

- Relationship to other items—the absence of a deduction for interest expense when real estate taxes are claimed may be significant. Similarly, the lack of dividends reported when the return shows sales of stock may also be significant.

According to a declassified handbook, the IRS looks for the following in selecting returns for an audit: exemptions claimed by noncustodial parents; losses claimed on rental property recently converted from a residence; and high receipt, low net profit business schedules for nonitemizers. The above deductions are listed as higher priority items than large medical expenses of large families or older taxpayers, home mortgage interest, auto expenses of users of the standard mileage rate, or transportation expenses of construction workers who work at more than one job site for more than one employer (*The Classification Handbook*, IRMO 41(12)0).

In September 2002, the Internal Revenue Service announced it was shifting its audit priorities to concentrate on "key areas" of tax law noncompliance by high-income taxpayers.

As part of a broader, agency-wide plan, the IRS said it will place "top priority on pursuing promoters of abusive schemes, shelters and trusts" and on identifying participants in the schemes.

The IRS increased audit resources, starting in fiscal year 2003, and used all available tools, the agency said, including "summons enforcement, injunctions and criminal investigation of promoters" and "civil audits of participants."

The strategy focused on six key areas of noncompliance:

- offshore credit card users,
- high risk, high-income taxpayers,
- abusive schemes and promoter investigations,
- high-income nonfilers,
- unreported income, *and*
- the National Research Program, the agency's compliance study involving 50,000 tax returns.

The Internal Revenue Service expects its management to use employee time productively. Therefore, each year, top administrators will "target" taxpayers in specific professions or with incomes from unusual sources where the highest potential monetary recovery may be found. For example, dentists, doctors, lawyers, and even accountants may receive much of their income in cash payments. The Internal Revenue Service believes that this permits them to "forget" to report all of their receipts. The Service also believes that the incentive to underreport would be greatly dulled if these professionals knew that, as a class, they were more likely to be audited. Therefore, as a class, they *are* more likely to be audited.

The IRS audit manual, *The Policies of the Internal Revenue Service Handbook,* set as the "primary objective" in selection of tax returns "*the highest possible revenue yield from the examination man hours expended,* and the examination of as many returns as is feasible for the maintenance of a high degree of voluntary taxpayer compliance" (author's italics).

Our federal income tax rates are imposed on a graduated progressive schedule. When you earn $1 more than the top of the previous bracket, a higher percentage of that *additional* dollar will be taken as taxes. Therefore, the more money you earn, the higher the potential return is likely to be on the time invested by the Internal Revenue Service in the case. If an agent denies a $100 deduction to a taxpayer in the 35 percent bracket, the United States Treasury receives $35, as opposed to only $10 from a taxpayer in the 10 percent bracket.

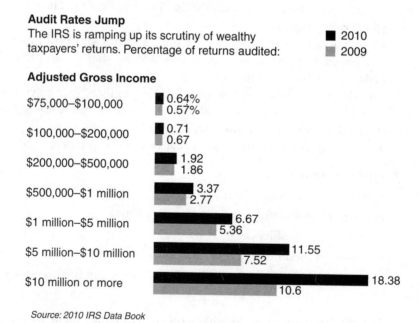

Audit Rates Jump
The IRS is ramping up its scrutiny of wealthy taxpayers' returns. Percentage of returns audited:

■ 2010
▨ 2009

Adjusted Gross Income

	2010	2009
$75,000–$100,000	0.64%	0.57%
$100,000–$200,000	0.71	0.67
$200,000–$500,000	1.92	1.86
$500,000–$1 million	3.37	2.77
$1 million–$5 million	6.67	5.36
$5 million–$10 million	11.55	7.52
$10 million or more	18.38	10.6

Source: 2010 IRS Data Book

One out of every twelve individuals with $1 million or more in total positive income was audited in fiscal year 2010. For 2011 and 2012, it jumped to one out of eight.

The Internal Revenue Service has found that returns filed by people who make over $100,000 provide fertile grounds for audit reviews. Other groups watched closely include taxpayers with a second or sideline business, those who report hefty capital gain income, and all who might be involved in a partnership tax shelter.

The IRS has adopted a more efficient system for classifying individual taxpayers of similar economic circumstances in order to select returns for an audit. In the past, returns were selected on the basis of adjusted gross income. Under that old system, individuals were selected for audit by separating business and non-business returns, grouping them into examination classes according to adjusted gross income, and running each class through the mathematical "discriminant function" formula to identify returns with high audit potential.

This system had definite drawbacks from the Internal Revenue Service's perspective, because adjusted gross income is determined *after* deductions and adjustments, which are of primary interest to auditors. A return showing a high gross income but large offsetting deductions (as from tax shelters) would present a relatively low adjusted gross income. Therefore, it would be assigned to a low adjusted gross income examination class, would generally receive light audit coverage, and would be scored under a "discriminant function" formula not geared to test its true audit potential.

The IRS's new classification system is based upon total positive income, relying on the total income of a taxpayer *before* adjustments or deductions. This is the sum of all positive items on your return. Any negative items—for instance, losses from tax shelters—are treated as zero. As a result of this reclassification, suspicious deductions and adjustments will not escape notice in, or distort the voluntary compliance level of, an examination class designed for lower-income taxpayers.

RATTING TO THE IRS

There is an additional reason why your return might be chosen for an audit. While the Internal Revenue Service does not publicly encourage tax informers, its representatives admit that many investigations could not be successfully conducted without the use of paid informants or the direct purchase of evidence. Most informers are former employees of a business that has been underreporting its income. A disgruntled employee who does not "rat" on the business itself may "rat" on its owner, or on a disliked manager.

But a neighbor who objects to your loud stereo at midnight or becomes jealous of your new car each year may just as quickly turn informer. These unofficial "agents" are used extensively in cases where the taxpayer under investigation is allegedly engaged in illegal activity. Tax informers were normally rewarded with up to 10 percent of the additional tax collected up to a $75,000, 5 percent of the next $25,000, and 1 percent of any additional amount. The maximum reward was $10 million. Informants fill out Form 211 which they can get by calling 1-800-TAX FORM. Rewards can be paid to any person, other than a present or former federal employee. Even payments to police officials are allowed. The IRS does not divulge the identity of its informants, (see *Whistleblower 14106–10 W v. Commissioner,* 2011), but such rewards are fully taxable. However, the grant of a reward was discretionary, not mandatory (*Krug v. U.S. Fed Ct.,* No. 96-62IT, 5/27/98). In fact, the IRS's denial of an award to an informant is not even reviewable by a court (*Destefano v. U.S.,* 2002), *Cooper v. Commissioner of Internal Revenue,* 136 T.C. 30 (2011).

Since the late 1960s, only about 8 percent of claims from tipsters has been judged worthy of a reward. To informers, though, the money is often secondary to revenge. You should, therefore, keep two rules in mind:

1. Never cheat on your income taxes.
2. If you do, never anger anyone who might know about it.

The Tax Relief and Health Care Act of 2006 changed the rules to encourage more reports. Now we have two tiers of rewards—the old discretionary system above and a new mandatory system. Here are the rules for mandatory rewards:

Q. What is the maximum reward you can receive?

A. Under the new law, which was effective as of December 26, 2006, for cases involving $2 million in taxes, penalties, fines, and interest, there is no longer a cap on the maximum reward that can be obtained. For cases in which less than $2 million is at issue, there is a $10 million cap on rewards.

Q. What is the reward based upon?

A. The IRS reward is based upon the taxes, reduction in overpayment credits, civil but not criminal fines, penalties, and **interest** that the IRS collects as a result of the information provided to it. Criminal penalties don't count.

Q. What percentage of the IRS collection will you receive?

A. Under new law, which was effective as of December 26, 2006, for cases involving $2 million in taxes, penalties, fines, and interest and at least $200,000 in gross income (if an individual), the IRS will pay **between 15 percent and 30 percent** of the monies recovered. For cases in which less than $2 million is at issue the percentage of the reward will vary from 1 percent to 15 percent depending upon how much the information provided assists the IRS in its investigation.

Q. What determines the percentage of the Reward that you will receive?

A. The quality and specificity of the information and how helpful your information was to the IRS in its investigation determines in large part the percentage of the reward. The more specific your evidence and the more compelling your presentation of an IRS violation, the higher the reward will generally be. If the IRS is already aware of the violation, the less the reward will typically be.

Q. Will your name be kept confidential by the IRS?

A. The IRS keeps the name of the individual providing information confidential and will not disclose your name at anytime during its investigation. However, there are some exceptional circumstances under which the whistleblower's identity could be revealed. You should discuss these circumstances with your lawyer.

Q. Will the IRS use your information in a criminal or civil case?

A. Your information could be used in a civil or criminal case or both, depending upon the type of IRS violations and the type of information provided.

Q. What determines whether the IRS will use your information to conduct an investigation?

A. The quality of the information determines in large part whether the IRS will use your information to start an investigation. The more specific your evidence and the more compelling your presentation of an IRS violation, the more likely the IRS will use your evidence to conduct an investigation.

Q. Does the IRS have to pay a Reward if it uses your information?

A. Prior to the new legislation enacted on December 26, 2006, the IRS had the discretion to determine whether a reward should be paid and whether the reward should be anywhere from 1 percent to 15 percent. The new law provides that if the IRS uses your information in matters involving $2 million or more in taxes, penalties, fines, and interests, the IRS must pay a reward between 15 percent and 30 percent.

The new system seems to be working. For fiscal year 2009 the IRS received leads on 1,900 taxpayers, up from 1,246 in fiscal year 2008. Dozens of the tips involve purported tax losses of $100 million or more. In fiscal year 2010, the IRS collected $464.6 million as a result of tips, more than twice what it collected in the prior year. A CPA was awarded $4.5 million by the IRS on April 7, 2011, for a tip on a Fortune 500 company.

However, whistleblowers and their attorneys complained that the IRS has been slow to process whistleblower claims and in many cases refused to acknowledge them. The IRS paid fewer than 100 whistleblowers in 2011, about half the number it paid 2 years earlier, even though it received more than twice the number of whistleblower cases.

As of April 2011, about 66 percent of the claims submitted in fiscal 2007 and 2008 were still in process. Pressured by Senator Grassley, who held up the confirmation of high Treasury officials, the IRS got the hint and paid over 90 awards between October 2011 and the end of July 2012. In September 2012, whistleblower Bradley Birkenfeld was awarded $104 million by the IRS. In 2012, the IRS collected a total of $592.5 million from whistleblowers and paid informants $125.4 million on those claims.

If you see tax fraud, please call the IRS Tax Fraud Hotline at 1-800-829-0433. It takes an average of over 7 years to collect.

THE OTHER SIDE OF THE STORY

Despite its image as a bureaucracy of terror, in all fairness another side of the IRS story must be told. Staff turnover has been one of the IRS's biggest problems, according to the internal study mentioned at the start of this chapter. More than 50 percent of the agency's file clerks had less than 12 months of experience in their positions, and 36 percent of managers had been in their jobs less than 1 year. Moreover, many employees were in the lowest civil service pay grades, and, as one IRS employee quoted in the study put it, "We lose them to Hardee's," the fast-food franchise.

In 1999, the IRS reported losing more than 15,000 people over the prior 5 years and was still losing about 450 tax examiners a year! In one 4-year period, the IRS hired just 28 new revenue agents—total!

An April 2001 study conducted by the Syracuse University Transactional Records Access Clearinghouse (TRAC) found that the IRS's permanent staff, after reaching a high of 119,000 in 1988, declined 31 percent to 82,000 in 2000. At the same time, the study noted, corporate and individual tax returns increased 20 percent, returns of individuals with $100,000 of income had quadrupled, and returns of the largest corporations had doubled.

As of April 2002, the IRS was operating with 15,000 fewer staff members than it had in the early 1990s. Processing had to be maintained, so cuts went to auditing and collection.

Between 1996 and 2002, the number of revenue agents, revenue officers, and criminal investigations personnel declined by 25 percent.

The attrition rate among revenue agents for 2006 was 20 percent. But the IRS has replaced bodies to stop the bleed. In fiscal 2006, it hired 670 auditors for the Large and Mid-Size Division alone.

But experienced auditors were leaving, and many of those left were needed to train new agents.

Even before the so-called Tax Simplification Act of 1978, the Service was responsible for interpreting and administering codes, regulations, and revenue manuals that filled over 32 shelf-feet with an incredible 40,000 pages of the most arcane, unintelligible gobbledygook ever written. There have been many

Enforcement Revenue Collected[1]

(Dollars in Billions)	FY 2002	FY 2003	FY 2004	FY 2005	FY 2006	FY 2007	FY 2008	FY 2009	FY 2010	FY 2011	FY 2012
Collection	$24.4	$24.8	$25.7	$26.6	$28.2	$31.8	$31.1	$26.9	$29.1	$31.10	$30.44
Examination	$ 5.7	$ 8.8	$12.5	$13.8	$13.0	$15.2	$15.8	$12.6	$16.9	$12.40	$10.20
Appeals[2]	$ 2.2	$ 1.9	$ 2.2	$ 3.9	$ 4.3	$ 8.3	$ 4.8	$ 4.8	$ 6.7	$ 6.50	$ 4.20
Document Matching	$ 1.8	$ 2.2	$ 2.7	$ 3.1	$ 3.3	$ 3.9	$ 4.7	$ 4.6	$ 4.9	$ 5.20	$ 5.27
Total[3]	$34.1	$37.6	$43.1	$47.3	$48.7	$59.2	$56.4	$48.9	$57.6	$55.20	$50.20

Staffing for Key Enforcement Occupations[4]

	FY 2002	FY 2003	FY 2004	FY 2005	FY 2006	FY 2007	FY 2008	FY 2009	FY 2010	FY 2011	FY 2012
Revenue Officers	5,502	5,076	5,156	5,249	5,627	5,662	5,492	5,451	6,042	5,619	5,186
Revenue Agents	11,743	11,780	11,811	12,192	12,778	12,816	12,599	12,958	13,888	13,867	13,021
Special Agents	2,868	2,834	2,778	2,771	2,780	2,709	2,631	2,650	2,780	2,698	2,661
Total	20,113	19,691	19,746	20,211	21,185	21,187	20,722	21,059	22,710	22,184	20,868

Notes:

[1] Enforcement revenue collected in a fiscal year includes tax, interest, and penalties from multiple tax years. Some enforcement activities can take more than a year to close and may generate revenue over several years, so it is generally inappropriate to compare revenue collected in a given fiscal year to the staffing available for that same year.

[2] Includes any revenue collection attributable to IRS Appeals activities.

[3] Includes the Information Reporter Program (IRP) and the Automated Underreporter (AUR) Program.

[4] Enforcement staffing levels presented in Full Time Equivalents (FTE). FTE funded directly by the Enforcement appropriation and by reimbursements are included.

"tax reform" bills since 1978. The law is so complex, so convoluted, that it is incomprehensible. As former Citicorp Chairman Walter B. Wriston pointed out: "All the Congress, all the accountants and tax lawyers, all the judges and a convention of wizards cannot tell for sure what the income tax law says." Between 1985 and 1996 Congress changed more than 3,000 sections of the tax code and created more than 100 new forms. Asked to perform an impossible function, it's not surprising that the IRS agent often fails. In December 1990, former IRS Commissioner Lawrence B. Gibbs noted that the numerous complex changes in the Internal Revenue Code in recent years have resulted in "confusion and frustration within the IRS and among taxpayers and their representatives." In November 2002, IRS National Taxpayer Advocate Nina Olson found taxpayers to be "frustrated" and "confused." Surprise!

That may account for an average of 16 percent of the total IRS workforce dropping out of the agency every year as revealed in June 2008. A TIGTA report from about the same time forecast the loss of 51 percent of the agency's executives and managers by 2010.

In 2009, the TIGTA reported that the IRS had made a significant effort to recruit new employees. But with an attrition rate for mission critical operations of 6.8 percent throughout the agency over the last several years, the agency has been unable to replace all the employees being lost. More than half of IRS employees and managers were age 50 or older, and 39 percent of IRS executives and 20 percent of managers were already eligible for retirement.

In 2009, the IRS hired 1,600 new revenue agents, 1,100 revenue officers, and 400 tax compliance officers. But as reported, roughly 20 percent of IRS employees in managerial roles became eligible to retire in 2010. To keep up, the IRS will have to recruit one manager a day for the next 10 years according to the TIGTA.

In 2010 the IRS added nearly 1,300 revenue agents and tax compliance officers. But the increased hiring did not make up for the growing IRS workload or pace of attrition.

Budget cuts and mission creep continue to weaken the IRS. Recent tax changes have expanded the IRS's role in administrating social, non-tax-related programs. Each dollar cut from the IRS budget costs as much as $200 in lost revenue. As of the end of 2011, more than half of IRS employees and managers have reached 50 years old and 39 percent of IRS executives were already eligible for retirement.

The IRS budget is down $1 billion since 2012, despite the increased responsibility from combating identity theft and implementing new laws. The Service is nearly 10,000 employees below in 2013 where it was during the 2010 filing season. Key enforcement jobs dropped 6 percent from 2012 to 2013 and more than 3,000 IRS employees are currently working on identity theft—double the figures from the prior year. Forty percent of IRS staff becomes eligible for retirement in the next 5 years said the TIGTA in February 2013. Finding qualified people will be a problem.

IRS EVALUATED—CONFUSION AND COMPLEXITY

Such confusion has been documented by Ralph Nader's Tax Reform Research Group. They prepared 22 identical tax reports based on the fictional economic plight of a married couple with one child, and these 22 identical copies were submitted to 22 different IRS offices around the country. Each office came up with an entirely different tax figure. The results varied from a refund of $811.96 recommended in Flushing, New York, to a tax-due figure of $52.14 derived by the tax office in Portland, Oregon.

In 1983, *USA Today* took an informal telephone survey of IRS tax-assistance offices in 15 major cities across the United States. Seven questions were picked that private tax consultants agreed were common and difficult but fair. For each question, interviewers called 10 IRS telephone tax assistants—70 phone calls in all. In 20 cases—28.6 percent of the time—the Internal Revenue Service's answers were wrong. In 5 more cases, the Internal Revenue Service's answers were only partly correct, bringing the total of incorrect or incomplete answers to 35.7 percent.

Furthermore, getting through to the Internal Revenue Service by phone was close to impossible. In the *USA Today* study, it was found that the IRS telephone line was busy 9 times out of 10 in New York City. When it did ring, the phone often went unanswered. On one try it rang 48 times before being picked up, and twice it rang 25 times to no avail.

On February 12, 1985, the *Wall Street Journal* asked the same four tax law questions of 17 IRS offices. Two questions, involving the casualty loss deduction and one-time diesel credit, were answered correctly most of the time. The other two, involving the medical expense deduction and the wash sale rules, resulted in totally or partially wrong answers most of the time. Walter M. Alt, Director of the IRS Taxpayers' Services Division, told the *Journal* that he was "dismayed and unhappy" about the errors. IRS advice is not binding—whether oral or in print. In fact, the IRS is not bound by statements contained in its own publications, including *Your Federal Income Tax*, the IRS's free instruction booklet (*Thomas R. Underwood*, T.C. Memo 1983–99; *Harvey Richard Bennett*, T.C. Memo 1983–183; see also *Sundermeier*, T.C. Memo 1987–50, wherein taxpayers were not permitted to rely on an IRS publication, even though their local IRS office advised them that there was no other information available).

According to U.S. District Court Judge Michael M. Mihm, in his opinion in *Sinn Oil Company, et al. v. United States:* "The case law has girded the Internal Revenue Service with a nearly impregnable shield against the people it serves.

Beginning with a Code which in its complexity is well nigh unfathomable to the average citizen...the judicial coup de grace is executed with the insistence that, if the taxpayer could find the relevant section and if he could be assured that there is not some supervening or nullifying regulation elsewhere and if he could then read and understand it, his reliance on the verbal representations of an agent [is] unreasonable."

The General Accounting Office did a study of its own: It checked out a sample of 2,543 tax returns in which the Internal Revenue Service had found 3,720 errors in arithmetic. Unfortunately, the General Accounting Office noted that the Internal Revenue Service itself had made nearly two-thirds of the errors. The General Accounting Office said that 33 million errors were found on the 94 million individual income tax returns processed in the fiscal year 1981, of which 37 percent were made by taxpayers and *63 percent* were made by employees of the IRS!

Another General Accounting Office survey in February and March of 1987 also faulted the accuracy of the IRS taxpayer telephone assistance program. The GAO found that taxpayers who called the Internal Revenue Service with tax law questions got inaccurate or incomplete answers more than one-third of the time. The survey showed that the IRS assistors provided correct answers to basic questions posed by callers from the General Accounting Office 63 percent of the time, correct but incomplete answers 15 percent of the time, and incorrect answers 22 percent of the time.

One year later things had not improved. A 1989 GAO report found that more than one-third of the answers that IRS telephone assistors provided were inaccurate. The GAO said that assisters provided the correct answer to a group of 20 questions only 64 percent of the time. According to House Ways and Means Committee Oversight Subcommittee Chairman J. J. Pickle of Texas, "Calling the IRS for tax advice is a real crap shoot."

Things didn't get better in 1999. In a GAO report issued in December, 1999, they reported that despite having assistors available 24 hours a day, 7 days a week, "The service did not improve. Instead it deteriorated."

Things were no better when the IRS took the time to write. A GAO review dated May 24, 1988, found that IRS centers issued incorrect, incomplete, unresponsive, or unclear correspondence half the time. The GAO considered IRS errors in 30 percent of this correspondence critical; these letters each contained at least one instance in which the Adjustment/Correspondence Branch either provided incorrect information, failed to address all the taxpayer's questions, or acted incorrectly in adjusting or failing to adjust the taxpayer's account.

Things had improved in 1990 when 77 percent of the telephone questions were answered correctly compared to 64 percent in 1989. However, while the questions asked by taxpayers were answered correctly more often than in 1989, fewer taxpayers were able to reach IRS personnel for assistance. IRS answered about 34 percent of the calls it received in 1990, while the balance either reached busy signals or hung up after being placed on hold, GAO said. In 1989, 58 percent of the incoming calls were answered.

The IRS's performance in handling calls from taxpayers deteriorated in 1992, according to the General Accounting Office. About 7 out of every 10 calls to the IRS between January 1 and April 25 went unanswered, the congressional watchdog agency says. That was up from 6 out of 10 calls in 1991. On the bright side, IRS helpers correctly answered 85 percent of questions posed by anonymous IRS test callers, up from 84 percent the prior year.

The "most significant" decline was in the timeliness with which IRS filled GAO's test mail and phone orders, the report noted. For example, GAO received only 33 percent of the mail-ordered items within IRS' 14-day goal, as compared to 74 percent the previous year, the report said.

However, Internal Revenue Service data, as of April 8, 1992, showed that 9 out of the 10 IRS service centers had met or exceeded IRS' 98 percent refund accuracy goal, and that all 10 service centers met IRS' goal of issuing taxpayers refunds in an average of 40 days or less, GAO said in the report (*Tax Administration: IRS' 1992 Filing Season Was Successful but Not without Problems,* GAO/GGD-92-132).

According to the GAO, taxpayers who called the IRS in 1993 had only a one in four chance of getting through—worse than in 1992. It found IRS efforts to communicate with taxpayers by mail littered with "delayed, inaccurate, incomplete, and confusing responses" to taxpayer questions.

In 1995, according to IRS data, telephone assistors answered 11 percent more calls than the IRS anticipated and provided accurate answers to 91 percent of the questions asked. However, the General Accounting Office reported that the IRS received many more calls than it was able to answer—only about 9 percent of the calls made during the study period were answered. In 1996, as a result of 119 million fewer calls, the IRS increased its rate of calls answered to 20 percent.

Moreover, the IRS, the auditor of us all, failed its own audit. The General Accounting Office in 1995 reported that it could not verify the reliability of the IRS's internal financial statements for 1993 and 1994 because of "poor accounting practices." They could not even verify either total revenue collected nor tax refunds paid!

In 1997, the GAO reported that at several facilities it inspected, the IRS could not account for about 6,400 missing tapes, cartridges, and other magnetic storage devices that could contain taxpayer data.

In a 1999 GAO audit, the IRS was found to continue to suffer from "serious financial management system deficiencies and internal control weaknesses. . . ."

Things weren't much better in March 2000, when the GAO reported that the "IRS cannot complete some of the basic accounting and recordkeeping tasks it expects from American taxpayers."

The good news in 1998 was that the GAO found that the IRS "met or exceeded most" of its 1997 tax-filing season goals, such as making it easier for taxpayers to reach the agency by phone. Perhaps the tide is beginning to turn. Perhaps not—in 1999, the chances of a taxpayer actually getting through to the IRS were only 54 percent, lower than in 1998, and, according to Commissioner Rossotti, "May not improve in 2000." Why?—Budget limitations!

In a May 2001 report by the Treasury Inspector General for Tax Administration, IRS employees charged with helping taxpayers at walk-in sites (now called Taxpayer Assistance Centers) around the United States provided incorrect or insufficient answers 73 percent of the time. The report found that taxpayers seeking help were sometimes denied service, told to return at another time or another day, had to wait excessive lengths of time to obtain help, and were occasionally subjected to IRS practices that may have confused, embarrassed, or angered them. Another report, released in July 2002, showed a vast improvement, but 20 percent of the answers were still incorrect.

In a January 2001 report, the General Accounting Office noted that major problems continued to persist. "Longstanding material weaknesses" remain in the IRS's systems and internal controls, says the report that focuses on fiscal 1999. Among the problem areas: "fundamentally deficient operational and financial systems" and "inadequate internal controls, policies, and procedures."

On May 15, 2002, the Federal Performance Project gave the IRS an overall grade of B minus in assessing the agency's management. In February, the GAO had issued an unqualified audit opinion for the second consecutive year on the IRS's financial statements. In addition, the GAO found, in May that five of the six IRS compliance programs and both of the IRS's collection programs have suffered "large and pervasive" declines.

According to then-Commissioner Rossotti, on September 24, 2002, the IRS was "winning the battle but losing the war." Rossotti reported that over the previous 5 years, the number of income tax returns increased by 12 million, while 19 tax bills were passed that changed 292 tax code sections and required 575 changes to forms and instructions.

Moreover, fixing IRS mistakes can take a long time. In one case, the IRS wrongly entered a taxpayer's $4,668 adjusted gross income as $466,800. "As a result, the taxpayer was assessed over $160,000 in taxes when he was actually due a refund," the GAO said. "It took 18 months for IRS to abate this erroneous assessment even though documentation in the case file indicated that IRS personnel believed the assessment was erroneous 10 months before they corrected the report." An IRS official says the agency agrees "on the whole" with the GAO report's recommendations for improvement.

By 2003, things were still mixed. The General Accounting Office concluded in reviewing the 2002 tax filing season, that ". . . IRS's performance included issuing almost all refunds on time, providing more accurate telephone service than 2001, and meeting many of its 2002 performance goals in all areas." The IRS customer service representatives answered 1.6 million more calls than in 2001. But, that was 2.6 million less than service's 2002 goal.

A December 2003 report from the Treasury Inspector General revealed that during a survey of assistance sites across the country, IRS employees incorrectly prepared 19 of 23 tax returns.

Some things did get better in 2003 when the GAO found that the IRS improved its filing season performance in key areas involving returns processing, refunds, electronic services, and taxpayer assistance. The IRS even improved its phone service—providing 872,000 more toll-free services than the prior year. But, 6.7 million taxpayers got disconnected.

So, how are they doing now? Since then, government studies have found:

- The IRS is not always following guidelines when conducting seizures. In 2007, 17 of the 50 cases it studied had violations.
- The time needed to resolve a taxpayer problem by the Taxpayer Advocate Service more than doubled from fiscal 1998 to 2003, from 37 to 76 days. This was despite no decrease in staff or increase in workload.
- The IRS Centralized Authorization file contained incomplete or incorrect information in about 40 percent of the records reviewed.
- The IRS system designed to uncover unauthorized access to IRS electronic data continues to malfunction.
- The IRS failed to release tax liens on nearly 23,000 taxpayers with no liability (32 percent of all liens).
- 21 percent of taxpayers were not at all satisfied with IRS customer service in 2004, up from 19 percent in 2003.
- A 2005 study concluded that the IRS had "serious weaknesses" in its ability to protect sensitive taxpayer and financial data.
- A 2006 TIGTA report found a 27 percent error rate at IRS taxpayer assistance centers. That might explain a 2007 study showing visits to such centers down by more than 1.9 million, a 22 percent decrease.
- The IRS system that is used to detect fraudulent returns had "significant security vulnerabilities" in a 2007 TIGTA study.
- Telephone inquiries were inaccurate as much as 10 percent of the time in 2006 as per a GAO study.

But there was some "good" news.

- For the 2004 filing season, the IRS gave taxpayers complete and accurate information regarding their accounts during 94 percent of all monitored calls. So 6 percent still got their accounts wrong.
- The accuracy of answers to tax questions at IRS offices improved to 67 percent in 2004. Still, 33 percent wrong?!
- In 2005 questions were answered correctly 66 percent of the time. That's still 34 percent wrong.
- But phone accuracy in 2005 jumped from 79.5 percent the year before to 89.5 percent. It surged to almost 90 percent in 2006.
- That's better if you can get through. Unfortunately phone accessibility slidded to 82 percent—18 percent couldn't even connect to ask a question.
- In 2006 telephone answers were still wrong about 10 percent of the time.
- In 2007 telephone answers were wrong only 9 percent of the time.
- Customer satisfaction for 2007 was up to 94 percent, at least for the 82 percent that actually got through.
- A 2009 TIGTA study found errors and legal violations in nearly half the IRS property seizures it studied.
- The IRS still needs help with the phone. In 2009, 5 million taxpayers received busy signals, and almost 18 million callers hung up before getting through.
- The GAO in 2009 found the IRS computer network still vulnerable to internal threats.
- After another 2009 study by the TIGTA, it was concluded that unauthorized and insecure Web servers placed both the computers and the entire IRS network at risk of unauthorized access to taxpayer and personally identifiable information.
- The IRS spent nearly 2 years and $19.5 million to develop its new Web portal, but it cancelled the project 6 months before its scheduled completion date.
- As of December 2008, the IRS had implemented only 81 percent of the security settings mandated by the Office of Management and Budget.
- The level of services on toll-free lines in 2009 was 71 percent, up from 53 percent in 2008. That's still 29 percent of calls not answered.
- A 2010 TIGTA report found that the IRS failed to follow statutory taxpayer rights when filing tax liens.
- Let's not even think about how the IRS handled the home buyer credit. The TIGTA identified more than 19,000 electronic returns claiming credit

in excess of $139 million for homes not yet bought and 580 taxpayers under age 18 who reported to be first-time home buyers.

- In 2010, the TIGTA concluded that the IRS had lost $695,115 in interest due to slow processing of paper checks.

- Another 2010 TIGTA report found that the IRS was not authenticating taxpayers who called toll-free assistance lines before giving out confidential tax account information.

- IRS employees did not work well with others. Two Covington, Kentucky, service center workers were charged with stealing money orders, and a California IRS agent was indicted for filing false tax returns, helping others to file false tax returns, and threatening to kill tax agents who were investigating him.

- Even volunteers had it rough, with a government audit finding that on 3.5 million returns filed, there was an accuracy rate of only 59 percent, in 2009, down from 69 percent in 2008.

- With the new IRS2Go 2.0 smartphone app, you can apply for a transcript, get the latest IRS news, or watch IRS YouTube videos.

- They are happy. Seventy-five percent of IRS employees were either "very satisfied" or "satisfied" with their jobs in 2011, up from 74 percent in 2010 and 55 percent in 2002. The fact that they actually had jobs may have been an influence.

- We are happy. In September 2011, TIGTA found IRS management in compliance with the law on employee evaluation standards. It found that the IRS did *not* use quota or tax enforcement results records to evaluate employee performance.

- In fiscal 2012, the IRS detected 3 million fraudulent returns totaling $20 billion, up from $14 billion in the prior year.

- The accuracy rate for the IRS Volunteer Program increased to 49 percent in 2012, up from 39 percent in 2011. That's still 51 percent wrong!

- The TIGTA in March 2013 found the IRS information technology system more than 2 years behind schedule, leaving taxpayers' information vulnerable to hackers.

- The IRS telephone service level in 2012 declined to 68 percent and 40 percent of the paper correspondence received by the IRS failed to be responded to within 45 days of receipt.

- In fiscal 2012, IRS employees used 573,319 hours on union activity, equivalent to 23,888 days!

- In fiscal 2012 and 2013, the IRS spent over $1 million on travel expenses for union activity.
- The IRS spent over $4.8 million in fiscal 2011 and $4.7 million in fiscal 2012 for executive travel.
- In a 2012 study, the TIGTA found that the IRS did not comply with legal seizure guidelines in 15 cases out of a random sampling of 50 seizures.
- According to TIGTA, the IRS is doing a poor job with identity theft reports. Many identity theft victims, including some visitors to IRS assistance centers, incorrectly used Form 3949-A to notify the IRS. That form is supposed to be used to report suspected fraudulent tax activity of individuals and businesses. Adding insult to injury, the Service destroyed about 3,000 forms filed by identity theft victims. If you believe you might be a victim of identity theft, call the IRS at 800-908-4490.
- Good news! The IRS has decided not to audit a taxpayer for more than 5 consecutive years. On the other hand, you may qualify for Examination Technique Code 4. That's where an audit can be closed after the initial appointment with a taxpayer.

The law is so complicated that it is difficult to fault the IRS on their incorrect answers, even when a taxpayer call goes through. In a 1988 study done by *Money* magazine, 50 tax professionals, including attorneys and CPAs, were asked to complete a tax return for a hypothetical family. The results were "unnerving"—no two preparers computed the same tax due and, worse, the answers varied by as much as 50 percent! In a second study by *Money*, done one year later, the answers were even more off the mark. Again, each participant computed a different tax for the family. And the bottom line ranged astonishingly from a low of $12,539 to a high of $35,813. The *Money* studies have continued each year with different bottom lines computed each year. The *minimum* spread was 50 percent in 1988; it was nearly 1,000 percent in 1991.

A 2006 GAO undercover investigation revealed poor performance at 19 tax-prep chain operations. Among the problems were micalculated refunds resulting in unwarranted extra refunds or incorrectly figured losses; unreported business income; faulty calculation of earned income credit; failure of preparers to take the most advantageous post-secondary education tax benefit; and improper itemization of deductions or failure to claim all available deductions.

The complexity and its confusion continue. Tax Analysts created a fictitious profile for a taxpayer in 2009 and filled out several free file tax returns. Each company calculated a different refund amount for the taxpayer, ranging from $1,201 to $3,400! Personally, I'd file the return with the $3,400 refund.

The IRS's office of professional responsibility has revealed that even tax practitioners who have been convicted of *tax crimes* continued to represent entities before the IRS. In a statistical survey, it was found that 4.5 percent of practitioners were noncompliant regarding their own individual tax obligations.

Thankfully, former IRS Commissioner Lawrence Gibbs, in a hearing of the Senate Finance Committee on Private Retirement Plans and IRS Oversight, stated that the IRS would not impose penalties on taxpayers who relied on incorrect information supplied by IRS telephone taxpayer assistance personnel. Nevertheless, the tax itself would not be forgiven, and the taxpayer would have the burden of maintaining a record of the name of the IRS employee who supplied the incorrect information as well as the date of the conversation.

Even though the Internal Revenue Service may not always be accurate, it strives always to be prepared. The IRS has revised IRM 1(16)00—Physical, Document, and Computer Systems Security—to include two former policy statements, P-1-165 and P-1-166. Both statements cover national emergency operations. The first statement discusses the function of the "IRS in the Event of a National Emergency—Especially Resulting from a Nuclear Attack." In case of an emergency, the primary duty of the IRS "is to support the Secretary of the Treasury." To this end, the duties of the IRS "will consist of analyzing and reporting on emergency tax legislation, prescribing regulations in forms, and issuing rulings and technical information of an emergency nature." The second statement specifies that, in the event of an emergency, the IRS will focus on operations that, given the circumstances, would yield the greatest revenue. "On the premise that the collection of delinquent accounts would be most adversely affected, and in many cases would be impossible in a disaster area, the Service will concentrate on the collection of current taxes," the manual said. Given the real possibility of a nuclear attack, I, for one, feel a lot more comfortable.

THE AUDIT

Internal Revenue Code Section 7605(a) gives the IRS the authority to fix the time and place of an audit as is reasonable under the circumstances. The Internal Revenue Manual states that IRS examiners should endeavor to make appointments at a time and place convenient for the taxpayer (IRM 4261.2). (See also Temp Reg. Section 301.7605-IT.)

Generally, the office that handles your audit will be determined by your domicile—where you live. However, the Internal Revenue Service will approve a request for a transfer of an audit if your domicile has changed before or during the exami-nation or if you have died and your legal representative is in another district. The following rules for audit location generally apply:

1. A request for a transfer to a district closer to your residence will normally be approved.

2. If you live in one district, work in another, and are not represented by a Power of Attorney, you will be examined in the district where you reside.

3. If you are called for an audit in one district but live in another district that is within commuting distance (not defined) of the first, and are represented by a Power of Attorney within that distance, the audit will normally take place in the district where you reside.

4. If you live in one district and are represented by a Power of Attorney doing business in another district that is within commuting distance of the first, you will be audited in the district where you live.

5. If you live in another district outside commuting distance of the district where your return is scheduled for audit and are represented by a Power of Attorney in the other district, you will have a transfer request approved.

6. If you reside in the district where the audit is scheduled and are represented by a Power of Attorney in a district outside commuting distance of the first, you may obtain a transfer if the receiving district agrees.

Each IRS district office is made up of four divisions. Each division is subdivided into branches, the titles of which describe what is done in each branch. The four divisions are Administration, Collection, Audit, and Intelligence.

The Administration Division handles such matters as personnel, training, and facilities management of all types—from selection of the site of the office to ordering pens and paper.

The Collection Division is the bill-collecting arm of the Internal Revenue Service. It is represented in the field by Revenue Officers and in the Office Branch. The Collection Division also has a section known as the Taxpayer Service Section, which is a year-round information center manned by Taxpayer Service Representatives.

The Intelligence Division is the branch of the Internal Revenue Service that handles criminal investigations. It is staffed with Special Agents, who are enforcement officers and whose work is primarily technical. The main objective of an investigation by a Special Agent is to determine whether or not there should be criminal prosecution—as contrasted with an Internal Revenue Agent's objective, which is to determine the proper tax to be paid.

The Audit Division is charged with verifying the accuracy of tax returns filed, regarding both the substance of the law and the validity of the amounts reported. The major branches of the Audit Division are Field Audit, Office Audit, Review, and Audit Service. They have been renamed Examinations Branch. Field Audit

IRS STRATEGIC PLANNING FRAMEWORK

MISSION

Provide America's taxpayers top quality service by helping them understand and meet their tax responsibilities and by applying the tax law with integrity and fairness to all.

GUIDING PRINCIPLES

- Understand and solve problems from taxpayer's point of view

- Enable managers to be accountable — knowledge, responsibility, authority, action

- Align measures of performance at all organizational levels.

- Foster open, honest communication

- Insist on total integrity

- Demonstrate effective stewardship of assets and information entrusted to the IRS

STRATEGIC GOALS and OBJECTIVES

Service to Each Taxpayer
- Make filing easier
- Provide first quality service to each taxpayer needing help with his or her return or account
- Provide prompt, professional, helpful treatment to taxpayers in cases where additional taxes may be due

Service to All Taxpayer
- Increase fairness of compliance
- Increase overall compliance

Productivity through a Quality Work Environment
- Increase employee job satisfaction
- Hold agency employment stable while economy grows and service improves

MODERNIZATION PROGRAMS

Fundamental long-term improvement in way IRS works

Organizational Modernization
- Customer-focused organizational structure
- Clear management roles and responsibilities

Business Systems Modernization
- Develop enterprise vision and architecture
- Revamp all major business practices
- Reengineer technology

Balanced Measures
- Align with strategic goals

Modernization Projects

Strategic Measures
- For major taxpayer segments
- Agency as a whole

Operational Measures
- For each operational program or activity

MAJOR STRATEGIES

How IRS will achieve goals in near term (2–3 years)

Operational Priorities
- Specific areas of emphasis to achieve strategies and goals

Improvement Projects
- Focused, near-term improvements in business practices and technology

Program Plans
- Program activities and resources
- Operational measures

IRS MISSION

Provide America's taxpayers top-quality service by helping them understand and meet their tax responsibilities and by applying the tax law with integrity and fairness to all.

STRATEGIC GOALS AND OBJECTIVES

Service to Each Taxpayer	Service to All Taxpayer	Productivity through a Quality Work Environment
• Make filing easier • Provide first quality service to each taxpayer needing help with his or her return or account • Provide prompt, professional, helpful treatment to taxpayers in cases where additional taxes may be due	• Increase fairness of compliance • Increase overall compliance	• Increase employee job satisfaction • Hold agency employment stable while economy grows and service improves

IRS Balanced Measures System | **Organizational Performance**

SERVICEWIDE and MAJOR CUSTOMER SEGMENT STRATEGIC MEASURES

• Overall customer satisfaction • Burden	• Payment compliance • Filing compliance • Reporting compliance	• Overall employee satisfaction • Productivity/Workload index

OPERATING UNIT OPERATIONAL MEASURES

• Customer satisfaction with specific products and services	• Quality of work products and services produced • Quality, accuracy and timeliness of products and services provided	• Organizational unit and Work group employee satisfaction

DIAGNOSTIC and WORKLOAD INDICATORS

• Diagnostic data that is helpful in understanding what influences and impacts operational and strategic measures

• Workload data used to project expected levels of activity for an organizational unit or program

INDIVIDUAL MEASURES

• Performance plans or agreements for executives, managers, and management officials aligned with strategic goals and balanced measures of customer satisfaction, employee satisfaction, and business results

• Critical job elements for front-line employees aligned with the goals of balanced measures

employs Internal Revenue Agents and Estate Tax Examiners, and they are charged with auditing the more complex tax returns filed. Office Audit is staffed with Tax Auditors, who primarily audit individual returns. The Review staff is composed of former Field Agents and Tax Auditors, who check the accuracy of the audits made by the examining officers. Audit Service maintains the files on prior reports by examining officers and is a control center for cases under audit or cases that have been audited.

The charts on pages 657 and 658 detail the 2001 IRS strategic planning framework.

Victims of IRS errors now have a form on which to claim reimbursement. Such a claim is allowable under 31 U.S.C. Section 3732 but is limited to $1,000 and must be submitted within 1 year of its accrual. Filers of new Form 8489, Claim for Reimbursement for Expenses Incurred Due to Service Error, are instructed to submit substantiating documentation and are cautioned not to claim expenses for telephone calls, mileage or parking, lost wages, postage, or other nonreimbursable costs of the kind that are common to any disputed bill.

The scope of an audit will depend on various factors, but according to a recent addition to the IRS Manual, there are four items that *must* be reviewed by an agent:

1. Income probes, including bank statement analysis, bartering schemes, sale of assets, prizes, alimony, pensions, income tax refunds, etc.

2. Determination of the results of previous audits, including when the last took place, the results, and any recent correspondence the taxpayer may have had with the IRS.

3. Examination of subsequent and prior years' returns to make sure whether they were filed on time, where similar adjustments to the year under examination are necessary, and whether there are other issues that should be probed.

4. Determination of whether penalties have been previously assessed and whether they should be assessed as a result of the current examination.

The IRS Manual instructs the agents to comment on these items in their workpapers or to document the reasons why they were not examined.

According to IRS guidelines, unless specific recordkeeping requirements must be met, statements by the taxpayer, or others, may serve as adequate evidence in an audit. The IRS Manual notes that adequate evidence does not require complete documentation (IRM 4231, Audit Guidelines for Examiners, 330[2]).

Because the law is so vague in spots and so complicated, an intensive review and appeals procedure is available to you. Once your audit has been completed, the agent will present a Revenue Agent's Report stating recommendations and advising of any additional tax you owe. You will then be asked to sign a waiver indicating that you agree with the assessment. At this point you have three choices:

1. You can accept the adjustments, sign the waiver, and pay the tax.
2. You can pay the tax and file for a refund of the disputed amount.
3. You can request a conference with the IRS Appellate Division.

Prior to October 2, 1978, you could have taken a dispute with a revenue agent to a district conference. If an agreement was not reached there, a second hearing was available at the appellate division level. Alternatively, you could have elected to go directly to the appellate division. Under the present system the Internal Revenue Service maintains appeals offices at all locations where full-time district conferees and regional appellate offices were formerly located. The theory of eliminating the district conference is that, according to the Internal Revenue Service, the two-level system of administrative review was a costly duplication, for both the taxpayer and the Service.

It is almost universally agreed that it is best to settle at the agent level, if possible. If the tax deficiency involved is small, it may not justify the cost in time and dollars of pursuing your case to a higher level. Moreover, if the agent has missed items that you don't want questioned, your best approach may be to pay the deficiency and run. But *never* settle or concede any issue until the audit is completed. When the agent's cards are on the table, you have more leeway in planning your negotiation strategy.

For a psychological advantage, where appropriate, you may wish to tape-record the audit proceedings. The Internal Revenue Service has revised the table of contents for, and added new text to, IRM 7600, Processing Determination Letter Applications. The new text, IRM 7610, Verbatim Recording of Conversations during Determination Proceedings, provides that verbatim recordings of Determination Proceedings will be permitted ordinarily with group manager approval (Manual Transmittal 7600-50 [11-18-83]; *Mott*, 214 F. Supp. 20 [N.D. Cal. 1963]; 1 Audit, CCH Internal Revenue Manual 4245). The absolute right to audiorecord a taxpayer interview was codified in Section 7520, enacted as part of the Omnibus Taxpayer Bill of Rights (you can even record an appeals hearing, *Keene v. Commissioner*, July 9, 2003), but see *Huehne*, 83-2345 (October 23, 1983), wherein the Court ruled that the taxpayer did not have a right to videotape the audit. However, in 2012, Taxpayer Advocate Nina Olson recommended that the IRS set up the technology to conduct virtual face-to-face audits via video-conference.

If you disagree with the agent's assessment, you will receive a copy of the revenue agent's report with a preliminary note advising you that you have

30 days to appeal. If you ignore this letter, you will then receive a "90-day" letter advising you to pay or to petition the tax court for redetermination.

After receiving the 30-day letter, but before receiving the 90-day letter, you may request a hearing by notifying your IRS regional appeals office. If the original audit was conducted by a tax auditor at an IRS office or by correspondence, you do not have to file a written protest to begin the appeal process. In the past, if the disputed amount was $2,500 or less, the same was true of a field examination conducted at your place of business; and if your field audit resulted in a disputed amount over $2,500, a written protest was necessary. These rules were changed by the IRS. Now, a written protest is required for field examinations only if the amount at issue for any tax year exceeds $25,000. (If the amount at issue does not exceed $25,000 but exceeds $2,500, a brief written statement of disputed issues is required [IA-85-91, 9/17/93].) As under prior law, no brief written statement or written protest is required to obtain an appeals office conference, in-office interview, or correspondence examination. An oral request will still suffice. The protest should be filed in duplicate and should contain the following:

a) your name and address;

b) the date and case reference symbols on the letter from the Internal Revenue Service transmitting the findings that you are protesting;

c) the tax years or periods involved;

d) an itemized schedule of adjustments or findings with which you do not agree;

e) a statement that you want to appeal the findings of the revenue agent;

f) a statement of factual evidence supporting your position in the contested issues, which should be sworn to as true, under penalties of perjury; *and*

g) a statement outlining the law or other authority upon which you are relying.

In response to your protest, an appellate conferee will meet with you at the regional office to discuss the disputed issues. While such a hearing is an informal procedure, you must remember that the burden of proof is still on you to provide clear and convincing evidence that the revenue agent's report should be amended. While oral statements and evidence will be considered, the best evidence is documentary—books, records, worksheets, journals, and so forth.

To help you with the appeals process, the IRS has created an appeals customer service program. You can call the following numbers to get help with any appeals matter:

Telephone Directory—National (Toll-Free) 877-457-5055

Appeals Customer Service Representation

Office (Location)	Customer Service Representatives (Not A Toll-Free Number)
NORTHEAST REGION	
Brooklyn *(Hempstead)*	516-539-6259
Connecticut-Rhode Island *(East Hartford)*	860-390-4055
Manhattan *(New York City)*	212-298-2430
Michigan *(Detroit)*	313-226-2314 ext. 62344
New England *(Boston)*	617-565-7962
New Jersey *(Newark)*	973-645-6288
Ohio *(Cleveland)*	216-623-2047
Pennsylvania *(Philadelphia)*	215-597-2177 ext. 160
Upstate New York *(Buffalo)*	716-551-5330 ext. 21
SOUTHEAST REGION	
Delaware-Maryland *(Baltimore)*	410-962-9354
Georgia *(Atlanta)*	404-338-7335
Gulf Coast *(New Orleans)*	504-558-3177
Indiana *(Indianapolis)*	317-226-6778
Kentucky-Tennessee *(Nashville)*	615-250-5613
North Florida *(Jacksonville)*	904-665-0962
North-South Carolina *(Greensboro)*	336-378-2309
South Florida *(Ft. Lauderdale)*	305-982-5377
Virginia-West Virginia *(Richmond)*	804-771-2302 ext. 19
MIDSTATES REGION	
Oklahoma-Arkansas *(Oklahoma)*	405-297-4941
Houston *(Houston)*	281-721-7255
Illinois *(Chicago)*	312-886-5736 ext. 652
Kansas-Missouri *(St. Louis)*	314-612-4652
Midwest *(Milwaukee)*	414-297-4120
North Central *(St. Paul)*	651-290-3867 ext. 351
North Texas *(Dallas)*	972-308-7329
South Texas *(Austin)*	512-499-5650
WESTERN REGION	
Central California *(San Jose)*	408-817-4622
Los Angeles *(Los Angeles)*	213-894-4700 ext. 129
Northern California *(San Francisco)*	415-744-9255

Office (Location)	Customer Service Representatives (Not A Toll-Free Number)
Northern California *(San Francisco)*	415-744-9255
Pacific Northwest *(Seattle)*	206-220-6054
Southern California *(Laguna Niguel)*	949-360-6380
Southwest *(Phoenix)*	602-207-8167
Rocky Mountain *(Denver)*	303-844-1951

For additional information, contact:
National Office *(Washington, DC)*
Office of Alternative Dispute Resolution and Customer Service Progrmas: Tom Louthan (202) 694-1842, Frederick L. Gavin (616)235-1280 or Darlene Marshall (202)694-1875
Regional Coordinators
Northeast Region (New York City): Ellen Wassong (212)298-2361
Southeast Region (Atlanta): Janell Gadd (404)338-7706
Midstates Region (Dallas): Leonard Horton (972)308-7495
Western Region (San Francisco): Dennis Malone (415)575-7313

The informality of the conference hearing is designed to save time and trouble for all parties. You may represent yourself, or you may be represented by an attorney, CPA, or an enrolled agent, an individual licensed to practice before the Internal Revenue Service. The aim of this stage of the appeals process is to resolve the issues with as little difficulty as possible. The objective here is to *settle!* In fiscal 1979 IRS agents at this level proposed to assess $1,900,124,000 in added tax and penalties. They *closed* these cases for $1,161,977,000—about 61 percent of the proposed assessments. In 1982, appeals officers heard more than 50,000 cases covering an estimated 150,000 separate tax returns in over 500 locations. According to Howard T. Martin, director of the Appeals Division, "Appeal officers have more flexibility, and we never give up the idea of resolving a case." A 1982 survey by the General Accounting Office found that extra taxes and penalties were reduced or eliminated in 84 percent of the cases in appeals. Unlike agents at the audit level, Appeals Officers can settle cases based on "hazards of litigation." Thus, in Appeals, it is possible to split or trade issues.

The Internal Revenue Service tells its Appellate personnel to negotiate settlements "on a basis which is fair to both the Government and the taxpayer. Strive to close on an agreed basis the highest possible number of cases." They are to maintain an overall agreement rate of at least 85 percent in cases not yet docketed for trial in the Tax Court except for certain tax shelter, protestor, and similar cases. In docketed cases, the Internal Revenue Service wants to "maximize" settlements, with the aim to maintain or improve the agreement rate achieved in the previous year.

In July 2007, the IRS revealed that of the roughly 100,000 appeals cases reviewed each year, 80 percent are successfully resolved.

On December 29, 1999, the IRS announced a two year test when the taxpayer and the IRS can request binding arbitration on *factual* issues in dispute with Appeals (Announcement 2000-4). Legal issues are not allowed. Mediation for appeals cases was expanded by announcement 2001-9 through January 2002. This arbitration process is no longer a pilot program, but rather "business as usual" (IR 2006-163).

The Internal Revenue Service Small Business/Self-Employed Division (SB/SE) has available Fast Track Mediation, a new service to assist you in resolving disputes that arise from examination or collection actions.

Fast Track Mediation can be offered even with disputes not yet before a court. The program is designed to assist in resolving tax disputes arising from an examination, an offer in compromise, a Collection Due Process, or a trust fund recovery penalty.

You can choose either fast track mediation or the normal appeals process. You don't forgo any appeal rights during mediation and can withdraw from mediation. If you withdraw from mediation, the dispute would follow the normal appeals process. Either you or the IRS can request mediation, but both must agree to mediate. On average, the mediation process should be started and completed within about 30–40 days. The normal appeals process can take months.

A specially trained IRS mediator from the Appeals Division will conduct the mediation session at a mutually agreed upon site. The mediator will discuss the dispute with both sides and can request additional information from either side. The mediator will not decide anything regarding the dispute. The mediator cannot impose a resolution and will not have settlement authority. The mediator will work to resolve the dispute between you and the IRS. You and IRS must both agree to any proposed resolution.

Fast track mediation was made permanent in June of 2003 (IR-2003-72 and Rev. Proc. 2003-41). Call (972)308-7330 for further details and how to initiate the process.

If you want to stop the running of interest on any potential deficiency, you are entitled to make what is known as a "deficiency deposit." Such a deposit should be made before the mailing of a deficiency notice and designated in writing as a "deposit in the nature of a cash bond." If you request a part or all of your deficiency deposit to be returned before the assessment of any tax, the request will be granted—unless the Internal Revenue Service determines that the deposit should be applied against a jeopardy assessment or another tax liability. No interest will be paid or allowed with respect to an amount returned to you.

There's one additional avenue of administrative redress for taxpayer problems. In 1977, the IRS instituted "problem resolution offices" (PROs) (now under the National Taxpayer Advocate's Office) to handle problems that have not been resolved through normal channels. Such problems include not only complaints by disgruntled taxpayers but lost, stolen, or delayed refund checks, billing errors, and hardship situations. The following table lists the addresses and telephone numbers of the Taxpayer Advocate Offices (TAO). For each district, address correspondence to the Taxpayer Advocate Officer, Internal Revenue Service.

ALABAMA
Birmingham Office
Taxpayer Advocate
801 Tom Martin Dr.
Birmingham, AL 35211
205-912-5631

ALASKA
Anchorage Office
Taxpayer Advocate
949 East 36th Ave.,
Stop A-405
Anchorage, AK 99508
907-271-6877

ARIZONA
Phoenix Office
Taxpayer Advocate
210 E. Earll Drive,
Stop 1005-PHX
Phoenix, AZ 85012
602-207-8240

ARKANSAS
Little Rock Office
Taxpayer Advocate
700 West Capitol St.,
Stop 1005-LIT
Little Rock, AR 72201
501-396-5978

CALIFORNIA
Laguna Niguel Office
Taxpayer Advocate
24000 Avila Road-
Room 3362
Laguna Niguel, CA 92677
949-389-4804

Los Angeles Office
Taxpayer Advocate
300 N. Los Angeles St.
Stop 1005-LA Room 5119
Los Angeles, CA 90012
213-576-3140

Oakland Office
Taxpayer Advocate
1301 Clay St. # 1540S
Oakland, CA 94612
510-637-2703

Sacramento Office
Taxpayer Advocate
4330 Watt Ave.
N. Highlands, CA 95660
916-974-5007

San Jose Office
Taxpayer Advocate
55 S. Market St.,
Stop HQ000-4
San Jose, CA 95113
408-817-6850

COLORADO
Denver Office
Taxpayer Advocate
600 17th St.,
Stop 1005-DEN
Denver, CO 80202-2490
303-446-1012

CONNECTICUT
Hartford Office
Taxpayer Advocate
135 High St., Stop 219
Hartford, CT 06103
860-756-4555

DELAWARE
Wilmington Office
Taxpayer Advocate
1352 Marrows Rd.
Newark, DE 19711-5445
302-286-1643

DISTRICT OF COLUMBIA
Baltimore Office
Taxpayer Advocate
31 Hopkins Plaza
Baltimore, MD 21201
410-962-2082

FLORIDA
Ft. Lauderdale Office
Taxpayer Advocate
7850 SW 6th Court
Plantation, FL 33324
954-423-7677

Jacksonville Office
Taxpayer Advocate
841 Prudential Dr.,
Suite 100
Stop: TA:SE/INT:JAX
Jacksonville, FL 32207
904-665-1000

GEORGIA
Atlanta Office
Taxpayer Advocate
401 W. Peachtree
St., NW,
Summit Building
Stop 202-D
Atlanta, GA 30308
404-338-8099

HAWAII
Honolulu Office
Taxpayer Advocate
Stop H-405
300 Ala Moana Blvd.,
#50089
Honolulu, HI 96850
808-539-2870

IDAHO
Boise Office
Taxpayer Advocate
550 West Fort St., Box 041
Boise, ID 83724
208-387-2827

ILLINOIS
Chicago Office
Taxpayer Advocate
230 S. Dearborn St.
Stop 1005-CHI
Chicago, IL 60604
312-566-3800

Springfield Office
Taxpayer Advocate
320 W. Washington St.
Stop 1005-SPD
Springfield, IL 62701
217-527-6382

INDIANA
Indianapolis Office
Taxpayer Advocate
575 N. Pennsylvania St.,
Stop TA770
Indianapolis, IN 46204
317-685-7840

IOWA
Des Moines Office
Taxpayer Advocate
210 Walnut St.,
Stop 1005-DSM
Des Moines, IA 50309
515-564-6888

KANSAS
Wichita Office
Taxpayer Advocate
271 W. 3rd St., North
Stop 1005-WIC
Wichita, KS 67202
316-352-7506

KENTUCKY
Louisville Office
Taxpayer Advocate
600 Dr. MLK Jr. Place
Federal Building-Room 622
Louisville, KY 40202
502-582-6030

LOUISIANA
New Orleans Office
Taxpayer Advocate
600 South Maestri Pl.,
Stop 2
New Orleans, LA 70130
504-558-3001

MAINE
Augusta Office
Taxpayer Advocate
68 Sewall St., Room 313
Augusta, ME 04330
207-622-8528

MARYLAND
Baltimore Office
Taxpayer Advocate
31 Hopkins Plaza
Baltimore, MD 21201
410-962-2082

MASSACHUSETTS
Boston Office
Taxpayer Advocate
25 New Sudbury St.
Boston, MA 02203
617-316-2690

MICHIGAN
Detroit Office
Taxpayer Advocate
McNamara Federal
Building
477 Michigan Ave. -
Room 1745
Detroit, MI 48226
313-628-3670

MINNESOTA
St. Paul Office
Taxpayer Advocate
Stop 1005-STP
316 North Robert St.
St. Paul, MN 55101
651-312-7999

MISSISSIPPI
Jackson Office
Taxpayer Advocate
100 W. Capitol St.,
Stop JK31
Jackson, MS 39269
601-292-4800

MISSOURI
St. Louis Office
Taxpayer Advocate
Robert A. Young Building
1222 Spruce Street,
Stop 1005-STL
St. Louis, MO 63103
314-612-4610

MONTANA
Helena Office
Taxpayer Advocate
Federal Building
301 S. Park, Stop 1005-HEL
Helena, MT 59626-0023
406-441-1022

NEBRASKA
Omaha Office
Taxpayer Advocate
1313 Farnam St.,
Stop 1005-OMA
Omaha, NE 68102
402-221-4181

NEVADA
Las Vegas Office
Taxpayer Advocate
110 City Parkway Blvd.
Stop 1005-LVG
Las Vegas, NV 89106
702-868-5179

NEW HAMPSHIRE
Portsmouth Office
Taxpayer Advocate
Federal Office Building
80 Daniel St.
Portsmouth, NH 03801
603-433-0571

NEW JERSEY
Springfield Office
Taxpayer Advocate
955 S. Springfield Ave.
Springfield, NJ 07081
973-921-4043

NEW MEXICO
Albuquerque Office
Taxpayer Advocate
5338 Montgomery Blvd.
N.E.
Stop 1005-ALB
Albuquerque, NM 87109
505-837-5505

NEW YORK
Albany Office
Taxpayer Advocate
Leo O'Brien Federal
Building
1 Clinton Square
Albany, NY 12207
518-427-5413

Brooklyn Office
Taxpayer Advocate
10 Metro Tech Center
625 Fulton St.
Brooklyn, NY 11201
718-488-2080

Buffalo Office
Taxpayer Advocate
201 Como Park Blvd.
Buffalo, NY 14227
716-686-4850

Manhattan Office
Taxpayer Advocate
290 Broadway - 7th Floor
New York, NY 10007
212-436-1011

NORTH CAROLINA
Greensboro Office
Taxpayer Advocate
320 Federal Place,
Room 125
Greensboro,
NC 27401
336-378-2180

NORTH DAKOTA
Fargo Office
Taxpayer Advocate
657 2nd Ave, N.,
Stop 1005-FAR
Fargo, ND 58102
701-239-5141

OHIO
Cincinnati Office
Taxpayer Advocate
550 Main St.,
Room 3530
Cincinnati,
OH 45202
513-263-3260

Cleveland Office
Taxpayer Advocate
1240 E. Ninth St.,
Room 423
Cleveland,
OH 44199
216-522-7134

OKLAHOMA
Oklahoma City Office
Taxpayer Advocate
55 N. Robinson,
Stop 1005-OKC
Oklahoma City,
OK 73102
405-297-4055

OREGON
Portland Office
Taxpayer Advocate
1220 S.W. 3rd Ave.,
Stop O-405
Portland, OR 97204
503-326-2333

PENNSYLVANIA
Philadelphia Office
Taxpayer Advocate
600 Arch St.
Philadelphia,
PA 19106
215-861-1304

Pittsburgh Office
Taxpayer Advocate
1000 Liberty Ave.
Pittsburgh,
PA 15222
412-395-4769

RHODE ISLAND
Providence Office
Taxpayer Advocate
380 Westminster St.
Providence,
RI 02903
401-525-4200

SOUTH CAROLINA
Columbia Office
Taxpayer Advocate
1835 Assembly St.
MDP 03
Columbia, SC 29201
803-253-3029

SOUTH DAKOTA
Aberdeen Office
Taxpayer Advocate
115 4th Ave.
Southeast
Stop 1005-ABE
Aberdeen, SD 57401
605-226-7248

TENNESSEE
Nashville Office
Taxpayer Advocate
801 Broadway,
Stop 22
Nashville, TN 37203
615-250-5000

TEXAS
Austin Office
Taxpayer Advocate
300 E. 8th St.,
Stop 1005-AUS
Austin, TX 78701
512-499-5875

Dallas Office
Taxpayer Advocate
1114 Commerce St.
10th Floor MC1005
Dallas, TX 75242
214-413-6500

Houston Office
Taxpayer Advocate
1919 Smith St.,
Stop 1005-HOU
Houston, TX 77002
713-209-3660

UTAH
Salt Lake City Office
Taxpayer Advocate
50 South 200 East,
Stop 1005-SLC
Salt Lake City,
UT 84111
801-799-6958

VERMONT
Burlington Office
Taxpayer Advocate
Courthouse Plaza
199 Main St.
Burlington,
VT 05401
802-859-1052

VIRGINIA
Richmond Office
Taxpayer Advocate
400 North 8th St.
Richmond, VA 23240
804-916-3501

WASHINGTON
Seattle Office
Taxpayer Advocate
915 2nd Ave.,
Stop W-405
Seattle, WA 98174
206-220-6037

WEST VIRGINIA
Parkersburg Office
Taxpayer Advocate
425 Juliana St.
Parkersburg, WV 26101
304-420-8695

WISCONSIN
Milwaukee Office
Taxpayer Advocate
211 West Wisconsin Ave.
Stop 1005-MIL
Milwaukee, WI 53203
414-231-2390

WYOMING
Cheyenne Office
Taxpayer Advocate
5353 Yellowstone Rd.
Stop 1005-CHE
Cheyenne, WY 82009
307-633-0800

National
877-777-4778
Toll-free

TAXPAYER ADVOCACY PANEL REPRESENTA-TIVE
888-912-1227
Toll-free

TAXPAYERS LIVING ABROAD OR IN U.S. TERRITORIES
A/C International
Taxpayer Advocate
7 Tabonuco Street

San Patricio Office
Building
Room 200
Guaynabo, Puerto Rico
00966
or
P.O. Box 193479
San Juan, Puerto Rico
00919-3479
787-622-8940 English
787-622-8930 Spanish

CENTERS
Andover Center
Taxpayer Advocate
P.O. Box 9055, Stop 121
Andover,
MA 01810-9055
978-474-5549

Atlanta Center
Taxpayer Advocate
P.O. Box 48-549,
Stop 29A
Doraville, GA 30362
770-936-4500

Austin Center
Taxpayer Advocate
P.O. Box 934,
Stop 1005-AUSC
Austin, TX 78767
512-460-8300

Brookhaven Center
Taxpayer Advocate
P.O. Box 960, Stop 102
Holtsville, NY 11742
631-654-6686

Cincinnati Center
Taxpayer Advocate
P.O. Box 1235,
Stop 11-G
Cincinnati,
OH 45201-1235
859-292-5316

Fresno Center
Taxpayer Advocate
P.O. Box 12161,
Stop 01
Fresno, CA 93776
559-442-6400

Kansas City Center
Taxpayer Advocate
333 W. Pershing
Stop 1005
Kansas City, MO 64108
816-291-9000

Memphis Center
Taxpayer Advocate
P.O. Box 30309 AMF,
Stop 13M
Memphis, TN 38130
901-395-1900

Ogden Center
Taxpayer Advocate
P.O. Box 1640
Stop 1005
Ogden, UT 84402
801-620-7168

Philadelphia Center
Taxpayer Advocate
11601 Roosevel Blvd.
Stop SW-820
Philadelphia, PA 19154
215-516-2499

An Internal Revenue Manual Supplement (MT 1279-57, May 25, 1988) provides complete guidelines for the operation of the program at all levels of the agency. The IRS adopted 11 separate categories of rights to which taxpayers are entitled. Some of these categories include:

- the right to prompt, courteous, and impartial treatment that includes the assumption that "each taxpayer wants to comply" with the tax code;

- the right to a reasonable amount of time to produce requested documentation;

- the right to receive copies of their returns from IRS Service Centers and any other tax information, such as examination, criminal investigation, and collection division work papers; *and*

- generally, the right to have a case transferred to a specific district office.

DEFICIENCY NOTICES

When the Internal Revenue Service determines that a deficiency exists, it must first send you a notice of the deficiency determination. You are then allowed a specific period—normally 90 days, beginning with the mailing of the notice—in which to file a petition for redetermination with the Tax Court. At that point the Internal Revenue Service is prohibited, with certain exceptions, from undertaking any assessment or collection activity until the deficiency notice has been mailed, the specified period has expired, and, if a Tax Court petition has been timely filed, the decision has become final [Section 6213(a)]. During the time this prohibition is in force, it is expressly provided that any assessment or collection activity by the IRS is subject to injunctive relief, notwithstanding the Anti-Injunction Act.

An *assessment* is, in essence, a bookkeeping notation that occurs when the IRS establishes an account against a taxpayer on the tax rolls. Technically, the assessment is made by an assessment officer for the district or regional service center by signing the summary record of assessment, which, through supporting records, provides the taxpayer's identification, the type of tax and taxable period, and the amount of the assessment. The date of the assessment is the date of the signing.

As soon as practical, and within 60 days after making the assessment, the IRS must give you notice of the unpaid amount and demand its payment by leaving the notice at your dwelling or usual place of business or by mailing it to your last known address. If you neglect or refuse to pay within 10 days after notice and demand, the IRS can proceed to collect the amount owed by levy. A *levy* includes the power of distraint and seizure by any means [IRC Section 6331(b)]. Ordinarily, a levy requires written notice of intent to levy at least 30 days prior to the day of levy, either in person or by leaving it at the dwelling or usual place of business or by certified or registered mailing to the last known address of the taxpayer [IRC Section 6331(d)(1), (2)]. In circumstances where you neglect or refuse to pay the tax after demand, a lien is created in favor of the United States on all property owned by you. The lien arises from the date of the assessment and is effective as against certain persons upon proper filing of a notice of lien. The Internal Revenue Service possesses additional power, subject to certain limitations, to sell property that it has seized (see IRC Sections 6335 and 6336). Remember, however, that a petition to the Tax Court, timely filed, will prevent the Internal Revenue Service from proceeding with any of these potential administrative actions.

If you are not satisfied at the administrative level, you must go to court. Even if the law is probably in favor of the Internal Revenue Service, it may pay for you to move a case into the judiciary if the dollar amount is large enough. This is because it provides an additional opportunity for you to compromise the case. When you go to court, the case is removed from the jurisdiction of the Internal Revenue Service district office, which started the investigation, and placed in the hands of the regional counsel. While agents in the district office are primarily concerned with the letter of the law, the regional counsel's staff is more concerned with disposing of cases. Remember, it costs the Internal Revenue Service time and money to litigate a case, just as it costs you. If there is no special reason, such as emphasizing an IRS stand on a particular issue for contesting a case, the regional counsel may offer a settlement just to save the trouble of going to court. Even if the offer is only 10 percent of an amount that the district office disallowed completely, you may still come out ahead.

The general rule is that a taxpayer will lose who attempts to sue an IRS agent for harrassment. In *Pope v. Organ*, 82-2 USTC Par. 9613, 50 AFTR 2d 82-5273 (DC Texas, 1982), the court held that an agent would be immune from prosecution if both of the following conditions were met: (1) the action was taken with the belief that it was lawful and without malicious intent to cause deprivation of constitutional rights, and (2) given the discretion of the official and the circumstances, it was reasonable to believe that there was a right to take the action.

However, on April 11, 1983, the U.S. Court of Appeals for the Fifth Circuit ruled that a taxpayer *could sue* an IRS agent as a federal official, acting under color of federal law when he allegedly violated taxpayers' constitutional rights to due process by willfully and maliciously assessing them for taxes they did not owe and harrassing them into paying those taxes (*Rutherford* 83-1 USTC Par. 9289, 51 AFTR2d 83-1084). The Court allowed suit for compensatory damages for mental anguish and for the legal fees incurred in resisting the government's claim as well as punitive damages in retribution for the agent's abuses of authority. (See also *Miklautsch v. Comm*, No. A89-291 Civil, 11/6/90 where it was held that the taxpayers have the right to bring action for unreasonable actions taken by IRS employees.) In 1998, Elvis E. "Johnny" Johnson was awarded $3.5 million when the IRS improperly publicized details of his tax situation.

EMPLOYEE DISCIPLINARY ACTION

The IRS has recognized the problem of employees' misconduct and has responded. IRS workers and the public may call 800-366-4484 to report IRS employee misconduct. Calls also may go to 800-826-0407 to reach the Treasury Inspector General's Office, which investigates senior IRS managers. In 1997, 172 IRS employees were fired or otherwise separated from the agency due to "administrative actions related to employee violations"—i.e., as a result of complaints, misuse of position or authority, or rude or discourteous conduct. In 1998, the IRS investigated 3,100 complaints against IRS employees. Of those one-third led to disciplinary action, including 200 criminal prosecutions.

Between July 1998 and September 2002, the IRS fired 71 employees after investigating 3,512 allegations and finding 419 violations. Other employees faced penalties or resigned. For fiscal 2007, the IRS took disciplinary action against more than 2,000, or 2.3 percent of its employees.

OFFERS IN COMPROMISE

Before you go to court (or even afterward), you have one more alternative option. An offer in compromise is a contract (Form 656) with the Internal Revenue Service whereby you recognize your liability but offer to satisfy it for less than its full amount. Such offers will be entertained only when there is doubt regarding either the taxpayer's liability or the collectibility of the amount assessed. Offers based on "equity and hardship factors" are also accepted for "effective tax administration."

According to the IRS District Director's letter, before the IRS will accept an offer in compromise, it will almost always require the taxpayer to enter into a collateral agreement to make payments from future income. Where liability has been established by a valid court judgment, the IRS will not compromise the liability. An offer in compromise is made on Form 656 and must be accepted in writing by the Internal Revenue Service.

The advantages of an offer in compromise are:

1. You may be able to satisfy the liability by paying less than the full amount.
2. You can defer payment over a number of years, thus reducing the immediate tax burden.
3. Making an offer will delay collection action, even if the offer is not accepted.
4. The compromise offer fixes your liability for the period once it is accepted.
5. If the offer is accepted, and you live up to it, there will be no surprise collection action by the IRS.
6. If you enter into a collateral agreement to make payments from future income, the IRS normally will release any tax liens that have been filed on your property.

Alternatively, the rejection of an offer can result in immediate collection action by the IRS. In addition, the offer requires the submission of detailed financial statements, which will aid the IRS Collection Division should the offer not be accepted; the offer requires a waiver of the statute of limitations; and when an offer is made, you will usually be required to make a cash deposit. This deposit will not draw interest, and it is subject to collection in case the offer is rejected.

In May 2004, National Taxpayer Advocate Nina Olson called the IRS OIC program "inflexible" and "mechanistic," with taxpayers treated as "inventory."

If the debt can be paid in 15 years, it's considered a "full pay" case. She discussed the case of a 75-year-old man who was ill. He was turned down for an OIC because he was deemed a full pay case!

The backlog of offers keeps increasing. The number of unresolved offers tripled from 32,300 to 94,900 cases between fiscal 1997 and 2001. It took, on average, 10 months to get a determination. According to the IRS in 2002, 37 percent of offers were settled within 6 months, and 74 percent within 1 year. By 2005, settlement time dropped to an average of 6 months for a single offer and about 22 months for repeat offers. As of October 25, 2011, there were 7,472 *unassigned* offers in the holding queues waiting to be looked at. Why? More offers and less IRS personnel.

As of November 1, 2003, the IRS charges a $150 "user fee" ($186 as of January 1, 2014) to process offers. The fee will be waived for offers based "solely" on doubt as to liability and for offers from "low income" taxpayers. A "low income" taxpayer is one with income at or below 250 percent of the poverty guidelines set by the Department of Health and Human Services. Get current levels from www.atdn.org/access/property.html.

The fee will be applied to your offer or refunded if:

- an offer is accepted to promote effective tax administration, *or*
- there is doubt as to collectability, and collecting an amount greater than the offer would create economic hardship.

The Tax Increase Protection Act of 2005 changed the rules again. Effective for all offers received starting July 16, 2006, you must make a 20 percent nonrefundable upfront payment for lump sum offers.

Taxpayers submitting requests for periodic-payment OICs must include the first proposed installment payment with their application. A periodic payment OIC is any offer of payments made in six or more installments. The taxpayer is required to pay additional installments while the offer is being evaluated by the IRS. All installment payments are nonrefundable.

Under the new law, taxpayers qualifying as low-income or filling an offer based solely on doubt as to liability qualify for a waiver of the new partial payment requirements.

If the IRS cannot make a determination on an OIC within two years, then the offer will be deemed accepted. If a liability included in the offer amount is disputed in any court proceeding, that time period is omitted from calculating the two-year timeframe.

See T.D. 9086 dated August 15, 2003 and IR-2006-106, dated July 11, 2006 for further details.

In 2012, the IRS made qualifying for the OIC program more flexible by:

- Revising the calculation for a taxpayer's *future income*. The IRS will now look at only 1 year (instead of 4 years) of future income for offers paid in 5 or fewer months; and 2 years (instead of 5 years) of future income for offers paid in 6 to 24 months. All OICs must be paid in full within 24 months of the date the offer is accepted.

- Allowing taxpayers to repay their *student loans*. Minimum payments on student loans guaranteed by the federal government will be allowed for the taxpayer's post–high school education. Proof of payment must be provided.

- Allowing taxpayers to pay *state and local* delinquent *taxes*. When a taxpayer owes delinquent federal and state or local taxes and does not have the ability to fully pay the liabilities, monthly payments to state taxing authorities may be allowed in certain circumstances.

- Expanding the *Allowable Living Expense* allowance. Standard allowances incorporate average expenses for basic necesssities for citizens in similar geographic areas. These standards are used when evaluating installment agreements and offer-in-compromise requests. The *National Standard* miscellaneous allowance has been expanded. Taxpayers can use the allowance to cover expenses such as credit card payments and bank fees and charges.

For instructions on making an offer in compromise, go to www.irs.gov/prod/ind_info/oic/index.html.

It is important to recognize that *oral* compromise agreements and unsigned settlements will not bind the Internal Revenue Service (see *Boulez*, 87-1 USTC Par. 9177, 59 AFTR 2d 87-608 [CA-D.C., 1987] and *Estate of Oman*, TCM 1987-71).

INSTALLMENT AGREEMENTS

A negotiated agreement to pay in monthly installments over a lengthy period of time is now within the recognized policy guidelines of the IRS. IRS Policy Statement P-5-14 (approved on March 3, 1976) states: "Although there is no specific authority for allowing a taxpayer to liquidate a delinquent account by installment payments, installment agreements are to be considered, and may be entered into, when appropriate." IRM 5223: (4)(g) states that "the amount to be paid monthly on an installment agreement payment will be the difference between the taxpayer's net income and allowable expenses rounded down to the nearest $5.00 increment." The 1998 Tax Reform Act, however, made installment agreements mandatory under certain circumstances if the liability, with interest and penalties, is not more than $10,000. However, the IRS generally will accept installment offers on tax debts up to $50,000, and have gone higher. You can actually get an agreement online—with no financial statements needed—at www.irs.gov up to $50,000 if you can pay in full within 72 months. If you owe $25,000 or less, you don't ever have to provide financial statements.

When you are unable to pay all of your taxes on time, you should file Form 1127. It's called "Application for Extension of Time for Payment of Tax" and it will give you up to 6 months from the due date to pay the tax you owe. In order to qualify, you must be able to show that you cannot borrow money to pay your tax bill except under terms that would cause severe loss and hardship. If you are granted an extension, all late payment penalties will be excused. However, you will still owe the IRS interest on the late-paid tax. In addition, the IRS now charges a $105 user fee ($120 as of January 1, 2014) for entering into a non-direct-debit installment agreement ($52 for direct-debit agreements or $43 if your income is within poverty guidelines) and a $45 user fee ($50 as of January 1, 2014) for restructuring or reinstating an installment agreement (IR 94-118).

GOING TO COURT

In entering the judiciary, you have three basic options:

1. *The U.S. Tax Court.* The U.S. Tax Court was first established in 1923. It is made up of 19 judges who travel around the country and hear cases in major cities on a regular basis. It handles only tax litigation and consists exclusively of tax experts. The major advantage of choosing this court is that it will decide the case **before** you have to pay the tax. When you receive the 90-day letter, if you file a petition with the U.S. Tax Court within 90 days of the date of the letter, the Internal Revenue Service may not initiate any further tax collection mechanics until after the case is decided. Be careful: Your letter must be postmarked within 90 days after the *date* of the IRS letter, not after you receive it.

   To get complete instructions on how to file a petition, write to the Clerk, United States Tax Court, 400 2nd Street, N.W., Washington, DC 20217, or call 202-376-2754. Although you may represent yourself at the Tax Court, it is best to have an attorney specializing in taxation to handle the case.

   If the disputed tax is $50,000 or less for any taxable year, a simplified alternative procedure is now available. Here you may want to represent yourself. Upon your request and with approval of the Tax Court, your case can be handled by the Small Claims Division, under the small tax case rules, at little cost to you in time or dollars. Cases in the Small Claims Division are heard by "special trial judges." If you want to use this procedure, write to the previously given address and ask that the clerk send you the small tax case division filing form, Petition, Form 2. You must file the original and two copies of the petition, a copy of the 90-day letter, and a fee of $60, along with your pick of one of the more than 100 cities in which the Small Claims Division of the Tax Court sits. The fee for cases that are not small claims cases is also $60. The case is heard informally by a trial judge and the formal rules of evidence do not apply. One special caveat, however: If you lose your case before the Small Claims Division, you cannot appeal. Their decision is final and binding.

Several final comments must be made about the Tax Court. First, while the disputed tax is not paid until after the trial, or until the case is settled, any tax found due will be paid with interest. This interest, however, is no longer tax deductible. Second, remember that the Tax Court consists exclusively of expert judges. There are no jury trials before the Tax Court. Therefore, if you have a case where the equities are strongly on your side, but the law itself is against you, you might be better advised to stay out of the Tax Court. Finally, don't expect quick action if you file a case in the Tax Court. The court is struggling to cope with a massive and ever-growing backlog of pending cases at a time when it also faces financial woes. Taxpayers in some large cities must now wait as long as a year and a half for their cases to come to trial. Furthermore, experts have predicted the problem will intensify, reflecting the complexity of new laws and confusing tax shelter controversies.

In Rev. Proc. 82-42, the Internal Revenue Service announced new procedures for processing Tax Court cases in an attempt to facilitate earlier disposition through trial or settlement. Docketed cases will be referred by district counsel to the Appeals Division for settlement unless counsel determines it unlikely that even a partial settlement will be reached there. Cases involving deficiencies of more than $10,000 (including tax and penalties for a period) will then be promptly returned to counsel when it appears that no progress toward a settlement has been made, unless counsel agrees to extend the period for the Appeals Division's consideration. Cases involving deficiencies of $10,000 or less (including small claims cases) will stay in the Appeals Division for 6 months or until receipt of notice of trial in regular cases, or 15 days before the trial calendar call in small claims tax cases if that is earlier. Again, counsel may extend the period in Appeals Division if it appears that a settlement may be reached.

2. *The U.S. District Court.* The U.S. District Court, which is part of the federal judiciary system, is the only place where a jury trial is available. These courts hear all kinds of litigation involving federal laws and any kind of law, state

or federal, if the litigants are citizens of different states. You can represent yourself in a district court, but the judges frown upon it. The advantages of going to the district court include the availability of a sympathetic jury and the fact that the judge may be more sympathetic to the equities of your case than to the letter of the tax law. To get into a U.S. District Court, however, you must first pay your tax deficiency and then file a claim for a refund with the Internal Revenue Service. Though the Internal Revenue Service has 6 months to act on your claim, chances are it will reject the claim promptly and you can then file suit for a refund in your district court. You can obtain information about the procedures for filing suit in a U.S. District Court by calling or writing the Clerk of the Court in the district in which you reside. See page 684 for the address of your area's office.

3. *The U.S. Claims Court.* The U.S. Claims Court is a special court that hears all sorts of claims against the United States, including the claim of overpaying taxes and wanting the money back with interest. Here, too, the tax has to be paid in advance. The major advantage of the claims court is that it does not have to follow the same precedents as do the Tax Court and district courts. If the other courts appear unfavorable, this may be your best avenue of appeal.

Currently, judges of the claims court usually hear case argument only in Washington, DC. However, before the argument, there is a fact-finding hearing before a trial judge of the claims court. This hearing will be conducted by the trial judge in a city near where you live. The trial judge will file the findings and the recommended decision. If either you or the Internal Revenue Service disagree, the case will come on for arguments before the full court in Washington. Legal briefs, which must be printed, are also required of both parties. Here the major disadvantage is the substantial expense of litigation. For information on filing suit here, contact the Clerk of the Court of Claims, 1717 Madison Place, N.W., Washington, DC 20005.

Appeals from both the Tax Court and the U.S. district courts go to the U.S. courts of appeals. The United States is divided geographically into 12 judicial circuits, each with its own court of appeals. District and tax court decisions in each circuit must follow the precedents of that circuit's court of appeals. Note, however, that decisions of the claims court do not have to follow such precedents. Furthermore, the courts of appeals in different circuits do not have to agree with each other. And if one circuit's court of appeals has not ruled on an issue, the lower courts may disagree among themselves. This means that a supereffective tax planning strategy for tax appeals is to file your case, whenever possible, in a judicial circuit whose precedents support your position.

Appeals from U.S. courts of appeals go directly to the Supreme Court. In addition, if you lose in the claims court, your appeal is directed first to the Federal Circuit Court of Appeals, then the Supreme Court, which may or may not accept such an appeal. As a practical matter, it accepts very few tax appeals from the claims court, or from appeals courts. Usually, it will only agree to do so where two U.S. courts of appeals have reached opposite results on a similar issue of fact and law.

One final note about going to court: Under Internal Revenue Code Section 7430, enacted by Section 292(a) of the Tax Equity and Fiscal Responsibility Act of 1982, Public Law 97-248 (September 3, 1982), the Tax Court is enabled to award *reasonable litigation costs* to a prevailing party who establishes that the position of the IRS commissioner was unreasonable. That means if you exhaust administrative remedies, go to court, and win, and the position of the Internal Revenue Service was not "reasonable," your costs, including what you have to pay to your attorney, will be reimbursed by the Treasury. The Tax Reform Act of 1986 changed the "not reasonable" requirement to one where the taxpayer must establish that the government's position was "not substantially justified." The 1996 Taxpayer's Bill of Rights 2 reversed the burden. If you win in court, the IRS must now prove that *it* was "substantially justified." These awards are now being given—see *Ashburn*, D.C. Alabama, June 15, 1983 and *Marlar Inc. v. U.S.*, W.D. Wash., No. C95–0729L, 5/18/99. In the case of *David Kaufman v. Roscoe Egger*, on March 19, 1985, the First Circuit Court of Appeals ruled that "unreasonable" IRS conduct, even prior to a suit, can be considered. Examining the underlying congressional committee reports, the Court concluded "that Congress intended IRS' liability to be triggered by unreasonable IRS conduct regardless of which stage in the proceedings such conduct occurs." Moreover, the purpose of the provision would be frustrated if the Internal Revenue Service, "after causing the taxpayer all kinds of bureaucratic grief at the administrative level, could escape attorney's fee liability by merely changing its tune after the initiation of a suit by the taxpayer." These litigation costs can be awarded without limit at a rate of $110 per hour[2] (indexed for inflation after 1996) (unless the court finds justification for a higher rate)! Moreover, this provision applies to suits not only in the District Court but also in the Tax Court (suits in the U.S. Claims Courts are covered only between February 28, 1983, and December 31, 1985—see the Tax Reform Act of 1984, Section 714[c]).

---

2. $180 per hour (indexed) for 2012, and $190 for 2013.

Section 7430(a)(1) now permits the recovery of reasonable administrative costs incurred in an administrative proceeding with the IRS in connection with the determination, collection, or refund of any tax, interest, or penalty. Such costs, under Prop. Reg. 301.7430-4, include the following:

1. A representative's fee
2. IRS administrative fees or similar charges
3. Costs of studies, analyses, etc., incurred in preparing the taxpayer's case

A taxpayer must meet the following conditions to be eligible for an award of administrative costs:

1. The underlying issues are not now, and were never, before a court.
2. The taxpayer is the prevailing party.
3. The taxpayer did not unreasonably prolong the portion of the proceeding for which recovery of costs is sought.
4. The application procedures of the Proposed Regulations were followed.

To be a prevailing party, you must:

1. Establish that the Service's position was not justified.
2. Substantially prevail in the dispute.
3. Meet certain size and net worth limitations.

Administrative awards are available to estates and individuals only if their net worth is not over $2 million ($4 million for joint returns as per the Tax Relief Act of 1997) (based on cost, not fair market value, *Swanson v. Comm.*, No. 21203-92, 106 T.C. No. 3, 2/14/96) on the administrative proceeding date. Businesses, whether incorporated or not, and most other organizations cannot have a net worth of more than $7 million and 500 employees.

The procedures for claiming an award are detailed in Prop. Reg. 301. 7430-2(c).

In general, a request must be made within 90 days of the mailing of the Service's final decision.

The claim must be filed with the Service employee who decided that issue, or the district office that considered the matter, if the employee's identity is unknown. The request must contain the following provisions:

1. A statement that neither the underlying issue or issues nor the claim for reasonable administrative costs is, or has been, before a court

2. A clear and concise assertion as to why the Service's position was not substantially justified

3. A declaration that the taxpayer prevailed with respect to the amount in controversy or the most significant issue or set of issues

4. A statement that the taxpayer did not unreasonably prolong the proceeding

5. An affidavit giving the nature and amount of each recovery item and a copy of the representative's billing records, if fees are requested

6. Another affidavit stating that the taxpayer meets the net worth and size limitations

7. An address where the taxpayer may be located

If your request is denied, you can appeal to the Tax Court.

The IRS Office of Chief Counsel issued a notice (CC-2010-007) dated April 2, 2010, that explained, under the "qualified offer rule," a taxpayer who meets certain net worth requirements and has used all of his administrative remedies may recover reasonable administrative and litigation costs from the IRS if the taxpayer's liability in a court proceeding is equal to or less than the liability the taxpayer would have had if the IRS had accepted the taxpayer's qualified offer.

One effect of the qualified offer rule, the notice explained, is that it eliminates the IRS's defense that its position was substantially justified.

CRIMINAL SANCTIONS

To survive an audit you must be able to document all deductions and you should demand the audit agent to document any claims of fact or law alleged. Alternatively, some tax practitioners have advised, "When in doubt, deduct." The rationale behind this perspective is that even if your deductions are disallowed, your maximum exposure is to pay the tax you would have paid originally plus about 3 percent interest (this rate will change every 6 months; the next change is scheduled for January 1, 2014). Remember, however, that your focus must be on tax avoidance rather than tax evasion. The focus of this book, as well, has been on avoidance—the completely legal objective of minimizing your taxes. You should *never* intentionally attempt to defraud the government with reference to your taxes. Such actions can bring about *criminal* penalties. In fact, a competitive writer, the author of *Pay No Income Taxes without Going to Jail*, went to jail. He also lost a big Tax Court case in which it was found that he treated employees as independent contractors, wrote checks in nonphotocopiable ink, did not report all his income, and did not file returns for several years (*Fry*, T.C. Memo 1991-51). However, the Internal Revenue Service has told its agents not to pursue criminal prosecution of most tax cheaters unless the underpayments average at least $2,500 a year for 3 straight years. Under these guidelines, a married person earning $20,000 a year and not itemizing deductions could file no return at all and not risk a felony prosecution, although civil penalties would probably be sought.

Further IRS internal guidelines with reference to criminal penalties include the following:

- Do not recommend felony prosecution in complex tax evasion schemes requiring difficult methods of proof unless the total amount of unpaid taxes is at least $10,000, including at least $3,000 for any single year.
- Do not recommend felony prosecution for willful failure to file or for filing a false return unless the average yearly unpaid tax involved is at least $2,500 over a 3-year period.
- Do not recommend misdemeanor prosecution for delivery or disclosure of false returns or documents unless the unpaid tax involved is more than $500.

The preceding guidelines contain exceptions for "flagrant or repetitious conduct," which would allow IRS agents to ignore the minimum dollar amounts. These exceptions are more likely to be used against celebrities whose prosecution would be covered by the news media and therefore serve as a deterrent to others. If a doctor were to be prosecuted, for example, they would probably select one who had just written a popular diet book. Alternatively, if they were to look at an attorney, they would want someone well known, particularly a tax lawyer.

Taxpayers in some communities are 10 times more likely to face criminal charges by the Internal Revenue Service than those living in others, but IRS recommends such action for only 17 per million taxpayers, according to an analysis of internal government records released April 13, 1996 by Syracuse University's Transactional Records Access Clearinghouse (TRAC).

TRAC said it found the chances of facing IRS criminal charges were higher in the federal judicial districts of Tulsa and Oklahoma City, Louisville, Wheeling, and Charleston, W.Va., New York's Manhattan and Bronx boroughs and northern suburbs, Pittsburgh, Miami, and Indianapolis. Among the least active, it added, were Madison, Wis., Montgomery, Ala., Topeka,

(continues on page 688)

Criminal Investigations

Prosecutions Recommended

By Source	FY 2002	FY 2003	FY 2004	FY 2005	FY 2006	FY 2007	FY 2008	FY 2009	FY 2010	FY 2011	FY 2012
Tax and Tax Related	991	1,336	1,439	1,434	1,343	1,423	1,293	1,269	1,511	1,622	1,846
Nontax (illegal)	483	521	719	658	756	866	804	769	864	989	1,073
Narcotics	659	684	879	767	621	548	688	532	659	799	782
Total	**2,133**	**2,541**	**3,037**	**2,859**	**2,720**	**2,837**	**2,785**	**2,570**	**3,034**	**3,410**	**3,701**
	FY 2002	FY 2003	FY 2004	FY 2005	FY 2006	FY 2007	FY 2008	FY 2009	FY 2010	FY 2011	FY 2012
Overall Conviction Rate	91.5%	91.5%	92.2%	91.2%	91.5%	90.20%	92.30%	87.20%	90.2%	92.70%	93.00%
	FY 2002	FY 2003	FY 2004	FY 2005	FY 2006	FY 2007	FY 2008	FY 2009	FY 2010	FY 2011	FY 2012
Average Sentence[1]	19	19	21	22	22	22	24	24	27	25	32
	FY 2002	FY 2003	FY 2004	FY 2005	FY 2006	FY 2007	FY 2008	FY 2009	FY 2010	FY 2011	FY 2012
Investigations initiated	3,906	4,001	3,917	4,269	3,907	4,211	3,749	4,121	4,706	4,720	5,125
Information & indictments[2]	1,924	2,128	2,489	2,406	2,319	2,323	2,547	2,335	2,645	2,998	3,390

[1] Average sentence in months for tax and tax-related cases.

[2] Both "information" and "indictments" are accusations. "Information" means an accusation made by law enforcement without the intervention of a grand jury, whereas an "indictment" is an accusation made by a prosecutor and issued by a grand jury.

Federal District Courts

ALABAMA
Northern District
104 Federal Courthouse
Birmingham, AL 35203

Middle District
P.O. Box 711
Montgomery, AL 36101

Southern District
P.O. Box 2625
Mobile, AL 36652

ALASKA
Federal Building
701 C Street
Anchorage, AK 99513

ARIZONA
Room 1400
U.S. Courthouse
& Federal Building
230 N. 1st Avenue
Phoenix, AZ 85025

ARKANSAS
Eastern District
P.O. Box 869
Little Rock, AR 72203

Western District
P.O. Box 1523
Fort Smith, AR 72902

CALIFORNIA
Northern District
U.S. Courthouse
P.O. Box 36060
San Francisco, CA 94102

Eastern District
2546 U.S. Courthouse
650 Capitol Mall
Sacramento, CA 95814

Central District
U.S. Courthouse
312 N. Spring Street
Los Angeles, CA 90012

Southern District
940 Front Street
San Diego, CA 92189

COLORADO
Room C-145
U.S. Courthouse
1929 Stout Street
Denver, CO 80294

CONNECTICUT
141 Church Street
New Haven, CT 06510

DELAWARE
Lockbox 18
Federal Building
844 King Street
Wilmington, DE 19801

DISTRICT OF COLUMBIA
U.S. Courthouse
3rd & Constitution
Ave., N.W.
Washington, DC 20001

FLORIDA
Northern District
110 East Park Avenue
Tallahassee, FL 32301

Middle District
P.O. Box 53558
Jacksonville, FL 32201-3558

Southern District
301 N. Miami Avenue
Miami, FL 33128-7788

GEORGIA
Northern District
75 Spring Street, S.W.
2211 U.S. Courthouse
Atlanta, GA 30335

Middle District
P.O. Box 128
Macon, GA 31202

Southern District
P.O. Box 8286
Savannah, GA 31412

GUAM
6th Floor
Pacific News Building
238 O'Hara Street
Agana, Guam 96910

HAWAII
P.O. Box 50129
Honolulu, HI 96850

IDAHO
U.S. Courthouse
P.O. Box 039
550 West Fort Street
Boise, ID 83724

ILLINOIS
Northern District
U.S. Courthouse
219 South Dearborn St.
Chicago, IL 60604

Central District
P.O. Box 315
Springfield, IL 62705

Southern District
U.S. Courthouse &
   P.O. Building
P.O. Box 677
Benton, IL 62812

INDIANA
Northern District
Federal Building
Rm 305, 204 S. Main St.
South Bend, IN 46601

Southern District
U.S. Courthouse
Room 105
46 East Ohio Street
Indianapolis, IN 46204

IOWA
Northern District
Federal Building
P.O. Box 4411
Cedar Rapids, IA 52407

Southern District
U.S. Courthouse
Room 200
E. 1st & Walnut Streets
Des Moines, IA 50309

KANSAS
204 U.S. Courthouse
401 N. Market
Wichita, KS 67202

KENTUCKY
Eastern District
P.O. Box 741
Lexington, KY 40586

Western District
230 U.S. Courthouse
601 West Broadway
Louisville, KY 40202

LOUISIANA
Eastern District
U.S. Courthouse
500 Camp Street
Chambers C-151
New Orleans, LA 70130

Middle District
Room 139, 707 Florida Ave.
Federal Building &
   U.S. Courthouse
Baton Rouge, LA 70801

Western District
106 Joe D. Waggonner
   Federal Building
500 Fannin Street
Shreveport, LA 71101

MAINE
P.O. Box 7505 DTS
Portland, ME 04112

MARYLAND
U.S. Courthouse
101 W. Lombard Street
Baltimore, MD 21201

MASSACHUSETTS
1525 Post Office &
   Courthouse Building
Boston, MA 02109

MICHIGAN
Eastern District
U.S. Courthouse
Room 133
Detroit, MI 48226

Western District
458 Federal Building
110 Michigan Street, N.W.
Grand Rapids, MI 49503

MINNESOTA
708 Federal Building
316 N. Robert Street
St. Paul, MN 55101

MISSISSIPPI
Northern District
P.O. Box 727
Oxford, MS 38655

Southern District
P.O. Box 769
Jackson, MS 39205

MISSOURI

Eastern District
U.S. Court & Custom
   House
1114 Market Street
St. Louis, MO 63101

Western District
U.S. Courthouse
811 Grand Avenue
Room 201
Kansas City, MO 64106

MONTANA
Rm 5405, Federal Bldg.
316 N. 26th Street
Billings, MT 59101

NEBRASKA
P.O. Box 129
Downtown Station
Omaha, NE 68101

NEVADA
300 Las Vegas Blvd., S.
Las Vegas, NV 89101

NEW HAMPSHIRE
P.O. Box 1498
Concord, NH 03301

NEW JERSEY
U.S. Post Office &
   Courthouse
P.O. Box 419
Newark, NJ 07102

NEW MEXICO
P.O. Box 689
Albuquerque, NM 87103

NEW YORK

Northern District
Box 950
Albany, NY 12201

Southern District
U.S. Courthouse
Foley Square
New York, NY 10007

Eastern District
U.S. Courthouse
225 Cadman Plaza East
Brooklyn, NY 11201

Western District
604 U.S. Courthouse
Buffalo, NY 14202

NORTH CAROLINA

Eastern District
P.O. Box 25670
Raleigh, NC 27611

Middle District
P.O. Box V-1
Greensboro, NC 27402

Western District
P.O. Box 92
Asheville, NC 28802

NORTH DAKOTA
P.O. Box 1193
Bismarck, ND 58501

**NORTHERN MARIANA
ISLANDS**
P.O. Box 687
Saipan, 96950

OHIO

Northern District
102 U.S. Courthouse
201 Superior Avenue, NE
Cleveland, OH 44114

Southern District
328 U.S. Courthouse
85 Marconi Blvd
Columbus, OH 43215

OKLAHOMA

Northern District
411 U.S. Courthouse
333 W. 4th Street
Tulsa, OK 74120

Eastern District
P.O. Box 607
U.S. Courthouse
Muskogee, OK 74401

Western District
Room 3210
U.S. Courthouse
Oklahoma City, OK 73102

OREGON
516 U.S. Courthouse
620 S.W. Main Street
Portland, OR 97205

PENNSYLVANIA

Eastern District
2609 U.S. Courthouse
Independent Mall West
601 Market Street
Philadelphia, PA 19106

Middle District
P.O. Box 1148
Scranton, PA 18501

Western District
P.O. Box 1805
Pittsburgh, PA 15230

PUERTO RICO
P.O. Box 3671
San Juan, PR 00904

RHODE ISLAND
119 Federal Building
& U.S. Courthouse
Providence, RI 02903

SOUTH CAROLINA
P.O. Box 867
Columbia, SC 29202

SOUTH DAKOTA
Room 220
Federal Building &
U.S. Courthouse
400 South Phillips Ave.
Sioux Falls, SD 57102

TENNESSEE
Eastern District
P.O. Box 2348
Knoxville, TN 37901

Middle District
800 U.S. Courthouse
801 Broadway
Nashville, TN 37203

Western District
950 Federal Building
167 North Main Street
Memphis, TN 38103

TEXAS
Northern District
U.S. Courthouse
1100 Commerce Street
Room 15C22
Dallas, TX 75242

Southern District
P.O. Box 61010
Houston, TX 77208

Eastern District
309 Federal Building &
U.S. Courthouse
211 W. Ferguson Street
Tyler, TX 75702

Western District
Hemisfair Plaza
655 E. Durango Blvd.
San Antonio, TX 78206

UTAH
P.O. Box 45390
Salt Lake City, UT 84145

VERMONT
P.O. Box 945
Burlington, VT 05402

VIRGINIA
Eastern District
307 U.S. Courthouse
600 Granby St.
Norfolk, VA 23510

Western District
P.O. Box 1234
Roanoke, VA 24006

VIRGIN ISLANDS
P.O. Box 720
Charlotte Amalie
St. Thomas, VI 00801

WASHINGTON
Eastern District
P.O. Box 1493
Spokane, WA 99210

Western District
308 U.S. Courthouse
Seattle, WA 98104

WEST VIRGINIA
Northern District
P.O. Box 1518
Elkins, WV 26241

Southern District
P.O. Box 2546
Charleston, WV 25329

WISCONSIN
Eastern District
Room 362
U.S. Courthouse
Milwaukee, WI 53202

Western District
P.O. Box 432
Madison, WI 53701

WYOMING
P.O. Box 727
Cheyenne, WY 82001

Kan., Detroit, Boston, Milwaukee, St. Louis, Philadelphia, Houston, and Des Moines, Iowa.

See the table on page 683 for a summary of prosecutions and investigations from 2002 through 2012.

WHAT ARE YOUR CHANCES?

The odds of facing criminal charges by the IRS depend on where you live. Of the 90 IRS offices, these are the top and bottom five by number of referrals to prosecutors in 1994 per million population.

IRS District Office	Per Capita Referrals
Washington, DC	71
Tulsa, Okla.	65
Louisville, Ky.	60
Oklahoma City	55
Charleston, W. Va.	45
Topeka, Kan.	5
Montgomery, Ala.	4
Madison, Wis.	4
Concord, N.H.	4
Burlington, Vt.	3

Source: Transactional Records Access Clearinghouse, Syracuse University.

According to Mark E. Matthews, Deputy Assistant Attorney General in the Tax Division, ". . . the certainty of prison time is generally faced only when the loss amount exceeds \$40,000." This is not ". . . a realistic threat to many taxpayers." Do NOT, however, take this as a license to cheat up to \$40,000!

You can access the IRS criminal investigation Website at www.treas.gov/irs/ci for fraud and scam alerts.

REFUNDS

If you are due a refund and if you file by April 15, that refund must be paid by June 1 or else the IRS must pay you interest. Interest on your refund starts accruing 45 days after the return's due date or the date on which you actually filed, whichever is later, and ends accruing 30 days before the date on which the IRS makes out a check to you. The status of a refund may be checked by calling the IRS during regular business hours on a special number available in 27 cities. Under this system, 10 weeks after the return is filed, you may dial the special automated service, then dial your Social Security number and the amount of the expected refund. You will then be advised when to expect a check. The numbers to call are listed below:

New Jersey	1-800-0-554-4477	St. Louis, MO	314-241-4700
Phoenix, AZ	602-261-3560	Newark, NJ	201-624-1223
Los Angeles, CA	213-617-3177	Brooklyn, NY	212-858-4461
Oakland, CA	415-839-4245	Buffalo, NY	716-856-9320
Denver, CO	303-592-1118	Manhattan, NY	212-406-4080
Washington, DC	202-628-2929	Cincinnati, OH	513-684-3531
Jacksonville, FL	904-353-9579	Cleveland, OH	216-522-3037
Atlanta, GA	404-221-6572	Portland, OR	503-294-5363
Chicago, IL	312-886-9614	Philadelphia, PA	215-592-8946
Indianapolis, IN	317-634-1550	Nashville, TE	615-242-1541
Baltimore, MD	301-244-7306	Dallas, TX	214-767-1792
Boston, MA	617-523-8602	Houston, TX	713-850-8801
Detroit, MI	313-961-4282	Seattle, WA	206-343-7221
St. Paul, MN	612-224-4288	Milwaukee, WI	414-886-1615

You can also check the status of your refund on the IRS Website, www.irs.gov, or by calling 1-800-829-1954, or after 4 weeks, 800-829-4477.

COLLECTIONS

If you have not read this book carefully, you may lose an audit and have to go into Collections. As of September 1, 1995, the IRS has implented new procedures which provide a consistent framework for evaluating a taxpayer's

Collection

Enforcement Actions

	FY 2002	FY 2003	FY 2004	FY 2005	FY 2006	FY 2007	FY 2008	FY 2009	FY 2010	FY 2011	FY 2012
Levies	1,283,742	1,680,844	2,029,613	2,743,577	3,742,276	3,757,190	2,631,038	3,478,181	3,606,818	3,748,884	2,961,162
Liens	482,509	544,316	534,392	522,887	629,813	683,659	768,168	965,618	1,096,376	1,042,230	707,768
Seizures	296	399	440	512	590	676	610	581	605	776	733

maximum ability to pay. The procedural changes center around allowable expenses—specifically, the types and amounts of expenses that are allowed.

The new procedures establish national standards for reasonable amounts for five necessary expenses: (1) food, (2) housekeeping supplies, (3) apparel and services, (4) personal care products and services, and (5) miscellaneous. All standards, except miscellaneous, are derived from the Bureau of Labor Statistics (BLS) Consumer Expenditure Survey. The miscellaneous standard has been established by the Service.

Local standards will be established for housing and transportation. Utilities are included under housing. "Other" expenses, not covered under the national or local standards (e.g., health care, job-related education), will be allowed if they meet the necessary expense test.

CONCLUSION

In conclusion, it is important to reiterate that this book has not taught you how to evade taxes but rather how legally, within the full ambit of our tax code, to reduce your taxes to zero. According to a 1987 report issued by the American Bar Association's Commission on Taxpayer Compliance, one-third of all taxpayers deliberately fail to claim tax deductions to which they believe they are entitled. (Reasons for not taking these deductions include concern that they might not be correct, ignorance or forgetfulness, insufficient records, perceptions that the deduction was too trivial or too complicated, and fear of audits.) If you want to pay more in taxes than the law requires, you may. In 1983, 3,500 taxpayers voluntarily coughed up a total of $300,000 in voluntary donations to the Internal Revenue Service in an attempt to reduce the national debt. In fiscal 1984, the government received 2,513 gifts, totaling $405,007. Through July 27, 1985, the Internal Revenue Service counted an additional 2,205 voluntary—and deductible—gifts, totaling $350,394, to help Uncle Sam reduce the public debt. Americans donated $1,697,366 to the Bureau of the Public Debt in fiscal 1986 for the Debt Reduction Fund. Of this amount, $1.1 million came via the Internal Revenue Service, thanks to a note in tax return instructions. An additional $719,516 arrived in the 6 months ending March 31, 1987, bringing the then-to-date total since 1961 to $13,138,462. Through fiscal 1993, the total was $38.6 million. If you want to pay more taxes, you therefore have the opportunity to do so. See the following chart showing donations made to pay off the national debt.

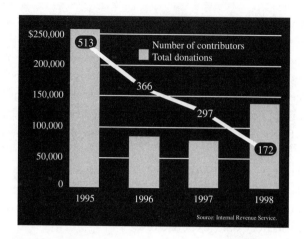

A great deal has been written and said on the question of the morality of tax saving in general, and on those who save taxes in particular. Perhaps the best statement on tax avoidance—the legal minimization of your tax liability—was written by Judge Learned Hand:

> If I understand the Commissioner, he wishes us to consider that these deeds may have been a preliminary step in a reprehensible scheme to lessen . . . income taxes. There is not the faintest ground for imputing any such purpose to the parties at bar; and if there were, it ought not to count. Over and over again courts have said that there is nothing sinister in so arranging one's affairs as to keep taxes as low as possible. Everybody does so, rich or poor; and all do right, for nobody owes any public duty to pay more than the law demands; taxes are enforced exactions, not voluntary contributions. To demand more in the name of morals is mere Cant. (*Commissioner v. Neuman*, 159 F. 2d 848.)

February 20, 1947

CHANCES OF AN AUDIT

Here's a quick and dirty on your chance of being audited.

For the fiscal year ended September 30, 2000, the IRS audited 0.49 percent of individual tax returns filed. This was less than one-third of the 1.67 percent of returns audited for fiscal 1996. Fiscal 2001 crawled up to 0.58 percent. In 2002, it was 0.57 percent, growing to 0.65 percent in 2003, 0.77 in 2004, 0.93 percent in 2005, 0.97 percent for 2006, and 1.03 percent for 2007. It dropped to 1.01 percent for 2008 and increased to 1.03 percent in 2009, and increased again in 2010 to 1.11 percent, where it stayed in 2011.

The IRS audited 1,564,690 individual tax returns in the fiscal year ending September 30, 2011. But only 25 percent of the returns were face-to-face audits. The rest were correspondence examinations. Of those, nearly 45 percent related to the earned income credit for the poor.

In fiscal year 2012, the audit rate dropped to 1.03 percent with total audits falling to 1,481,966. Only 2.4 percent were not correspondence audits.

Of returns showing income of $200,000 or more, the audit rate was 3.70 percent, down from 2011's 3.93 percent, but up from 3.10 percent in fiscal 2010 and 2.89 percent in 2009.

PENALTIES AND INTEREST

Late Filing of a Return: There is a penalty of 5 percent of the unpaid tax for each month or fraction thereof that the return is late, up to a maximum of 25 percent. For example, assume you owe $2,000 on your Form 1040, which you file on April 20 (5 days late). The late filing penalty is $100. There is a minimum late *filing* penalty of the lesser of $135 or the tax due if the return is not filed within 60 days of the prescribed due date.

Understatement of Taxes: In IRS Ruling 8802003, the Internal Revenue Service ruled that a taxpayer was liable for a 25 percent substantial understatement penalty even though his tax liability had been satisfied through withholding or estimated payments. In this case, the tax returns for more than 3 years were filed only after numerous contacts and inquiries by IRS personnel. The IRS ruled that the substantial underpayment penalty is imposed if an underpayment of taxes is attributable to an understatement that exceeds the greater of 10 percent of the tax required to be shown on the return or $5,000. An understatement is generally the excess of the amount of tax required to be shown on a tax return over the actual amount of tax shown on the return. The IRS concluded that for this purpose, the amount of tax shown on the return did not include any additional tax shown on a return filed *after* the Internal Revenue Service had contacted the taxpayer about the liability for the year. Moreover, the amount of tax required to be shown on the return is the tax *without* regard to any payments of tax or estimated tax by the taxpayer.

However, the Tax Court has held that the 25 percent penalty on a tax underpayment attributable to a substantial understatement of tax applies to the unpaid amount of tax after reduction by the amount of federal taxes withheld from a taxpayer's wages. (See *W.A. Woods, II*, C.C.H. Dec. 44903 91 T.C., No. 11.) The substantial understatement penalty is now 20 percent.

Negligence: There is a negligence penalty of 5 percent of the underpaid tax, plus 50 percent of the interest due on the portion of the underpayment attributable to negligence or intentional disregard. This 50 percent of the interest charge is a penalty and cannot be deducted from federal taxes.

Examination—Individual Return Closures and Coverage Rates

Total Individual Returns	FY 2002	FY 2003	FY 2004	FY 2005	FY 2006	FY 2007	FY 2008	FY 2009	FY 2010	FY 2011	FY 2012
Field	205,134	206,457	197,388	247,235	302,785	311,339	310,429	326,249	342,762	391,621	359,750
Correspondence	538,747	642,839	810,486	968,073	981,165	1,073,224	1,081,152	1,099,639	1,238,632	1,173,069	1,122,216
Total Examinations	743,881	849,296	1,007,874	1,215,308	1,283,950	1,384,563	1,391,581	1,425,888	1,581,394	1,564,690	1,481,966
Returns Filed in Prior CY*	129,444,947	130,341,159	130,134,277	130,576,852	132,275,830	134,542,879	137,849,635	138,949,670	142,823,105	140,837,499	143,399,737
Coverage	0.57%	0.65%	0.77%	0.93%	0.97%	1.03%	1.01%	1.03%	1.11%	1.11%	1.03%

Income Under $200,000	FY 2004	FY 2005	FY 2006	FY 2007	FY 2008	FY 2009	FY 2010	FY 2011	FY 2012
Field	n/a	n/a	266,726	267,699	256,854	269,865	284,241	313,229	290,015
Correspondence	n/a	n/a	929,666	1,011,315	1,003,976	1,010,870	1,144,178	1,076,607	1,012,898
Total Examinations			1,196,392	1,279,014	1,260,830	1,280,735	1,428,419	1,389,836	1,302,913
Returns Filed in Prior CY*			128,875,395	130,600,177	133,407,479	133,924,956	137,892,685	136,387,547	138,554,470
Coverage			0.93%	0.98%	0.95%	0.96%	1.04%	1.02%	0.94%

Income $200,000 and Higher	FY 2004	FY 2005	FY 2006	FY 2007	FY 2008	FY 2009	FY 2010	FY 2011	FY 2012
Field	n/a	n/a	36,059	43,640	53,575	56,384	58,521	78,392	69,735
Correspondence	n/a	n/a	51,499	61,909	77,176	88,769	94,454	96,462	109,318
Total Examinations			87,558	105,549	130,751	145,153	152,975	174,854	179,053
Returns Filed in Prior CY*			3,400,435	3,942,702	4,442,156	5,024,714	4,930,420	4,449,952	4,845,267
Coverage			2.57%	2.68%	2.94%	2.89%	3.10%	3.93%	3.70%

Income $1 Million and Higher	FY 2004	FY 2005	FY 2006	FY 2007	FY 2008	FY 2009	FY 2010	FY 2011	FY 2012
Field	5,857	7,166	9,459	12,259	12,233	15,730	16,509	20,475	17,826
Correspondence	3,719	5,669	4,728	10,941	9,641	12,619	15,985	15,947	23,139
Total Examinations	9,576	12,835	14,187	23,200	21,874	28,349	32,494	36,422	40,965
Returns Filed in Prior CY*	190,372	210,280	270,161	339,138	392,776	441,715	388,763	291,831	337,477
Coverage	5.03%	6.10%	5.25%	6.84%	5.57%	6.42%	8.36%	12.48%	12.14%

* CY = calendar year.
n/a = not available

Examination—Business Return Closures and Coverage Rates[1]

	FY 2002	FY 2003	FY 2004	FY 2005	FY 2006	FY 2007*	FY 2008	FY 2009	FY 2010	FY 2011	FY 2012
Total Returns Examined	40,287	38,299	29,445	47,593	52,149	59,516	59,823	58,144	58,067	62,445	70,265
Returns Filed in Prior CY*	7,576,681	7,849,109	8,141,645	8,373,880	8,722,410	9,072,828	9,530,662	9,951,648	9,941,289	9,869,358	9,950,784
Coverage	0.53%	0.49%	0.36%	0.57%	0.60%	0.66%	0.63%	0.58%	0.58%	0.63%	0.71%
Small Corporation Returns (Assets Under $10 Million)											
Returns Examined	14,655	13,608	7,294	17,858	17,849	20,020	20,580	18,298	19,127	19,697	21,164
Returns Filed in Prior CY*	2,329,479	2,327,272	2,310,279	2,249,416	2,230,024	2,171,144	2,166,197	2,146,400	2,041,474	1,931,008	1,896,158
Coverage	0.63%	0.58%	0.32%	0.79%	0.80%	0.92%	0.95%	0.85%	0.94%	1.02%	1.12%
Large Corporation Returns (Assets $10 Million and Higher)											
Returns Examined	8,443	7,125	9,523	10,829	10,578	9,644	9,406	9,536	10,207	10,459	10,752
Returns Filed in Prior CY*	59,602	58,974	56,883	54,091	56,847	57,357	61,641	65,546	61,570	59,291	60,489
Coverage	14.2%	12.1%	16.7%	20.0%	18.6%	16.8%	15.26%	14.55%	16.58%	17.64%	17.78%
Subchapter S Returns (Form 1120-S)											
Returns Examined	11,646	9,695	6,402	10,417	13,970	17,657	16,634	17,455	16,327	18,519	21,658
Returns Filed in Prior CY*	3,022,589	3,191,108	3,369,122	3,523,934	3,715,249	3,909,730	4,155,830	4,390,857	4,414,662	4,444,154	4,469,329
Coverage	0.39%	0.30%	0.19%	0.30%	0.38%	0.45%	0.40%	0.40%	0.37%	0.42%	0.48%
Partnership Returns (Form 1065)											
Returns Examined	5,543	7,871	6,226	8,489	9,752	12,195	13,203	12,855	12,406	13,770	16,691
Returns Filed in Prior CY*	2,165,011	2,271,755	2,405,361	2,546,439	2,720,290	2,934,597	3,146,994	3,348,845	3,423,583	3,434,905	3,524,808
Coverage	0.26%	0.35%	0.26%	0.33%	0.36%	0.42%	0.42%	0.38%	0.36%	0.40%	0.47%

[1] Business returns include small and large corporation returns and Subchapter S and partnership pass-through returns.

* CY = calendar year.

Examination—Large Corporation Return Closures and Coverage Rates

Assets $10 Million and Higher	FY 2002	FY 2003	FY 2004	FY 2005	FY 2006	FY 2007	FY 2008	FY 2009	FY 2010	FY 2011	FY 2012
Total Returns Examined	8,443	7,125	9,523	10,829	10,578	9,644	9,406	9,536	10,207	10,459	10,752
Returns Filed in Prior CY*	59,602	58,974	56,883	54,091	56,877	57,357	61,641	65,546	61,570	59,291	60,489
Coverage	14.2%	12.1%	16.7%	20.0%	18.6%	16.8%	15.3%	14.5%	16.6%	17.6%	17.78%

By Asset Class	FY 2002	FY 2003	FY 2004	FY 2005	FY 2006	FY 2007	FY 2008	FY 2009	FY 2010	FY 2011	FY 2012
$10 Million < $50 Million											
Returns Examined	2,540	1,987	2,864	3,535	4,218	4,473	3,833	3,473	4,307	4,059	3,266
Coverage	7.8%	6.2%	9.4%	12.3%	14.2%	15.0%	11.7%	10.1%	13.4%	13.3%	10.48%
$50 Million < $100 Million											
Returns Examined	865	782	965	1,148	999	801	893	1,158	1,259	1,442	1,543
Coverage	10.7%	9.8%	12.9%	16.4%	13.8%	11.4%	11.7%	14.3%	16.2%	18.9%	20.74%
$100 Million < $250 Million											
Returns Examined	1,289	1,026	1,308	1,287	1,085	946	1,026	1,134	1,191	1,289	1,854
Coverage	16.0%	12.9%	16.9%	17.5%	14.0%	12.1%	12.8%	13.6%	14.7%	16.6%	23.19%
$250 Million and Higher											
Returns Examined	3,749	3,330	4,386	4,859	4,276	3,424	3,654	3,771	3,450	3,669	4,089
Coverage	34.4%	29.8%	39.8%	44.1%	35.2%	27.2%	27.4%	25.7%	25.3%	27.6%	29.41%

* CY = calendar year.

Examination—Tax Exempt Organization Return Closures

	FY 2002	FY 2003	FY 2004	FY 2005	FY 2006	FY 2007	FY 2008	FY 2009	FY 2010	FY 2011	FY 2012
Total Returns Examined	5,278	5,754	5,800	4,953	7,079	7,580	7,861	10,187	11,449	11,699	10,743
Returns Processed in Prior Calendar Year	783,582	809,223	863,494	849,342	849,227	867,696	888,412	823,087	776,300	858,865	798,903
Coverage	0.67%	0.71%	0.67%	0.58%	0.83%	0.87%	0.88%	1.24%	1.47%	1.36%	1.34%

Taxpayer Service

Electronic Filing (e-File) Rate—Individual Returns

FY 2002	FY 2003	FY 2004	FY 2005	FY 2006	FY 2007	FY 2008	FY 2009	FY 2010	FY 2011	FY 2012
36%	40%	47%	51%	54%	57%	58%	66%	69%	77%	81%

Toll-Free Assistor Level of Service

FY 2002	FY 2003	FY 2004	FY 2005	FY 2006	FY 2007	FY 2008	FY 2009	FY 2010	FY 2011	FY 2012
69%	80%	87%	83%	82%	82%	53%	70%	74%	70%	68%

Toll-Free Tax Law Accuracy

FY 2002	FY 2003	FY 2004	FY 2005	FY 2006	FY 2007	FY 2008	FY 2009	FY 2010	FY 2011	FY 2012
84%	82%	80%	89%	91%	91%	91%	93%	93%	93%	93%

Toll-Free Customer Satisfaction Rating

FY 2002	FY 2003	FY 2004	FY 2005	FY 2006	FY 2007	FY 2008	FY 2009	FY 2010	FY 2011	FY 2012
n/a	93%	94%	94%	94%	94%	93%	93%	92%	94.0%	92%

Web Page Visits on IRS.Gov (in millions)

FY 2002	FY 2003	FY 2004	FY 2005	FY 2006	FY 2007	FY 2008	FY 2009	FY 2010	FY 2011	FY 2012
n/a	102.6	152.7	176.5	197.1	217.8	329.4	266.7	304.8	319.3	372.5

Online Refund Status Checks Through "Where's My Refund" (in millions)

FY 2002	FY 2003	FY 2004	FY 2005	FY 2006	FY 2007	FY 2008	FY 2009	FY 2010	FY 2011	FY 2012
1.1	12.4	14.9	22.1	24.7	32.1	39.2	54.30	66.9	78.0	132.3

Moreover, in Technical Advice Memorandum 8527012, the Internal Revenue Service ruled that a 5 percent negligence penalty may be imposed in the case of a taxpayer who was entitled to a refund on a late-filed return where the late filing was due to negligence or intentional disregard of the rules and regulations. According to the TAM, "the failure to file a timely tax return in itself can constitute the negligence or intentional disregard of rules and regulations." Whether this Technical Advice Memorandum can withstand the test of judicial scrutiny, however, is arguable.

Late Payment of Tax: There is a penalty of .5 percent (increasing to 1 percent on the tenth day after the date a notice of levy is given) of the tax due for each month or fraction thereof that the payment is late, up to a maximum of 25 percent. For example, assume you owe $2,000 on your Form 1040, which you filed timely, but did not pay the tax due until April 30. The late *payment* penalty is $10. In the event that the return is neither timely *filed* nor timely *paid*, both penalties will apply for the first 5 months, but the combined monthly penalty cannot exceed 5/(5.5) percent. After the 5-month period, the late payment penalty continues at .5 percent per month until the maximum 25 percent is reached. Obviously, if you are short of cash and cannot pay the tax due at the filing date, you should still file the return. Remember that an extension of time avoids a penalty for failure to file but does not extend the time to pay the tax. These penalties apply to most types of returns, such as income, payroll, and fiduciary tax returns. They will be waived only if the failure to file or failure to pay is due to "reasonable cause," such as illness or incapacity. If you enter into an installment agreement with the IRS, the 0.5 percent penalty falls to 0.25 percent per month.

To assist those in need, the IRS granted a 6-month grace period from the failure to pay penalty for tax year 2011 only if the tax, interest, and any other penalties were fully paid by October 15, 2012.

The penalty relief was available to two categories of taxpayers:

- Wage earners who have been unemployed at least 30 consecutive days during 2011 or in 2012 up to the April 17 deadline for filing a federal tax return in 2012.

- Self-employed individuals who experienced a 25 percent or greater reduction in business income in 2011 due to the economy.

This penalty relief was subject to income limits. A taxpayer's income must not exceed $200,000 if he or she files as married filing jointly or not exceed $100,000 if he or she files as single or head of household. This penalty relief was also restricted to taxpayers whose calendar year 2011 balance due does not exceed $50,000.

Taxpayers meeting the eligibility criteria needed to complete Form 1127A to seek the 2011 penalty relief.

Interest: In addition to the penalties, interest will compound daily on any taxes and penalties due until they are paid. The current interest rate, about 3 percent, will change on January 1, 2014. The rate is adjusted quarterly and calculated on the basis of the short-term federal rate plus 3 percent as of the first month of each quarter, effective as of the *following* calendar quarter.

For example, assume the short-term federal rate during January 2014 is 2 percent. Therefore, an underpayment rate of 5 percent will be established for the calendar quarter beginning April 1, 2014. Note that rates of interest paid by the IRS to corporate taxpayers for overpayments are always 1 percent lower than the rates paid to the Internal Revenue Service for underpayments. For noncorporations, the rates are the same. The personal interest paid and the penalties are both now not deductible.

Failure to File Information Returns: There is a $50 penalty for failure to file required information returns and statements with the IRS. There is an additional $50 penalty for failure to provide a copy to the payee. Thus, a failure *both* to file the information return with the IRS and to provide a copy to the payee results in a penalty of $100 per failure, with a total aggregate maximum penalty of $200,000. Every person engaged in a trade or business (including nonprofit organizations) must file an information return for payments of employees' salaries, rent and royalties, nonemployee compensation (independent contractors), interest, and dividends. Information returns are required if payments to a single individual total $600 or more, except for interest and dividends, where the limit is $10. Of course, all employee wages and salaries are reported on Form W-2 regardless of amount paid.

Stopping Interest: Interest on taxes owed is compounded daily, and charging interest on interest is allowed. In Revenue Proclamation 84-58, I.R.B. 1984-33, 9, the IRS detailed the steps that should be taken to stop the running of interest on a contested IRS determination. You may stop the running of interest by prepaying the amount contested, without jeopardizing your right to contest the issue, or by posting a cash bond. The prepayment would draw interest and the bond would not. However, the bond could be withdrawn at any time before assessment. Note, however, that a payment response to a proposed liability—e.g., as a result of a revenue agent's report—will be treated as a payment of tax, rather than a cash bond, unless you specifically designate the remittance as a "deposit in the nature of a cash bond." A remittance that is made before liability is proposed, however, will be treated as a cash bond. If the cash bond exceeds the amount of tax ultimately determined, you may have it applied against other liabilities, either assessed or unassessed. Furthermore, you may make a partial payment, but you must designate the part of the liability that is proposed to be satisfied. If the IRS cannot tell whether the payment is a partial payment of tax or a cash bond, it will treat it as being in the latter category. Moreover, the bond must include interest to date in order to stop the further running of interest on any interest accrued.

Partial Payments: If you do not pay the entire amount owed to the Internal Revenue Service, a partial payment generally will be applied first to tax, then to penalty, and finally to the interest that is owed.

Frivolous Tax Penalty: A frivolous tax penalty of up to $25,000 can be assessed on a taxpayer who institutes a Tax Court proceeding primarily to delay payment or for frivolous reasons. Moreover, a $25,000 penalty can be imposed upon any taxpayer who, in furtherance of a frivolous position or with a prima facie intent to delay or impede administration of the tax law, files a purported return that fails to contain information from which the correctness of a reported tax liability can be determined, or that clearly indicates that the tax liability shown must be substantially incorrect.

In fact, the IRS can assess a penalty against a taxpayer who files a return that it deems frivolous even when no taxes are owed and a return is not required to be filed. For example, in *Bradley v. U.S.* (No. 85-2445, May 22, 1987, CA9), the taxpayer wrote a statement to the IRS saying that he refused to pay taxes because of the government's intervention in Central America and filed that statement with his Form 1040. The taxpayer owed no tax and was not required to file a return. However, a notice was sent to Bradley informing him that he had filed a frivolous return and that a penalty was being assessed. The court upheld the penalty because the Form 1040 that Bradley returned purported to be a tax return but lacked the information on which the substantial correctness of the self-assessment could be judged and took a frivolous position.

Interest on Erroneous Refunds: Normally, if you receive an erroneous refund, the Internal Revenue Service will require that you pay it back with interest. However, in Delegation Order No. 231, published in *The Federal Register* on July 11, 1988, the IRS delegated authority to district service center directors to determine administratively that interest is not due on erroneous refunds under certain circumstances. These circumstances include the following:

1. Documentation is present that leaves no doubt that an IRS error caused the erroneous refund to be issued.
2. Documentation is present that substantiates that repayment of the refund has been made in full.
3. The official is satisfied—after considering the relative size of the erroneous refund, the amount of the interest involved, the circumstances surrounding

any delay in the repayment of the refund, and the handling and collection cost that would be entailed—that a waiver would be fair and equitable to the government and the taxpayer.

PENALTY ABATEMENT

You may be entitled to penalty abatement, if the IRS follows the rules.

The TIGTA found that many taxpayers did not receive an abatement of the failure to file (FTF) and failure to pay (FTP) penalties even though they qualified under the *First-Time Abate* (FTA) criteria. The IRS waives the FTF and FTP penalties for some taxpayers who have demonstrated full compliance over the prior 3 years in the FTA program to reward past compliance and promote future compliance. However, many taxpayers with compliant tax histories were not offered and did not receive the FTA waiver. The unabated penalties totaled more than $181 million. You must request the abatement to get it.

STATE TAXES

To aid in the filing of state tax returns, see page 708 for a list of telephone numbers and addresses for obtaining out-of-state income tax forms.

CREDIT CARD PAYMENTS

If you want to pay your tax with a credit card, call either 800-272-9829 or 888-255-8299. Any mileage earned could offset any fees charged, and the fees are now deductible.

THE TAXPAYER'S BILL OF RIGHTS

The Technical and Miscellaneous Revenue Act of 1988 (TAMRA) created a consolidated statutory system that addressed a wide range of procedural subjects, including extensive changes in collection procedures. The intent of the Taxpayer's Bill of Rights is to provide a better balance between taxpayers' rights and the IRS's authority in administering the federal tax system. The Bill enhanced many safeguards and remedies previously available to taxpayers and established several new restrictions on the procedures governing the assessment and collection of taxes by the Internal Revenue Service.

The provisions of the Bill included the following: The Internal Revenue Service must provide taxpayers with a written statement of taxpayer rights and the obligations of the Internal Revenue Service during audit, repeals, refund, and collection processes when taxpayers are contacted regarding determinations or collections of tax.

Original Income Tax Return, 1913

Form 1040.

INCOME TAX.

THE PENALTY

FOR FAILURE TO HAVE THIS RETURN IN
THE HANDS OF THE COLLECTOR OF
INTERNAL REVENUE ON OR BEFORE
MARCH 1 IS $20 TO $1000.

(SEE INSTRUCTIONS ON PAGE 4.)

UNITED STATES INTERNAL REVENUE.

RETURN OF ANNUAL NET INCOME OF INDIVIDUALS.

(As provided by Act of Congress, approved October 3, 1913.)

RETURN OF NET INCOME RECEIVED OR ACCRUED DURING THE YEAR ENDED
DECEMBER 31, 191____

(FOR THE YEAR 1913, FROM MARCH 1 TO DECEMBER 31.)

TO BE FILLED IN BY COLLECTOR.

List No. ....

.... District of ....

Date received ....

TO BE FILLED IN BY INTERNAL
REVENUE BUREAU.

File No. ....

Assessment List ....

Page .... Line ....

Filed by (or for) .... of ....
　　　　　　　(Full name of individual.)

in the City, Town, or Post Office of .... State of ....
　　　　　　　　　　　　　　　　　　　　　　　　　　　　　　　(Street and No.)

(Fill in pages 2 and 3 before making entries below.)

1. GROSS INCOME (see page 2, line 12)	$		
2. GENERAL DEDUCTIONS (see page 3, line 7) ...	$		
3. NET INCOME	$		

Deductions and exemptions allowed in computing income subject to the normal tax of
1 per cent.

(continues)

4. Dividends and net earnings received or accrued, of corporations, etc., subject to like tax. (See page 2, line 11) .... $ ....

5. Amount of income on which the normal tax has been deducted and withheld at the source. (See page 2, line 9, column A) ....

6. Specific exemption of $3,000 or $4,000, as the case may be. (See Instructions 3 and 19) ....

Total deductions and exemptions. (Items 4, 5, and 6) .... $ ....

7. TAXABLE INCOME on which the normal tax of 1 per cent is to be calculated. (See Instruction 3). .... $ ....

8. When the net income shown above on line 3 exceeds $20,000, the additional tax thereon must be calculated as per schedule below:

INCOME		TAX
1 per cent on amount over $20,000 and not exceeding $50,000	$	$ ....
2 " " " 50,000 " " 75,000	....	....
3 " " " 75,000 " " 100,000	....	....
4 " " " 100,000 " " 250,000	....	....
5 " " " 250,000 " " 500,000	....	....
6 " " " 500,000	....	....

Total additional or super tax .... $ ....

Total normal tax (1 per cent of amount entered on line 7) .... $ ....

Total tax liability .... $ ....

704

Within 1 year after November 10, 1988, the IRS must prescribe standards for selecting a reasonable time and place for taxpayer interviews. These regulations should provide that it is not reasonable to require an interview at a service office other than the one closest to the taxpayer's home. Moreover, it is unreasonable for the IRS to audit a taxpayer at his or her place of business if the business is so small that doing so effectively requires the taxpayer to close the business, except where facts, such as inventory, must be verified by a direct visit.

The Internal Revenue Service must prescribe procedures for a taxpayer to make an audio recording of an interview at his or her own expense. The IRS can also record an interview, provided that the taxpayer is given advance notice and a transcript or copy of the recording upon request and payment of costs. These changes largely codify existing practices.

The IRS must notify a taxpayer that an interview may be suspended at any time if the taxpayer clearly states the desire to consult with an authorized representative—that is, an attorney or accountant. Moreover, the IRS cannot require a taxpayer to accompany an authorized representative to an interview unless it issues an administrative summons.

The IRS must abate any portion of penalties on tax attributable to erroneous written advice provided by the IRS. However, the Bill does not require abatement of interest on deficiencies arising from such erroneous advice. The new provision applies (1) if the advice was given in response to a specific written request made after 1988, (2) if the advice was reasonably relied upon, and (3) if the penalty or addition did not result from the taxpayer's failure to provide full and accurate information to the IRS.

The Bill extended the time period within which levies can be issued by the IRS and within which banks must respond to a levy. The required minimum period of time between the IRS's issuance to a taxpayer of a notice of levy and the actual levy was increased from 10 to 30 days. Similarly, banks must now wait 21 days before surrendering deposits in response to a levy. The amount to be surrendered includes any interest that accrues during the escrow period.

Any notice of levy must contain a statement describing the statutory provisions and administrative procedures relating to the levy, sale and redemption of property, the administrative appeals available to contest the levy, and the alternatives available to the taxpayer (including an installment payment agreement) for preventing the use of a levy. This statement must be written in simple and nontechnical terms.

The Bill prohibits the use of a levy if the IRS estimates that the expenses that will be incurred for the levy and sale of the property will exceed the property's fair market value at the time of the levy.

Moreover, the Bill expanded the types and amounts of property exempt from levy. The exemption for wages and salary was increased from $75 plus $25 for each dependent, per week, to a weekly amount equal to the taxpayer's standard deduction and allowable personal exemptions, divided by 52. The exemption for fuel, provisions, furniture, and personal effects was also increased from $1,500 to $1,550 in 1989 and $1,600 thereafter. Similarly, the exemptions for books, tools, and personal effects was increased from $1,000 to $1,050 in 1989 and $1,100 thereafter. A new exemption was created for the principal residence of a taxpayer, except in jeopardy cases or where the district director or assistant district director personally approves the levy in writing. New exemptions were also created for certain public assistance and job training partnerships payments.

The Bill directed that the IRS provide an accelerated appeals process to determine whether any seized personal property used in a trade or business should be released from levy on any appropriate statutory grounds. Such grounds would include the taxpayer's entering into an installment agreement with respect to the liability or an IRS determination that the levy "is creating an economic hardship due to the financial condition of the taxpayer."

The owner of seized property now has the right to request that that property be sold within 60 days after such a request.

The Bill required the IRS to issue regulations under which taxpayers may obtain a review of a publicly filed notice of lien. The taxpayer will be able to correct erroneous filings—for example, when the underlying tax liability has been satisfied or the assessment was untimely or improperly made.

Regardless of whether a taxpayer challenges the lien, the IRS is required to issue a special certificate of release whenever a lien is found to be erroneously filed. The certificate must be filed expeditiously—"if practicable, within 14 days"—after the error is determined. It must also include a statement that the filing of the notice was erroneous.

The Bill codified the current IRS practice of entering into installment agreements when taxpayers are unable to satisfy a tax delinquency in full. However, the IRS is given the authority to alter, modify, or terminate an agreement if it determines that the financial condition of the taxpayer has significantly changed. The IRS must give the taxpayer at least 30 days' notice prior to the action and must provide the reason for its determination.

The Bill allows the IRS's taxpayer ombudsman to issue taxpayer assistance orders (TAOs) that may include releasing taxpayers from levies of property and directing the IRS to cease collection attempts, though such orders can be modified or rescinded by certain other IRS officials. The issuance of a TAO will suspend any applicable period of limitation from the date of the taxpayer's application until the date of the ombudsman's decision on the application.

The Bill expanded the jurisdiction of the Tax Court to intercede when the IRS decides to seize taxpayer property immediately if a taxpayer petition has been filed with the court. Effective November 10, 1988, the Tax Court has concurrent jurisdiction with the taxpayer's local district court to enjoin the assessment or collection of a tax that is the subject of a timely filed petition with the Tax Court. Note that taxpayers who are the subject of a premature assessment or collection activity but who have not yet filed a petition with the Tax Court must still pursue their injunctive remedy in a district court.

Moreover, the Tax Court now has jurisdiction, upon motion by a taxpayer, to order a refund if the IRS has failed to make a refund within 120 days after the court's decision becomes final. This provision is effective for overpayments not refunded by February 8, 1989.

In addition, the Tax Court is granted limited jurisdiction to consider disputes concerning the interest due on deficiencies that it has determined. The jurisdiction of both the Tax Court and the district courts to hear certain causes of action arising from jeopardy assessments and levies has also been expanded.

The Bill created a new cause of action for damages against the United States in district courts for the reckless or intentional disregard of the Code or Regulations by an IRS employee in connection with the collection of any tax. However, to be eligible for a recovery, a taxpayer must exhaust all administrative remedies. This civil action must be commenced within 2 years after the date the right of action accrued, and the liability of the government under this provision is limited to the lesser of $100,000 or the sum of the "actual, direct economic damages, sustained as a proximate cause" of the reckless or intentional actions of the employee, plus the costs of the action.

Note that the court has the right to assess damages up to $10,000 against a taxpayer who the court determines to have instituted or maintained a frivolous or groundless action under this provision.

The Bill also created a new cause of action for damages against the United States in a federal district court for an IRS failure to release a lien after 1988. Both the exhaustion of administrative remedies and the period of limitations are the same as the above newly created cause of action.

Reasonable litigation costs were available to prevailing taxpayers prior to the Bill. TAMRA creates an expanded remedy to permit taxpayers to recover reasonable administrative costs incurred for certain administrative proceedings. Such costs include costs incurred on or after the earlier of (1) the date the taxpayer receives a notice of deficiency or (2) the date the taxpayer received the decision notice from the IRS Office of Appeals. In order to collect, the taxpayer must be a "prevailing party," and the taxpayer retains the burden of proof that the position of the government was not substantially justified. "The position of the U.S." means the position taken by the IRS after the dates referred to above. If neither date is applicable, then the position of the United States is the position taken in litigation.

The Bill contained provisions that prevent temporary regulations from remaining in effect longer than 3 years.

The Bill contained provisions preventing the IRS from using tax enforcement results as a basis for evaluating its employees or for imposing or suggesting production goals or quotas for its employees to meet. Each district director must certify quarterly, in a letter to the commissioner, that tax enforcement records are not being used in a prohibited manner.

The Bill provided for a statutorily required position as second assistant commissioner responsible for Taxpayer Services.

The Bill created a new civil penalty against tax return preparers who disclose any information obtained in preparing a return or who use such information for any purpose other than preparing a return. This penalty was $250 for each such disclosure, up to a maximum of $10,000 per calendar year. The criminal penalty for such disclosures is modified to apply only when the prohibited disclosure is done knowingly or recklessly.

The creation of the Taxpayer's Bill of Rights represented a significant advance in the direction of tax equity and fairness. Further advances were achieved by the Taxpayer's Bill of Rights 2 passed in 1996, which created what is now the Office of the Taxpayer Advocate, and 3, passed in 1998, which provided enhanced "innocent spouse" relief.

State Tax Departments

ALABAMA
205-262-1112
State Dept. of Rev
 Income Tax Division
P.O. Box 327410
Montgomery, AL
 36132-7410

ALASKA
907-465-2302
Dept. of Rev.
S.O.B. Box SA
Juneau, AK 99811

ARIZONA
602-542-4260
Dept. of Rev.
Attn: Forms
1600 W. Monroe
Phoenix, AZ 85007

ARKANSAS
501-682-7255
Dept. of Finance and
 Administration
Rev. Division
P.O. Box 3628
Little Rock, AR 72203

CALIFORNIA
916-635-8023
Franchise Tax Board
Tax Forms Request
P.O. Box 942840
Sacramento, CA
94240-0070

COLORADO
303-534-1408
Dept. of Rev.
1375 Sherman Street
Denver, CO 80261

CONNECTICUT
203-566-8520
State Tax Dept.
Dept. of Rev. Services
92 Farmington Avenue
Hartford, CT 06105

DELAWARE
302-571-3300
Dept. of Finance
Division of Rev.
Delaware State Building
820 N. French St.
Wilmington, DE 19801

FLORIDA
904-487-3107
Dept. of Rev. Supply Dept.
501 S. Calhoun St.
Tallahassee, FL
323/99-0100

GEORGIA
404-656-4293
Income Tax Unit
Dept. of Rev.
Trinity-Washington Bldg.
Atlanta, GA 30334

HAWAII
808-548-3270
First Taxation District
830 Punch Bowl St.
P.O. Box 259
Honolulu, HI 96809

IDAHO
208-334-7660
State Tax Commission
700 W. State St.
P.O. Box 36
Boise, ID 83722

ILLINOIS
217-782-3336
Dept. of Rev.
101 W. Jefferson
Springfield, IL 62708

INDIANA
317-232-2189
Dept. of Rev.
100 N. Senate Ave.
Room 113
Indianapolis, IN
46204-2253

IOWA
Dept. of Rev.
Hoover State Office
 Building
Des Moines, IA 50319

KANSAS
913-296-305
Dept. of Rev.
Division of Taxation
Box 12001
Topeka, KS 66612-2001

KENTUCKY
502-564-3658
Rev. Cabinet
Property and Mail Service
Frankfort, KY 40620

LOUISIANA
504-925-7532
Dept. of Rev.
P.O. Box 201
Baton Rouge, LA 70821

MAINE
207-289-3695
Bureau of Taxation
Income Tax Section
Station 24
Augusta, ME 04333

MARYLAND
301-974-3117
Comp. of the Treasury
Income Tax Division
Annapolis, MD 21401

MASSACHUSETTS
617-727-4392
Income Tax Bureau
Services and Supplies
 Section
100 Cambridge Street
Boston, MA 02204

MICHIGAN
517-335-1144
Dept. of Treasury
Treasury Building
430 W. Allegan St.
Lansing, MI 48922

MINNESOTA
612-296-3781
Minnesota Dept. of Rev.
Tax Division
Mail Station 4451
St. Paul, MN 55145

MISSISSIPPI
601-359-1105
State Tax Commission
P.O. Box 960
Jackson, MS 39205

MISSOURI
314-751-4866
Dept. of Rev.
P.O. Box 3022
Jefferson City, MO 65102

MONTANA
406-444-2981
Income Tax Division
Sam Mitchell Building
Helena, MT 59620

NEBRASKA
402-471-2971
Dept. of Rev.
Box 94818
Lincoln, NE
68509-4818

NEVADA
702-885-4892
Dept. of Taxation
Capitol Complex
Carson City, NV 89710

NEW HAMPSHIRE
603-271-2191
Dept. of Rev.
61 S. Spring St.
P.O. Box 457
Concord, NH 03302

NEW JERSEY
609-292-6400
Division of Taxation
50 Barrack St.
Trenton, NJ 08646-0269

NEW MEXICO
505-827-0700
Rev. Division
P.O. Box 630
Santa Fe, NM 87509-0630

NEW YORK CITY
718-935-6000
Dept. of Finance
Forms Information
25 Elm Place, 3rd Floor
Brooklyn, NY

NEW YORK STATE
518-457-2772
Dept. of Taxation and
  Finance
Taxpayer Service
Harriman Campus
State Office Building
Albany, NY 12227

NORTH CAROLINA
919-733-3991
Dept. of Rev.
Box 25000
Raleigh, NC 27640

NORTH DAKOTA
701-224-3450
State Tax Commission
State Capitol
Bismarck, ND 58505

OHIO
614-433-7750
Dept. of Taxation
Forms Request
P.O. Box 2679
Columbus, OH 43270

OKLAHOMA
405-521-3108
Income Tax Division
2501 Lincoln Blvd
Oklahoma City, OK
  73194-0020

OREGON
503-3-371-2244
Dept. of Rev.
955 Center St., N.E.
Salem, OR 97310

PENNSYLVANIA
717-986-4621
Dept. of Rev.
Bureau of Admin.
  Services
Dept. 281200
Harrisburg, PA
17128-1200

RHODE ISLAND
401-277-3934
Division of Taxation
289 Promenade St.
Providence, RI 02908

SOUTH CAROLINA
803-737-5000
Tax Commission
Individual Income Tax
  Division
P.O. Box 125
Columbia, SC 29214

SOUTH DAKOTA
605-773-3311
Dept. of Rev.
700 Governors Dr.
Pierre, SD 57501-2276

TENNESSEE
615-741-3133
Dept. of Rev.
Andrew Jackson
  State Office Bldg.
Room 807
500 Deaderick St.
Nashville, TN 37242

TEXAS
512-463-4600
Comptroller's Office
Capitol Station
Austin, TX 78774

UTAH
801-530-6306
Heber Wells Building
160 East, 300 South
Salt Lake City,
UT 84134

VERMONT
802-828-2545
Pavillion Office Bldg.
Dept. of Taxes
Montpelier,
VT 05602

VIRGINIA
804-367-8055
Dept. of Taxation
P.O. Box 1317
Richmond, VA
  23210-1317
Attn: Forms Request
  Unit, P.O. Box 3784

WASHINGTON
206-753-5540
Dept. of Rev. AX-02
Olympia, WA 98504

WASHINGTON, D.C.
202-727-6104
District of Columbia
Finance Office Rev. Div.
Room 1046
300 Indiana Ave., N.W.
Washington, D.C. 20001

WEST VIRGINIA
304-348-3333
State Tax Dept.
Taxpayer Service Division
P.O. Box 3784
Charleston, WV
25337-3784

WISCONSIN
608-266-1961
Dept. of Rev.
P.O. Box 8903
Madison, WI 53708

WYOMING
307-777-7378
The State of Wyoming
  Secretary of State
Capitol Building
Cheyenne, WY
  82002-0020

IRS PICKS UP SPEED ON INFORMATION SUPERHIGHWAY

With a computer and a modem, you can get federal tax forms and information online.

"This is another way the IRS is keeping its promise to serve our customers more efficiently and change the way we do business," said Bob Wenzel, IRS Chief of Strategic Planning and Communications.

The address for the IRS homepage on the World Wide Web is www.irs.gov.

To check the status of a refund, call 800-829-1954 or 800-829-4477.

To pay your taxes using the Internet, go to www.eftps.com or call 800-555-4477 or 800-945-8400.

To get an extension, call 888-796-1074.

For the Tax Practioners Priority Service for correspondence audits, call 866-860-4259.

State Tax Department Internet Sites

Alaska Department of Revenue	www.revenue.state.ak.us/
Arizona Department of Revenue	aspin.asu.edu/aztax/
California Franchise Tax Board	www.ftb.ca.gov/
Colorado Department of Revenue	www.state.co.us/gov_dir/revenue_dir/home_rev.html
Delaware Division of Revenue	www.state.de.us/govern/agencies/revenue/revenue.htm
Florida Department of Revenue	fcn.state.fl.us/dor/revenue.html
Hawaii Department of Taxation	www.hawaii.gov/icsd/tax/tax.html
Idaho State Tax Commission	www.state.id.us/apa/idapa35/taxindex.htm
Illinois Department of Revenue	www.revenue.state.il.us/
Indiana Department of Revenue	www.state.in.us/sic//HTML/revenue.html
Iowa Department of Revenue and Finance	www.state.ia.us/government/drf/index.html
Kansas Department of Revenue	www.ink.org.public/kdor/
Kentucky Revenue Cabinet	www.state.ky.us/agencies/revenue/rev.home.htm
Louisiana Department of Revenue Taxation	www.rev.state.la.us/
Maine Bureau of Taxation	www.state.me.us/taxation
Maryland Comptroller of the Treasury	www.inform.umd.edu:8080/UMS+State/MD_/Resources/COT/
Massachusetts Department of Revenue	www.magnet.state.ma.us/dor/
Michigan Department of Treasury	info.migov.state.mi.us/depts/treasury/treasury.html
Minnesota Department of Revenue	www.state.mn.us/ebranch/mdor/
Missouri Division of Taxation and Collection	www.state.mo.us/dor/tax
Nebraska Department of Revenue	www.nol.org/home/NDR/
Nevada Department of Taxation	www.state.nv.us/inprog.htm
New Hampshire Department of Revenue	www.state.nh.us/agency/drabbs.htm
New Jersey Division of Taxation	www.state.nj.us/treasury/taxation/
New Mexico Taxation and Revenue Department	www.state.nm.us/tax/

State Tax Department Internet Sites *(continued)*

New York State Department of Taxation and Finance	www.tax.state.ny.us/forms/
North Carolina Department of Revenue	www.dor.state.nc.us/DOR/
Ohio Department of Taxation	www.odh.ohio.gov/tax/
Oklahoma Tax Commission	www.state.ok.us/~tax/
Oregon Department of Revenue	www.dor.state.or.us/
Pennsylvania Department of Revenue	www.revenue.state.pa.us/
South Carolina Department of Revenue	www.state.sc.us:80/dor/
South Dakota Department of Revenue	www.state.sd.us/state/executive/revenue/revenue.html
Tennessee Department of Revenue	www.state.tn.us/revenue/
Texas Comptroller of Public Accounts	www.window.texas.gov/
Utah State Tax Commission	txdtm01.tax.ex.state.ut.us/
Virginia Department of Taxation	www.state.va.us/tax/tax.html
Washington Department of Revenue	www.wa.gov/DOR/wador.htm
Wisconsin Department of Revenue	badger.state.wi.us/agencies/dor/
Wyoming Department of Revenue	www.state.wy.us/state/government/state_agencies/text_revenue.html

STATE-BY-STATE SUMMARY OF ELECTRONIC FILING OPPORTUNITIES

State	Tax[1]	Website
Alabama	Personal Income Sales and Use Withholding	www.ador.state.al.us
Alaska	None	www.revenue.state.ak.us
Arizona	Personal Income	www.revenue.state.az.us
Arkansas	Personal Income Sales and Use Motor Fuel Corporate Franchise Tax	www.accessarkansas.org/dfs

(continues)

STATE-BY-STATE SUMMARY OF ELECTRONIC FILING OPPORTUNITIES *(continued)*

State	Tax[1]	Website
California	Personal Income Sales and Use Withholding Motor Fuel	www.ftb.ca.gov
Colorado	Personal Income Sales and Use	www.taxcolorado.com
Connecticut	Personal Income Sales and Use Business Use Withholding	www.drs.state.ct.us
Delaware	Personal Income Gross Receipts Withholding (S Corporation)	www.state.de.us/revenue
District of Columbia	Personal Income Corporate Franchise Sales and Use Withholding Personal Property	www.cfo.dc.gov/etsc/ main.shtm
Florida	Sales and Use Motor Fuel Withholding Intangible Personal Property Communication Services	sun6.dms.state.fl.us/dor
Georgia	Personal Income	www2.state.ga.us/ Departments/DOR
Hawaii	Personal Income Corporate Income Sales and Use Withholding	www.state.hi.us/tax/tax.html
Idaho	Personal Income Sales and Use Withholding Motor Fuel	www2.state.id.us/tax/index.html

STATE-BY-STATE SUMMARY OF ELECTRONIC FILING OPPORTUNITIES *(continued)*

State	Tax[1]	Website
Illinois	Personal Income Sales and Use	www.revenue.state.ll.us
Indiana	Personal Income Corporate Income Sales and Use Withholding (Fuel Tax available soon)	www.state.in.us/dor
Iowa	Personal Income	www.state.la.us/tax
Kansas	Personal Income Sales and Use Withholding Motor Fuel	www.ink.org/public/kdor
Kentucky	Personal Income	www.state.ky.us/agencies/ revenue
Louisiana	Personal Income Sales and Use Withholding	www.rev.state.la.us
Maine	Personal Income Sales and Use Withholding	www.state.me.us/revenue
Maryland	Personal Income Sales and Use (telefile) Withholding (telefile)	www.comp.state.md.us
Massachusetts	Personal Income Corporate Estimated Income Sales and Use (telefile) Withholding (telefile)	www.dor.state.ma.us
Michigan	Personal Income Motor Fuels Tax Single Business	www.treas.state.mi.us

(continues)

STATE-BY-STATE SUMMARY OF ELECTRONIC FILING OPPORTUNITIES *(continued)*

State	Tax[1]	Website
Minnesota	Personal Income Sales and Use Withholding	www.taxes.state.mn.us
Mississippi	Personal Income	www.mstc.state.ms.us
Missouri	Personal Income Sales and Use Withholding	www.dor.state.mo.us
Montana	Personal Income Withholding	discoveringmontana.com/ revenue/css/default.asp
Nebraska	Personal Income Sales and Use Withholding	www.revenue.state.ne.us/ index.html
Nevada	None	www.tax.state.nv.us
New Hampshire	In development	www.state.nh.us/revenue
New Jersey	Personal Income Sales and Use	www.state.nj.us/ treasury/taxation
New Mexico	Personal Income	www.state.nm.us/tax
New York	Personal Income Sales and Use Withholding Motor Fuel Petroleum Business	www.tax.state.ny.us
North Carolina	Personal Income Sales and Use Withholding in 2003	www.dor.state.nc.us
North Dakota	Personal Income Sales and Use Withholding Oil and Gas	www.state.nd.us/taxdpt
Ohio	Personal Income Natural Gas	www.state.oh.us/tax

STATE-BY-STATE SUMMARY OF ELECTRONIC FILING OPPORTUNITIES *(continued)*

State	Tax[1]	Website
Oklahoma	Personal Income Sales and Use Withholding	www.oktax.state.ok.us
Oregon	Personal Income	www.dor.state.or.us
Pennsylvania	Personal Income Corporate Estimated Income Sales and Use Withholding Fuel Tax	www.revenue.state.pa.us
Rhode Island	Personal Income Sales and Use Withholding	www.tax.state.ri.us
South Carolina	Personal Income Corporate Estimated Income Withholding Sales and Use (telefile)	www.sctax.org
South Dakota	Sales and Use Contractor's Excise	www.state.sd.us/revenue/ revenue.html
Tennessee	Sales and Use Hall Income Tax (on dividends and interest)	www.state.tn.us/revenue
Texas	Sales and Use Withholding Motor Fuel Natural Gas International Fuel Tax Agreement	www.window.state.tx.us
Utah	Personal Income Sales and Use Withholding IFTA	www.tax.ex.state.ut.us
Vermont	Personal Income	www.state.vt.us/tax

(continues)

STATE-BY-STATE SUMMARY OF ELECTRONIC FILING OPPORTUNITIES *(continued)*

State	Tax[1]	Website
Virginia	Personal Income Sales and Use Withholding	www.tax.state.va.us
Washington	Sales and Use Business Excise Taxes	www.dor.wa.gov
West Virginia	Personal Income	www.state.wv.us/taxdiv
Wisconsin	Personal Income Sales and Use Motor Fuel (EFT)	www.dor.state.wi.us
Wyoming	Sales and Use Mineral Tax	revenue.state.wy.us

[1] This chart does not include less significant taxes such as lodging or tourism tax. Also, many states, including those that do not offer e-filing, allow payment of business taxes, such as withholding and motor fuels tax, through electronic funds transfer.

Tax-Related Websites

www.aicpa.org—	The AICPA's Website, rated highly by professionals and non-CPAs alike. This site gives AICPA Tax Division members access to the online version of *The Tax Advisor*.
www.taxsites.com— or www.el.com/elinks/taxes	Probably the only other tax Website you'll really need, since either is a "metasite" (a site whose sole purpose is to provide links to other Websites of the same topic).
www.irs.gov—	Homesite of the Internal Revenue Service, helpful for accessing and downloading Federal forms, instructions, and other IRS materials.
www.ssa.gov—	The Social Security Administration's Website, which includes the text of totalization agreements the U.S. has with various foreign countries.
www.mtc.gov—	This site is a must for practitioners who service multistate clients. Here, the Multistate Tax Commission keeps you informed on the state uniformity of nexus issues.
www.ipl.org—	Even the Internet has a public library, and this is it. A great source for links to background information and numerous online publications.

Tax-Related Websites *(continued)*

The Big Six and national firms sites—	Although designed to market the firm's products and services, these sites offer useful information with their respective tax pages and links:

www.arthurandersen.com	www.bdo.com	www.ey.com
www.colybrand.com	www.gt.com	www.pw.com
www.us.deloitte.com	www.kpmg.com	

Other sites—	The larger firms aren't the only ones in the game; some smaller practitioners are offering their own blend of creative and informative tax sites. Some to try: www.taxman.com; www.taxwizard.com

Governmental Sites

Internal Revenue Service: *www.irs.gov*

Joint Committee on Taxation: *www.house.gov/jct*

Department of Treasury: *www.ustreas.gov*

Federal Register reflecting latest information on pending legislation: *www.access.gpo.gov/su_docs/aces/aces140.html*

Supreme Court and appellate court cases: *law.house.gov/6.htm*

IRS Bulletins: *www.fedworld.gov*

Highlights of latest revenue rulings, court opinions, legislation, and other tax topics: *www.ppcinfo.com/5-min.htm*

Tax Code Online: *www.law.cornell.edu/uscode*

Federal Web Locator: *www.law.vill.edu/Fed-Agency/fedwebloc.html*

Library of Congress: *lcweb.loc.gov/homepage/lchp.html*

SEC database of corporate information: *www.sec.gov/edgarhp.html*

General Accounting Office: *www.gao.gov*

U.S. Tax Court: *www.ustaxcourt.gov*

Criminal activity: *www.treas.gov/irs/ci*

IRS appeals: *www.irs.gov/prod/indinfo/appeals*

(continues)

Governmental Sites *(continued)*

IRS telephone directory: The main directory is located at www.irs.gov/prod/bus_info/tax_pro/iod/index.html; the state-by-state directory at www.irs.gov/prod/where_file/index.html; the practitioner hotline directory at www.irs.gov/prod/bus_info/tax_pro/prac-htln.html; and the Centralized Authorization File (CAF) Unit fax directory at www.irs.gov/prod/bus_info/tax_pro/caf.html. The filing locations by processing site are available at www.irs.gov/prod/bus_info/tax_pro/svc-cntr2001.html; and find the service center directory at www.irs.gov/prod/bus_info/tax_pro/svc-cntrstate.html.

SPECIAL REPORT—TAXES AND TERRORISM

Special tax consideration has been voted on for victims of terrorism, even those outside of the immediate disaster areas:

The Victims of Terrorism Relief Act of 2001 provided a 1-year exemption from federal income taxes for individuals who were killed or who died as a result of a terroristic attack.

For specific questions, call the IRS toll-free at 866-562-5527.

For donation questions, go to www.abanet.org/tax or www.guidestar.org.

See also IRS Pub. 3920 and Pub. 3991 for additional details. Both can be downloaded from www.irs.gov.

Mission Statement

"The Internal Revenue Service has adopted a new mission statement:

Provide America's taxpayers top quality service by helping them understand and meet their tax responsibilities and by applying the tax law with integrity and fairness to all.

Taxpayers have the right to be treated fairly, professionally, promptly and courteously by Internal Revenue Service employees. Our goal at the IRS is to protect the rights of taxpayers and ensure the highest confidence in the integrity, efficiency and fairness of our tax system. To make sure that taxpayers always receive such treatment, you should know about the many rights you have at each step of the tax process.

1. Receive an explanation of the examination and collection processes and taxpayers' rights under these processes before or at the initial interview for the determination or collection of tax.

2. Have representation at any time during these processes by a person who may practice before the IRS, except in certain criminal investigations.

3. Make an audio recording or receive a copy of such a recording of an interview for the determination or collection of tax.

4. Reasonably rely on written advice of the IRS that was provided in response to a specific written request.

5. File an application for relief with the IRS National Taxpayer Advocate or Local Taxpayer Advocate in a situation in which the taxpayer is suffering or about to suffer a significant hardship as a result of the manner in which the IRS is administering the tax laws.

6. Receive a written notice of levy, no less than 30 days prior to enforcement, that explains in nontechnical terms the levy procedures and the administrative appeals and alternatives to levy that are available."

April 19, 1999

"Activities engaged in by a citizen to prevent the Government from confiscating the fruits of his labor are the noblest endeavors of man."

BENJAMIN FRANKLIN

Appendix A

Cost Recovery/Depreciation

The Tax Reform Act of 1986 created a new accelerated depreciation system, which grouped property in the following classes:

- 3-year class—asset depreciation range (ADR) midpoints of 4 years and less, except that automobiles and light trucks are excluded and present law for horses that are in the 3-year class is retained. The method is 200 percent declining balance, switching to straight line.

- 5-year class—ADR midpoints of more than 4 years and less than 10 years, adding automobiles, light trucks, qualified technological equipment, computer-based central office switching equipment, renewable energy and biomass properties that are small power production facilities, and research and experimentation property. The method is 200 percent declining balance.

- 7-year class—ADR midpoints of 10 years and more but less than 16 years, adding single-purpose agricultural and horticulture structures and property with an ADR midpoint that is not classified elsewhere. The method is 200 percent declining balance.

- 10-year class—ADR midpoints of 16 years and more but less than 20 years. The method is 200 percent declining balance.

- 15-year class—ADR midpoints of 20 years and more but less than 25 years, including sewerage treatment plants and telephone distribution plants and related equipment used for the two-way exchange of voice and data communications. The method is 150 percent declining balance.

- 20-year class—ADR midpoints of 25 years and more, other than real property with an ADR midpoint of 27.5 years and more, and including sewer pipes. The method is 150 percent declining balance.

- 27.5 years—residential real property. The method is straight line.

- 31.5 years—nonresidential real property (real property that is not residential rental property and does not have an ADR midpoint of less than 27.5 years). The method is straight line.

To find appropriate ADR class lives, see Rev. Proc. 87-56, 1987-2 C.B. 674.

For personal property, both the first and last depreciation allowances for an asset reflect the one-half-year convention. The prior law mid-month convention applies to real property, and a midquarter convention applies to taxpayers who place more than 40 percent of their property in service during the last quarter of the taxable year.

Generally, the effective date for all depreciation provisions is for property placed in service on or after January 1, 1987. However, the Act allowed taxpayers to start using the new system for property placed in service after July 31, 1986

Note that OBRA '93 changed nonresidential real estate from a 31.5-year basis to a 39-year basis for property placed in service on or after May 13, 1993 unless there was a binding contract or construction began prior to May 13, 1993.

The following tables list percentages for property in the 3-, 5-, 7-, 10-, 15-, and 20-year classes.

TABLE 1. General Depreciation System
Applicable Depreciation Method: 200 or 150 Percent
Declining Balance Switching to Straight Line
Applicable Recovery Periods: 3, 5, 7, 10, 15, 20 Years
Applicable Convention: Half-Year

If the Recovery Year Is:	and the Recovery Period Is:					
	3-Year	5-Year	7-Year	10-Year	15-Year	20-Year
	the Depreciation Rate Is:					
1	33.33	20.00	14.29	10.00	5.00	3.750
2	44.45	32.00	24.49	18.00	9.50	7.219
3	14.81	19.20	17.49	14.40	8.55	6.677
4	7.41	11.52	12.49	11.52	7.70	6.177
5		11.52	8.93	9.22	6.93	5.713
6		5.76	8.92	7.37	6.23	5.285
7			8.93	6.55	5.90	4.888
8			4.46	6.55	5.90	4.522
9				6.56	5.91	4.462
10				6.55	5.90	4.461
11				3.28	5.91	4.462
12					5.90	4.461
13					5.91	4.462
14					5.90	4.461
15					5.91	4.462
16					2.95	4.461
17						4.462
18						4.461
19						4.462
20						4.461
21						2.231

TABLE 2. General Depreciation System
Applicable Depreciation Method: 200 or 150 Percent
Declining Balance Switching to Straight Line
Applicable Recovery Periods: 3, 5, 7, 10, 15, 20 Years
Applicable Convention: Mid-Quarter
(Property Placed in Service in First Quarter)

If the Recovery Year Is:	and the Recovery Period Is:					
	3-Year	5-Year	7-Year	10-Year	15-Year	20-Year
	the Depreciation Rate Is:					
1	58.33	35.00	25.00	17.50	8.75	6.563
2	27.78	26.00	21.43	16.50	9.13	7.000
3	12.35	15.60	15.31	13.20	8.21	6.482
4	1.54	11.01	10.93	10.56	7.39	5.996
5		11.01	8.75	8.45	6.65	5.546
6		1.38	8.74	6.76	5.99	5.130
7			8.75	6.55	5.90	4.746
8			1.09	6.55	5.91	4.459
9				6.56	5.90	4.459
10				6.55	5.91	4.459
11				0.82	5.90	4.459
12					5.91	4.460
13					5.90	4.459
14					5.91	4.460
15					5.90	4.459
16					0.74	4.460
17						4.459
18						4.460
19						4.459
20						4.460
21						0.557

TABLE 3. General Depreciation System
Applicable Depreciation Method: 200 or 150 Percent
Declining Balance Switching to Straight Line
Applicable Recovery Periods: 3, 5, 7, 10, 15, 20 Years
Applicable Convention: Mid-Quarter
(Property Placed in Service in Second Quarter)

If the Recovery Year Is:	and the Recovery Period Is:					
	3-Year	5-Year	7-Year	10-Year	15-Year	20-Year
	the Depreciation Rate Is:					
1	41.67	25.00	17.85	12.50	6.25	4.688
2	38.89	30.00	23.47	17.50	9.38	7.148
3	14.14	18.00	16.76	14.00	8.44	6.612
4	5.30	11.37	11.97	11.20	7.59	6.116
5		11.37	8.87	8.96	6.83	5.658
6		4.26	8.87	7.17	6.15	5.233
7			8.87	6.55	5.91	4.841
8			3.33	6.55	5.90	4.478
9				6.56	5.91	4.463
10				6.55	5.90	4.463
11				2.46	5.91	4.463
12					5.90	4.463
13					5.91	4.463
14					5.90	4.463
15					5.91	4.462
16					2.21	4.463
17						4.462
18						4.463
19						4.462
20						4.463
21						1.673

TABLE 4. General Depreciation System
Applicable Depreciation Method: 200 or 150 Percent
Declining Balance Switching to Straight Line
Applicable Recovery Periods: 3, 5, 7, 10, 15, 20 Years
Applicable Convention: Mid-Quarter
(Property Placed in Service in Third Quarter)

If the Recovery Year Is:	and the Recovery Period Is:					
	3-Year	5-Year	7-Year	10-Year	15-Year	20-Year
	the Depreciation Rate Is:					
1	25.00	15.00	10.71	7.50	3.75	2.813
2	50.00	34.00	25.51	18.50	9.63	7.289
3	16.67	20.40	18.22	14.80	8.66	6.742
4	8.33	12.24	13.02	11.84	7.80	6.237
5		11.30	9.30	9.47	7.02	5.769
6		7.06	8.85	7.58	6.31	5.336
7			8.86	6.55	5.90	4.936
8			5.53	6.55	5.90	4.566
9				6.56	5.91	4.460
10				6.55	5.90	4.460
11				4.10	5.91	4.460
12					5.90	4.460
13					5.91	4.461
14					5.90	4.460
15					5.91	4.461
16					3.69	4.460
17						4.461
18						4.460
19						4.461
20						4.460
21						2.788

TABLE 5. General Depreciation System
Applicable Depreciation Method: 200 or 150 Percent
Declining Balance Switching to Straight Line
Applicable Recovery Periods: 3, 5, 7, 10, 15, 20 Years
Applicable Convention: Mid-Quarter
(Property Placed in Service in Fourth Quarter)

If the Recovery Year Is:	and the Recovery Period Is:					
	3-Year	5-Year	7-Year	10-Year	15-Year	20-Year
	the Depreciation Rate Is:					
1	8.33	5.00	3.57	2.50	1.25	0.938
2	61.11	38.00	27.55	19.50	9.88	7.430
3	20.37	22.80	19.68	15.60	8.89	6.872
4	10.19	13.68	14.06	12.48	8.00	6.357
5		10.94	10.04	9.98	7.20	5.880
6		9.58	8.73	7.99	6.48	5.439
7			8.73	6.55	5.90	5.031
8			7.64	6.55	5.90	4.654
9				6.56	5.90	4.458
10				6.55	5.91	4.458
11				5.74	5.90	4.458
12					5.91	4.458
13					5.90	4.458
14					5.91	4.458
15					5.90	4.458
16					5.17	4.458
17						4.458
18						4.459
19						4.458
20						4.459
21						3.901

The following tables show recovery percentages for residential and non-residential real property.

TABLE 6. General Depreciation System
Applicable Depreciation Method: Straight Line
Applicable Recovery Period: 27.5 Years
Applicable Convention: Mid-Month

Recovery Year Is:	and the Month in the First Recovery Year the Property Is Placed in Service Is:											
	1	2	3	4	5	6	7	8	9	10	11	12
	the Depreciation Rate Is:											
1	3.485	3.182	2.879	2.576	2.273	1.970	1.667	1.364	1.061	0.758	0.455	0.152
2	3.636	3.636	3.636	3.636	3.636	3.636	3.636	3.636	3.636	3.636	3.636	3.636
3	3.636	3.636	3.636	3.636	3.636	3.636	3.636	3.636	3.636	3.636	3.636	3.636
4	3.636	3.636	3.636	3.636	3.636	3.636	3.636	3.636	3.636	3.636	3.636	3.636
5	3.636	3.636	3.636	3.636	3.636	3.636	3.636	3.636	3.636	3.636	3.636	3.636
6	3.636	3.636	3.636	3.636	3.636	3.636	3.636	3.636	3.636	3.636	3.636	3.636
7	3.636	3.636	3.636	3.636	3.636	3.636	3.636	3.636	3.636	3.636	3.636	3.636
8	3.636	3.636	3.636	3.636	3.636	3.636	3.636	3.636	3.636	3.636	3.636	3.636
9	3.636	3.636	3.636	3.636	3.636	3.637	3.636	3.636	3.636	3.636	3.636	3.636
10	3.637	3.636	3.637	3.637	3.636	3.636	3.637	3.637	3.636	3.637	3.636	3.636
11	3.636	3.637	3.636	3.636	3.637	3.636	3.636	3.637	3.637	3.636	3.637	3.637
12	3.637	3.637	3.637	3.637	3.636	3.637	3.636	3.636	3.636	3.636	3.636	3.636
13	3.636	3.636	3.636	3.636	3.636	3.636	3.637	3.637	3.637	3.637	3.637	3.637

14	3.637	3.637	3.637	3.637	3.637	3.637	3.636	3.636	3.636	3.636	3.636	3.636
15	3.636	3.636	3.636	3.636	3.636	3.636	3.637	3.637	3.637	3.637	3.637	3.637
16	3.637	3.637	3.637	3.637	3.637	3.637	3.636	3.636	3.636	3.636	3.636	3.636
17	3.636	3.636	3.636	3.636	3.636	3.636	3.637	3.637	3.637	3.637	3.637	3.637
18	3.637	3.637	3.637	3.637	3.637	3.637	3.636	3.636	3.636	3.636	3.636	3.636
19	3.636	3.636	3.636	3.636	3.636	3.636	3.637	3.637	3.637	3.637	3.637	3.637
20	3.637	3.637	3.637	3.637	3.637	3.637	3.636	3.636	3.636	3.636	3.636	3.636
21	3.636	3.636	3.636	3.636	3.636	3.636	3.637	3.637	3.637	3.637	3.637	3.637
22	3.637	3.637	3.637	3.637	3.637	3.637	3.636	3.636	3.636	3.636	3.636	3.636
23	3.636	3.636	3.636	3.636	3.636	3.636	3.637	3.637	3.637	3.637	3.637	3.637
24	3.637	3.637	3.637	3.637	3.637	3.637	3.636	3.636	3.636	3.636	3.636	3.636
25	3.636	3.636	3.636	3.636	3.636	3.636	3.637	3.637	3.637	3.637	3.637	3.637
26	3.637	3.637	3.637	3.637	3.637	3.637	3.636	3.636	3.636	3.636	3.636	3.636
27	3.636	3.636	3.636	3.636	3.636	3.636	3.637	3.637	3.637	3.637	3.637	3.637
28	1.970	2.273	2.576	2.879	3.182	3.485	3.636	3.636	3.636	3.636	3.636	3.636
29	0.000	0.000	0.000	0.000	0.000	0.000	0.152	0.455	0.758	1.061	1.364	1.667

TABLE 7. General Depreciation System
Applicable Depreciation Method: Straight Line
Applicable Recovery Period: 31.5 Years
Applicable Convention: Mid-Month

Recovery Year Is:	and the Month in the First Recovery Year the Property Is Placed in Service Is: the Depreciation Rate Is:											
	1	2	3	4	5	6	7	8	9	10	11	12
1	3.042	2.778	2.513	2.249	1.984	1.720	1.455	1.190	0.926	0.661	0.397	0.132
2	3.175	3.175	3.175	3.175	3.175	3.175	3.175	3.175	3.175	3.175	3.175	3.175
3	3.175	3.175	3.175	3.175	3.175	3.175	3.175	3.175	3.175	3.175	3.175	3.175
4	3.175	3.175	3.175	3.175	3.175	3.175	3.175	3.175	3.175	3.175	3.175	3.175
5	3.175	3.175	3.175	3.175	3.175	3.175	3.175	3.175	3.175	3.175	3.175	3.175
6	3.175	3.175	3.175	3.175	3.175	3.175	3.175	3.175	3.175	3.175	3.175	3.175
7	3.175	3.174	3.175	3.175	3.175	3.175	3.175	3.175	3.175	3.175	3.175	3.175
8	3.175	3.175	3.175	3.174	3.175	3.174	3.175	3.175	3.175	3.175	3.175	3.175
9	3.174	3.175	3.174	3.175	3.174	3.175	3.174	3.175	3.175	3.175	3.175	3.175
10	3.175	3.174	3.175	3.174	3.175	3.174	3.175	3.174	3.175	3.175	3.174	3.175
11	3.174	3.175	3.174	3.175	3.174	3.175	3.174	3.175	3.174	3.174	3.175	3.174
12	3.175	3.174	3.175	3.174	3.175	3.174	3.175	3.174	3.175	3.175	3.174	3.175
13	3.174	3.175	3.174	3.175	3.174	3.175	3.174	3.175	3.174	3.174	3.175	3.174

14	3.175	3.174	3.175	3.174	3.175	3.174	3.175	3.174	3.175	3.174	3.175	3.174
15	3.174	3.175	3.174	3.175	3.174	3.175	3.174	3.175	3.174	3.175	3.174	3.175
16	3.175	3.174	3.175	3.174	3.175	3.174	3.175	3.174	3.175	3.174	3.175	3.174
17	3.174	3.175	3.174	3.175	3.174	3.175	3.174	3.175	3.174	3.175	3.174	3.175
18	3.175	3.174	3.175	3.174	3.175	3.174	3.175	3.174	3.175	3.174	3.175	3.174
19	3.174	3.175	3.174	3.175	3.174	3.175	3.174	3.175	3.174	3.175	3.174	3.175
20	3.175	3.174	3.175	3.174	3.175	3.174	3.175	3.174	3.175	3.174	3.175	3.174
21	3.174	3.175	3.174	3.175	3.174	3.175	3.174	3.175	3.174	3.175	3.174	3.175
22	3.175	3.174	3.175	3.174	3.175	3.174	3.175	3.174	3.175	3.174	3.175	3.174
23	3.174	3.175	3.174	3.175	3.174	3.175	3.174	3.175	3.174	3.175	3.174	3.175
24	3.175	3.174	3.175	3.174	3.175	3.174	3.175	3.174	3.175	3.174	3.175	3.174
25	3.174	3.175	3.174	3.175	3.174	3.175	3.174	3.175	3.174	3.175	3.174	3.175
26	3.175	3.174	3.175	3.174	3.175	3.174	3.175	3.174	3.175	3.174	3.175	3.174
27	3.174	3.175	3.174	3.175	3.174	3.175	3.174	3.175	3.174	3.175	3.174	3.175
28	3.175	3.174	3.175	3.174	3.175	3.174	3.175	3.174	3.175	3.174	3.175	3.174
29	3.174	3.175	3.174	3.175	3.174	3.175	3.174	3.175	3.174	3.175	3.174	3.175
30	3.175	3.174	3.175	3.174	3.175	3.174	3.175	3.174	3.175	3.174	3.175	3.174
31	3.174	3.175	3.174	3.175	3.174	3.175	3.174	3.175	3.174	3.175	3.174	3.175
32	1.720	1.984	2.249	2.513	2.778	3.042	3.175	3.174	3.175	3.174	3.175	3.174
33	0.000	0.000	0.000	0.000	0.000	0.000	0.132	0.397	0.661	0.926	1.190	1.455

Table 8 lists depreciation rates for nonresidential real property placed in service after 5/13/93, unless there was a binding contract prior to that date.

TABLE 8. Depreciation Rates for Nonresidential Real Property Placed in Service After May 13, 1993, Unless There Was a Binding Contract Prior to May 13, 1993

Mid-Month Convention

Straight Line—39 Years

Year	Month Property Placed in Service											
	1	2	3	4	5	6	7	8	9	10	11	12
1	2.461%	2.247%	2.033%	1.819%	1.605%	1.391%	1.177%	0.963%	0.749%	0.535%	0.321%	0.107%
2–39	2.564	2.564	2.564	2.564	2.564	2.564	2.564	2.564	2.564	2.564	2.564	2.564
40	0.107	0.321	0.535	0.749	0.963	1.177	1.391	1.605	1.819	2.033	2.247	2.461

Appendix B

Business Use of "Listed Property"

Prior to 1984, computers, automobiles, and other types of personal property were eligible for annual depreciation deductions with accelerated rates and recovery periods. Where such property was partly used for business purposes and partly used for personal purposes, the allowable amount of the otherwise available depreciation deduction was determined on the basis of the proportion of business use.

In 1984, Congress drew a sharp distinction between property used more than 50 percent for business purposes as compared to property having business use of 50 percent or less. Furthermore, for automobiles, additional restrictions have been imposed upon the maximum amount of yearly depreciation deductions.

The property covered by the stricter rules is referred to as "listed property" and includes the following:

a) passenger automobiles weighing 6,000 pounds or less,

b) other transportation property,

c) property used for entertainment, recreation, or amusement,

d) computers and peripheral equipment, *and*

e) "other" property to be specified by regulations.

For *all* categories of the above listed property used 50 percent or less for business purposes, depreciation is to be determined on the straight-line method over a period of years that is longer than the minimum period otherwise provided.

In addition, satisfaction of the 50 percent test will be determined solely with reference to the use of the property in a *trade or business*. Use of the property in connection with the production of investment income is not taken into account for this purpose. Once it is determined, however, on the basis of business use, whether the property is to be treated under the more than 50 percent or the 50 percent or less rule, the use of the property in investment activities will be taken into account in determining the proportion of the tax benefits that are allowable.

For example, assume a computer is used 40 percent in the conduct of a trade or business and 30 percent for investment activities. The more than

50 percent business use test is *not* satisfied. Depreciation will be determined on the straight-line method. However, *70* percent of that depreciation so determined will be allowable.

Except for *automobiles*, the depreciation deductions for listed property used *more* than 50 percent in a trade or business will be determined under prior law. The accelerated rates and periods under 1987 modified ACRS may be used to determine depreciation and then the percentage of business use will be combined with the percentage of use in investment activities to determine the portion of the total amount of depreciation that will be allowable.

For automobiles, however, including those with more than 50 percent business use, there are additional restrictions and limitations. Depreciation deductions are limited for each year. These fixed limitations apply to all depreciation deductions, not just depreciation under the accelerated method.

If business use is less than 100 percent, you are entitled to claim the portion of the depreciation deduction allowable which corresponds to your business use percentage.

Moreover, leasing an automobile will not avoid the limitations. Lessees of property will be subject to restrictions on lease payments. These restrictions are comparable to the limitations on depreciation that would apply if the automobile were owned instead of leased. The percentage of lease payments allowable will be calculated pursuant to tables published by the Treasury. These restrictions, however, do not apply to the tax benefits available under prior law to the lessors of property regularly engaged in the business of leasing property.

Employees

If you are an employee, the rules are even more stringent. *No* depreciation will be allowable for listed property owned by employees unless the property is:

a) required for the convenience of the employer, *and*

b) required as a condition of employment.

These requirements will *not* be satisfied merely by an employer's statement that the property is required as a condition of employment. It is intended that the property must be required in order for an employee to properly perform the duties of his/her employment.

Furthermore, if in years subsequent to the year of purchase, there is a reduction of the percentage of business use, that reduction could have triggered an investment credit recapture. If the business use declines to 50 percent or less of the use of the property in the subsequent year, the *entire* amount of the investment credit was recaptured. However, the Treasury can provide a rule that a *de minimus* reduction in the business use of the property will not trigger any recapture.

In addition to the existing rules governing the recapture of depreciation, the law requires recapture in the event property used more than 50 percent for business in the year it is placed in service declines to 50 percent or less of business use in a subsequent year. The amount of the recapture will be based upon the difference between the depreciation allowed in prior years and the amount that would have been allowed if the applicable accelerated rate and period of ACRS had not been available in such years. The Treasury has been instructed to provide for comparable recapture requirements applicable to lessees whose business use declines in subsequent years.

In IRS Letter Ruling 8615024, the IRS ruled that an employee's use of a personal computer did *not* meet the convenience of the employer and condition of employment tests. In denying any deduction or credit, the Internal Revenue Service said that to meet the convenience of the employer test, the employee must be *required* to purchase the computer to properly perform the duties of her employment. In that case, the taxpayer was not "required" to purchase the computer to properly perform her duties. Although the benefits of the taxpayer's use of the computer may inure to her employer, the purchase of a computer was clearly not required as a condition of employment. The facts of the case suggested that computer use, although work-related, was not inextricably related to proper performance of the taxpayer's job. Moreover, there appeared no evidence in the facts that those employees who did not purchase a computer were professionally disadvantaged. See *Mulne v. Commissioner*, T.C. Memo 1996-320 for an example of how to meet both tests.

In IRS Letter Ruling 871009, this position was reiterated. Here the Internal Revenue Service held that an insurance agent's use of a portable computer as an aid in selling financial products did not meet the convenience of the employer test. They concluded that the taxpayer, who used the computer exclusively for business purposes, must be required to purchase the computer to properly perform the duties of his employment in order to take the deduction. The computer purchase was optional rather than mandatory. "The facts indicate that computer use, although work-related, is not inextricably related to the proper performance of 'the taxpayer's' job. Further, there appears no evidence that those employees who do not purchase computers are professionally disadvantaged." (See also Rev. Rul. 86-129, 1986-45 IRB 4 and Letter Rul. 8725067.)

As of January 1, 2010, the Small Business Jobs Act of 2010 removed cell phones as "listed property."

Luxury Cars

The Tax Reform Act of 1986 defined a *passenger automobile* as any four-wheeled vehicle that is manufactured primarily for use on public streets, roads, and highways and is rated at 6,000 pounds *unloaded* gross vehicle weight or less. For *trucks* or *vans*, the rule becomes *loaded* gross vehicle weight—its maximum recommended weight for the vehicle, fuel, passengers, and all cargo. Sport Utility Vehicles (SUVs) are classified under trucks. The Act requires that fixed limitations on automobile deductions be conformed to the new recovery period, so that the price range of affected cars is unaffected. Depreciation deductions are limited for each year. These fixed limitations apply to all depreciation deductions, not just depreciation under the accelerated method.

Limitations on Luxury Auto Depreciation Deductions

Date of Purchase	Yearly Maximum 1	2	3	4 and After
6/19/84 to 4/2/85[a]	$4,000 (25%)	$6,000[b] (38%)	$6,000[b] (37%)	$6,000[b]
4/3/85 to 12/31/86[a]	3,200 (25%)	4,800 (38%)	4,800 (37%)	4,800
1987 to 12/31/88[c]	2,560 (20%)	4,100 (32%)	2,450 (19.2%)	1,475 (11.52%)
1989 to 12/31/90[c]	2,660 (20%)	4,200 (32%)	2,550 (19.2%)	1,475 (11.52%)
1991[c]	2,660 (20%)	4,300 (32%)	2,550 (19.2%)	1,575 (11.52%)
1992[c]	2,760 (20%)	4,400 (32%)	2,650 (19.2%)	1,575 (11.52%)
1993	2,860 (20%)	4,600 (32%)	2,750 (19.2%)	1,675 (11.52%)
1994	2,960 (20%)	4,700 (32%)	2,850 (19.2%)	1,675 (11.52%)
1995	3,060 (20%)	4,900 (32%)	2,950 (19.2%)	1,775 (11.52%)
1996	3,060 (20%)	4,900 (33%)	2,950 (19.2%)	1,775 (11.52%)
1997	3,160 (20%)	5,000 (33%)	3,050 (19.2%)	1,775 (11.52%)
1998	3,160 (20%)	5,000 (33%)	2,950 (19.2%)	1,775 (11.52%)
1999	3,060 (20%)	5,000 (33%)	2,950 (19.2%)	1,775 (11.52%)
2000	3,060 (20%)	4,900 (33%)	2,950 (19.2%)	1,775 (11.52%)
2001	3,060 (20%)[d]	4,900 (33%)	2,950 (19.2%)	1,775 (11.52%)
2002	3,060 (20%)[d]	4,900 (33%)	2,950 (19.2%)	1,775 (11.52%)
2003	10,710 (20%)[e]	4,900 (33%)	2,950 (19.2%)	1,775 (11.52%)

[a]Year of disposition: zero.

[b]The limit is $6,200 if placed in service after 12/31/84 and before 4/3/85.

[c]Year of disposition: half-year.

[d]The first-year writeoff limit is increased by $4,600 for a total of $7,660 for cars placed in service after September 10, 2001 and before September 11, 2004.

[e]Including first-year bonus depreciation of $7,650—i.e., $3,060 + $7,650 = $10,710—as per the 2003 Tax Act.

THE 2004 LIMITS

Depreciation Limitations for Passenger Automobiles (That Are Not Bonus Depreciation Passenger Automobiles, Trucks, Vans, or Electric Automobiles) Placed in Service by the Taxpayer During Calendar Year 2004

Tax Year	Amount
1st tax year	$2,960
2nd tax year	$4,800
3rd tax year	$2,850
Each succeeding year	$1,675

Depreciation Limitations for Trucks and Vans That Are Bonus Depreciation Passenger Automobiles Placed in Service by the Taxpayer During Calendar Year 2004

Tax Year	Amount
1st tax year	$10,910
2nd tax year	$5,300
3rd tax year	$3,150
Each succeeding year	$1,875

Depreciation Limitations for Bonus Depreciation Passenger Automobiles (That Are Not Trucks, Vans, or Electric Automobiles) Placed in Service by the Taxpayer During Calendar Year 2004

Tax Year	Amount
1st tax year	$10,610
2nd tax year	$4,800
3rd tax year	$2,850
Each succeeding year	$1,675

Depreciation Limitations for Electric Automobiles (That Are Not Bonus Depreciation Passenger Automobiles) Placed in Service by the Taxpayer During Calendar Year 2004

Tax Year	Amount
1st tax year	$8,880
2nd tax year	$14,300
3rd tax year	$8,550
Each succeeding year	$5,125

Depreciation Limitations for Trucks and Vans (That Are Not Bonus Depreciation Passenger Automobiles) Placed in Service by the Taxpayer During Calendar Year 2004

Tax Year	Amount
1st tax year	$3,260
2nd tax year	$5,300
3rd tax year	$3,150
Each succeeding year	$1,875

Depreciation Limitations for Electric Automobiles That Are Bonus Depreciation Passenger Automobiles Placed in Service by the Taxpayer During Calendar Year 2004

Tax Year	Amount
1st tax year	$31,830
2nd tax year	$14,300
3rd tax year	$8,550
Each succeeding year	$5,125

THE 2005 LIMITS:

Depreciation Limitations for Passenger Automobiles Placed in Service by the Taxpayer During Calendar Year 2005

Tax Year	Amount
1st tax year	$2,960
2nd tax year	$4,700
3rd tax year	$2,850
Each succeeding year	$1,675

THE 2006 LIMITS:

Depreciation Limitations for Passenger Automobiles Placed in Service by the Taxpayer During Calendar Year 2006

Tax Year	Amount
1st tax year	$2,960
2nd tax year	$4,800
3rd tax year	$2,850
Each succeeding year	$1,775

Depreciation Limitations for Trucks and Vans Placed in Service by the Taxpayer During Calendar Year 2005

Tax Year	Amount
1st tax year	$3,260
2nd tax year	$5,200
3rd tax year	$3,150
Each succeeding year	$1,875

Depreciation Limitations for Trucks and Vans Placed in Service by the Taxpayer During Calendar Year 2006

Tax Year	Amount
1st tax year	$3,260
2nd tax year	$5,200
3rd tax year	$3,150
Each succeeding year	$1,875

Depreciation Limitations for Electric Automobiles Placed in Service by the Taxpayer During Calendar Year 2005

Tax Year	Amount
1st tax year	$8,880
2nd tax year	$14,200
3rd tax year	$8,450
Each succeeding year	$5,125

Depreciation Limitations for Electric Automobiles Placed in Service by the Taxpayer During Calendar Year 2006

Tax Year	Amount
1st tax year	$8,980
2nd tax year	$14,400
3rd tax year	$8,650
Each succeeding year	$5,225

THE 2007 LIMITS:

Depreciation Limitations for Passenger Automobiles Placed in Service by the Taxpayer During Calendar Year 2007

Tax Year	Amount
1st tax year	$3,060
2nd tax year	$4,900
3rd tax year	$2,850
Each succeeding year	$1,775

Depreciation Limitations for Trucks and Vans Placed in Service by the Taxpayer During Calendar Year 2007

Tax Year	Amount
1st tax year	$3,260
2nd tax year	$5,200
3rd tax year	$3,050
Each succeeding year	$1,875

Note: Expanded Limits for electric cars expired on December 31, 2006.

Depreciation Limitations for Passenger Automobiles (that are not trucks or vans) Placed in Service by the Taxpayer in Calendar Year 2007, for which the 50 percent additional first-year depreciation deduction does not apply

Tax Year	Amount
1st tax year	$2,960
2nd tax year	$4,800
3rd tax year	$2,850
Each succeeding year	$1,775

THE 2008 LIMITS:

Depreciation Limitations for Passenger Automobiles (that are not trucks or vans) Placed in Service by the Taxpayer in Calendar Year 2008, for which the 50 percent additional first-year depreciation deduction applies

Tax Year	Amount
1st tax year	$10,960
2nd tax year	$4,800
3rd tax year	$2,850
Each succeeding year	$1,775

Depreciation Limitations for Trucks and Vans Placed in Service by the Taxpayer in Calendar Year 2008, for which the 50 percent additional first-year depreciation deduction does not apply

Tax Year	Amount
1st tax year	$3,160
2nd tax year	$5,100
3rd tax year	$3,050
Each succeeding year	$1,875

Depreciation Limitations for Trucks and Vans Placed in Service by the Taxpayer in Calendar Year 2008, for which the 50 percent additional first-year depreciation deduction applies

Tax Year	Amount
1st tax year	$11,160
2nd tax year	$5,100
3rd tax year	$3,050
Each succeeding year	$1,875

THE 2009 LIMITS:

Depreciation Limitations for Passenger Automobiles (that are not trucks or vans) Placed in Service by the Taxpayer in Calendar Year 2009, for which the 50 percent additional first-year depreciation deduction does not apply

Tax Year	Amount
1st tax year	$2,960
2nd tax year	$4,800
3rd tax year	$2,850
Each succeeding year	$1,775

Depreciation Limitations for Trucks and Vans Placed in Service by the Taxpayer in Calendar Year 2009, for which the 50 percent additional first-year depreciation deduction does not apply

Tax Year	Amount
1st tax year	$3,060
2nd tax year	$4,900
3rd tax year	$2,950
Each succeeding year	$1,775

Depreciation Limitations for Passenger Automobiles (that are not trucks or vans) Placed in Service by the Taxpayer in Calendar Year 2009, for which the 50 percent additional first-year depreciation deduction applies

Tax Year	Amount
1st tax year	$10,960
2nd tax year	$4,800
3rd tax year	$2,850
Each succeeding year	$1,775

Depreciation Limitations for Trucks and Vans Placed in Service by the Taxpayer in Calendar Year 2009, for which the 50 percent additional first-year depreciation deduction applies

Tax Year	Amount
1st tax year	$11,060
2nd tax year	$4,900
3rd tax year	$2,950
Each succeeding year	$1,775

THE 2010 LIMITS:

Rev. Proc. 2010-18 Table 1

Depreciation Limitations for Passenger Automobiles (That Are Not Trucks or Vans) Placed in Service in Calendar Year 2010

Tax Year	Amount
1st tax year	$ 3,060
2nd tax year	$ 4,900
3rd tax year	$ 2,950
Each succeeding year	$ 1,775

Rev. Proc. 2010-18 Table 2

Depreciation Limitations for Trucks and Vans Placed in Service in Calendar Year 2010

Tax Year	Amount
1st tax year	$ 3,160
2nd tax year	$ 5,100
3rd tax year	$ 3,050
Each succeeding year	$ 1,875

THE 2011 LIMITS:

Rev. Proc. 2011-21 Table 1

Depreciation Limitations for Passenger Automobiles (that are not trucks or vans) Placed in Service in Calendar Year 2011, for which the §168(k) additional first-year depreciation deduction applies

Tax Year	Amount
1st tax year	$11,060
2nd tax year	$4,900
3rd tax year	$2,950
Each succeeding year	$1,775

Rev. Proc. 2011-21 Table 2

Depreciation Limitations for Trucks and Vans Placed in Service in Calendar Year 2011, for which the §168(k) additional first-year depreciation deduction applies

Tax Year	Amount
1st tax year	$11,260
2nd tax year	$5,200
3rd tax year	$3,150
Each succeeding year	$1,875

Rev. Proc. 2011-21 Table 3

Depreciation Limitations for Passenger Automobiles (that are not trucks or vans) Placed in Service in Calendar Year 2011, for which the §168(k) additional first-year depreciation deduction does not apply

Tax Year	Amount
1st tax year	$3,060
2nd tax year	$4,900
3rd tax year	$2,950
Each succeeding year	$1,775

Rev. Proc. 2011-21 Table 4

Depreciation Limitations for Trucks and Vans Placed in Service in Calendar Year 2011, for which the §168(k) additional first-year depreciation deduction does not apply

Tax Year	Amount
1st tax year	$3,260
2nd tax year	$5,200
3rd tax year	$3,150
Each succeeding year	$1,875

Rev. Proc. 2011-21 Table 7

Depreciation Limitations for Passenger Automobiles (that are not trucks or vans) Placed in Service in Calendar Year 2010, for which the §168(k) additional first-year depreciation deduction applies

Tax Year	Amount
1st tax year	$11,060
2nd tax year	$4,900
3rd tax year	$2,950
Each succeeding year	$1,775

Rev. Proc. 2011-21 Table 8

Depreciation Limitations for Trucks and Vans Placed in Calendar Year 2011 for which the §168(k) additional first-year depreciation deduction applies

Tax Year	Amount
1st tax year	$11,160
2nd tax year	$5,100
3rd tax year	$3,050
Each succeeding year	$1,875

THE 2012 LIMITS:

Rev. Proc. 2012-23 Table 1

Depreciation Limitations for Passenger Automobiles (that are not trucks or vans) Placed in Service in Calendar Year 2012, for which the §168(k) additional first-year depreciation deduction applies

Tax Year	Amount
1st tax year	$11,160
2nd tax year	$5,100
3rd tax year	$3,050
Each succeeding year	$1,875

Rev. Proc. 2012-23 Table 2

Depreciation Limitations for Trucks and Vans Placed in Service in Calendar Year 2012, for which the §168(k) additional first-year depreciation deduction applies

Tax Year	Amount
1st tax year	$11,360
2nd tax year	$5,300
3rd tax year	$3,150
Each succeeding year	$1,875

Rev. Proc. 2012-23 Table 3

Depreciation Limitations for Passenger Automobiles (that are not trucks or vans) Placed in Service in Calendar Year 2012, for which the §168(k) additional first-year depreciation deduction does not apply

Tax Year	Amount
1st tax year	$3,160
2nd tax year	$5,100
3rd tax year	$3,050
Each succeeding year	$1,875

Rev. Proc. 2012-23 Table 4

Depreciation Limitations for Trucks and Vans Placed in Service in Calendar Year 2012 for which the §168(k) additional first-year depreciation deduction does not apply

Tax Year	Amount
1st tax year	$3,360
2nd tax year	$5,300
3rd tax year	$3,150
Each succeeding year	$1,875

THE 2013 LIMITS:

Rev. Proc. 2013-21 Table 1

Depreciation Limitations for Passenger Automobiles (that are not trucks or vans) Placed in Service in Calendar Year 2013, for which the §168(k) additional first-year depreciation deduction applies

Tax Year	Amount
1st tax year	$11,160
2nd tax year	$5,100
3rd tax year	$3,050
Each succeeding year	$1,875

Rev. Proc. 2013-21 Table 2

Depreciation Limitations for Trucks and Vans Placed in Service in Calendar Year 2013, for which the §168(k) additional first-year depreciation deduction applies

Tax Year	Amount
1st tax year	$11,360
2nd tax year	$5,400
3rd tax year	$3,250
Each succeeding year	$1,975

Rev. Proc. 2013-21 Table 3	
Depreciation Limitations for Passenger Automobiles (that are not trucks or vans) Placed in Service in Calendar Year 2013, for which the §168(k) additional first-year depreciation deduction does not apply	
Tax Year	**Amount**
1st tax year	$3,160
2nd tax year	$5,100
3rd tax year	$3,050
Each succeeding year	$1,875

Rev. Proc. 2013-21 Table 4	
Depreciation Limitations for Trucks and Vans Placed in Service in Calendar Year 2013, for which the §168(k) additional first-year depreciation deduction does not apply	
Tax Year	**Amount**
1st tax year	$3,360
2nd tax year	$5,400
3rd tax year	$3,250
Each succeeding year	$1,975

A van or light truck is not subject to the annual limit on the depreciation deduction for passenger autos if it is a qualified nonpersonal use vehicle (T.D. 9133, July 2004).

SUVs are listed property, so they are subject to limits. An SUV built on a truck chassis is considered a truck for these purposes.

Businesses can currently expense up to $500,000 (for 2013) of the cost of pickup trucks that have a loaded gross vehicle rate weighing in excess of 14,000 pounds. Though post-2006 expensing has been cut to $25,000 for SUVs with loaded weight between 6,000 and 14,000 pounds, heavy pickups are exempt from that limit. For 2010, you deducted $25,000 plus 50 percent of the remainder as bonus business depreciation. So on a $50,000 purchase, $25,000 plus $12,500 plus the 20 percent first-year normal allowance on the remaining $12,500 was deducted. That was a total $40,000 first-year deduction! In 2012 and 2013, the bonus depreciation is 50 percent. If you buy a *new* $60,000 SUV with a loaded gross weight over 6,000 pounds, you can expense the first $25,000. Half the remaining $35,000 cost ($17,500) qualified as bonus depreciation. You also get 20 percent of the leftover basis ($17,500) or $3,500 as regular depreciation. Use the car 100 percent for business and you get a $46,000 first-year deduction. *Used*, heavy SUVs do not get the bonus depreciation.

To qualify, the vehicle must have a cargo area at least 6 feet in length separate from the passenger compartment. The cargo hold can be capped. Heavy vans and small buses also get the higher expensing limit. An eligible van cannot have seating behind the driver seat, and no part of the body can protrude more than 30 inches in front of the windshield. Small buses must have at least nine seats behind the driver's seat. For 2011, the 100 percent bonus depreciation allowed the cost of 100 percent business-use heavy SUVs to be expensed. The bonus depreciation for 2012 and 2013 is 50 percent.

Note that the 1986 law put automobiles in the 5-year class. However, if the amount limitation prevents full use of the percentage depreciation in any year, the recovery period will be extended. Any unrecovered cost will be treated as an automobile expense subject to the annual limitation in taxable years after the end of the ordinary recovery period. The annual depreciation deduction, assuming the 200 percent declining-balance method, therefore, will be the lesser of the expense deduction or the percentage depreciation.

If qualified business use in the year the automobile is placed in service does not exceed 50 percent, then the basis must be recovered over 5 years using the straight-line method and the half-year convention. If qualified business use falls to 50 percent or less of total use during any part of the recovery period, part of the depreciation claimed in prior years must be included in the taxpayer's income, and a switch must be made to straight-line depreciation.

Appropriate limitations with respect to comparable dollar caps will be applicable to leased automobiles. Lessees of luxury automobiles used in business will be required to have income included to reflect the reduction in their deduction for lease payments. This income inclusion will be based on special tables provided by the Treasury after netting out the repeal of the investment tax credit. See Appendix C for inclusions required.

Appendix C

Auto Leases

Lessors of automobiles having a cost of more than $11,250 had to include in their 1986 income an amount based on tables in Announcement 85-127 that was equal to the value of the limitations imposed by the 1985 law change. For example, a lessee(s) (including an employer or self-employed individual) who leased a car worth $14,300 that was first used on September 1, 1985, and was used 90 percent for business, included approximately $61 in income ($204 times 122/365 of a year times 90 percent business use).

For any passenger automobile leased after April 2, 1985, the inclusion amount is based on the fair market value of the automobile, the lessee's amount of business use, and the quarter of the taxable year during which the automobile was first used under the lease.

The inclusion amount is based upon the following tables and is computed as follows:

1. For the appropriate range of fair market values, find the dollar amount from the column for the quarter of the taxable year in which the automobile is first used under the lease.

2. Prorate the dollar amount for the number of days of the lease term included in the taxable year.

3. Multiply the prorated dollar amount by the percentage of business use for the taxable year.

   Here are the Tables for the last decade:

REV. PROC. 2004-20
Dollar Amounts for Passenger Automobiles (That Are Not Trucks, Vans, or Electric Automobiles) with a Lease Term Beginning in Calendar Year 2004

Fair Market Value of Passenger Automobile		Tax Year During Lease				
Over	Not Over	1st	2nd	3rd	4th	5th and Later
$17,500	$18,000	$11	$ 23	$ 33	$ 42	$ 48
18,000	18,500	13	26	40	49	56
18,500	19,000	14	31	46	55	65
19,000	19,500	16	35	51	63	73
19,500	20,000	18	39	57	70	81
20,000	20,500	20	43	63	77	89
20,500	21,000	22	47	69	84	97
21,000	21,500	23	51	75	91	106
21,500	22,000	25	55	81	98	114
22,000	23,000	28	61	90	109	126
23,000	24,000	32	69	102	123	142
24,000	25,000	35	77	114	137	159
25,000	26,000	39	85	126	151	176
26,000	27,000	43	93	137	166	192
27,000	28,000	46	101	149	180	209
28,000	29,000	50	109	161	194	225
29,000	30,000	54	116	174	208	242
30,000	31,000	57	125	185	223	257
31,000	32,000	61	133	197	237	274
32,000	33,000	64	141	209	251	291
33,000	34,000	68	149	221	265	307
34,000	35,000	72	157	232	280	323
35,000	36,000	75	165	244	294	340
36,000	37,000	79	173	256	308	357
37,000	38,000	83	181	268	322	373
38,000	39,000	86	189	280	337	389
39,000	40,000	90	197	292	351	405
40,000	41,000	94	204	304	365	423
41,000	42,000	97	213	316	379	438
42,000	43,000	101	221	327	394	455
43,000	44,000	105	228	340	408	471

REV. PROC. 2004-20
Dollar Amounts for Passenger Automobiles (That Are Not Trucks, Vans, or Electric Automobiles) with a Lease Term Beginning in Calendar Year 2004 *(continued)*

Fair Market Value of Passenger Automobile		Tax Year During Lease				
Over	Not Over	1st	2nd	3rd	4th	5th and Later
$ 44,000	$ 45,000	$108	$237	$351	$ 422	$ 488
45,000	46,000	112	245	363	436	504
46,000	47,000	115	253	375	451	520
47,000	48,000	119	261	387	464	538
48,000	49,000	123	269	398	479	554
49,000	50,000	126	277	411	493	570
50,000	51,000	130	285	422	508	586
51,000	52,000	134	292	435	522	603
52,000	53,000	137	301	446	536	619
53,000	54,000	141	309	458	550	636
54,000	55,000	145	316	471	564	652
55,000	56,000	148	325	482	578	669
56,000	57,000	152	333	493	593	685
57,000	58,000	155	341	506	607	701
58,000	59,000	159	349	517	622	718
59,000	60,000	163	357	529	636	734
60,000	62,000	168	369	547	657	759
62,000	64,000	176	384	571	686	792
64,000	66,000	183	401	594	714	825
66,000	68,000	190	417	618	743	857
68,000	70,000	197	433	642	771	890
70,000	72,000	205	448	666	800	923
72,000	74,000	212	465	689	828	956
74,000	76,000	219	481	713	856	990
76,000	78,000	227	496	738	884	1,022
78,000	80,000	234	513	760	914	1,055
80,000	85,000	247	540	803	963	1,112
85,000	90,000	265	580	862	1,035	1,194
90,000	95,000	283	621	921	1,105	1,277
95,000	100,000	301	661	980	1,177	1,359

(continues)

REV. PROC. 2004-20

Dollar Amounts for Passenger Automobiles (That Are Not Trucks, Vans, or Electric Automobiles) with a Lease Term Beginning in Calendar Year 2004 *(continued)*

Fair Market Value of Passenger Automobile		Tax Year During Lease				
Over	Not Over	1st	2nd	3rd	4th	5th and Later
$100,000	$110,000	$328	$ 721	$1,069	$1,284	$1,482
110,000	120,000	365	800	1,189	1,426	1,646
120,000	130,000	401	881	1,307	1,568	1,811
130,000	140,000	438	960	1,426	1,711	1,975
140,000	150,000	474	1,041	1,544	1,853	2,140
150,000	160,000	511	1,120	1,663	1,996	2,304
160,000	170,000	547	1,200	1,782	2,138	2,468
170,000	180,000	583	1,281	1,900	2,280	2,633
180,000	190,000	620	1,360	2,020	2,422	2,797
190,000	200,000	656	1,440	2,139	2,564	2,962
200,000	210,000	693	1,520	2,257	2,707	3,126
210,000	220,000	729	1,600	2,376	2,849	3,291
220,000	230,000	765	1,681	2,494	2,991	3,455
230,000	240,000	802	1,760	2,613	3,134	3,619
240,000	250,000	838	1,840	2,732	3,276	3,784

REV. PROC. 2004-20
Dollar Amounts for Trucks and Vans with a Lease
Term Beginning in Calendar Year 2004

Fair Market Value of Passenger Automobile		Tax Year During Lease				
Over	Not Over	1st	2nd	3rd	4th	5th and Later
$18,000	$18,500	$ 7	$ 15	$ 21	$ 26	$ 30
18,500	19,000	9	18	28	33	38
19,000	19,500	11	22	34	40	47
19,500	20,000	13	26	39	48	55
20,000	20,500	14	31	45	54	63
20,500	21,000	16	35	51	61	72
21,000	21,500	18	38	58	68	80
21,500	22,000	20	42	63	76	88
22,000	23,000	23	48	72	87	100
23,000	24,000	26	57	83	101	117
24,000	25,000	30	64	96	115	133
25,000	26,000	34	72	108	129	149
26,000	27,000	37	81	119	143	166
27,000	28,000	41	88	132	157	183
28,000	29,000	44	97	143	172	198
29,000	3,0000	48	104	155	187	215
30,000	31,000	52	112	167	201	231
31,000	32,000	55	121	178	215	248
32,000	33,000	59	128	191	229	264
33,000	34,000	63	136	203	243	281
34,000	35,000	66	145	214	257	298
35,000	36,000	70	152	227	271	314
36,000	37,000	74	160	238	286	330
37,000	38,000	77	169	249	301	346
38,000	39,000	81	176	262	314	364
39,000	40,000	84	185	273	329	379
40,000	41,000	88	192	286	343	396
41,000	42,000	92	200	298	357	412
42,000	43,000	95	209	309	371	429
43,000	44,000	99	216	322	385	445
44,000	45,000	103	224	333	400	462

(continues)

REV. PROC. 2004-20
Dollar Amounts for Trucks and Vans with a Lease
Term Beginning in Calendar Year 2004 *(continued)*

Fair Market Value of Passenger Automobile		Tax Year During Lease				
Over	Not Over	1st	2nd	3rd	4th	5th and Later
$ 45,000	$ 46,000	$106	$233	$ 345	$ 413	$ 479
46,000	47,000	110	240	357	428	495
47,000	48,000	114	248	369	442	511
48,000	49,000	117	257	380	457	527
49,000	50,000	121	264	393	471	544
50,000	51,000	125	272	404	486	560
51,000	52,000	128	280	417	499	577
52,000	53,000	132	288	428	514	593
53,000	54,000	135	297	440	527	610
54,000	55,000	139	304	452	542	626
55,000	56,000	143	312	464	556	643
56,000	57,000	146	321	475	571	659
57,000	58,000	150	328	488	585	675
58,000	59,000	154	336	499	600	691
59,000	60,000	157	345	511	613	708
60,000	62,000	163	356	529	635	733
62,000	64,000	170	372	553	663	766
64,000	66,000	177	389	576	692	798
66,000	68,000	185	404	600	720	832
68,000	70,000	192	420	624	749	864
70,000	72,000	199	436	648	777	897
72,000	74,000	206	453	671	805	931
74,000	76,000	214	468	695	834	963
76,000	78,000	221	484	719	863	996
78,000	80,000	228	501	742	891	1,029
80,000	85,000	241	528	785	940	1,087
85,000	90,000	259	568	844	1,012	1,168
90,000	95,000	277	609	902	1,084	1,250
95,000	100,000	296	648	962	1,155	1,333
100,000	110,000	323	708	1,052	1,261	1,456
110,000	120,000	359	788	1,171	1,403	1,620
120,000	130,000	396	868	1,289	1,546	1,785

REV. PROC. 2004-20

Dollar Amounts for Trucks and Vans with a Lease

Term Beginning in Calendar Year 2004 *(continued)*

Fair Market Value of Passenger Automobile		Tax Year During Lease				
Over	Not Over	1st	2nd	3rd	4th	5th and Later
$130,000	$140,000	$432	$ 948	$1,406	$1,688	$1,949
140,000	150,000	469	1,028	1,526	1,831	2,113
150,000	160,000	505	1,108	1,645	1,973	2,278
160,000	170,000	541	1,188	1,764	2,115	2,443
170,000	180,000	578	1,268	1,882	2,258	2,607
180,000	190,000	614	1,348	2,001	2,400	2,771
190,000	200,000	651	1,428	2,120	2,542	2,936
200,000	210,000	687	1,508	2,239	2,684	3,100
210,000	220,000	724	1,588	2,357	2,827	3,264
220,000	230,000	760	1,668	2,476	2,969	3,429
230,000	240,000	796	1,748	2,595	3,112	3,593
240,000	250,000	833	1,828	2,713	3,254	3,758

REV. PROC. 2004-20

Dollar Amounts for Electronic Automobiles with a Lease

Term Beginning in Calendar Year 2004

Fair Market Value of Passenger Automobile		Tax Year During Lease				
Over	Not Over	1st	2nd	3rd	4th	5th and Later
$53,000	$54,000	$33	$ 72	$106	$127	$147
54,000	55,000	37	79	118	142	164
55,000	56,000	40	88	130	155	180
56,000	57,000	44	96	141	170	197
57,000	58,000	48	103	154	184	213
58,000	59,000	51	112	165	199	229
59,000	60,000	55	120	177	213	245
60,000	62,000	60	132	195	234	270
62,000	64,000	68	147	219	263	303

(continues)

REV. PROC. 2004-20
Dollar Amounts for Electronic Automobiles with a Lease
Term Beginning in Calendar Year 2004 *(continued)*

Fair Market Value of Passenger Automobile		Tax Year During Lease				
Over	Not Over	1st	2nd	3rd	4th	5th and Later
$ 64,000	$ 66,000	$ 75	$ 164	$ 242	$ 291	$ 336
66,000	68,000	82	180	266	320	369
68,000	70,000	90	195	290	348	402
70,000	72,000	97	211	314	377	435
72,000	74,000	104	228	337	405	468
74,000	76,000	111	244	361	434	500
76,000	78,000	119	259	385	462	534
78,000	80,000	126	275	409	491	566
80,000	85,000	139	303	451	540	624
85,000	90,000	157	343	510	612	706
90,000	95,000	175	384	569	682	788
95,000	100,000	193	424	628	754	870
100,000	110,000	221	483	718	860	994
110,000	120,000	257	563	837	1,003	1,158
120,000	130,000	294	643	955	1,145	1,323
130,000	140,000	330	723	1,074	1,288	1,486
140,000	150,000	366	804	1,192	1,430	1,651
150,000	160,000	403	883	1,311	1,573	1,815
160,000	170,000	439	963	1,430	1,715	1,980
170,000	180,000	476	1,043	1,549	1,857	2,144
180,000	190,000	512	1,123	1,668	1,999	2,309
190,000	200,000	548	1,203	1,786	2,142	2,473
200,000	210,000	585	1,283	1,905	2,284	2,637
210,000	220,000	621	1,363	2,024	2,426	2,802
220,000	230,000	658	1,443	2,142	2,569	2,966
230,000	240,000	694	1,523	2,261	2,711	3,131
240,000	250,000	730	1,603	2,380	2,854	3,294

REV. PROC. 2005-13 TABLE 4

Dollar Amounts for Passenger Automobiles (That Are Not Trucks, Vans, or Electric Automobiles) with a Lease Term Beginning in Calendar Year 2005

Fair Market Value of Passenger Automobile		Tax Year During Lease				
Over	Not Over	1st	2nd	3rd	4th	5th and Later
$15,200	$15,500	$ 3	$ 6	$ 9	$ 11	$ 13
15,500	15,800	4	9	13	17	19
15,800	16,100	5	12	18	22	26
16,100	16,400	7	15	22	27	32
16,400	16,700	18	18	27	32	39
16,700	17,000	9	21	32	38	44
17,000	17,500	11	25	38	45	52
17,500	18,000	14	30	45	54	63
18,000	18,500	16	35	52	63	73
18,500	19,000	18	40	60	72	83
19,000	19,500	20	46	67	80	94
19,500	20,000	23	50	75	90	104
20,000	20,500	25	55	82	99	115
20,500	21,000	27	61	89	108	125
21,000	21,500	30	65	97	117	135
21,500	22,000	32	70	105	125	146
22,000	23,000	35	78	116	139	161
23,000	24,000	40	88	131	156	182
24,000	25,000	44	98	146	175	202
25,000	26,000	49	108	161	192	223
26,000	27,000	54	118	175	211	244
27,000	28,000	58	128	191	228	265
28,000	29,000	63	138	205	247	285
29,000	30,000	67	149	220	264	306
30,000	31,000	72	159	234	283	326
31,000	32,000	77	168	250	300	348
32,000	33,000	81	179	265	318	367
33,000	34,000	86	189	279	336	389
34,000	35,000	90	199	295	354	409
35,000	36,000	95	209	309	372	430
36,000	37,000	99	219	325	389	451

(continues)

REV. PROC. 2005–13 TABLE 4
Dollar Amounts for Passenger Automobiles (That Are Not Trucks, Vans, or Electric Automobiles) with a Lease Term Beginning in Calendar Year 2005 *(continued)*

Fair Market Value of Passenger Automobile		Tax Year During Lease				
Over	Not Over	1st	2nd	3rd	4th	5th and Later
$37,000	$38,000	$104	$229	$339	$ 408	$ 471
38,000	39,000	109	239	354	426	491
39,000	40,000	113	249	370	443	512
40,000	41,000	118	259	384	462	533
41,000	42,000	122	269	400	479	554
42,000	43,000	127	279	414	497	575
43,000	44,000	132	289	429	515	595
44,000	45,000	136	299	444	533	616
45,000	46,000	141	309	459	551	636
46,000	47,000	145	320	473	569	657
47,000	48,000	150	329	489	587	678
48,000	49,000	154	340	504	604	699
49,000	50,000	159	350	518	623	719
50,000	51,000	164	360	533	640	740
51,000	52,000	168	370	548	659	760
52,000	53,000	173	380	563	676	781
53,000	54,000	177	390	578	694	802
54,000	55,000	182	400	593	712	823
55,000	56,000	186	410	609	729	844
56,000	57,000	191	420	623	748	864
57,000	58,000	196	430	638	766	884
58,000	59,000	200	440	653	784	905
59,000	60,000	205	450	668	802	925
60,000	62,000	212	465	691	828	957
62,000	64,000	221	485	721	864	998
64,000	66,000	230	506	750	900	1,039
66,000	68,000	239	526	780	935	1,081
68,000	70,000	248	546	810	971	1,123
70,000	72,000	258	566	839	1,008	1,163
72,000	74,000	267	586	869	1,044	1,204
74,000	76,000	276	606	899	1,079	1,247

REV. PROC. 2005-13 TABLE 4

Dollar Amounts for Passenger Automobiles (That Are Not Trucks, Vans, or Electric Automobiles) with a Lease Term Beginning in Calendar Year 2005 *(continued)*

Fair Market Value of Passenger Automobile		Tax Year During Lease				
Over	Not Over	1st	2nd	3rd	4th	5th and Later
$ 76,000	$ 78,000	$ 285	$ 626	$ 930	$1,114	$1,288
78,000	80,000	294	646	960	1,150	1,329
80,000	85,000	310	682	1,011	1,213	1,402
85,000	90,000	333	732	1,086	1,303	1,504
90,000	95,000	356	782	1,161	1,392	1,608
95,000	100,000	379	832	1,236	1,481	1,712
100,000	110,000	413	908	1,347	1,616	1,867
110,000	120,000	459	1,009	1,496	1,795	2,073
120,000	130,000	505	1,109	1,646	1,974	2,280
130,000	140,000	551	1,210	1,795	2,153	2,486
140,000	150,000	597	1,310	1,945	2,332	2,693
150,000	160,000	642	1,411	2,094	2,511	2,900
160,000	170,000	688	1,512	2,243	2,690	3,106
170,000	180,000	734	1,612	2,392	2,870	3,313
180,000	190,000	780	1,713	2,541	3,048	3,520
190,000	200,000	826	1,813	2,691	3,227	3,727
200,000	210,000	871	1,914	2,840	3,407	3,933
210,000	220,000	917	2,015	2,989	3,585	4,141
220,000	230,000	963	2,115	3,139	3,764	4,347
230,000	240,000	1,009	2,216	3,288	3,943	4,554
240,000	and up	1,055	2,316	3,437	4,123	4,760

REV. PROC. 2005-13 TABLE 5
Dollar Amounts for Trucks and Vans with a Lease
Term Beginning in Calendar Year 2005

Fair Market Value of Truck or Van		Tax Year During Lease				
Over	Not Over	1st	2nd	3rd	4th	5th and Later
$16,700	$17,000	$ 3	$ 6	$ 8	$ 10	$ 11
17,000	17,500	4	10	14	17	20
17,500	18,000	7	15	21	26	30
18,000	18,500	9	20	29	35	40
18,500	19,000	11	25	37	43	51
19,000	19,500	14	30	44	52	61
19,500	20,000	16	35	51	62	71
20,000	20,500	18	40	59	71	81
20,500	21,000	20	45	67	79	92
21,000	21,500	23	50	74	88	103
21,500	22,000	25	55	81	98	113
22,000	23,000	28	63	92	111	129
23,000	24,000	33	73	107	129	149
24,000	25,000	38	83	122	147	169
25,000	26,000	42	93	137	165	190
26,000	27,000	47	103	152	183	210
27,000	28,000	51	113	167	201	231
28,000	29,000	56	123	182	218	253
29,000	30,000	60	133	197	237	272
30,000	31,000	65	143	212	254	294
31,000	32,000	70	153	227	272	314
32,000	33,000	74	163	242	290	335
33,000	34,000	79	173	257	308	355
34,000	35,000	83	184	271	326	376
35,000	36,000	88	193	287	344	397
36,000	37,000	93	203	302	361	418
37,000	38,000	97	214	316	380	438
38,000	39,000	102	223	332	397	459
39,000	40,000	106	234	346	415	480
40,000	41,000	111	244	361	433	500
41,000	42,000	115	254	376	451	521

REV. PROC. 2005-13 TABLE 5
Dollar Amounts for Trucks and Vans with a Lease
Term Beginning in Calendar Year 2005 *(continued)*

Fair Market Value of Truck or Van		Tax Year During Lease				
Over	Not Over	1st	2nd	3rd	4th	5th and Later
$42,000	$43,000	$120	$264	$ 391	$ 469	$ 542
43,000	44,000	125	274	406	487	562
44,000	45,000	129	284	421	505	583
45,000	46,000	134	294	436	523	603
46,000	47,000	138	304	451	541	624
47,000	48,000	143	314	466	558	645
48,000	49,000	148	324	481	576	666
49,000	50,000	152	334	496	594	687
50,000	51,000	157	344	511	612	707
51,000	52,000	161	355	525	630	728
52,000	53,000	166	364	541	648	748
53,000	54,000	170	375	555	666	769
54,000	55,000	175	385	570	684	789
55,000	56,000	180	394	586	701	811
56,000	57,000	184	405	600	720	830
57,000	58,000	189	415	615	737	852
58,000	59,000	193	425	630	755	873
59,000	60,000	198	435	645	773	893
60,000	62,000	205	450	667	800	924
62,000	64,000	214	470	697	836	966
64,000	66,000	223	490	727	872	1,007
66,000	68,000	232	510	757	908	1,048
68,000	70,000	241	531	786	944	1,089
70,000	72,000	251	550	817	979	1,131
72,000	74,000	260	571	846	1,015	1,172
74,000	76,000	269	591	876	1,051	1,213
76,000	78,000	278	611	906	1,087	1,254
78,000	80,000	287	631	936	1,123	1,296
80,000	85,000	303	666	989	1,185	1,368
85,000	90,000	326	717	1,063	1,274	1,472
90,000	95,000	349	767	1,137	1,365	1,575

(continues)

REV. PROC. 2005-13 TABLE 5
Dollar Amounts for Trucks and Vans with a Lease
Term Beginning in Calendar Year 2005 *(continued)*

Fair Market Value of Truck or Van		Tax Year During Lease				
Over	Not Over	1st	2nd	3rd	4th	5th and Later
$95,000	$100,000	$ 372	$ 817	$1,212	$1,454	$1,678
100,000	110,000	406	893	1,324	1,588	1,833
110,000	120,000	452	993	1,474	1,767	2,040
120,000	130,000	498	1,094	1,623	1,945	2,247
130,000	140,000	544	1,194	1,772	2,125	2,454
140,000	150,000	590	1,295	1,921	2,304	2,660
150,000	160,000	636	1,395	2,071	2,483	2,867
160,000	170,000	681	1,496	2,220	2,662	3,074
170,000	180,000	727	1,597	2,369	2,841	3,281
180,000	190,000	773	1,697	2,519	3,020	3,487
190,000	200,000	819	1,798	2,668	3,199	3,694
200,000	210,000	865	1,898	2,817	3,379	3,900
210,000	220,000	910	1,999	2,967	3,557	4,107
220,000	230,000	956	2,100	3,115	3,737	4,314
230,000	240,000	1,002	2,200	3,265	3,916	4,520
240,000	and up	1,048	2,301	3,414	4,094	4,728

REV. PROC. 2005-13 TABLE 6
Dollar Amounts for Electric Automobiles with a Lease
Term Beginning in Calendar Year 2005

Fair Market Value of Electric Automobile		Tax Year During Lease				
Over	Not Over	1st	2nd	3rd	4th	5th and Later
$45,000	$46,000	$ 5	$ 11	$ 18	$ 21	$ 25
46,000	47,000	10	21	33	39	45
47,000	48,000	14	31	48	57	66
48,000	49,000	19	41	63	75	86
49,000	50,000	23	52	77	93	107
50,000	51,000	28	61	93	111	127

REV. PROC. 2005-13 TABLE 6
Dollar Amounts for Electric Automobiles with a Lease
Term Beginning in Calendar Year 2005 *(continued)*

Fair Market Value of Electric Automobile		Tax Year During Lease				
Over	Not Over	1st	2nd	3rd	4th	5th and Later
$ 51,000	$ 52,000	$ 33	$ 71	$ 108	$ 129	$ 148
52,000	53,000	37	82	122	147	169
53,000	54,000	42	92	137	164	190
54,000	55,000	46	102	152	183	210
55,000	56,000	51	112	167	200	231
56,000	57,000	55	122	182	218	252
57,000	58,000	60	132	197	236	272
58,000	59,000	65	142	212	254	293
59,000	60,000	69	152	227	272	314
60,000	62,000	76	167	250	298	345
62,000	64,000	85	187	280	334	386
64,000	66,000	94	208	309	370	427
66,000	68,000	104	227	339	406	469
68,000	70,000	113	247	369	442	510
70,000	72,000	122	268	398	478	551
72,000	74,000	131	288	428	514	593
74,000	76,000	140	308	458	550	634
76,000	78,000	149	328	489	585	675
78,000	80,000	159	348	518	621	717
80,000	85,000	175	383	571	683	789
85,000	90,000	197	434	645	773	892
90,000	95,000	220	484	720	863	995
95,000	100,000	243	534	795	952	1,099
100,000	110,000	278	610	906	1,086	1,254
110,000	120,000	323	711	1,055	1,266	1,460
120,000	130,000	369	811	1,205	1,444	1,668
130,000	140,000	415	912	1,354	1,623	1,874
140,000	150,000	461	1,012	1,504	1,802	2,081
150,000	160,000	507	1,113	1,652	1,982	2,287
160,000	170,000	553	1,213	1,802	2,161	2,494

(continues)

REV. PROC. 2005–13 TABLE 6
Dollar Amounts for Electric Automobiles with a Lease
Term Beginning in Calendar Year 2005 *(continued)*

Fair Market Value of Electric Automobile		Tax Year During Lease				
Over	Not Over	1st	2nd	3rd	4th	5th and Later
$170,000	$180,000	$598	$1,314	$1,951	$2,340	$2,701
180,000	190,000	644	1,415	2,100	2,519	2,908
190,000	200,000	690	1,515	2,250	2,698	3,114
200,000	210,000	736	1,616	2,399	2,877	3,321
210,000	220,000	782	1,716	2,549	3,055	3,528
220,000	230,000	827	1,817	2,698	3,235	3,734
230,000	240,000	873	1,918	2,847	3,413	3,942
240,000	and up	919	2,018	2,997	3,592	4,148

REV. PROC. 2006-18 TABLE 4
Dollar Amounts for Passenger Automobiles (That Are Not Trucks, Vans, or Electric Automobiles) with a Lease Term Beginning in Calendar Year 2006

Fair Market Value of Passenger Automobile		Tax Year During Lease				
Over	Not Over	1st	2nd	3rd	4th	5th and Later
$15,200	$15,500	$ 4	$ 6	$ 10	$ 10	$ 10
15,500	15,800	6	10	16	18	18
15,800	16,100	8	15	22	25	28
16,100	16,400	9	19	29	33	36
16,400	16,700	11	24	35	40	45
16,700	17,000	13	28	42	48	53
17,000	17,500	16	34	50	58	66
17,500	18,000	19	41	61	71	80
18,000	18,500	23	48	71	84	95
18,500	19,000	26	55	82	96	110
19,000	19,500	29	62	93	109	125
19,500	20,000	32	70	103	122	139
20,000	20,500	36	76	114	135	154
20,500	21,000	39	84	124	148	168

REV. PROC. 2006-18 TABLE 4

Dollar Amounts for Passenger Automobiles (That Are Not Trucks, Vans, or Electric Automobiles) with a Lease Term Beginning in Calendar Year 2006 *(continued)*

Fair Market Value of Passenger Automobile		Tax Year During Lease				
Over	Not Over	1st	2nd	3rd	4th	5th and Later
$21,000	$21,500	$ 42	$ 91	$135	$160	$184
21,500	22,000	45	98	146	173	198
22,000	23,000	50	109	162	192	220
23,000	24,000	57	123	183	218	250
24,000	25,000	63	138	204	243	279
25,000	26,000	70	152	225	269	309
26,000	27,000	76	166	247	294	339
27,000	28,000	83	181	268	319	368
28,000	29,000	90	195	289	345	397
29,000	30,000	96	209	311	371	426
30,000	31,000	103	223	332	397	455
31,000	32,000	109	238	353	422	485
32,000	33,000	116	252	374	448	515
33,000	34,000	122	267	395	473	545
34,000	35,000	129	281	417	498	574
35,000	36,000	135	295	439	523	604
36,000	37,000	142	309	460	549	633
37,000	38,000	148	324	481	575	662
38,000	39,000	155	338	502	601	691
39,000	40,000	161	353	523	626	721
40,000	41,000	168	367	545	651	750
41,000	42,000	175	381	566	677	780
42,000	43,000	181	396	587	702	810
43,000	44,000	188	410	608	728	839
44,000	45,000	194	424	630	753	869
45,000	46,000	201	438	651	770	898
46,000	47,000	207	453	672	805	927
47,000	48,000	214	467	694	830	956
48,000	49,000	220	482	715	855	986
49,000	50,000	227	496	736	881	1,016

(continues)

REV. PROC. 2006-18 TABLE 4

Dollar Amounts for Passenger Automobiles (That Are Not Trucks, Vans, or Electric Automobiles) with a Lease Term Beginning in Calendar Year 2006 (*continued*)

Fair Market Value of Passenger Automobile		Tax Year During Lease				
Over	Not Over	1st	2nd	3rd	4th	5th and Later
$50,000	$51,000	$233	$ 510	$ 758	$ 906	$1,045
51,000	52,000	240	525	778	932	1,075
52,000	53,000	246	539	800	958	1,104
53,000	54,000	253	553	821	984	1,133
54,000	55,000	259	568	842	1,009	1,163
55,000	56,000	266	582	864	1,034	1,192
56,000	57,000	273	596	885	1,080	1,221
57,000	58,000	279	611	906	1,085	1,251
58,000	59,000	286	625	927	1,111	1,281
59,000	60,000	292	639	949	1,136	1,311
60,000	62,000	302	661	981	1,174	1,354
62,000	64,000	315	690	1,023	1,225	1,413
64,000	66,000	328	718	1,066	1,276	1,473
66,000	68,000	341	747	1,108	1,328	1,531
68,000	70,000	354	776	1,151	1,378	1,590
70,000	72,000	367	804	1,194	1,429	1,649
72,000	74,000	380	833	1,236	1,481	1,707
74,000	76,000	393	862	1,278	1,532	1,767
76,000	78,000	407	890	1,321	1,583	1,825
78,000	80,000	420	919	1,363	1,634	1,884
80,000	85,000	443	969	1,438	1,723	1,987
85,000	90,000	475	1,041	1,544	1,851	2,135
90,000	95,000	508	1,112	1,651	1,978	2,282
95,000	100,000	541	1,184	1,757	2,106	2,429
100,000	110,000	590	1,291	1,917	2,297	2,650
110,000	120,000	655	1,435	2,130	2,552	2,944
120,000	130,000	720	1,579	2,342	2,807	3,239
130,000	140,000	786	1,722	2,555	3,062	3,534
140,000	150,000	851	1,865	2,768	3,317	3,829
150,000	160,000	916	2,009	2,980	3,573	4,123
160,000	170,000	982	2,152	3,193	3,828	4,417

REV. PROC. 2006-18 TABLE 4
Dollar Amounts for Passenger Automobiles (That Are Not Trucks, Vans, or Electric Automobiles) with a Lease Term Beginning in Calendar Year 2006 *(continued)*

Fair Market Value of Passenger Automobile		Tax Year During Lease				
Over	Not Over	1st	2nd	3rd	4th	5th and Later
$170,000	$180,000	$1,047	$2,295	$3,406	$4,083	$4,712
180,000	190,000	1,112	2,439	3,619	4,337	5,007
190,000	200,000	1,178	2,582	3,832	4,592	5,301
200,000	210,000	1,243	2,726	4,044	4,848	5,595
210,000	220,000	1,309	2,869	4,257	5,103	5,890
220,000	230,000	1,374	3,012	4,470	5,358	6,185
230,000	240,000	1,439	3,156	4,682	5,613	6,480
240,000	and up	1,505	3,299	4,895	5,868	6,774

REV. PROC. 2006-18 TABLE 5
Dollar Amounts for Trucks and Vans with a Lease Term Beginning in Calendar Year 2006

Fair Market Value of Truck or Van		Tax Year During Lease				
Over	Not Over	1st	2nd	3rd	4th	5th and Later
$16,700	$17,000	$ 4	$ 8	$ 12	$ 14	$ 16
17,000	17,500	6	14	20	24	29
17,500	18,000	9	21	31	37	43
18,000	18,500	13	28	42	49	58
18,500	19,000	16	36	52	62	72
19,000	19,500	19	43	63	75	87
19,500	20,000	23	50	73	88	102
20,000	20,500	26	57	84	101	116
20,500	21,000	29	64	95	113	131
21,000	21,500	32	72	105	126	146
21,500	22,000	36	78	116	139	161
22,000	23,000	41	89	132	158	183

(continues)

REV. PROC. 2006-18 TABLE 5
Dollar Amounts for Trucks and Vans with a Lease
Term Beginning in Calendar Year 2006 (*continued*)

Fair Market Value of Truck or Van		Tax Year During Lease				
Over	Not Over	1st	2nd	3rd	4th	5th and Later
$23,000	$24,000	$ 47	$104	$153	$183	$213
24,000	25,000	54	118	174	209	242
25,000	26,000	60	132	196	235	271
26,000	27,000	67	146	217	261	300
27,000	28,000	73	161	238	286	330
28,000	29,000	80	175	260	311	359
29,000	30,000	86	190	281	336	389
30,000	31,000	93	204	302	362	418
31,000	32,000	99	219	323	388	447
32,000	33,000	106	233	344	413	478
33,000	34,000	112	247	366	439	506
34,000	35,000	119	261	387	465	536
35,000	36,000	125	276	408	490	566
36,000	37,000	132	290	430	515	595
37,000	38,000	139	304	451	541	624
38,000	39,000	145	319	472	566	654
39,000	40,000	152	333	493	592	684
40,000	41,000	158	347	515	618	712
41,000	42,000	165	362	536	642	743
42,000	43,000	171	376	557	669	772
43,000	44,000	178	390	579	694	801
44,000	45,000	184	405	600	719	831
45,000	46,000	191	419	621	745	860
46,000	47,000	197	434	642	770	890
47,000	48,000	204	448	663	796	919
48,000	49,000	210	462	685	822	948
49,000	50,000	217	476	707	847	977
50,000	51,000	224	490	728	872	1,008
51,000	52,000	230	505	749	898	1,037
52,000	53,000	237	519	770	924	1,066
53,000	54,000	243	534	791	949	1,096

REV. PROC. 2006-18 TABLE 5
Dollar Amounts for Trucks and Vans with a Lease
Term Beginning in Calendar Year 2006 *(continued)*

Fair Market Value of Truck or Van		Tax Year During Lease				
Over	Not Over	1st	2nd	3rd	4th	5th and Later
$54,000	$55,000	$ 250	$ 548	$ 813	$ 974	$1,125
55,000	56,000	256	563	833	1,000	1,155
56,000	57,000	263	577	855	1,025	1,184
57,000	58,000	269	591	877	1,051	1,213
58,000	59,000	276	605	898	1,077	1,243
59,000	60,000	282	620	919	1,102	1,272
60,000	62,000	292	641	951	1,141	1,316
62,000	64,000	305	670	994	1,191	1,375
64,000	66,000	318	699	1,036	1,242	1,435
66,000	68,000	331	728	1,078	1,293	1,494
68,000	70,000	344	756	1,121	1,345	1,552
70,000	72,000	358	784	1,164	1,395	1,612
72,000	74,000	371	813	1,206	1,447	1,670
74,000	76,000	384	842	1,249	1,497	1,729
76,000	78,000	397	871	1,291	1,548	1,788
78,000	80,000	410	899	1,334	1,600	1,846
80,000	85,000	433	949	1,409	1,688	1,950
85,000	90,000	465	1,021	1,515	1,816	2,098
90,000	95,000	498	1,093	1,621	1,944	2,244
95,000	100,000	531	1,164	1,728	2,071	2,392
100,000	110,000	580	1,272	1,887	2,263	2,612
110,000	120,000	645	1,416	2,099	2,518	2,907
120,000	130,000	711	1,559	2,312	2,773	3,202
130,000	140,000	776	1,702	2,525	3,028	3,497
140,000	150,000	841	1,846	2,738	3,283	3,791
150,000	160,000	907	1,989	2,950	3,539	4,085
160,000	170,000	972	2,132	3,164	3,793	4,380
170,000	180,000	1,037	2,276	3,376	4,049	4,674
180,000	190,000	1,103	2,419	3,589	4,303	4,969
190,000	200,000	1,168	2,563	3,801	4,559	5,263

(continues)

REV. PROC. 2006-18 TABLE 5
Dollar Amounts for Trucks and Vans with a Lease
Term Beginning in Calendar Year 2006 *(continued)*

$200,000	$210,000	$1,233	$2,706	$4,015	$4,813	$5,558
210,000	220,000	1,299	2,849	4,227	5,069	5,853
220,000	230,000	1,364	2,993	4,440	5,324	6,147
230,000	240,000	1,430	3,136	4,652	5,580	6,441
240,000	and up	1,495	3,279	4,866	5,834	6,736

REV. PROC. 2006-18 TABLE 6
Dollar Amounts for Electric Automobiles with a Lease
Term Beginning in Calendar Year 2006

Fair Market Value of Electric Automobile		Tax Year During Lease				
Over	Not Over	1st	2nd	3rd	4th	5th and Later
$45,000	$46,000	$ 4	$ 8	$ 11	$ 12	$ 12
46,000	47,000	10	22	33	37	42
47,000	48,000	17	36	54	63	72
48,000	49,000	24	51	74	89	101
49,000	50,000	30	65	96	114	131
50,000	51,000	37	79	118	139	160
51,000	52,000	43	94	139	165	189
52,000	53,000	50	108	160	190	219
53,000	54,000	56	123	181	216	248
54,000	55,000	63	137	202	242	277
55,000	56,000	69	151	224	267	307
56,000	57,000	76	165	245	293	337
57,000	58,000	82	180	266	318	367
58,000	59,000	89	194	288	343	396
59,000	60,000	95	209	309	369	425
60,000	62,000	105	230	341	407	470
62,000	64,000	118	259	383	459	528
64,000	66,000	131	288	425	510	587
66,000	68,000	144	316	469	560	646
68,000	70,000	158	345	510	612	705
70,000	72,000	171	373	554	662	764

REV. PROC. 2006-18 TABLE 6
Dollar Amounts for Electric Automobiles with a Lease
Term Beginning in Calendar Year 2006 *(continued)*

Fair Market Value of Electric Automobile		Tax Year During Lease				
Over	Not Over	1st	2nd	3rd	4th	5th and Later
$ 72,000	$ 74,000	$ 184	$ 402	$ 596	$ 713	$ 823
74,000	76,000	197	431	638	765	881
76,000	78,000	210	459	682	815	940
78,000	80,000	223	488	724	866	1,000
80,000	85,000	246	538	798	956	1,103
85,000	90,000	278	610	905	1,083	1,250
90,000	95,000	311	682	1,011	1,211	1,397
95,000	100,000	344	753	1,118	1,338	1,544
100,000	110,000	393	861	1,277	1,529	1,766
110,000	120,000	458	1,004	1,490	1,785	2,060
120,000	130,000	524	1,147	1,703	2,040	2,354
130,000	140,000	589	1,291	1,915	2,295	2,649
140,000	150,000	654	1,435	2,127	2,551	2,943
150,000	160,000	720	1,578	2,340	2,806	3,237
160,000	170,000	785	1,721	2,553	3,061	3,532
170,000	180,000	850	1,865	2,766	3,315	3,827
180,000	190,000	916	2,008	2,979	3,570	4,122
190,000	200,000	981	2,151	3,192	3,826	4,416
200,000	210,000	1,046	2,295	3,404	4,081	4,711
210,000	220,000	1,112	2,488	3,617	4,386	5,005
220,000	230,000	1,177	2,581	3,830	4,591	5,390
230,000	240,000	1,243	2,725	4,042	4,846	5,594
240,000	and up	1,308	2,868	4,255	5,102	5,888

REV. PROC. 2007-30 TABLE 3
Dollar Amounts for Passenger Automobiles
(That Are Not Trucks or Vans) with a Lease
Term Beginning in Calendar Year 2007

Fair Market Value of Passenger Automobile		Tax Year During Lease				
Over	Not Over	1st	2nd	3rd	4th	5th and Later
$15,500	$15,800	$ 2	$ 5	$ 11	$ 11	$ 13
15,800	16,100	4	10	17	19	22
16,100	16,400	6	14	24	28	31
16,400	16,700	9	18	31	35	41
16,700	17,000	11	23	37	43	50
17,000	17,500	13	29	46	54	62
17,500	18,000	17	37	56	68	77
18,000	18,500	20	44	68	81	93
18,500	19,000	24	51	80	94	108
19,000	19,500	27	59	90	108	124
19,500	20,000	30	67	101	121	139
20,000	20,500	34	74	113	134	154
20,500	21,000	37	82	123	148	170
21,000	21,500	41	89	135	161	185
21,500	22,000	44	97	146	174	201
22,000	23,000	49	108	163	194	224
23,000	24,000	56	123	185	221	255
24,000	25,000	63	138	207	248	285
25,000	26,000	70	153	229	275	316
26,000	27,000	77	168	251	302	347
27,000	28,000	83	183	274	328	378
28,000	29,000	90	198	296	355	409
29,000	30,000	97	213	318	382	439
30,000	31,000	104	228	341	408	470
31,000	32,000	111	243	363	435	501
32,000	33,000	118	258	385	461	532
33,000	34,000	125	273	407	488	563
34,000	35,000	131	288	430	515	593
35,000	36,000	138	303	452	542	624
36,000	37,000	145	318	474	568	656

REV. PROC. 2007-30 TABLE 3
Dollar Amounts for Passenger Automobiles
(That Are Not Trucks or Vans)with a Lease
Term Beginning in Calendar Year 2007 *(continued)*

Fair Market Value of Passenger Automobile		Tax Year During Lease				
Over	Not Over	1st	2nd	3rd	4th	5th and Later
$37,000	$38,000	$152	$333	$ 496	$ 595	$ 686
38,000	39,000	159	348	519	621	717
39,000	40,000	166	363	541	648	748
40,000	41,000	172	378	564	674	779
41,000	42,000	179	393	586	701	810
42,000	43,000	186	408	608	728	840
43,000	44,000	193	423	630	755	871
44,000	45,000	200	438	652	782	902
45,000	46,000	207	453	674	809	933
46,000	47,000	213	468	697	835	964
47,000	48,000	220	483	719	862	995
48,000	49,000	227	498	742	888	1,025
49,000	50,000	234	513	764	915	1,056
50,000	51,000	241	528	786	942	1,087
51,000	52,000	248	543	808	969	1,117
52,000	53,000	254	558	831	995	1,148
53,000	54,000	261	573	853	1,022	1,179
54,000	55,000	268	588	875	1,049	1,210
55,000	56,000	275	603	897	1,076	1,241
56,000	57,000	282	618	920	1,102	1,271
57,000	58,000	289	633	942	1,128	1,303
58,000	59,000	296	648	964	1,155	1,334
59,000	60,000	302	663	987	1,182	1,364
60,000	62,000	313	685	1,020	1,222	1,411
62,000	64,000	326	716	1,064	1,276	1,472
64,000	66,000	340	746	1,108	1,329	1,534
66,000	68,000	354	775	1,154	1,382	1,595
68,000	70,000	367	806	1,198	1,435	1,657
70,000	72,000	381	836	1,242	1,489	1,719
72,000	74,000	395	865	1,287	1,543	1,780

(continues)

REV. PROC. 2007-30 TABLE 3
Dollar Amounts for Passenger Automobiles
(That Are Not Trucks or Vans) with a Lease
Term Beginning in Calendar Year 2007 *(continued)*

Fair Market Value of Passenger Automobile		Tax Year During Lease				
Over	Not Over	1st	2nd	3rd	4th	5th and Later
$ 74,000	$ 76,000	$ 408	$ 896	$1,331	$1,596	$1,842
76,000	78,000	422	926	1,376	1,649	1,903
78,000	80,000	436	955	1,421	1,703	1,965
80,000	85,000	460	1,008	1,498	1,796	2,074
85,000	90,000	494	1,083	1,610	1,929	2,228
90,000	95,000	528	1,158	1,721	2,063	2,382
95,000	100,000	562	1,233	1,833	2,196	2,536
100,000	110,000	614	1,346	1,999	2,396	2,767
110,000	120,000	682	1,496	2,222	2,663	3,075
120,000	130,000	750	1,646	2,444	2,931	3,383
130,000	140,000	819	1,796	2,667	3,197	3.692
140,000	150,000	887	1,946	2,890	3,464	4,000
150,000	160,000	956	2,096	3,112	3,731	4,308
160,000	170,000	1,024	2,246	3,335	3,998	4,616
170,000	180,000	1,093	2,396	3,557	4,266	4,924
180,000	190,000	1,161	2,546	3,780	4,532	5,233
190,000	200,000	1,229	2,696	4,003	4,799	5,541
200,000	210,000	1,298	2,846	4,225	5,067	5,848
210,000	220,000	1,366	2,996	4,448	5,333	6,157
220,000	230,000	1,435	3,146	4,671	5,600	6,465
230,000	240,000	1,503	3,296	4,893	5,867	6,774
230,000	240,000	1,503	3,296	4,893	5,867	6,774
240,000	and up	1,571	3,446	5,116	6,134	7,082

REV. PROC. 2007-30 TABLE 4
Dollar Amounts for Trucks and Vans with a Lease
Term Beginning in Calendar Year 2007

Fair Market Value of Truck or Van		Tax Year During Lease				
Over	Not Over	1st	2nd	3rd	4th	5th and Later
$16,400	$16,700	$ 2	$ 4	$ 8	$ 10	$ 11
16,700	17,000	4	9	15	17	21
17,000	17,500	6	15	24	28	33
17,500	18,000	10	22	35	42	48
18,000	18,500	13	30	46	55	64
18,500	19,000	17	37	57	69	79
19,000	19,500	20	45	68	82	94
19,500	20,000	24	52	80	95	109
20,000	20,500	27	60	90	109	125
20,500	21,000	30	67	102	122	141
21,000	21,500	34	75	113	135	156
21,500	22,000	37	82	124	149	171
22,000	23,000	42	94	140	169	194
23,000	24,000	49	109	163	195	225
24,000	25,000	56	123	186	222	256
25,000	26,000	63	138	208	249	286
26,000	27,000	70	153	230	276	317
27,000	28,000	77	168	252	302	349
28,000	29,000	83	184	274	329	379
29,000	30,000	90	199	296	356	410
30,000	31,000	97	214	318	383	440
31,000	32,000	104	228	342	408	472
32,000	33,000	111	243	364	435	503
33,000	34,000	118	258	386	462	534
34,000	35,000	125	273	408	489	564
35,000	36,000	131	289	430	515	595
36,000	37,000	138	304	452	542	626
37,000	38,000	145	318	475	569	657
38,000	39,000	152	333	497	596	688
39,000	40,000	159	348	520	622	718
40,000	41,000	166	363	542	649	749

(continues)

REV. PROC. 2007-30 TABLE 4
Dollar Amounts for Trucks and Vans with a Lease
Term Beginning in Calendar Year 2007 *(continued)*

Fair Market Value of Truck or Van		Tax Year During Lease				
Over	Not Over	1st	2nd	3rd	4th	5th and Later
$41,000	$42,000	$172	$ 379	$ 563	$ 676	$ 780
42,000	43,000	179	394	586	702	811
43,000	44,000	186	409	608	729	842
44,000	45,000	193	423	631	756	872
45,000	46,000	200	438	653	783	903
46,000	47,000	207	453	675	810	934
47,000	48,000	213	469	697	836	965
48,000	49,000	220	484	719	863	996
49,000	50,000	227	499	741	890	1,026
50,000	51,000	234	514	764	916	1,057
51,000	52,000	241	528	787	943	1,088
52,000	53,000	248	543	809	969	1,119
53,000	54,000	254	559	831	996	1,150
54,000	55,000	261	574	853	1,023	1,180
55,000	56,000	268	589	875	1,050	1,211
56,000	57,000	275	604	897	1,076	1,243
57,000	58,000	282	618	920	1,103	1,273
58,000	59,000	289	633	943	1,129	1,304
59,000	60,000	296	648	965	1,156	1,335
60,000	62,000	306	671	998	1,196	1,381
62,000	64,000	319	701	1,043	1,249	1,443
64,000	66,000	333	731	1,087	1,303	1,504
66,000	68,000	347	761	1,131	1,357	1,566
68,000	70,000	361	791	1,176	1,410	1,627
70,000	72,000	374	821	1,221	1,463	1,689
72,000	74,000	388	851	1,265	1,517	1,751
74,000	76,000	402	881	1,309	1,570	1,813
76,000	78,000	415	911	1,354	1,624	1,874
78,000	80,000	429	941	1,399	1,676	1,936
80,000	85,000	453	994	1,476	1,770	2,044
85,000	90,000	487	1,069	1,587	1,904	2,198

REV. PROC. 2007-30 TABLE 4
Dollar Amounts for Trucks and Vans with a Lease
Term Beginning in Calendar Year 2007 *(continued)*

Fair Market Value of Truck or Van		Tax Year During Lease				
Over	Not Over	1st	2nd	3rd	4th	5th and Later
$ 90,000	$ 95,000	$ 521	$1,144	$1,699	$2,037	$2,352
95,000	100,000	555	1,219	1,810	2,171	2,506
100,000	110,000	607	1,331	1,977	2,371	2,737
110,000	120,000	675	1,481	2,200	2,638	3,045
120,000	130,000	744	1,631	2,423	2,904	3,354
130,000	140,000	812	1,781	2,646	3,171	3,662
140,000	150,000	880	1,932	2,867	3,439	3,970
150,000	160,000	949	2,081	3,091	3,705	4,279
160,000	170,000	1,017	2,232	3,313	3,972	4,586
170,000	180,000	1,086	2,381	3,536	4,239	4,895
180,000	190,000	1,154	2,532	3,758	4,506	5,203
190,000	200,000	1,222	2,682	3,981	4,773	5,511
200,000	210,000	1,291	2,831	4,204	5,040	5,820
210,000	220,000	1,359	2,982	4,426	5,307	6,128
220,000	230,000	1,428	3,131	4,649	5,575	6,435
230,000	240,000	1,496	3,282	4,871	5,841	6,744
240,000	and up	1,565	3,431	5,095	6,108	7,052

REV. PROC. 2008-22 TABLE 5
Dollar Amounts for Passenger Automobiles (That Are Not Trucks or Vans)
with a Lease Term Beginning In Calendar Year 2008

Fair Market Value of Passenger Automobile		Tax Year During Lease				
Over	Not Over	1st	2nd	3rd	4th	5th and Later
$18,500	$19,000	$ 20	$ 42	$ 62	$ 73	$ 84
19,000	19,500	22	47	71	83	94
19,500	20,000	25	53	78	93	106
20,000	20,500	27	58	87	102	117
20,500	21,000	30	63	95	112	128
21,000	21,500	32	69	103	122	139
21,500	22,000	34	75	111	131	151
22,000	23,000	38	83	123	146	167
23,000	24,000	43	94	139	165	190
24,000	25,000	48	105	155	185	212
25,000	26,000	53	115	172	204	235
26,000	27,000	58	126	188	223	257
27,000	28,000	63	137	204	243	279
28,000	29,000	68	148	220	262	302
29,000	30,000	73	159	236	282	324
30,000	31,000	78	170	252	301	347
31,000	32,000	83	181	268	321	368
32,000	33,000	88	192	284	340	391
33,000	34,000	93	202	301	359	414
34,000	35,000	98	213	317	379	436
35,000	36,000	103	224	333	398	459
36,000	37,000	108	235	349	418	481
37,000	38,000	113	246	365	437	503
38,000	39,000	118	257	381	457	525
39,000	40,000	123	268	397	476	548
40,000	41,000	128	279	413	495	571
41,000	42,000	133	289	430	515	593
42,000	43,000	137	301	446	534	615
43,000	44,000	142	312	462	553	638
44,000	45,000	147	323	478	573	659
45,000	46,000	152	333	495	592	682

REV. PROC. 2008-22 TABLE 5
Dollar Amounts for Passenger Automobiles (That Are Not Trucks or Vans) with a Lease Term Beginning In Calendar Year 2008 *(continued)*

Fair Market Value of Passenger Automobile		Tax Year During Lease				
Over	Not Over	1st	2nd	3rd	4th	5th and Later
$ 46,000	$ 47,000	$157	$ 344	$ 511	$ 611	$ 705
47,000	48,000	162	355	527	631	727
48,000	49,000	167	366	543	650	750
49,000	50,000	172	377	559	670	772
50,000	51,000	177	388	575	689	794
51,000	52,000	182	399	591	709	816
52,000	53,000	187	410	607	728	839
53,000	54,000	192	420	624	747	862
54,000	55,000	197	431	640	767	884
55,000	56,000	202	442	657	785	906
56,000	57,000	207	453	673	805	928
57,000	58,000	212	464	689	824	951
58,000	59,000	217	475	705	844	973
59,000	60,000	222	486	721	863	996
60,000	62,000	229	502	746	892	1,029
62,000	64,000	239	524	778	931	1,074
64,000	66,000	249	546	810	970	1,118
66,000	68,000	259	567	843	1,008	1,164
68,000	70,000	269	589	875	1,047	1,209
70,000	72,000	279	611	907	1,086	1,253
72,000	74,000	289	633	939	1,125	1,298
74,000	76,000	299	654	972	1,164	1,342
76,000	78,000	309	676	1,004	1,203	1,387
78,000	80,000	319	698	1,036	1,242	1,432
80,000	85,000	336	736	1,093	1,309	1,511
85,000	90,000	361	791	1,173	1,406	1,623
90,000	95,000	386	845	1,255	1,503	1,734
95,000	100,000	410	900	1,335	1,600	1,846
100,000	110,000	448	981	1,457	1,745	2,014
110,000	120,000	497	1,090	1,619	1,939	2,238
120,000	130,000	547	1,199	1,780	2,133	2,462

(continues)

REV. PROC. 2008-22 TABLE 5
Dollar Amounts for Passenger Automobiles (That Are Not Trucks or Vans) with a Lease Term Beginning In Calendar Year 2008 *(continued)*

Fair Market Value of Passenger Automobile		Tax Year During Lease				
Over	Not Over	1st	2nd	3rd	4th	5th and Later
$130,000	$140,000	$ 597	$1,308	$1,942	$2,327	$2,685
140,000	150,000	646	1,417	2,103	2,521	2,910
150,000	160,000	696	1,526	2,265	2,715	3,133
160,000	170,000	745	1,635	2,427	2,908	3,357
170,000	180,000	795	1,744	2,588	3,103	3,581
180,000	190,000	845	1,853	2,750	3,296	3,805
190,000	200,000	894	1,962	2,912	3,490	4,028
200,000	210,000	944	2,071	3,073	3,684	4,252
210,000	220,000	994	2,179	3,235	3,878	4,476
220,000	230,000	1,043	2,289	3,396	4,072	4,700
230,000	240,000	1,093	2,397	3,559	4,265	4,924
240,000	and up	1,142	2,507	3,720	4,459	5,148

REV. PROC. 2008-22 TABLE 6
Dollar Amounts for Trucks and Vans with a Lease
Term Beginning in Calendar Year 2008

Fair Market Value of Truck or Van		Tax Year During Lease				
Over	Not Over	1st	2nd	3rd	4th	5th and Later
$19,000	$19,500	$ 17	$ 37	$ 54	$ 65	$ 73
19,500	20,000	20	42	63	73	85
20,000	20,500	22	48	70	84	96
20,500	21,000	25	53	79	93	107
21,000	21,500	27	59	86	103	118
21,500	22,000	30	64	95	112	130
22,000	23,000	33	72	107	128	146
23,000	24,000	38	83	123	147	168
24,000	25,000	43	94	139	166	191
25,000	26,000	48	105	155	186	213
26,000	27,000	53	116	171	205	236
27,000	28,000	58	127	187	225	258
28,000	29,000	63	138	204	243	280
29,000	30,000	68	148	221	263	302
30,000	31,000	73	159	237	282	325
31,000	32,000	78	170	253	301	348
32,000	33,000	83	181	269	321	370
33,000	34,000	88	192	285	340	393
34,000	35,000	93	203	301	360	414
35,000	36,000	98	214	317	379	437
36,000	37,000	103	225	333	399	459
37,000	38,000	108	235	350	418	482
38,000	39,000	113	246	366	437	505
39,000	40,000	118	257	382	457	526
40,000	41,000	123	268	398	476	549
41,000	42,000	128	279	414	496	571
42,000	43,000	133	290	430	515	594
43,000	44,000	137	301	447	534	616
44,000	45,000	142	312	463	553	639
45,000	46,000	147	323	479	573	661

(continues)

REV. PROC. 2008-22 TABLE 6
Dollar Amounts for Trucks and Vans with a Lease
Term Beginning in Calendar Year 2008 *(continued)*

Fair Market Value of Truck or Van		Tax Year During Lease				
Over	Not Over	1st	2nd	3rd	4th	5th and Later
$ 46,000	$ 47,000	$152	$ 334	$ 495	$ 592	$ 684
47,000	48,000	157	345	511	612	705
48,000	49,000	162	356	527	631	728
49,000	50,000	167	366	544	651	750
50,000	51,000	172	377	560	670	773
51,000	52,000	177	388	576	689	796
52,000	53,000	182	399	592	709	817
53,000	54,000	187	410	608	728	840
54,000	55,000	192	421	624	748	862
55,000	56,000	197	432	640	767	885
56,000	57,000	202	443	656	787	907
57,000	58,000	207	453	673	806	929
58,000	59,000	212	464	689	825	952
59,000	60,000	217	475	705	845	974
60,000	62,000	224	492	729	874	1,008
62,000	64,000	234	513	762	913	1,052
64,000	66,000	244	535	794	951	1,098
66,000	68,000	254	557	826	990	1,142
68,000	70,000	264	579	858	1,029	1,187
70,000	72,000	274	600	892	1,067	1,232
72,000	74,000	284	622	924	1,106	1,276
74,000	76,000	294	644	956	1,145	1,321
76,000	78,000	304	666	988	1,184	1,366
78,000	80,000	314	687	1,021	1,222	1,411
80,000	85,000	331	726	1,077	1,290	1,489
85,000	90,000	356	780	1,158	1,387	1,601
90,000	95,000	381	835	1,238	1,484	1,713
95,000	100,000	405	889	1,320	1,581	1,825
100,000	110,000	443	971	1,440	1,727	1,993
110,000	120,000	492	1,080	1,602	1,921	2,216
120,000	130,000	542	1,189	1,764	2,114	2,440

REV. PROC. 2008-22 TABLE 6
Dollar Amounts for Trucks and Vans with a Lease
Term Beginning in Calendar Year 2008 *(continued)*

Fair Market Value of Truck or Van		Tax Year During Lease				
Over	Not Over	1st	2nd	3rd	4th	5th and Later
$130,000	$140,000	$ 592	$1,297	$1,926	$2,308	$2,665
140,000	150,000	641	1,407	2,087	2,502	2,888
150,000	160,000	691	1,515	2,249	2,696	3,112
160,000	170,000	740	1,625	2,410	2,890	3,336
170,000	180,000	790	1,733	2,573	3,083	3,560
180,000	190,000	840	1,842	2,734	3,278	3,783
190,000	200,000	889	1,951	2,896	3,472	4,007
200,000	210,000	939	2,060	3,058	3,665	4,231
210,000	220,000	989	2,169	3,219	3,859	4,455
220,000	230,000	1,038	2,278	3,381	4,053	4,678
230,000	240,000	1,088	2,387	3,542	4,247	4,903
240,000	and up	1,137	2,496	3,704	4,441	5,126

REV. PROC. 2009-24 TABLE 5
Dollar Amounts for Passenger Automobiles (That Are Not Trucks or Vans) with a Lease Term Beginning in Calendar Year 2009

Fair Market Value of Passenger Automobile		Tax Year During Lease				
Over	Not Over	1st	2nd	3rd	4th	5th and Later
$18,500	$19,000	$ 9	$ 19	$ 28	$ 34	$ 38
19,000	19,500	10	21	32	38	43
19,500	20,000	11	24	36	42	48
20,000	20,500	12	27	39	46	54
20,500	21,000	13	29	43	51	58
21,000	21,500	15	31	47	55	64
21,500	22,000	16	34	50	60	68
22,000	23,000	17	38	56	66	76
23,000	24,000	20	42	64	75	86
24,000	25,000	22	47	71	84	96
25,000	26,000	24	52	78	93	107
26,000	27,000	26	58	85	101	117
27,000	28,000	29	62	93	110	127
28,000	29,000	31	67	100	119	138
29,000	30,000	33	72	108	128	147
30,000	31,000	35	77	115	137	157
31,000	32,000	38	82	122	146	167
32,000	33,000	40	87	129	155	178
33,000	34,000	42	92	137	163	188
34,000	35,000	44	97	144	172	199
35,000	36,000	47	102	151	181	208
36,000	37,000	49	107	159	189	219
37,000	38,000	51	112	166	199	228
38,000	39,000	53	117	173	208	239
39,000	40,000	56	122	180	216	250
40,000	41,000	58	127	188	225	259
41,000	42,000	60	132	195	234	269
42,000	43,000	62	137	203	242	280
43,000	44,000	65	141	210	252	290
44,000	45,000	67	146	218	260	300
45,000	46,000	69	151	225	269	311

REV. PROC. 2009-24 TABLE 5
Dollar Amounts for Passenger Automobiles (That Are Not Trucks or Vans)
with a Lease Term Beginning in Calendar Year 2009 *(continued)*

Fair Market Value of Passenger Automobile		Tax Year During Lease				
Over	Not Over	1st	2nd	3rd	4th	5th and Later
$ 46,000	$ 47,000	$ 71	$157	$232	$278	$ 320
47,000	48,000	74	161	240	286	331
48,000	49,000	76	166	247	296	340
49,000	50,000	78	171	255	304	351
50,000	51,000	80	176	262	313	361
51,000	52,000	83	181	269	322	371
52,000	53,000	85	186	276	331	381
53,000	54,000	87	191	284	339	392
54,000	55,000	89	196	291	349	401
55,000	56,000	92	201	298	357	412
56,000	57,000	94	206	306	365	423
57,000	58,000	96	211	313	375	432
58,000	59,000	98	216	320	384	442
59,000	60,000	101	221	327	393	452
60,000	62,000	104	228	339	406	467
62,000	64,000	109	238	353	424	488
64,000	66,000	113	248	368	441	509
66,000	68,000	118	258	382	459	529
68,000	70,000	122	268	397	476	550
70,000	72,000	127	277	413	493	570
72,000	74,000	131	288	427	511	590
74,000	76,000	136	297	442	529	610
76,000	78,000	140	307	457	546	631
78,000	80,000	145	317	471	564	651
80,000	85,000	152	335	497	595	686
85,000	90,000	164	359	534	639	737
90,000	95,000	175	384	570	683	789
95,000	100,000	186	409	607	727	839
100,000	110,000	203	446	662	793	916
110,000	120,000	226	495	736	881	1,018
120,000	130,000	248	545	809	970	1,119

(continues)

REV. PROC. 2009-24 TABLE 5
Dollar Amounts for Passenger Automobiles (That Are Not Trucks or Vans)
with a Lease Term Beginning in Calendar Year 2009 *(continued)*

Fair Market Value of Passenger Automobile		Tax Year During Lease				
Over	Not Over	1st	2nd	3rd	4th	5th and Later
$130,000	$140,000	$271	$ 594	$ 883	$1,058	$1,220
140,000	150,000	293	644	956	1,146	1,322
150,000	160,000	316	693	1,030	1,234	1,424
160,000	170,000	338	743	1,103	1,322	1,526
170,000	180,000	361	792	1,177	1,410	1,628
180,000	190,000	383	842	1,250	1,498	1,730
190,000	200,000	406	891	1,324	1,586	1,831
200,000	210,000	428	941	1,397	1,675	1,932
210,000	220,000	451	990	1,471	1,762	2,035
220,000	230,000	473	1,040	1,544	1,851	2,136
230,000	240,000	496	1,089	1,618	1,939	2,238
240,000	And up	518	1,139	1,691	2,027	2,340

REV. PROC. 2009-24 TABLE 6
Dollar Amounts for Trucks and Vans with a Lease
Term Beginning in Calendar Year 2009

Fair Market Value of Truck or Van		Tax Year During Lease				
Over	Not Over	1st	2nd	3rd	4th	5th and Later
$18,500	$19,000	$ 8	$ 17	$ 25	$ 30	$ 35
19,000	19,500	9	19	29	35	40
19,500	20,000	10	22	33	38	45
20,000	20,500	11	25	36	43	50
20,500	21,000	12	27	40	48	55
21,000	21,500	13	30	43	52	60
21,500	22,000	15	32	47	56	66
22,000	23,000	16	36	52	64	72
23,000	24,000	18	41	60	72	83
24,000	25,000	21	45	68	81	93
25,000	26,000	23	50	75	90	103
26,000	27,000	25	56	82	98	114
27,000	28,000	27	61	89	107	124
28,000	29,000	30	65	97	116	134
29,000	30,000	32	70	104	125	144
30,000	31,000	34	75	112	134	154
31,000	32,000	36	80	119	143	164
32,000	33,000	39	85	126	151	175
33,000	34,000	41	90	134	160	184
34,000	35,000	43	95	141	169	195
35,000	36,000	45	100	148	178	205
36,000	37,000	48	105	155	187	215
37,000	38,000	50	110	163	195	226
38,000	39,000	52	115	170	204	236
39,000	40,000	55	120	177	213	246
40,000	41,000	57	125	185	221	256
41,000	42,000	59	130	192	231	266
42,000	43,000	61	135	199	240	276
43,000	44,000	64	139	207	249	286
44,000	45,000	66	144	215	257	296
45,000	46,000	68	149	222	266	307

(continues)

REV. PROC. 2009-24 TABLE 6
Dollar Amounts for Trucks and Vans with a Lease
Term Beginning in Calendar Year 2009 *(continued)*

Fair Market Value of Truck or Van		Tax Year During Lease				
Over	Not Over	1st	2nd	3rd	4th	5th and Later
$ 46,000	$ 47,000	$ 70	$155	$229	$274	$ 317
47,000	48,000	73	159	237	283	327
48,000	49,000	75	164	244	292	338
49,000	50,000	77	169	251	301	348
50,000	51,000	79	174	259	310	357
51,000	52,000	82	179	266	318	368
52,000	53,000	84	184	273	328	378
53,000	54,000	86	189	281	336	388
54,000	55,000	88	194	288	345	399
55,000	56,000	91	199	295	354	408
56,000	57,000	93	204	302	363	419
57,000	58,000	95	209	310	371	429
58,000	59,000	97	214	317	381	439
59,000	60,000	100	219	324	389	450
60,000	62,000	103	226	336	402	465
62,000	64,000	107	236	351	420	485
64,000	66,000	112	246	365	438	505
66,000	68,000	116	256	380	455	526
68,000	70,000	121	266	394	473	546
70,000	72,000	125	276	409	491	566
72,000	74,000	130	286	423	509	586
74,000	76,000	134	296	438	526	607
76,000	78,000	139	305	454	543	627
78,000	80,000	143	316	467	561	648
80,000	85,000	151	333	493	592	684
85,000	90,000	163	357	531	635	735
90,000	95,000	174	382	567	680	785
95,000	100,000	185	407	604	724	836
100,000	110,000	202	444	659	790	912
110,000	120,000	225	493	733	878	1,014
120,000	130,000	247	543	806	966	1,116

REV. PROC. 2009-24 TABLE 6
Dollar Amounts for Trucks and Vans with a Lease
Term Beginning in Calendar Year 2009 *(continued)*

Fair Market Value of Truck or Van		Tax Year During Lease				
Over	Not Over	1st	2nd	3rd	4th	5th and Later
$130,000	$140,000	$270	$ 592	$ 880	$1,054	$1,218
140,000	150,000	292	642	953	1,143	1,319
150,000	160,000	315	691	1,027	1,230	1,421
160,000	170,000	337	741	1,100	1,319	1,522
170,000	180,000	360	790	1,174	1,407	1,624
180,000	190,000	382	840	1,247	1,495	1,726
190,000	200,000	405	889	1,321	1,583	1,828
200,000	210,000	427	939	1,394	1,671	1,930
210,000	220,000	450	988	1,468	1,759	2,031
220,000	230,000	472	1,038	1,541	1,847	2,134
230,000	240,000	495	1,087	1,615	1,935	2,235
240,000	and up	517	1,137	1,688	2,024	2,336

REV. PROC. 2010-18 TABLE 3
Dollar Amounts for Passenger Automobiles
(That Are Not Trucks or Vans) with a Lease
Term Beginning in Calendar Year 2010

Fair Market Value of Passenger Automobile		Tax Year During Lease				
Over	Not Over	1st	2nd	3rd	4th	5th and Later
$16,700	$17,000	$ 3	$ 7	$ 10	$ 11	$ 14
17,000	17,500	4	8	13	15	16
17,500	18,000	5	10	16	19	21
18,000	18,500	6	13	18	23	26
18,500	19,000	7	15	22	26	31
19,000	19,500	8	17	25	30	35
19,500	20,000	9	19	29	34	39
20,000	20,500	10	21	32	38	44
20,500	21,000	11	23	35	42	48
21,000	21,500	12	26	38	45	53
21,500	22,000	13	28	41	50	57
22,000	23,000	14	31	46	56	63
23,000	24,000	16	36	52	63	73
24,000	25,000	18	40	59	71	81
25,000	26,000	20	44	66	78	90
26,000	27,000	22	49	71	86	100
27,000	28,000	24	53	78	94	108
28,000	29,000	26	57	85	101	118
29,000	30,000	28	61	92	109	126
30,000	31,000	30	66	97	117	135
31,000	32,000	32	70	104	125	144
32,000	33,000	34	74	111	132	153
33,000	34,000	36	79	117	140	161
34,000	35,000	38	83	123	148	171
35,000	36,000	40	87	130	156	179
36,000	37,000	42	92	136	163	188
37,000	38,000	44	96	143	170	198
38,000	39,000	46	100	149	179	206
39,000	40,000	48	105	155	186	215
40,000	41,000	50	109	162	194	224

REV. PROC. 2010-18 TABLE 3
Dollar Amounts for Passenger Automobiles
(That Are Not Trucks or Vans) with a Lease
Term Beginning in Calendar Year 2010 *(continued)*

Fair Market Value of Passenger Automobile		Tax Year During Lease				
Over	Not Over	1st	2nd	3rd	4th	5th and Later
$41,000	$42,000	$ 52	$113	$169	$201	$233
42,000	43,000	54	118	174	210	241
43,000	44,000	56	122	181	217	251
44,000	45,000	58	126	188	225	259
45,000	46,000	60	131	194	232	269
46,000	47,000	61	135	201	240	277
47,000	48,000	63	140	207	248	286
48,000	49,000	65	144	213	256	295
49,000	50,000	67	148	220	263	304
50,000	51,000	69	153	226	271	313
51,000	52,000	71	157	232	279	322
52,000	53,000	73	161	239	287	331
53,000	54,000	75	166	245	294	340
54,000	55,000	77	170	252	302	348
55,000	56,000	79	174	258	310	358
56,000	57,000	81	178	265	318	366
57,000	58,000	83	183	271	325	375
58,000	59,000	85	187	278	333	384
59,000	60,000	87	191	284	341	393
60,000	62,000	90	198	294	352	406
62,000	64,000	94	207	306	368	424
64,000	66,000	98	215	320	382	443
66,000	68,000	102	224	332	398	460
68,000	70,000	106	232	346	413	478
70,000	72,000	110	241	358	429	496
72,000	74,000	114	250	371	444	513
74,000	76,000	118	258	384	460	531
76,000	78,000	122	267	396	476	549
78,000	80,000	126	276	409	491	566
80,000	85,000	132	291	432	518	598

(continues)

REV. PROC. 2010-18 TABLE 3
Dollar Amounts for Passenger Automobiles
(That Are Not Trucks or Vans) with a Lease
Term Beginning in Calendar Year 2010 *(continued)*

Fair Market Value of Passenger Automobile		Tax Year During Lease				
Over	Not Over	1st	2nd	3rd	4th	5th and Later
$ 85,000	$ 90,000	$142	$313	$ 464	$ 556	$ 643
90,000	95,000	152	334	497	594	687
95,000	100,000	162	356	528	634	731
100,000	110,000	177	388	577	691	798
110,000	120,000	196	432	641	768	887
120,000	130,000	216	475	705	846	976
130,000	140,000	236	518	770	922	1,065
140,000	150,000	256	561	834	1,000	1,154
150,000	160,000	275	605	898	1,077	1,243
160,000	170,000	295	648	963	1,153	1,333
170,000	180,000	315	691	1,027	1,231	1,421
180,000	190,000	334	735	1,091	1,308	1,510
190,000	200,000	354	778	1,155	1,386	1,599
200,000	210,000	374	821	1,220	1,462	1,688
210,000	220,000	393	865	1,284	1,539	1,777
220,000	230,000	413	908	1,348	1,617	1,866
230,000	240,000	433	951	1,413	1,693	1,956
240,000	and up	453	995	1,476	1,771	2,044

REV. PROC. 2010-18 TABLE 4
Dollar Amounts for Trucks and Vans with a Lease
Term Beginning in Calendar Year 2010

Fair Market Value of Truck or Van		Tax Year During Lease				
Over	Not Over	1st	2nd	3rd	4th	5th and Later
$ 17,000	$ 17,500	$ 3	$ 6	$ 9	$ 10	$ 11
17,500	18,000	4	8	12	14	16
18,000	18,500	5	10	15	18	21
18,500	19,000	6	12	19	22	24
19,000	19,500	7	15	21	26	29
19,500	20,000	8	17	25	29	34
20,000	20,500	9	19	28	33	38
20,500	21,000	10	21	31	37	43
21,000	21,500	11	23	35	41	47
21,500	22,000	12	25	38	45	51
22,000	23,000	13	29	42	51	58
23,000	24,000	15	33	49	58	67
24,000	25,000	17	37	56	66	76
25,000	26,000	19	42	62	73	85
26,000	27,000	21	46	68	82	93
27,000	28,000	23	50	75	89	103
28,000	29,000	25	55	81	97	111
29,000	30,000	27	59	88	104	121
30,000	31,000	29	63	94	113	129
31,000	32,000	31	68	100	120	138
32,000	33,000	33	72	107	127	148
33,000	34,000	35	76	114	135	156
34,000	35,000	37	81	119	143	165
35,000	36,000	39	85	126	151	174
36,000	37,000	41	89	133	158	183
37,000	38,000	43	94	139	166	191
38,000	39,000	45	98	145	174	201
39,000	40,000	47	102	152	182	209
40,000	41,000	49	106	159	189	218
41,000	42,000	51	111	164	198	227
42,000	43,000	53	115	171	205	236
43,000	44,000	55	119	178	213	245
44,000	45,000	57	124	184	220	254
45,000	46,000	59	128	190	228	263

(continues)

REV. PROC. 2010-18 TABLE 4
Dollar Amounts for Trucks and Vans with a Lease
Term Beginning in Calendar Year 2010 *(continued)*

Fair Market Value of Truck or Van		Tax Year During Lease				
Over	Not Over	1st	2nd	3rd	4th	5th and Later
$ 46,000	$ 47,000	$60	$133	$197	$235	$272
47,000	48,000	62	137	203	244	280
48,000	49,000	64	142	209	251	290
49,000	50,000	66	146	216	259	298
50,000	51,000	68	150	223	266	308
51,000	52,000	70	154	229	275	316
52,000	53,000	72	159	235	282	325
53,000	54,000	74	163	242	290	334
54,000	55,000	76	167	249	297	343
55,000	56,000	78	172	254	305	352
56,000	57,000	80	176	261	313	361
57,000	58,000	82	180	268	320	370
58,000	59,000	84	185	274	328	378
59,000	60,000	86	189	280	336	388
60,000	62,000	89	195	291	347	401
62,000	64,000	93	204	303	363	418
64,000	66,000	97	213	315	379	436
66,000	68,000	101	221	329	394	454
68,000	70,000	105	230	341	410	472
70,000	72,000	109	239	354	424	490
72,000	74,000	113	247	367	440	508
74,000	76,000	117	256	380	455	526
76,000	78,000	121	264	393	471	543
78,000	80,000	125	273	406	486	561
80,000	85,000	131	289	428	513	592
85,000	90,000	141	310	461	552	636
90,000	95,000	151	332	492	591	681
95,000	100,000	161	353	525	629	726
100,000	110,000	176	386	573	686	793
110,000	120,000	195	430	637	763	882
120,000	130,000	215	473	701	841	971

REV. PROC. 2010-18 TABLE 4
Dollar Amounts for Trucks and Vans with a Lease
Term Beginning in Calendar Year 2010 *(continued)*

Fair Market Value of Truck or Van		Tax Year During Lease				
Over	Not Over	1st	2nd	3rd	4th	5th and Later
$130,000	$140,000	$235	$516	$ 766	$ 918	$1,059
140,000	150,000	255	559	830	995	1,149
150,000	160,000	274	603	894	1,072	1,238
160,000	170,000	294	646	958	1,150	1,326
170,000	180,000	314	689	1,023	1,226	1,416
180,000	190,000	333	733	1,087	1,303	1,505
190,000	200,000	353	776	1,151	1,381	1,594
200,000	210,000	373	819	1,216	1,457	1,683
210,000	220,000	392	863	1,280	1,534	1,772
220,000	230,000	412	906	1,344	1,612	1,861
230,000	240,000	432	949	1,409	1,689	1,949
240,000	250,000	452	992	1,473	1,766	2,039

REV. PROC. 2011-21 TABLE 5
Dollar Amounts for Passenger Automobiles (That are not Trucks or Vans)
with a Lease Term Beginning in Calendar Year 2011

Fair Market Value of Passenger Automobile		Tax Year During Lease				
Over	Not Over	1st	2nd	3rd	4th	5th and Later
$18,500	$19,000	$ 3	$ 8	$11	$ 13	$ 16
19,000	19,500	4	9	13	15	18
19,500	20,000	4	10	15	17	20
20,000	20,500	5	11	16	19	23
20,500	21,000	5	12	18	21	25
21,000	21,500	6	13	19	24	26
21,500	22,000	6	14	21	26	29
22,000	23,000	7	16	23	29	32
23,000	24,000	8	18	27	32	37
24,000	25,000	9	20	30	36	42
25,000	26,000	10	23	33	40	46
26,000	27,000	11	25	36	44	51
27,000	28,000	12	27	40	48	55
28,000	29,000	13	29	43	52	60
29,000	30,000	14	31	47	55	65
30,000	31,000	15	34	49	60	69
31,000	32,000	16	36	53	63	73
32,000	33,000	17	38	56	68	77
33,000	34,000	18	40	60	71	82
34,000	35,000	19	42	63	75	87
35,000	36,000	20	45	66	79	91
36,000	37,000	21	47	69	83	96
37,000	38,000	22	49	73	87	100
38,000	39,000	23	51	76	91	105
39,000	40,000	24	53	80	94	110
40,000	41,000	25	56	82	99	114
41,000	42,000	26	58	86	102	119
42,000	43,000	27	60	89	107	123
43,000	44,000	28	62	93	110	128
44,000	45,000	29	64	96	114	133

REV. PROC. 2011-21 TABLE 5
Dollar Amounts for Passenger Automobiles (That are not Trucks or Vans)
with a Lease Term Beginning in Calendar Year 2011 *(continued)*

Fair Market Value of Passenger Automobile		Tax Year During Lease				
Over	Not Over	1st	2nd	3rd	4th	5th and Later
$ 45,000	$ 46,000	$ 30	$ 67	$ 98	$119	$137
46,000	47,000	31	69	102	122	141
47,000	48,000	32	71	105	127	145
48,000	49,000	33	73	109	130	150
49,000	50,000	34	76	111	134	155
50,000	51,000	35	78	115	138	159
51,000	52,000	36	80	118	142	164
52,000	53,000	37	82	122	146	168
53,000	54,000	38	84	125	150	173
54,000	55,000	39	87	128	153	178
55,000	56,000	40	89	131	158	182
56,000	57,000	41	91	135	161	187
57,000	58,000	42	93	138	166	191
58,000	59,000	43	95	142	169	196
59,000	60,000	44	98	144	174	200
60,000	62,000	46	101	149	179	207
62,000	64,000	48	105	156	187	216
64,000	66,000	50	109	163	195	225
66,000	68,000	52	114	169	203	234
68,000	70,000	54	118	176	211	243
70,000	72,000	56	123	182	218	253
72,000	74,000	58	127	189	226	262
74,000	76,000	60	132	195	234	270
76,000	78,000	62	136	202	242	279
78,000	80,000	64	140	209	250	288
80,000	85,000	67	148	220	264	304
85,000	90,000	72	159	237	283	327
90,000	95,000	77	170	253	303	350
95,000	100,000	82	181	269	323	372
100,000	110,000	90	198	293	352	406
110,000	120,000	100	220	326	391	452

(continues)

REV. PROC. 2011-21 TABLE 5
Dollar Amounts for Passenger Automobiles (That are not Trucks or Vans)
with a Lease Term Beginning in Calendar Year 2011 *(continued)*

Fair Market Value of Passenger Automobile		Tax Year During Lease				
Over	Not Over	1st	2nd	3rd	4th	5th and Later
$120,000	$130,000	$110	$242	$359	$430	$ 497
130,000	140,000	120	264	392	469	543
140,000	150,000	130	286	424	509	588
150,000	160,000	140	308	457	548	633
160,000	170,000	150	330	490	587	679
170,000	180,000	160	352	523	626	724
180,000	190,000	170	374	555	666	769
190,000	200,000	180	396	588	705	815
200,000	210,000	190	418	621	744	860
210,000	220,000	200	440	654	784	904
220,000	230,000	210	462	687	823	950
230,000	240,000	220	484	719	863	995
240,000	and up	230	506	752	902	1,040

REV. PROC. 2011-21 TABLE 6
Dollar Amounts for Trucks and Vans with a
Lease Term Beginning in Calendar Year 2011

Fair Market Value of Truck or Van		Tax Year During Lease				
Over	Not Over	1st	2nd	3rd	4th	5th and Later
$19,000	$19,500	$ 3	$ 7	$ 9	$ 12	$ 13
19,500	20,000	3	8	11	14	15
20,000	20,500	4	9	13	15	18
20,500	21,000	4	10	15	17	20
21,000	21,500	5	11	16	20	22
21,500	22,000	5	12	18	22	24
22,000	23,000	6	14	20	24	29
23,000	24,000	7	16	24	28	32
24,000	25,000	8	18	27	32	37
25,000	26,000	9	20	31	36	41
26,000	27,000	10	23	33	40	46
27,000	28,000	11	25	37	43	51
28,000	29,000	12	27	40	48	55
29,000	30,000	13	29	43	52	60
30,000	31,000	14	31	47	56	64
31,000	32,000	15	34	49	60	69
32,000	33,000	16	36	53	63	74
33,000	34,000	17	38	56	68	78
34,000	35,000	18	40	60	71	83
35,000	36,000	19	43	62	76	87
36,000	37,000	20	45	66	79	92
37,000	38,000	21	47	69	83	97
38,000	39,000	22	49	73	87	101
39,000	40,000	23	51	76	91	105
40,000	41,000	24	54	79	95	109
41,000	42,000	25	56	82	99	114
42,000	43,000	26	58	86	103	118
43,000	44,000	27	60	89	107	123
44,000	45,000	28	62	93	110	128
45,000	46,000	29	65	95	115	132
46,000	47,000	30	67	99	118	137
47,000	48,000	31	69	102	123	141
48,000	49,000	32	71	106	126	146
49,000	50,000	33	73	109	130	151
50,000	51,000	34	76	112	134	155

(continues)

REV. PROC. 2011-21 TABLE 6
Dollar Amounts for Trucks and Vans with a
Lease Term Beginning in Calendar Year 2011 *(continued)*

Fair Market Value of Truck or Van		Tax Year During Lease				
Over	Not Over	1st	2nd	3rd	4th	5th and Later
$51,000	$52,000	$ 35	$ 78	$115	$138	$160
52,000	53,000	36	80	118	143	164
53,000	54,000	37	82	122	146	169
54,000	55,000	38	84	125	150	173
55,000	56,000	39	87	128	154	177
56,000	57,000	40	89	131	158	182
57,000	58,000	41	91	135	162	186
58,000	59,000	42	93	138	166	191
59,000	60,000	43	95	142	169	196
60,000	62,000	45	99	146	175	203
62,000	64,000	47	103	153	183	212
64,000	66,000	49	107	160	191	221
66,000	68,000	51	112	166	199	229
68,000	70,000	53	116	173	206	239
70,000	72,000	55	121	179	214	248
72,000	74,000	57	125	186	222	257
74,000	76,000	59	129	192	231	266
76,000	78,000	61	134	198	239	275
78,000	80,000	63	138	205	246	285
80,000	85,000	66	146	217	260	300
85,000	90,000	71	157	233	280	322
90,000	95,000	76	168	250	299	345
95,000	100,000	81	179	266	319	368
100,000	110,000	89	196	290	348	402
110,000	120,000	99	218	323	387	447
120,000	130,000	109	240	355	427	493
130,000	140,000	119	262	388	466	538
140,000	150,000	129	284	421	505	583
150,000	160,000	139	306	454	544	629
160,000	170,000	149	328	487	583	674
170,000	180,000	159	350	519	623	719

REV. PROC. 2011-21 TABLE 6
Dollar Amounts for Trucks and Vans with a
Lease Term Beginning in Calendar Year 2011 *(continued)*

Fair Market Value of Truck or Van		Tax Year During Lease				
Over	Not Over	1st	2nd	3rd	4th	5th and Later
$180,000	$190,000	$169	$372	$552	$662	$ 765
190,000	200,000	179	394	585	701	810
200,000	210,000	189	416	618	740	856
210,000	220,000	199	438	651	779	901
220,000	230,000	209	460	683	819	946
230,000	240,000	219	482	716	858	992
240,000	and up	229	504	749	897	1,037

REV. PROC. 2012–23 TABLE 5
**Dollar Amounts for Passenger Automobiles (that are not trucks or vans)
with a Lease Term Beginning in Calendar Year 2012**

Fair Market Value of Passenger Automobile		Tax Year During Lease				
Over	Not Over	1st	2nd	3rd	4th	5th and later
$18,500	$19,000	$ 2	$ 4	$ 5	$ 6	$ 8
19,000	19,500	2	4	7	7	9
19,500	20,000	2	5	8	8	10
20,000	20,500	3	5	9	10	11
20,500	21,000	3	6	9	12	12
21,000	21,500	3	7	10	12	14
21,500	22,000	3	8	11	13	16
22,000	23,000	4	8	13	15	17
23,000	24,000	4	10	15	17	20
24,000	25,000	5	11	17	19	23
25,000	26,000	6	12	19	21	26
26,000	27,000	6	14	20	24	28
27,000	28,000	7	15	22	26	31
28,000	29,000	7	16	25	28	33
29,000	30,000	8	18	25	32	35
30,000	31,000	9	19	27	34	38
31,000	32,000	9	20	30	36	41
32,000	33,000	10	21	32	38	43
33,000	34,000	10	23	33	41	46
34,000	35,000	11	24	35	43	49
35,000	36,000	12	25	37	45	52
36,000	37,000	12	27	39	47	54
37,000	38,000	13	28	41	49	57
38,000	39,000	13	29	43	52	59
39,000	40,000	14	30	45	54	62
40,000	41,000	14	32	47	56	65
41,000	42,000	15	33	49	58	68
42,000	43,000	16	34	51	61	70
43,000	44,000	16	36	52	63	73
44,000	45,000	17	37	54	66	75
45,000	46,000	17	38	57	67	78

REV. PROC. 2012–23 TABLE 5
Dollar Amounts for Passenger Automobiles (that are not trucks or vans)
with a Lease Term Beginning in Calendar Year 2012 *(continued)*

Fair Market Value of Passenger Automobile		Tax Year During Lease				
Over	Not Over	1st	2nd	3rd	4th	5th and later
$ 46,000	$ 47,000	$18	$ 39	$ 59	$ 70	$ 80
47,000	48,000	19	40	61	72	83
48,000	49,000	19	42	62	75	86
49,000	50,000	20	43	64	77	89
50,000	51,000	20	45	66	79	91
51,000	52,000	21	46	68	81	94
52,000	53,000	21	47	70	84	96
53,000	54,000	22	48	72	86	99
54,000	55,000	23	49	74	88	102
55,000	56,000	23	51	76	90	104
56,000	57,000	24	52	78	92	107
57,000	58,000	24	54	79	95	110
58,000	59,000	25	55	81	97	113
59,000	60,000	26	56	83	100	115
60,000	62,000	26	58	86	103	119
62,000	64,000	28	60	90	108	124
64,000	66,000	29	63	94	112	129
66,000	68,000	30	66	97	117	135
68,000	70,000	31	68	102	121	140
70,000	72,000	32	71	105	126	145
72,000	74,000	33	74	109	130	151
74,000	76,000	35	76	113	135	156
76,000	78,000	36	78	117	140	161
78,000	80,000	37	81	120	145	166
80,000	85,000	39	86	127	152	176
85,000	90,000	42	92	137	163	189
90,000	95,000	45	98	147	175	202
95,000	100,000	48	105	155	187	215
100,000	110,000	52	115	170	203	235
110,000	120,000	58	127	189	227	262
120,000	130,000	64	140	208	250	288

(continues)

REV. PROC. 2012–23 TABLE 5
Dollar Amounts for Passenger Automobiles (that are not trucks or vans) with a Lease Term Beginning in Calendar Year 2012 *(continued)*

Fair Market Value of Passenger Automobile		Tax Year During Lease				
Over	Not Over	1st	2nd	3rd	4th	5th and later
$130,000	$140,000	$ 70	$153	$227	$272	$315
140,000	150,000	75	166	246	296	340
150,000	160,000	81	179	265	318	368
160,000	170,000	87	192	284	341	394
170,000	180,000	93	204	304	364	420
180,000	190,000	99	217	323	387	446
190,000	200,000	105	230	342	409	473
200,000	210,000	111	243	361	432	499
210,000	220,000	116	256	380	455	526
220,000	230,000	122	269	399	478	552
230,000	240,000	128	282	418	501	578
240,000	And up	134	294	437	524	605

REV. PROC. 2012–23 TABLE 6
Dollar Amounts for Trucks and Vans with a Lease
Term Beginning in Calendar Year 2012

Fair Market Value of Truck or Van		Tax Year During Lease				
Over	Not Over	1st	2nd	3rd	4th	5th and later
$19,000	$19,500	$ 1	$ 4	$ 5	$ 6	$ 7
19,500	20,000	2	4	6	7	9
20,000	20,500	2	5	7	8	10
20,500	21,000	2	5	8	10	11
21,000	21,500	3	6	9	10	13
21,500	22,000	3	6	10	12	14
22,000	23,000	3	8	11	14	15
23,000	24,000	4	9	13	16	18
24,000	25,000	4	10	15	19	21
25,000	26,000	5	11	17	21	24
26,000	27,000	6	12	19	23	26
27,000	28,000	6	14	21	25	29
28,000	29,000	7	15	23	27	32
29,000	30,000	7	17	24	30	34
30,000	31,000	8	18	26	32	37
31,000	32,000	9	19	28	34	40
32,000	33,000	9	20	31	36	42
33,000	34,000	10	21	33	39	44
34,000	35,000	10	23	34	41	48
35,000	36,000	11	24	36	44	50
36,000	37,000	12	25	38	46	53
37,000	38,000	12	27	40	48	55
38,000	39,000	13	28	42	50	58
39,000	40,000	13	29	44	53	60
40,000	41,000	14	31	45	55	63
41,000	42,000	14	32	48	57	66
42,000	43,000	15	33	50	59	69
43,000	44,000	16	34	52	61	72
44,000	45,000	16	36	53	64	74
45,000	46,000	17	37	55	66	77
46,000	47,000	17	38	58	68	79

REV. PROC. 2012–23 TABLE 6
Dollar Amounts for Trucks and Vans with a Lease
Term Beginning in Calendar Year 2012 *(continued)*

Fair Market Value of Truck or Van		Tax Year During Lease				
Over	Not Over	1st	2nd	3rd	4th	5th and later
$ 47,000	$ 48,000	$18	$ 40	$ 59	$ 70	$ 82
48,000	49,000	19	41	61	73	84
49,000	50,000	19	42	63	75	87
50,000	51,000	20	43	65	78	89
51,000	52,000	20	45	66	80	93
52,000	53,000	21	46	68	83	95
53,000	54,000	21	48	70	84	98
54,000	55,000	22	49	72	87	100
55,000	56,000	23	50	74	89	103
56,000	57,000	23	51	76	92	105
57,000	58,000	24	52	78	94	108
58,000	59,000	24	54	80	96	111
59,000	60,000	25	55	82	98	114
60,000	62,000	26	57	85	101	118
62,000	64,000	27	60	88	106	123
64,000	66,000	28	62	93	110	128
66,000	68,000	29	65	96	115	134
68,000	70,000	30	67	100	120	139
70,000	72,000	32	70	103	125	144
72,000	74,000	33	72	108	129	149
74,000	76,000	34	75	111	134	155
76,000	78,000	35	78	115	138	160
78,000	80,000	36	80	119	143	165
80,000	85,000	38	85	125	151	175
85,000	90,000	41	91	135	163	187
90,000	95,000	44	98	144	174	201
95,000	100,000	47	104	154	185	214
100,000	110,000	52	113	169	202	234
110,000	120,000	57	127	187	225	261
120,000	130,000	63	139	207	248	287
130,000	140,000	69	152	226	271	313
140,000	150,000	75	165	245	294	339

REV. PROC. 2012–23 TABLE 6
Dollar Amounts for Trucks and Vans with a Lease
Term Beginning in Calendar Year 2012 *(continued)*

Fair Market Value of Truck or Van		Tax Year During Lease				
Over	Not Over	1st	2nd	3rd	4th	5th and later
$150,000	$160,000	$ 81	$178	$264	$316	$366
160,000	170,000	87	190	283	340	392
170,000	180,000	92	204	302	362	419
180,000	190,000	98	216	322	385	445
190,000	200,000	104	229	340	409	471
200,000	210,000	110	242	359	431	498
210,000	220,000	116	255	378	454	524
220,000	230,000	122	267	398	477	551
230,000	240,000	127	281	416	500	577
240,000	And up	133	294	435	523	603

REV. PROC. 2013–21 TABLE 5
Dollar Amounts for Passenger Automobiles
(that are not trucks or vans) with a Lease
Term Beginning in Calendar Year 2013

Fair Market Value of Passenger Automobile		Tax Year During Lease				
Over	Not Over	1st	2nd	3rd	4th	5th and later
$19,000	$19,500	$ 2	$ 4	$ 6	$ 7	$ 8
19,500	20,000	2	5	6	9	9
20,000	20,500	2	5	8	9	11
20,500	21,000	3	6	8	10	12
21,000	21,500	3	6	10	11	13
21,500	22,000	3	7	10	13	14
22,000	23,000	4	8	11	14	16
23,000	24,000	4	9	14	16	18
24,000	25,000	5	10	15	18	21
25,000	26,000	5	12	16	21	23
26,000	27,000	6	12	19	23	25
27,000	28,000	6	14	20	25	28
28,000	29,000	7	15	22	27	30
29,000	30,000	7	16	24	29	33
30,000	31,000	8	17	26	31	35
31,000	32,000	8	19	27	33	38
32,000	33,000	9	20	29	35	40
33,000	34,000	10	21	31	37	43
34,000	35,000	10	22	33	39	45
35,000	36,000	11	23	35	41	48
36,000	37,000	11	25	36	43	50
37,000	38,000	12	26	38	45	53
38,000	39,000	12	27	40	47	55
39,000	40,000	13	28	42	49	58
40,000	41,000	13	29	44	52	59
41,000	42,000	14	30	45	54	63
42,000	43,000	14	32	47	56	64
43,000	44,000	15	33	48	59	67
44,000	45,000	15	34	51	60	69
45,000	46,000	16	35	52	63	72

REV. PROC. 2013–21 TABLE 5
Dollar Amounts for Passenger Automobiles
(that are not trucks or vans) with a Lease
Term Beginning in Calendar Year 2013 *(continued)*

Fair Market Value of Passenger Automobile		Tax Year During Lease				
Over	Not Over	1st	2nd	3rd	4th	5th and later
$ 46,000	$ 47,000	$17	$ 36	$ 54	$ 65	$ 74
47,000	48,000	17	38	55	67	77
48,000	49,000	18	39	57	69	79
49,000	50,000	18	40	59	71	82
50,000	51,000	19	41	61	73	84
51,000	52,000	19	42	63	75	87
52,000	53,000	20	43	65	77	89
53,000	54,000	20	45	66	79	92
54,000	55,000	21	46	68	81	94
55,000	56,000	21	47	70	84	96
56,000	57,000	22	48	72	85	99
57,000	58,000	22	50	73	88	101
58,000	59,000	23	51	75	90	103
59,000	60,000	24	52	76	92	106
60,000	62,000	24	54	79	95	110
62,000	64,000	25	56	83	99	115
64,000	66,000	27	58	87	103	120
66,000	68,000	28	60	90	108	125
68,000	70,000	29	63	93	112	130
70,000	72,000	30	65	97	117	134
72,000	74,000	31	68	100	121	139
74,000	76,000	32	70	104	125	144
76,000	78,000	33	73	107	129	149
78,000	80,000	34	75	111	133	154
80,000	85,000	36	79	117	141	162
85,000	90,000	39	85	126	151	174
90,000	95,000	41	91	135	162	186
95,000	100,000	44	97	144	172	199
100,000	110,000	48	106	157	188	217
110,000	120,000	53	118	174	210	241

(continues)

REV. PROC. 2013–21 TABLE 5
Dollar Amounts for Passenger Automobiles
(that are not trucks or vans) with a Lease
Term Beginning in Calendar Year 2013 *(continued)*

Fair Market Value of Passenger Automobile		Tax Year During Lease				
Over	Not Over	1st	2nd	3rd	4th	5th and later
$120,000	$130,000	$ 59	$129	$193	$230	$266
130,000	140,000	64	141	210	252	290
140,000	150,000	70	153	227	273	315
150,000	160,000	75	165	245	294	339
160,000	170,000	80	177	263	315	363
170,000	180,000	86	189	280	336	388
180,000	190,000	91	201	298	357	412
190,000	200,000	97	212	316	378	436
200,000	210,000	102	224	333	400	461
210,000	220,000	107	236	351	420	486
220,000	230,000	113	248	368	442	509
230,000	240,000	118	260	386	463	534
240,000	And up	124	272	403	484	558

REV. PROC. 2013–21 TABLE 6
Dollar Amounts for Trucks and Vans with a
Lease Term Beginning in Calendar
Year 2013

Fair Market Value of Truck or Van		Tax Year During Lease				
Over	Not Over	1st	2nd	3rd	4th	5th and later
$19,000	$19,500	$ 1	$ 3	$ 4	$ 5	$ 6
19,500	20,000	2	3	5	6	7
20,000	20,500	2	4	6	7	8
20,500	21,000	2	5	7	8	9
21,000	21,500	2	5	8	9	11
21,500	22,000	3	6	8	10	12
22,000	23,000	3	7	10	11	14
23,000	24,000	4	8	11	14	16
24,000	25,000	4	9	14	16	18
25,000	26,000	5	10	15	18	21
26,000	27,000	5	12	17	20	23
27,000	28,000	6	13	18	23	25
28,000	29,000	6	14	20	25	28
29,000	30,000	7	15	22	27	30
30,000	31,000	7	16	24	29	33
31,000	32,000	8	17	26	31	35
32,000	33,000	8	19	27	33	38
33,000	34,000	9	20	29	35	41
34,000	35,000	10	21	31	37	43
35,000	36,000	10	22	33	39	46
36,000	37,000	11	23	35	41	48
37,000	38,000	11	25	36	43	51
38,000	39,000	12	26	38	45	53
39,000	40,000	12	27	40	48	55
40,000	41,000	13	28	42	49	58
41,000	42,000	13	29	44	52	60
42,000	43,000	14	30	46	54	62
43,000	44,000	14	32	47	56	65
44,000	45,000	15	33	48	59	67
45,000	46,000	15	34	51	60	70

(continues)

REV. PROC. 2013–21 TABLE 6
Dollar Amounts for Trucks and Vans with a
Lease Term Beginning in Calendar
Year 2013 *(continued)*

Fair Market Value of Truck or Van		Tax Year During Lease				
Over	Not Over	1st	2nd	3rd	4th	5th and later
$ 46,000	$ 47,000	$16	$ 35	$ 52	$ 63	$ 72
47,000	48,000	17	36	54	65	74
48,000	49,000	17	38	55	67	77
49,000	50,000	18	39	57	69	79
50,000	51,000	18	40	59	71	82
51,000	52,000	19	41	61	73	84
52,000	53,000	19	42	63	75	87
53,000	54,000	20	43	65	77	89
54,000	55,000	20	45	66	80	91
55,000	56,000	21	46	68	81	94
56,000	57,000	21	47	70	84	96
57,000	58,000	22	48	72	86	98
58,000	59,000	22	50	73	88	101
59,000	60,000	23	51	75	90	103
60,000	62,000	24	52	78	93	108
62,000	64,000	25	55	81	97	113
64,000	66,000	26	57	85	101	118
66,000	68,000	27	60	88	106	122
68,000	70,000	28	62	92	110	127
70,000	72,000	29	64	96	114	132
72,000	74,000	30	67	99	118	137
74,000	76,000	31	69	103	122	142
76,000	78,000	32	72	105	127	147
78,000	80,000	34	73	110	131	151
80,000	85,000	35	78	116	138	160
85,000	90,000	38	84	124	149	172
90,000	95,000	41	90	133	160	184
95,000	100,000	44	95	142	171	196
100,000	110,000	48	104	156	186	214
110,000	120,000	53	116	173	207	240

REV. PROC. 2013–21 TABLE 6
Dollar Amounts for Trucks and Vans with a
Lease Term Beginning in Calendar
Year 2013 *(continued)*

Fair Market Value of Truck or Van		Tax Year During Lease				
Over	Not Over	1st	2nd	3rd	4th	5th and later
$120,000	$130,000	$ 58	$128	$191	$228	$264
130,000	140,000	64	140	208	249	288
140,000	150,000	69	152	226	270	313
150,000	160,000	75	164	243	292	336
160,000	170,000	80	176	261	312	361
170,000	180,000	85	188	278	334	386
180,000	190,000	91	199	296	355	410
190,000	200,000	96	211	314	376	434
200,000	210,000	101	223	332	397	459
210,000	220,000	107	235	349	418	483
220,000	230,000	112	247	367	439	507
230,000	240,000	118	259	384	460	532
240,000	And up	123	271	401	482	556

Index

Note: A page number followed by a roman f indicates figures; a roman t indicates tables; and a roman n indicates notes.

About the Author

Jeff A. Schnepper, Esq., is the author of multiple books on finance and taxation, including all 30 previous editions of *How to Pay Zero Taxes*. He is a financial, tax, and legal advisor for Estate Planning of Delaware Valley and operates a tax, accounting, and legal practice in Cherry Hill, New Jersey. Schnepper formerly was Microsoft's MSN MONEY tax expert and a professor of accounting, finance, and taxation at the American College in Bryn Mawr, Pennsylvania. He currently is an economics editor for *USA Today* and tax counsel for Haran, Watson & Company.